Praise for *Mourning Lincoln*

Editor's Choice, *New York Times Book Review*

An "elegant and nuanced study."—Patrick T. Reardon, *Chicago Tribune*

"Engrossing reading. . . . A layered, nuanced work."—*Kirkus Reviews*

"This book is a timely reminder that wars rarely end on the battlefield. Through the lens of Lincoln's death, Martha Hodes vividly portrays a scarred and bitter nation that had laid down its arms yet embarked on a conflict that endures 150 years after Appomattox."—Tony Horwitz, author of *Confederates in the Attic: Dispatches from the Unfinished Civil War*

"In *Mourning Lincoln*, Martha Hodes's ingenious approach and graceful execution succeed in deepening our knowledge of a calamity that will never fully end."—Thomas Mallon, author of *Henry and Clara* and *Mrs. Paine's Garage*

"*Mourning Lincoln* is an original and important book. . . . Through extensive research, Martha Hodes has discovered voices that are both moving and surprising. The result is an illuminating work that allows us for the first time to understand fully the meaning of Lincoln's death at the time."—Louis P. Masur, author of *Lincoln's Hundred Days*

"This is a book full of things you think you know—and the opposite. The author has discovered much that is new and unknown."—Liz Smith, *NewYorkSocialDiary.com*

Mourning
Lincoln

Mourning
Lincoln

Martha Hodes

Yale

UNIVERSITY PRESS

NEW HAVEN AND LONDON

Published with assistance from the Mary Cady Tew Memorial Fund.

Yale University Press books may be purchased in quantity for educational, business, or promotional use. For information, please e-mail sales.press@yale.edu (US office) or sales@yaleup.co.uk (UK office).

Designed by Lindsey Voskowsky.
Set in Bulmer MT type by Integrated Publishing Solutions.
Printed in the United States of America.

Library of Congress Control Number: 2014952310
ISBN 978-0-300-19580-4 (hardcover)
ISBN 978-0-300-21975-3 (pbk.)

Catalogue records for this book are available from the
Library of Congress and the British Library.

10 9 8 7 6 5 4 3 2 1

For Linda
and
As ever, for Bruce

Contents

Mourning
Lincoln

Good Friday, 1865

THE PLAY HAD ALREADY STARTED when the Lincolns arrived. As the honored guests made their way up the stairway to the dress circle, the actors stopped and the audience cheered. As the band struck up "Hail to the Chief," the president took an impromptu bow. It was Good Friday, April 14, 1865.

The *Washington Evening Star* had carried a front-page advertisement for Laura Keene's appearance at Ford's Theatre in the lighthearted comedy *Our American Cousin,* and an announcement inside indicated that the president and Mrs. Lincoln would be attending that night. The Lincolns had extended an invitation to General Ulysses S. Grant and his wife, Julia, and when they declined, to Assistant Secretary of War Thomas Eckert, who declined as well. Next down the list were Clara Harris and Major Henry Rathbone, who happily accepted. She was the daughter of a New York senator, and he, Clara's stepbrother and fiancé. It was an evening that would ruin their lives.

The presidential box, personally decorated by one of the Ford brothers for the occasion, hovered above stage left. Lincoln lowered himself into the walnut rocking chair, with Mary seated to his right. At perhaps a quarter past ten, the audience roared with laughter as the actor Harry Hawk, in the role of the backwoods American cousin of British relatives, uttered the

John Wilkes Booth fires into the back of Lincoln's head. This 1865 lithograph shows
Clara Harris seated next to Mary Lincoln while Henry Rathbone attempts to stop the
assassin. Lincoln's hand is grasping the drapery fashioned from an American flag.
LC-USZ62-2073, Prints and Photographs Division, Library of Congress.

line, "Well, I guess I know enough to turn you inside out, old gal—you
sockdologizing old mantrap!" Then came a pistol crack. Was it part of the
play? An accidental firing by a soldier in the audience? Now a man leapt
to the stage—was *that* part of the script? But he'd jumped from the president's box and caught one foot in the decorative swags, waving a knife.
Some heard him shout, "Sic semper tyrannis!"—*Thus always to tyrants.*
Some heard, "The South is avenged," and others heard nothing at all. It
didn't seem like a play anymore, and for a split second everything froze. By
the time the audience jolted from their seats, the gunman had vanished.

Up in the presidential box, Clara Harris's hands and face were covered
with blood, her clothes saturated. Henry Rathbone hadn't seen or heard
a thing until the shot rang out. He had tried to prevent the assailant from
vaulting to the stage, provoking the man to slash his arm from elbow nearly
to shoulder. After that, Rathbone could only shout, "Stop that man!" Then
Mary Lincoln thought that the blood all over Harris was her husband's and
kept screaming, "My husband's blood, my dear husband's blood!" Now
came shouts from the audience about murder and calls for doctors. People
rushed the stage. Women fainted. Soldiers hurried in with bayonets.

John Wilkes Booth lands on the stage at Ford's Theatre after jumping from the presidential box. In this engraving, Mary Lincoln and Clara Harris assist the wounded president while men in the audience jump to their feet, pointing at the assassin.
McLellan Lincoln Collection, John Hay Library, Brown University.

At 10:30 p.m., from Tenth Street outside Ford's Theatre, the news traveled through the darkness, people shouting, rapping on windows, pounding on doors. Mounted patrols galloped through throngs of frightened people, with soldiers, sailors, and policemen everywhere. Members of the audience had recognized the intruder as the well-known Shakespearean actor John Wilkes Booth, and his name spread rapidly. Word came as well about Secretary of State William Seward: another man had knocked on the door of his Washington home at about 10:00 p.m., forced his way upstairs, and assaulted Seward right in his bed, where he was recuperating from a recent carriage accident. As the city embarked on a manhunt for the killer and his accomplices, trains and ferries were ordered halted, and guards stood posted at all roads leading out of the capital.

Booth and his recruited conspirators had at first planned to abduct the president and hold him hostage in exchange for wartime prisoners, but after Confederate general Robert E. Lee surrendered at Appomattox on April 9, they changed the scheme from kidnapping to murder. Simultaneous with Booth's deed, three other men were set to carry out two related missions. George Atzerodt would kill Vice President Andrew Johnson in his suite at the Kirkwood House Hotel on Pennsylvania Avenue, and Lewis Powell would kill Seward while David Herold, on horseback, held Powell's waiting horse for the escape. Atzerodt lost his nerve at the last minute, and Powell's plan went awry when his ruse of delivering medicine to the ailing secretary of state failed. Instead, Powell violently fought his way into the Seward residence, where he shot Seward's grown son (he would recover), then stabbed the intended victim in his bed (he too would recover) before another son intervened. Powell managed to break free, but Herold, flustered by the screams coming from inside the house, had already galloped off on his own horse. Later that night, Herold would meet up with Booth, the two disappearing together into the surrounding countryside. Among the other conspirators were a carpenter at Ford's Theatre, who briefly held on to Booth's horse in the back alley; Dr. Samuel Mudd, who later that night would treat the broken bone Booth had sustained from his leap to the stage; and Mary Surratt, a widow who ran a Washington boardinghouse near the theater and owned a Maryland tavern, both of which were implicated in the conspiracy.

Unlike his collaborators, John Wilkes Booth had executed his portion of the plot nearly flawlessly. Three days earlier, on Tuesday, April 11, the twenty-six-year-old actor had stood among a crowd gathered outside the White House, listening to Lincoln deliver a victory speech about reconstructing the nation. When the president spoke of voting rights for black men, Booth was roused to fury. "That means nigger citizenship," he uttered, according to a companion. "Now, by God, I'll put him through." When Booth entered the box at Ford's Theatre, he stood directly behind the president, aimed his derringer, and fired one shot into the back of Lincoln's head.

When the audience's moment of motionless shock passed, and after people raced outside to tell the world what had happened, three doctors and four soldiers took charge of the unconscious president. With no stretcher available, and the half-mile to the White House too far to travel, they crossed the street to a boardinghouse run by a German tailor named William Petersen. (In years to come, an impossible number of men would claim to have carried the president's body out of the theater that night.) At Petersen's, the men maneuvered Lincoln's gangly frame into a first-floor chamber, placing him diagonally across the small bed. The president's eld-est son, twenty-one-year-old Captain Robert Lincoln, soon arrived, as did Secretary of War Edwin Stanton, who right there in the back parlor directed the search for Booth and his conspirators. Mary Lincoln had followed, but eventually those in charge could no longer withstand the sounds of her torment and insisted that she move from the back bedroom into the front parlor. All through the night and past dawn, the cramped space hosted a somber parade of statesmen and friends, lingering, departing, and return-ing, alongside the doctors trying to save the president's life, even as his head wound bled on. Death came at twenty-two minutes past seven o'clock in the morning. At that moment, Edwin Stanton said something. Some heard the words, "Now he belongs to the ages." Others heard, "Now he belongs to the angels." Ages or angels, history or heaven, Lincoln belonged to both.

It was Saturday, April 15, 1865. Word spread across the telegraph wires, north, south, and west. Soon, with dispatches read aloud to gathering by-standers, glances at newspaper headlines, and the sight of stricken faces at front doors, millions across the country knew.[1]

THE STORY OF THE NATION'S first presidential assassination has been told many times over, in biographies of Lincoln and inquiries into the con-spiracy, in chronicles of the Civil War and textbooks of American history. These accounts often portray the nation's (and the world's) response by looking to newspapers, sermons, formal expressions of condolence, and the phenomenal crowds that turned out for religious services and civic ceremonies. The outlines of that portrait are consistent, describing shock, grief, and anger. But how well does that familiar picture capture the full range of responses? And how universal were the experiences captured in those public sources?

Two personal experiences of collective catastrophe prompted me to ask: How did people respond—at home, on the street, at work, with their fami-lies, by themselves—when they heard the news that Abraham Lincoln had been assassinated?

September 11, 2001, was the first day of the fall semester at New York University. When I set out to teach my 9:30 a.m. class, I'd already heard a phenomenal boom, though I had no idea what it was. In the streets of

Greenwich Village, I joined a knot of people gazing skyward toward the fractured North Tower of the World Trade Center a mile and a half downtown, thick smoke streaming from the upper windows. Then, as the second plane crashed from the other side, I saw an orange ball of fire burst from the South Tower. It astonishes me now that I went on to class, that the students—they too had seen the burning towers—arrived on time and sat in their chairs. Not until someone opened our classroom door with news of the buildings' collapse did I dismiss the students, all of us just beginning to comprehend the magnitude of the event.

Out on the street, people looked into one another's faces to verify that it wasn't a terrible nightmare, then rushed home to confirm everything by television. Most important was to communicate with loved ones, at least until the phone lines and Internet went dead. Especially for those who lost family and friends, life would never again be the same, but the world did not stop that morning. Even those separated from the flames, ash, and bodies by as little as a mile walked their dogs or finished up work that seemed important. At the same time, the city's residents began to create makeshift shrines, amassing thousands of candles, flowers, flags, and signs. The cellophane-wrapped bouquets made clear that people in flower shops and corner delis were still at work.

At sunrise the next day, I walked north in search of a newspaper—another way to confirm what still seemed like a dream. I fell in step with a neighbor on the same mission, passing through a police checkpoint and continuing on for dozens of blocks before we found an open newsstand. "U.S. ATTACKED," read the *New York Times* headline. Across the country that day, headlines universalized the nation's reaction: DEVASTATION, read the *Baltimore Sun;* OUTRAGE, cried the *Atlanta Journal-Constitution.* UNTHINKABLE, proclaimed the *Salt Lake City Tribune.*

People put their feelings into words by chalking messages onto sidewalks and taping up handwritten or hastily printed signs. Some imparted information that testified to the disaster: "Vigil in park @ dusk" or "For obvious reasons our screening this evening has been cancelled." The signboard outside a bar read, "Sports Today: None." Many posters revealed a spirit of unity, thanking police and firefighters, offering compassion, or asking for prayers—in English, Spanish, German, Chinese, Japanese, Hebrew, and Arabic. Others revealed more confusion than conviction: "I don't know how to feel," read one; a slip of paper, posted in multiple locations, read simply, "Why?"

It felt as if the whole world was grieving and in shock, yet evidence of tension and contention could be read everywhere. One sign called for peace, another for "peace after payback." Messages calling for harmony were defaced with calls to war, in turn answered with cries for justice without revenge. Some signs spewed fury at the peacemakers; others warned mourners to distrust the media.

I began right away to gather tokens and relics: along with the newspapers from that day, I bought special issues of magazines paying tribute to the lost, and searched for postcards of the city skyline with the Twin Towers intact. As if in a trance, I dropped off an armload of warm clothes and helped prepare a meal for rescue workers. Three days later, as I rode a train out of New York, I found myself startled at the conversation in the seats just ahead: someone was talking about something unrelated to September 11.

Hazier in my memory (and undocumented in my personal archives) is the assassination of President John F. Kennedy, about which Americans continue to ask one another, or their elders, "Where were you when you found out?" My sole recollection of that day in November 1963, when I was five years old, consists of walking up Third Avenue in the Murray Hill neighborhood of New York with Mary Gallagher, the devout Catholic woman who took care of us while my father was at work. Schools had been dismissed early, and Mary and I were going to pick up my sister. How Mary loved Kennedy! His murder might as well have been the crucifixion, my father would say later—or if he was not quite Jesus, then JFK felt to Mary like a brother or a son, and she must have asked God why, struggling to find spiritual consolation. Up the avenue we walked, tears streaming down Mary's face as she pressed a transistor radio to her ear. Other grown-ups on the street must have been weeping too, searching one another's faces to make sure the awful tidings were true. In my sister's first-grade classroom, the loudspeaker had crackled with an announcement that the president had been shot. At a Ford dealership on the West Side, my father had been paying for auto parts when the man behind the counter gruffly announced the news to his customers, then turned the volume up high on his backroom radio. Along with everyone else at the counter, my father completed his purchase.

If I'd been watching our small black-and-white television that after-noon, I'd have seen Walter Cronkite break into a soap opera broadcast to announce the shooting. When the camera switched to the CBS affiliate in Dallas, viewers saw the hotel ballroom where so many had gathered to hear President Kennedy deliver a speech. For a long moment, the lens trained on an African American man in waiter's vest and bowtie, wiping his eyes repeatedly with a linen napkin. The Texas reporter soon passed on the emergency room's unofficial pronouncement of death, informing viewers that the doctor himself was in tears. Minutes later, from the New York stu-dio, Cronkite told his audience that Kennedy had died at 1:00 p.m. central standard time. Looking into the camera, he struggled just a bit to remain composed.

The grown-ups around me knew they were part of history-in-the-making that day, yet the world had not stood still then either. The next day, my father taught his dance class at the Martha Graham School, and Mary, still stricken, came to work. Soon I joined the one hundred million viewers watching the funeral on television. Surely it felt as if the shock and sorrow were universal, yet I now know that despite the overwhelming grief, there were also disagreements and anger, even fistfights between mourners and exulters. Indeed, just before Walter Cronkite officially announced Kenne-dy's death on air, he told the nation that Dallas had called out an extra four hundred policemen owing to "fears and concerns" for the president.

THESE EXPERIENCES, ENCOMPASSING ONLY A fraction of the range of reactions to transformative events, led me to wonder what stories we might find if we listened for immediate personal responses to Lincoln's assassination: of northerners and southerners, Yankees and Confederates, African Americans and whites, soldiers and civilians, men and women, rich and poor, the well known and the unknown. What would we find by read-ing extensively through the diaries people kept and the letters they wrote during the momentous hours, days, weeks, and months that followed the crime at Ford's Theatre? Here was a key moment of confusion and con-flict that has been left out of the story or glossed over with generalities. The record of personal responses overlaps with public pronouncements, but the two are not the same, as individual writings reveal experiences that cannot be recovered elsewhere. Drawing on evidence from hundreds of letters, diaries, and other sources that disclose personal responses, *Mourning Lincoln* delves into the moment of Lincoln's assassination to uncover a profusion of real-time sentiments, creating a multivocal narrative history that takes us far beyond the headlines to tell the story, and illuminate its meanings, on a human scale.

In the quest for raw reactions, I have bypassed memoirs. Although all private writings are in some respects written from memory, responses to Lincoln's assassination from the spring and summer of 1865 differ considerably from the polished reminiscences of burnished recollections. Consider the diary of Union soldier Henry Gawthrop, who lay in an army hospital in Virginia. In April 1865, Gawthrop recorded that President Lincoln had stopped by to shake hands with the wounded soldiers. Some fifty years later, the veteran elaborated on this memory, writing that Lincoln had greeted a Confederate soldier with the words, "I hope you will soon be well and return to your home." It's hard to tell whether Gawthrop neglected to record that scene at the time or if he embellished his memory bit by bit over the years until he came to believe it had happened that way. The fact is, the words that Gawthrop later attributed to Lincoln make the most sense in the context of white North-South reconciliation, fully under way by the early twentieth century.[2]

Many memoirs, moreover, comfortably corroborate a static portrait of a weeping nation. In September 2001 and November 1963, many perceived the whole world to be in grief, and so did Lincoln's mourners in April 1865. When the bereaved wrote about the immediate aftermath of the assassination, they tended toward extravagant descriptions of *everyone, everywhere,* of universal grief and worldwide sorrow. When church bells chimed on a hillside, it felt as if bells were tolling across the land. With every building in a village draped in black, it seemed the whole country must be shrouded. Sharing feelings of shock and horror, out on the street or in church, it was easy to envision the entire nation in a state of distress, the whole world under the same spell of gloom.

None of this was literally true, and personal responses from the spring of 1865 make that eminently clear. Grieving men and women described a nation and a world in mourning, but it was they who constructed that universality, nourished by personal rituals: spreading the word to neighbors, tacking black drapery to windows, crowding together into church pews. All of those actions made the calamitous crime both more real and more bearable, and illusions of collective grief served the same purpose. As a black preacher in upstate New York put it, "No deeper sorrow ever filled the universal heart of the country." In the words of a white Washington correspondent from California, horror "swept over the land," while "from sea to sea a smitten nation wept." People made the same kinds of observations in their personal writings. The shock, a mourner wrote to her brother, was soothed by the "universal feeling of one sorrow that overcame all." After four years of bloody conflict, moreover, the bereaved were ready to see all enmity between Union and Confederate suddenly evaporated. "North & South are weeping together," a woman wrote to her husband. Around the globe, the chorus echoed. In the West Indies, it seemed to a Christian missionary that even the most bitter sentiments of secession had melted away. In South Africa, a U.S. diplomat thought that "even those who never sympathized with our holy cause" were "overwhelmed with horror." As the English novelist Elizabeth Gaskell insisted, "*Everyone* is feeling the same. I never knew so universal a feeling." Accordingly, black worshippers in San Francisco resolved to "join our grief with that of the World."[3]

In fact, though, not everyone was included in this vision of a monolithic grieving nation, nor did everyone wish to be. Even as many of Lincoln's mourners were eager to universalize their responses, their own accounts contradicted that very yearning. Grand and impressive as the public ceremonies might have been, this end-of-war moment was less a time of unity and closure and much more a time of ongoing dissension. And no matter how comforting was the thought of universal grief, mourners knew that others responded to the assassination with gratitude and glee. Indeed, despite the common invocation of the Civil War as a conflict between North and South, regional boundaries prove inadequate, since the populations of neither section were of one mind. Lincoln's supporters encompassed black southerners and black northerners and the majority of white northerners. Lincoln's opponents encompassed the majority of white southerners and a significant minority of white northerners, the so-called Copperheads. In the pages that follow, I thus avoid the popular usage of *the North* and *the South,* writing instead about Lincoln's mourners, Union supporters, and

Yankees on the one hand, and Confederates, rebels, and Lincoln's antagonists on the other.

THE CIVIL WAR WAS A revolutionary war, and Lincoln's assassination complicated its ending. The strife provoked by conflicting political stakes at war's end was inseparable from irreconcilable personal responses to Lincoln's assassination. No single moment can by itself explain the war's meaning, and responses to the startling burst of violence in Ford's Theatre cannot explain what lay in the future any more than can the Emancipation Proclamation, the military turning point at the Battle of Gettysburg, or the president's stirring second inaugural address. If one legacy of the war was an extraordinary moment of black freedom and equality during radical Reconstruction that foreshadowed the Civil Rights Movement, we can find the beginnings of that historical development in the post-assassination determination of African Americans and their white allies. If another legacy was a replication of the violent and oppressive conditions of racial slavery that lasted well into the twentieth century, we can find the roots of that trajectory in the Confederate defiance that followed Lincoln's death.

Responses to the crime at Ford's Theatre were intertwined with different understandings of the war that had just ended and, in turn, different hopes and fears about what would come next. When Lincoln was assassinated, mourners cast him as the best friend Confederates could have hoped for, and some Confederates reluctantly agreed, as Union victory and the end of black slavery seemed to usher in their subjugation to tyrannical Yankees. Whether they imagined Lincoln as merciful or malicious, defeated white southerners hoped the assassination was God's plan to vindicate their downfall, looking back to the days when military victory and independence had seemed certain, and farther back to the lost world of white mastery. When Confederates looked ahead, it was to a day when God would ultimately prove their cause right and righteous, or at least to a time when they could wreak vengeance upon their conquerors.

Lincoln's mourners, by contrast, wanted to believe that the assassination was part of God's plan to render the outcome of the four-year conflict more meaningful and long-lasting. They had just experienced the exhilaration of victory, and for African Americans and white abolitionists, that triumph encompassed the remarkable achievement of black freedom. With the overthrow of secession and slavery, and now with a martyred chief, the victors looked optimistically toward a reconstructed nation, to God's graces for themselves, and to divine punishment for their enemies, out of whose ranks had emerged the assassin. Yet catastrophe and crisis can breed contradiction, and in shaping visions for the future, Lincoln's mourners portrayed their slain leader in two different ways. On the one hand, they pointed to evidence of the president's moderation and lenience; on the other, they drew attention to hints of his political radicalism. If the lenient Lincoln was an ally of Confederates, the radical Lincoln was an ally to African Americans. Had Lincoln lived, he could hardly have been both, but while President Andrew Johnson recoiled from demands for equal rights, Lincoln's martyrdom permitted black Americans and their white friends to invoke his name in the quest for post-emancipation equality. Amid fears for the future, they looked to Lincoln's most admirable actions—and to what little he had said on the subject in his last days—to fortify their impassioned calls for justice.

MOURNING LINCOLN BEGINS WITH THE fall of the Confederate capital and the surrender of General Robert E. Lee in early April 1865. The story continues through the execution of four of the conspirators in early July, concluding with a brief look at the postwar decades. Each chapter tells a story, and together the chapters complicate the larger story of the assassination, charting the optimism evinced by the victors-turned-mourners and exposing the formidable challenges to visions of a unified nation, including fissures between black and white mourners.

The experiences of three protagonists, for whom surviving records are particularly rich, open each chapter and serve as a template for broader investigations. The first two, husband and wife Sarah and Albert Browne, were white abolitionists from Salem, Massachusetts, who despaired mightily at Lincoln's death. The third, Rodney Dorman, was a Confederate lawyer living in Jacksonville, Florida, who delighted in Lincoln's murder. The Brownes and Dorman represent two ends of the ideological spectrum and two of the most powerful ideologies of the Civil War era—abolitionism on the one hand and diehard rebeldom on the other—and thus together serve as excellent conduits through which to understand the conflicts that raged on after Union victory and Lincoln's death. Although the Brownes and

Albert Browne Sr. and Sarah Browne, about 1865.
Browne Family Papers, The Schlesinger Library, Radcliffe Institute, Harvard University.

Dorman never met, at times they seem to be talking directly to each other. Here I introduce them more fully.

The Brownes lived within a passionate ideological universe of abolitionist Protestant ethics. Though not radicals like the followers of William Lloyd Garrison—the man who publicly burned a copy of the U.S. Constitution for its complicity with slavery—they were liberal Christians (first Congregationalists, then Unitarians) who prayed for black freedom and demanded suffrage for black men. Steeped in convictions about the virtues of individual striving in a burgeoning capitalist nation, Sarah and Albert dedicated themselves to the moral superiority of free labor, a central tenet of the new Republican Party that had risen from the ashes of the antebellum Whigs. In this promising view, work was an inherently noble and dignified enterprise, and unfettered opportunity guaranteed that hard work would bring uplift and upward mobility.

When they looked to the South, antislavery Republicans like the Brownes saw both an un-Christian evil and a backward civilization of economic exploitation and stagnation. Slave labor, the exact opposite of free labor, permitted no incentive or chance for improvement and, worst of all, degraded the very act of work, thereby spreading indolence and immorality throughout the population, black and white, rich and poor. The problem was that the Brownes' brand of free-labor ideology glorified landownership just when the northern landscape was seismically shifting from farm to factory. As the North saw a steadily growing and increasingly divided population of employers and wageworkers (the latter including women and children), the Brownes held fast to their ideals, pressing for the transfer of southern land from former masters to former slaves in order to emulate a northern economic system that was already rapidly breaking down. At the same time, a conventional brand of paternalistic racism marred their earnest professions of equality.

Albert Browne was a rope manufacturer, a partner with Whiton, Browne, and Wheelwright, a maritime supply dealer in Salem and Boston. Between 1863 and 1865, he worked for the Union army, as an agent of the U.S. Treasury Department, taking charge of abandoned enemy property in South Carolina, Georgia, and Florida. General William Tecumseh Sherman remembered Albert as a "shrewd, clever Yankee," crediting him with the idea of sending a telegram about the fall of Savannah to President Lincoln in December 1864; that advice resulted in Sherman's then-and-now famous message to the president, "I beg to present you as a Christmas-gift the city of Savannah." Albert made his southern home in the town of Beaufort, on Port Royal Island in the South Carolina Sea Islands. When the Union occupied the islands early in the war, much of the native white population fled, and Beaufort's gracious homes stood empty. Along the streets, Albert likely encountered only Yankee soldiers and former slaves—one visitor saw black children playing happily, "now that the dark shadow of slavery hangs over them no more." Albert's job included raiding expeditions that yielded mostly bales of cotton left behind by fleeing Confederates, though he and his men seized everything from scrap iron to buried silver. They also halted blockade running and personally informed African Americans of their freedom.[4]

Back home in the dynamic port town of Salem, Sarah Browne tended their spacious residence at 40 Summer Street on the corner of Broad. She managed the household, including directing a group of servants (likely Irish immigrants) who lightened her day-to-day burdens considerably. Sarah sewed, tended to the family's health, and taught her younger son French and Latin. She advised her husband on professional matters, visited neighbors, and received guests. She worked hard, though with plenty of time for reading and the luxury of lying down midday whenever she felt tired. In the spring of 1865, Sarah was living with Edward, nearly twelve (two more sons had died in infancy), and Alice, in her early twenties. The eldest child, Albert Jr., had graduated from Harvard College in 1853, at eighteen the youngest member of his class. Through the war, Albert Jr. served as military secretary to Massachusetts governor John Andrew, making frequent visits home to his mother and siblings. Nellie, the Brownes' other daughter, had died the year before, at the age of twenty-two.[5]

Sarah Browne avidly kept up with the war news. Salem had supplied the Union with more than three thousand soldiers and sailors over the course of four years (out of a population of just over twenty thousand). Black residents served in the Fifty-Fourth and Fifty-Fifth Massachusetts regiments, and white residents served as their officers. Salem men fought at Bull Run and Antietam, Fredericksburg and Chancellorsville, Gettysburg and Cold Harbor. They also stepped in to quell the New York City draft riots in 1863 and marched through Georgia and the Carolinas with General Sherman. Men from Salem entered the fallen Confederate capital of Richmond at war's end, and some were present for Lee's surrender at Appomattox. When the war was over, more than a hundred came home wounded, and more than two hundred never came home at all.

Sarah and Albert's antislavery sentiments emerged even more strongly in some of their children. As a law student, Albert Jr. had gotten himself arrested for participating in a violent fight outside the Boston courthouse on behalf of a fugitive slave. At school, Nellie Browne befriended Charlotte Forten, the daughter of a well-to-do black family in Philadelphia. Forten had moved to Salem at sixteen, eager for an education unavailable in the segregated classrooms of her native city. Boarding with a family of prominent black abolitionists, she nonetheless found life trying in the "conservative, aristocratic old city of Salem," as she put it, for African Americans in and around Boston still suffered "insulting language" and could be treated as pariahs. Girls at school might be "kind and cordial," Forten confided to her diary, while out on the street "they feared to recognize me." In her journal, Forten referred to Nellie Browne as *Brownie.* "There is one young girl and only one," she wrote of Nellie, "who I believe thoroughly and heartily appreciates anti-slavery, *radical* anti-slavery and has no prejudice against color." In 1855, when Charlotte was eighteen and Nellie fourteen, the two went together to join the Salem Female Anti-Slavery Society. When Nellie left Salem to attend school in Cambridge in 1856, Charlotte missed her white friend. "More lonesome than ever now," she wrote one day, longing for Nellie's company, and on another day, "Feel sorry that *Brownie* has gone."[6]

Beginning in 1858, Sarah Browne kept a diary that would continue through 1884, the year before she died. In pocket-sized annual journals, she captured her activities and thoughts in neat handwriting. The wartime separation of husband and wife meant that the couple also wrote each other long letters during those years, and Albert's, often addressed to the whole family, were particularly loquacious, serving nearly as his own diary. In the Brownes' experiences, we find not only the complexities of shock, sorrow, and ferocious anger over Lincoln's assassination but also a record of preoccupation with private loss: the death of Nellie Browne in 1864.

IN JACKSONVILLE, RODNEY DORMAN COULD count himself a devotee of the most virulent proslavery ideology to emerge in the antebellum South, characterizing the enslavement of African Americans as economically efficient and benevolent, rooted as it was in white superiority and black inferiority. Dorman further understood black people as incapable of desiring or fighting for freedom and thus blamed meddling white abolitionists for everything that proved otherwise. For Dorman, the entire Civil War was an act of Yankee aggression that unlawfully interfered with the natural and constitutional rights of white southerners, and he rapidly became a diehard rebel, utterly despising the enemy and conceding no possibility of reconciliation. The only satisfactory sequel to Confederate defeat would be retribution and ultimate redemption.

Jacksonville lay on the Saint Johns River in the northeast corner of Florida, just inland from the Atlantic, and Dorman had arrived there as a young man, from up north. That this zealous Confederate was a native of western Massachusetts who spent part of his boyhood in Ohio is not surprising. With other economically ambitious New Englanders, Dorman had come to Florida in the late 1830s. Many such men made their fortunes in the lumber business, but Dorman became a prosperous attorney and never looked back. In 1850, nearly half the city's population was enslaved, and Dorman owned a forty-year-old black man, whom he likely hired out to the sawmills. Also in Dorman's household in 1850 lived a free black woman, listed in the census as his servant, and it's possible that their relationship encompassed sexual exploitation in return for legal freedom. Ten years later, on the eve of the Civil War, Dorman no longer owned a slave or had a live-in servant, though his personal wealth had increased five times over. He never married.[7]

Yankees had done well in northern Florida through the booming 1850s, but as sectional hostilities heated up, fierce secessionists began to accuse them of abolitionism. Maybe that's why Dorman told the census-taker in 1860 that he was born in South Carolina; by then he had so thoroughly become a southerner that he wanted no one to mistake him for anything else. In the months leading up to Lincoln's election that year, even silence could be construed as disloyalty to the Confederate cause, and self-appointed vigilance committees in Jacksonville harassed the Unionists in their midst, sometimes violently. In January 1861, Florida became the third state to secede from the Union, following South Carolina by three weeks and Mississippi by a day. (Alabama, Georgia, Louisiana, and Texas departed next, followed in the spring by Virginia, Arkansas, Tennessee, and North Carolina.)

Dorman's home, which included his law office, stood downtown on Pine Street (present-day Main Street), just west of the intersection of Ocean and Bay. Over the course of the war, Jacksonville changed drastically. The Union blockade of the Saint Johns halted the city's lively river trade, and the Confederate army claimed most of its young white men. Slaves either escaped or were forced by their masters into the interior, and many of the northerners who clung to Unionist sentiments fled as well. The homes and churches that lined the once elegant, gaslit streets soon stood empty and shuttered. Weeds choked the sidewalks, the railroad depot lay abandoned, and merchants' once crowded shelves held precious few goods.[8]

Even as other well-to-do Confederate men departed with their families, Rodney Dorman stayed, and for him the pivotal event of the Civil War was the third of four Union occupations of Jacksonville. This mission, cut short after a mere three weeks in March 1863, had been intended as a grand one. Two months earlier, Lincoln had issued the Emancipation Proclamation, declaring legal freedom for all slaves in areas in rebellion against the United States and providing for the enlistment of black men into the Union army. Now the Florida expedition was to be undertaken by the First and Second South Carolina regiments, the first black units of the Civil War, recruited from the ranks of former slaves and led by white abolitionists. Colonel Thomas Wentworth Higginson, commanding the First South Carolina, envisioned the assignment as a moral and political endeavor to prove the capabilities of black soldiers and to help destroy slavery: the presence of black troops would facilitate freedom, as slaves in the Deep South escaped to Union lines. It's possible that the slave once owned by Rodney Dorman fought with these first black regiments; some of the men were from northern Florida, and as Higginson noted, "Many were owned here & do not love the people." Indeed, the expedition's other explicit purpose was to unsettle local whites. A black woman who traveled with the regiment remembered Jacksonville Confederates as "bitterly against our people," and Dorman accordingly called them "Higginson's nigger occupation."[9]

Rodney Dorman was apoplectic as the occupiers took over his city and threatened imprisonment for any white resident who refused to take an oath of allegiance to the United States. At some point, Dorman left home to live with other refugees west of the city, near enough to make his way in and out of the main streets as he pleased (though he would never take the oath). Then, just when Colonel Higginson decided to raid the interior, higher-ups suddenly ordered the Union regiments out of Jacksonville, probably because white troops were needed in Charleston and the black regiments could not sustain the Florida operation alone. Most observers agreed that it was the white soldiers who set fire to the city, just before leaving. Some said that black men helped out or at least watched with satisfaction as the spring breezes fanned the flames. When the vessels left the docks, a good third of Jacksonville was burning. Fire consumed Dorman's entire home and law office, scorching even his fences and shrubbery. Sure that the Union forces had invaded his property before they set the building aflame, Dorman declared his losses in a claim filed with the Confederate government: more than sixteen thousand dollars' worth of property, either stolen or burned. In the same distinctively flat and wide handwriting found in his journals, Dorman itemized everything, from furniture, firearms, and fishing equipment to a gold watch, a chess set, and a silk umbrella—even a hat brush and a dog whistle. Most egregious of all was the destruction of his nearly four-hundred-volume law library.[10]

Union forces, including the black men of the Fifty-Fourth Massachusetts, returned to occupy Jacksonville in early 1864, and this time they

Newly free African Americans in Jacksonville, Florida, pose in front of the building appro-
priated as the Union Provost Marshal's office, in 1864. The presence of freedpeople and
Union army soldiers, especially black soldiers, continually infuriated Rodney Dorman.
Courtesy of Jacksonville Historical Society, with assistance of Dr. Daniel R. Schafer.

stayed. One soldier described the city as "heaps of ashes." Another saw
former slaves meeting hungry former mistresses in the sutler stores and
noted the once grand homes of white people serving as hospitals for his
comrades. In early April, President Lincoln conveyed his pleasure to the
abolitionist general David Hunter. "I am glad to see the accounts of your
colored force at Jacksonville," he wrote. "It is important to the enemy that
such a force shall not take shape and grow and thrive in the South, and
in precisely the same proportion it is important to us that it *shall.*" Still,
Rodney Dorman declined to leave, for Jacksonville was the only home he
knew. Just to walk in and out of town, he now needed a pass, which he felt
sure Union officials would deny him in light of his refusal to take the oath.
But Dorman managed to exempt himself from declaring allegiance to the
United States by having someone vouch for him—probably his brother, the
better-known lawyer Orloff Dorman, who had moved from New England
to Chicago to Saint Augustine. Orloff, who had remained a Unionist and
served as a paymaster for the Union army in the Department of the South
(the Civil War did indeed pit brother against brother), likely assured the
occupying authorities that Rodney generally minded his own business.[11]

By the time the Confederacy surrendered, Rodney Dorman lived a mostly isolated life. Though he recorded occasional interactions with like-minded locals, his journal was his steadiest companion. The first extant tome (the volume covering 1862 and 1863 was destroyed in the fire) opens in 1864, and six more take him through 1886. Each notebook, free of printed dates, contains hundreds of pages of writing. The third and fourth volumes comprise the year 1865 and run nearly seven hundred pages apiece. Dorman later entitled his wartime journals "Memoranda of Events that transpired at Jacksonville, Florida, & in its vicinity; with some remarks & comments thereon," the last phrase referring to the fact that he inserted additional commentary when he copied them over in the postwar years. Dorman penned lengthy meditations on legal and historical subjects, but the diaries also gave him a place to vent his fury, sheltering extended rants against the federal government, the enemy army, President Lincoln, northern politicians, and especially Yankee abolitionists—people just like Sarah and Albert Browne.

LONG AFTER I SELECTED MY protagonists, I discovered that the Brownes and Rodney Dorman had crossed paths, if obliquely, during the Civil War. In the spring of 1864, Dorman wrote angrily about a "cow-stealing raid" up the Saint Johns River led by one General Birney. He mentioned a local newspaper account of the raid, written by the U.S. treasury agent, a man named Browne (spelled with an *e,* he noted), a tale Dorman found infuriatingly self-aggrandizing, not to mention self-incriminating. Indeed, Albert Browne had been part of that expedition. Moreover, Sarah, Eddie, Alice, and Nellie had left New England that April for an extended visit south, and while Albert was off on his raid, the rest of the family made an excursion to Jacksonville. Sarah found the city disappointing, wrecked as it was by the "havoc of war," but they all nonetheless had a lovely time as guests of the Union commanders, touring the splendid mansion appropriated for army headquarters, enjoying teatime on the veranda, taking leisurely boat rides, and visiting the men of the U.S. Colored Troops. The family also visited with one Lyman Stickney, the U.S. tax collector to whom Rodney Dorman would later write an angry letter in reference to his destroyed property. When Albert Browne returned in soiled and tattered clothing, he regaled the family with accounts not only of captured cattle and cotton but also of black people whom he and his men had alerted to emancipation. A year later, Sarah sorted through a parlor closet in Salem during spring cleaning, arranging "little mementoes from Beaufort, St. Augustine—Jacksonville."[12]

FOR SARAH AND ALBERT BROWNE and for Rodney Dorman—just as for so many others—thinking about, articulating, and documenting their responses to the assassination of President Abraham Lincoln became part of working out an understanding of the war. The polyphonic din that followed that night at Ford's Theatre pointed toward long-lasting legacies that remain part of our world today.

We begin as the battlefield war drew to a close, in early April 1865. At that moment, the call to find meaning had already taken on a new urgency. How would Union victory play out? What did Confederate defeat portend? What kind of nation would the people and their leaders create? Black freedom had been seized and delivered, but would it last? Peace would soon be declared, but could it endure? How could Confederates be brought back into the citizenry? Where and how would former slaves live and work? Could they become citizens too? The pages that follow explore the thoughts, feelings, beliefs, convictions, and questions of Lincoln's mourners and his antagonists as they confronted an event that transformed both the Civil War and the nation's history.

1

Victory and Defeat

SARAH BROWNE WAS EXUBERANT. Exclamation points marched across the pages of her diary, four in a row. In the first hours of Monday, April 3, 1865, news had come into the Salem telegraph office reporting General Grant's probable victory at Petersburg. Soon after Sarah heard the ringing bells at four o'clock that afternoon, she learned that the Union army had entered Richmond. Telegrams reported the city burning and Grant pursuing Lee, and the next day's papers told of a crowd gathering in Washington to listen to Secretary of War Edwin Stanton announce the fall of the Confederate capital. That intelligence merited another four exclamation points. From the newspaper columns, Sarah selected particular facts. "Rebels flying toward Lynchburg. Our losses less than 7,000," she wrote. "Sheridan has headed off Lee!!" By Friday, April 7, the headline of the *Boston Evening Transcript* declared the news glorious: six rebel generals captured, Mobile likely to fall, Lee's troops cut off from Lynchburg, and President Lincoln in Richmond, walking among the Union soldiers and now-free black population. "All over the North are wild with joy," Sarah wrote. "Joy—Joy every where!" To continue with her usual household tasks seemed nearly impossible.[1]

At four o'clock in the morning on Monday, April 10, the Browne household was roused by bells and gunfire, followed by voices calling out that Lee and his entire army had surrendered. Sarah and the children hurried out of bed to illuminate the outdoor gaslights and unfurl a flag from an upstairs window. In the predawn darkness, neighbors blew horns and tossed firecrackers. In the daylight, walking through Salem, Sarah exchanged happy greetings with everyone who had come outdoors to celebrate, and the news garnered eight exclamation points in her diary. At a special service that week, the minister at church spoke boldly of black suffrage, and Sarah felt grateful to God. It was only when she read through the speech President Lincoln had delivered from the White House on April 11, laying out his ideas for reconstructing the nation, that her mood shifted. "I am much disappointed at finding it unmistakably conservative," she sighed. "Why can't he cut down the whole tree, instead of lopping off the branches?"[2]

Down south, at the same moment, Albert Browne was marveling over the fall of Richmond. "How fast I have lived these past two years," he exulted. "What a grand period in history is the present moment." The South, Albert believed, could now emerge from feudalism into the "glorious splendor of the nineteenth century." And to think of the elevation of Negroes! "A man is a man, be he black, white, or grey," he wrote to his family up north.[3]

After Lee's surrender, came the re-raising of the Union flag over Fort Sumter in South Carolina, where Confederates had won the first battle of the war. Albert was there now, four years later, among those listening reverently to the abolitionist New York minister Henry Ward Beecher, and it was a day he would never forget, a day he hoped his children and grandchildren would never forget, a day "most grand, imposing and soul inspiring." The battered walls of the fort. The defiant, high-flying flag. The triumph. The glory. Albert described everything in a letter home, even the way the chairs were arranged for the speakers. That was the easy part—it was his emotions that he couldn't convey, for everything was "*unspeakable*" (he underlined that word). Late into the night, lying awake, Albert heard the public prayers of hundreds of former slaves gathered in the streets of Charleston, praising God for freedom. How unabashedly symbolic was the return to Sumter to raise the Union flag once again over the fort, bringing full circle the revolutionary changes wrought by four years of terrible war! "The sights I have seen," Albert Browne told his wife and children, "are written with a piece of steel on my memory."[4]

AS APRIL ARRIVED IN JACKSONVILLE, Rodney Dorman was in despair over the city's unsanitary conditions: the torn-up sidewalks layered thickly with sand and soil, the heaps of foul trash and fish carcasses fermenting under the southern sun. Worse, though, were the enemy occupiers. If they didn't pack up soon, and take their "nonsensical, outrageous-to-humanity dogmas & knavery" with them, Dorman wrote in his journal, he would have to find a way to leave. Most horrific of all, the gunboats from Fernandina and Charleston brought in the northern newspapers proclaiming Confederate defeat. The Union men in his midst cheered and hugged, fired a two-hundred-gun salute, lit rockets, set barrels of tar afire, and got drunk, all of which sent Dorman into a rage, the flames from their tar barrels perhaps conjuring visions of his own torched home. The black soldiers irked him the most, even though he was sure their white comrades and the northern missionaries had put them up to their insolent behavior, since the white Yankees were, he fumed into his diary, "blacker than the negroes." Why should he believe the news, anyway? After all, there had been a dozen false reports that Richmond had fallen. Still unconvinced, even in the face of the carousing Yankees, Dorman wrote the words "if the North succeeds in this war." Soon enough, he was confronted with a jubilant meeting of African Americans at the Methodist church led by, he could only scowl, "some negro, abolitionist incendiary chaplain." If only, he pled, "a thunder bolt would grind the whole of them to powder."[5]

Dorman then turned his thoughts to Abraham Lincoln, whose name he always wrote as *Lincon,* intentionally misspelling the second syllable to emphasize the scoundrel's wily nature. The collapse of the Confederacy was, he reasoned, akin to the Roman defeat of Carthage or the English defeat of the Irish: a tyrant had gotten his military victory, but now he had a badly fractured country on his hands, one he would never be able to control. Turning pensive for only a moment, Dorman paused his tirade. "Summer is coming on now, & I don't know what I am going to do," he wrote. "It will be intolerable to spend it here, & I don't know where else I can go." Jacksonville had become hell incarnate, and he no longer had a home.[6]

Dorman read all about the Union flag raising at Sumter in those late-arriving New York newspapers too—"some kind of a tom-foolery celebration" by a bunch of "fools & knaves," he called it. How Dorman hated Henry Beecher, leading the festivities in South Carolina, gabbling to his geese, more wicked than the devil himself. That Beecher wasn't a radical like William Lloyd Garrison made no difference. It was all the same, the Yankee preacher's shameful charisma and activism having spread antislavery ideology like wildfire. For Rodney Dorman, not even "a hundred hangings" would be enough for Henry Ward Beecher.[7]

RICHMOND HAD FALLEN! ON SUNDAY, April 2, 1865, the white congregation at Saint Paul's Church watched as the sexton entered to deliver a message, then watched President Jefferson Davis slip out of his pew. The worshippers soon learned that the telegram, from Robert E. Lee, had alerted Davis that the city would shortly come under Union control. Davis left the Confederate capital that night, soon to be followed by the rest of his government. With impending occupation, white residents could stay or go, and the streets were chaotic, crowded with loaded-down horses, carriages, and wagons. Rebel troops would burn parts of the city on their way out.

When Union troops marched in the next morning, they sang "Babylon Is Fallen." Union soldiers, black and white, met crowds of black men and women who shook their hands, blessed them, and thanked God for answering their prayers. "You've come at last," they said. "We've been looking for you." Their people had fought for freedom, and now they were free. The elderly praised God that they had lived to see the day. Right from the start, the runaway slave and abolitionist Frederick Douglass had proclaimed the Civil War "a war for and against slavery," and from the start, black men had pressed the federal government to let them fight. But even now, for some, the downfall of Richmond could barely avenge generations of enslavement. "They sold my father, they murdered my mother," one freedman said. Another looked around at the wounded Confederates, wanting to do violence to every one of them.[8]

Meanwhile, when the news reached a black school in Norfolk, the boys and girls gave three cheers, then sang "Colored Volunteer" and "Battle Cry of Freedom," enunciating the words *Not a man shall be a slave* and *Union forever*. When they came to "John Brown's Body," with the words *We'll hang Jeff Davis from the sour apple tree,* a little girl named Rose wanted to know if the Confederate president had been sent to the gallows. A little boy announced he was "glad Uncle Sam beat the Secesh," and with the help of the missionary teachers from up north, the children made wreathes and banners for the upcoming parade. They talked of finding parents or siblings who had been sold away or forced by their masters to leave the city during the war. Rose felt indignant when she learned that Jefferson Davis was still alive, but Union victory now seemed certain, and that meant freedom forever.[9]

The next day, Tuesday, April 4, President Lincoln arrived in Richmond, holding the hand of his twelve-year-old son, Tad, as he walked among the people. All along the route to the former executive mansion—where Lincoln would sit at the desk of the fleeing Jefferson Davis—thousands of overjoyed African Americans encircled and followed, spreading word of Lincoln's presence. Some of the city's middling and poorer whites joined in, but it was the black residents who shouted praises to God, calling the president "father" or "master Abraham." The black Philadelphia journalist Thomas Morris Chester was already referring to his people as citizens in his dispatches. At a jubilee celebration, black families filled every church pew and aisle. Outside, people climbed up to the windows, the crowd so immense that many stood too far away to hear a single word.[10]

"We thought Lincoln was risking too much to go into Richmond," wrote Annie Dudley, a white woman who worked at the Bureau of Indian Affairs in Washington, "very much afraid he would get killed by some of those defeated arch rebels."[11]

The news of Richmond's fall came to Union troops by telegram, with mounted officers galloping along the lines, or by northern newspapers delivered by passing locomotives or docking steamers. The men threw their hats in the air and cheered. "By jove I never thought men had such lungs," exclaimed a Michigan soldier. They threw their shoes in the air too, fired muskets and cannons, lit firecrackers, jumped up and down, and danced to the music of regimental bands. Soldiers who got word at nine in the morning reveled till past midnight, gulping whiskey and malt liquor. "Glory to God!" an Ohio man wrote in the pages of the address book he used as a wartime diary. In Tennessee, a bunch of soldiers repeatedly fired a cannon in front of a Confederate residence until every pane of glass was smashed,

President Lincoln walks through the streets of Richmond, Virginia, just after the Confederate capital fell to the Union. In this 1866 drawing, Lincoln holds the hand of his twelve-year-old son, Tad, while African Americans celebrate their freedom and pay tribute to their "best friend."

Picture Collection, The Branch Libraries, The New York Public Library, Astor, Lenox and Tilden Foundations.

then joked that the burning building could now pass for an illuminated Unionist home. When word arrived at the Union hospitals, the sick and wounded could all of a sudden "bear their pain better."[12]

Wild. Crazy. Agog. That's how people described the mood when the news reached the northern home front. In Wilmington, New York, Cincinnati, Chicago, Sacramento, and everywhere in between, it was huzzas, songs, speeches, pealing church chimes and clanging fire bells, tooting steam whistles and roaring guns and cannons. Crowds collected around the newspaper and telegraph offices. Classroom doors burst open as teachers dismissed school. Washington was in an intoxicated uproar all day April 3 and for three days afterward, the White House "resplendent with candles," the Capitol dome decorated with "tiers of lights." The War Department and Post Office were lit up too, and in front of the Patent Office, gas jets spelled the word *Union* in enormous letters.[13]

"Richmond has fallen," Emilie Davis wrote in her Philadelphia diary. The young woman's words were spare but the occasion grand, for her brothers had fought with black units in the war, she had attended an emancipation celebration in 1863, and she had listened to Frederick Douglass deliver a lecture only a few months earlier. Young folks in the city, both black and white, took in the illuminations on Chestnut, Walnut, and Arch Streets, and to sixteen-year-old Margaret Howell, the night felt like "New Year's Eve, Christmas Eve, and Fourth of July all combined." In Boston, boys piled into a wagon, waving flags and handkerchiefs, shaking rattles and banging drums, stopping in front of each house to shout the news and catch an answering cheer in return. At the state legislature, the men adjourned and broke into "Old John Brown." When the news reached the California mining town of Weaverville, the workers quit and took their families dancing at the local theater late into the night. Across the Atlantic, the U.S. consul and future novelist William Dean Howells had been entertaining American guests at his home in Venice when word came (it was late April by then), prompting exultation and "great handshaking."[14]

Like Emilie Davis, and like Sarah and Albert Browne, those who counted themselves foes of slavery were immeasurably overjoyed. At eighty-seven years old, John Prentiss of New Hampshire had prayed he would live to see the day. The rebels had fought for slavery as their "*Corner Stone*," the elderly white man wrote in his diary, referring to the 1861 "cornerstone speech" of Alexander Stephens, in which the Confederate vice president had proclaimed the "great truth that the negro is not equal to the white man," that enslavement was his natural condition. Now, Prentiss rejoiced, the slaveholders were "doomed *forever*." Abolitionists knew this was the work of God.[15]

TO THE VICTORS, THE ENTIRE nation appeared to be celebrating, but that impression was accurate only if they ignored the evidence of Confederate distress. For Secretary of the Navy Gideon Welles it seemed the "entire population" was celebrating in the streets of Washington, even as he noted in his diary that all secessionists living in the capital "must have retired." Notably, the Confederates themselves refrained from describing scenes of universal celebration; Henry Berkeley, an imprisoned private from Lee's army, named the revelers only as "all yankeedom." True, some of Richmond's white residents joined in the festivities, but most stayed inside. Union soldiers could read their "sour faces," reflecting both anguish and apprehension. Thomas Morris Chester could see them standing silently at their front steps or peering from their windows. He knew it was an occasion they had scarcely ever imagined, and for the vanquished it was frightening indeed. Henri Garidel, in town from Louisiana, watched as black people greeted his conquerors amid billowing Union flags. Listening to their hurrahs, his heart felt "heavy as a mountain." Lincoln's carriage, it seemed to Garidel, was "followed by the entire Negro population of Richmond," and now his own heart was breaking. Nor was every white person up north thrilled—one New Yorker surmised that the "contemptable Copperheads" were keeping quiet out of fear, some even deceitfully waving flags, despite their hatred of Lincoln, black people, and the whole Civil War.[16]

For Lee's men, the last months in the Army of Northern Virginia had been an ordeal of despair and exhaustion accompanied by steady desertion. A member of the Richmond Howitzers, watching the bursting mortar shells through the night, thought "the world would fall to pieces." Civilians invoked the language of doom too. "Every body is dying with the blues," Amanda Edmunds wrote from her family's thousand-acre Virginia plantation. Diehard rebels tried mightily to keep up their spirits, but Yankee glee made it worse, or maybe it was their pious gratitude. Seventeen-year-old Emma LeConte had been living in Columbia, South Carolina, in February, when the combined actions of Union soldiers, slaves, evacuating Confederates, and escaped prisoners set the city afire, sparing the college campus where her father taught. The family also owned a large plantation, and now LeConte had to suffer heretofore unknown hardships, reading by candlelight instead of gas and wearing undergarments cut from rough cloth. Still, anything was worth avoiding surrender. "The South *will* not give up," she wrote in her diary. "I can not think that." As for President Lincoln, the Richmond papers echoed the people's sentiments. He was a fool and a tyrant.[17]

Unthinkable or not, rumors of surrender—originating from speculation, a wish, a worry, or a lie—began the day after Richmond fell. A Union soldier had to discard a jubilant letter announcing the capitulation of Lee's whole army; "as it isn't so," he wrote, "I begin again, crestfallen." Michigan soldiers in camp near Detroit heard that Robert E. Lee had surrendered, then that it was only Fitzhugh Lee, cavalry commander in his uncle's army. On the home front, Wilmington Unionists celebrated surrender until the evening papers set the record straight. In Boston, a postman stopped Anna Lowell on the street to impart the thrilling news of final victory, which all too soon, she lamented, "proved *bogus.*" Rumors also overtook the Confederates. Prisoners at Fort Delaware heard talk of the "heartsickening" possibility, while rebel soldiers in Texas heard that Robert E. Lee had been killed.[18]

When the real news came, the most critical part was that Lee had surrendered his entire army, with not a remnant left to fight. Just days after the fall of Richmond, the general and his escaping troops had found themselves surrounded and trapped by the forces of Generals Ulysses S. Grant and Philip Sheridan. Lee had been hoping to meet up with General Joseph E. Johnston in North Carolina, but by the evening of April 6, as Confederate desertion continued apace, the Army of the Potomac overpowered the men at a place called Sayler's Creek, ending in more than seven thousand Confederate casualties and prisoners. On April 7, Grant proposed the enemy's surrender, and over the next two days, messengers conveyed a series of exchanges through the lines, until the two generals agreed to convene in the Virginia village of Appomattox Court House, about a hundred miles west of Richmond. The morning of April 9 saw a brief and ultimately futile Confederate assault, and soon Lee arrived to concede defeat. The surrender of the Army of Northern Virginia was not technically synonymous with Confederate surrender, since fragments of other armies remained in the field, and through late May there would be skirmishes from North Carolina to Texas. But it didn't matter anymore. The *entire army:* that was the phrase Grant used in his communication to Sherman, and that was the point Sherman passed on to the officers and soldiers. It was the part that echoed over and over, from the lips of Tennessee farmers to the pens of abolitionist Boston ladies. Lee's surrender made inevitable the end of the Confederacy.[19]

Rippling outward, beginning that day and extending for weeks into the remotest corners of the nation, word traveled. At Appomattox, African Americans lined the road to honor Union soldiers. Something so long prayed for, "yet it seems impossible that it has come," wrote Thomas Morris Chester in Richmond, as he watched elderly men and women weep, pray in gratitude, and call out their jubilations. In that once capital city, former slaves congregated—some well dressed, others in field-hand rags—to promenade and sing about John Brown. Children jumped rope and rolled hoops. To the heartbroken Confederate Henri Garidel, the "shouts of joy of the Negroes" made the city "tremble as much as the cannon." On Roanoke Island off North Carolina, freedmen and women bowed their heads in prayer, then gave three cheers and sang "The Star-Spangled Banner." The city of Charleston was "wild with rejoicing" as black celebrants sang "Glory to God."[20]

Black and white Union soldiers mostly expressed their elation with deafening noise. The men of a Connecticut regiment had been advancing on the rebel army when an aide-de-camp rode beside the line to relay the news, prompting instant cheers "from a hundred thousand throats." A Vermont soldier at Appomattox found himself among acres of troops yelling and discharging weapons amid "Toasts and cheers and music," followed by "music cheers and Toasts." At City Point, Virginia, General George Meade rode down the line in a carriage, tossing his hat in the air, turning a weary march of the 139th New York into a euphoric parade. In camp in North Carolina, soldiers formed an obedient row to hear an officer read a telegram, then went wild. When word arrived via northern newspapers delivered to a dock or a depot, the reaction was the same.[21]

Everywhere, the men "kicked up" and "hurrahed good." They did handstands, rolled in the springtime mud, and drank whatever liquor was at hand ("I could dance a double shuffle for 6 hours if I had half a pint," claimed a limping soldier). Regimental musicians—fife and drum, brass bands—kept up the bedlam. In Raleigh it sounded as though "every tree in the surrounding woods was screaming." In East Tennessee, the all-night roar of the musketry resonated across the landscape just the same as a battle. From army hospital beds, even the most mangled soldiers reveled in the news. A week later, it still seemed "almost incredible," as if the men would wake up to find their enemies as determined as ever. Thinking of Robert E. Lee, one man "had a sort of impression that we should fight him all our lives." Marching in North Carolina, white Union soldiers tore down a slave whipping post and set it on fire.[22]

WHITE SOUTHERNERS EVERYWHERE, like Rodney Dorman in Jacksonville, reacted with astonishment of an entirely different order. A retreating officer likened the turn of events to "a thunderbolt from heaven." For the Confederate army, Lee's surrender completed the gloom of Richmond's downfall. The imprisoned private Henry Berkeley described a "most intense mental anxiety." Already heavy hearts sank faster with each crack of celebratory Yankee gunfire. One Virginia lieutenant called it the "*saddest day of my life*," underlining each word. For a Tennessee private, the whole world had stopped. "Minutes seem days, and days are months," he wrote in his diary. In Texas, an army surgeon found himself haunted by "rivers of blood, Southern blood," flowing through a ruined landscape of mourning widows and orphaned children. A few of the men refused to believe it was true. "Sick at heart, but not conquered yet," wrote the Tennessee private. Or as a Virginia rebel retorted to a Yankee, "It ain't over yet." For most, though, the war was indeed over, at least for now. Across two pages of his journal, Captain Henry Chambers of the Forty-Ninth North Carolina poured out his "bitter, bitter humiliation." With Yankees, including Negro soldiers, in the role of taunting conquerors, all hope of southern independence was "blasted!" When rain fell, Chambers picked up on the metaphor. "Nature weeps over Liberty's death," he wrote, diligently ignoring emancipation, since liberty was for white people only.[23]

If rain felt like nature's tears, Confederate men joined in, unembarrassed. At Appomattox, everyone from privates to officers "broke down and wept like little children," one man recorded, "and Oh, Lord! I cried too." When General Lee bade his men good-bye, "not a dry eye could be seen," another wrote, and many "sobbed aloud in uncontrollable anguish." The man didn't know how long this ritual went on, for as soon as he shook hands with Lee, he left the scene, "almost blind of tears." For Henri Garidel, the grief of defeat took a toll on his body. "My heart was so heavy that I was almost suffocating," he wrote the day after Lee's surrender, his symptoms spreading to include a stomach ailment and heartburn. "Unhappiness," he reported, "is going to kill me."[24]

Gloom and anger engulfed the Confederate home front. In Richmond, Lucy Fletcher had seen the crowds of black people in the streets (deceived by the Yankees into leaving their masters, she felt sure), actually "enjoying themselves," she spluttered, "negro & Yankee, Yankee & negro, ad nauseum." After Union victory, she sat alone inside a shattered church, unable to quiet the "anxious forebodings," as she pled with God to "overrule this terrible calamity." Time felt distorted, just as it had for men in the field. For nineteen-year-old Mary Cabell in Lynchburg, the shock turned weeks into years, then compressed years into days. When Cabell thought back to the rebel victory at Fort Sumter and the jubilee that had followed Virginia's secession five days later, surrender felt like "a wild, dreadful, bewildering dream." The mood around Eliza Andrews in Mayfield, Georgia, was one of "complete revulsion," with no more talk of "fighting to the last ditch," since, she conceded, "the last ditch has already been reached." Emma Le-Conte was simply incredulous: "*We* give up to the *Yankees!* How *can* it be?" Why, if the problem was inferior numbers, then Jefferson Davis should have called out the women, for "we would go and *fight,* too." The future was impossible to imagine, unless you thought about leaving the United States altogether, or maybe committing suicide.[25]

Unionists in the border states of Delaware, Maryland, Kentucky, and Missouri, where the white population had divided sharply over the war, marked the occasion in ways that reflected local dissension. To Anna Ferris in Wilmington, the pealing bells seemed to be ringing in a thousand years of peace, while in Lexington, a small crowd of soldiers, poor whites, and African Americans remained subdued. In Baltimore, bells rang and cannons fired, but many white residents refused even to place a candle in their windows. One black man at first thought all the nighttime noise signaled a rebel attack. "Surrender of Lee and his whole Caboodles," he wrote when definitive word came. "Bully for Grant."[26]

Up north, it was easier for the victors to imagine their own exhilaration as universal. Sextons rang church bells, women rang dinner bells, men fired the town cannons, boys burst firecrackers, and housewives and servants got to work sewing bunting, cutting streamers from white flannel, and searching for scraps of complementary red and blue. In Washington, from the White House to the humblest homes of freedpeople, "light answered light," wrote Julia Shepard, taking in the calcium illumination on public buildings, the bonfires and bursting rockets in the streets, and the windows lit up by a million candles that made midnight look like noontime. Downtown Chicago blazed with bonfires at eleven o'clock at night, and in Hartford a street carnival lasted till dawn. In New York the next morning, a newsboy breathlessly hawked the extra, calling out, "Surrender of Lee's army, ten cents and no mistake."[27]

When Mary Peck heard the church bells ringing off schedule, she at first thought someone had died in her tiny town near Albany. When she wrote the word "victory" in a letter to her husband at the front, she underlined it and added two exclamation points; the words "Lee has surrendered" merited a triple underline. Pausing from her domestic chores, Peck watched as farmers passing along the road threw their caps in the air and cheered. How she longed to join them, but "I am a woman," she wrote, "so I only said *Thank God!* & went in the house—& *cried.*" With her young son shouting, "Mama we've whipped the rebels," the family's two black servants quit work and took the boy into town to celebrate. In Cincinnati, African Americans hoisted a sign reading, "All men are born equal." In Sacramento, residents burned Jefferson Davis in effigy. In Iowa, Hattie Schenck thought she could see the horses making merry, and in New Hampshire, Henry Thacher thought even "inanimate matter" was filled with joy. Everywhere, Union supporters prayed, for victory was a sure sign of God's graces.[28]

Prayer was more trying for Confederates, who had convinced themselves all through the war that God favored their cause. Now as they asked for reversal and retribution, they could attribute the outcome only to divine mystery or maybe to their own sins. Ardent rebel Ellen House surmised that her people had "depended too much" on General Lee and "too little on God." In Norfolk, twenty-one-year-old Cloe Whittle made herself read the Bible before she could bring herself to think about God's will. Even then, she couldn't fathom the Lord's purposes, and neither could anyone she knew. It wasn't simply that the Confederacy had lost. It was that black men had fought in the uniforms of the conquering army, and now black people were free. God was working out his plan, she recited, as if by rote, but it was "so hard, hard, very hard" to make sense of it. After all, didn't the Bible condone slavery? For Whittle, as for so many of her compatriots, the quest to understand became an ongoing spiritual endeavor. In mid-June, she would still be begging God for guidance. "I feel in a measure calmed & soothed by leaving the fate of my beloved country in my Father's hands," she ventured, still thinking of the failed nation as her homeland. Yet the sight of Yankees occupying the streets made it impossible to stifle the humiliation and bitterness.[29]

Abraham Lincoln had invoked God's will, alongside the horrors of slavery, in his second inaugural address only a month before the Confederacy's end, calling North and South alike guilty in sustaining human bondage. God, Lincoln had said then, would make the war continue "until every drop of blood drawn with the lash, shall be paid by another drawn with the sword." Now abolitionists readily connected victory to the end of human bondage, recording the final overthrow of the "hell-born slave-holders' rebellion" and proclaiming the American flag a symbol of freedom for people "of every color." At the same time, at least some white victors assumed the conquered rebels to be acquiescent. Because Union army chaplain Hallock Armstrong felt sure the southern planters were "more than eager to give up slavery," he also believed that the North should "forgive and forget." Quaker Anna Ferris likewise shunned a "cruel or vindictive triumph," advocating "pity & mercy for the fallen foe." Union success, she reasoned, was Confederate salvation, and both sides would regenerate together through policies of moderation and magnanimity.[30]

But images of a united nation moving forward came more readily to white people. Black abolitionists, for their part, sounded notes of caution. "If we feel less disposed to join in the shouts of victory which fill the skies," the editors of the *New York Anglo-African* wrote, "it is because with the cessation of the war our anxieties begin." That was an ominous assertion in the face of euphoric festivities, but the end of bondage, they made clear, nevertheless left "an immense margin for oppressions akin to slavery." At Faneuil Hall in Boston, Frederick Douglass sounded a similar note, informing his listeners on April 4 that "hereafter, at the South, the negro will be looked upon with a fiercer and intenser hate than ever before."[31]

Skeptical Union supporters also interrupted their revelry to ponder the mild, even indulgent, terms of Confederate surrender. White abolitionist Lydia Maria Child felt "weary of seeing the U.S. bow before those arrogant rebels," for it seemed to her that Robert E. Lee had conducted himself more like a righteous conqueror than a defeated traitor. Indeed, she worried that the lenient terms of surrender would only make Confederates "*more* arrogant." In Boston, Mary Putnam was indignant that Lee and his officers could take their sidearms home, and Caroline Dunstan took every flag out of her New York windows, "mortified at what I consider Grants surrender to Lee," she wrote. One soldier in the field deplored the release of Confederate prisoners who swore loyalty to the Union; watching Virginia men "squirm considerably" as the provost marshal administered the oath of allegiance on April 9, he judged every one of the pledgers "a rebel at heart," suddenly in need of protection from the government they had fought to overthrow. General John Wolcott Phelps expressed disgust that Lee's farewell to his troops mentioned duty to "*their country*" and invoked inferior numbers as the sole cause of defeat. "There was no admission of error or wrong," Phelps fumed, with Lee evincing an "unbroken spirit" and appearing to reserve the possibility of "future opposition." Perhaps the editors of the *Anglo-African* said it best: Confederates would "lay down their arms to-day in the hope of taking them up again at a future day," with "larger hopes of success." Confederate women too, the black journalists warned, "brood rebellion," teaching their children to hate the Yankees.[32]

EVEN AS THE VICTORS REJOICED, few dispensed with the doings of everyday life. As fourteen-year-old Sarah Putnam told her diary, "Mr. Charles Mills is killed. Oh! dear! Lillie Jackson is engaged to Mr. Henry Winsor. *Richmond is surrendered to us!!!!!* Everybody is happy with the news. Grandma Upham came to tea." Putnam's ingenuous sentences intertwined the momentous war tidings with ever-present news of battlefront casualties and an imminent marriage that signaled the forward march of daily life. She also took a moment to record something much more mundane: teatime with her grandmother. Someone, whether Grandma Upham or a servant, had to brew and serve that tea, and for northern women, neither the news of Richmond's fall nor that of Lee's surrender suspended their domestic duties. Accordingly, after a night sitting up with the baby, Rachel Cormany ironed, made the beds, mended, and bordered a shawl. Only after recording those chores did she note in her diary the firing of guns in honor of Petersburg and Richmond. A week later, Elizabeth Cabot followed the exclamation "Lee's army surrender!" with "I put up furs and woolens all day." Laboring men also blurred the glorious and the humdrum, like John Orton of Kalamazoo, Michigan, who remembered April 14 with a diary entry that read, "Took little load of stove wood to Lockport, sold hams at 20, Government has ordered recruiting stopped, Lee having Surrendered. Split rails." Men in the service did the same. From the Spanish port city of Cádiz, escaped slave and Union navy sailor William Gould was a kindred spirit to Sarah Putnam, recording the mail's tidings this way: "Heard of the marrage of Miss R.K. to V.R.," followed by, "Heard of the Surrender of Lee to Grant of his entire force."[33]

None of that diminished the import of the historic news. It was more that everyday life persisted in tandem with even the grandest of national and global events. If victory made it feel momentarily as if all the world had stopped, in fact it had not stopped at all, a truth made especially apparent in the continuing casualties. Like Sarah Putnam with her consternation ("Mr. Charles Mills is killed. Oh! dear!"), Sophia Perry was about to celebrate Lee's capitulation by illuminating her Maine home when a friend came in with the news that a neighbor's husband had been killed in battle. "I took far less pleasure than I anticipated," Perry wrote. "I could not keep his poor wife out of my mind." The man had been home on furlough so recently, she lamented, "and now—can never come again."[34]

Still, comfort came to the victors in the knowledge not only that the toll of battlefield deaths would soon cease, but also that no life had been given in vain. For Confederates, by contrast, the persistence of everyday life felt far different. Mississippi planter Alden Forbes wrote in his diary about the difficulty of planting potatoes in the rain, then recorded that he had ridden into town and "heard of the surrender." All that week, Forbes charted the progress of his farm labor, occasionally adding news of the war, until he came to: "worked on fence all day. News of an armistice with the Federal

Govt. rec'd to day & I think the Confederacy has gone up." Forbes had no choice but to maintain an account of his crops, since one season's results mattered for the next, even if visions of those future seasons were now filled with great uncertainty.[35]

DESPITE THE CONTINUITIES IN PEOPLE'S lives, a great deal was about to change, in ways no one could yet fathom. On Tuesday evening, April 11, 1865, President Lincoln stood on the White House balcony, speaking to an initially rapturous crowd gathered below. To the dismay of some, the president dispensed with the expected triumphal speech, offering instead something of a policy statement about what was to come. He spoke briefly of "speedy peace," General Grant, and God, but mostly Lincoln talked about reconstructing the nation, an endeavor, he admitted, that would be "fraught with great difficulty." Soon the president brought up the subject of the reconstructed state government of Louisiana. The Thirteenth Amendment, abolishing slavery, had been passed by Congress in January, and Louisiana's voters—largely moderate Unionists who had taken the oath of allegiance—had already ratified it. But African American men wanted the right to vote, and the white men who wrote the state constitution declined to include them. That evening, Lincoln offered the opinion ("I would myself prefer" is how he put it) that suffrage should be extended to black men who had fought for the Union and those deemed (by whom he did not say) "very intelligent."[36]

Reactions were mixed. Pennsylvania soldier Franklin Boyts, in the audience, thought the president a noble man, equal to none less than George Washington. Abolitionists were, like Sarah Browne, more circumspect. Confederates, unsurprisingly, were wholly unmollified. John Glenn, a well-to-do Marylander, thought Lincoln a despot, his talk of black rights plainly demonstrating that the South would be "kept in subjugation by armed Negroes."[37]

Listening to Lincoln that evening was the aggrieved actor and proslavery Confederate sympathizer John Wilkes Booth. Conspirator David Herold later testified that Booth muttered about "nigger citizenship" as the president spoke, but whatever he said aloud that night, Booth had already written down his conviction that "this country was formed for the *white* not for the black man." Now Booth was angrier than ever, as he witnessed what he would turn into Lincoln's last public speech.[38]

ON THURSDAY, APRIL 13, WASHINGTON remained "all alive with enthusiasm," a magnificent illumination making every street and square "one continuous blaze of light" as darkness fell. Walking with his wife and daughter, the white minister James Ward saw a "blaze of glory" that was "brilliant and splendid beyond the powers of words to describe." The next day was Good Friday, and still the capital's streets were jammed, every house and public building "blazing with candles from top to bottom," everyone still "wild with excitement" and "crazy with joy."[39]

Friday, April 14, offered the occasion for yet another celebration: the re-raising of the flag over Fort Sumter. Four years earlier, on April 12, 1861, the first shots of the Civil War were fired in the waters off South Carolina. Sumter, a federal fort, had been running out of food that spring, prompting President Lincoln to give notice to his enemies that he would send unarmed ships bearing provisions for the soldiers stationed there. Interpreting the resupply mission as an act of aggression, Confederates fired on the fort. Lincoln had prepared for that reaction, but his waiting warships were thwarted by mixed-up orders and high seas. After some thirty hours of bombardment, Sumter fell to the Confederacy. Now, four years later, the victors returned to re-raise the rightful flag over the fort's ruins—the very same flag, in fact, the one shot through with bullet holes.

The 1865 observances took place at Sumter and across the harbor in the city of Charleston, which had fallen to the Union just two months before Lee's surrender. The lineup of luminaries included Robert Smalls, a former South Carolina slave and future U.S. congressman who had won his freedom by piloting a Confederate vessel into the hands of the Union navy; Martin Delany, abolitionist and black nationalist, writer, physician, recruiter of black soldiers, and major in the Union army; and the son of Denmark Vesey, whose enslaved father had been hanged for plotting an uprising for freedom more than forty years earlier. The famous white abolitionist William Lloyd Garrison was also there, as generals, senators, congressmen, Supreme Court justices, and their families converged, packing the parade grounds and stands, along with black and white soldiers and sailors.

There were prayers and psalms, the singing of the national anthem, a reading of the dispatch announcing the fort's fall in 1861, and a one-hundred-gun salute. President Lincoln had asked the Reverend Henry Ward Beecher to orate, and now Beecher fashioned the American flag into a character. Torn down by the Confederates four years earlier, it had brooded and cried out to God. Now again it gazed over the bay with "starry eyes." No longer, Beecher proclaimed to great applause, would that banner wave over slavery, for in the restored nation, slavery would be "utterly and for ever abolished!" The planter class was to blame for everything, Beecher told his listeners. Aristocratic slaveholders, those "arrogant instigators of war," had provoked the common white folk, bribed them with lies against their own interests, and for that they should suffer "endless retribution" ("Amen! Amen!" shouted the crowd). As to those duped white folk, the victors should let "not a trace of animosity remain," Beecher counseled. But neither should "aimless vengeance" against the planter class sully the hearts of the conquerors, who must not forget the enemy's sorrow ("Millions mourn for millions slain," he preached). The best policy, Beecher concluded, was pardon "but no concession," amnesty "but no honied compromises."[40]

African American men, women, and children paraded, made speeches, and yet again sang "John Brown's Body." When Garrison, elated to witness their celebrations of freedom, talked about Abraham Lincoln, the people cheered. When Massachusetts senator Henry Wilson mentioned Lincoln's name, the crowd waved their hats and hurrahed. Southern slaves had been loyal to the United States, Wilson proclaimed, and their old masters were now powerless (more cheers). The U.S. government, the English abolitionist George Thompson told the freedpeople, "regards you as equally entitled, with Abraham Lincoln himself, to exercise the rights and privileges of citizenship." The sentiments at Sumter and Charleston reverberated north and west, as Union soldiers in the field echoed the hundred-gun salute, and towns and cities staged their own parades, complete with speeches, songs, and fireworks. Everywhere, the victors recorded the day's event. It was the "very *same flag*," thrilled Wilmington farmer Samuel Canby; the same flag, wrote Boston businessman Daniel Child, once torn down by "slaveholding traitors."[41]

The unending combination of merriment and solemnity taxed the vanquished. "I suppose the Yankees are holding a great jubilee in Charleston today," scoffed Emma LeConte, "raising their wretched *flag* over noble old Sumter." Wistfully she recalled the day four years earlier: how the bells began to ring, how her family had run to the veranda and front gate to gather tidings of the fallen fort, everyone in a tumult of excitement. "Poor old Sumter—dear old fort!" she wrote now. "What a degradation!"[42]

The Sumter festivities capped twelve days that propelled Union supporters into a palpable sense of participation in history. "Your letters are all carefully saved," Nathan Seymour wrote from Ohio to his son volunteering among former slaves in Richmond, for the nation could endure such a trial only "once in five hundred years." Caroline White wrote down that Appomattox marked a week "unparalleled in the annals of this war," maybe even in all of history. The wealthy merchant Amos Lawrence literally inscribed victory in stone, instructing his workmen to engrave the new chimney of his Boston home with the appropriate dates and the Latin phrases for "Richmond taken" and "Confederate army surrendered." By the same token, Confederates wrote history into their letters and journals, using similar language with exactly the opposite meaning. "How fast I have lived these past two years," Albert Browne had declared. In the words of Confederate Emma LeConte, "What changes—what a lifetime we have lived in the four years past!" Albert Browne had described the sights he had seen as "written with a piece of steel on my memory." For Confederate Mary Cabell, the day of Lee's surrender was "written on my brain in letters of fire." These were days Albert Browne wanted his descendants never to forget. For a Virginia woman, the day that orders came for the evacuation of Richmond was one "never to be forgotten," whether or not she or anyone else wanted to remember it.[43]

If the sense of participating in history was interchangeable between Yankee and Confederate, nothing else was. With the long war on the battlefield drawing to a close, Union supporters spoke the language of gratitude and jubilation, white southerners the language of incredulity and misery. At Sumter, after sundown on Friday evening, lanterns and bursting rockets lit up the fort. At home in Salem, Sarah Browne felt keenly aware of springtime's beauty, surveying the buds and flowers, leaves and green grass. "Above the clouds how plainly visible the divine hand!" she wrote in her diary. Sarah was certain that with the battlefield war concluded, the nation had already seen the triumph of justice. She did not know then that the laying down of arms could not end the war in people's hearts. Nor did she know just how soon Yankees and Confederates would exchange the moods of glee and gloom. No one did. Amos Lawrence did not know that he would soon request a third inscription from his stonecutters: "The joy of the people succeeded by the greatest grief."[44]

Rumors

AMONG THE SOLDIERS, THE TALK started on Saturday, April 15. People were saying that President Lincoln had been shot, but soldiers were accustomed to untrustworthy news. Even in an age of swift communications, where it seemed the telegraph could instantaneously set everything straight, rumors always flew faster than dispatches arrived. The soldiers called it the "grapevine telegraph," joshing about "the latest grape" and "Madam Rumor." People were saying Grant had been killed too, or maybe it was Secretary of War Edwin Stanton, or Secretary of State William Seward, or Seward's son Frederick. Some said Lincoln and his son Tad had both been killed.[1]

"Lincoln is said to have been shot and Seward's throat cut, but dont believe it yet," wrote an Iowa soldier in Mobile Bay that morning. It was the same for Ohio soldiers in Tennessee, for the news "could be traced to no reliable source." As another man put it, "I don't hardly believe the story, for it seems too absurd." The unreliable reports continued through Easter Sunday— "Hope it is not so," yet another soldier jotted in his diary that day. At Appomattox the men swore at the preposterousness of it all, and at Nottoway Station, even after General Philip Sheridan read a dispatch aloud, the men still weren't sure. It was circulating around Richmond by noon, but Union supporters dismissed it as a secessionist concoction, and Confederates didn't know what to think. When word came to the 114th U.S. Colored Troops near Petersburg on Monday (they heard that Lincoln, Seward, and Seward's son had all been killed), the men talked about it into the evening, trying hard to "treat it as a camp story." In North Carolina, the soldiers who passed on the news were branded "rumor makers." When the 149th New York heard that Lincoln had been killed in Richmond, one man recorded the deed in his diary, then told himself, "No no it is only a rumor I'm sure of it." The next day came confirmation ("Lincoln is dead & a nation mourns"), only to be contradicted that afternoon ("Lincoln is alive & well"). Illinois soldiers down south heard the bad news via the telegraph, but when northern papers arrived with no mention, they were sure that rebels had "operated the wires."[2]

Among Confederate prisoners in Virginia, reports circulated for two or three days, while the men attributed the lowered flags on passing ships to the death of some high-ranking Union officer. Near Greensboro, North Carolina, on Wednesday, April 19, people heard that Lincoln and Seward had been murdered, along with rumors that the federals had granted southern independence, with slavery intact, for the next five or ten or maybe twenty years. On Friday, in a small town in Georgia, a man thrust his head into the window of an arriving train, shouting that Lincoln had been assassinated, only to be answered with laughter and a cry that April Fools was over. In Mississippi, a planter heard the first intimation on April 21 but didn't believe it, since no one he knew even believed that Lee had surrendered—in fact, rumor had it that Lee and Joseph Johnston had united forces and whipped Sherman. Next came stories that Vice President Andrew Johnson was dead too, or maybe that Johnson had ordered Lincoln's assassination. In upcountry South Carolina, Confederates treated the news as simply too "theatric and improbable" to take seriously. In Griffin, Georgia, people heard that Lincoln had been murdered but assumed it to be just as mythical as the reports that France, England, Spain, and Austria had recognized the Confederacy or, for that matter, just as mythical as reports that Robert E. Lee had surrendered to the Yankees.[3]

Into the next week, Pennsylvania soldiers in the Deep South were having trouble deciding what news to trust, since so many half-truths and untruths "float from mouth to mouth," as one man wrote. Toward the end of April,

Union prisoners on the march in Georgia and Florida got the news of Lincoln's death from their captors, but an Iowan dismissed it with the words, "All kinds of rumors in camp." When a black regiment in Louisiana heard talk of assassination, the men "discussed the unlikeliness of the affair," hoping the next editions of the papers would report a contradiction. On the last day of April, a white South Carolina family received word of Lincoln's murder alongside a report that "the Yankee Congress had a row, and Andy Jonson was killed." Into May, the men of a Tennessee regiment in Alabama found themselves in the thick of stories that Lincoln had been assassinated and the Confederacy had won the war. One young private prayed to God that both pieces of information "may not prove a myth."[4]

In Washington it began earliest, with unconfirmed stories on the night of April 14. James Tanner, a War Department clerk, was watching a play about Aladdin's lamp at Grover's Theatre when someone opened the playhouse doors and shouted that the president had been assassinated over at Ford's. Then someone else shouted for everyone to sit down—it was only a ruse perpetrated by pickpockets. Annie Dudley was awakened at her boardinghouse by the voices and footfalls of men running through the streets, and another lodger said that William Seward had been murdered—which made no sense since Seward was in bed recovering from an accident. On the north side of Lafayette Square, the secretary of the navy had been drifting off to sleep when his wife alerted him to someone outside. When Gideon Welles stuck his head out the window, he found his personal messenger in a state of extreme agitation, incoherently relating that Lincoln, Seward, and Seward's son had all been killed. Very improbable, Welles thought—indeed, rather melodramatic—especially since the messenger mentioned Ford's Theatre, and everyone knew that Seward was home in bed.[5]

John Stonehouse, a Union army officer, was about to retire for the night when someone ran into his house breathlessly inquiring which theater President Lincoln was attending that night—he had to know because William Seward had just been murdered. Hurrying outside, Stonehouse encountered the crowds coming from Ford's. People were saying Lincoln had been killed, and when Stonehouse reached the theater, he saw that it was neither improbable nor theatrical. By the light of the glowing gas lamp on Tenth Street, he watched men carrying the president's unmistakably long body out of the auditorium and across the street.[6]

2

Shock

LINCOLN HAD BEEN DEAD FOR little more than an hour when Sarah Browne heard. Over breakfast on Saturday morning, April 15, she and the children were talking about the anniversary at Fort Sumter and picturing the festivities Albert had attended when a neighbor came to the door. Thinking that he might have picked up letters for her at the post office, Sarah greeted him happily, then saw immediately, in the man's face, that something was wrong. He said it all at once.

"There is very bad news, Sarah, this morning. President Lincoln was shot at Ford's Theatre last evening." Perhaps Sarah pressed him to see if he were sure, and perhaps he offered proof in the form of a newspaper or telegraph dispatch, for right away she knew it was not a rumor.

"What a shock!" Those were the words Sarah wrote in her diary—"like a thunder clap it came and no words could express enough of horror and grief at this unparalleled outrage." *Horror. Grief. Outrage.* Sarah Browne's description encapsulated the emotions of many: first shock, then sorrow, then anger. She copied down parts of the official account by Secretary of War Stanton from the morning newspapers: the time of the shooting, who else had been sitting in the presidential box, Booth's leap to the stage, the attack on Secretary of State William Seward and his son Frederick (serving as assistant secretary of state). As Sarah walked through Salem over the following days—so different from the walk she had taken earlier that week, when neighbors had joyously congratulated one another over Union victory—she saw that neighborhood women had hastily sewn black borders onto the flags recently unfurled to celebrate triumph. "Almost every house shows something to symbolize deep grief," she recorded, noticing as well the miniature black-trimmed flags pinned to children's clothing.

Sarah did not write to Albert for five days, wanting to be absolutely sure that he had already heard, that she would not be the one to convey the news. "By this time, the *atrocious deed* must have been made known to you," she wrote then, imagining her husband's state of mind: "*Your* heart as a part of the heart of *our* Nation must be distracted by feelings of honor and indignation." Then Sarah helped Albert imagine the scene at home in Salem. She described the black-bordered flags and the black and white bunting on the houses and public buildings. After that, she attempted to convey something of her own experience. "The terrible news came to us in the midst of our great rejoicing," she wrote, "on the very day too when the eyes of the nation were turned towards Fort Sumter—what a change! from frantic joy to frantic grief!" Unable to bring herself to rehearse the details, she bundled up the newspapers, adding a perfunctory, "I refer you to the daily press." Later that day, Sarah wrote to Albert again, realizing that she had told him nothing else about herself or the family. "We have not recovered from the terrible shock," she explained, adding that they all remained haunted by visions of the scene in the theater.[1]

Albert Browne was among a party of dignitaries accompanying Henry Ward Beecher when the telegram arrived at Saint Helena Island, between Charleston and Savannah, on Tuesday, April 18. The message was addressed to Senator Henry Wilson of Massachusetts and contained, Albert told Sarah, the "astonishing intelligence of the assassination of Mr. Lincoln." Beecher decided to return to New York at once, and so the two bade farewell with sentiments restrained. "I took his hand in mine, he took mine in his," Albert wrote, "and we parted without saying goodbye." Stoic silence was an acceptable reaction to devastating news, comporting with conventions of manly behavior, as were the responses Sarah had imagined for her husband: identification with the nation and indignation for national honor. Even more than Sarah, Albert could find few words to express his feelings on paper, settling for a sentence with less emotion than his wife's horror, grief, and outrage: "I cant say more & am too full." Emotion crept in only when he once again recorded his sense of participation in history: "O how much I have lived in these few days!"[2]

Events in Charleston better permitted Albert to articulate his shock and sorrow. The Union-occupied city was draped and flags were lowered, while officers wore black bands on their left arms, as ordered by the War Department. Although he took in the "unmistakable evidence of its truth," the whole thing still seemed truly unbelievable, coming as it did amid the celebrations at Sumter. "The reaction has been so sad so sudden, as to take from me the power of just thought," Albert wrote to his family.[3]

THE MURDER OF GREAT LEADERS is at least as old as Julius Caesar, and death threats and attempts had not been unknown to Abraham Lincoln. But the assassination of an American president seemed nearly unimaginable before it happened. The shock professed by Sarah and Albert Browne echoed through the Union, as new questions became suddenly pressing. How would the nation be reconstructed now? How would President Andrew Johnson contend with the Confederates? What would become of Lincoln's Emancipation Proclamation? Would black suffrage come to pass? What would happen the next day?

If Lincoln's mourners everywhere felt themselves in a state of amazement, those who had been inside Ford's Theatre had to cope as well with the trauma of witnessing the crime. None had a closer view than those in the presidential box. "Henry has been suffering a great deal with his arm, but it is now doing very well," Clara Harris wrote to a friend, sheltered in her father's home off Lafayette Square, a half-mile from Ford's and just down the street from the White House. "The knife went from the elbow nearly to the shoulder inside—cutting an artery, nerves & veins," she explained, describing the wound inflicted on her fiancé by the assassin. "He bled so profusely as to make him very weak." As for herself, she felt tremendously unsettled, unable to undertake even the slightest task. Harris recounted how her clothes had been "saturated literally with blood, & my hands & face—." But she couldn't go on so drew a dash instead, adding only, "you may imagine what a scene." She was haunted too by Mary Lincoln's screams, recalling how the First Lady had stared at the blood from Henry Rathbone's gashes, thinking it had gushed from the gunshot to her husband's head. Harris hadn't intended to write so many details, it was just that she couldn't think about anything else. "I cannot sleep & really feel wretchedly," she confessed to her friend, doubly panicked that John Wilkes Booth remained at large and might still be in Washington. Harris and Rathbone would marry two years later. He enjoyed a successful career with the U.S. military, they had three children and later moved to Germany, with Rathbone posted at the American consulate in Hanover. Yet he never fully recovered from the mental anguish of his encounter with Lincoln's assassin. Years later, Rathbone would murder his wife and end his life in an asylum.[4]

Some of the theatergoers that night were Washington residents, others visitors to the city. Some had reserved seats in advance, expressly to view the president, while others had gone to the play on a whim. Afterward, either they couldn't sleep at all or their dreams were nightmares. Julia Shepard's brother had died in the Battle of Cold Harbor, and she had come to the capital to accompany his body home to upstate New York. On her way out of the theater that night, she tried not to step on the blood that was all over the stairs. "Sleeping or waking, that terrible scene is before me," she wrote to her father, finding herself unable to be alone. Frederick Sawyer, a Massachusetts man, had come to Washington from Charleston, where he was teaching school. "I cannot sleep," he wrote from his room at Willard's Hotel at one o'clock in the morning, completely agitated. The city around him remained in an uproar, and, he knew, "only horrid dreams await my slumbers."[5]

Word spread quickly through the night, as people rushing out of the theater told people walking by on the street. Someone had awakened the vice president with the news, and Andrew Johnson now paid a brief visit to the dying executive at Petersen's boardinghouse. Officers made the rounds to the homes of other high-ranking men, and after a colonel told Minerva Meigs, wife of the quartermaster general, her nephew guarded the door with pistol in hand. At the sprawling Armory Square Hospital on the mall, an elderly ward master hoarsely called out to the soldier patients, "Have you heard the terrible news? The president was assassinated tonight at the theater." On the streets outside the hospital windows, people were screaming and shouting—a nurse made out the words *awful* and *horrible*. News of the attack on William Seward spread too.[6]

Guards stand outside Ford's Theatre on Tenth Street in Washington, D.C., after the assassination, with black mourning crape festooned in the windows. The gas lamp (lower-left corner) illuminated the way for Lincoln's body to be carried out of the theater, then illuminated the street's commotion through the night.
LC-DIG-ppmsca-23872, Prints and Photographs Division, Library of Congress.

Infantry and cavalry tried to control the growing commotion outside Ford's as crowds gathered on the street between theater and boardinghouse. Half a mile away, thousands of the city's black residents, men and women, young and old, congregated in front of the White House. Some looked through the iron fence toward the mansion, now heavily guarded, while others sat on the curb or the sidewalk. Some asked passing soldiers if the president was dead. Others wondered aloud if Lincoln's death meant a return to slavery.[7]

"My good president! My good president!" a tearful woman lamented. "I would rather have died myself!" Young black men showed their despair with martial spirit, another form of honorable manly behavior. "If the North would just leave *us* to finish this war!" said one. Said another, "Just let them leave the rebels to us!"[8]

At Petersen's, one of the doctors eventually described the president as "dead to all intents," and Secretary of the Navy Gideon Welles watched

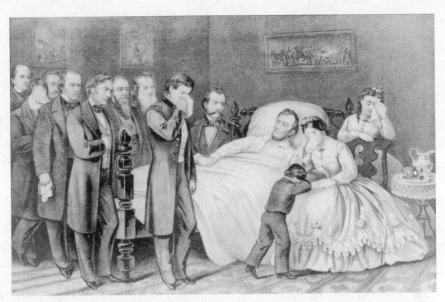

Lincoln dies at Petersen House. This 1865 lithograph shows a highly idealized version of the deathbed, with Mary Lincoln, Tad Lincoln, and Robert Lincoln weeping as a doctor holds Lincoln's hand and a line of statesmen look on. In reality, Mary Lincoln was not present when her husband died, Tad never entered the room, the space was far too cramped for such a crowd, and Lincoln lay diagonally across the small bed, his head resting on a bloody pillow and his face showing the effects of the gunshot wound. *LC-USZ62-43633, Prints and Photographs Division, Library of Congress.*

as one eye swelled and Lincoln's face changed color. At six in the morning, Welles stepped out for air, though the day was turning out to be dark and damp. The crowds were more black than white, he noticed, as people stopped him to ask about the president's condition. Everywhere Welles saw "intense grief," but the Negroes appeared especially "painfully affected." Back at Petersen's an hour later, Welles witnessed Robert Lincoln break down, and soon the doctors officially pronounced Lincoln dead. He was fifty-six years old. The hour and minute of death—7:22 a.m.—would be enshrined in headlines and then again in the personal writings of mourners. Soon, in the parlor of the Kirkwood House Hotel, Chief Justice Salmon Chase swore in Andrew Johnson as president of the United States.[9]

For the horse-drawn ride to the White House, Lincoln's body rested inside a flag-draped casket, inside a hearse. In a guest bedroom on the second floor, doctors sawed off the top of his head, removed the brain, and watched the assassin's bullet clatter into a basin. Meanwhile, Benjamin

Brown French, the city's commissioner of public buildings, began to give orders for the ordeal ahead: draping the White House and Capitol Rotunda in mourning fabric, designing and building the catafalque on which the coffin would rest while lying in state, and preparing the city for a massive funeral. By afternoon, French had a terrific headache. Unable to put his feelings into words, he could only borrow from Shakespeare's *Macbeth:* "O horror, horror, horror! Tongue nor heart / Cannot conceive nor name thee!"[10]

PEOPLE HAD RUN STRAIGHT FROM Tenth Street to the telegraph office, spreading word beyond the capital. The government-owned telegraph was central to Civil War military operations, with its speedy transmission over great distances, and Lincoln had spent hours at the office every week, waiting for communications from the front and conversing with the operators, who received and delivered messages day and night. Early transmissions about the crime at Ford's were not entirely clear as to the president's state, but in time official confirmation of death reached communities wherever the wires ran. Newspapermen wrote headlines from the dispatches, and printers hurried through their mechanical tasks. Newsboys scooped up the bundles of papers or sheaves of "extras" and set out on their rounds, calling out the tidings. The *Berkshire Courier* extra in Great Barrington, Massachusetts, with a 10:00 a.m. dateline, read "TERRIBLE NEWS! LINCOLN DEAD! He is Shot by an Assassin!"[11]

Beyond Washington on Saturday morning, April 15, laborers and servants were among the first to know. Night watchmen, coal shovelers, and lamplighters passed the news along to one another, as cooks in kitchens, up at dawn preparing breakfast, and valets, building fires in their masters' bedrooms, stepped outside to investigate the ruckus of shouting and hurried footsteps.

"Oh, Ma'am, President Lincoln was murdered last night in the Washington theater by an actor!" cried Ellen Kean's maid, entering the bedroom of the English actress who was playing in New York.

"Oh, Mr. Clapp, there is a policeman downstairs, and he says President Lincoln has been killed." Boston editor William Clapp wasn't yet dressed when his servant Kate burst into his room, in tears.

"Tell Mrs. Dall Lincoln and Seward have been assassinated," the milkman ordered a servant in the vestibule of Caroline Dall's Boston home.

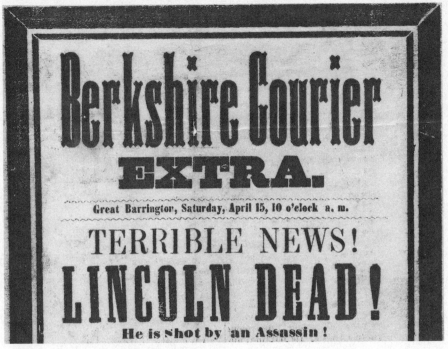

Berkshire Courier

EXTRA.

Great Barrington, Saturday, April 15, 10 o'clock a. m.

TERRIBLE NEWS!

LINCOLN DEAD!

He is shot by an Assassin !

Less than three hours after Lincoln was pronounced dead on Saturday morning, April 15, 1865, the *Berkshire Courier* in Great Barrington, Mass., published this "extra." The black edging signified mourning.
Call #AB85.L6384.Y865b, Houghton Library, Harvard University.

"Nonsense," retorted Dall, who had gone to bed happily thinking of victory.

"I wonder what they will say next," marveled fifteen-year-old Sadie Dall, as she and her mother descended to breakfast. That's when Sadie picked up the newspaper on the doorstep, turned pale, shrieked, and began to cry. Soon the bells began to toll. Northerners were used to turning to the morning paper's "telegraphic column" for the latest war news, and for many that Saturday, the headlines explained the confusing off-hour chimes. For others, like the Dalls, the bells confirmed the seemingly inconceivable headlines.[12]

Passing on the news became a first act of mourning. Saying the words aloud was one way to make it more real, and telling someone else meant you didn't have to be alone with it. Just as laborers out on the street had informed one another, and just as servants passed the news to their employers, now those at home began to knock on neighbors' doors and call into windows.[13]

"Have you heard the terrible news?" the man at the front stoop asked Charles Mallory in Mystic, Connecticut. It was Mr. Woodward, Mallory's blind neighbor, and he was crying. "They have killed our good president."

"Oh! Horrible, horrible news!" Those were the words Lucy McKim heard as she readied to catch the nine o'clock train out of Philadelphia. Her cousin Annie had just spoken with a neighbor and was now sobbing.[14]

Everywhere, people gathered, and everywhere they searched one another's faces for verification. Just as Sarah Browne had instantly absorbed the distress on the visage of the man at her door, mourners read the meaning in eyes, brows, lips, and complexions, telling of genuine consternation, alarm, and woe. For one's face to reflect sincere feelings was an ideal that had become increasingly untenable in middle-class Victorian culture, with the growing acceptance of artful cosmetics and fashion, but at this cataclysmic moment, all masks seemed to fall away, as people turned earnestly to the countenances around them, not simply to affirm the news but also for guidance about how to respond to such an unprecedented event.

To authenticate the news further, people had to leave the house in order to engage with others. Out on Boston's State Street, Caroline Dall saw the bare heads of men buried in newspapers and realized that they had rushed outside too quickly even to put on their hats.

Anna Lowell ordered her driver to take her through the streets of Boston in her horse and buggy, from where she "could see people looking at me & at each other."

"Is it true what they say, that our president—" called out a man in a passing wagon.

"Yes—murdered!" Lowell called back.

"Oh dear, oh dear!" the man moaned, driving on.

Boston businessmen headed to the Merchants' Reading Room, where members gathered spontaneously to pray together, while women accepted guests at home and paid visits to neighbors.[15]

On that Saturday morning, news of the crime reached small towns in northern New England and the Mid-Atlantic, as well as Chicago, Kansas, and Salt Lake City. In Sacramento, the first mentions arrived at nine in the morning, local time. That afternoon, outside the telegraph office in a northern California mining town, a crowd gathered to listen to a public reading of the telegram, "word by word" as it arrived. By the next day, smaller cities in Ohio, Wisconsin, and Minnesota knew. Where no telegraph lines ran, people wouldn't know until newspapers arrived by mail—Santa Fe and the remoter parts of Utah Territory didn't hear until May. Speed of transmission to the South varied, what with rail lines cut by the Union army and newspaper offices abandoned by fleeing Confederates. Some small towns received telegrams that same Saturday. New Orleans got the news four days later, via newspaper. More than a week after the assassination, some Texans were just hearing rumors of the fall of Richmond, and Iowa soldiers in Alabama got word at the end of April. For some freedpeople, both adults and children, the first announcement came in the classroom, from Yankee teachers or school superintendents. Confederates might see the occupiers' flags flying at half-mast. Verification then came in letters and newspapers arriving on steamships from the North.[16]

On the water, word passed from ship to ship, as U.S. vessels ordered other boats to lower their flags. Across the oceans, steamships arrived with bundles of telegrams and newspapers. On the day Lincoln died, William Gould, the Union navy runaway slave, was in Cádiz, Spain, just learning of the fall of Richmond. The timing was the same in London; as Lincoln's funeral was under way in Washington, the legation there was crowded with elated Americans congratulating themselves on Richmond's fall, and a week after Lincoln's death, they had just begun to celebrate Lee's surrender. In Jamaica, news of victory and the assassination arrived simultaneously at the end of April, obliging residents to "rejoice with trembling." Gould and his fellow sailors were en route to Lisbon in early May when a U.S. vessel brought the "awful tidings," he wrote in his diary. The news reached Sierra Leone and China in mid-June, Australia in late June.[17]

For Lincoln supporters who heard of the assassination long after, the feelings and rituals were the same. Charles Hale, U.S. consul in Egypt, had been enjoying himself in the diplomats' stand at early May horse races in Alexandria, cooling off with ices, savoring bonbons, and accepting felicitations over Union victory, when a woman called out, "Come here, Mr. Hale, here's some news for you." She had just gotten word from Constantinople, where the telegraph connected with London, and as this particular dispatch had it, Lincoln had been shot in Richmond. Shaken, and thinking the interruption "thoughtlessly abrupt," Hale returned to his seat, "very much overcome," even as he wondered if it could possibly be true. The news was later confirmed and corrected via ships from Malta and Italy, and in a batch of mail from Marseille that included letters from home, a copy of the official telegram from Edwin Stanton, and the April 15 editions of the New York and Boston newspapers. Hale stayed up most of the night and into the next day, poring over the "tale of horror," making himself believe what everyone at home had known for weeks.[18]

ASTONISHED. ASTOUNDED. STARTLED. Stupefied. Thunderstruck. A calamity. A catastrophe. A dagger to the heart. A thunderbolt. A thunderclap from a clear blue sky. The feelings that had engulfed the Confederates less than a week earlier now overtook their conquerors. It was "too horrible to be true" and "too terrible to believe." It was simply impossible to "realize"—that was a favored nineteenth-century locution, meaning *to make real,* and over and over again people invoked that word; "I can scarcely realize it." "I cannot realize it." "But how can we realize it?" People could not and would not believe it. "I cannot have it so," one woman wrote; "it must not be so."[19]

Disbelief was most intense for African Americans, whose stake in the war's outcome and promise was so tangible. Freedpeople in the tiny settlement of Frogmore on Saint Helena Island off the South Carolina coast refused to mourn until they were certain. As the black minister there explained, "They could not think that was the truth, and they would wait and see." For the soldiers of the Fifty-Fourth Massachusetts, the news was "too overwhelming, too lamentable, too distressing" to comprehend. Many of the men of the Twenty-Fifth U.S. Colored Troops likewise "refused to believe the report" until absolutely confirmed. On Bienville Street in New Orleans, Elizabeth Clark felt very much "agitated," while her neighbor Mary Jones felt "very much worried" as she sat outside her door so as not to miss any further information. Mattie Jackson, an escaped slave from Missouri, called the assassination "an electric shock to my soul." Again, the reading of countenances commenced the process of turning the incredible into the credible, of validating feelings and expression of those feelings. In Louisville, "distress was visible in every colored person's face."[20]

For some, it took a long time to concede. Like Confederates who felt time distorted and reality displaced when they learned of defeat and surrender, Lincoln's mourners thought it must be a lie or, as freedpeople in a Virginia classroom put it, "a secesh lie." In Baltimore, Edward Greble, a white man, was riding an omnibus when he heard someone say that the president had been assassinated, which he quickly dismissed as "a canard." Back at his hotel, the proprietor had just been to the telegraph office, and Greble watched as the other guests remained so incredulous as to think it a joke. To Boston merchant Charles French, it all seemed like a sensational getup. It felt like a "dreadful dream," people said, a "horrible dream" or a play on a stage. To Elizabeth Agassiz, who got the news while traveling in Brazil, it felt like "the last scene in a five act tragedy," then "a gigantic street rumor," then a bad dream. "Stunning," the women's rights reformer Susan B. Anthony wrote from Leavenworth, Kansas. Walt Whitman would soon capture these feelings in a tribute poem to the president, casting Lincoln as a ship captain, writing, "It is some dream that on the deck, / You've fallen cold and dead." A lie or a joke, a sham or mere gossip, a nightmare or a show: that was how it felt. A deception, an illusion, a performance—the words people invoked conveyed all manner of the unreal. Today we might say, *I felt like I was in a movie.*[21]

Magnifying the shock was the crime's timing—Sarah Browne's "frantic joy" turned into "frantic grief." In Norfolk, the freedpeople's schools, already closed for victory celebrations, now remained shuttered for the rituals of mourning. In Nashville, Unionists changed the city from its "*gala* appearance" into a cheerless scene, cannons now booming in sorrow instead of jubilation. Yankee soldiers there had been strutting in a parade when the news came "like a crash," prompting the musicians to switch from quicksteps to death marches. In New Bern, North Carolina, Mary Ann Starkey looked around her contraband camp, filled with fellow former slaves. Had she written only a few days earlier, she confessed in a dictated letter, "I should only have rejoiced over the *glorious* news"; among the war refugees she assisted as head of the Colored Women's Union Relief Association, Starkey now saw "little heart left." In Charleston, the men of the black Fifty-Fifth Massachusetts had just enjoyed the company of Henry Ward Beecher and William Lloyd Garrison. Soon they lowered flags, fired guns, tolled bells, and draped headquarters, all their actions "feeble expressions of feeling, for so great a loss." It was, wrote a northern teacher in Virginia, the "*most Joyous,* yet saddest month our country has ever known."[22]

A group of two hundred prominent New Yorkers had chartered a steamer to take them to the flag-raising at Fort Sumter and as yet knew nothing as they sailed toward Fortress Monroe, Virginia, one of the stops on their post-celebration tour of Civil War sites. Early on Tuesday, April 18, the passengers were breakfasting when a pilot boat with a lowered flag came into view.

"What's the news?" someone called out.

"President Lincoln is dead!" came the response, prompting the diners to drop their silverware. Had the president "at last worn himself out," they wondered? Soon other passing ships conveyed the facts, and the New York, Baltimore, and Richmond papers waiting at Fortress Monroe contained the details. The New York revelers canceled their itinerary and headed straight home.[23]

Up north, with fireworks and victory parades barely over, the outpourings of joy abruptly ceased and reversed course, some victory parties quite literally interrupted. In Chicago, happy shouts and the noise of tin horns subsided into solemnity. In a Maine town, the bells kept ringing, one moment "chiming merrily," the next "tolling a requiem." It was "more dreadful by the contrast," wrote an Ohio man; "all the darker for the previous light," wrote a woman in Massachusetts. All in the same day, Caroline White recorded in her diary, "the sun rose upon a nation jubilant with victory" and set "upon one plunged in deepest sorrow." Over and over, people tried to articulate the nature of the change. Edward Everett Hale could not believe he was "in the same world, and in the same week." A Connecticut soldier in Virginia thought back to his regiment's victory observances, only to realize that "while we were having such a fine time here, the President was being murdered." How sad the timing was too for President Lincoln himself, another soldier wrote to his parents, "to be shot just as he was about to see the war closed," when peace was just about to "crown his honest and earnest efforts."[24]

If passing on the news was one way to make sense of the senseless, another was to make a record of the deed. Michael Shiner, a former slave and laborer in the Washington navy yard, noted in his journal a set of details

Saturday, Apl. 15th 1865. — We have the saddest tidings this morning that ever shocked our Country. It almost chills my heart's blood to record it. President Lincoln was murdered at Ford's Theater last night !!! The dwelling house of Mr. Seward, Secretary of State, was also entered about the same time, and an attempt made to assassinate

The Washington minister James Ward expressed shock and dismay in his diary on April 15, 1865. "*We have the saddest tidings this morning that ever shocked our Country*," he wrote. "It almost chills my heart's blood to record it. *President Lincoln was murdered at Ford's Theater last night!!!*"
James Thomas Ward diary, April 15, 1865, Manuscript Division, Library of Congress.

that a great many would write down: the day, date, and place of the shooting, and the date of Lincoln's death. Connecting himself personally to the event, Shiner added that the Lincolns had visited the navy yard on the very day of the assassination. The white Washington minister James Ward embellished his own record with underlinings and exclamation points. "*We have the saddest tidings this morning that ever shocked our Country*," he wrote. Then, like Shiner, he recorded the main fact: "*President Lincoln was murdered at Ford's Theater last night!!!*" When Sarah Putnam, fourteen years old, heard the news at her Boston breakfast table, she drew a picture of her feelings—a face with two wide, round eyes and a wider circle for a mouth—thereby preserving the essence of the visible expressions that helped make the news believable (the girl would grow up to be a portrait painter). Putnam vowed to her diary to report the facts "without any sentiment," but when she wrote, "Now president L. is *dead*," her double underline, along with the face she had rendered, betrayed her emotions.[25]

People flipped back the pages of their diaries in efforts to create an accurate chronological account. A Union soldier who had noted drills, a dress parade, and a package from home on April 14 now squeezed in the words, "President Lincoln shot in Ford's Theatre." When the news reached England, *Punch* journalist Shirley Brooks turned back the sheets of his diary twelve days to write, "This evening President Lincoln was killed," as if he had gotten the news that same night. People wrote long letters, then asked for them to be returned; "send it back, for I have no other record," Caroline Dall instructed the recipient of a long missive in which she set down all the details.[26]

People preserved their reactions on paper in all kinds of ways. They drew heavy black lines to signal the separation of everything that came before the assassination from everything that would come after. They recorded the deed, then drew a box around the words to make them stand out on the page. People drew pictures of graves or penned the facts in beautiful calligraphy. Annie Hillborn wrote the word "Died" at the top of the page, then wrote "April 15" in the left margin and "1865" in the right margin. Beneath that came the words, "Our Loved President" and "At 22 min past 7 O'clock AM." She added Lincoln's birth date and age, followed by "A martyr to Justice & Liberty. Killed by the hand of an assassin." A seamstress in New York City, without the time and supplies available to Hillborn, crammed a record of the event onto a page in her account book, fitting the words around her list of purchases. "The Pres. was assassinated in his seat at Ford's Theatre," she wrote, "a ball pass through his brain."[27]

Sarah Browne had referred her husband to the newspapers, unable to bring herself to write out the particulars, but unlike Sarah, many mourners drank up and dwelled on the details. Some cut out newspaper columns and pasted them into their journals, while others copied out the facts, refashioning official reports into personal records. Either way, it was a means both to preserve history and to face what still felt incomprehensible, as the act of assembling, organizing, and composing formed another step in the confounding process of "realization."

They wrote down everything. How the president's bodyguard went ahead to the theater but was nowhere to be found when the assassin approached. How the president's personal valet unwittingly let the assassin by. That the assassin was the actor John Wilkes Booth. How Booth entered the anteroom and looked through a peephole in one of the doors that led directly to the box. How he had earlier carved that peephole himself, since he was permitted access to the theater as a recognized actor. How he opened the door and wedged it shut from the inside. How he shot the president once in the back of the head. How Mary Lincoln screamed. How Booth broke his ankle on his clumsy vault to the stage. How he cried out, "Sic semper tyrannis!"—the motto of the state of Virginia—as he leapt, or

In his diary on April 15, 1865, Bostonian Francis Brooks drew an upside-down American flag at half-mast, decorated with a mourning ribbon, flying over a grave with a skull and crossbones signaling the assassination's danger to the nation.
Francis Brooks Journal, April 15, 1865. Courtesy of the Massachusetts Historical Society.

maybe he said, "The South is avenged." How the president was conveyed across the street to the Petersen boardinghouse. How another conspirator attacked the Sewards. That the president expired at twenty-two minutes past seven o'clock the next morning.

Every detail recorded and absorbed made it less a hallucinated nightmare or a theatrical drama, less a lie or a hoax. After eleven-year-old Grenville Norcross wrote in his diary that President Lincoln was "shot through the head by J. W. Booth," the boy used up four pages transcribing every word of a newspaper article. Anna Lowell selected particular facts: that Lincoln laughed at the play yet looked sad; that Mrs. Lincoln tried to rouse her husband after Booth pulled the trigger. A woman in New Hampshire described the bullet's entrance, "three inches back of the left ear." A man in Washington recorded that Lincoln had entered Ford's Theatre "from the *dress circle* through a narrow corridor some three feet wide and eight or ten long" and that the room at Petersen's was "about 9 feet by 15, with two windows and three doors." In the two days following, Charles French wrote down all the specifics, from Lincoln's decision to attend the theater that night to a description of the suit the president would wear inside his casket. Every fact made it more possible that it had truly come to pass.[28]

Just as the victors had imagined their exultation as universal less than a week earlier, as mourners they now envisioned their grief the same way. If recording the facts helped them cope with their shock, so too did observing and preserving the public scenes of reaction. Many noted not only the desolation etched onto every face, but also the pervasive mood of despondency, thereby fitting their own despair into something larger: a whole village, an entire city. Just as Sarah Browne imagined the feelings of her husband down south, mourners everywhere imagined—and newspapers confirmed—that their own feelings were multiplied across the nation and around the globe. White people who lived or worked near black people tended to record those emotions, like Gideon Welles in Washington who documented the grief of the capital's large wartime African American population. Some who didn't know any black people but who associated Lincoln with emancipation conjured those feelings, like the northern New England woman who envisioned "how the poor Freedmen will mourn over the dreadful calamity so suddenly fallen upon us!"[29]

Newspaper reports, from which mourners gathered so much of their information, also helped the bereaved put unspeakable feelings into words. When a Pennsylvania soldier wrote of the "greatest National calamity that ever befell the American people," he likely borrowed that description from a journalist. When sixteen-year-old Margaret Howell recorded that she was awakened with the "startling news of the assassination of our noble and beloved President," she no doubt meant every word, even if the adjectives she chose—*startling, noble, beloved*—were ubiquitous in the papers. When she wrote, "'Tis the saddest day in our History," she was also likely echoing the papers, invoking a reporter's words in order to give voice to her own emotions.[30]

Excitement and *gloom.* Those were the two words people wrote down again and again, the first emanating from within, the second seeming to descend from the atmosphere. In the nineteenth century, to *excite* meant to elicit strong emotions of any sort. At Ford's Theatre, "everybody was excited," and then the capital had been "thrown into the most intense excitement." Cities were in "a state of great excitement," indeed the whole Union was in a state of the "most intense excitement ever known." People also invoked the word to describe their own sense of being unnerved, like eyewitness Frederick Sawyer who pronounced himself "so excited by what has occurred to night."[31]

Gloom, in counterpoint, implied melancholy, shadows, and darkness, all of which endured after the state of excitement died down. Among the freedpeople of Wilmington, North Carolina, wrote a white teacher, the news caused "a dreadful gloom to settle in our midst." In Brookline, Massachusetts, white men stood together, talking in low voices, while "gloom & dismay were pictured upon every countenance"—again, the reading of faces worked to convince observers that they were not mistaken. John Nicolay, Lincoln's private secretary, described the gloom in Washington as "heavy and ominous," as if "some greater calamity still hung in the air, and was about to crush and overwhelm every one." Soldiers in camp felt it keenly, many remaining quiet in keeping with masculine protocol. For the members of a black regiment that had entered Richmond, the news arrived on a lovely spring day, casting "a gloom over every thing." When an officer gave word to an Illinois regiment in Virginia, "a silent gloom fell upon us like a pall," wrote Daniel Chisolm. "No one," he explained, "spoke or moved." There was no drill or dress parade, "No Nothing, all quiet, Flags at half mast." The next day, after the troops packed up to move across the railroad tracks, the men "lay around," Chisolm wrote in his notebook, "mostly in our tents all quiet and lonesome," a "Silent Gloom" hovering over the camp.[32]

Mourners found confirmation of the catastrophic event and of the universal grief they imagined as they soaked up and participated in public rituals. Cities, towns, and villages seemed instantaneously drenched in black drapery, complemented by white, the two traditional colors of nineteenth-century mourning. Businesses that had opened early on Saturday soon began to close—stores, theaters, bars—with the exception of shops that carried anything that could be fashioned into a mourning decoration. By the end of the day on Saturday, A. T. Stewart's department store in New York had sold a hundred thousand dollars' worth of black goods. Sundown brought the rituals of illumination—now in sorrow instead of joy—combining burning candles in residential windows, kerosene and gas lamps all aglow, and bonfires lighting up the streets (always accompanied by the worry of spreading flames). The death of a statesman also warranted the donning of mourning emblems, some with likenesses or mottoes, others fashioned more plainly from the ubiquitous crinkly fabric called *crape,* pinned to bonnets, collars, or sleeves. Shopkeepers began selling the badges on the morning of April 15 and kept up a steady business all through the spring.[33]

The near-immediate shrouding of public buildings, which to privileged observers seemed to have been accomplished by magic, in fact fell to workingmen, just as the draping of private homes fell to wives and servants ("If you have not already draped our flags with mourning, have it done," a man told his wife, his words indicating that she should direct a domestic laborer). Washington was the first to be transformed, as workers followed orders to cloak the White House, the Capitol, the War Department, Treasury Department, Post Office, and Patent Office. Servants meanwhile created elaborate displays on the exteriors of the city's poshest residences ("I had our house fixed early in the day," Elizabeth Blair Lee wrote to her husband). African Americans, many of them poor, along with the city's poorer whites, displayed their sentiments with as much black cloth as they could scare up, and soon the city was shrouded in "miles upon miles of material," as a federal clerk put it, or as Julia Shepard described the scene, the drapery went "on and on," the streets presenting "only the blackness of darkness."[34]

Beyond the capital, mourners worked just as hard. Women transformed the victory flags, sewing black trim along the edges or tying black ribbon to the poles. A man traveled nearly five miles to procure a half-yard of black crape. A woman who didn't get to the shops quickly enough had to festoon a window with her own black shawl, and widows lent their personal mourning attire to drape local church altars. A shopkeeper used lace collars to display the words "The dead still live." Poor people everywhere tacked up black rags, while Anna Lowell instructed her servants to decorate the portico of her home with black alpaca and white cotton, accented with black and white rosettes. At the Winter Garden Theatre in New York, someone covered over the name of Edwin Booth, the assassin's brother, who had just ended a run as Hamlet. Across the continent the labor continued for more than a week, "hammers & stepladders everywhere," black and white bunting concealing the facades, columns, window frames, and door frames of city halls, churches, banks, department stores, shops, hotels, libraries, schools, and houses from tenement to mansion. Up went the bordered flags, the swags and streamers, the bows and ribbons, banners pronouncing the nation in mourning, and photographs of the slain president, their frames fringed in black.[35]

In the defeated Confederacy, freedpeople, Yankee occupiers, and Unionists got to work too. In Charleston and New Orleans, black residents decorated houses and clothing. In Savannah and Norfolk, the homes of even the most impoverished African Americans had "a bit of black suspended upon door or window," and the smallest children wore mourning badges. On the Sea Islands, freedwomen made their children "little crape rosettes," and the children crafted wreaths of roses tied with dark crape, while white teachers distributed scraps of fabric to those who had none. On Saint Helena, one little girl cut her black bonnet into pieces small enough that she "supplied the whole school." By order of the War Department, Union soldiers and officers set to the task of draping their military posts. One soldier had to travel into the nearest town, inquiring of every merchant and any person along the way if they had any makeshift mourning goods to sell or donate. Union officers meanwhile saw to it that the only trade conducted, most especially among local Confederates, was in mourning goods.[36]

All these rituals were carried out amid shock, the same state of mind so recently entered by defeated Confederates. Yet Lincoln's supporters had not truly exchanged places with their enemies, for the president's assassination did not reverse Union victory, and Confederates remained the ones for whom the war had been fought in vain. Nonetheless, the crime compounded the uncertainty of what would happen next for the triumphant nation. This was true most especially for African Americans: recall the freedpeople in Washington who wondered right away if Lincoln's demise would jeopardize freedom. Although black leaders had criticized the president's hesitancy regarding emancipation early in the war, Lincoln had over time been deeply influenced by the convictions of black and white abolitionists, including the more radical members of his own party. For many African Americans in the spring of 1865, Abraham Lincoln was the Great Emancipator (the "bondman's saviour," wrote a member of the U.S. Colored Troops), and his death brought very real forebodings. In Charleston, black men and women expressed apprehension about the murder, fearing "the result of it to themselves." On the Sea Islands, some wondered if the white northerners who were running the old plantations as free-labor experiments would now depart, prompting their former masters to return. Others wondered if, with Lincoln gone, the whole Union government was dead too. Like those outside the gates of the White House on Saturday morning, adults and children in the South articulated the terrible question: Would they be slaves again?[37]

Free African Americans up north meanwhile felt the loss of hope they had built so high: hope built on the escape of slaves to Union lines, on the Emancipation Proclamation affirming those actions, and on Confederate surrender affirming it decisively. Writing to the black-owned *Christian Recorder*, correspondents relayed the mood around them. In Chicago, "We felt as if all our hopes were lost." In Indiana, "The hope of our people is again stricken down." White mourners expressed fear as well, though theirs was more amorphous, less concrete: "visions of disaster and desolation, & national ruin," in the words of a Pennsylvania man. Or as Anna Ferris wrote from Delaware, "We seem groping in thick blackness & look at each other in fear & dread." Others wrote of a future filled with evil and anarchy. But for Lincoln's black mourners alone was shock accompanied by the most raw anxiety.[38]

In the days afterward, it felt to Sarah Browne that everyone shared her sense of horror, grief, and outrage. The crime, she wrote, "froze the blood of the nation, which now flows in one current." Sarah didn't count the Confederates—those "aiders and abettors of treason"—as part of that single current. Nor did she count those in her own New England city who defied the solemnity. She'd heard of a dissenter thrown off a Salem streetcar, another "compelled to salute the Flag," people even tarred and feathered for their refusal to mourn for Lincoln. Without hesitation, Sarah endorsed these violent actions against the enemies in her midst. "All this is right," she wrote to Albert.[39]

Sarah Browne wrote in her diary and letters about universal shock, but

across the Confederacy and across the Union, the reaction to Lincoln's assassination was not all horrific disbelief, excitement and gloom, mourning
drapery and badges, fear and dread. For some, Lincoln's murder was an
occasion for celebration. The Yankee president murdered! It was almost
too good to be true.

Men Weeping

PLENTY OF MEN KEPT THEIR feelings in check, conserving their words or remaining silent in grief and anger. Extreme circumstances, however, could snap codes of conduct, and the end of the Civil War was just such an occasion: when Garland White and his fellow black soldiers entered the fallen city of Richmond, White found himself "overcome with tears." The higher a man's social status, the more constricted he felt in displaying emotion, but now it barely mattered. For Union men, black and white, rich and poor, victory had been worthy of weeping with joy, and news of the assassination likewise brought tears of sorrow. Just as Confederate men had wept openly in the shock and bitterness of defeat, it was now the turn of Union men to break the rules of masculine deportment.[1]

That grown men cried—a staple of news reports and memoirs—is proven in the leaves of private journals. Some, like George Templeton Strong, swallowed hard, as his eyes kept filling, and the corners of his mouth kept twitching, "in spite of all I could do," he wrote in his diary. Walking through the Broadway throngs in New York, one woman saw that her husband could "scarcely keep back the tears." Others didn't bother to try. As black soldiers in camp in Pennsylvania listened to a sermon on Lincoln's death, many wept freely, the same as on city and village streets, where white men were "sobbing and crying bitterly." In Philadelphia, weeping men grasped hands, while in Saco, Maine, men talked in groups, "wiping their eyes." At a church service for Americans in Paris, the minister got through the service only with a "violent effort of self-control," his voice breaking at the closing prayer for the slain president.[2]

Men, one woman wrote, were "not *ashamed* of their tears." To be sure, many who recorded the sobs of their male companions made sure to call those men strong, in an effort to distinguish them from excusably weak women. In the post office in New York, one woman found "the Clerks & every one so sad—*strong men in tears,*" just as a minister in Buffalo spoke of the "unusual spectacle of strong men in tears." Others portrayed the men as shedding tears of fury. Inside Ford's Theatre, one witness wrote, "strong men wept, and cursed, and tore the seats in the impotence of their anger." Some men recorded their own emotions obliquely, bypassing the use of first-person singular. "We think it no shame to weep here to-day," wrote a federal clerk in Washington. Others put it more directly. A man riding on the streetcars in New York found it "impossible to control my tears," then found himself face to face with another weeping gentleman, the reality of the terrible crime once again verified in an exchange of glances that revealed befitting emotions. As a white officer in a black regiment told his mother, "I never wept so much over the death of any person."[3]

Because the sight of men crying in public was far from common, some observers felt obliged to describe them as children, thereby casting their actions as something more familiar. At a Quaker meeting in Philadelphia, a woman watched as a man cried out, "Oh no! no! it *cannot* be" and "wept as a child." Aggrieved Union soldiers in Raleigh were subdued, some "weeping like children." Of course those men were still strong. On the street outside Ford's Theatre, wrote one eyewitness to the murder, "strong men throw their arms around each other's necks and cry like children." Anson Henry, Lincoln's physician and friend, had come to Washington immediately on hearing the news. When he laid eyes on the president's lifeless body, "the fountain of tears was broken up," he wrote, "and I wept like a child refusing to be comforted, remaining riveted to the spot." To his wife, he confided, "I had never before realized the luxury of tears."[4]

3

Glee

THE PRESIDENT HAD BEEN DEAD for a week when a navy ship came into Jacksonville, Florida, carrying the April 15 issue of the *New York Herald.* "IMPORTANT: ASSASSINATION OF PRESIDENT LINCOLN," read the headline, and below that, "SECRETARY SEWARD DAGGERED IN HIS BED." Here was Rodney Dorman's moment of triumphal vengeance. Good riddance to them, he crowed, presuming that Seward hadn't survived, for both men were "nuisances to the earth," and "a thousand deaths each could not atone for their cruelty, crimes & wickedness." A Union soldier in the city's occupying forces surmised that local Confederates were "making merry," even if they remained silent in public, and no doubt Dorman confined his sentiments to the pages of his diary. There he relished the news, grateful to both God and the assassin. Whoever the killer was, he was "a great public benefactor."[1]

The next evening came further confirmation via another vessel (with no contradiction of Seward's demise), fanning Dorman's glee, alongside his ever-present ire. How glorious that neither man could any longer "exult & gloat over the South, & the ruin & devastation they have caused," he wrote. Among Dorman's other targets were Henry Ward Beecher (along with all meddling northern ministers), New York newspaperman Horace

Greeley, radical Republican senator Charles Sumner of Massachusetts, and other such "disgraces to humanity & the world." All these evil people—who Dorman thought of as a "sanctimonious band of self satisfied villians & hypocrites"—should now live in fear that God would strike them down too.[2]

The gratification that Rodney Dorman expressed at Lincoln's assassination stemmed from the same convictions that drove his reactions to Union victory: fury, inflamed by the humiliation of defeat. During the war, fellow Confederates and the rebel press had fed that anger, casting Abraham Lincoln as a tyrant who deserved death for barbaric actions like arming the enslaved men of the South. Dorman had always considered Lincoln the quintessential wicked northerner imposing his decrees on the white South, beginning with a party platform that wanted slavery excluded from all future states carved out of the western territories. The Yankee chief's dictatorship extended to his administration's abridgment of civil liberties, notably the wartime suspension of the writ of habeas corpus. Now, after the assassination, Dorman seethed as he read in the northern papers about the arrest of those who expressed approval of Lincoln's murder. "A general hanging of the whole batch of officials, as userpers & outlaws, would be but slight redress to the outraged laws of the country," he fumed, "yet they talk of treason & traitors with reference to others." The same kind of corruption prevailed in Jacksonville, and the demagogues in the Yankees' sham republican government with its phony laws "ought to have their brains blown out immediately." That is, Dorman added, "if they have any brains." And speaking of tyranny, the Emancipation Proclamation alone constituted an illegal usurpation of power for which President Lincoln—*Lincon*—"deserved assassination." Only public execution would have been better.[3]

Dorman's satisfaction at Lincoln's death was interrupted only by the sight of mourners in his midst. Just as he had so painfully observed celebrations of Union victory all around him, he now watched as black people and Yankee occupiers wept and prayed, lowered their American flags ("hanging out rags," he called it), and draped the city's churches. Even worse was the behavior of local whites. They may have been Unionists or they may have been poorer residents who had never much supported the Confederate effort, but either way their sycophantic public laments were nauseating.

As far as Dorman was concerned, any white southerner who mourned for Lincoln was either a fool or insane.[4]

LINCOLN'S MOURNERS INSISTED ON DESCRIBING to themselves and one another a "universal" grief, imagining a once divided nation now united by the assassination of its leader, even as they saw evidence to the contrary. Contradictory evidence aside, mourners nonetheless built an optimistic vision of a nation rising from Union victory, a healed nation to which the vanquished would willingly return as patriots. Perhaps those were the hopes of Union officer Oscar Ireland, who wrote home from Virginia, claiming that "all over the land seems to be the same mind." Everywhere he looked, he saw "mourning and regret for the loss of the President" and "hatred and scorn for the fiendishness and utter folly of the assassins." Maybe Ireland intended to include the freshly defeated Confederates in his vision, or maybe he was writing prescriptively (*Here is what everyone ought to be feeling*) or perhaps just hopefully. Lincoln's mourners contradicted themselves all the time when they wrote about the grief of "the nation," sometimes seeming to conjure the entire population of North and South alike, other times clearly excluding the Confederates, and much of the time writing in sweeping phrases too vague to interpret one way or the other.[5]

Thornier questions stood behind such pronouncements. How could white southerners be subsumed into the victorious Union—or should they be? Should recalcitrant Confederates be coerced into patriotism—or could they be? Should the privileges of citizenship be extended to the defiant among them? These were the questions that would trouble Lincoln's mourners in the weeks and months to come, most especially black mourners and their white abolitionist allies. From the other side, a white South Carolina journalist wrote that the assassination would "hardly affect the relations of the two countries," truculent words that defined the Confederacy as a separate nation-state, even after conquest and surrender. Cries of despair in the diaries of the southern elite attest to the same conviction. "Alas! for my poor Country," wrote a former slave owner in Mississippi. "Oh! my poor Country," wrote a Louisiana planter. "What have you yet to suffer?" The fact was, for Confederates, Lincoln's assassination was a different matter altogether. For one thing, most of them hated Lincoln. They had hated Lincoln when he ran for president in 1860, and they hated him through all four years of war. In the rebel press, in textbooks, cartoons, verse, and the theater, Confederates had painted the Yankee executive as a boorish frontier oaf, a buffoon and a drunk, an ape, a gorilla, and a baboon, a bastard and a coward, a warmonger and a butcher, a monster and a tyrant, a Negrophile and a Negro himself. And to think that this creature had walked through the streets of their capital city in triumph, surrounded by free black people who worshipped him as a god![6]

When Lincoln was assassinated, Confederates had just stepped into the long grief of surrender, and it was surrender that remained immediate and disastrous, producing apprehension and anxiety, fear and distress, melancholy and depression. Surrender had destroyed their world, including the enslavement of black people, a system that had been central to southern society for nearly two hundred years. Accordingly, whereas African Americans worried about the revival of legal slavery, Confederates agonized over its demise. True, Lincoln's assassination shifted the mantle of gloom and offered Confederates an unexpected reprieve in the form of their conquerors' woe. True too, a lone few fantasized that the assassination would reverse defeat, perhaps "produce anarchy in Yankeedom," which would then make southern independence possible. But most knew that the assassination could not undo defeat. They knew the difference between their own rejoicings at Lincoln's death and the rejoicings of the Yankees at Union victory. Theirs was nothing more than a temporary lifting of the shadows, a mere postponement of long-term despair. All knew, too, that the steady pain of humiliation had not transferred to the Union. Rodney Dorman's moment of triumphal vengeance was just that: a moment. What was more, the war's casualties were colossal—the numbers for the losing side proportionally even greater than for the victors—and now came the crushing awareness that all those losses had been for nothing. For Confederates, the unthinkable calamity, the heart-sinking, time-stopping, faith-defying cataclysm was defeat.[7]

Preoccupied as they were, then, many white southerners seemed barely to register the assassination. Confederate officer John Taylor Wood noted the news in his often-detailed diary this way: "Heard of Lincoln's death. Mobile & Columbus lost" (the Alabama city had fallen to the Union army two days before Booth shot Lincoln, the Georgia city on Easter Sunday).

Captain Henry Chambers of the Forty-Ninth North Carolina had recently covered two pages of his journal with morose reflections on the "bitter, bitter humiliation" of surrender, waxing poetic about the rain falling like nature's tears for the loss of white freedom. Now Chambers squeezed in the words "rumors of Lincoln's death," and the next day squeezed in "Lincoln's assassination confirmed." Others referenced the news as no more than an irritant. A woman in New Orleans, delayed in trying to procure a fashionable hat for a friend in Natchez, explained that "unfortunately on account of Pres. Lincoln's death, the stores were closed in the city," the misfortune being the shuttered shops. A Tennessee farmer expressed exasperation at the interruption to planting corn, what with all the fuss, and a young Confederate in Philadelphia worried about getting home to Baltimore, with all trains stopped while the assassin remained at large. "My troubles never cease," she complained to her diary. In a letter from Richmond, Emmy Welford likewise filled two pages with descriptions of the fallen capital and the mortifying presence of black soldiers, followed by a single line: "Of course you have heard of the assassination of Lincoln." Confederates "grieved dreadfully," she added, "at our defeat."[8]

Some made no mention at all. The news had already arrived at Fort Delaware when Confederate soldier James McMichael wrote only about the disgrace of losing the war and his *"long, dark* and *miserable* year in prison." When Mary Bethell, a North Carolina plantation mistress, picked up her diary after a two-month hiatus, she recorded surrender, the end of slavery, and the return of her two sons from the army but not a word about the assassination. Even more pointed, when a Confederate woman wrote of the "deplorable events" of April 14 and 15, she described how she had watched from her Virginia porch as Union gunboats landed and Yankees marched through the streets. They had come into her very own yard, and eventually her former slaves had departed with them. For her, those events, not the crime at Ford's Theatre up in Washington, were the tragedies of April 14 and 15, 1865.[9]

Unadorned narrations or studious silences could reflect fears of committing one's true sentiments to paper that might pass through Yankee hands, and no doubt some Confederates censored their reactions. In the Yankee capital, William Owner had entitled his diary "Notes & Incidents of the B.R. War To Subjugate the South And Steal Niggers." *B.R.* stood for "Black Republican," a common epithet for antislavery politicians, and during the war Owner wrote reams of vitriol to match that phrase, including gleefully celebrating the news of William Seward's carriage accident in early April. When Lincoln was shot, though, Owner recorded nothing beyond the bare facts. More to the point, for many Confederates there was simply no contest: their own defeat and the destruction of slavery easily trumped the death of the Yankee president. When Confederates did write in greater detail about the assassination, many added their trepidations to the record. "I fear it bodes no good for the south," wrote Marmaduke Shannon, former editor of the *Vicksburg Whig,* to his daughter. Lucy Fletcher despaired that the man who had once been a "living buffoon" was now a martyr, fretting likewise that his murder "bodes no good to us." During the war, Mary Chesnut's plantation-class friends had caricatured Lincoln as a baboon, and even as they continued to do so after the assassination, Chesnut felt afraid. "This foul murder will bring down worse miseries on us," she confided to her diary, revealing a sense of unease about both the crime and its effects on her circle. A Confederate officer in a Union prison summed up his people's anxiety most accurately: "The principal cause of our feeling the matter so strongly," he wrote, "is the question of how it will affect us."[10]

In their own way, then, Confederates mourned for Lincoln too. Paradoxically, or perhaps hypocritically, despite their relentless assertions of the president as a tyrant, they felt uneasy precisely because they suspected that Lincoln would ultimately have treated them with lenience, a view that followed logically from the comparative moderation he demonstrated all during the war. "Horrible news!" Margaret Wight wrote in her diary, for without Lincoln, Confederates could expect only "the hardest terms." A state senator wrote to his sweetheart that Lincoln "would have been more liberal to the Southern people than any one else," while another agitated Confederate agreed that he "would have shown *mercy* & pardon." A North Carolina slave owner spoke for many when he wrote that Lincoln's death was "to us politically disastrous," letting slip his genuine regret when he explained that "old Abe with all his apeishness, was a kind hearted man and disposed to treat us generously." Many Union supporters accordingly understood that when Confederates wept for Lincoln, it was largely because "they know their loss," because "they could not hope for a more lenient chief ruler," because they had "lost a friend."[11]

Out in public, Confederates in Union-occupied areas often found silence to be the most prudent response, for despite surrender, it felt a lot like the war was still on. On the home front, tensions with the occupying troops were palpable. "We were all right uneasy," an imprisoned soldier confided to his diary, "lest the Yankees might retaliate on us." In Vicksburg, where bells tolled and black Union soldiers displayed their mourning badges, the defeated exercised caution. "No guests tonight," one woman recorded. "We are all going to bed early." In Raleigh, rumors of reprisal swirled. "How uneasy we were!" wrote Bessie Caine; "frightened to death," she and her comrades filled their pockets with valuables and slept in their clothes. As for those who dared to mingle outside, they carefully expressed regret at the crime, afraid that nightfall would bring the complete destruction of their city. Likewise in New Orleans, the "*Rebs* had to keep very quiet," Union men observed, even if they were "secretly rejoicing."[12]

Again, Lincoln's mourners looked into the faces of those around them, now with rancor and mistrust, searching for what might lie behind mute masks, looking for attitudes that could destroy hopes of a healed nation unified in sorrow. In Charleston, as flags were lowered and guns fired, the white residents stayed aloof, and with good reason, a northern missionary asserted, since "every native is looked at suspiciously." In Richmond, Union soldiers "looked sharp at those who passed." In Savannah, the soldiers walked the streets, "looking each man in the face" for traces of "so much as a smile." In Raleigh, it was a good thing the Confederates stayed "mighty mum," since "they would have been served the same way"—as the slain Lincoln, that is—"if they had shown any pleasure about it."[13]

Silence and absence were harder to read definitively, but it was the matter of black drapery that proved most vexing. As much as Lincoln's mourners wanted to read the festooned buildings around them as the whole world's bereavement, they worried that mourning crape could make for a relatively effortless deception of true feelings, and they knew that such displays of fabric did not always indicate genuine loyalty or grief. Even as a Washington correspondent wrote that "a smitten nation wept" from "sea to sea," the capital's mourners knew otherwise. Secessionists, one noted, "*all* draped their houses in crape." The secesh, another explained, "fling out their mourning through fear." On the waters, a Confederate gunboat sailed in broad daylight with American flags slung at half-mast until it had passed the federal fleet, whereupon the sailors completely lowered the enemy flag and hoisted their own. In Baltimore, more subtly, some Confederate sympathizers draped their homes with the "scantiest possible amount of mourning," while conversely in New Orleans, observed Confederate Sarah Morgan, "the more thankful they are for Lincoln's death, the more profusely the houses are decked with the emblems of woe." Even those who "hated Lincoln with all their souls" decorated their homes out of fear. As one of Morgan's neighbors cried, "This vile, *vile* old crape!"[14]

Swayed by the dream of post-victory unity, some of Lincoln's mourners took Confederate laments as sincere. A Baltimore Unionist thought the secessionists around her showed the "strongest feelings of sympathy," and in Montgomery, Alabama, even though grieving Confederates had been "*bitter rebels,*" a Union observer willingly embraced their about-face. Skepticism was the order of the day for most mourners, however, with African Americans the least inclined to attribute authentic grief to white southerners (many former slaves, after all, knew personally that their masters had displayed a duplicitous paternalism to the world). Black men in Richmond who saw Confederate officers wearing crape on their uniforms declared themselves the only ones who wore such badges as "truthful expressions." The best assessment came from the pen of Thomas Morris Chester, the black Richmond journalist. Rebel officers sporting black crape signified either "feigned regret for the assassination" or "sincere sorrow for the death of the Southern Confederacy." Morris was right: Confederates were grieving, but not for President Lincoln.[15]

Neither apprehensions about their own future nor fear of Union vengeance stopped Confederates from reveling privately, and Rodney Dorman was hardly alone in gloating over Lincoln's murder as retribution for conquest. "Pity it hadn't been done years ago," one rebel soldier wrote. Another thought Booth had committed the "best *act* of his life," adding that the assassin's cry of "Sic semper tyrannis" should be translated as "Bully for Booth." When William Ellis, marching home from Lee's army, got the news from trains passing through South Carolina, he wrote in his diary, "Thus passeth from earth one of the greatest monsters who ever lived."

In Texas, a doctor wrote to his son-in-law, overjoyed at the "killing of the cold hearted tyrant Lincoln," hoping the assassin would live to "burst the sculls" of a few more despots (the doctor signed his letter "Thine in Christ"). Fire-eating secessionist and proslavery proselytizer Edmund Ruffin rejoiced privately at home, enjoying a rare interruption to his consuming depression over defeat. While Lincoln's grieving supporters earnestly copied down the details of the assassination, Ruffin perused the northern papers with a different purpose. Like Dorman, he believed that the Yankee president deserved death for the destruction of slavery, and thus did he find the details of the crime to be "entertaining reading."[16]

Gleeful expressions filled the personal writings of Confederate women on the home front too. Secure in their lack of full citizenship, and perhaps construing themselves as powerless in the wake of a war that had in fact empowered them at home, they felt even less constricted in recording sentiments offensive to the victors. The day before she got word of the assassination, seventeen-year-old Emma LeConte had been "sick at heart," wondering "what fresh misfortune will I have to chronicle tomorrow?" When the news arrived the next day, during a German lesson, LeConte positively cheered. "Hurrah!" she wrote. "Old Abe Lincoln has been assassinated!" The lesson forgotten, everyone around her was "so excited," talking endlessly about the wonderful surprise. Soon LeConte took off, "trembling and my heart beating with excitement," mixed with "gratified revenge." She stopped first at her aunt Josie's, where everyone shouted, "Isn't it splendid?" A similar scene of jubilation awaited her at home. As for the "*vile* Seward," LeConte was disappointed only that he had escaped death. Best of all was picturing the abrupt end to Union victory celebrations. Stopping for a moment to wonder if it was all a "Yankee lie," she added, "If it is *only* true!"[17]

Cloe Whittle prayed that God would prevent her from "feeling *glad* at this awful & most horrible transaction," but most Confederates prayed in the other direction. Clara Dargan wrote in her diary about the assassination and the attack on Seward, calling the two victims a "Royal Suite of the Imperial Apes" and thanking God fervently for a "first gleam of light in this midnight darkness." Twenty-one-year-old Sarah Wadley was likewise "electrified" by the tidings, which readily shook her out of her surrender-induced melancholy. Wadley took comfort in the assassin's motto, hoping his words would "find an echo in every southron's heart." More laconic expressions were no less sincere. "I glory in the *assassinator*," wrote a Texas woman, while another in South Carolina called the news "very cheering."[18]

This kind of spiteful gratification rose from the ongoing war in hearts and minds, in which Lincoln's violent death avenged the destruction of the Confederate nation and its precious institution of slavery. It was not simply that Lincoln had been killed, it was also that Confederates could now return the humiliating glee that Yankees had expressed in the process of conquering their land. For Amanda Edmunds, the despised Lincoln and Seward had now "felt the suffering which they have inflicted on our Southern people." Kate Stone, who had lost two brothers in the war, honored Booth in her journal, naming him the "brave destroyer" of the tyrant Lincoln, who could no longer "rejoice in our humiliation." Should Booth escape to the South, Stone felt sure he would "meet with a warm welcome."[19]

Public delight in the assassination could be safely manifested where there was no Union presence to interfere. When the news arrived at a Georgia train station just north of where Sherman's army had marched to the sea, Confederates laughed and clapped. But white southerners did not have to be isolated to react honestly. From the moment of victory, the joy coursing through black communities in the South had been tempered by unease, with wartime hostilities further stirred up. "We are surrounded by a people who hate us with a deadly hatred," wrote a northern teacher working among former slaves in Natchez, Mississippi. The night schools for freedpeople in Hampton, Virginia, had to be suspended, another teacher explained, because of all the paroled rebel soldiers "let loose here to prowl around the country, threatening the lives of Union men and colored people." In Richmond, the "*wrath* and hatred" of former masters, who watched their own former slaves (for some, their biological children) walk freely to church and school, was "*terrible, terrible.*"[20]

Lincoln's assassination only exacerbated this antagonism, even more vividly giving the lie to mourners' deluded, if soothing, assertions of a nation united by the terrible crime. While Confederates feared retaliation from angry mourners, worries went both ways. In Portsmouth, Virginia, it was dangerous to venture out at night "since the assassination of the Pres. and since the return of so many Rebel prisoners," wrote a northern missionary. As soldiers from Lee's defunct army filled the streets of Richmond, no more would Thomas Seymour, a young white man working with freedpeople, amble over to the telegraph office at night, since "by the citizens we are known to be Yankees." In Saint Augustine, Florida, downhearted rebels brightened at news of the assassination, "taunting the colored people" about reenslavement, and in Lexington, Kentucky, a white man named Thomas Outten assaulted a black man, calling out, "Old Lincoln is dead, and I will kill the goddamned Negroes now." When news of the assassination arrived in New Orleans, Patrick Shields, whose slaves had left during the war, pointed to the newspaper being passed among his black neighbors and laughed in approval. Shields attracted a crowd of black and white onlookers as he proclaimed that "all the niggers" would now "go home to their masters." Jefferson Davis, he went on, was coming to "hang all the niggers to the trees."[21]

Merrymakers weren't necessarily deterred by the presence of black Union soldiers either, and some were downright emboldened, aiming their actions directly at them. Confederates in Key West demonstrated "expressions of joy" in front of the black troops, and a white woman in Jacksonville asked black men if they were "going to celebrate." Extra soldiers were called out to patrol the streets of New Orleans after dark, "fearing some trouble with the Negroe Regiment stationed here," and black occupiers in Petersburg witnessed paroled officers "strutting about" with their swords and pistols, making known "the most jubilant manifestations of satisfaction." In Tennessee, a white woman jeered at African American soldiers, telling them, "Your father is dead." Gleeful rebels ignored white enemies too. Unionists in Baltimore saw returning Confederate soldiers "partying it about," while a Richmond Unionist reported local women exulting over the assassination.[22]

For all that, Confederates who expressed glee in public did not always get away with it, and any such demonstration might become a symbolic battlefield on which to put down unfinished rebellion. In a variant of "hard war," in which the Union understood Confederate soldiers, leaders, and civilians alike as enemy and target, authorities might react with violence to any impudent or imprudent act in the wake of Lincoln's assassination. As Albert Browne wrote home from Charleston, "Woe be to him who should dare to utter one word of jubilation." In prison camps in particular, Union officials saw little reason to withhold retaliatory discipline. When one inmate in Chicago responded to the news with the words, "That's bully," a Yankee commenced "kicking him about like a brute," then hung him twenty feet off the ground for hours, with irons tied to both legs. At Fort Delaware, a prisoner who called Lincoln a "goddamned old nigger-loving son of a bitch" was knocked down and slapped by a Union general, hung by his hands for an hour, and ordered whipped by a black man. When prisoners at Fort Jefferson, Florida, cheered Lincoln's death, they were tied up and suspended, their feet barely touching the ground. The men begged and prayed and cursed to no avail, prompting remorse from some of their captors; other Union men, though, wanted to shoot them right there.[23]

Civilians who refused to censor their anti-Lincoln sentiments in public could also find themselves in trouble. Suspicious of a man observed doing no more than laughing on his porch, Yankees searched his house and threatened to burn it down. When locals in Alexandria, Virginia, refused to obey orders to drape their homes, some were assaulted with brickbats and stones. "The fate of our President has so enraged the soldiers at St. Louis," a northerner observed, "that several persons have been shot who have said things in the wrong direction." Surrender or no surrender, rebels remained defiant, and Yankees responded with violence. Legal action could also be a consequence. Union authorities in Huntsville, Alabama, announced that anyone rejoicing at the assassination would be tried for treason, and elsewhere jubilant Confederates were in fact arrested: in Chattanooga for "expressing pleasure" at the assassination; in Mobile for declaring that Lincoln was "not worth the powder that shot him"; in Nashville for joking that the headlines should have read "Glorious News!" When two stricken Union men brought a newspaper into a cigar store on Magazine Street in New Orleans, only to hear the proprietor say, "I am glad of it, I hope it is true," they had the offender taken into custody. In Washington, when a black woman reported a secessionist thanking God for Booth, authorities seized the man. At least some of these arrests resulted from more than words, including that of Patrick Shields, who harassed his black neighbors in New Orleans, and Thomas Outten, who assaulted a black man in Lexington. As a northern teacher wrote to her parents from Charleston, "More than one man was arrested for expressing his joy at the news," and there was "considerable apprehension as to the safety of the Northerners."[24]

Whether Confederates remained silent, gloated in private, or expressed themselves in public with or without retaliation, they knew their joy was fleeting. Even the exuberant young Emma LeConte understood that Lincoln's death could not reverse defeat. "There seems no reason to exult, for this will make no change in our position," she sighed amid her family's happy acclamations. When Georgia plantation mistress Caroline Jones considered that Lincoln could no longer "raise his howl of diabolical triumph," she knew it was only "one sweet drop among so much that is painful." In South Carolina, Mary Chesnut listened to the men around her talk about "a nation in mourning," with no reference to Lincoln. The Confederacy was her nation, and its downfall her people's tragedy; "glorious young blood poured out like rain on the battlefields," Chesnut wrote. "For what?" When Rodney Dorman poured his elation into his private journal, it was tinged with the same question.[25]

ALTHOUGH CONFEDERATES CONTRADICTED COMFORTING visions of universal grief, Lincoln's mourners could at least wave them away as the stubborn enemy and bitter losers. But northerners who declined to mourn—or, worse, openly celebrated—proved more irksome to the loyal bereaved. It was these subversives who most uncomfortably disrupted the idea of a unified victorious and grieving nation at war's end, for these antagonists dwelled within the Union states, among the mourners, in their own towns and cities, some even right next door.

Named by their opponents after a poisonous snake, these were the *Copperheads,* members of the northern Democratic Party who disagreed with the whole premise of a civil war over slavery. As the most virulent faction of the so-called Peace Democrats (they were against the war, but not because they were pacifists), Copperheads renounced the conflict as an unconstitutional raising of arms. Many who identified as such—they soon took the name for their own—had come from slave states or emigrated from Ireland or Germany, joining the northern working classes. Their common denominator was hostility to the antislavery cause, often accompanied by intense racism. Lines of dissent and treason blurred during wartime, but most Copperheads were not strictly traitors, since they did not support secession or hope for Confederate victory. Their desire, rather, was to restore the pre–Civil War nation, but since Confederates were fighting to preserve slavery via secession and independence, that position made little sense. If Lincoln gave in to his northern enemies and gave up on the war, there would be two nations, not one, a problem the Copperheads avoided addressing.

Copperheads had made known their anti-Lincoln sentiments at the outbreak of war, and in late 1862 they again spoke up loudly when President Lincoln introduced his plans for the Emancipation Proclamation. The pinnacle of their influence came in the summer of 1864, with mounting Confederate victories, a rising Union death toll, and tensions over the northern draft. Their nadir came that autumn, with the fall of Atlanta to Sherman's army, followed by Sheridan's Shenandoah Valley campaign, both of which ensured Lincoln's handy reelection in November. Then, the assassination unleashed the Copperheads again, as they spewed enough glee to make clear that they had never melted away. Now mourners had to contend not only with defiant Confederates but also with a faction of northern citizens who turned the Union home front into a battleground. At the literal battlefront too, loyal Union soldiers confronted outspoken disloyal brethren in blue.

Not all of Lincoln's northern adversaries felt free to speak their minds. The same as fearful southern whites, some Copperheads just kept quiet. In upstate New York, locals known for their anti-Lincoln sentiments all played the parts of "good Union men," and in a northern California town, any rejoicing among them had to take place "in their own Houses & among themselves." Where Union supporters and Confederate sympathizers had once gotten along out west by steering clear of war talk, such toleration was simply not possible after the assassination; one mourner decided then and there to "quit all social intimacy" with those on the other side. Like nervous Confederates, some Copperheads also hid their hatred of Lincoln in deceptive public displays. In Chicago, an abolitionist schoolteacher noticed that "strong Democrats now mourn with the rest." In Saco, Maine, everyone paid tribute to Lincoln, "even those who were against him politically." The city of Trenton, with a reputation for disloyalty, was soon "draped in mourning from one end to the other," and in Brooklyn there were "plenty of Traitors & copperheads hanging out mourning," wrote one of the aggrieved, scoffing at those "compelled by public feeling to act the Hypocrite." A sergeant in the Fifteenth New Jersey likewise painfully admitted that many in his company had "secretly rejoiced" at the news; none had "dared to cheer," he added, though he felt sure that "if some Rebel had proposed it there were plenty ready to join in."[26]

Still, many Copperheads, like many Confederates, refused to disguise their true sentiments. Private or semiprivate conversations proved the least dangerous. In Bloomington, Indiana, a woman declared her intention to "give a grand dinner" to mark the occasion. In Saint Peter, Minnesota, a young woman told a Union soldier that she "expected to have a good time" at a local ball "because Lincoln was killed" (the man promptly withdrew his invitation). In Boston, an Irish cook made her politics known in front of her employer by "laughing all day" when the news arrived. In another northern household, the Irish servants made clear that they were "*so glad* Lincoln was dead!" As their mistress explained it to herself, "They hate him for emancipating the negroes, fearing we shall employ them, & reduce the wages." Meanwhile, a New York hotel fired its Irish waiters for their "Celtic talk approving Lincoln's murder."[27]

Mixing race and racism into their post-assassination utterances, Copperheads fanned another ongoing conflict on the northern home front: that between abolitionists, black and white, who wanted equal rights for African Americans, and those who wanted no such thing. One soldier said he approved of Lincoln's death because the president was an abolitionist who had caused "thousands of innocent men being killed." Private Elijah Chapman was angry that the president had doffed his hat to black people, and Private Henry Peters told another soldier in the washroom of a Saint Louis boardinghouse that he applauded the assassination because Lincoln was "for the Negro." At Philadelphia's naval hospital, a sailor hoped aloud that "the next president will put the niggers where they ought to be," while in camp in Alabama a Union soldier declared the murder justified since Lincoln permitted "white men to be slaughtered for the nigger." Like Confederates, Copperheads also directed their taunts directly at African Americans. A Union soldier from Indiana, in camp in Nashville, boasted of telling a black man that he rejoiced in Lincoln's death. "Goddamn him," the soldier added, "he ought to have been killed long ago." On Saint Helena Island, a sneering Union army boatswain told the deckhands, "Come up here you damned black sons of bitches, your best friend is dead." Even more disconcerting, Copperheads extended threats of white-on-black violence into the North, as far up as Canada. A black minister in Ontario, shattered at news of the assassination, heard a group of boys delighting that "the nigger's friend was dead." Spying the minister, they turned on him, exclaiming, "There is one of his nigger friends now."[28]

This flare-up of Copperhead sentiments provoked violent thoughts among grieving civilians. A Massachusetts farmer described the reaction of the bereaved as "bloodthirsty," while a Pennsylvania woman declared indignant mourners "ready to go to war *now*." Told of a man exulting over the assassination, a Baltimore mourner wanted the offender "dangling from a lamp post." Passing men on the streets of Boston who didn't appear to be mourning, Caroline Dall "could have killed them." Female offenders might be spared, perhaps because their talk (like that of Confederate women) did not seem sufficiently threatening. In Chicago, a woman seen tearing down mourning drapery was quickly surrounded by an "indignant crowd," then left alone after she slipped into a shop. When gossip circulated in an upstate New York town that Susan Hews had clapped and cheered at the news, citizens ordered her exiled, but Hews denied the reports. One angry mourner called her a "dirty low-minded ignorant disloyal contemptable *Thing*," making clear that had she "been a *man*," she would never have gotten away with her alleged behavior. Still, femininity was not always a safeguard, at least not in the eyes of female mourners. Em Cornwall, disgusted by insincere drapery in her Connecticut town, wanted to "knock every one of the mean, nasty, slimy, reptiles into the dust," whether they wore "petticoats or pantaloons."[29]

Nor was it all wishes and warnings. Menacing crowds forced some transgressors into exile and made others take back their insults, as in Brattleboro, Vermont, where neighbors forced a man to mount a wagon and recant. In New York, mourners tarred an undraped house, and in Germantown, Pennsylvania, three men swore at a neighborhood traitor so menacingly that a black-bordered flag soon floated from his window. Copperhead expressions could also induce a warlike atmosphere. In Boston, reports of anti-Lincoln behavior prompted an increase in the police force. In Indianapolis, Union soldiers who expressed satisfaction with the president's death were so violently threatened that they were put under the protection of military authorities. In San Francisco, mourners attacked Democratic newspaper offices, and the militia was called out, with the city under siege for days.[30]

Tarring and Feathering at Swampscott, Mass., of a Justifier of the Assassin.

New Englanders react in fury to a man who expressed glee over Lincoln's death. This woodcut from an April 1865 issue of the *National Police Gazette,* entitled "Tarring and Feathering at Swampscott, Mass., of a Justifier of the Assassin," shows the tarred and feathered victim paraded through the streets with an American flag planted next to him. The mob includes a bonneted woman (far right) and a young boy (far left).
National Police Gazette, April 29, 1865, Lincoln Collection Publications and Newspapers, Special Collections Research Center, University of Chicago Library.

Just as Lincoln's mourners copied out the facts of the night at Ford's Theatre in their personal writings, so too did they copy down reports of Copperhead expressions and the violence that ensued, whether gleaned from newspaper notices or captured in swirling rumors. From the Boston area came stories of a store mobbed and cleaned out, a man tarred and feathered, people "roughly handled," factory workers assaulted by fellow laborers. Word came that a man joking that Lincoln "had as much brain now as he ever had" was nearly killed by a mob. New Yorkers offered accounts of gloating Irish immigrants igniting "violent demonstrations," a young boy beaten, a man carried "almost dead" to the police station. Rumors circulated of a Copperhead in Pennsylvania quickly "crushed into a jelly"; a man in Washington shot by Union cavalry for proclaiming the assassination "good enough for the black rascal"; an offender in Chicago "shot dead" for exulting in the murder; a fellow in Minnesota hanged from a tree as "a warning to all future traitors."[31]

To preserve the details of Copperhead actions in their personal writings, to express outrage about such actions, and in particular to record the retaliations helped to preserve mourners' imagined visions of a victorious nation united in grief by declaring that there was no place for such sentiments. Most who recorded these incidents and their consequences, like Sarah Browne, did so without voicing objection ("All this is right," she wrote), and some capped their narratives with a retributive *served him right*. "I do not believe in mob law," wrote the antislavery and women's rights reformer Martha Coffin Wright in upstate New York, where she had heard about a forced exile, but neither did she object to what she called "a *quiet drumming out of town*." An Ohio man insisted that the nation must be "thoroughly purged of the unclean," and a New Englander even defended reports of the murder of Copperheads by asserting that no one who reacted violently was "quite sane in this moment of horror." To demand the exile, purge, and death of those in the Union who celebrated Lincoln's assassination was to mark them as outsiders, brazen misfits, deranged deviants.[32]

"Secretary Stanton has ordered that all persons expressing treasonable sentiments shall be placed under arrest," a Philadelphia man wrote in his journal, and citizens of the Union indeed faced legal consequences for demonstrations of glee. In this sense as well, the war was not over, for the army still sought out traitors and prosecuted sedition. In Baltimore, a man was found guilty for proclaiming, "They were building another part in hell for Abe Lincoln"; another for declaring, "The damned old son of a bitch is dead at last." Both were sentenced to thirty days in jail. In West Virginia, a man was sentenced to a year in prison for stating that Lincoln had ruined the country and that "a few more of our leaders ought to be strung up." Trouble could come far from the war too. In a Los Angeles saloon, Chat Helms was playing a drinking game when news of the assassination arrived, upon which he announced that "he would walk a thousand miles to have the pleasure of shitting on the president's grave." Helms was apprehended under General Order No. 27 of the Department of the Pacific, which called for the arrest of those who celebrated Lincoln's death, on the theory that they were "virtually accessories after the fact" and therefore threats to the social order. Helms was found guilty, though released with the explanation that he was no more than "an ignorant person, occupying no social position."[33]

Members of the Union armed forces who publicly delighted in the assassination were especially subject to violent treatment, and whether or not authorities brought formal charges, fellow soldiers and sailors frequently took informal retribution upon themselves. These were often public shaming rituals (supposedly rarer in northern culture, compared to the more honor-based culture of white southerners). When a man in the Seventeenth Maine "expressed satisfaction at the murder," his compatriots hauled him off to a nearby pond, where they dunked him almost to the point of drowning ("He was taken from the water more dead than alive, coated with green slime"). In an Indiana regiment, officers intervened to prevent the drowning of an offender but let the men whip him severely, along with another guilty party. "Searved him right," a witness wrote to his wife. "I hope they will shoot both of them."[34]

Union troops and their officers were expected by law to demonstrate loyalty, and the War Department issued orders requiring expressions of "profound sorrow" over the assassination. Charges varied for those who disobeyed. Sometimes court cases named violation of the Fifth Article of War, which mandated trial by court-martial for speaking of the president with contempt. More often, courts brought charges of disrespectful, disloyal, treasonable, seditious, or mutinous language, disloyal conduct, or (in a regularly invoked phrase) "conduct prejudicial to good order and military discipline." Quietly declining to wear crape could get you arrested, as could declaring the assassination inconsequential—not particularly sad or "a damned small loss." A lieutenant colonel from Wisconsin (known to call Lincoln a fool and an imbecile when alive) was arrested for announcing that the country would "suffer nothing" by his death. At Camp Fry in Washington, D.C., Private Elijah Chapman similarly proclaimed that "a damned sight better men than Abraham Lincoln ever was, has died, and not as much fuss made about it." But the more common alleged offense was public delight. A sergeant in Fort Preble, Maine, said it was "too good to believe," and the army boatswain on Saint Helena said he'd celebrate if he had a bottle of whiskey. Offensive conduct included laughter, cheering, waving one's cap, and general joviality. When the news interrupted the victory celebrations of the 182nd Ohio, Private Eli Smith proceeded to sing anti-Lincoln ditties. In camp in Tennessee, a private shouted, "Hip, hip, hurrah, Lincoln is dead."[35]

Copperhead soldiers and sailors let loose all kinds of inflammatory remarks that resulted in arrest. They damned Lincoln and said he'd gone to hell. They called him a cur, a son of a bitch, a damned son of a bitch, "a long slab-sided Yankee son of a bitch," and a "damned old whoremaster." Like the saloon patron in Los Angeles, a Union mate on the Mississippi River said he would find Lincoln's grave and "shit on it." Praise for the assassin constituted an offense as well. Docked at the Brooklyn navy yard, the crew of a vessel clamored for the April 15 edition of the *New York Sun,* then expressed shock when Captain Thomas Jackson called the murderer a bold and brave man. At camp in Illinois with the Twenty-Fourth Michigan, John Largest was in the privy when another soldier bellowed the news through the door, only to hear Largest retort that the assassin had done right. A Union soldier aboard a ship in Haiti was "only sorry that Jeff Davis did not kill him," and an Ohio soldier asserted that if Jefferson Davis and Abraham Lincoln "were put up for a target," he'd "shoot Old Abe first." All of these naysayers were placed under arrest.[36]

Ambiguous circumstances could also land an offender in jail. For James Tozier, on a naval ship off Norfolk, what began as a playful prank ended with legal charges. When a newspaper extra arrived on board, the men crowded around in high spirits, expecting good news. Someone asked Tozier to read the dispatch aloud, "Johnny fashion"—that is, as a Confederate "Johnny Reb" would do. Thus did Tozier announce Lincoln's assassination in elated tones, substituting "glorious news" where the bulletin read "sad news," and calling on the men to give three cheers. Even when someone told Tozier to quit, he persisted, "dancing around the deck holding the hand-bill up and waving it." Act or no act, Tozier was sentenced to a year in prison. Other trials resulted in dishonorable discharge or military prison terms, ranging from a month to two years or the remainder of one's term of service. Most included confinement by ball and chain, hard labor, or both. For Lincoln's antagonists, these military punishments for treasonous expressions only reinforced the unwelcome expanding power of the federal government as an outgrowth of the war.[37]

Copperheads had always disrupted visions of a unified Union during the war, and now they did so again, confounding an imagined community of northern mourners. Yet in the face of all this nettlesome evidence, coming from as far north as Maine and as far west as California, many of Lincoln's mourners continued to paint portraits of collective grief. African Americans everywhere and white Unionists in the border states better understood the tenuousness of this proposition. When black residents of Washington met just after the assassination to compose resolutions, they crafted the phrase, "we, in common with all other loyal citizens," the word *loyal* pointedly excluding northern dissenters. Communications issued by residents of the border states likewise referred to Kentucky's "loyal community" and "loyal Missourians." Otherwise, most white mourners insisted upon sweeping statements, and many, like Sarah Browne, recounted Copperhead offenses right alongside pronouncements of universal bereavement. Immediately after recording the anti-Lincoln outbursts of a local woman, a resident of upstate New York wrote, "I think the sorrow is universal. If Cooperstown is an example the whole country mourns." From Massachusetts, Henry Thacher asserted that "there are few indeed who do not sincerely mourn at this time," adding, "Even the genuine Copperheads are remarkably quiet." Thacher's slippage is telling, since keeping quiet hardly equaled sincerity. Yet this kind of fabricated cohesion served both as a command about acceptable behavior to outliers and as a soothing fiction, since Lincoln's supporters knew full well that white northerners had never entirely united behind the president and the war. Now especially, in the immediate aftermath of the assassination, did the victors-turned-mourners yearn for an uncomplicated unity.[38]

Together, Confederates and Copperheads disrupted the illusion of a continent convulsed by sorrow. Neither the majority of white southerners nor a vocal minority of white northerners belonged to the conjured nation-in-shock. Both groups earned the wrath of Lincoln's mourners, not only because the mourners loved Lincoln, but also because the words and actions of the subversives played havoc with visions of the nation at the exact moment in which the Union had triumphed, at least on the battlefield.

ALONG WITH CONFEDERATES AND COPPERHEADS, there was one other segment of the population that was, if far from gleeful over the assassination, nonetheless not entirely sorry that President Lincoln had been removed as head of state. These were the most radical members of Lincoln's own Republican Party, whose anguish came mixed with a strain of relief. Along with Frederick Douglass and other African American leaders who had advocated untiringly for emancipation, radical Republicans had criticized Lincoln all through the war and right through surrender, concerned at hints of overly conciliatory policies to come. In the aftermath of the assassination, while African Americans north and south genuinely lamented the loss of Lincoln, some of these white radicals expressed quiet satisfaction, as yet unaware of the troubles that would so soon arise with President Andrew Johnson. Indiana congressman George Julian (who had criticized Lincoln and Seward as "great leaders in the policy of mercy") found himself surprised and even disgusted at the forthright hostility toward Lincoln expressed by his fellow radicals after the murder. The "universal feeling among radical men here," Julian wrote in his diary, "is that his death is a godsend." More diplomatically, radical Republican senator Zachariah Chandler of Michigan wrote to his wife that God had allowed Lincoln to remain in office "as long as he was usefull & then substituted a better man to finish the work." That was a sentiment that many white mourners would soon express, for unlike African Americans, they looked toward the elevation of the vice president with great hope.[39]

With Lincoln gone, his antagonists, north and south, asked the same questions as his mourners: about the path of reconstruction and the fate of the vanquished—for Confederates, that meant their own fate. Like Lincoln's mourners, his antagonists also wondered what would happen the next day. Lincoln had died on Saturday, April 15, and as it turned out, the next day was Easter Sunday.

Public Condolences

A TORRENT OF CONDOLENCES FROM across the British Empire bombarded Charles Francis Adams, the Boston Brahmin who served as the U.S. minister in London. From England, Scotland, and Ireland, from "British Jews" to "Mauritian colored residents," came cards, letters, resolutions, and telegrams, and it was his burden to respond to every single one of them. At the same time, Adams and Assistant Secretary Benjamin Moran saw their offices crowded with weeping Americans and Britons, including one elderly fellow who, Moran wrote with exasperation, "cried like a child." Moran also expressed irritation at the hordes, "nearly all of them bores," he added. Adams and Moran were in fact taken by surprise at encountering any mourners at all, since, as Adams marveled, many of the British had quite recently considered Lincoln "an ignorant boor" and William Seward "an ogre." Adams promptly returned a condolence letter from the Confederate Aid Society in Manchester, and as for the Confederate-sympathizing *London Times,* the newspaper had, sniffed Moran, "made a complete somersault."[1]

Not that anti-Lincoln sentiments had gone entirely underground with the assassination, for Moran recorded "much secret exaltation among our enemies," while Adams read a letter from a worker in Hull who castigated his town's Confederate sympathizers. There was the case too of the Londoner who shouted vindictively about the murder while wishing for an earthquake to "swallow up the whole north." Adams's mailbag also held anonymous anti-Lincoln doggerel, including a verse portraying the late president conversing with the devil on his way down to hell ("My Dear Abe Lincoln, I'm glad beyond measure / This visit unlooked for, gives infinite pleasure"). Back across the Atlantic, mourners accordingly read the English newspapers and scoffed at the "*crocodile tears* of the Rebel Sympathisers." Even Confederates mocked the sudden "bootlicking tones" of the English journalists.[2]

Charles Francis Adams held in his hands plentiful evidence of divided reactions, yet (perhaps unsurprisingly) when he fulfilled his diplomatic duty to spread news of the assassination to British consulates across the globe, he felt compelled to write of "regret universally felt," and when he forwarded messages of condolence to Mary Lincoln, he assured her that those sentiments were "felt universally in this Kingdom." Adams was far from alone in the words he chose for his formal communications.[3]

From across the Continent and the world, official tributes poured in to Washington. From Europe and the Mediterranean, Central and South America, Liberia, Russia, China, and Japan, the testimonials came from lords and princes, prime ministers and presidents; the church, the press, and universities; temperance societies, ladies' societies, and secular societies; cotton brokers, railroad companies, and workers' associations. From groups as disparate as Creoles of African descent in Guadeloupe and Polish refugees in Switzerland, nearly all such messages invoked the language of universality. News of the assassination produced "throughout the civilized world a sentiment of indignation and of horror" (a French minister), insured that "all the political factions" spoke in "one unanimous cry" of denunciation (the Italian Chamber of Deputies), and caused "horror and indignation wherever it has gone" (the Hanseatic Republics). Right in the U.S. capital, where secessionists and Copperheads alike could be seen and heard, a group of mourning German immigrants drew up resolutions calling the assassination "shocking to all mankind."[4]

4

❦

God

IN JACKSONVILLE, THE ENEMY HAD been thanking God endlessly since the fall of Richmond, and now it was Rodney Dorman's turn to pay tribute to the Almighty. "Their time had come," he puffed into his diary, with news of the assassination. "Thank God!" While Yankee occupiers and black residents fretted over the mysteries of divine intention, Dorman laughed in their faces. "What will they say to that?" he smirked. "Is it not God's work?" For Dorman, the assassination was an indisputable moment of spiritual certainty, for if Yankees were so sure that God had orchestrated Union victory, had he not also directed the assassination of President Lincoln? Surely if it wasn't God who had cut down their leader at the exact moment of Confederate defeat, then there was no God at all. Of course, the blind and ignorant Yankees would never discern divine intention in the assassination, for it was only in their "perverted, prostituted" ways and their phony Christianity, he wrote, that "they pretend to see his doings." At the very least, the sanctimonious hypocrites should tremble and repent.[1]

Dorman was incensed too that white ministers in the Confederacy were getting in trouble for neglecting to mention Lincoln in their prayers. What sycophancy on the part of those who obeyed!—why, Lincoln, that "ill shapen, deformed, & most evil minded person," would be "damned to

94

Hell," whether anyone prayed for him or not, and the quicker he and his friends got there, the better. Looking toward the future, Dorman composed a prayer of his own. When those in authority were not fit to govern, he exhorted God, "remove them forthwith, in such a manner as, in thy pleasure, may serve as an example to other aspirants & for the good of the people." He asked God to punish "false teachers & leaders" for "every userpation & excess of power." With either humility or hubris, Dorman asked God to answer his prayer "for the sake of mankind." He hoped that the assassination was just the beginning of God's retribution against those who now ruled over his land, and all through the spring and into summer, Dorman continued to pray, if less formally, for a time when the despots in his midst would be "swallowed in one overwhelming gulp."[2]

LIKE MANY ABOLITIONISTS, BOTH BLACK and white, Sarah and Albert Browne vacillated between spiritual trust and uncertainty in the days and weeks following Lincoln's assassination. It was easier for Sarah, more sure-footed in her faith. The pulpit of Salem's Unitarian North Church was draped in mourning and decorated with beautiful flowers, and there she prayed to the "Giver of all good," grateful to him for the fact that President Lincoln had lived to see victory. Through sorrow and anger, Sarah held fast to her confidence in God's mysterious plan for the nation.[3]

Down south, Albert struggled more. With Lee's surrender, he had readily invoked the glory of God ("the God of righteousness has done this"), but Albert was never as comfortable as his wife in the realm of faith. Now he tried to find solace in the mystery of divine ways, hoping for good to emerge out of such patent evil. Writing home, he quoted Matthew 10:29, about no sparrow falling to the ground without God's knowledge and consent, and asked his family to pray for the future, asserting freedom and justice as the war's ultimate outcome. Albert had "not a shadow of doubt" about that, he told Sarah, even as he wrestled with both shadows and doubt. "If I believe at all, I must believe in predestination," he wrote, straying from liberal Christianity as he tried to convince himself that the "omniscient being whom we call God" had a "plan or scheme, call it what you will," for without such a plan—even one that was beyond human comprehension—there could be only dark and dismal chaos. Filled with "gloomy doubts," Albert wondered if he was asserting his faith only because it was "more difficult not to believe." Still, he couldn't keep himself from fretting that perhaps the assassination was a form of divine punishment. While Sarah thought of Lincoln as a Christlike man, Albert could only hope that the president had finished his work on earth. He didn't want to articulate any "reproach of Mr. Lincoln," he hedged, but perhaps the president had "erred in too much leniency" toward the rebels. Maybe that was why God had taken him away right after Union victory.[4]

LIGHT IN THE DARKNESS: THAT'S how Lincoln's assassination felt to the downcast Confederates. Like Rodney Dorman, many of those who expressed glee also expressed gratitude to God for arranging the deed. Recall Clara Dargan (she had named Lincoln and Seward a "Royal Suite of the Imperial Apes"), who thanked God for Lincoln's death, which she called the "first gleam of light in this midnight darkness." Confederates in Nashville likewise prayed in appreciation to God, who had "*at last* shed the Light of His Countenance upon their cause." The fact that Good Friday was meant to be a day of thanksgiving for Union victory seemed definitive proof. Surely it had been a divine act against the wicked Yankees, asserted Elizabeth Alsop, to orchestrate Lincoln's murder on "the very day appointed as a time of *rejoicing* for our misfortunes." What clearer sign could there be, she asked, of providence "visiting their sins upon their own heads"?[5]

Providence: that's how it felt too. All through the war, both sides had judged the outcome of each skirmish and battle, each advance and setback, in terms of God's purposes, and for the Confederates, the previous weeks, even months, had offered no sign of divine favor. Now the "state of alarm" into which the victorious Yankees were so suddenly thrown, a Richmond resident reasoned, pointed clearly to a "visitation of Providence." Some appealed for more of the same—Eleanor Cohen, in Charleston (among the small number of Jewish Confederates), prayed that God would make "all our foes perish!" A few even hoped that a reversal of the war's outcome was imminent. Cloe Whittle thought God wanted to make the assassination "of use to the South," and Eliza French believed that God's warning to the victors "may work out yet for our good." Up north and out west, Copperheads and Confederate sympathizers expressed many of the same thoughts. In New York, some Irish immigrants referred to the assassination as the "judgment of God for political & religious crimes," and a man in California felt sure that God had once again remembered the Confederates and "was on their side." Perhaps, after all, the gloom would lift.[6]

Good cheer could not be sustained, though, as the realities of defeat persisted, even in church. With the surrender of Robert E. Lee, Union authorities had ordered Confederate clergymen to cease their prayers for Jefferson Davis and to pray for President Lincoln instead. Some obeyed, but even after the assassination many refused, and there were reports that in Charleston and Tallahassee, ministers got in trouble for omitting the slain executive from their services. Elsewhere, Union authorities closed down houses of worship whose ministers would not comply, and those who followed the rules did so only with contempt. One minister prayed first for rebel soldiers, then mouthed the decreed prayer by spitting out the words *United States,* "as if it was a bitter pill," to which "there were hardly five responses in the whole room."[7]

Fantasies of divine payback proved short-lived, and Easter Sunday in the defeated Confederacy was a bleak day indeed. Parishioners in a Richmond church found it hard to celebrate without their pew cushions (appropriated by a nearby hospital) or their bells (melted down for cannonballs by the Confederate army). A woman in Georgia could only unhappily recall the "sunny Easter Sundays" she had once spent with those "now gone forever." If any grim satisfaction remained, it came in imagining the spiritual struggles of the conquerors, suddenly forced to confront more complicated theories about God's hand in the Civil War. As Rodney Dorman put it, "What will they say to that?"[8]

SHOT ON GOOD FRIDAY AND dead on Saturday: the timing of the assassination made Easter Sunday 1865 a particularly important—and confusing—occasion, as shocked mourners came to church for what should have been a day of rejoicing over both the resurrection of Christ and military victory. The reversal of fortunes was manifested materially, as churchwomen rearranged the colorful springtime displays they had readied. Easter decoration had become something of a commercial enterprise by the mid-nineteenth century, with elaborate presentations meant to reflect religious devotion. Flowers played a central role, and now the women highlighted the white blossoms as they searched for black fabric to cover railings and arches, chancel and altar, pulpit and organ, and placed portraits of the late president amid the myrtle, tea roses, and heliotrope. As a congregant in Boston recorded, grappling with the juxtaposition of joy and sorrow, "This glorious Easter morn our Church put on the garb of mourning."[9]

The crowds were phenomenal. Pews always filled to capacity on Easter, but no one had ever seen anything like April 16, 1865. Wherever the news had arrived, from the East Coast to the Midwest to the Pacific Ocean, black churches and white churches were jammed. Aisles and galleries were full, choir steps packed tight. Men carried in extra settees and benches, leaving not an inch of floor space to spare. Many who spilled out the doors strained to hear the service, and those at the back of the outdoor crowds stood too far away to hear anything at all. The same was true in army camps, where Union officers and soldiers gathered in unprecedented numbers to listen to whoever was preaching and however many sermons were offered. The same as the day before, mourners craved company in order to absorb the tragic event. The shock had not yet dissipated, and just as in the streets on Saturday, on Sunday people observed the grief of their neighbors in church or their comrades in camp, reading the faces around them for confirmation that it was not, after all, a hoax or a dream.[10]

Very sad: those two words conveyed the heavy sorrow that had mixed with the initial shock from the first moment Lincoln's supporters had counted the news as credible. In Baton Rouge, a Union army chaplain found the hundreds of freedpeople "all very sad." In Minnesota, "the people all feel very sad," a soldier wrote in his diary. It was, Mary Emerson wrote from Paris, in her *petit souvenir journalier,* the "saddest saddest news we ever heard." Others employed more vivid vocabulary. The news "threw a mantle of sadness over every heart," or people were "struck down" in anguish, "crest fallen and agitated." One soldier thought even the defeat of Sherman or Grant would have brought less gloom to camp. Just as mourners had draped their churches, so too did they imagine nature attired in grief. Where it rained, people saw the clouds "weeping copiously," where skies were blue, "the very sunshine looked mournful." A former slave in Washington said that even the trees were weeping for Lincoln.[11]

For communities of freedpeople across the South, grief washed through like a tidal wave. From Norfolk and Portsmouth, Beaufort and Charleston came the most "heartfelt sorrow," "troubled countenances," and "*very great*" grief. Everywhere, children cried audibly and grown-ups wept bitterly. Some cried all night, others just felt numb. One woman described herself as "nearly deranged" with grief. Black soldiers were utterly bereft. Edgar Dinsmore of the Fifty-Fourth Massachusetts felt "a loss irreparable." One man compared the circumstances to a horrific scene he had witnessed as a slave: a mother whipped forty lashes for weeping when white people took away her children. The violence had traumatized him, "but not half so much as the death of President Lincoln," he confessed. Some white officers in black regiments felt the sense of loss magnified. "Oh how Sad, How Melancholy," James Moore wrote to his wife. Such intense sorrow overcame him that it seemed "an impossibility to rally from it." In Petersburg, Thomas Morris Chester saw both "unfeigned grief" and an "undisguised feeling of horror," for the question hadn't gone away: Would they "have to be slaves again"?[12]

African Americans claimed for themselves a special place in the outpouring of sorrow, and the prayers and sermons of Easter Sunday magnified Lincoln's role as the Great Emancipator. A New Orleans minister asserted that his people felt "deeper sorrow for the friend of the colored man," and black clergymen in the North allowed that their people felt the loss "more keenly" and "more than all others." Journalists singled out the "dusky-skinned men of our own race" as the "chief—the truest mourners," and black soldiers maintained that "as a people none could deplore his loss more than we." Frederick Douglass, speaking extemporaneously in Rochester on Saturday, told the overflowing crowd that he felt the loss "as a personal as well as national calamity" because of "the race to which I belong." Even the most stricken white mourners conceded the point. Secretary of the Navy Gideon Welles thought the "colored people" to be the "truer mourners." In the words of one minister, "We who are white know little of the emotions which thrill the black man's heart to-day," and as another told his congregation, "intense as is our grief," no white person could "fathom the sorrow" of black people. White mourners also pondered this difference in their personal writings. "How I pity the poor colored people," wrote one, "who share *perhaps most* deeply in our *great calamity!*"[13]

From the moment the news arrived, Lincoln's mourners cried as they recorded their emotions, smudging the ink in their journals and letters. Up Broadway in New York, with black drapery obscuring all facades, everything "looked so—sorrowful—& sad," Emily Watkins wrote haltingly to her husband, her dashes perhaps standing in for intermittent sobs. In a small town in Indiana, a young southern Unionist likewise drew dashes (and comforted herself with imagined universality): "The horror and the sorrow are intense—Tears are in all eyes—sobs in every voice—old men and children—rich and poor, white and black." By the rules of American culture (which applied most strictly to the middle and upper classes), expressions of grief were meant to be properly bounded: too much, and one was overly self-indulgent; too little, and one was not quite sensitive enough. Still, the antebellum decades had witnessed a new sentimentalization of death, as the harshness of the Puritan legacy crumbled, and communities and families increasingly attended to the emotions of earthly survivors. On this particular day, all societal pressure lost its power, and most mourners made little effort to conceal their feelings. For the second day in a row, men wept openly, including clergymen. One minister "broke down & the tears rolled down his cheeks." Children saw their male Sunday school teachers barely able to get through a prayer. "Even the boys," Anna Lowell wrote, appeared stricken through the hymns.[14]

Finding words to speak aloud or write down could be a challenge. Frederick Douglass, who had met President Lincoln for the third time only weeks earlier, had "scarcely been able to say a word" to friends who had grasped his hands and looked into his eyes. A black soldier in Florida saw sorrow and misery on every face, yet still "none could express their feelings." Silence, allowed another black mourner in the South, was the "sure sign of sorrow, and when the heart is full it is difficult to speak." The same was true for white mourners. After recording facts and details, many stumbled in their attempts to articulate their sentiments on paper. "I cannot express my feelings" and "I cannot describe my feelings" became common refrains for men and women alike. Some conveyed the point more poetically. A Philadelphia man felt a "dull & stupefied sense of calamity." The British writer Edward Peacock found himself stymied, since any description of genuine emotion would appear "wildly exaggerated."[15]

Others couldn't write anything at all. "I have heard such dreadful news today that I feel totally unfit for writing a letter," a Massachusetts woman confessed to her mother. From the battlefront, General Carl Schurz explained to his wife that he would have written earlier had he been able to "shake off the gloom." At the same time, those who routinely committed but few words to paper betrayed their sorrow by writing more than usual. Whereas Unitarian minister George Ellis normally kept a bare roster of church doings and dining companions, he now added two descriptive words to his log: "awful consternation." The perfunctory journal of Elizabeth Childs, usually home to memos like "Fanny dined here," now carried the notation, "Sad day."[16]

Complete listlessness could take over from the inability to speak or write. "Do not feel like doing anything," wrote sixteen-year-old Margaret Howell in Philadelphia (she then crossed out the word *thing*, and changed it to "work or sewing"). For a Union soldier in Alabama, the news made him feel "so bad," he told his wife, "that I went to bed and I have not felt like getting up since." For others, it was just the opposite. "Sleep was out of the question!" wrote a disconsolate Englishwoman. Grief affected people's physical well-being too, in all kinds of ways: lightheadedness or debilitating headaches, prolonged trembling, "prostration of the nervous system," even days of indefinable sickness. The declaration of victory had enabled Moses Cleveland, serving outside Mobile, to bear his poor health more easily, but the assassination brought him back to the army surgeon, who dispensed medicine and orders to rest. Henry Gawthrop's body reacted the other way around; suffering in a Virginia field hospital with an amputated foot and a bleeding stomach, he found that the terrible tidings made him "almost forget bodily pain." From the start of the ordeal, from the first moments the shock began to wear away to reveal the truth of President Lincoln's murder, in rushed overwhelming sorrow.[17]

MOURNERS CAME TO CHURCH ON Easter Sunday to affirm their sorrow and to make the assassination more believable, but they also came prepared for strenuous religious reflection, longing to make sense of what felt incomprehensible. Grief without faith was impossible for most nineteenth-century Americans, but the graceful acceptance of such a cataclysmic event proved a formidable challenge. Foremost in the minds of many Christian mourners loomed the conundrum of evil. How to explain the existence of evil in the lives of the faithful was a persistent religious problem, but the question also took particular forms at specific historical moments. Before the Civil War, slaves and abolitionists confronted the problem of evil in the

These two badges expressed common sentiments of sorrow among Lincoln's mourners, the first portraying the slain president as a beloved family member, the second assuming the sense of loss to be shared universally.
Call #MS Am 2605, Houghton Library, Harvard University.

institution of human bondage. During the war, both Union and Confederate confronted the problem of evil in the horrors of the battlefield. Then, with surrender, Union supporters had celebrated victory, the end of the fighting, and the end of slavery all at once, vindicating the terrible war. Now, less than a week later, they faced evil all over again. Lincoln's death had to be the design of God, but how could it be? How could a good God be the source of such a terrible deed? The bereaved came to church to wrestle with faith and doubt. Some came to wrestle with the meaning of war and death, maybe even the meaning of life itself.

The spiritual dilemmas of April 1865 came in the context of religious change. Orthodox Calvinism preached an immovable and mysterious God, human depravity, and salvation predestined from birth, in which only the elect few would be saved and only God knew who would go to heaven or hell. In a nation of increasingly democratic ideals, Protestant theologians, ministers (Henry Ward Beecher among them), and worshippers began to reject those premises, insisting instead on a more benevolent God who had endowed human beings with reason and free will along with the prospect of renewal through Jesus Christ. Liberal Protestantism also entered the realm of politics in a peculiarly American "civil religion," in which citizens understood God as deeply concerned with the fate of the nation, calling on his believers to fulfill divine intention through civic action. Lincoln himself had advocated this idea at Gettysburg in the summer of 1863. In his address at the battlefield cemetery in Pennsylvania, Lincoln spoke of the nation's "new birth of freedom," upholding the promise of human beings in control of their own moral destiny, in a "government of the people, by the people, for the people."[18]

But if human beings were responsible for their own salvation through their own moral agency, then the problem of evil became even more nettlesome. What had the victors done that made God take Lincoln away? The puzzle was so overwhelming that some liberally minded mourners (like Albert Browne, in his invocation of predestination) could only turn back toward the rigidity of Calvinism. Mourners also found comfort looking back to the Calvinist tones of Lincoln's second inaugural address, delivered just six weeks before his death—which stood in tension with what the president had earlier implied about human beings controlling moral destiny. No one had expected the war to go on for so long, Lincoln reflected at his second inauguration, vividly invoking the sin of slavery, but "the Almighty has His own purposes." Conversely, invoking the sin of slavery may have been Lincoln's way of suggesting that the length of the war was due to human failing, thereby making God's actions more understandable. Now the assassination brought liberal Protestants up against the same question: of seemingly unfathomable divine purpose on the one hand and punishment for human sinfulness (clearly slavery) on the other.[19]

The line between acceptance of God's will and the effort to understand God's will was a fine one, and nearly every utterance on the subject could be read both ways: assertions of faith shot through with ambivalence, or assertions of uncertainty shot through with trust in God. Where mourners recorded a struggle, they also asserted faith. Where they asserted faith, they hinted at inner conflict. Like Albert Browne, many entertained doubt. "I *Cannot* believe it was for the best," a Union soldier admitted, stumped as to why God would take away the nation's leader at just this moment. A white captain in the Twenty-Second U.S. Colored Infantry (his regiment had welcomed Lincoln to Richmond) wondered if God had forsaken them all and the nation was "drifting into Anarchy." For Quaker Anna Ferris, Lincoln's death was such an "incredible atrocity" that she couldn't tell "whether love & mercy still reign in Heaven." Even those who proclaimed spiritual certainty betrayed themselves. Abolitionist and reformer Lydia Maria Child wrote of a trust in God so strong that the assassination "did not shake that faith for an instant," yet a sentence later she described herself as one who "trusted in Providence till the breeching broke" and the horse ran away.[20]

No matter how confusing and distressing were the questions, Lincoln's mourners did find solace at church, as they listened for affirmations of what they struggled to believe. Outside the White House on the morning of April 15, Gideon Welles had passed African Americans in mourning, then recorded in his diary their "hopeless grief." But hopelessness was not quite the right description for many black mourners. The idea, as a letter-writer to the *San Francisco Elevator* put it, was to "draw some consolation out of this great calamity." The loss of Lincoln, Jacob Thomas told his congregation in upstate New York, was "more than we can bear"—strong words indeed, but Thomas reminded his flock that "in God is our consolation" and asked them to "hope for the best." The task was to mourn without losing trust, to mourn without losing hope, as Philip Alexander Bell, editor of the *Elevator,* implored his readers. Chauncey Leonard, one of the few black chaplains in the Union army, knew that Lincoln had piloted the soldiers through the war in order to achieve "Liberty, and Equal Political right," and yet he knew too that God, "in his wise Providence," had taken Lincoln away.[21]

Hopelessness was not the state of mind of most white mourners either.

A woman who at first felt that "all was over" and "anarchy would follow" soon soothed herself with her minister's "trust & confidence in God." Like Albert Browne, many repeated the formulaic phrases. Mourners wrote about leaving all affairs to God, "who doeth all things well," that it was by God that "all things are permitted." They wrote about God's "wise purpose," exhorting themselves to "acquiesce in His will," and they asked themselves to accept the "unfathomable designs of Providence." Formulaic or not, such words could hold off despair. As one woman wrote on Easter Sunday, "Everybody here seems trying to remember that God will bear us safely through this new & terrible trial, if we are faithful."[22]

That was the key: remaining steadfast in one's faith. Steadfastness of faith required resignation to God's incomprehensible ways, which if sincerely achieved turned out to be the most spiritually satisfying stance, precisely because it consigned evil to the hands of a deity in control of all, for the purpose of eventual good. That did not exactly contradict liberal Christian ideas about human moral agency and control, because God's will still stemmed from the choices made by human beings on earth. Rather, resignation served as a consoling alternative to thoughts of untethered evil beyond divine rule.

For the faithful, then, a divine explanation of Lincoln's tragic death would become clear at some point in the nation's future. Frederick Douglass conveyed this conviction, with only a touch of uncertainty: "It may be," he told the crowd in Rochester the day before Easter, "that the blood of our beloved martyred President will be the salvation of our country." Wavering sentiments like that could be heard everywhere among lay mourners. A northern missionary among the freedpeople thought that "in *some way* God will bring good out of it." A New England woman offered just a tad more certitude. "There is doubtless good to come from this great calamity and wickedness," she wrote, "but as yet it is impossible to see." Nor did spiritual confidence preclude acknowledging the terrible deed. The way a Vermont man tried to see it, God had lowered "a cloud of more than midnight darkness," yet that cloud would eventually rise, revealing "His will concerning this great Republic."[23]

Sad as people were, it helped to keep in mind that grief by its very nature was a form of resistance to God's will, thereby reinforcing the conviction that only resignation would bring consolation in the form of God's mercy. Jews made this point too: "stricken with sorrow," the members of a California synagogue nonetheless "most resignedly and most humiliatingly" bowed to "divine decree." Yet uncertainty crept in everywhere, forcing mourners to struggle with a sense that their heartfelt grief cast them as disobedient to God. "It must be all right as God permitted it," reflected North Carolina freedwoman Mary Ann Starkey, before allowing that "it does seem very hard to us." That Lincoln's death was a matter of divine intention was "the view taken by almost every public speaker," wrote a New England woman, "and every time it is expressed it meets the approval of the audience." That approval, however, was given in front of religious authorities; in private, doubt lingered. After church on Easter Sunday, Charlotte Blech prayed to "understand & have reason to rejoice even in view of this dark dispensation." The president's death, Georgia Treadway mused, after coming home from two Easter services, "seems to be looked upon as Providential," her uncertain language revealing her spiritual ambivalence.[24]

It was a tall order for clergymen, forced to dispense with their prepared sermons. On a day's notice, they had to find a way to address the palpable sorrow without entirely jettisoning Easter season rejoicing. They had to think about the problem of calamitous evil in the world God had created, and they had to make sense of Union victory and the end of slavery, followed by the president's murder. As Unitarian minister Edward Everett Hale wrote to his brother on Saturday, Lincoln's assassination represented the "triumph of Palm Sunday" on the one hand and the "wretchedness and agony of the crucifixion" on the other. James Ward, the Methodist minister in Washington, mulled over in his diary whether the assassination foreshadowed the "dawn of the glorious day" or "a renewed darkness" that would continue on for a long time to come.[25]

From the pulpit, the men spoke candidly of the people's sorrow and intently of God's unerring will. With the victorious Union's claim of divine favor now complicated by Lincoln's death, preachers strived to convey that this very complication added even greater meaning to the war's outcome. Implicit, if unspoken directly, was the idea that a puzzling and mysterious message from God (taking Lincoln away at such a crucial moment) was more powerful and significant than the mere fulfillment of what the faithful had always expected to happen (Union victory by God's decree). On Easter Sunday, ministers strove to make their congregants understand that the assassination should intensify faith in God's ultimate plan precisely *because* it was so mysterious. For the most part, this message met a cooperative—if still mystified—audience. When mourners went to church, they heard sermons that put into words what they had been trying to tell themselves and one another from the first moment the news arrived (the Easter service, wrote a woman in Chicago, "expressed my feelings this morning").[26]

The best way to make sense of the catastrophe was to incorporate it into Union victory. But Lincoln's assassination as the will of God did not necessarily constitute a complete answer—after all, vindictive Confederates explained the assassination the same way. Putting your faith in divine intention prompted one further question, a question even some of the most devoted could not stop themselves from asking: *Why?*

"Where was God when he let the people kill Abraham Lincoln?" asked a freedman in Washington.

"O why did God permit this awful thing to occur?" Lizzie Moore wrote to her husband.

"Why did God let them kill him?" asked twelve-year-old Lettie Lindsley.

"O God! Our God! What does it mean?" cried Lettie's older sister, Maggie.[27]

The very drive to ask the question implied the certainty of an eventual resolution. Some were satisfied with a plain assertion of God's mysterious ways, while others craved deeper explanations. Either way, attempting to answer the question helped the grief-stricken not only to persist in the duties and trials of life on earth but also to undertake future civic actions directed by God for the sake of the nation.

One answer could be found in the idea that the Almighty had imparted a painful lesson to humankind for some wrongdoing. "God knows our affliction, and when we are sufficiently punished, and the Nation sufficiently humbled, He will send deliverance," reasoned Henry Thacher. As for identifying that wrongdoing, Lizzie Moore speculated that perhaps the nation had sinfully worshipped the president more than God. Her husband, at the front, concurred. "Had Lincoln lived no doubt we should all have thought too much of him," he wrote back. As another mourner explained, precisely because the Union had put its full trust in the president, God had taken him away so that the people would be forced to confirm their "trust in a higher power." A white teacher in Norfolk told the black children in her classroom that God could "save the nation without Mr. Lincoln, as well as with him." In this light, God had permitted Lincoln's assassination as punishment for the fickle victors.[28]

Slavery was also the people's sin, and another compelling answer could be found there. Though this explanation echoed the idea of the judgmental Calvinist God, it also came wrapped in the optimism of liberal Protestantism, for if God had taken Lincoln as punishment for the national sin of slavery, then Lincoln was also a martyr to slavery. A letter writer to the *San Francisco Elevator* told his fellow black readers that Lincoln's life had been sanctified by the *"Freedom of the Bondmen,"* that every drop of Lincoln's blood "redeemed a bondman" and foretold a time when "the whole earth shall be free." The tide of freedom was thus unstoppable, and if that wasn't "cheering and consoling," then nothing was. In the Christian tradition of millennialism—the belief that there would be a thousand-year reign of peace and prosperity on earth upon the second coming of Christ—Frederick Douglass, like other black leaders, believed that slavery simply could not be sustained, given God's ultimate direction of human affairs. To loud applause, Douglass told his listeners that although the president had been murdered, "the nation is saved and liberty established forever." White abolitionists offered similar messages. The assassination, one man wrote in his diary, would "inspire the world with a deeper abhorrence of Slavery," and the abolitionist Wendell Phillips asserted that because God took Lincoln for the cause of antislavery, his death would "seal the sure triumph of the cause."[29]

Spiritual consolation could be found as well in the related idea that the president had finished his work on earth, the hope Albert Browne invoked in his despairing letter home. In the Protestant idea of a "calling," the work of every individual, lowly or great, contained a purpose designated by God. Why, then, had the president been "killed when most needed"? one mourner asked. "Who can take his place?" another wondered. "Why could he not have been spared until it was all settled up?" yet another implored. Answers came in the assurance that Lincoln's labor had been completed when he died. "I can only reconcile it by thinking that the Lord saw that Abraham Lincoln's work was done," Lizzie Moore told her husband. Here was God's providence for the victors-turned-mourners. Lincoln's actions had been intended to carry out a particular divine plan for human history, and once it was accomplished there was no more need for the president to remain on earth. Edgar Dinsmore, with the Fifty-Fourth Massachusetts, took comfort ("some slight consolation" is how he phrased it) in a different facet of this conviction: that Lincoln had been "rewarded for his labours here" and now rested in a land without sin or sorrow.[30]

Assumptions about Lincoln's political lenience figured strongly in these formulations. Just as some Confederates lamented the assassination because they believed Lincoln would have treated them with mercy, so too did Union supporters invoke this vision when they spoke of God's providence. Perhaps the most convincing of all spiritual explanations, this one reached directly into the realm of civil religion and pointed concretely toward a bright future for the nation. Many mourners in fact agreed with the radical Republicans that if Lincoln had a single fault, it was his generous spirit. Right before the assassination, at the Fort Sumter celebrations, William Lloyd Garrison had observed "much anxiety" occasioned by the president's "disposition to be lenient with the conquered rebels." Now the conviction that Lincoln had finished his work on earth implied that had he lived, his policies would have compromised the glory of Union victory. An Indiana soldier told his mother that it was "providential that he died when and as he did," for God had called Lincoln away "before he could tarnish his illustrious name." As Lizzie Moore phrased it more simply, God took Lincoln because he "might have grown weak."[31]

Ministers put forth two opposing ideas: Lincoln's generosity of spirit as a positive attribute on the one hand and his presumed lenience toward the enemy as a fatal flaw on the other. Either way, he was simply not the right man to reconstruct the nation, this line of spiritual reasoning went, and mourners elaborated at length on the fact that such an undertaking had never been his calling. Lydia Maria Child could only conclude that the assassination was one of the "wonderful manifestations of Providence," since the "kind-hearted" Lincoln would have offered the rebels "too easy terms." Lincoln's only fault, wrote Washington telegrapher David Homer Bates, was being "too lenient with the vile traitors," and thus had come the "hand of Providence." The president, Anna Ferris wrote in her diary, was struck down while embarking on "a policy so benign that his enemies could ask for nothing more." On the Sunday after Easter, Wendell Phillips proclaimed that God took Lincoln "when his star touched its zenith."[32]

DEATH AT JUST THE RIGHT moment, many mourners believed, served the nation—and Lincoln—best, and indeed the timing and circumstances made for nearly instantaneous deification, swiftly erasing almost all criticisms that had once been advanced by Union supporters. Even some who had recently condemned the president's moderation were quick to characterize him, in death, as noble and courageous. But not all. Although the editors of the *San Francisco Elevator* praised the slain president, they did not hesitate to remind their readers that "we have sometimes thought Mr. Lincoln too slow" in "the elevation of our race." More pointedly, an emigrant in Liberia wrote critically of the late president's treatment of African Americans as "cast off and forsaken" (the mourner himself was one such exile). In a different vein, a white college professor criticized the late president as a "sorry intellect" (if honest and hardworking); the Emancipation Proclamation was Lincoln's greatest act, this man believed, but it had been forced on him by others more farsighted than he.[33]

Still, these voices—mourners rationalizing the demise of the man they were mourning—made up only a quiet chorus. Confederates noticed with contempt that Union supporters now glossed over Lincoln's faults. The bereaved, John Glenn wrote in his Maryland diary, were "prepared to make a demigod of Lincoln," willfully blind to the flaws they had so recently recognized. "The infatuation of the people is certainly extraordinary," he sniffed. As for the ardent secessionist Edmund Ruffin, glancing through the reprinted sermons in the northern newspapers, he found himself "utterly disgusted" by the "man-worship." Worship it was, as mourners both anticipated and echoed the clergymen and journalists, dispensing with nuance in a flood of laudatory adjectives. An Ohio soldier summed up the tone echoing across so many letters and diaries when he described the slain chief as noble, patriotic, wise, honest, sincere, generous, kind, unpretending, decisive, and just.[34]

Lofty comparisons soon followed. George Washington was invoked most commonly, as mourners pronounced Lincoln the greatest president since the nation's first. Like Washington, Lincoln deserved a towering memorial for his immortal statesmanship (the Washington Monument had been under construction since 1848). If Washington was the father of the country, claimed the poet John Greenleaf Whittier, then Lincoln was its savior. A few thought Lincoln superior, since he was much more a "man of the people," and some specifically distinguished Lincoln from the slave-holding founder, proclaiming him the father of liberty—indeed the Emancipation Proclamation meant that Lincoln would live on in American memory long after Washington had been forgotten. The president's connection to black freedom also prompted mourners to invoke Moses, with Philip Alexander Bell calling the late president the "Moses of his age," even as Bell criticized him for straggling in the "elevation of our race." Ministers both black and white pointed out that God had permitted Moses to lead his people to the Promised Land but not to enter it. Listening to her pastor make this comparison, Lizzie Moore thought it "a beautiful coincidence."[35]

Death on Good Friday made parallels with Jesus inescapable, not to mention a Christian understanding that saw the president's recent entry into the enemy capital as parallel to Jesus's entry into Jerusalem before crucifixion. Lincoln, wrote the black editors of the *Elevator*, was "but one degree inferior" to Christ. A former slave in Virginia claimed that the president had been "more than anybody else to us," with the exception of God, and a freedman on Saint Helena Island went even further: "Lincoln died for we, Christ died for we," he said, and the two were the same man. Some white mourners drew the same comparison. "Mankind has lost its best friend since the crusifiction of Christ," wrote an army officer, and a Wisconsin soldier thought no equal to Christ had lived on earth until President Lincoln.[36]

Comparisons with Jesus stemmed from more than parallels of circumstance, for Christian mourners also invoked their savior as another means to envision a luminous future for the nation—again, not despite the assassination but precisely because of it. Lincoln's demise, like that of Christ, was the result of controversial ideas and actions, wrote the editors of the *New York Anglo-African*, and thus would the assassination *"benefit that cause"*—of black freedom. The white Unitarian minister James Freeman Clarke (who called the death of Christ an assassination) spoke of a "dark future," yet made clear that just as the crucifixion had appeared to be the "direst calamity" at the time, so much good had followed. As a layman put it, Lincoln's death would no more harm the Union than "the Crucifixion destroyed Christianity." The idea that the enemy had killed Lincoln but could not destroy God was oft-repeated. "They killed our best friend," said a black woman at Fortress Monroe. "But God be living yet. They can't kill Him." Or as a white New Englander put it, "Abraham Lincoln is dead, but God *lives*." Just as they did all through the war, Lincoln's mourners now found consolation in faith, and with Lincoln gone, they both deified him and reckoned with the fact that the godlike Lincoln was only a mortal.[37]

There was something else too. Just as the president had spoken of "malice toward none" and "charity for all" in his second inaugural address in March 1865, so had Christ spoken the words, "Father forgive them for they know not what they do," in his crucifixion prayer. But if the message of Easter was one of forgiveness, the message for Lincoln's mourners, in church on Easter Sunday, was decidedly more confusing. Ironically, it was Lincoln's propensity for forgiveness—the very quality that made him most Christlike—that served as one of the most satisfying explanations as to why God had taken him away immediately after victory. If God had removed the president because he was too generous to deal properly with the vanquished enemy, then God also presumably wanted the victors to hold their enemies accountable for slavery, secession, and war.

THE GLOOM THAT DESCENDED ON Lincoln's supporters was overwhelming, and yet they ultimately looked forward, in faith, to the post–Civil War world. A providential view of history contained within it an inherent optimism, even if believers had to suffer all along the way, and in this spirit mourners embraced the idea that Lincoln's assassination would make Union victory even better. Indeed, for African Americans it was impossible not to continue celebrating the destruction of slavery despite such profound loss. The president had been dead for less than a week when 250 black men, who had taken flight in order to evade Confederate impressment, celebrated Union victory and their own liberty by marching and singing in front of Yankee soldiers. No more than a week after the assassination, a group of former slaves, overjoyed to come into contact with Union men sailing north from Mobile, were seen "jumping about & swinging their hands" in joy. Slavery had torn the Union apart, and now with victory—even without President Lincoln—the Union was safe, and slavery appeared to be no more. When Lincoln died, all hope at first seemed lost, wrote Garland White, runaway slave and chaplain of the Twenty-Eighth U.S. Colored Infantry, to his friend William Seward, the wounded secretary of state. Soon, though, White felt sure that the nation was "again Safe from the powers that sought to devide distroy & sink it in Eternal Shame." For George Gaskell, a white officer, and his men of the Eleventh U.S. Colored Heavy Artillery, the war's outcome would not be diminished. "Aside from this great calamity," Gaskell wrote to his sister, "the prospects are bright." Frederick Douglass had already made the same point on the very day the president died, at least when it came to the integrity of the nation: "Though Abraham Lincoln dies, the Republic lives."[38]

Victory could not long be overshadowed for white soldiers either, no matter their views on slavery. The British-born John Burrud, fighting with the 160th New York, felt sure that "the Calamity will not Change the result of the War," for with Confederate defeat, he wrote to his wife, "the Country is Safe." Mourners on the home front agreed. "How full of promise is the future!" enthused Samuel Haven after the assassination. When Haven, who had lost a son in the war, explained that the world seemed "brighter on account of the blackness of darkness" which had recently descended, he may have meant Lincoln's death, all four years of war, or both. As another white man wrote in his diary, "The nation still lives & cannot be assassinated."[39]

But manifestations of shock and grief persisted alongside this optimism. "Splitting headache and no wonder," wrote the minister Edward Everett Hale in the days after Easter Sunday. On the Tuesday after Easter, Anna Lowell still felt "very tired & exhausted in mind & body." At her Sunday school class the following week, her heart still felt so full that she wasn't ready to divert attention from the assassination. When the men in Rudolph Rey's company received news that Confederate general Joseph Johnston had surrendered to Sherman in late April, not a cheer went up, for the soldiers had "not got over morning for there late *President*." Even with peace formally declared, "not a solitary cheer was hird from the wole army," Rey noted. Elizabeth Blackwell, a doctor in New York City, thought that mourning for Lincoln would "hang always on a never fading memory."[40]

All through the spring, mourners would ponder God and the assassination. "We bow with meek and humble resignation to his Divine will, because He does all things well," wrote the black Union officer and radical

abolitionist Martin Delany in late May. Weeks after Lincoln's death, Lydia
Maria Child reasoned that "even the removal of kind and honest 'old Abe'"
had been "necessary for the completion of the great work." Whereas for
Rodney Dorman and other Confederates, God's purpose was plain—the
Good Friday crime was retribution for Union victory (even if that left
plenty of unanswered questions about why God had not orchestrated
Confederate victory in the first place)—for Sarah Browne and other Union
supporters, the theological questions yielded all kinds of contradictions.
Amid their spiritual puzzlement, Lincoln's mourners looked also toward
more earthly realms for answers to why the president had been slain. Who,
exactly, they wanted to know, was responsible for the murder?[41]

Love

PEOPLE *LOVED* ABRAHAM LINCOLN. That was the word they used. "I never felt before how deep a hold he had on the hearts of the people," wrote a Union soldier, and women tended to describe such feelings with greater effusion. "O that good, great man, whom we so loved & revered!" Anna Lowell fretted. "It seemed strange to love so much one whom we have never seen—but we did." President Lincoln had blurred the boundaries between leader and loved one, and at his death the categories blurred yet more.[1]

Whereas a beloved intimate could never be replaced, in a democracy one esteemed leader would always be succeeded by another. Though astounded by Lincoln's death, Theodore Lyman nevertheless reasoned that "we have fought with success for four years, and I do not believe the shooting of one man is going to trouble us much now." True, reflected Frederick Sawyer (he had been at Ford's Theatre that night), "no man on the continent can do just what Mr. Lincoln could have done," but God would never leave a nation's work in the hands of a single person. Or as freedpeople in Virginia put it, "God raised us up one friend and He will raise us up another."[2]

The trouble with these rationalizations was that people thought of Lincoln as far more than a statesman, and many mourners felt—as one put it—"personally afflicted" by his death. Some invoked similes, mourning "as if for a dear friend." For others, no simile or metaphor was necessary. To the readers of San Francisco's black newspaper, the president had been a "beloved friend." For "us of the U.S. colored army," wrote a white officer, "the death of Lincoln is indeed the loss of a friend." Even more, Lincoln felt to many like family. A white captain in a black regiment felt as if he had lost "some near kindred." Union soldiers, a white man wrote, "could not of felt any worse if evry one of them had lost their nearest reletave." Mourners saw this sentiment all around: "Everywhere it seemed as if the death were of one near and dear in the family" or "as though a private grief had come to each family." In Chicago, mused one mourner, "almost every family circle seems to be broken."[3]

In particular, people thought of Lincoln as a father, a symbol that held religious as well as familial meaning. An elderly freedwoman called the slain president "a mighty good father to us," and a white soldier told his brother that the men "all claimed him as a father" (Union soldiers had long spoken of Lincoln as "Father Abraham"). Lincoln's mourners, one woman mused, were like orphans, a term defined in the nineteenth century as fatherless children. Symbolic as this imagery may have been, Lincoln's mourners felt moved to compare their feelings to more literal personal losses. "I could not have been *more* shocked had it been my Father," wrote a Pennsylvania businessman. An American in Paris mourned for Lincoln "as sorrowfully and far more bitterly than I mourned for my dear father." Even more, when a freedwoman in North Carolina got word, she felt as if both her father and mother had died at the same time.[4]

As for the vanquished (who held ambivalent feelings for President Jefferson Davis by war's end), they gave their love to General Robert E. Lee. On the morning of April 9, 1865, Lee had said he would "rather die a thousand deaths" than surrender to Grant. Lee had done the deed and had not died, but to his admirers surrender felt akin to death, which only elevated the general more. After Appomattox, one Confederate soldier called Lee an "illustrious chieftain" superior to Washington and Napoleon, vowing that southern babies would be taught to lisp his name. "Dear noble old man," mused a Virginia woman, invoking words that Lincoln's mourners used to describe their late leader. "I love & revere him now more than ever."[5]

5

❧

Blame

FOR SARAH BROWNE, THE "UNPARALLELED outrage" of Lincoln's assassination was "enough to rouse up the spirit of the meekest angel." Grieving and in shock, Sarah was also angry. She wanted the assassin and his conspirators to suffer, but it wasn't they alone who were guilty. She also wanted the "Fathers" of the rebellion to suffer, for she believed that Confederate political and military leaders had made the actions of Booth and the conspirators possible. The many middling and poor white people of the South, for their part, had been drawn into the war "against the dictates of their hearts and Consciences," Sarah believed, and thus deserved gentler treatment.[1]

Sarah expressed grief more vividly than anger, while Albert vented a fury more easily permitted to men, enraged at the Confederates around him in the South, those "dastardly cowardly wretches" with their "devilish purposes." Slavery, Albert proclaimed, had caused the murder of President Lincoln (the "tree of Slavery," he wrote, had "borne fruit" in the assassination), and the terrible crime was the "culmination of the teachings from the Southern pulpit and press," not to mention the leadership of Jefferson Davis and all of "Southern Society." When it came to the "poor deluded ones"—the white southerners whom Sarah excused—Albert agreed that they should be pardoned freely, as long as their leaders were hanged or forever banished from the nation. The anger Albert Browne felt at Lincoln's assassination turned him into a savage, he confessed. Subjugate them, humiliate them, exterminate them, he cried, underlining the word *exterminate*. "We have played with this serpent long enough now," he wrote; "let us kill the monster and all its infernal brood." If Sarah thought he had spewed enough bile, Albert assured her there was "a heap left."[2]

FOR RODNEY DORMAN, GLEE WAS fleeting and anger enduring. As far as Dorman was concerned, John Wilkes Booth alone was responsible for the murder of Abraham Lincoln, but of course the Yankees would "molest a great many people" who had nothing to do with the deed, acting with revenge, "against all law" and with "total disregard of all rights." Unlawful power exercised by the conquerors infuriated Dorman no end—how the Yankees did "beshit & befoul" all they touched in their "fraudulent, forceable, unwarranted, contemptible manner," he wrote in his diary. As for Booth, he should be honored for his manly bravery, just as in ancient Greece, Harmodius and Aristogeiton were honored for saving Athens by murdering a tyrant.[3]

The Yankees said that slavery had killed Lincoln, but in Rodney Dorman's view, slavery was a force of good: a benevolent institution in which masters loved and provided for their "servants," who in turn loved and needed their subjugators. "In some instances," Dorman conceded, slaves had "not been treated as they ought," but those instances were exceptional. In his version of American history, wicked white northerners had stolen Africans from their native lands (here he called the victims "slaves," rather than "servants"), sold them to white southerners, then stole them back by "force & fraud" during the Civil War, making for a "double crime, aggravated!" Indeed, at times Dorman reserved greater hostility for white northerners than he did for the freedpeople, for without white instigators, he felt sure, black people would have remained content with enslavement. It was those blasted abolitionists who had awakened the desire for liberty, and the black soldiers he saw in Jacksonville—the literal embodiment of that liberation—were thus intolerable or, in Dorman's words, "beyond the powers of endurance of man." All during the spring and summer of 1865,

Rodney Dorman seethed at the Yankees. "The only remedy," he confided to his journal, would be "a general extermination of the whole of them."[4]

LINCOLN'S MOURNERS WERE ANGRY, very angry. Reconciliation to the will of God and acceptance of the assassination as part of a divine plan for the nation's glorious future did not exempt the guilty parties from facing justice.

Anger was a complicated emotion for nineteenth-century Americans. Long associated with a deplorable lack of self-control, anger, particularly men's anger, had been likened to barbarism, unbecoming to civilized people. These cultural assumptions had recently begun to change, with the idea that well-moderated fury could be put to good use, and even savage rage like Albert Browne's was understandable in particularly abominable circumstances. That permission extended almost exclusively to white men of the middling and upper classes, while women were meant never to be angry, under any circumstances. But with Lincoln's murder, these social rules evaporated, just as had the dictates against men weeping, and mourners embraced their fury without compunction. As one man wrote in his diary, describing a pervasive state, "Wrath flashes through the gloom."[5]

A vitriol of stunning intensity runs through the record of personal responses to Lincoln's assassination. *Indignation.* That was one way mourners described their feelings, as if they had personally been victims of an unjust act (recall that Sarah Browne had pictured Albert's initial feelings as "honor and indignation"). At a meeting of black San Franciscans, poet and plasterer James Madison Bell spoke of pain "mixed with indignation." A white woman in Boston juggled "amazement, horror, indignation, and a feeling of personal bereavement." *Rage.* That word was even more commonly invoked. On a New England street on the day Lincoln died, people wept, "fired with rage." On Easter Sunday in Philadelphia, a woman watched her brother-in-law "crushed with sorrow" yet "savage with rage." In Washington on Sunday too, people appeared "wild with grief and rage." Down south, the sorrowing hearts of Union soldiers and officers filled up with hatred and fury.[6]

Wartime is a powerful catalyst to acceptable anger, requiring as it does the demonization of the enemy. If surrender had softened those feelings among the victors, Lincoln's assassination recalled them, then multiplied the demonization a hundredfold. General Joseph Keifer had been counseling moderation and magnanimity, rationalizing that the war was over and bitterness an unchristian sentiment, but now he regretted that he'd ever treated a rebel well. From Virginia, he wrote to his wife that he was ready to take an "oath of eternal enmity." The day before the assassination, a Union soldier allowed that he could have "forgiven all of those wretches of Rebels"; the day after, he wanted only to "crush them." Women expressed similar thoughts, if in gentler and more religious language. "We were preparing in peace and forgiveness to smooth over and forget," a mourner in Connecticut wrote to her sister, but now "God has given us a sword again." Men and women alike depicted the violence against Lincoln with adjectives that suggested an otherworldly brutality. It was a "murderous *devilish* malignity," wrote one; "infernal, diabolical Devillish, demoniacal," wrote another. It "caps the climax of inhuman atrocity," a soldier wrote home. From there, it was easy to dehumanize the wider Confederate population. They were miscreants and fiends, malicious, bloodthirsty, vile, venomous, base, and barbarous. They were savages, and savages must be met with equal—nay, overpowering—ferocity.[7]

From the front came cries for vengeance. "Is there a man in the Army, or out of it that will not Seek revenge?" asked an Iowa soldier, answering his own question: "*no* not *One*." Union officer Newton Perkins felt himself enveloped in a gloom pierced by a "*spirit* of *vindictiveness* and *vengeance*." Even on Easter Sunday, he wrote to his mother, he couldn't find "*one* spark of *Christianity* left in me towards *traitors*." Lee's soldiers should have been butchered, not paroled, another fumed. Had the black soldiers at the siege of Fort Blakeley, Alabama—a battle fought on the day of Lee's surrender—known the assassination was imminent, a white officer surmised, they would have chanted King Lear's chorus, "Kill, kill, kill, kill, kill, kill!"[8]

Visions of a speedy peace receded as the men imagined the actions they would take should they find themselves in another engagement with the enemy. Many in fact hungered for just such an encounter—recall the words of young black men outside the White House on the night the president died: "Just let them leave the rebels to us!" White soldiers who supported Lincoln felt the same way, no matter what they made of black freedom. All thoughts of returning home were forgotten, an officer observed, as his men begged to fight any remaining remnant of armed rebels. When it appeared that General Joseph E. Johnston, still in the field, might surrender to Sherman, Union soldiers in North Carolina were dismayed. "We wish that the fight were not over yet!" they exclaimed around the campfire. "Don't let him surrender," they repeated over and over, hoping to be "let loose" on the enemy in order to "revenge the President's murder." Some felt sure the war would now be prolonged—"& it better last until they are all killed," one man added.[9]

Should another battle in fact come to pass, the men vowed to wage brutal warfare. A black soldier in Florida would fight until the enemy was "driven into humble submission." The men of a black regiment that had marched triumphantly into Richmond wanted fervently to "burn, kill, & distroy." They would make "a monument of dead rebells," one of their white officers wrote to his sister, for Lincoln's life was worth more to them than all the rebels in the whole state. If another battle ensued, it would be "a Sory day" for Confederates, a white soldier told his parents. As for Newton Perkins of the Thirteenth Connecticut, he would inscribe the word *Lincoln* on a banner, and shout, "Boys, Slay and spare not!" What was more, he promised his mother, those enemy soldiers would wish "they had never been *born.*" General Carl Schurz thought the Confederates should thank God the war had ended; had his army marched again, he told his wife, the campaigns would have rivaled those of Attila the Hun.[10]

Laws of war and honorable wartime conduct held no place in mourners' fantasies. Union soldiers wanted to meet Confederates on the battlefield because they wanted to exterminate them—Albert Browne was far from alone in that wish. "Extirminate—yes that is the word," wrote a man in the Forty-Fourth Indiana to his wife—"let *extirmination* be our watchword," for "the sooner the world is rid of those vile creatures, the better it will be for mankind." At this point, he explained, any mercy would be akin to warming up a cold viper, "only to be stung to death with its venomous fangs." Stationed in South Carolina, the men of the Fifty-Fourth Massachusetts told one another, "Now there is *no more* peace, let us turn back, again load our muskets and if necessary exterminate the race that can do such things." For these black men, the Confederates seemed a wholly separate race, and whites used the same language—one called the enemy a "badly whipped race." Union officer Alonzo Pickard also advocated "*extermina-*

tion" (like Albert Browne, he underlined the word); if that directive seemed "barbarous," Pickard assured his brother-in-law that it barely matched the murder of Lincoln. Forget taking them as prisoners—Union soldiers at Fort Spanish, Alabama, were for "exterminating the Rebels altogether," eager just to "shoot them down." Francis Barnes, a white lieutenant with a black regiment, also wanted the paroled Confederates in Mobile exterminated and was "willing to fight all the rest of my life" to make it happen.[11]

Angry campfire talk and imagined retribution could be converted into action. Near Ford's Theatre on the night of April 14, "mutterings & threats of vengeance" could be heard everywhere, and with soldiers "threatening death to all rebels or their sympathizers," several paroled Confederates ended up "severly handled." When news of the assassination arrived at the Union prison at Fort Delaware, a Yankee lieutenant got drunk, found himself a five-foot club, and went into the barracks, striking right and left, inflicting blows on the few who didn't get out of his way fast enough. In fact any handy Confederate man, including a civilian, would do. "Very hard feeling toward the Rebs," a Union soldier jotted in his Richmond diary; "afraid there will be blood shed." In Vicksburg, Union soldiers and African Americans planned to take revenge on white residents ("get up a row and murder the citizens" is how one man put it) before officers put a stop to it. When the news came to Raleigh, Union soldiers expressed such fury that Yankee authorities ordered encircling guards to keep the city from destruction. Patrols were doubled and a curfew imposed, because, wrote General Schurz to his wife, it seemed the soldiers would "vent their rage by setting fire to the city."[12]

Mourners on the northern home front called for retaliation too, beginning on the streets of Washington on the night of the assassination, where the tears of all those weeping men fell as much in anger as in sorrow. The people could "hardly contain their wrath," and the next day residents of the capital shouted to burn down the military prisons as armed guards watched over the enemy inmates. A federal official had never witnessed "so earnest and determined a cry for vengeance," including one group who wanted to lynch all incarcerated Confederate officers. Calls for reprisal were directed at southern civilians too. The San Francisco poet James Madison Bell rhymed the line "Exterminate! shall be our cry" with "Rebellion's hated brood shall die!" and included "Fathers and sons, and wives and daughters" as the targets of his decree. George Comfort, though a Quaker, found himself filled with "a feeling of bitter and unrelenting hatred" that would be satisfied only by the "speedy and utter extermination" of the enemy population. As an Illinois man admitted to his own Confederate relative, "I actually thirst for blood and vengeance." Women joined the chorus, if again more obliquely and in more spiritual guises. Trusting in God's providence, Anne Neafie told her husband at the front that she wouldn't object if the soldiers exchanged "ill judged clemency" for greater punishment. Just as Sarah Browne wished for the guilty parties to be crushed, some women expressed their anger more directly, even if they could not enact the vengeance themselves. When Mary Butler cried "*death to all traitors,*" she included her Confederate beau, Frank, whom she decided then and there never to see again. "I hope he will meet the fate he deserves," she told her mother, careful to repeat exactly what she meant: "death to the traitors."[13]

Anger rang out from the pens and pulpits of mourning ministers as well. Sharing and reflecting the ire of their congregants, these men intertwined pleas to accept God's will with calls for reprisal. Churchgoing mourners thus heard confusing messages, an inconsistent brew of mercy and vengeance. Invoking the wrathful God of the Old Testament, clergymen made clear that only retribution, albeit always guided by reason, would pave the way toward justice. "Traitors beware! Vengeance fills the air," wrote the black minister Thomas Ward in California. A white Congregationalist minister in the Union army made the same point in different words: "Mercy is dead now: justice rules alone." The fact was, messages of submission to God's will could be understood in contradictory ways. On the one hand, Union supporters could find comfort in God's ultimate plans for the nation, even if those plans were impossible to discern. On the other hand, God had intended the assassination precisely to forestall lenience by rousing Union wrath against the enemy. One seemed to cancel out the other, making for a thorny tangle of imperatives.[14]

FOR ALL THE RAGE, AND for all the contradictory directives from clergymen, whom exactly did the grieving blame for Lincoln's murder? When a mourner wrote to her daughter that "the feeling against all those implicated in the assassination of the President was deep & vengeful," what did she

mean by *all those implicated?* When a missionary among the freedpeople
hoped that "those who merit punishment receive their deserts," who exactly were *those who merit punishment?* When a barely literate New Hampshire laborer wrote of "the Presdants death" and his wish to "dam" those
who carried it out, whom exactly did he include? Who or what had killed
Abraham Lincoln?[15]

Within hours of the crime at Ford's Theatre, and continuing for two
weeks afterward, federal authorities made hundreds of arrests, eventually
charging seven men and one woman with taking part in the conspiracy. The
eight suspects were held in a Washington penitentiary, awaiting a trial that
would begin in early May. There was George Atzerodt, who failed in his assignment to murder Vice President Andrew Johnson, and there was Lewis
Powell, who succeeded in wounding Secretary of State William Seward
and one of his sons. There was David Herold, Powell's accomplice waiting
outside the Seward home, and there was Dr. Samuel Mudd, who set the
bone that John Wilkes Booth had broken when he jumped to the stage.
There were also Samuel Arnold and Michael O'Laughlen, who had helped
plan the scheme, and Edman Spangler, the carpenter who worked at Ford's
Theatre. The lone woman was the widowed Mary Surratt, whose Washington boardinghouse and Maryland tavern were linked to the conspirators.
Also wanted was Surratt's son John, who worked for the Confederate secret service; he had not been in Washington on the appointed evening and
soon escaped to Canada, then to England, then Rome, then Egypt. But it
was the man who pulled the trigger on Lincoln—still at large—who domi-
nated the minds of mourners.

In the immediate aftermath, gleeful Confederates had exalted John Wilkes
Booth, with Rodney Dorman calling him a "great public benefactor" and
others cheering him on and welcoming him to the South. At the same time,
however, Confederates were careful to lay the blame squarely on Booth,
keen to confine the guilt to a single perpetrator and his lone circle of collaborators. Even as rebels gloried in the killer's actions, it was important
to separate him from all who had fought for the just and noble cause of
the Confederacy, and it was equally important to exempt themselves from
Union wrath. One way to accomplish this was by casting Booth—despite
his heroic status—as mentally unstable. A Georgia woman worried that the
Yankees would blame the whole Confederacy when the assassination was

nothing more than the "crazy deed of a madman." A New Orleans planter believed it had been an act of "some private revenge, and not at all political," undertaken by a "crazy play Actor." It was the "work of a lunatic," others said, the efforts of a man "imbued with tyrannicidal monomania." As for the larger conspiracy, it was the work of "a few poor fanatics" or "desperadoes."[16]

A smaller number of Confederates removed Booth from their orbit entirely, instead implicating the Copperheads up north. "I do not believe this to be the work of Southerners," asserted Cloe Whittle. "I believe it is Northern men who have done it." A minority of Lincoln's mourners likewise turned their anger on Copperheads, not only for their public expressions of glee but also as directly responsible for the crime. Caroline Dunstan placed at least some of the blame on the "Northern traitors" she saw around her in New York City. A white lieutenant with the U.S. Colored Troops noticed "how the soldiers curse the Copperheads at home," and a white soldier named the "traitors up North" as "aiding the South every day," sure they had "killed President Lincoln to aid this Rebelion." John Burrud, the Englishman fighting with a New York regiment, peppered letters to his wife with especially intense anti-Copperhead rants. Familiar with Lincoln's antagonists in his upstate hometown, Burrud claimed to hate Copperheads more even than he hated Confederates. The "meanest and most degraded Southern Rebel," according to Burrud, was "a *Saint* compared with one of those Copperhead Pipers." They were fools, idiots, reptiles, and "Black hearted Slavery loveing Demons," every one of whom should be hanged and sent to hell for the atrocity of Lincoln's assassination. If they had joined the Confederate army in the first place, Burrud seethed, Union forces could have "rid the Earth of Their poluted carcasses," but the miscreants were too cowardly, and now Burrud wanted them exterminated (that word again). For their part, Copperheads unsurprisingly agreed with Confederates that the actions of John Wilkes Booth had nothing to do with anyone but himself. As one anti-Lincoln northerner told his friends, gathered at a New York City hotel on the day of Lincoln's death, the assassin's act was likely the consequence of a "drunken after dinner boast."[17]

Confederates and Copperheads alike must have found some relief in the fact that most of Lincoln's mourners trained a good portion of their wrath on Booth. Editors at the *San Francisco Elevator* called him vile and a wretch, but mourners didn't need journalists to tell them that—they readily cast the assassin as a scoundrel, a fiend, a dog, and a demon. To capture John Wilkes Booth alive was the hope of many mourners, since death was a "gift to martyrs," and it was the president who should be martyred, not his murderer. The bereaved wanted to see Booth suffer, and with blood boiling (mourners invoked that phrase to describe their anger), they devised the means. Like many, seventeen-year-old Clara Allen believed that hanging would be too mild and that Booth should be "tortured in some way." Outside Ford's Theatre on the night of April 14, people were already exchanging suggestions for the particulars: Hang him from the first lamppost available or cut him to pieces before a lamppost could even be found. Flog him. Shoot him like a dog. Burn him alive slowly. Hang him until almost dead, then "resuscitate him and repeat the procedure for several days." In Cincinnati, where another Booth brother was appearing at the opera house, the theater had to be closed on the morning of Lincoln's death, in the face of a furious mob, as Junius Brutus Booth Jr. hurried out of town on an early train.[18]

The War Department printed up "wanted" posters for John Wilkes Booth, promising a reward of a hundred thousand dollars, but imagining one's own participation in Booth's torment offered special satisfaction beyond a monetary reward. Troops gathered around campfires, conjuring their actions should they personally catch the guilty party. Some wanted to operate the hangman's noose themselves. A white soldier wanted to chain up Booth and place four black men ready to brand him with hot irons if he tried to sleep, "till he died dead," while Billy Patterson of the Seventeenth Maine wanted to "fry his liver before his very eyes." Such scenes were influenced by popular travel accounts that purported to disclose the brutal violence of honor and vengeance in the southern backwoods, entertaining readers with depictions of gouged eyes and severed limbs. John Worthington, an upstate New York banker, bested all the soldiers' plans for Booth when he told his sister that he wanted to "tear him slowly in pieces, kill him by inches, pull out his toe-nails & pick out his rascally eyes with a fork. Cut out his tongue, break his arms & leg's & at last hang him on a nail by one eyelid."[19]

Although Lincoln's mourners envisioned such tortures for Booth in particular, they did not confine their vindictive thoughts to the killer and

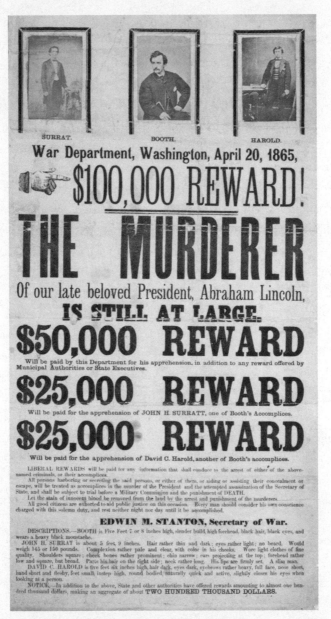

The War Department's "wanted" poster promised a reward for the capture of the assassin of the "late beloved President," displaying an image of John Wilkes Booth, along with conspirators John Surratt and David Herold (with both their names misspelled). *LC-USZ62-11193, Rare Book and Special Collections Division, Library of Congress.*

his immediate circle, not by far. Rather, the Confederacy as a whole had emboldened Booth to commit the deed, and as a rational criminal, he had acted in the spirit of the rebels, including the violation of law and the U.S. Constitution. From Virginia, black Civil War correspondent Thomas Morris Chester explained the assassination as "another one of the infamous crimes which logically followed the efforts of treason to dismember the Union." According to a Maryland Unionist, Booth had been spurred on by all who had ever prayed for Lincoln's death, even by anyone who had ever so much as called the president a despot. In the pages of her spare diary, African American servant and night-school student Emilie Davis called Booth the "Confederate villain," thereby plainly associating him with the rebels, and white schoolgirl Sarah Putnam likewise named all Confederates as guilty when she wrote, "The rebels only hurt their own cause when they assassinated dear old Lincoln."[20]

The bigger culprit was something mourners called the southern "system." All secessionists were guilty, explained Francis Lieber, legal adviser to the Lincoln administration (and one-time southern slaveholder), because Booth was the servant of a "devilish system and doctrine." Others invoked the same word: Lincoln was the victim of a "thug system." The act of assassination comported exactly with "their whole system." Racial slavery was at the heart of that system. When Union army authorities appealed to African Americans in the greater Washington area to assist with the capture of the assassin, the official bulletin announced that Lincoln had been murdered "because he was your friend." Though Booth grasped the pistol, the message read, it was "fired by the hands of treason and slavery," and Lincoln might have been spared had he been "unfaithful to you and to the great cause of human freedom." In those words were implicated not only all treasonous rebels but also the cause of that treason: slavery.[21]

Blaming slavery for the assassination was not necessarily the same as upholding racial equality, since Union supporters fought a war against slavery for a variety of reasons, ranging from the moral opposition of abolitionists to much more broadly based economic objections that saw slave labor as competing unfairly with the freedom of white wageworkers. Vermont soldier George Mellish, for one, deeply mourned Lincoln, even as he recorded his hatred of the black people he encountered down south. Mellish supported emancipation, he explained, but he wanted the freedpeople sent off to Africa. Likewise, Pennsylvania soldier John Smith mourned Lincoln and hated Confederates, while he also hated abolitionists and black people (he was going to bring his gun home, he told his mother, "to shoot nigers"). Conversely, to believe in black inferiority and subordination was not necessarily to endorse the institution of slavery, and in fact mourners all along the political spectrum invoked slavery as the cause of the president's murder. Abolitionists certainly made this cry, but more moderate Union supporters did so too. An eyewitness at Ford's Theatre, writing out his experiences on the night of April 14, exclaimed, "How many more martyrs to slavery!" At seven o'clock in the morning in New York City, even before Lincoln was pronounced dead, Francis Lieber wrote to Union general Henry Halleck, "It is Slavery, Slavery!" All day Saturday, the accusations continued. Lincoln had been sacrificed to slavery, taken by "an agent of that accursed system of Slavery and State Rights." It was the fault of "all the hate, wickedness, & guilt of Slavery." In London, with the official telegram from Secretary of War Edwin Stanton at hand, Charles Francis Adams was stunned, but soon, he confessed to his diary, he understood the crime as the "fruit of the seed that was sown in the slavery of the African race."[22]

In church on Easter Sunday, ministers affirmed these convictions. "It was slavery that killed our President," pronounced Joseph Prime, a black minister in upstate New York. For a white minister in Cincinnati, "Booth was the Agent but Slavery was the murderer." Abolitionist clergymen explained that God had taken Lincoln in order to punish the nation for its sins, and that included the North, which was complicit in slavery. At a black church in San Francisco, mourners agreed that Lincoln's death would "expiate a nation's guilt" and listened to a disquisition on the national, rather than sectional, "sin of slavery." Indeed, Lincoln himself had articulated that idea in his second inaugural address, first singling out the South (slavery was "localized in the Southern part" of the nation and "constituted a peculiar and powerful interest") but also implicating the North (God brought war to both sections, as punishment to "those by whom the offence came").[23]

No matter if both sections of the country were implicated, all through the weeks afterward, as mourners thought and talked about the relation between slavery and the assassination, they focused their anger on the Confederacy. The crime, asserted African Americans north and south, was the "natural fruit" of the "barbarous institution of slavery" and the "natural outcrop" of slavery's cruelty. Whites agreed that whether or not Booth was a slaveholder (he was not) mattered little, since he had acted on behalf of slaveholders' interests. As one man put it, "Slavery, Rebellion and Assassination form but one word." A woman "deepley afflicted" by Lincoln's death sent ten dollars to a charity for work among the freedpeople so that the "last vestage of slavery" would be "swept from the earth." A freedwoman in Maryland put it most directly of all, telling her former mistress, "You are the slayer of my deliverer!"[24]

On the most straightforward level, mourners insisted that Lincoln had died because he was a foe of slavery. On deeper levels, slave-ownership and the workings of the institution led whites to depravity, which led to the assassination. Slavery, wrote Francis Lieber, ruminating on the murder, had "perverted the minds of the Southerners," turning them into "fiends and fools." Mourners crafted their official proclamations to make the same point in more lyrical language. The citizens of Pennsylvania detected in the assassination "but another illustration of the diabolical spirit of American slavery." The citizens of Ohio perceived in the crime an "appalling exhibition of the brutalizing and relentless spirit engendered by slavery." Men of the Union League Club of Philadelphia loathed equally the "pistol and dagger of the assassin" and the "lash of the slave-driver." The malevolence, violence, brutality, heartlessness, and treachery of slavery, they wrote, were all "embodied in that miserable assassin."[25]

THE COMPLICITY OF ALL WHITE southerners might have been implied in such assertions but, like Sarah and Albert Browne, Lincoln's mourners often pointed in particular to the Confederate leadership. Lincoln's supporters had all along blamed rebel leaders and powerful slaveholders for secession and war, believing that their poorer compatriots had been coerced into supporting the conflict. Just before the outbreak of fighting, Lincoln himself had put forward the idea that the majority of white southerners would demonstrate loyalty to the Union—after all, the majority of white southerners did not own slaves—thereby foiling secession. Wrong as Lincoln had been, the vision of Confederate leaders as responsible for the assassination was a logical extension of the idea that the rebel government and elite slaveholders were ultimately responsible for the war.[26]

Right there at Petersen House, as President Lincoln breathed his last, Secretary of War Stanton began to collect accounts from eyewitnesses for the criminal investigation, working from the premise that Confederate authorities, with Jefferson Davis at the top, had hatched the plot and sent Booth as their emissary. Judge Advocate General Joseph Holt, who would soon take over from Stanton and serve as chief prosecutor at the trial of the conspirators, agreed with the secretary of war (though Holt would ultimately be unable to prove the involvement of the Davis administration). On the day Lincoln died, mourners likewise pointed to Confederate officials, naming "the Jeff Davis crew," as one put it, or in the words of another, "some Black hearted Rebel Hireling of the Tyrant Jeff Davis."[27]

Clergymen confirmed this idea, focusing largely on leaders and elites, as they cast John Wilkes Booth as product and symbol of the slave South. Take the particularly angry sermon preached by Alonso Quint on Easter Sunday in New Bedford, Massachusetts. Quint, a white man, fired up his congregation with calls for black citizenship and the confiscation of rebel property, characterizing the generic southern white person as lazy, ignorant, deceitful, greedy, licentious, and barbaric (thereby turning the tables on white stereotypes of black people). Yet Quint was speaking of slaveholders only, evident in his imagery of whips and chains. By the same token, some ministers advocated the death penalty, not only for the assassin, but also for Jefferson Davis, Robert E. Lee, and other higher-ups. In New Haven, Georgia Treadway attended two Easter services, both of which placed Davis, along with Lee and other Confederate generals, "on the same level as the *murderer.*" Journalists also singled out Confederate authorities, with the *New York Anglo-African* hoping to see such men tried in the courtroom. Once their "connection with the murder of the President" was proven, the black editors wrote, it would be "impossible to save their necks."[28]

Unsurprisingly, Confederates expressed dismay that their conquerors would think to place blame anywhere beyond Booth and his accomplices or the Copperheads. "I dont see why they should take revenge on us," an imprisoned private wrote in his diary, while Edmund Ruffin—the zealous secessionist known for firing a shot in Charleston harbor at the war's outset—was infuriated to read a sermon in the New York papers

that equated Booth with the "spirit which fired on Fort Sumter." Eliza Andrews, believing Booth alone to be guilty, called the "wanted" handbills for
Jefferson Davis "villainous slander."[29]

Lincoln's mourners meanwhile kept up a steady chorus, naming as guilty
the "leading men," the "secession party," the "upper classes of the South,"
and the "hot-headed leaders." As a black man in California claimed, "The
leaders of the rebellion have always aimed at one thing, and that is the destruction of the Chief Magistrate," while a white woman in Vermont wanted
Jefferson Davis hanged from the same gallows as John Brown. In the two
days after Easter, lawyer George White recorded in his diary a long list
of Confederates potentially responsible for the assassination. Along with
Davis and Lee, he identified Judah Benjamin (secretary of state), John
Breckinridge (secretary of war), John Campbell (assistant secretary of
war), Robert Toombs (previous secretary of state), James Mason and John
Slidell (diplomats), Robert Hunter (Virginia senator, and peace commissioner in early 1865), Jacob Thompson (agent to Canada), and Generals
P. G. T. Beauregard, Richard Ewell, A. P. Hill, and Joseph E. Johnston.
Women of the slaveholding classes held an uncertain position in these assertions. Mostly they went unmentioned, though the minister Quint saw fit
to pity them as suffering widows. Occasionally a mourner implicated them
fully, like the man who fumed over "shedevils" or the one who pronounced
Confederate ladies even "worse than the Men in their Sentiments."[30]

Blaming the Confederate leadership for Lincoln's assassination meant
exempting white southerners outside the planter classes, but when mourners invoked phrases like "the masses," it was never entirely clear who exactly fell into that category. From its founding in the 1850s, the Republican
Party had envisioned the white population of the South as slaveholding
elites in conflict with a degraded class of impoverished and powerless ple-
beians whose chances for upward mobility were squelched by slave labor.
All through the war, white northerners imagined just such a simplistically
divided Confederacy, unwilling to differentiate among the majority of white
southerners who fell outside the category of large plantation owners. That
left a great deal of ambiguity. Where was the dividing line between large
and small planters, between small planters and yeoman farmers (who might
own a few slaves), and between struggling yeoman farmers and poverty-
stricken white families? Just such ambiguity was apparent in the speech

Henry Ward Beecher had delivered at Fort Sumter, right before Lincoln's assassination, in which he blamed the war squarely on southern slaveholders, accusing them of sweeping "common people" into their ranks with lies "against interests as dear to them as their own lives" and implored fellow victors to treat the deceived masses with mercy. Even if they had cast their wartime lot with their powerful neighbors, Beecher believed, the whole of the ignorant rank and file should be welcomed back into the Union.[31]

Beecher spoke for most white northerners, who believed not only that the institution of slavery oppressed white people outside the master class, but also that those oppressed whites had always harbored antislavery sentiment. At war's end, many white Union supporters believed that the majority of white southerners would act on their long-smoldering resentment of aristocratic slaveholders and reveal themselves as natural allies of the Yankees. After the fall of Richmond, Henry Thacher was waiting for "the *people*" to turn their wrath from the Union to their own leaders, once they discovered "the game the Chivalry are playing." For Union army chaplain Hallock Armstrong, confirmation came from common southern whites themselves, who told him that the Civil War was "a war of the Aristocracy of the South," prompting Armstrong to project that victory would "knock off the shackles from millions of poor whites." Passing through Virginia on his way home, Edward Benham and his fellow soldiers were cheered by African Americans, but it was the white natives who startled them, convincing Benham that with the war over, they would now "think for themselves." From the other side, a soldier in Lee's army was shocked that the "miserably poor" whites he met in North Carolina expressed delight at the coming of the Yankees. Some of the Union troops, though, voiced skepticism, wondering whether those exulters had given up on the Confederate cause only after the war became too oppressive on the home front. After the fall of Richmond, one Union soldier thought white people were happy to encounter the enemy, "not because they were *Union* from principle, but because they were *Union* by being whipped & tired out by the war." After surrender, another noticed that the women of destitute white families welcomed Yankees because they were starving yet still defended the Confederate cause.[32]

Despite any evidence to the contrary, most of Lincoln's white mourners only amplified their portraits of innocent poor whites in the defeated Confederacy. Leave the "ignorantly deluded" alone, Alonso Quint pled in his Easter Sunday sermon, and they would "learn better by and by." In Springfield, Illinois, when the Reverend Matthew Simpson singled out Confederate leaders, he simultaneously extended forgiveness to the "deluded masses." A Union soldier in Raleigh warned his compatriots to take care in their treatment of the "unwilling, reluctant, enforced accessories" of the wicked leaders, and a Maryland Unionist brought the slain president into the picture, blaming Lincoln-hating Confederates for "inflaming the minds of humbler individuals."[33]

Where Confederate soldiers fit into this stark division was less clear. Immediately following the assassination, Union troops had fantasized about brutally attacking their already vanquished enemies on the battlefield, and a few explicitly named the rebel rank and file as culpable. Alfred Neafie, for one, pronounced guilty every soldier who remained loyal to the rebellion after Lincoln's murder. Alonzo Pickard made the same point more violently. "I was always very lenient in my feelings towards all except the leaders," he wrote from Virginia, but now he wanted everyone exterminated, leader and follower alike. Yet apart from the anger that flared, especially among Union soldiers, in the immediate aftermath of the assassination, the great majority of Lincoln's white mourners continued to speak in sweeping terms about the blameless poor white people of the South.[34]

Trouble was, if the majority of southern whites resented the slaveholding aristocracy, they did not appreciate black freedom either. During the secession crisis and then during the war, the planter classes had indeed taken care to suppress, sometimes with violence, any heterodox antislavery ideas among whites in their midst, and poor and middling folk certainly benefitted from remaining in the good graces of those who held political and social power. But southern whites outside the planter classes allied with the rich not merely out of fear. Comradeship with a wealthy slaveholder could provide a gin to clean their few bales of cotton, a slave or two to borrow for a particularly arduous task, even the opportunity to work as a plantation overseer. Many poor whites also shared an antagonism toward federal power. And though the destruction of slavery might break the cross-class bonds of southern white people, racism easily persisted across class lines.

This was the problem that Lincoln's white mourners elided. By exempting those beyond the planter classes, they let slide the fact that the vast majority of white southerners in 1865 remained loyal to white supremacy.

Though African Americans had joined the chorus that blamed the Confederate leadership for secession, war, and the assassination, they were also among the few who raised the problem of racism among the so-called white masses of the South. In the speech he delivered in Rochester on the day Lincoln died, Frederick Douglass pointedly divided the South into two distinct populations: not rich and poor but, rather, black friends and white foes, mindful of the fact that all white southerners held a sturdy stake in black subjugation. A writer for the *New York Anglo-African* likewise wrote that "poor and ignorant" white people in the slave states should be emancipated from the "tyranny of the rich and educated" but doubted that they could be "emancipated from negro-hate." A writer for the *Christian Recorder* wrote of the "class of ignorant white loyalists" who also believed that his people were "made to be slaves."[35]

When this complication occurred to Lincoln's white mourners, they tended only to expand their idealism. Hallock Armstrong admitted that "poor white trash" in the South appeared to hate black people (he believed they craved "somebody more degraded than themselves"), yet he confidently imagined that by treating them with benevolence, the occupying Yankees could embark on the mission of "regenerating the misguided millions." Just as the followers of William Lloyd Garrison had once imagined themselves ending slavery purely through the moral suasion of slaveholders, white mourners now imagined themselves enlightening poorer white southerners out of their racism. On the home front, in the days following the assassination, Anna Lowell attended a meeting of Bostonians who wished to "instruct & civilize," not only freedpeople, but also poor whites, who "needed it even more." The "white trash" of the South, John Greenleaf Whittier wrote in the *Liberator* (he put the phrase in quotation marks), looked toward African Americans "with a bitter hatred," yet education, he believed, would cure the racism of these pitiable "misguided masses"—note the contrast with the black writer who described the Negro-hating wealthy classes of the South as "educated," aware that education made no difference.[36]

These convictions about moral uplift were sincere, part and parcel of deep-rooted ideas about the social mobility inherent in a system built on capital and labor, standing in turn on a foundation of faith in the inevitable progress of human civilization. Yet by implying that the institution of slavery alone fueled racism, these white mourners exempted themselves from their own paternalism and prejudices.

GRIEVING CLERGYMEN CALLED FOR VENGEANCE, but they also helped diffuse anger with concurrent calls for mercy. Some mourners may have come home from church on Easter Sunday with their initial fury fanned, yet many found greater comfort in commands to forgive. For Anna Ferris, "the feeling of indignation & rage melted away" after Sunday services, replaced by an understanding of Jesus's prayer "Father forgive them for they know not what they do." On each successive Sunday after Easter, the assassination-themed sermons became less harsh, and vengeful human feelings paled before the knowledge that God would serve as the final judge of the criminals. As the Washington minister James Ward wrote in his diary, "It is God, to whom alone vengeance belongeth," and as Caroline Laing wrote to her daughter, paraphrasing Romans 12:19 (and likely a sermon she had heard), "Vengeance is mine saith the Lord."[37]

Wrestling with blame and forgiveness, people turned to President Lincoln's second inaugural address. Drawn to the words "malice toward none" and "charity for all," and to Lincoln's directive to "bind up the nation's wounds," mourners came to two different conclusions. Some invoked these words to demonstrate that the president's lenience would have made him unfit to reconstruct the nation, hence God had taken him away at just the right moment. Others invoked the same words to prove that mercy constituted the proper attitude toward their vanquished enemies, since that was what the slain president would have wanted (and some invoked both interpretations at the same time). Even though the very fact of the assassination only further complicated those words—if Lincoln had advocated for clemency when he was alive, did that still hold true after the Confederate system had murdered him?—many nonetheless focused on the message of forgiveness. Black minister Jacob Thomas told his Easter Sunday listeners that Lincoln had shown Christian grace by exercising mercy "even toward his foes," and white writer J. G. Holland refrained from speaking aloud the vengeance he felt inside, for Lincoln's kind spirit spoke of charity and "Christian forbearance." *With malice toward none* and *with charity for all* were the words that mourners frequently chose to inscribe onto their signs and banners in the wake of Lincoln's death.[38]

Yet if President Lincoln appeared to have been encouraging clemency, he had closed the second inaugural with a more complicated imperative: "to do all which may achieve and cherish a just, and a lasting peace." At the inauguration, Lincoln had reflected on divine judgment for the national sin of slavery, making clear that slavery was the cause of the conflict ("All knew," he said, that slavery was "somehow, the cause of the war"). All hoped and prayed the war would soon end, Lincoln went on, but if God willed the war to continue "until every drop of blood drawn with the lash, shall be paid by another drawn with the sword," so it must be. Lincoln was less clear about what, precisely, constituted the end of slavery—simply its legal demise or the fuller project of black citizenship and equality—and that was why his words were hard to interpret in light of the assassination. *Malice toward none* and *charity for all:* that was either why God had taken Lincoln (because of his lenience toward the enemy) or how Lincoln would have wanted the defeated enemies treated in his own absence (with mercy). *A just, and a lasting peace:* that implied that peace without enduring justice was not enough. Since these words followed Lincoln's reflections on slavery as the cause of the war, the idea of a democratic and egalitarian peace seemed to pertain especially to the future of the freedpeople.[39]

Many fewer mourners attended to this last point. Anna Lowell may have been thinking of the juxtaposition of the two imperatives when she read the address to her Sunday school students the week after Easter. Lincoln's words, she wrote in her diary, "almost sublimely mingle the ideas of Justice & Mercy." More direct were the words of a Chicago woman who signed herself only as "Ruth" in a letter to the black *Christian Recorder.* "We all remember well the late President's last Inaugural Address," she wrote, "and what he said about paying back the blood drawn by the lash." Yet Anna Lowell and Ruth were both unusual in calling up the second inaugural as a way to point toward Lincoln's desire, not only for black freedom, but also for justice—for equal political rights—after emancipation.[40]

If the ultimate meaning of Lincoln's second inaugural address was hard to decipher in the aftermath of the assassination, so too did clergymen preach multilayered messages of mercy and vengeance, and so too did Lincoln's lay mourners struggle with clashing impulses. For all the anger and calls to reprisal, for all the imagined and real violence toward the demonized enemy, for all the blame they placed on slaveholders and slavery,

Lincoln's mourners, both black and white, took at least a measure of refuge in their end-of-war optimism, nurtured by victory and emancipation. Now, amid sorrow and anger, they looked toward the president's funeral, hopeful that it would offer both resolution for their grief and a path forward for the postwar nation.

Best Friend

ENVISIONING LINCOLN'S GENEROSITY TOWARD THE defeated Confederates—contrasting him with the ruthlessness of Generals Sherman and Grant, or with President Andrew Johnson's hatred of the planter classes, and no doubt thinking of the words *with malice toward none*—the victors cast him as their enemy's best friend. As the "best friend of the *South*," a white mourner wrote in his diary on April 15, Lincoln would have leavened justice with love. A letter writer to the *New York Anglo-African* declared that the Confederates had "murdered their best friend," and the black editors of the *Christian Recorder* and the *San Francisco Elevator* likewise named Lincoln the best friend of the rebels. Ministers chimed in too, and mourners echoed the imagery from pulpit and press, ranging from cabinet members ("In the Murder of Lincoln the rebels have killed their best friend," Secretary of the Interior John P. Usher told his wife), to Union generals (Carl Schurz thought the assassin had "killed the best friend of the South"), to army officers ("They have lost their best friend," Francis Barnes wrote home from Alabama), to Union soldiers ("They murdered their best friend," wrote Franklin Boyts), to women on the home front ("The South have lost their *best* friend" and "murdered their *own* cause," Caroline Laing told her daughter). President Lincoln was the "best friend the South ever had," Albert Browne fairly gloated, "and how have the dastardly cowardly wretches repaid him."[1]

Rodney Dorman couldn't have disagreed more, for *Lincon* was no best friend of his people. Instead, the assassin and his conspirators were "among the greatest benefactors of mankind," and Dorman approved and applauded them as "killers of tyrants." Dorman was thus no doubt displeased with the considerable number of his compatriots who took up the best-friend chorus, whether sincerely or shrewdly. Confederates in New Orleans told a Union officer that "the South had lost their best friend." Hannah Turner, living in Philadelphia, with her husband in the rebel army, wrote that the president would have proven to be "a warm friend to the South," and Marylander Kate Johnson confided to her brother that the assassination was "too horrible to think of" because "we have lost our best friend."[2]

Lincoln's own contradictions—or maybe his magisterial skills as a statesman—emerge in the fact that mourning freedpeople made the same claim for themselves, calling Lincoln the "best friend ever I had" and their "best earthly friend." Bostonian George Ruffin, addressing his people in Richmond, called the slain leader the "Great Emancipator" and "our best friend." North and south, journalists chimed in. "Brothers mourn! sisters weep!" exclaimed the *New York Anglo-African,* "for our best friend has passed away." The *New Orleans Black Republican* called Lincoln the "greatest earthly friend of the colored race."[3]

Best friend of the freedpeople or best friend of the Confederates, perhaps Lincoln had been both—or at least he had made it appear that way as the war came to a close.

6

Funeral

WHEN RODNEY DORMAN READ THE coverage of Lincoln's funeral in the New York papers, he felt sickened all over again. It was utterly ridiculous, "gross & distorted," all "gas & bombast," with Lincoln lying in state as if the man were royalty or the pope. "Are they not aware of the satire & caricature?" he asked his diary. In complete "tom-foolery" on the day the funeral train was to arrive in Chicago, Union forces in Jacksonville fired a gun every half-hour from sunrise to sunset. "It is enough to make a dog sick," Dorman wrote, "even after eating his own vomit." This was Dorman's version of Proverbs 26:11, "As a dog returneth to his vomit, so a fool returneth to his folly."[1]

The funeral ceremonies for the Yankee chief disgusted Dorman, but at least he could extract a measure of satisfaction when he read about the lenient terms of surrender that Confederate general Joseph Johnston had negotiated with Sherman soon after the assassination. Dorman found this a "start in the right direction," so when he learned that President Andrew Johnson had rejected the terms entirely, his fury again surged against all those "dastardly scoundrels" up north. He grew impatient too as he read about the crackdown on freedom that accompanied the search for Lincoln's assassin. That no one could depart from the city of Washington he found entirely despotic. "But what does it matter about law, or the rights of citizens, when tyrants will otherwise?" he asked. The arrest of Mary Surratt, the sole woman among the conspirators, further inflamed him. "You sycophantic, time-serving knaves!" he thundered. "All of you!"[2]

SARAH BROWNE STAYED ANGRY TOO. At 11:30 on the morning of Wednesday, April 19, 1865, the bells began to toll in Salem. Services for the president commenced at noon, and Sarah took her place in a pew of the North Church, alongside her children Alice and Eddie. The pulpit remained draped in black and white, and again the mourners sought consolation and confirmation in one another's faces ("Eye met eye with the fixed expression of horror & sadness," Sarah wrote in her diary). After church, she and the children walked along Essex Street, joining the crowds to absorb the city's mourning decorations, and when she described the public mood that afternoon, she wrote not only of gloom and grief but also of ire. "Blood calls for an avenger," she asserted. "Let us unite together against all tyranny—all oppression—all outrage." Later, Sarah gazed at the fragrant white roses that she and the children had plucked from the church altar after the service. "We smiled as we looked at these flowers," she conceded, "but apart from them, all was dark—mysterious—terrible." She drew a heavy line of black ink across the page, perhaps hoping that the local funeral service would provide a point of closure from which to look ahead.[3]

Sarah's elder son, Albert Jr., who worked for the governor of Massachusetts, had traveled to Washington for Lincoln's funeral, and over the next two weeks Sarah followed the whereabouts of the president's body. She had already recorded when it was embalmed and brought to the White House. Now she described the ceremonies in the capital, read accounts of the funeral train's journey, and noted the whereabouts of Mary Lincoln and her sons. As Lincoln's body headed north and west, Sarah also kept up with the military news, expressing consternation over General Sherman's overly magnanimous negotiations with General Johnston. They were the "most astonishing—most outrageous—most humiliating agreements ever talked over!" she exclaimed, wondering if the hero and idol of the Union had lost his mind. Down south, Albert agreed, though he made light of the compromises. "Old Tecumpsy Sherman has made a mistake, a grievous mistake," he wrote home.

Sarah followed the whereabouts of John Wilkes Booth too, noting the assassin's escape from Ford's Theatre and the federal government's ongoing hunt. "Booth is supposed to be in Maryland," she wrote on April 25, the day before he was captured. "We wait with great interest for all news from the Capitol." In early May, Sarah documented Lincoln's burial at Oak Ridge Cemetery in his hometown of Springfield, Illinois. The grand formalities were over, but Sarah Browne's thoughts remained peppered with words and phrases like *fiends* and *horrible sin*.[4]

MOURNERS CAME TO WASHINGTON BY the thousands. They arrived on foot, on horseback, in carriages, and on special trains that the railroad companies added to their timetables. They filled every hotel and boardinghouse, slept in spare rooms, on floors, in their own conveyances, and out of doors. If anything was intended to affirm worldwide grief, it was the capital's funeral, and mourners wanted to count themselves part of that powerful, imagined universality. They came looking to participate in rituals that would help them understand God's purposes and the meaning of Lincoln's death. They came to take part in the making of history. They expected to be overawed, and they wanted the victorious nation to move forward into a glorious future.[5]

Early on Tuesday, April 18, people began lining up outside the heavily draped White House for the privilege of viewing the president's body, lying in state in the East Room, and many of those filling Pennsylvania Avenue (some observers thought most) were African Americans. When the doors opened at 9:30 a.m., viewers saw their own efforts at tacking up mourning drapery magnified a thousandfold. Dark fabric covered nearly every surface, with mantels, mirrors, columns, and light fixtures concealed. Hundreds of yards of black and white silk and ninety boxes' worth of the finest crape had been beautifully arranged. The catafalque, a confection of black alpaca, velvet, crape, and muslin, and black and white satin, stood so high—eleven feet including the canopy—that workmen had removed an entire chandelier to accommodate it. On the platform, amid wreaths of laurel, cedar, and camellia, rested the silver-handled walnut coffin. It was open to reveal the top third of the president's body, clad in the same black suit he had donned for his second inauguration, complemented by black bowtie and white gloves. His head rested on a white silk pillow. Inside, the coffin was strewn with roses, magnolias, and lilies.[6]

The undertakers had worked hard to preserve the president for public display, injecting an artery with chemicals to retard decay and paying special attention to the face. Booth's lead bullet had penetrated Lincoln's skull and brain, and after manipulating the protruding eyes back into their sockets, the embalmer arranged the features into a tableau of "quiet sleep": eyelids closed, beard shaved, visage dusted, and lips shaped into a glimmer of a smile. Benjamin Brown French, Washington's commissioner of public buildings, and the man in charge of the body, thought the face looked "perfectly natural," except for the bloodshot spot under the right eye. Although the science of embalming had improved during the war years, it was still a rudimentary art in 1865, and Lincoln's body would begin to decompose almost right away. A doctor would travel with the funeral train, continually repowdering the face to mask the inevitable darkening of the skin.[7]

Over the next eight hours, mourners waiting outside the White House divided into two lines to enter the East Room, climbing the steps on each side of the catafalque to file past. The scene was intended to be both serene and imposing, and many found it exactly so. "My last view of *ABRA-HAM LINCOLN*," one man recorded grandly in his diary that day. But just as mourners would discover all through the Washington funeral, and all through the journey of the funeral train that took the president back to Illinois, dissatisfaction punctuated the majesty. Here in the East Room, it was a "rush & jam." Rose Pickard, a Union hospital volunteer, was "jammed almost to death" before she even got in. Spectators were hurried along, each one given little more than a second to glance at the president, instructed not to linger, and prodded along by guards whose job it was to see that only as many people entered as exited. Helen McCalla could barely "wait a moment near the corpse," making it "impossible to obtain a satisfactory view." Others stood in line for hours, only to be turned away when the doors closed.[8]

Wednesday, April 19, was a beautiful spring day in the capital, the "saddest day of my life," wrote Anson Henry, Lincoln's physician and friend. The funeral service held in the East Room was for dignitaries only: President Johnson, cabinet members, generals, governors, senators and representatives, Supreme Court justices, ambassadors, and other eminent men. Elder son Captain Robert Lincoln was there, struggling to retain his composure, but Mary Lincoln stayed away, unable to bear it. Also missing was Secretary of State William Seward, still recovering from the wounds inflicted by one of Booth's conspirators. Only seven women stood among the crowd of about six hundred: four wives, two daughters, and the nurse who had cared for Willie Lincoln, Robert and Tad's brother, who had died in 1862 at the age of twelve. Mourners all over the world would later drink up the particulars of the East Room services, avidly reading the newspapers and copying down details.[9]

The Reverend Phineas D. Gurley delivered the sermon. He was minister of the Presbyterian church where the Lincoln family worshipped and had conducted the funeral service for Willie Lincoln too. Gurley offered comfort, but he did not brush aside the unfathomable. There was divine will, of course: Gurley invoked a striking image of God's hand hovering above the one that pointed the gun and pulled the trigger, permitting "whatsoever He pleased." But even as Gurley surmised that God intended Lincoln's death to humble the victors, he admitted the crime's incomprehensible nature ("a mystery that is very deep"). There was the imperative to submit but also the undeniable pain and sorrow ("We bow, we weep, we worship"). There were hints of anger when Gurley claimed that Lincoln had been the nation's "best hope." There was profound optimism (soon would come "a bright and glorious day, such as our country has never seen"), but then again dawn coexisted with darkness in the "stricken and weary land." There was a mixture of retribution and generosity ("We sing of mercy as well as of judgment"), and there was, finally, Abraham Lincoln's larger purpose in an abolitionist and emancipationist view of the war: the end of slavery and the hope of racial equality. Consolation ultimately lay in the assurance that freedom and union would last forever. Once again, men wept openly.[10]

Although most found the ceremony solemn and impressive, not everyone came away pleased. George Templeton Strong, New York lawyer and treasurer of the U.S. Sanitary Commission, thought the whole thing "vile and vulgar," the prayers uttered by Bishop Matthew Simpson "whining" and "most nauseous." For Easter Sunday, ministers had composed their remarks hurriedly, amid shock and grief; perhaps Strong, and others too, now found the language overwrought.[11]

The funeral of George Washington, in 1799, served as the model for the day's formalities. Men from the Veteran Reserve Corps removed Lincoln's coffin from the East Room and transferred it to the hearse that would carry it the mile and a half from the White House to the Capitol, where it would rest on a second custom-built catafalque in the Rotunda, also heavily draped. A carriage drawn by six horses and followed by one riderless mount, empty boots turned backward in the stirrups, conveyed the body. Many from the indoor service marched in the procession, joined by all manner of contingents: fraternal orders, workingmen, hospital convalescents, college students. First in the procession of infantry and cavalry were black soldiers, though not by design. The Twenty-Second U.S. Colored Troops, which had marched into Richmond, were called to Washington "to represent the Colored Soldiers." Arriving by boat in the nick of time, they had met the procession head-on. In a metaphorical reenactment of their service to the nation, the men turned about-face to lead the parade, just as they had run to Union lines before they were permitted to enlist, then turned about-face to fight when Lincoln issued the Emancipation Proclamation. Perhaps sixty thousand spectators, with a likely majority of African Americans, watched perhaps forty thousand marchers, from curbs and pavement, windows and balconies, rooftops and treetops. One white viewer was struck especially by the "negro & white troops" and the "white & black" civilians. Another described the "promiscuous motley procession headed & tailed by Ethiopian Americans."[12]

The gravity was palpable to many. George Templeton Strong brightened, grateful to be present for the "most memorable ceremonial this continent has ever seen." Another observer found it "a splendid sight and a mournful one," and a soldier listening from his hospital bed described an otherwise "solemn hush" over the whole city. Even a Confederate sympathizer, who regularly filled his diary with references to "nig suffrage" and "nig troops," noted the "great display."[13]

And yet how different everything felt from the days before. Out on the streets on the day Lincoln died, and in church on Easter Sunday, people had gathered spontaneously with family and friends to find and offer comfort. Now you either had to be invited or you had to plan carefully, and either way, you likely stood among strangers. A soldier in the Fourteenth Indiana thought it all the most imposing thing he'd ever seen, but "the biggest thing to me," he told his wife, "was that I had my pocket picked." One man recorded only that he "roasted in the sun" for hours, another that he found it "an Excellent opportunity to see distinguished officials." Those who stood too far back could follow along only by the gun salutes and clip-clop of horses' hooves. The well-orchestrated pomp and circumstance made it seem as if all the questions had been settled, when none had. As Sarah Browne put it after the services in Salem, everything remained "dark—mysterious—terrible."[14]

For mourners at home in their own cities, towns, and villages on April 19, the day felt less grand and more subdued, with a pall and a stillness replacing the customary weekday bustle. In Brattleboro, Vermont, everyone appeared "serious and thoughtful." In San Francisco, the morning seemed almost holy in its silence. Across the country, the drapery had been augmented for Wednesday's events, and again women provided much of the labor. Shock lingered; as one woman wrote, it was still "too dreadful to believe." For Anna Lowell, the day brought on one of her awful headaches, and for Caroline Dall, it all made her "faint & sick." Where the weather was fine, the contrast was painful. A "lovely day—*& yet so sad*," one mourner wrote.[15]

Beginning at eleven or noon, bells, guns, and cannon broke the stillness. In church, mourners saw the now-familiar dark drapery, white flowers, and portraits of Lincoln—that is, if they could see anything at all. Just as on Easter Sunday three days before, people crammed inside. Anna Lowell's church was so crowded that a minister friend "took hold of our hands & shoved us in," she wrote. Inside, the messages were the same. At Cincinnati's black Baptist church, the preacher reminded his congregants that ultimate judgment lay with the Lord. Choirs sang "Thy will be done" and "God Works in a Mysterious Way." Em Cornwall thought she had "got over it a little," but the gloom of the service prompted grief to "burst forth afresh." For Caroline Laing, it was the booming cannon announcing the start of services down in Washington. "I felt sad enough before, but at that sound I could control myself no longer & wept during the whole service," she confided to her daughter. Others stepped back from the intensity.

In Newport, Rhode Island, an ingenuous fifteen-year-old who attended two services in a row told her journal that she had "got a little too much" of it. After Quaker services, Annie Hillborn spent a "delightful afternoon" with friends in Philadelphia's Fairmount Park.[16]

Following the religious services came the ceremonies. In Altoona, Pennsylvania, four mourning-bedecked horses carried an empty, flag-draped coffin. In San Francisco, five hundred dapper black men joined the procession, followed by the city's Chinese merchants. In camp, Union soldiers polished their guns and boots for dress parade and did the women's work of trimming flags with black crape. In occupied southern cities, Yankees and black residents marched together. In Fernandina, Florida, the bells and cannon "told rebeldom their doom," a black soldier reported, and Sergeant Thomas Darling, once a slave, offered an oration that included "the claims of our race to all legal rights."[17]

Once again, both in Washington and beyond, it felt as if the whole world was mourning for Lincoln. In New York City, home to a sizable Copperhead population, Caroline Laing convinced herself that even Lincoln's "worst enemies" were "enemies no longer." In the border state of Delaware, Anna Ferris thought she had never seen "so universal & heartfelt a tribute of grief." Some were more judicious, speaking cautiously of free states or crafting phrases like "where the Union Element prevails." Partly the mourning felt omnipresent on Wednesday, April 19, because at least some dissenters stayed out of the way. In New York, a young secessionist studiously spent the day writing and rewriting her school composition; the like-minded "did not dare show their faces," she wrote to her brother, lest they be mobbed. In Baltimore, Confederate Louisa Mason purposely stayed inside unpacking a trunk, and down south, it was a good time for Lincoln's antagonists to keep their thoughts private, like the man who wrote in his diary of "Poor 'Old abe' the 'Ape.'" Some joined in the ceremonies despite their views—Democratic congressman John Pruyn bristled silently at the extolling of the Emancipation Proclamation at New York's Trinity Church. Still others feigned grief in efforts at self-protection—in Maryland, John Glenn draped a single windowsill for all of five hours ("during the time prescribed by Military orders for mourning," he explained). In Boston, a "bitter Copperhead" showed up at church to assure the minister that he was "entirely converted." Many just remained indifferent, like the Confederate prisoner who noted that no business would be transacted because of the funeral, adding that the day brought no news "of any importens." All such behavior eased the way for mourners to comfort themselves with the ideal of universally shared grief, however vaguely or inaccurately they may have defined that universality.[18]

ON THURSDAY, IT RAINED IN Washington, and forty thousand more people filed past the coffin in the Capitol Rotunda. The next morning, an escort carried Lincoln's body to the funeral train waiting at the New Jersey Avenue Station of the Baltimore and Ohio Railroad, where Phineas Gurley offered a last prayer to an enormous crowd. It was Friday, April 21, 1865, and the president's homeward journey was about to begin.

Cities and towns had petitioned for inclusion as stops along the route, countering the wishes of Mary Lincoln, who wanted a nonstop run to Springfield. Now the train's itinerary largely retraced, in reverse, the route that Lincoln had traveled to the White House four years earlier. On that journey, credible rumors of a secessionist assassination plot had marred Lincoln's passage through Baltimore, prompting a secretive switch of plans and a disguise that included discarding the signature stovepipe hat. In 1865, carrying the corpse of the slain chief, the funeral train would stop first in Baltimore, then continue to Harrisburg, Philadelphia, New York, Albany, Buffalo, Cleveland, Columbus, Indianapolis, and Chicago, before reaching Lincoln's hometown. But it was not just these cities that mattered, it was also the routes in between: the villages and hillsides at which mourners could gather to watch the locomotive pass. Just as they traveled to the nation's capital, just as they read about every detail of the ceremonies in the newspapers, just as they planned and participated in local observances, now again mourners were eager to make themselves part of the rituals that might answer the restless quest for the meaning of Lincoln's assassination. At the very least, they wanted to bid a formal good-bye and turn toward the future.

Planning and executing the funeral train proved a herculean effort. Roughly three hundred passengers would ride in the nine-car train during any given segment, including all manner of national and state officials, who traded places from city to city. Woodstoves would give warmth, and oil would shed light, but the train had to stop for most meals. All along the way, the cars had to be inspected and serviced, halting for water (for the boilers) and wood (for the stoves in cool spring weather). In the eighth car lay two coffins: that of the president and that of Willie Lincoln, who had been disinterred in Washington to be reburied with his father at home. At each major stop, guards would keep watch over the boy while Lincoln's body was removed for the ceremonies. Robert Lincoln rode to Baltimore, then returned to Washington to stay with his mother. He would join the mourning rituals again only in Springfield. Mary Lincoln stayed in the White House for the duration of the journey.

Transcontinental railroads were a product of the Civil War, and to many of the victors-turned-mourners, Lincoln's funeral train pointed the way to the triumph of industry and free labor (and, less happily, corruption and greed). The lack of a federal railroad system in 1865, though, meant that no single funeral train traveled the route from start to finish. Rather, over nearly seventeen hundred miles, planners had to coordinate as many as eighty different passenger cars from the Baltimore and Ohio Railroad, the Pennsylvania Railroad, the Hudson River Railroad, the Buffalo and Erie Railroad, the Columbus and Indianapolis Central Railroad, and the Chicago and Alton Railroad, among others. It was not just that different companies owned the cars, it was also that they had built tracks with different gauges, making it impossible for the same cars to travel continuously across the continent. Nor were time zones standardized in 1865, meaning that planners had to calculate arrivals and departures according to an array of schedules, in order to permit newspapers to print the local hour and minute of passage through each town and village—calculations that were hard enough within the same time zone. Residents of Swanville, Pennsylvania, for example, anticipated the train's appearance on Friday, April 28, at 2:42 in the morning, with its next appearance, at the Fairview station, at 2:49 a.m.

In the course of some four and a half hours on the morning of Friday, April 28, 1865, Lincoln's funeral train traveled about a hundred miles, beginning in Erie, Pennsylvania, crossing into Ohio at the town of Conneaut, and proceeding to Cleveland. Mourners gathered at every stop, even in the middle of the night. This commemorative ribbon displays the train schedule, capped by an image of a woman weeping over Lincoln's casket, flanked by mourning soldiers. Strict orders for punctuality appear below the schedule. *Lincoln Financial Foundation Collection, courtesy of the Indiana State Museum.*

CLEVELAND & ERIE RAIL ROAD.

TIME CARD

For Special Train, Friday, April 28th, 1865,

CONVEYING REMAINS OF ABRAHAM LINCOLN,

LATE PRESIDENT OF THE UNITED STATES,

AND ESCORT.

STATIONS.	Miles.	Miles.	Pilot Engine.	Cortege Train.	
			LEAVE	LEAVE	
Erie			2.15 A.M.	2.25 A.M.	
Swanville	8¼	8½	2.42	2.52	Pilot Engine & Cortege Train meets Stock Express No 1.
Fairview	11	2½	2.49	2.59	Pilot Engine & Cortege Train meets Stock Express No. 2.
Girard	15½	4½	3.05	3.15	
Springfield	20¼	4¾	3.17	3.27	
Conneaut	27¾	7½	3.39	3.48	Pilot Engine & Cortege Train passes Fast Freight No. 3.
Kingsville	35¼	7½	3.59	4.09	
Ashtabula	41	5¾	4.17	4.27	
Saybrook	45¾	4¾	4.30	4.40	
Geneva	50¼	4½	4.42	4.52	
Unionville	53½	3¼	4.51	5.01	
Madison	55¾	2¼	4.59	5.09	
Perry	61	5¼	5.13	5.23	
Painesville	66½	5½	5.31	5.41	
Mentor	72¾	6¼	5.47	5.57	
Willoughby	77	4¼	5.58	6.08	
Wickliffe	81¼	4¼	6.10	6.20	
Euclid	86	4¾	6.22	6.32	
Cleveland	95½	9½	6.50 A.M.	7.00 A.M.	
			ARRIVE.	ARRIVE.	

This Train and the Pilot Engine will have the POSITIVE RIGHT OF ROAD, and all Trains must be kept entirely out of their way.

Train and Pilot Engine must be run strictly to card time as possible.

Strict carefulness is enjoined upon Agents, Train Men, and all Employes. You must be on duty, and know that every thing is right when Pilot Engine and this Train is due.

Supt's Office C. & E. R. R., Cleveland, April 26, 1865. **H. NOTTINGHAM, Sup't.**

SANFORD & HAYWARD, PRINTERS, CLEVELAND.

With schedules distributed, communities drew up plans. Unlike the highly orchestrated ceremonies that would take place at the eleven major stops, the scale of in-between activities was more intimate. At various junctures, workers constructed temporary decorative arches over the tracks, intertwined with evergreens and adorned with flowers and flags. Citizens arranged for tolling bells, cannon blasts, gunshots, prayers, and dirges. Delegations of women in white dresses would greet the train, and schoolchildren would scatter flowers along the tracks. A few used the occasion to satisfy personal curiosity, like Charles Larrabee, who came by for the train's brief evening stop in Poughkeepsie. "I stood where I could see the *notables* as they were eating and finally got in amongst them," he wrote to his mother, amused to see that military and government men "*acted* like other folks." Most, though, created a more significant experience for themselves. Wherever the train puffed into view, people gathered to watch it traverse the landscape. Once again, mourners walked, rode their horses, drove their buggies—and boarded other, specially scheduled trains—to arrive at the closest venue at just the right moment. In deference, the funeral cars typically traveled at twenty miles an hour, slowing down considerably when passing overflowing station platforms. When the moment came, the mourners knelt, wept, prayed, doffed hats, removed bonnets, and held children aloft for a sight they would remember their whole lives. Where springtime rains fell, spectators got wet and stayed damp, shoes and hemlines caked with mud, flags and white handkerchiefs soggy. Where the train traveled in darkness, mourners built bonfires or lit lanterns and torches. Even when the train chugged through a village at three o'clock in the morning in a heavy downpour, throngs paid tribute, often by the thousands.[19]

Mourners also crowded into the eleven chosen cities, again arriving by any and every means possible, filling every room for rent, and sleeping in parks and streets. "This is a very lonesome day," wrote an Indiana woman who lived sixty miles north of the train route. "Every body almost has gone to Indianapolis to see the remains of A. Lincoln." Just as in Washington on April 19, spectators jammed avenues, windows, balconies, and rooftops and climbed trees for a better view. In Philadelphia, Anna Ferris observed a "living tide" gush through the streets. In New York, one man estimated a crowd of a hundred thousand lined up at two o'clock in the morning to view the body and a million and a half watching the procession, which took "7 hours in passing a given point." In Albany, pushing and shoving was the only way to ensure a place on the stifling outbound cars when the ceremonies ended, prompting people to faint in the middle of crowds. Mourners who made their way to Springfield toured Lincoln's home, law offices, church pew, even his barbershop, then slept outside or just walked the streets all night, waiting for the train's arrival. As in Washington, people performed the rituals of grief in the company of strangers.[20]

Drapery everywhere was thicker than it had been on Saturday, April 15, or on Easter Sunday, or Wednesday, April 19. Shopkeepers sold miles more fabric, as Philadelphians covered the Liberty Bell and New Yorkers decorated the twenty-foot windows of the Lord and Taylor department store in red, white, and blue silk, complemented by black and white bombazine. The weather was at its springtime best in New York, Albany, and Chicago, while heavy rains fell in Baltimore, Harrisburg, and Cleveland, drenching the train's black drapery and causing the dye of mourning fabric to bleed onto building facades. The rains were so torrential in Indianapolis that the procession accompanying the hearse to and from the State House had to be canceled. Everywhere, hawkers peddled likenesses of the president. Everywhere, banners—both official and homemade—told you how to feel, proclaiming sentiments in words both plain and poetic: "The Nation Mourns" or "The great heart of the Nation throbs heavily at the Portals of his Grave." Where a week or two earlier, mourners had searched one another's faces for the meaning of the tragedy, now they read the placards. Nearly everywhere they could see the words from Lincoln's second inaugural: *With malice toward none.*[21]

Lincoln's mourners made efforts to connect themselves to the grand and historic events all around them. At each of the major stops, a Veteran Reserve Guard of Escort, consisting of twenty-nine men who rode the entire route, hoisted the coffin to their shoulders and conveyed it to a locally supplied horse-drawn hearse that in turn transported the body to the venue where it would lie in state. Enormous crowds gathered to watch the transfer, then again to witness the elaborate ceremonies planned by local committees. For a man perched in a second-story window in New York, it was, he felt sure, "the most imposing thing I ever saw or ever expect to see again." In Indianapolis, a spectator thought the display "the most notable & worthy of the age & century." Still, the experience was far from perfect.

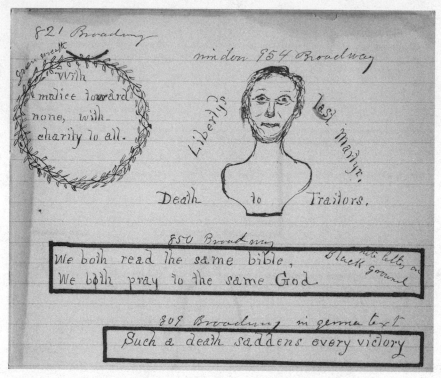

An anonymous sketcher walked the streets of New York City after the assassination, recording the signs and banners displayed in shop windows and on building facades. This page, with Broadway addresses recorded, documents magnanimous sentiments, taken from Lincoln's second inaugural address in March 1865 ("With malice toward none, with charity to all"), alongside more vengeful statements ("Death to Traitors").
McLellan Lincoln Collection, John Hay Library, Brown University.

Mourners pushed, shoved, and fainted, while pickpockets collected wallets and watches and thieves worked the empty houses. For some, the extensive preparations took a toll on the occasion's gravity. English actress Ellen Kean detected entirely too much gaiety (women smiling in their spring dresses!) and not enough dignity (Lincoln's remains shuttled about "to gratify the morbid curiosity of the idle"). A critic in the Midwest thought the ceremonies amounted to "more of a show than respect for Lincoln." Sometimes it was just exhausting. In Chicago, a woman held up her baby girl to see the parade until the child seemed to weigh a ton.[22]

Miscalculations and blunders were inevitable, given the scale of the endeavor. The New York procession straggled, with marchers forming pathetic-looking lines that were "twenty a-breast, and only two deep." In

Philadelphia, everything was running late, and as dusk turned to darkness, no one could see much of anything. Annie Hillborn and her friends stood in a "*Sea* of people" through bursts of rain that occasioned the raising of "thousands of umbrellas," and after a four-hour wait, they could "scarcely distinguish the procession from the spectators." For Anna Ferris, straining her eyes, only the "flash of a street lamp revealed the coffin for an instant." Soon the frustrated viewers became unruly, prompting policemen to "beat the people back with their clubs." Near Independence Hall, male spectators were "fumbling the women." Lucy McKim was among the very few to record the occasion without sentimental revision, one of the few to document the impersonal nature of the formal rituals. On Broad Street between Spruce and Arch, McKim pushed against a solid wall of people, "every available perch being black with a seething mass of human beings." Moving inside at Ninth and Arch, she and her companions waited until after sunset for the procession to appear, at which point a group of boys let out an unseemly cheer. It could hardly be called marching, McKim scoffed, with the lines gaping and no music to be heard. "Play up! Play up!" people shouted at the bands. When the hearse finally appeared, it "bobbed & jolted," unable to provoke the intended awe. So "entirely ludicrous" was it all, McKim recounted to her fiancé, that she actually burst out laughing. The whole thing was no more than "a miserable, showy, superficial, irreverent farce."[23]

No matter how satisfying or unsatisfying were the rituals, many of Lincoln's mourners had come for a single objective: to view the president's body up close. Again, the contrast with the immediacy of learning the news was unmistakable. In those moments and hours, mourners had gazed at the stricken brows and falling tears across so many countenances for confirmation and comfort, whereas now they came to gaze upon a single face only. For many, to be sure, that turned out to be a reverent experience. In Philadelphia, African American student and servant Emilie Davis anticipated Lincoln's arrival, recording the upcoming event the day before, then again the next morning. "The President comes in town this afternoon," she wrote in her diary, as if Lincoln were still alive. Davis's first two attempts to view the body failed because the crowds were so great, and the next day she waited several hours for a turn. Yet even that briefest glimpse was, for her, "a sight worth seeing." In Indianapolis, Mattie Jackson was among the last few hundred viewers to glimpse the president, since African Americans were relegated to the back of the line. Jackson, who had escaped from slavery in Missouri, went to see the body expressly because she wouldn't believe Lincoln was dead until she set her own eyes on the lifeless corpse.[24]

Persistence paid off for Emilie Davis and Mattie Jackson, but not all mourners found what they hoped for in the viewing ritual. Just as in Washington, workers at each venue had built elaborate catafalques for the coffin. Everywhere the lines were frightfully long and time permitted in the casket's presence astonishingly short. In New York, more than 100 people filed by each minute, in Cleveland perhaps 180 per minute across fifteen hours. In Philadelphia, some 300,000 caught a glimpse. In Chicago, 7,000 people saw the body each hour the coffin remained open, in Columbus, 8,000. All in all, perhaps a million people glanced at Lincoln, each for no more than a second or two. A soldier in Philadelphia who felt "rushed right through" returned to the queue twice more. To see the body in New York, mourners had to make their way through a basement and a set of narrow, poorly lit stairs. One man made "3 ineffectual attempts," then lined up at one o'clock in the morning before he got a quick look. "The whole live long night the crowd poured through," he wrote to his sister, the line as long at three o'clock in the morning as it had been at noon.[25]

Even those who stole an extra moment or lined up more than once might come away disappointed. The fact was, the one face that mourners had waited so long to see was faded and decayed, powdered and worked over. By the time the funeral train got to New York, the discoloration was evident, with viewers describing it either as "wan and shrunken" or "shrunken & dark." In Albany, mourners noticed the putrefying, lead-colored skin. By Chicago, the face had darkened nearly beyond repair. People there expressed surprise at its thinness and retreating chin, disillusioned that Lincoln didn't look "as they fancied great men did." Even before full deterioration set in, the face seemed more a mask of artful disguise than anything else—eyes shut and mouth artificially set—unable to impart either emotion or meaning to those hurrying past. A few figured this out beforehand. "Sally & Annie Kennedy asked me to go with them," a Washington woman wrote in her diary, but she declined, preferring to remember Lincoln "as I saw him last," orating at his second inauguration. Some avoided the capital's ceremonies altogether. "Funeral of President Lincoln," the nurse Clara Barton wrote in her diary. "I remained in doors all day." When William

THE BODY OF THE MARTYR PRESIDENT, ABRAHAM LINCOLN.
LYING IN STATE AT THE CITY HALL, N.Y. APRIL 24 & 25 1865.

Mourners file past Lincoln's body at New York's City Hall on April 24 and 25, 1865. The real scene was not nearly as orderly as depicted in this 1865 lithograph.
LC-USZC2-1982, Prints and Photographs Division, Library of Congress.

Webster lined up in Philadelphia at eight in the morning, he was told he wouldn't reach the coffin until three that afternoon. "I am glad I did not go on," he wrote to his brother. "I shall remember Mr. L. as I saw him in Trenton, with that bright smile playing in his face." The glances and glimpses could not accomplish anything close to that, making it harder still to extract meaning or find closure.[26]

AS THE FUNERAL CAPTIVATED AND frustrated mourners, there was still the war to distract them from any illusion of unbroken solemnity. Now, during the journey of the funeral train, came the matter of General William Tecumseh Sherman's negotiations with Confederate general Joseph Johnston, which Rodney Dorman found encouraging and Sarah Browne pronounced outrageous.

By mid-March 1865, much of the Confederacy had been transformed into a ruined landscape with a shattered economy and rapidly deserting soldiers. The only slim-as-thread possibility to stave off defeat lay in combining the forces of Robert E. Lee and Joseph E. Johnston, the latter commanding the remnants of the Army of Tennessee. But Lee postponed that plan, thereby forming two parallel contests: Grant versus Lee in Virginia and Sherman versus Johnston in North Carolina. Then, when Johnston got news of Lee's surrender, he told Jefferson Davis in no uncertain terms that the war was over, that his men could not and would not fight any longer, for it was simply impossible to conquer Sherman. Johnston communicated with Sherman too, requesting a meeting under a flag of truce, and in the two days between Easter Sunday and the Washington funeral, the generals conferred at a North Carolina farmhouse, agreeing to terms on April 18, the day mourners lined up to view Lincoln's body at the White House. If Sherman had his way, the United States would recognize fully restored governments for the former Confederate states, contingent on no more than officials taking an oath of allegiance; amnesty would be granted to former Confederates, including the restoration of property rights—the terms contained no qualification, not even to disallow the return of property in slaves. Sherman believed that he was acting on the wishes of the late executive, but in fact he had significantly overreached his position by effectively engaging in reconstruction policy. Indeed, the terms Sherman proffered far exceeded those to which Grant and Lee had agreed at Appomattox.

As Caroline White wrote in her diary, Sherman was "confounding all his friends & former admirers" by "treating with rebels on subjects quite beyond & foreign to his powers."[27]

Mourners engrossed in the progress of the funeral train now shook themselves back into the world of formal politics, forced to choose between the two contradictory interpretations of Lincoln's political sensibilities. Either Lincoln's kindheartedness stood supreme (*with malice toward none* and *charity for all*) or it was precisely such generosity of spirit that had prompted God to take Lincoln away. As much as mourners had copied those merciful words onto their funeral banners, in this instance most chose to draw upon the opposite conviction. "Shermans inglorious treat with Johnston," a Michigan soldier jotted in his diary on the day of Lincoln's funeral in Washington. On April 21, the day the funeral train departed from the capital, President Andrew Johnson rejected the agreement, but the firestorm among mourners continued. Anna Lowell thought Sherman's behavior "startling & alarming." Henry Thacher thought the assassination itself "hardly more astounding" than Sherman's actions. If others didn't go quite so far, they nonetheless sympathized. It was a "stupendous blunder." Sherman had "made an ass of himself." He was the "most astonishing ignoramus of the age," as Anne Neafie put it to her husband. Francis Lieber compared Sherman's actions to the fall of a virtuous woman, and Lydia Maria Child found herself using "language quite too muscular for polite circles."[28]

In a future without Lincoln, those who wanted to honor his legacy would have to navigate between mercy and justice, and at least in this instance, the choice was clear. On Wednesday, April 26, as the president's body left Albany, the two generals met again at the same farmhouse, this time for Johnston's surrender under the same terms agreed to by Grant and Lee. Still the excoriation of Sherman continued, mourners unwilling to forget his misstep. A Wisconsin soldier hoped to be home by the Fourth of July, "if Sherman does not hold any more peace conferences," he wrote. From Alexandria, Egypt, Charles Hale, the U.S. consul, joked that it appeared Sherman had "proclaimed himself President of the Confederacy."[29]

As Lincoln's funeral train headed west toward Buffalo, another worldly event intruded, this one even more disruptive. After leaping from the Lincolns' box at Ford's Theatre, John Wilkes Booth had galloped off on a

waiting horse, eluding the uncoordinated searches of federal and munic-
ipal authorities. On April 26, after a twelve-day manhunt, and on the same
day as Johnston's proper surrender, men of the Sixteenth New York Cavalry closed in on Booth, who was hiding in a barn in northern Virginia
along with one of his accomplices. David Herold was the man who had
stood outside the Seward home, holding onto Lewis Powell's horse while
Powell tried to kill the secretary of state, then taken flight when he heard
the screams inside. Herold now surrendered, but Booth was armed and
refused to yield, even after the captors set the barn on fire. At that moment,
one of the soldiers decided to shoot, mortally wounding Lincoln's assassin. The men then sewed Booth's body into a blanket and loaded it onto a
steamer bound for Washington. It was Secretary of War Edwin Stanton's
idea to bury Booth beneath the floor of a room in the Washington Arsenal,
even as the press reported an ignominious burial at sea. At all costs, Stanton did not want Booth's grave to become a shrine to Lincoln's enemies.

Passengers on the funeral train got word the very next day, and as the
news spread, both glee and anger welled up; for most, *charity for all* by
no means extended to John Wilkes Booth. Some rejoiced, glad that the
assassin had been "shot and thrown away" into oblivion. "Well done! Rest
in obscurity forever," exclaimed one mourner. "Let him die and be forgotten," said another. Some regretted the foreclosure of retributive justice. He
should have been hanged or, better yet, tortured and then hanged, and in
the most cruel manner possible. How terrible, an aggrieved woman pointed
out, that Booth had died "in the same way as his illustrious victim." Some
did heed Lincoln's imperative, and in fact it was the ardent abolitionists,
especially the women among them, who most strenuously took up the cry
for mercy. "I dare say the wretched crazy fool had suffered enough in his
attempt to escape from justice," wrote Sarah Hale, sure that the "execration
of the world" constituted quite enough retaliation. Martha Coffin Wright
expressed even greater sympathy, suffering several "restless nights" thinking about Booth, disturbed by the calls for torture, and relieved that he was
finally "at rest." For their part, Confederates didn't have much to say on the
matter. One hoped the shooting would subdue Lincoln's "fanatical parti-
sans," while another felt sorry about the killing only because she couldn't
bear the breast-beating Yankee triumph of it all.[30]

Yankee triumph was indeed the order of the day. While sorrowfully worshipping the president's body, most also happily celebrated the handling of the dead assassin. The stark difference between the treatment of the two corpses, one extravagantly revered for two carefully planned weeks, the other disposed of unceremoniously after a nearly two-week search, offered a satisfying symbolic gesture of putting the past to rest and looking toward the nation's future.

WHEN THE NEWS OF LINCOLN'S assassination first arrived, mourners wrote down all the particulars of the evening at Ford's Theatre, from Booth's every motion to the measurements of the room in which the president expired. In the days afterward, they made note of the drapery and flags, the shuttered businesses and immense crowds, the subdued silences, doleful bells, and cannon roar. With Booth's capture, they painstakingly wrote out narratives of the stand-off, the shooting, and the disposition of the body. During the journey of the funeral train, people set themselves as well to preserving the details. From New York, James Williams told his sister that it was all too upsetting to "think or talk about," then launched into everything he had seen; when he wrote that the police made sure no one so much as stepped off the curb, he described the granite cubes that paved the street. In the same vein, Elon Lee wrote to his family from Chicago, explaining that the coffin "rested on a slightly inclined plane." Those who couldn't attend any of the ceremonies took the journey vicariously, through the newspapers and telegraph dispatches, noting the train's arrival and departure times, the numbers of viewers, and the order of processions. Mourners pored over reprinted eulogies and snipped out articles to mail to friends or paste into scrapbooks.[31]

Whether written from their own observations or gleaned from newspapers, the accounts held the same purposes: to substitute descriptive narratives when it was too hard to find words for emotions, to help Lincoln's mourners "realize" the terrible event, and to insert themselves into the passage of history. "Thus ends a most eventful month," Martha Anderson wrote in her Massachusetts diary, considering the span of time between the fall of Richmond on April 3 and Lincoln's upcoming burial on May 4. In between came Lee's surrender, the re-raising of the flag over Fort Sumter, the assassination, Johnston's surrender, and the capture and killing of Booth. Now the grand funeral would soon bring the president's body "to its resting place." Or as a woman wrote in her diary after attending the Chicago ceremonies, "So now we have seen the last of Abr. Lincoln that we can ever see on earth." Such recapitulations and flourishes offered yet another version of turning symbolically from past to future.[32]

If the funeral and funeral train intermittently implied a vision of universal mourning that pointed toward a reunited nation, the ceremonies simultaneously offered evidence of strife, both present and future. Many antagonists stayed away or kept quiet during the long series of events, but not all. In camp in Virginia, on the day of the funeral in Washington, a Copperhead private in the Thirty-Sixth Ohio loudly damned Lincoln and praised the assassin. With the train at Philadelphia, a Copperhead soldier in Richmond proclaimed that the president should have been shot four years ago and named Jefferson Davis "a better man than Old Abe ever dared to be." While residents of Columbus were mourning over Lincoln's body, James Hall was drinking in a Baltimore saloon, telling his companions that John Wilkes Booth had "done right," prompting one patron to throw down his playing cards in fury, while others shouted, "Knock him down!" In West Virginia that same day, John Craig announced in public that he was damn glad the president had been killed, and with the president's remains in Chicago, Captain David Parsons in upstate New York hoped aloud that John Wilkes Booth would "sit on the right hand of God." These incidents inflamed an answering wrath in Lincoln's mourners. Even where no antagonists made their voices heard, one escorting soldier felt his hatred for the rebels "added to tenfold."[33]

There were strains and tensions among the mourners too. Though one journalist swore no exaggeration in reporting that blacks and whites "leaned forth from the same windows" with "no consciousness of any difference of color," such romanticized accounts of racial unity were contradicted from the start. On Market Street in San Francisco, Irish soldiers broke through the April 19 procession, cutting off black mourners from the rest of the parade. African Americans who came to view the president's body were often directed to the back of the line, and when officials gave them a place in the processions, it was usually at the end. In New York's Union Square, George Bancroft delivered an oration that singled out the Emancipation Proclamation as the war's most important outcome, yet not two years earlier white city residents, largely Irish immigrants, had rioted over the draft, brutally attacking black New Yorkers. Now city officials wanted to bar black people from the procession altogether, but African Americans protested so strongly that Secretary of War Stanton reversed the decree. Ellen Kean accordingly found it a "curious satire" that black marchers had to be guarded by the police—"Do they not say they have been fighting for the negro?" she asked. Nativism joined racism in slicing through the wished-for communal grieving. Kean herself expressed annoyance at the marching Irish ("in *inconceivable numbers,* they were *never ending*"), not to mention the irritating presence of Scots and Germans, Jews and Roman Catholics. Tensions rose too between African Americans and Confederate sympathizers. With the train stopped at Baltimore, John Glenn fumed that it was "utterly impossible to keep servants in the house or to get any work out of them." Despite the yearned-for universality, mourners could find signs all through the grand funeral ceremonies that reconstruction would come hard to the postwar nation.[34]

THURSDAY, MAY 4, WAS AN UNUSUALLY hot day in Springfield. Lincoln's body traveled in a lavish hearse drawn by six black horses, preceded by an Illinois regiment, and accompanied by a choir, gun salutes, and drumbeats. Robert Lincoln followed, and African Americans brought up the rear, as the procession marched past the Lincoln home at Eighth and Jackson, then proceeded to Oak Ridge Cemetery. After two weeks and nearly seventeen hundred miles, the president would rest in a vault alongside a stream, with the much smaller coffin of Willie Lincoln beside him.

Services at the cemetery opened with a prayer that invoked grief for the slain chief and acknowledged that millions had "come out of bondage." In his funeral oration, Bishop Matthew Simpson, from Washington (the same man who had so irritated George Templeton Strong at the White House services), spoke of "sadness inexpressible" and "anguish unutterable," of God's will and of mercy—"with malice toward none." Already Lincoln's words had become the scripture of civil religion; another minister had recited the whole second inaugural before the sermon, adding his own phrasing, "free from all feelings of personal vengeance, yet believing that the sword must not be borne in vain, let us go forward even in painful duty." Simpson now forgave the "deluded masses" of the Confederacy, promising to "take them to our hearts" as the nation went forward "to work out a glorious destiny." After the tomb was closed, African Americans continued to reserve for themselves a special place among the bereaved. One man in Springfield asserted that "none mourn more sincerely than our race, who have lost their Moses."[35]

Across the nation, mourners read about the burial and recorded its details. Some preserved the facts only: "To day the funeral of our President Abraham Lincoln took place in Springfield Illinois" or "The remains of the President have found their resting place in the West." Some wrote more ritualistically, like Washington minister James Ward, who noted that the obsequies had begun in his own city on April 19 and "continued from day to day in the cities on the route to his old home-place." Now it had all come to an end, Ward recorded in his diary, as Lincoln's "mortal remains were deposited in the earth." Others, more often women, recorded their emotions. "Oh! how our hearts *ache* when we think of the cruel deed which ended his noble life," Caroline White wrote on May 4. Others were willing to think of Lincoln, finally, as a replaceable leader. His influence would be mighty, Elon Lee acknowledged from Chicago, yet "the world will move on," he believed, "with other men" to "guide our national affairs."[36]

Confederates once again had to contend with the Lincoln worship they so despised. In Chattanooga on May 4, Union authorities closed businesses, lowered flags, and draped doors. Anyone acting "at all noisy and boisterous"—in fact, anyone so much as caught laughing—could be arrested. In Alexandria, Virginia, Confederates had to listen to the gun blasts from Washington all day. "I do hope it is the last we are to hear of President Lincoln," wrote Anne Frobel, exasperated that "the yanks have been dragging him about for exhibition," wasting money on "that miserable old carcass"—why, she had never even heard of a *catafalque* before and figured Lincoln wouldn't have known that word either. May 4 was also the day Confederate general Richard Taylor surrendered the last forces in the Department of Alabama, Mississippi, and East Louisiana, though intermittent skirmishing would continue.[37]

In Washington, less than a week after the burial, Benjamin Brown French thought the city had settled down into an "old jog trot mood that interests nobody." In Danville, Illinois, where Lincoln had once had a law office, his death had been the "all absorbing theme" for three full weeks, wrote one resident, but by mid-May it was "quickly wearing off." Cities that had hosted the president's remains left their mourning decorations in place long after the train departed. Drapery still hung from Philadelphia's Independence Hall in late April, and soldiers passing through Indianapolis in late May noticed the faded bunting. Imagined universality, hopes for closure, and dreams of a bright future aside, it wasn't as if anybody knew just how the nation would heal. All the while, moreover, Lincoln's mourners and antagonists alike had to contend with the tasks and trials of their everyday lives.[38]

Springtime

FOR THE VANQUISHED, SPRINGTIME among the ravaged southern landscape offered varied messages. "It is humiliating, very indeed to be a conquered people," wrote Georgia plantation mistress Ella Thomas in her diary, "but the sky is so bright, the air so pure, the aspect of nature so lovely that I can but be encouraged, and hope for something which will benefit us." For a Confederate nurse in Georgia, the brilliant colors of the meadows and woodlands arrived just in time to soothe her people's "troubled spirits." The warm weather, in tandem with the end of war, also promised homecoming. "Life will be one long summer's day when you are once again with me," a woman wrote to her husband in a Yankee prison. Others among the defeated, however, could eke out but little comfort. "Oh! that our national prospects were as bright & encouraging," cried a Virginia woman for whom springtime tried unsuccessfully "to woo us to be cheerful." For another, the "flowers & bright days" seemed "to mock our sorrow." To Rodney Dorman and his fellow diehard rebels, springtime made no difference at all.[1]

For Lincoln's mourners, the season's beauty stood in stark contrast to lingering grief. In late April, Lucretia Hale opened the windows and drank in the "loveliest day that was ever made," but she couldn't help feeling that "the President's terrible death casts such a shadow over all hopes." On a Sunday evening in mid-May, Union soldier Douglass Taylor wrote to his mother from Washington. It was a lush spring, the blooming trees and flowers incongruous with the "gloomy drapery" still hanging from the Capitol. Were it not for Lincoln's assassination, it would be the happiest spring he had ever known. Walt Whitman began composing his elegy "When Lilacs Last in the Dooryard Bloom'd" almost immediately after Lincoln's death, writing (though without direct mention of the president) of the rituals of mourning and nature's annual renewal. "I mourn'd," his poem announced, "and yet shall mourn with ever-returning spring."[2]

Whitman's poem was both sorrowful and hopeful, and many among the mourners saw affirmation of an optimistic future in springtime. For the victors, the season also served as a natural metaphor, marking the passage from wartime and winter's darkness to peace and vernal freshness. For women—wives, mothers, daughters, servants—the arduous work of spring cleaning also marked renewal as they labored to sweep away ashes and dirt. Union soldiers described nature's splendor during the funeral train's two-week journey, associating sweet-scented flowers or fields of clover with victory, peace, and home. A Massachusetts soldier in Virginia sat outside his tent one balmy morning, grateful for "the world & its beauty." While Delaware farmer Samuel Canby mournfully kept track of Lincoln's body, he also noted "everything so fresh & green." Women wrote particularly effusively. "I cannot describe to you how happy I feel this charming season," Unionist Harriet Williams wrote to her husband during those weeks, as she communed with nature in Maryland. Even Anna Lowell, among the few who wrote about Lincoln's death long into May, noticed the "exquisite verdure & rich blossoms." For the victors, the spring of 1865, the first in four years not overtaken by war, conjured regeneration. For Sarah Browne, the symbolism of the weather helped. Amid the tasks of spring cleaning in Salem, she marveled at the bright sun, green leaves, fragrant flowers, and singing birds creating "a life of beauty," for which she gave credit to God.[3]

7

Everyday Life

ON WEDNESDAY, APRIL 19, 1865, Sarah Browne absorbed a funeral sermon in Salem's North Church, then gazed upon a friend's new baby, "all sweetness—all Joy," she wrote, the infant "realizing nothing of the great events which were transpiring in the turbulent world." Sarah herself would remain preoccupied that spring: with anti-Lincoln sentiments in her own city, Jefferson Davis's part in the conspiracy, the suffering of Union soldiers in Confederate prisons, Albert Jr.'s trip to Washington for the funeral, and fears for her husband's safety down south. The next day, April 20, was Eddie Browne's twelfth birthday, and Albert wrote his son from Charleston, exhorting the boy to work hard in order to be "fitted to enter Cambridge" in the not-too-distant future (he must improve his penmanship and strive to be a good Christian). But up in Salem, the birthday turned out unhappily. Somewhere along the way Eddie misbehaved. It's easy to imagine the boy confused by nearly a week in which his mother and sister remained in shock, and men wept openly on streets shrouded in dark drapery, all the while his father far away. None of that mollified Sarah though. "It is Eddie's birth-day," she wrote to Albert, "but he has been naughty, so I shall not celebrate it." Soon Albert wrote to his son again, this time asking why he caused others so much pain when he possessed so many privileges.[1]

As April turned to May, Sarah continued to write in her diary about Lincoln's funeral train and Booth's capture. Eddie resumed being a good boy, studying his Latin and French and attending a happy May Day picnic. The local minister had separated from his wife, setting off a rush of gossip. Spring cleaning contributed to Sarah's sense of renewal, and now she interwove lingering sorrow and anger with matter-of-fact chronicles about organizing the parlor closet, supervising a thorough scrubbing of the house, and contending with the servants' demand for better wages. In her pages, the realm of war and politics met the affairs of everyday life. "A Proclamation has been issued by President Johnson recognizing the close of the rebellion," she wrote on May 10. "Alice & I still find enough work in rearranging bureau drawers."[2]

THE WAR HAD IMMEASURABLY INTERRUPTED Rodney Dorman's daily life, most especially when the Union army's 1863 occupation culminated in the burning of his home and law office. As an exile on the outskirts of Jacksonville, Dorman could provide himself only the "bare necessities," he wrote in his diary in the spring of 1865, and only with the "greatest difficulty." Now Dorman watched as white people filled up the city again. They were paroled soldiers, exchanged prisoners, and refugees returning from the interior, but many had nowhere to live and no money. "It keeps me melancholly," he wrote, for once putting aside his vitriol, to "see so much of the distresses & sufferings." Though Dorman's own troubles were considerable, it pained him yet more to observe his compatriots in such dire circumstances, with no prospect of better days ahead. "It would take an immense fortune to administer relief to all," he knew, frustrated that he couldn't help. If only he could wreak vengeance on the conquering enemy, he seethed, his anger returning with every thought of the Yankees' "cursed robbing, theiving, murdering & torturing."[3]

Everyday life for Rodney Dorman that spring and summer included active hatred of the Union victors, in particular the black and white Yankees in his midst. Those impudent, lying devils of the U.S. occupation forces spoke of protection, but he knew otherwise. "The only protection we ask or require of them, the fiends, is that they will clear out & keep away," he told his diary. More than anything, Dorman wished for a return to the lives he and his fellow rebels had known before the war. "What did the

Confederacy want but her own rights?" he inquired rhetorically. "They merely asked from the first but to be let alone," and now the Yankees, those "black-hearted, miserable cowards," were doing nothing short of sowing "revolution."[4]

Dorman was correct on that count. A revolution had indeed come to pass, for his whole world had been not merely disrupted but demolished. Dorman took some comfort in the "old, familiar faces" among what he called the "new trash" in his city, but he also saw white people begging for food, black men in soldiers' uniforms, and northerners teaching black men, women, and children to read and write. Clearly it was black freedom that had destroyed Dorman's old life in Jacksonville. "I really wish I could get away, somewhere, out of the turmoil," he wrote, displaying a second rare note of melancholy. "I can merely stay now as long as life lasts," he sighed, resigned to "little, if any comfort." The luxurious "enjoyment of life" he had once known now seemed entirely out of reach.[5]

LINCOLN'S ASSASSINATION STOPPED THE world. That's what mourners told themselves in the grip of shock and grief. "Nothing is thought excepting the *Horrible event* at Washington," one man wrote. No one could speak of anything else, a woman in New Haven assured a friend. Julia Shepard, worshipping in Washington after witnessing the crime at Ford's Theatre, felt, she told her father, "as though my heart had stopped beating." Clergymen relied on similar descriptions. At Lincoln's graveside in Springfield, the Reverend Matthew Simpson talked about the whole world coming to a halt. Men abandoned their plows in the field, he intoned, merchants closed their doors, and the hum of factories ceased. Or as the Unitarian minister Edward Everett Hale wrote to his brother, for nearly two weeks "all things stood still when the President was killed" and "no word was read or written that had not reference to him."[6]

Mourners indulged in the idea of a halted world. If time had frozen, perhaps it could also reverse course, and Lincoln's death would prove after all to be a dream, a ruse, or a staged play. Or if reversal proved impossible, a pause would at least permit the bereaved to lay aside every distraction and interference in order to absorb and make sense of the assassination.

Yet the world did not stand still after the assassination, and Lincoln's mourners well knew that. Union supporters had thought about, talked

about, and written about everyday matters all through the war, and when
victory came they kept at it, brewing tea, hauling wood, announcing wedding engagements. The same was true in the immediate aftermath of Lincoln's death, for it was impossible to keep everyday life at bay. Women
could not long neglect their duties, farmers remained concerned with
weather and crops, soldiers counted their rations and pay, laborers had to
report to work, and merchants looked impatiently toward the resumption
of commerce. Perhaps mourners made pronouncements about a halted
world precisely because they couldn't engage in the personal and collective
rituals of mourning full-time, and imagining a transfixed world lent greater
gravitas to the thoughts and actions they set aside for Lincoln.

The fact was, the amount of ink that mourners devoted to the doings of
daily life readily contradicted their own statements that they were too overwhelmed to think about anything but the president's death. If the assassination interrupted everyday life, then everyday life also intruded into the
assassination, for cataclysmic events never come to pass apart from daily
life, but only in the midst of it.[7]

JOURNALISTS AND MINISTERS CLAIMED that all labor ceased in the
aftermath of the tragic event, but women and girls knew that was patently
untrue. Female labor was burdensome in the mid-nineteenth century.
Ashes and soot had to be swept from stoves and fireplaces every day. Water
had to be hauled inside for washing and cooking, then back outside once
dirtied. Chamber pots had to be emptied. Soap had to be manufactured
from grease and lard. Linens and clothing had to be scrubbed on wash-
boards, hung up to dry, then pressed with leaden irons. Recall the New
York seamstress who crammed the astounding tidings into her account
book. "Funeral Obsequies of Pres. Lincoln in Washington—Stores closed
and business of all kind suspended," she wrote in a circle around the edges
of a page. "The Pres. was assassinated in his seat at Ford's Theatre—a ball
pass through his brain." The fact that she crowded those words onto a page
of her ledger (not even a diary) reveals not just the momentousness of the
event but also the centrality of daily labor for this working-class woman.[8]

Everywhere, mourning women wrote in their diaries simultaneously
about the assassination and domestic labor without comment or self-
consciousness, interweaving the terrible news and its aftermath into their

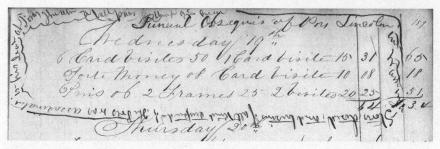

An anonymous seamstress recorded the funeral in Washington on Wednesday, April 19, 1865, fitting the words into a circle around a list of purchases and sales for that day, which included postcards ("Card Visites") and frames. "Funeral Obsequies of Pres. Lincoln in Washington—Stores closed and business of all kind suspended," she wrote. "The Pres. was assassinated in his seat at Ford's Theatre—a ball pass through his brain." *Anonymous account book, Anonymous Diaries and Account Books, The Schlesinger Library, Radcliffe Institute, Harvard University.*

records of planting gardens, darning socks, ironing clothes, whitewashing walls, dyeing cloth, sweeping chimneys, replacing parlor curtains, making mustard poultices, and tending to children's injuries. Typically, a Pennsylvania woman sandwiched a remark about the journey of Lincoln's body between two mundane incidents. "Tom ploughing to day," she wrote. "The Presidents body is to be taken to Baltimore to day. Fan coughed nearly all last night, & seemed very cranky."[9]

For some, the assassination offered the briefest reprieve. Lizzie Moore nearly fainted when she heard the news, then couldn't finish the day's baking (which only meant she would have more work the next day). Margaret Howell didn't "feel like doing anything" when she first heard, but the next day had to sew her pillowcases before going out to inspect the mourning drapery. Most women got no reprieve at all. As Caroline Dall wrote in her diary, capturing the ongoing cycle of domestic labor, "We are cleaning house, but I don't care." Yet it wasn't merely that women couldn't neglect the everyday. It was also that going through the motions of routine or onerous tasks could be a welcome distraction. As Caroline White wrote on Easter Sunday, "I keep busy about my household duties—going through with them mechanically." In Vermont, Harriet Canfield admitted to her husband that she "dare not think of the future" in the wake of the president's death. How much easier it was to ponder a new bedroom carpet than the fate of the nation, and indeed Canfield wrote as well about lambs and sheep, grain and hay, fences and manure. For Rachel Cormany, a young mother living with her Pennsylvania in-laws while her husband was away in the army, the ceaseless tasks of household labor felt overwhelming. "I nearly gave out before I got done," she wrote on the day Lincoln died, yet her burdens also allowed her to push aside the horror. "O! how dreadful it seems," she wrote that day. "My God what does it all mean—Is anarchy & destruction coming upon us?" When the funeral train arrived fifty miles away in Harrisburg, Cormany recorded only her work in the house, barn, and garden. "I nearly gave out," she wrote again. "I cannot stand it." Cormany's oppressive labor also kept away thoughts of the destruction of the world.[10]

Just as women could not abandon domestic labor, farmers could hardly abandon their plows in the field. To begin with, continuous records were essential to future agricultural cycles. Take the spare diary of Ebenezer Paul in Dedham, Massachusetts. On the day of Lincoln's assassination, Paul recorded only that he had planted peas and potatoes, an entry similar to those that came before and after. On April 19, Paul wrote the words, "funeral of president Lincoln," followed by "put out fire in woods." He never mentioned Lincoln again. Yet Ebenezer Paul was not unmoved. Every day for thirty-three years, this man wrote a line or two about his daily activities, and April 1865 was no different, except for that one day, that one line. The words "funeral of president Lincoln" were such an enormous disruption to an unbroken record of planted vegetables, carted wood, and dampened fires that it was as if he had walked down the streets of Dedham with tears streaming down his face (which in fact he may have done). If Lincoln's assassination had interrupted Paul's equilibrium, it could not interfere with his day-to-day undertakings. Those cycles were both compulsory and comforting, and most helpful of all, they pointed toward the future.[11]

Business concerns also clashed with full-fledged devotion to grief, and bereaved men in a variety of occupations intertwined the mundane and the grave without reservation. A shipbuilder punctuated his record of weather and wind, the planking of schooners, and the mending of brigs with a reference to the assassination. A lawyer fretted about delayed trials. A writer asked his publisher, "How about my 3d novel? Shall I commence it, or wait for a more favorable season?" (For a few, the assassination made business better, not worse. One man thought that Booth should burn in hell even as he anticipated considerable profits from engravings of the president. "Presume we shall sell thousands," he wrote.) At an auction house, it was business as usual: the announcement of Booth's capture prompted a round of applause, followed by the auctioneer's call, "And how much shall I have for lot 4367, gentlemen?"[12]

In military service, camp life became its own domestic sphere, where Union troops wove a record of the ordinary into their heartfelt expressions of grief. For many, the wartime diary—often a pocket-sized register providing a few lines for each printed date—was a bare-bones listing of activities and memos. Now the men interspersed mentions of the president's death among entries about picket and guard duty, camp inspections, and weather conditions. As one soldier put it on April 15, "Died at 7 o'clock A.M. Day cloudy and some rain. Detailed for duty on patrol on Martinsburg Road." A Wisconsin volunteer followed up news of the assassination with what mattered most: stretched rations, a shaded camping spot, letters at mail call. Nor could matters of health be left aside. "President was shot by an assassin and cannot live. I am suffering with a very lame back," one man wrote in his diary. Another reversed the order: "In Hospital. Comfortable. President Lincoln assassinated last night."[13]

William Gould, the runaway slave in the Union navy, received the appalling news from another ship while en route to Lisbon in early May. Docked at Lisbon, Gould made a record of the facts (the shooting, the gunman, the assault on Seward), adding that the men had commenced supplying the ship with coal. The next day, Gould described the sailors' flag-lowering ceremony in between his record of the continued coaling of the ship and a trip ashore to market. None of that diminished the significance of the loss; elsewhere in his diary, Gould wished for Jefferson Davis to be hanged and offered a vehement dissent against the deportation of freed slaves, indicating his immersion in wartime politics.[14]

When it came to the chronicling of events, mourners interwove ordinary life with the trauma of Lincoln's assassination even more seamlessly in letters than in diaries, moving with ease between the catastrophic and the everyday. Some of this fulfilled nineteenth-century convention, which called for opening one's letters with an acknowledgment of missives received, and Lincoln's assassination little disrupted this pattern—as a Union soldier wrote to his sister, "I recd a letter from Susie two or three days ago. I have not answered it yet. President Lincoln is dead." For letter writers, it was also a matter of resources. Time was often short, whether for servant, mistress, farmer, merchant, or soldier, and once you sat down to compose a letter, it was imperative to convey everything your correspondent needed to know, including details that seemed insignificant compared with the calamity at hand. The scarcity of paper and other writing supplies, especially for the working classes and troops in the field, likewise obligated correspondents to fill their sheets full, further prompting the inclusion of seemingly petty concerns.[15]

Soldiers' letters were less perfunctory than their diaries, as the men shared their grief and continued, as usual, to ask those at home for assistance with the challenges of camp life. An army officer expressed outrage at Lincoln's murder, then asked his wife to send undershirts and drawers, while another thanked his mother for sending maple sugar before turning to the assassination. Another held off on the national news until he had instructed his parents to fix a pair of ill-fitting boots, after which he imparted that he was "exceedingly saddened and surprised" at the president's murder. By the same token, letter writers wanted to know about daily life on the home front. Although Horace Gilmore communicated his shock and sadness to his wife, he also needed to know about their farm's grain and grass seed. Likewise, after mentioning the assassination, a sergeant inquired of a veteran friend, "Have you got your artificial Arm yet and if so how does it work?" Hardship and bravery were also important to convey to loved ones, and soldiers spun tales that easily trumped, in length and depth, their responses to Lincoln's assassination. One young man wrote in meticulous detail about his lost overcoat, after which he conceded, "We are all greatly grieved at the death of our President." Another, perhaps for the sake of his children, regaled his family with the story of an encounter with a "monstrous big black snake" before mentioning the funeral sermon he'd taken in.[16]

Well-to-do white women offered the most dizzying interweaving of the profound and the mundane. Letter-writing manuals consumed by the middling and upper classes in the nineteenth century directed them, after all, to "relate the little incidents of your domestic life," and this they did in their ample leisure time. Among the most voluble was a correspondent named

Rebecca (no last name survives), writing to a cousin traveling in China. In an effort to fit the most news into the least amount of postage, Rebecca never so much as indented a paragraph. Beginning with grief "too deep ever to be forgotten," she gave an account of Lincoln's funeral services in Boston, then listed the wedding presents received by a recent bride and hinted at the out-of-wedlock pregnancy of a neighbor ("To judge from some little things that have been said, I should think the engagement would not be a very long one"). Rebecca reported that Lincoln's mourning drapery had been removed from the church for another wedding, for which she described the bride's dress and veil, before adding, "That day we heard of Booth's capture and death." From an account of the conspirators' trial, Rebecca leapt to the issue of how hot a griddle should be when cooking buckwheat pancakes. Such interspersing of trivia need not indicate a vacuous mind. Ardent abolitionist and women's rights reformer Martha Coffin Wright didn't mention Lincoln's assassination until after she had written reams of minutiae to her daughter-in-law, elaborating on housepainting, wallpapering, and the merits and demerits of various servants. Yet Wright eventually expressed some of the most radical ideas about the political disempowerment of Confederates.[17]

Engaging in the activities of everyday life—and writing about them—also became part of the process of coping with the present and facing the future. Eyewitness Helen Du Barry, who had found herself "so nervous since that awful night" at Ford's Theatre, apprised her mother of her progress in sewing little more than a week later. "I have finished my green dress and it looks good as new," she reported. "I am on the pink plaid pineapple —putting a lining in the skirt & flouncing it." It wasn't that Du Barry had put the trauma behind her; far from it. It was just that everyday life intruded and distracted, and therefore served as comfort.[18]

True, a minority of mourners pled that they could think of nothing but the assassination. One man asked his mother's forgiveness for writing so much about it, explaining, "My heart is so full that I can scarcely turn my thoughts into a different channel." A woman likewise explained her inability to mention any other topic by declaring that "the pen refuses to write except of national affairs." A few mourners were entirely unable to go on with everyday life, like twenty-three-year-old Martha Thomas. When Thomas was admitted to an asylum in Washington, D.C., several years later for "chronic mania," doctors listed the cause as "Lincoln's Death" (perhaps she had been in the theater on the fateful night). For others, though, expressions of anguish proved no more than typical of their daily lives. When Emily Watkins heard the news on the morning of April 15, she filled a letter to her husband with a torrent of feverish lamentations. *"Our poor Country,"* she cried, "Oh! Oh!—what will become of us. . . . Oh—Dear.—What a calamity—what a loss.—What a dreadful event in our history." On and on she went, stopping at a last lament about "the death of poor Lincoln." Rather than reflecting disruption, however, these words are of a piece with a life of near-constant anguish. A month later, overburdened with helping her grown daughter plan a schoolroom pageant, Watkins felt "troubled & tormented & *wretched*" for lack of a letter from her husband, worrying that she would go crazy or die of the "suspense & torture." Though Watkins no doubt meant every overwrought word she penned about Lincoln, she had simply gone on with her everyday life, applying her usual litany of agonized expressions to the current national tragedy.[19]

Others, ambivalent about mingling the cataclysmic with the routine, found ways to separate one from the other. Some drew thick black lines across the page before turning from the assassination to more personal news. Others marked the transition with words, like the Boston woman who wrote solemnly about the president, then told her correspondent, "I will cease this subject and go back a little to tell you what we have been doing"—which gave her license to launch into cheerier events. Abby Briggs was "as funny as ever and kept us laughing," she wrote next. "You should have heard her talk French with Irène!" Helen Blake, an American traveling in Europe, put the distractions first, spending more than three pages arranging summer plans with a friend, discussing matters like the Swiss weather and foreign tipping customs. Then she paused. "I have written all this without saying one word of the dreadful news that stunned us all last week," she admitted, for once she made mention of it, she knew she could "write of nothing else." Blake looked to the future with trepidation, she told her friend, but promised to "spare you all my fears until we meet." By reserving thoughts of Lincoln's assassination for another time and place, Blake embraced the persistence of daily private life; indeed, the rest of her letter described her delightful surroundings and how much fun the children were having.[20]

Even mourners who claimed the trivia of daily life to be just that—trivial in the face of disaster—readily contradicted themselves. When Sarah Hale asserted that recent events (the fall of Richmond, Confederate surrender, and the assassination) "prevented people from thinking or talking much of any thing else," that assertion came on the fourth page of a letter positively crammed with seemingly idle local and family news. In another letter, after six pages of domestic and neighborhood anecdotes, Hale added, "All this is hardly worth writing but it is of such trifles that our life is made up." By admitting that it was impossible to jettison quotidian matters, Hale overruled the words that came both before (*hardly worth writing*) and after (*such trifles*).[21]

Even more striking are the claims of William Lloyd Garrison Jr., son of the famed abolitionist, whose diary betrayed his preoccupation with his wife's poor health. "Ellie sick again," he wrote on April 15, the day he received the "horrible news" of the assassination; "Ellie sick," he reiterated the next day. "Last week has been a hard one," Garrison wrote to his mother-in-law on Easter Sunday, referring not to Lincoln but to his wife, for with housecleaning and houseguests, she had "worked beyond her strength." When Garrison finally came to the great crime, he wrote—discrediting both his letters and his diary—"There is only one topic to-day & the feeling it excites is too deep to allow much else than a few, sad words of regret." Clearly there was more than *one topic* for Garrison, which he justified by claiming that the feelings called up by the assassination were too profound to articulate. With an ill spouse interfering, perhaps Garrison invoked the idea of profundity as a way to excuse himself from falling short of the ideal of complete engrossment in the devastating event. In part, both Hale and Garrison meant that nothing else merited attention in conventional public discourse. Where headlines, sermons, and words exchanged on the street were meant to be unswervingly devoted to the assassination, personal writings became a refuge from that imperative.[22]

Unable and unwilling to fulfill the ideal of complete absorption in Lincoln's death, mourners sometimes wrote about that very conflict, doubling back to dismiss their more mundane concerns. When Harriet Canfield wrote to her husband about the new bedroom carpet on Easter Sunday, she added, "It seems almost wrong to keep to business as though no such awful thing had happened." After a Brooklyn woman expended several hundred words describing the exhausting search for a new house to rent, she likewise conceded to her daughter, "But how trifling all this seems compared with the dreadful calamity which has fallen upon the Nation." James Garfield, future president of the United States (himself to be assassinated in 1881), was away from home to conduct property transactions, but, he wrote to his wife, it felt "sacrilege to talk of money or business now."[23]

More often, though, mourners moved effortlessly from the catastrophic to the everyday without worry. In the days following the "very sad" news of Lincoln's death, Emilie Davis, the African American servant, combined descriptions of the public arena with important fragments of daily life: attending school, visits with female friends, a sore throat, and whether or not her suitor had stopped by. As someone who had stood in line for hours across two days in order to catch a glimpse of Lincoln's body in Philadelphia, Davis made no pretense that the world had come to a halt, and those who wrote in greater detail display similar patterns.[24]

Nor did Lincoln's death keep his mourners from pursuing everyday amusements, any more than had four years of war. Immediately following the assassination, and all during the two weeks of the funeral train, bereaved men and women both recorded their grief and enjoyed themselves. They played whist, croquet, and jackstraws, went on shopping excursions, attended dances and balls, and went to the circus. The day after a "solemn & impressive" service for the fallen president, Mary Elliot played Chinese billiards with her friends, then played again the next day. Not only did people engage in such diversions, but most found nothing troubling in recording them right alongside news of the president's murder and their aggrieved responses. Mourners even went to the theater. A small number faulted Lincoln for that unchristian form of entertainment—even before the crime, the minister James Ward was mortified with the president's Good Friday plans at a "Temple of Evil" when he should have been in church, and afterward Ellis Hughes wished that Lincoln had saved his own life by resisting the wicked crowds known to frequent auditoriums. But most didn't give it a thought, and some followed in the late president's footsteps. As one woman scoffed at New York theatergoers who lined up to exchange their tickets for a future performance (all theaters had closed after the crime), "Grief or no grief they will flock to the play." She was right, but her interpretation was wanting. The ticket holders were mourning for Lincoln, but they were also diverting their sorrow and finding solace by participating in the ongoing flow of everyday life.[25]

Romance gave men and women alike an antidote to grief, but even more than that, it called them toward the future. The day after Lizzie Niles wrote in her diary of a weeping nation, she didn't hesitate to note down news of an entirely different order. "The funniest thing of all is that Nathaniel Bull and Abbie Sabin are *married*," she marveled. "Well I wonder what will happen next." Even as Maggie Wylie paid lip service to the idea that life had come to a halt ("We can talk or think of nothing else but the assassination"), she thought a great deal about her fiancé, Arthur Mellette, fighting with the Ninth Indiana. "I had such a plain dream of Arth," she wrote soon thereafter. "I never had such a one before—I thought we were married." Young men revealed similar preoccupations. Maryland Unionist Henry Shriver grieved for Lincoln, but evenings spent with his sweetheart overtook those thoughts. After church on Easter Sunday, their evening alone turned out to be, Shriver confided to his diary, the "most intensely delightful one that I ever spent." When romance turned out badly, the trouble not only intruded on the ideal of wholly focused mourning but also supplanted attention to the president. One Union supporter wrote the words "President Lincoln was assassinated" in her diary, then without so much as skipping a line, launched into a lament about a son who had run off with the wrong girl, concluding (of her son, not Lincoln), "O how sad & heart broken I feel about him." Happy or sad, the future still mattered precisely because the world had not stood still.[26]

Matters of the heart were a recurring topic in soldiers' letters, countering the dreariness of camp life and the ordeals of the battlefield, and the subject lost none of its power in the aftermath of Lincoln's assassination. Edgar Dinsmore, in Charleston with the Fifty-Fourth Massachusetts, was both deeply dismayed over the president's death and at once engaged in serious flirtation with a young woman named Carrie Drayton. How, Dinsmore asked, could he "express the pleasure that I experience this evening at the reception of your inexpressibly welcome and more than sweet letter?" He continued in the same vein at considerable length, at one point mentioning that the Fifty-Fourth had been "marching and fighting, for the good old cause—*Liberty*," but mostly Dinsmore detailed his joy at corresponding with Drayton and the prospect of returning home. When, after many pages, he declared, "We mourn for the loss of our great and good President as a loss irreparable," he immediately resumed his earnest wooing. Maybe Dinsmore didn't want to mar his courtship efforts with reference to the assassination. Maybe there was nothing left to say that the two African Americans didn't already know. No doubt both hoped that the president's death would not change the war's glorious outcome of union and freedom.[27]

White soldiers flirted too. William Mead first wrote of vengeance and justice, then teased Louisa White not to be jealous if he occasionally corresponded with another "fair, young, interesting, lovely, and k-i-s-s-a-b-l-e damsel." Some put that kind of banter first, like Nelson Palmer, who cheerfully related his diversions with a southern girl "of some 16 summers," before reporting that his regiment had fired seventy-six guns for the slain president. Away from the war, young men's thoughts also strayed from the terrible news. As Henry Adams (son of the U.S. minister in London) wrote from overseas to a male friend back home—in the same letter in which he reflected on Lincoln's assassination—"If you know Miss Montgomery (the blonde) tell her that she looks like the Venus of Medici."[28]

The promise of love proved to be among the best that everyday life could offer heartbroken mourners. On April 19, 1865, the day of Lincoln's funeral in Washington, a man named Frank sat down to write to his dear friend Henry Morgan, who had long ago chosen that date for his wedding. "I will shut my eyes to all tokens of mourning, and close my ears to all sorrowful tollings to-day," Frank wrote, "and hear only joy-bells because it is your wedding-day." Frank tried mightily to stay on the happy topic, though it had been "ghastly," he admitted, to be "plunged from the heights of joy" following Union victory to the "depths of sorrow by the horrible murder." Frank confessed that he was grateful for distraction, beseeching Morgan to tell him "all about the wedding, whether you behaved yourself or not," and "how many mistakes you made in the service." Indeed, Frank specifically requested information about the most quotidian details, asking about Morgan's new married life, including "how your rooms look" and "what you can see from their windows." Mourners like Frank, though bereft, self-consciously immersed themselves in the everyday, both as diversion and as a means to embrace the way forward.[29]

Participation in everyday life served to distract and to comfort, and to comfort by distraction. But that participation also signified something more. Not only did the hum of daily life give the lie to declarations that the world had come to a halt, but at the core of mourners' immersion in everyday life stood their tenacious optimism. Driven by Union victory and the conviction that the assassination would become part of a magnificent divine plan for the nation's future, Lincoln's mourners embraced the persistence of daily life—whether mundane, joyous, or distressing—because victory had brought them into a world they welcomed. From Virginia, Nathan Appleton, a Union officer and scion of a New England family of industrial wealth, found Lincoln's death a terrible blow, then a week later reflected with gusto on the juxtaposition of tragedy and the progress of the nation. "In the midst of our great excitement the game of life runs gaily on," he wrote home, as Lincoln's funeral train headed north. "What a marvelous country!" Henry Adams was touring in Italy when a midnight telegram brought him the news of Lincoln's murder. Writing to a chum, he rambled on for pages about the ordeal of traveling with his mother and siblings, cracking jokes about the weather in Florence and Dante's *Inferno,* before asserting that he was "much too strong an American" to think "we are going to be shaken by a murder." For African Americans in particular, chronicling everyday events like working for wages and spending those wages (for William Gould onboard a Union ship) and visits with friends (for Emilie Davis in Philadelphia) took on an added dimension: to be immersed in those activities meant to be free. Pursuing the commonplace activities of freedom served as a tribute to President Lincoln and to the future he had helped them bring about.[30]

Walt Whitman's 1865 poem about Lincoln's assassination, "When Lilacs Last in the Dooryard Bloom'd," is best known for its imagery of lilac, star, and songbird, but Whitman also noticed the persistence of everyday life for the president's mourners, offering an arresting image of "infinite separate houses, how they all went on, each with its meals and minutia of daily usages." In their grief over the slain president, Lincoln's mourners wished for resolution, and certainly the massive public funerals across the country made for a ritual that signaled a turn away from the past. But genuine closure is uneven at best, and any forward movement can come only amid the swirl of daily life.[31]

DEFEAT HAD WROUGHT CHANGES IN the lives of Confederates that no mourner of Lincoln could fathom. Where Union soldiers looked eagerly toward mustering out, thoughts of home were more confusing for boys and men in gray. "Blues awfully," wrote a Tennessee private in the final entry of his wartime diary. "Anxious thoughts of home." While Lincoln's mourners grieved for their leader, Confederates grieved for an entire world and way of life. It was a grief that disrupted the quotidian in ways that the assassination of President Lincoln could not.[32]

For white southerners whose lives had been upended by the war, romance supplied one of the few refrains of everyday life's persistence. In the same letter in which he celebrated Lincoln's murder, a Confederate soldier in Louisiana facetiously wished to be wounded, "so as to produce a reaction in the female hearts." Ellen House, despite her despair at surrender, described a May wedding in Knoxville that included a "delightful little dance" and flirtations all around. The same was true for an ardent rebel who detailed her gloom before adding, "Mr. Meade & Miss Leaton are—engaged!! & will be *married* in three weeks & go to Canada!" For Elizabeth Alsop, a friend's marriage proved a distraction, albeit a short-lived one. One night, Alsop stayed up with two friends until two o'clock in the morning, talking about the approaching wedding, but once the occasion had passed, she found herself again bereft. "My heart is so rebellious," she told her diary, "that instead of forgiving our enemies, I hate them more every hour of my life." Alsop spoke for many as she found the routines of daily life taking place against a steady state of misery and anger.[33]

The end of slavery constituted the most consequential disruption of all for the planter classes. Enslaved people had left their masters throughout the war, and Union victory both precipitated more departures and finalized the meaning of earlier ones. When white Mississippian Nancy Robinson recorded that "all are mourning & their hearts are crushed," President Lincoln was nowhere in her thoughts, for Robinson estimated that she had been deprived of sixty-five thousand dollars' worth of human chattel. When yet another former slave informed Robinson that she and her family would be leaving (emphasizing that "they were *Free*"), Robinson felt, she wrote, "restless with a dread I cannot describe." In Georgia, Eva Jones wrote to her mother about the "dark, crowding events of this most disastrous year," of "a life robbed of every blessing." She specifically meant emancipation and runaway slaves, which she called an "unprecedented robbery," expressing shock that those who left ("in search of freedom," she fully admitted) had neglected to say proper good-byes. Jones signed off in "an abyss of despair."[34]

Cornelia Spencer felt so distraught about all the changes in her day-to-day life in North Carolina that it seemed plausible she would lose her mind. She worried that marriages performed in the Confederate states would no longer be legally recognized, and she envisioned "a life of continued toil." Notably, the future she pictured for herself bore obvious parallels with the daily lives of slaves: marriage unrecognized and labor unending. Whether she was oblivious to those parallels or intended deliberately to portray masters as the slaves of Yankees, when Spencer described her home, she might as well have been describing a slave cabin: "not a chair . . . not a fork . . . nor a single set of table ware of any sort," she wrote, "not a carpet or a curtain or a napkin" and "*flies* every where in doors." How different from the imagery conjured by Henry Morgan's friend Frank, up north, picturing Morgan's cheerful life as a newly married man, including "how your rooms look" and "what you can see from their windows."[35]

Cornelia Spencer was not alone. Everyday life in a postwar, post-emancipation future became unbearable for some Confederates. Many of the vanquished, and veterans in particular, suffered anguish and torment manifested as apathy, humiliation, bitterness, and defiance. Combined with the physical wounds of the returning troops, the financial ruin of families and communities, and a racial world turned upside-down, unknown numbers faced lives of depression and mental instability, including alcoholism and family violence. For many there were no words to describe their feelings, much less adequate medical categories to define their conditions. And yet perhaps none at all could admit that their newfound hardships paled in comparison to legal enslavement, living day in and day out as a piece of property to be bought and sold, with the never-ending threat or reality of separation from loved ones, of sexual exploitation and horrific violence.

Nonetheless, when Confederates thought about the contours of daily life after the war, some drifted into suicidal broodings. "I think if I were sure of going to Heaven and it pleased God to take me to himself," Elizabeth Alsop wrote shortly after Lee's surrender, "I should be *glad to die.*" A despondent soldier thought an early May day's gloomy weather could "drive a morbid melancholy man to commit suicide." The desolation of defeat did in fact drive a number of Confederates to take their own lives. The best known was Edmund Ruffin, the fire-eating, proslavery secessionist. Ruffin, living on his farm near Richmond at war's end, expressed venom toward the Yankees in the pages of his diary as freely as did Rodney Dorman, choking on the "repulsive" and "disgusting" northern newspapers that compounded his "hatred & abhorrence" of Yankee rule. From the moment Richmond fell, Ruffin prepared for suicide, even envying his own son who had fallen in the war ("Would that I had died with him," he wrote). Were he himself younger, Ruffin reasoned, he might look forward to a reversal of fortunes in the future, but now it was his "earnest wish that I may not live another day," as he plainly put it. Ruffin consoled himself with the heterodox view that the Bible permitted the taking of one's own life, and shortly before he put the musket in his mouth, he once again recorded his "unmitigated hatred" of Yankees. Edmund Ruffin saw no future at all after defeat, and so when Confederate secession failed, he seceded from the world in the most radical way possible.[36]

In the ideal vision of the president's mourners, the world came to a halt when Lincoln died. Although it was impossible for events to reverse course, at least the illusion of suspended time permitted proper mourning for the slain chief, as a prelude to looking toward the future of the victorious nation. In the ideal vision of Lincoln's enemies, on the other hand, the world would stop and reverse course, taking them back, not to the world before the assassination, but much farther than that, to the antebellum South. For white southerners, the revolution wrought by the war altered everyday life too fundamentally to permit much distraction, amusement, or comfort, what with slaves gone, free black men in military uniforms patrolling their land, and white privilege seemingly vanished. Confederates wished now for the world to stop, but Lincoln's mourners knew that it would not: not for well-to-do New Englanders who put on their wedding finery and shared pancake recipes; not for black and white Union soldiers or the working classes, who kept on marching and laboring; and certainly not for former slaves who looked toward freedom.

There was one thing, though, that made looking toward the glorious future just as unbearable for Lincoln's mourners as it was for his antagonists: the death of loved ones, those who would never return home to rejoin the stream of daily life. In the Browne household, the loss of their daughter Nellie in 1864 unrelentingly overshadowed the assassination, and with the fearfully high toll of wartime deaths, similar devastation could be found in just about any family at the end of the Civil War.

Young Folk

CHILDREN ON THE UNION HOME front felt the devastation of Lincoln's assassination all around them, and none more so than those among the freedpeople. "Uncle Sam is dead," proclaimed a Virginia boy of five or six years old. When he asked an adult, "Have I got to go back to massas?" he echoed the question he'd been hearing all around him. In the southern classrooms where former slaves learned to read and write, children responded to the news by "ceasing from play" or expressed their grief with "tearful inquiries." Up north too, in an Ohio classroom, free black children "felt the weight of the sorrow," a teacher wrote, whispering to one another, "The president is dead! The president is dead!" As parents, instructors, and ministers spoke of black freedom, these young ones grasped the import of Lincoln's death, and no doubt white observers accurately captured their reactions. What went unrecorded, given that missionary teachers had a stake in portraying their charges as pious and serious, was the likelihood that the children remained immersed in their daily lives, the younger ones perhaps jumping rope or playing ball on their way home from school that day.[1]

Young white children who wrote their own narratives expose just such ingenuous absorptions. On the day of the president's funeral, nine-year-old Edward Martin wrote that his school had let out early, adding, "In the after noon I played ball." On the day he got the news of Lincoln's assassination, eleven-year-old Grenville Norcross traded adventure books with friends, lending *The Three Daring Trappers* and borrowing *The Pioneer Boy, and How He Became President;* if Grenville chose a book about the late executive on purpose, he wrote only, "All the houses are being hung in black on account of the *death of Abraham Lincoln.*"[2]

Like the grown-ups around them, children on the Union home front, both black and white, experienced grief at Lincoln's loss in the context of everyday life. Accordingly, a child might grasp the gravity by thinking of President Lincoln as a father, free of metaphorical meaning. When a Vermont mother explained to her five-year-old son that the slain president had two boys of his own, her son thought those bereft children might "try to die too." Or a young person might attempt to imitate the sorrow of her parents, like the little girl who refused to kiss her father because, she explained, "good President Lincoln's dead, and I feel *so* bad!" On the other hand, younger children might unwittingly break the spell of solemnity. One little girl, entranced by marching soldiers at the Chicago funeral, exclaimed, "Oh *ain't* it nice! I'm so glad I came," while another, filing past Lincoln's body at the Chicago courthouse, remarked frankly that she liked looking at "dead folks" so much that she wished she were the president's embalmer. Older children, or more precocious ones, understood more. In a Virginia classroom of freedpeople, some expressed anxieties about President Andrew Johnson's policies. In Nashville, the twelve-year-old daughter of an ardent white Unionist family paced up and down, wringing her hands over the assassin and his conspirators. "Catch the murderers!" she cried. "Oh, if *I* was only a *man,* I would kill the very last one of them!"[3]

But like Eddie Browne in Salem, some older white children rebelled against the grown-ups' grief. In Newport, Rhode Island, on the morning Lincoln died, Carrie Hunter, about fifteen, wrote to her sister in New York, describing everything as "rather dismal," what with all the prostrated adults, black drapery, and shut-up shops. Seeking the company of schoolmates, Carrie "could not help laughing to see Katey Powell & Fannie Ogden looking so dreadfully grave & solemn." When the three girls encountered another friend, they playfully instructed her that she "must look sober." Among the group was Georgiana King, who had learned of

Lincoln's death when someone rushed into her parents' home, "weeping and screaming," and she too was glad to get away. To her diary, Georgiana confessed how handsome she found John Wilkes Booth, before writing about the good-looking new boy in town, with whom she and her friends resolved to "have a *flirtation.*" Lincoln's assassination had intruded on the carefree lives of Newport's privileged youth, and they made sure to intrude right back. Indeed, at least some adults must have felt the same kind of impatience expressed by young folk like Carrie and Georgiana.[4]

Privileged young Confederates also found time for distraction amid the terrible gloom of defeat. Seventeen-year-old Emma LeConte, who had written gleefully about the assassination and poured the bitterness of conquest into the pages of her diary, brightened up a bit in May. With a group of contemporaries, including young men home from the army, Emma took walks in the woods, where, she wrote, "we sit and talk and laugh and tease each other till almost dark." Sometimes they had little parties—"How long it had been since any of us had danced!" she exclaimed, and how good it was to "throw off the trouble and gloom for a little while." Emma admitted that in a way it felt wrong to be happy, thereby illuminating an important difference with Lincoln's mourners—their lightheartedness could be excused by victory. Instead, Emma LeConte consoled herself that she and her friends had fun "only among ourselves" and offered a reasonable excuse: "Young people cannot be depressed and gloomy *all* the time."[5]

8

Everyday Loss

THE FUSS OVER THE SLAIN Yankee president infuriated Rodney Dorman, and not merely because he found it sickening to treat the despotic leader as royalty. Dorman also found the spectacular pageantry offensive because it detracted from the "thousands other slain, since the war began!" Casualties on both sides were enormous, but Dorman's anger no doubt sprang from the especially colossal death rate among the rebels—somewhere between two and three times higher than that for Union soldiers.[1]

The Confederate toll also prompted Dorman to pen a furious diatribe about Yankee prisons. "How many prisoners did they starve & freeze, in a land of plenty?" he asked his diary. "How many did they freeze to death?" Conditions in all Civil War prisons were deplorable, often horrific, though captured Union men tended to suffer greater material want because of the collapsing Confederate economy. To defend the sorry treatment of Union soldiers, Dorman explained to himself that the rebels were forced to crowd Yankees into camps as a result of President Lincoln's tyrannical policies—namely that prisoner exchange had broken down when Confederate authorities refused to include African Americans, on the theory that runaway slaves on the battlefield remained stolen property, which comported with Dorman's views exactly. The Yankees "put it beyond the power of the Confederacy to treat prisoners very well," he reasoned, yet "compelled them to hold them indefinitely! & then complained of the treatment!" It was "an outrage upon humanity," though only in keeping with the barbaric nature of his enemies. "How many did they wontonly murder?" Dorman asked. "Answer this, you murderers & thieves without a parallel in the history of the world." For Rodney Dorman, that so many Confederate men had died in the war was a result of Yankee savagery, both on and off the battlefield.[2]

ON A VISIT TO FORT WAGNER, in Charleston harbor, in the spring of 1865, Albert Browne happened upon bones, the "remains of our brave soldiers," he wrote, from the battle that took place there in 1863, in which so many men of the Fifty-Fourth Massachusetts had perished. This was the battle that had proven to skeptical white northerners that African Americans were capable of fighting. Now Albert's eyes alighted on part of a skeleton clad in a decayed blue uniform. "All these should be carefully gathered and buried," he wrote home.[3]

While Albert decried bones on the battlefield, he and his family had another, more personal, experience with death on their minds: less than a year before Lincoln's assassination, the Brownes' daughter Nellie had died at the age of twenty-two. In the spring of 1864, Sarah and the children had traveled from Massachusetts for an extended visit with Albert in Beaufort, South Carolina. With her sister, Alice, also in her early twenties, Nellie visited wounded soldiers at the Union hospital, went sailing and horseback riding, and socialized with other northern military families in the occupied Sea Islands. When the Brownes took an excursion to Jacksonville, Nellie Browne met and instantly fell in love with Captain Lewis Weld, provost marshal of the District of Florida and recruiter of black troops. Lewis was more than ten years Nellie's senior, and within two weeks the couple was privately engaged and planning to wed in June. "*Burn this letter,*" Nellie wrote to her older brother, Albert Jr., back in Boston, underlining every word. "*Keep everything secret*" (the last word got an extra underscore). When the Browne family returned to Beaufort, Nellie and Lewis wrote back and forth, expressing their longing for each other. Though her brother, and eventually her father, tried to dissuade Nellie from such recklessness, there was nothing the family could do to slow the impulsive romance.[4]

Then, in late May, Nellie suddenly fell ill. Doctors diagnosed poisoned blood and provided quinine, arsenic, and brandy. They ordered Nellie's hair shorn to relieve her brain. She recognized no one at her bedside but called for Lewis. Typhoid fever was the likely culprit, and on the sixth day of delirium, Albert tried to resign himself to his daughter's fate by appealing to God's will—"trying to deceive myself" is how he put it. The family had written to alert Lewis in Jacksonville, and now he wrote back with alarm. "Why did you get sick my darling," he asked his beloved. "I am terribly anxious about you." By the time Lewis wrote those words, Nellie was gone. She died on June 2, 1864.[5]

From that day forward, the Browne family began a mourning that would last their whole lives. They now looked toward Lewis with gratitude, reversing their earlier objections with the belief that God had sent him to make Nellie's last weeks on earth the happiest of her short life. Sarah, the inveterate diarist, left every page of her 1864 pocket journal blank between May 28 and June 5. "The sad task is over, amid tears and agony," she wrote on June 6, as the family prepared to sail north, taking Nellie's body home. After that, Sarah didn't write another word for nearly three weeks, living in an "aching void" of loneliness, as Alice disclosed to Lewis (taking that phrase from a hymn about death and mourning). Toward the end of June, Sarah recorded that Albert had placed flowers on Nellie's grave in Salem's Harmony Grove Cemetery and that she could feel her daughter's spiritual presence. Sarah neglected her diary again until the end of August, when she went to church for the first time since returning from the South. Albert, in a stupor of despair, had more trouble accepting God's will. His daughter's sudden death a stunning blow, his heart bitter and rebellious, he invoked an image that would later be repeated by so many of Lincoln's mourners: it felt like a "thunder bolt from so clear and unclouded a sky." Truth was, Albert's spiritual doubts left him with too little comfort in God's supposedly right and merciful ways. "I am past all that," he told the minister who attempted religious consolation. Unable to conjure a future "blessed reunion" in heaven, the thought that so sustained his wife, Albert was "wretchedly miserable."[6]

Through the jubilation of Union victory the next spring, Nellie Browne was never far from her parents' minds. "It is a comfort to talk with one who loved our dear Nellie," Sarah wrote a few days after the fall of Richmond, following a visit with friends. A week later, the Brownes found the death of

President Lincoln unfathomable, while the loss of Nellie remained unbearable. With the first anniversary approaching, and as Lincoln's funeral train neared its destination, Sarah tried hard to conjure her daughter's "sweet presence" in God's bright sunshine and greenery. "I cannot feel that Nellie is *dead—her* presence is ever with me," she wrote some weeks after Lincoln's burial. Nighttime always proved more trying, as desolation crept in, and particular days proved especially difficult. On May 14, 1865, in a letter to her husband, Sarah wrote down three words, twice: "A year ago a year ago—." Unable to complete the sentence, she drew a dash. One year before, Nellie had been well and happy, for May 14 was the day she had revealed her newfound romance, and now Sarah likely held that rapturous letter in her hands. Two weeks later, just before the anniversary of Nellie's death, Sarah confided to her diary, "I open my arms and drive back the phantom of mental agony but Oh! God I cannot drive away the feeling of loneliness."[7]

June 1, 1865, had been proclaimed a day of national mourning for Abraham Lincoln, and Albert Browne was grieving. "I cannot sleep," he wrote to Sarah from Charleston that evening, "but have arisen and throw open the blinds of my chamber." By the southern moonlight he continued, "I know full well that at this very moment our hearts and feelings are in accord, that we are each calling to mind the dear departed one." It wasn't President Lincoln that Albert was writing about, of course, but Nellie.[8]

THE WORLD DID NOT STOP when Lincoln was assassinated, and neither did the war's death toll. With high child mortality rates, low life expectancy, and the prevalence of epidemics, death was a part of everyday life for antebellum Americans. Yet the war's toll immeasurably escalated experiences of loss: all told, the Civil War claimed more than three-quarters of a million lives, comprising roughly 2 percent of the population, north and south—a figure that would translate into more than seven million in the present-day United States. Accordingly, in the spring of 1865, those who grieved for Lincoln also mourned for husbands, fathers, sons, brothers, sweethearts, friends, and neighbors. Just about everyone on both sides knew someone who had died. When Lincoln was assassinated, some were coping with fresh news of a passing, while others marked anniversaries of earlier losses or lived with continued anxiety over the missing. Personal sorrows both accompanied and competed with grief for the slain president.

In a photograph subtitled "A Harvest of Death," the corpses of Union soldiers lay strewn across a Pennsylvania field after the Battle of Gettysburg, in July 1863. With approximately 750,000 losses, virtually every family on both sides of the Civil War knew someone who had died.
LC-B8184-7964-A, Prints and Photographs Division, Library of Congress.

Americans in the nineteenth century constructed elaborate religious and cultural ideals centered around grief, and survivors increasingly expressed themselves in highly sentimentalized ways, creating a "cult of mourning" in which intentionally overwrought outpourings soothed their pain. Faith was meant to serve as the first realm of comfort, and all losses were to be reconciled to the will of God. Survivors should strive to accept, and even to embrace, the passing of a loved one, not only because it was imperative to submit to God's will, but also because the dead would find a land of glorious redemption in the hereafter. Heaven, understood as an enchanting land lying just above the clouds, would bring the joyous reunion of relatives and close friends, where love, marriage, and family life continued on. Ideally, then, death could be anticipated with complete serenity. Agonizing wounds and protracted illnesses aside, Americans tried hard to find consolation in this imagery as they coped with phenomenal wartime losses, combined with the customary march of death, including elderly parents, infants, and anyone in between.

Always came the question *Why?* addressed by the faithful to God. President Lincoln himself had pondered the war's immense death toll in his second inaugural address. "Fondly do we hope—fervently do we pray—that this mighty scourge of war may speedily pass away," he had said then. Yet if it was God's will, Lincoln continued, so be it ("every drop of blood drawn with the lash, shall be paid by another drawn with the sword"), for slavery offended God, and the bloody war was the price the nation must pay, on both sides. Many who listened to the address in Washington or later read the president's words in the newspapers had already lost loved ones in the war, and here Lincoln spoke of those losses in two different ways: first, as divine retribution for the sin of slavery (a sin, he made clear, for which North and South alike held responsibility), and second, for Union supporters, as deaths ennobled precisely because the war would continue on until human bondage was destroyed. Just so, in spite of the astonishment and devastation at Lincoln's assassination—in fact, because of that very astonishment and devastation—it was fitting for mourners to cast the president's death as part of God's mysterious plans. For some, Lincoln's assassination became the "ultimate death," symbolizing all soldier deaths and promising immortality for all. Immediately following Union triumph (and on Good Friday, at that), it signaled a divinely ordained future brighter than they could ever have imagined in all the jubilation of victory.[9]

But when God took away an intimate, as opposed to a statesman, the question *Why?* carried a different valence, even if that statesman could be cast as a symbolic father. The loss of a loved one mattered less for the future of the nation and the world, and much more for the rest of a family's life on earth. As the war came to an end, coping with private loss—whether at the battlefront or at home—was the one obstacle that made the resumption of everyday life impossible for victor and vanquished alike. Albert Browne Jr. captured this fact eloquently when he wrote to his sister's bereaved fiancé that the "hardest hours" were not those in the immediate aftermath of death but rather the time ahead, "when in the daily course of our life we shall miss Nellie, be lonely without her, and long for her." Heartache nearly always conflicted with the spiritual resignation of even the most faithful. These were the losses that stubbornly resisted closure and healing. When a neighbor brought word of Lincoln's death to Calvin Fletcher in Indianapolis on the morning of April 15, Fletcher thought it the "most apaling announcement" he had ever heard, "except," he wrote in his diary, for "the sudden death of my poor son Miles in 1862." The president's death was "horrid news" to Edward Lear, the English illustrator and poet, yet unmatched by the horror of a friend's suicide a few days later. That was the news that stopped Lear from working, that prompted "Distress & depression—all day." When the American consul in Marseille got word of Lincoln's assassination from Paris, he neglected his duty to send out official condolences. "I should have taken an earlier notice of your despatch," he explained to a fellow diplomat, "but for the loss of my little boy whose recent death temporarily unfitted me for the office."[10]

True, mourners sometimes tilted the comparison the other way. A freedwoman among the crowd in front of the White House on the morning of April 15 was heard to say that she would "rather have given the babe from my bosom!" and a Union soldier in Virginia ruminated that "never had the death of a relative so depressed me as that of our President." But these striking statements, rather than diminishing the import of private losses, worked by metaphor to conjure vividly the shock of the nation's first presidential assassination and the depth of mourners' esteem for President Lincoln.[11]

African Americans claimed Lincoln's assassination to be more crushing for themselves, and grieving whites did not contradict them. As a minister in Cincinnati intoned, "Take father, mother, sister, brother; but do not take the life of the father of this people." Away from the oratory of the pulpit, though, when the president's mourners, black as well as white, faced the death of relatives and intimates, whether on or off the battlefield, all found a desolation far beyond that provoked by the assassination. Emilie Davis's brother Alfred had served in the Union navy, and in late 1865 he died, perhaps from an illness contracted during the war. Yet the fact that her brother had fought for freedom could alleviate Davis's grief but little. Disclosing her intense sorrow in characteristically few words, Davis recorded that the news was "very sad," that the journey to her brother's funeral was "very sad" (the same phrase she had used in recording Lincoln's assassination), and that she was "so Sorry i Did not get to see him before he Died." Davis appealed to God for comfort, then wrote a sentence of understated devastation: "i hope i never will have another day like yesterday." For Emilie Davis, as for African Americans in North and South alike, Lincoln's assassination was shattering. Yet Davis's spare diary entries make clear that whereas the president's funeral in Philadelphia had been for her a grand and solemn occasion, the day of Alfred's funeral was (despite pride in her brother's contribution to the fight for black freedom) the worst day of her life.[12]

Union victory, wrote the journalist Thomas Morris Chester, constituted the "highest degree of happiness attainable upon earth" for his people, since victory included emancipation—and this made for a further dilemma. Throughout slavery, the afterlife had been the only possibility for genuine freedom, prompting African American communities in some measure to celebrate death. Now, with the victorious war for freedom on earth, the afterlife no longer offered the only realm of happiness. How much more unbearable, then, that the absent ones could not experience freedom during their lives, whether death came on home front or battlefront. How much more agonizing for Emilie Davis to endure her brother's death after the war was over and her people everywhere were free.[13]

MINISTERS SPOKE OF LINCOLN AS the last casualty of the Civil War, but that was true only symbolically. After surrender and the assassination, after the funeral and the funeral train, soldiers kept dying, in hospitals, in camp, and back at home from disease, infection, and mortal wounds. "President Lincoln assassinated last night," wrote a Massachusetts soldier in a Washington hospital. Over the following days and weeks, he added: "Five died in this ward," "The man next bed to me died," and "Another poor fellow relieved from all suffering." During the days that Lincoln's funeral train traveled across the country, two Pennsylvania sisters recorded funerals for a neighbor killed in battle and another neighbor's wounded brother, who "had his arm amputated & bled to death." During those same days, Walt Whitman, visiting patients at Armory Square Hospital in Washington, wrote to the mother of a young man who had just perished, trying to soothe the family's pain by describing the suffering boy as "perfectly resign'd."[14]

Soldiers were still dying after Lincoln's burial in early May. John Payne, who began his military career in the Tenth Louisiana Volunteers of African Descent, was thrilled that the Confederates had been "whipped and cowed" yet at the same time crushed by the death of a white comrade in late May, a man he called "perhaps the warmest personal friend of my youth." In late May too, when a soldier drowned while bathing near a dangerous current in a Virginia river, a devastated friend lifted the lifeless body, wondering why he himself had been spared. "One shall be taken and another left," he wrote home to his wife, who in turn asked why they were the ones "left to mourn." Here was another version of the *why* question addressed to God, this time dwelling on the puzzle of who survived the war and who did not. Abial Edwards, a Maine volunteer, suffered the death of his younger brother that autumn, while both young men were still in the field. He had never expected the war to "strike me so near," he confided to his sweetheart at home, and when Edwards asked God why, no answer felt satisfactory. Like Albert Browne wandering around Fort Wagner, soldiers continued to happen upon the bodies and bleached bones of their unburied comrades all through the spring and beyond. As the Washington minister James Ward wrote in his diary two weeks after Lincoln's assassination, cemeteries everywhere were filling up, creating "a world of death" all around.[15]

Men who lost their comrades were also haunted by visions of impending grief on the home front. "How sad it will be for his mother and the girls," a soldier sighed over a fallen man on Easter Sunday, perhaps finding it easier to imagine the feelings of womenfolk than to face his own emotions. A few days after Lincoln's burial, a Union soldier in Savannah likewise wrote home to New England, reflecting on the "many dark and dreary nights" during which wives and children had waited for word from husband and father, "only to hear that he was no more."[16]

Indeed, the distance of faraway wartime deaths made everything worse for families. Lincoln's funeral train delivered his body home to Springfield, but for the hundreds of thousands of Union troops who had died in battle, on the march, in camp, and in army hospitals, there would be no such return. From the start, the Civil War disrupted ideal visions of death, in which the expiring patient lay abed at home, surrounded by family and friends. Popular wartime songs portrayed the dying man, far from the hearth, with his mother standing as the symbol of home: "Break It Gently to My Mother" (in the dying soldier's voice) or "Let Me Kiss Him for His Mother" (in the voice of a kind stranger). Next best for families was to retrieve the body, not least for the purpose of verification, in an era when identification of battlefield corpses was woefully inadequate. But retrieval often entailed disinterment from a makeshift grave wherever a man had fallen, not to mention the expense of embalming and shipment. Unlike Lincoln's corpse, only a small number of the wartime dead would ever return

THE SOLDIER'S MEMORIAL.

A mourner on the home front weeps for a "brave and gallant soldier, and a true patriot."
In this 1863 lithograph, the blank spaces for name, regiment, and place and date of death
permitted bereaved families to imagine their own loved one identified on this imposing
tombstone. In reality, many of the fallen went unidentified and few families could afford
to bring bodies back home. Visible in the background are Union troops and a fluttering
American flag.
LC-USZ62-35580, Prints and Photographs Division, Library of Congress.

to their families, for there was simply not enough space, time, resources, or
labor for all the procedures of proper burial, let alone travel home.[17]

Sometimes the war took women away from the home front too, depriv-
ing them of any last days or moments with a dying loved one. Rose Pickard
was volunteering at a Union hospital in Virginia when her brother died in

upstate New York of an illness contracted in the army. Unable to reach her parents' house until after the burial, Pickard could only take in her brother's empty room, plagued by his lament: "Rose won't come. I shall never see her." Where Pickard had recently expressed shock at Lincoln's death ("It dont seem possible that it is really the President," she had written to her brother as Lincoln lay in state), now her despair shifted. "I cant realize that Byron is dead and buried," she wrote, suffering a grief that would never come to a close.[18]

News of the president's assassination also further provoked apprehension about loved ones at the battlefront. On Easter Sunday, when Mary Mellish wrote to her son in the Union army, she opened with "deep feelings of anxiety," wishing she could "feel assured that you are alive," then restlessly awaiting the day's newspaper casualty lists. Prominent Washingtonian Elizabeth Blair Lee felt the same way, with her husband in the Union navy. "I never thought of you more in my life," she wrote to him during the president's funeral in Washington. "I am blessed indeed to have you spared to me." In the other direction, a Union soldier down south who hadn't written to his parents since the assassination, now penned a letter to let them know "that I am a live." Those at home also worried about faraway loved ones, no matter where they were. With her husband away on business when Lincoln was shot, Emily Watkins checked the papers for accounts of accidents, then wrote to tell him, "*You are all the world to me*," double underlining each word.[19]

Just as those at home worried over news from the battlefield, so too did those at the front wonder about the well-being of loved ones at home. Away in the army three years, one man could only ponder the "many vacancies of which we cannot realize untill our return." When bad news arrived in letters, soldiers too had to contend with the inability to bid a loved one good-bye around the deathbed. William Gould, the North Carolina slave who ran away to the Union navy, was at sea in the spring of 1865 when he received word from his sister, "bringing me," he wrote, "the sad news of the death of Mother." Gould's ship was docked in England, and his mother had died more than two months earlier. "What sad news for me," he added to his diary entry. That same spring, a soldier in the Forty-Sixth Illinois read letters from his parents, grieving over the loss of his brother to an unexpected illness three months before. More than a month later, the dead boy's father still found it hard to get up in the morning, an unsurprising fact that speaks volumes about the difference between the loss of Lincoln and that of an intimate.[20]

Death on the home front also forced the president's mourners to revise any romantic thoughts of Lincoln's assassination as a final loss. On Saturday, April 15, before people received word of the assassination, they were already at funerals burying loved ones. Likewise, after preaching at Easter services the next day, Boston minister Edward Everett Hale called on a dying parishioner, and on the day of the president's funeral in Washington, Hale attended the funeral of a local woman, then another for a seventeen-year-old boy who had starved to death in a Confederate prison; the day after that, a parishioner's baby died. For some, a more personal loss resulted directly from the assassination, as for William Brooks, whose boyhood friend had already been "depressed," Brooks admitted, then hanged himself on hearing of Lincoln's murder.[21]

A home-front death meant that survivors could engage with the body, and those encounters differed considerably from the experiences of Lincoln's mourners rushing past the president's corpse in a crowd. In Philadelphia, Annie Hillborn watched Lincoln's body pass through her city, but only after she had attended the funeral of young Clementine Mifflin earlier the same day. The girl had died of an illness the night before, and Hillborn and her friends gazed for as long as they liked upon her white cashmere robes, the rosebuds arranged in her hands, and the flowers strewn about the coffin's interior. The same was true when a bereaved family could afford to have a soldier's body returned. Jennie Smith, whose dear friend Otis had been thrown from his army horse, stood by his body marveling that he "looked so *natural,*" with "his hair combed *beautifully*" and "such a *pleasant,* such a *sweet* expression" on his face. Not only could Smith spend time with Otis's body, but the corpse's return had been swift enough that the face remained well preserved, allowing her to commune with the departed in a way infinitely more satisfying than permitted by Lincoln's decaying visage. After writing five pages about the deceased young man, Smith turned to the assassination, composing more formulaic phrases about "*universal* mourning" and the "beautiful show of respect" by thousands when the funeral train passed through Syracuse at midnight.[22]

Throughout the spring, mourners interwove their thoughts about the president with the loss of intimates. On the Sunday after Easter, Anna Lowell thought a sermon preached for a deceased soldier contained passages "much applicable to our martyred chief." For William Brooks, with the funeral train nearing the end of its journey, "how vividly does the loss of our dear son George come before us," he wrote, adding that the boy had "died in a glorious cause." Even when death came far from the battlefield and apart from the war, those personal losses melded with Lincoln's assassination. On Saturday, April 15, residents of a Massachusetts town attended a burial for a ten-year-old girl who had succumbed to scarlet and typhoid fevers. "The funeral was doubly sad," one woman wrote, "for at noon we heard our President was dead and the bell was tolled for a long time." Annie Hillborn drew an even more direct parallel when she attended the funeral of Clementine Mifflin on the day Lincoln's body traveled through Philadelphia. "Here too is a great sacrifice!" Hillborn wrote, without compunction equating the girl's death with the president's murder.[23]

Anniversaries of personal losses also resonated in the aftermath of the assassination. Laura Lamson had just started her Saturday morning ironing when a neighbor brought the news of Lincoln. Dutifully, Lamson recorded the time of the president's death as 7:22 a.m., then drew a dash and added, "Two years ago today at 6 a.m. our little Willie died." For Sarah Gilpin, it was the anniversary of her mother's passing that preoccupied her. "These are very sad days to me," she wrote in her diary, as Lincoln's funeral took place in the capital. Gilpin noted New York's closed shops and dark drapery, but that wasn't her main concern. "I scarcely feel the public events," she admitted, "my mind is so filled by the associations of last year hour by hour." Gilpin noted when Lincoln's body was nearing her city, but she also found it trying that, with so much attention focused on the president, "no one else *seems* to remember."[24]

In a letter to her children, Sarah Hale skipped back and forth, reflecting first on the assassination, then passing on the news of the death of a friend's baby. "Other forms of grief and bereavement may be severe," she wrote, alluding to the assassination, but nothing, she insisted, could cause greater pain to a mother than the loss of an infant. Anne Neafie would have agreed. On the day Lincoln's funeral train left Albany, Neafie, in a small town eighty miles south, wrote to her husband in the army in Savannah. She commented on the "grief and rage" occasioned by the assassination, but she also had "family matters of importance" to convey: their young son might not survive scarlet fever. Now Alfred Neafie looked for his wife's letters with dread, and soon Anne wrote to tell him that "we have no longer a little boy on earth." Anne felt, she confessed to Alfred, "as if I could not take up again the burden of my life," and as she appealed to God, her "stricken heart" cried out in rebellion. In Savannah, Alfred recorded the date and hour of death on a photograph of his boy, then turned to God with an "aching void" in his heart—the same words Alice Browne had invoked after the death of her sister, Nellie. Just as for the Brownes, there was no solace or closure for the Neafies, with every glance at a toy or a piece of the boy's clothing tearing at Anne. "Oh, darling it is killing me," she wrote to her husband.[25]

For some, despair at the loss of an intimate eclipsed both Lincoln's assassination and Union victory. Louisa Hughes had watched her husband die of a long illness during the war; in a state of nearly suicidal grief, she found herself unable to accept God's will in the "months of weeping and desolation" that followed. In the spring of 1865, when Hughes recorded Confederate surrender in her Connecticut diary, she addressed her thoughts to her absent beloved. "Alas my husband," she wrote, "you are silent and feel nothing now." The joy of victory meant little, since she enjoyed no occasion "until I had shared it with you," she told his ghost. In church on Easter Sunday, gazing upon the flowers symbolizing the resurrection of Christ, Hughes found herself wishing it was her husband who could be raised from the dead—not Jesus Christ, not Abraham Lincoln, but her husband. Others, consumed by private shock and sorrow, made no mention of the assassination at all. In New Hampshire, Mary Russell wrote to her aunt Eunice Stone after Easter services, with a "heavy heart," not to impart reflections on the slain president, but because she had received news of the death of Stone's husband (in the case of this divided family, he died fighting for the Confederacy). When the fallen man's sister, an ardent Union supporter, wrote to the widow Stone on the day of the Washington funeral, she too had nothing to say about Lincoln. "Try and think it is the will of God," she advised, echoing the preaching ministers but referring instead to the husband's death. Just as men of the pulpit foretold a luminous future for the nation, she added, albeit more prosaically, "I hope there is better days in store for you."[26]

Terrible as Lincoln's death was for those who loved him as statesman and metaphorical friend or father, the loss of intimates was devastating in an entirely different way. Sarah and Albert Browne well knew this, and they were far from alone in a grief that could not be put to rest, for the death of a spouse, child, sibling, parent, or dear friend proved resistant to the comforts of divine design, whether that death came on the battlefield for a glorious cause, at home in bed, or anywhere else. The march of death in the spring and summer of 1865 made eminently clear to Lincoln's mourners that the assassination had brought neither life nor death to a halt.

AS WHITE SOUTHERNERS IN THE spring of 1865 confronted their own enormous death toll, the hardest part was the knowledge that every soldier seemed to have died in vain. That understanding was precisely what drove Rodney Dorman to such fury over the lost lives of Confederates in Union prisons. Over time, the grim thought of so many pointless deaths would be assuaged by "Lost Cause" ideology, first advanced by General Robert E. Lee in his farewell address to his troops the day after surrender. All rebel soldiers, Lee asserted, had fought bravely for independence, and defeat had resulted only from the Union's "overwhelming numbers and resources." Oft-repeated, Lee's formulation would quickly take root, nurturing the idea that every Confederate death was a noble one. But that spring, as the conquered asked God why their loved ones had died, nothing at all seemed noble. In South Carolina on the Sunday after Easter, plantation mistress Mary Chesnut listened to her compatriots putting the unfathomable outcome into words: "so many left dead on battlefields, so many dead in hospitals and prisons," others suffering "with hideous wounds and diseases" or "frozen to death—starved to death," leaving "brokenhearted women" everywhere. What Chesnut and her friends implied, Kate Stone articulated directly: "The best and bravest of the South sacrificed—and for nothing," she wrote in her Texas diary. "Yes, worse than nothing."[27]

Nor was it merely that each death had been in vain. It was that each death had been in vain because the Confederate nation had died too. Virginia planter William Gordon spent much of April consoling friends whose seventeen-year-old son had just fallen in the war, the boy's family "in the depth of wretchedness & despair." As for himself, Gordon hadn't picked up his journal for nearly a month, for he had "no heart to write down the particulars of our great calamity, culminating in the final overthrow." A Tennessee farmer was more explicit. "We Will sit down & Mourn in Sack Cloathes & ashes for many days, Weeks, Months, & years to come," he wrote in his diary. In the combination of lost lives and a nation defeated, there seemed no end to the mourning ahead.[28]

Indeed, defeat itself felt nearly like the loss of an intimate. Martha Crawford, serving as a Baptist missionary in China, received news of Lee's surrender in June, overwhelming her with grief. Shocked and shattered, she found it "bitterer than death." Equally devastated, Cornelia Spencer compared her feelings about defeat to those that had engulfed her upon the death of her husband, Magnus, several years earlier. "I feel a good deal as I did when my beloved M. died," she wrote from North Carolina, "as if something I had watched & loved & hoped & prayed for so long—was dead," as if she had "lost an incentive to prayer—or to exertion of any kind." A Virginia private who looked through his family's empty larder—no flour, corn, bacon—on his return home from a Yankee prison wondered what was to come. "Ah! what hardships, what sufferings, what trials, what deaths, what sorrows, what tears," he wrote, "what great losses both of men & of property." That last word, *property,* referred plainly to the slaves his family had once owned, their departure making clear the end of the Confederate aim of an independent, slaveholding republic.[29]

Confederate soldiers, like their Union counterparts, also had to contend with losses on the home front. When Samuel McCullough, in a Union prison in Ohio, saw a notice of his father's death in a newspaper, he was stunned. Truly, it seemed like a dream, he wrote, echoing the initial disbelief of Lincoln's mourners. "Language is too impotent to portray, & tongue too feeble to tell the indescribable sorrow & anguish," he elaborated, again echoing the experiences of Lincoln's mourners searching for ways to articulate their pain. Unlike the vast majority of the president's bereaved supporters, though, McCullough felt nearly suicidal with grief. Likely reacting to defeat as well, he confided to his brother that, were it not for the rest of the family, he would now "rather die than live."[30]

A few of the vanquished consoled themselves by casting Lincoln's assassination as vindication for their personal losses. Union authorities had convicted and hanged Confederate naval officer John Beall for spying, and after the president's death, a grieving relative felt sure that Beall's demise had been "avenged by the assassination of Lincoln." More commonly, solace came in thoughts of heavenly happiness, but that conviction had another, more somber dimension to it when the grieving took comfort that the departed would never know the horror of life on earth after Yankee victory. For Elizabeth Alsop, the death of a friend in the Appomattox campaign was "agony itself," yet at least the man would be "spared the sorrow of seeing our Country's degradation," she wrote in her diary. Some survivors even envied the wartime dead, just as the suicidal Edmund Ruffin envied his own fallen son. A private in the Army of Northern Virginia, making his way home in late June, gazed at the wreckage of Richmond, wondering if the "unreturning brave" were better off than he. A prisoner in a Yankee jail thought longingly of those around him who had died of starvation, and a woman on the home front "could not wish them back," she wrote of the dead, since they rested in peace, spared from "shame & humiliation." Cloe Whittle knew it was unchristian to think such thoughts, but she imagined that, had she been a soldier, she would have courted death on the battlefield, knowing that the alternative was to "drink the deadly cup of submission to the Yankees." When Whittle heard news of an explosion at the Charleston depot, she envied those killed in the blast.[31]

For Confederates, the loss of loved ones only magnified defeat, and defeat only compounded personal loss. For them, the end of their hoped-for slaveholding nation filled the future with uncertainty. Lincoln's mourners, on the other hand, found in the aftermath of the assassination a complicated alloy of devastation and optimism. When they called Saturday, April 15, 1865, the saddest day they had ever known, that was true only in the most collective, public, and communal sense. If the elaborate ceremonies staged for the president momentarily stood in for the absent bodies of loved ones, survivors still had to cope with terrible absences in their everyday lives. For all Union supporters who had suffered the loss of intimates in the war, the end of fighting called forth retrospective thoughts that intensified grief and yet soothed that grief in the security of victory.

The unbearable loss of the ordinary people they loved, and the unfathomable loss of their leader: both gained meaning from the context of victory. In that context too, Lincoln's mourners had to think concretely about reconstructing the nation without slavery—and without President Lincoln either.

Mary Lincoln

POOR MRS. LINCOLN. HOW OFTEN the president's mourners invoked that phrase, thinking of the great man's own loved ones! It was a thought that occurred more often to women, who could more readily imagine themselves in her place, but male mourners felt sorry for the president's widow too.

"Poor Mrs. Lincoln," wrote John Downing, eyewitness at Ford's Theatre, in a letter from Washington. "How I pity her."

"Poor Mrs. Lincoln has not left her bed," Helen Du Barry, another eyewitness to the crime, wrote to her mother on Easter Sunday.

"Poor Mrs. Lincoln, her utter desolation," wrote Sarah Hale from Boston, "and how many years she has got to struggle on."

"Poor Mrs. Lincoln," wrote Samuel Lee, whose wife was a close friend of the First Lady. "I feel very acutely for her great loss & her suffering under it."

"Poor Mrs. Lincoln!" cried a London socialite. "What a grief! what a horror for her!"

Even the wife of a New York Democratic judge (she had once referred to Lincoln as "Uncle Ape") couldn't help exclaiming into her diary, "Poor Mrs. Lincoln!"[1]

The president's mourners knew that if anyone's world had come to a halt in the aftermath of the assassination, it was that of Mary Lincoln, who shut herself up in a White House bedroom, unwilling to attend her husband's funeral, unwilling to accompany his body along the route of the funeral train, and unwilling to be present at his burial in Springfield. When Lizzie Moore wrote, "O, how sad it must be to those who knew him personally," she named the difference between mourning for a statesman and mourning for a loved one. Secretary of the Navy Gideon Welles recorded in his diary that at the White House on Saturday, the president's twelve-year-old son, Tad, had asked him, "Oh, Mr. Welles, who killed my father?" Strangers to the president thought about the boy too. "Poor little Tad," wrote Anna Lowell, recording (from the newspapers) how he was "overcome with grief" at his father's death. Some included the older son, Robert, in their thoughts as well. "The tears of sympathy flow for the widow & orphans of our martyred chief," Caroline White told her diary.[2]

Mourners also dwelled on the effects of the harrowing circumstances: the president's sudden, violent assassination before his wife's very eyes. "Poor Mrs. Lincoln," wrote the English novelist Elizabeth Gaskell, "it adds to the depth of the crime that it should be done in her presence." Another mourner wondered how she felt "as she sat by him, and saw him shot!" Unlike so many Civil War soldiers, Lincoln had not died in a place far away from his family, but neither had he died peacefully at home. Rather, he had passed his final hours in a too-small bed, in a cramped room at a random boardinghouse, with a steady stream of visitors coming and going, an investigation into his murder taking place in the very next room, even before he had breathed his last. As for the First Lady, the men who took charge soon excluded her from the bedroom where her husband lay dying, finding her state of extreme distress overly irritating. All in all, there was little comfort to be taken in being with her husband on that night, only devastation and lifelong trauma.[3]

Newspaper accounts of Mary Lincoln's screams in Ford's Theatre, and of her delirium during the long hours at Petersen House, troubled mourners too. One woman recorded Mrs. Lincoln's "agonizing inquiries" about her husband's life and the "heart rending response" she ultimately received. Men and women alike wrote down that Mary Lincoln couldn't bring herself to attend the Washington funeral and that she was too grief-stricken to travel with the funeral train. One man involved in the funeral preparations recorded that when the carpenters were setting up the East Room of the White House, the bedridden and shattered First Lady cried that each hammer blow sounded to her like a pistol shot. As Lincoln's body was carried west, a man in California generously suggested that his people, "the colored people of the United States," contribute a dollar each to buy a home for the president's widow.[4]

Grieving for their own loved ones, Lincoln's mourners wrote frequently about the afterlife of the departed, happy in heaven, "above all pain," in a "better world where war and sickness can never come." At a New England eulogy for the president, the writer J. G. Holland offered an image of Lincoln in the next world. "Ah, that other shore!" he said, visualizing the president in heaven "with his army." In "victory and peace," Holland continued, the commander-in-chief and the departed troops heard no groans of death or rumbles of cannon fire. Yet Lincoln's lay mourners rarely evoked images of the president happily reunited with loved ones in heaven, despite their chief's increasingly careworn expression over the course of four years, and despite the personal losses he and Mary had endured in the deaths of their sons, Eddie in 1859, and Willie in 1862. Some may have grappled with Lincoln's ambiguous relationship to Christianity, but for most mourners it was simply that the president was not theirs to meet or imagine in heaven. That was another indicator of the distinction they made between the loss of Lincoln and the loss of intimates. To envision reunion in that joyful realm above the clouds was a privilege reserved for Mary, Robert, and Tad.[5]

Many of those who sympathized with Mary Lincoln took the time to write to her, and letters of condolence poured in from around the world. Although Queen Victoria did not know the First Lady personally, she sent her a letter detailing her own despair on the death of her husband, Prince Albert, four years earlier. "No-one can better appreciate than I can who am myself *utterly broken hearted* by the loss of my own beloved Husband," Victoria wrote, "who was the *light* of my Life—my stay—*my all,*—what your sufferings must be." Nor was it only royalty and dignitaries who wrote to Mrs. Lincoln. When Charles Francis Adams, the U.S. consul in London, received a torrent of cards, letters, and telegrams from across the British Empire, he had to create an entirely separate catalog for the considerable accumulation of mail addressed to Mary.[6]

Elizabeth Blair Lee was one of the very few whom Mary Lincoln wished to see in the days and weeks following the murder. During that time, Lee stayed by Mrs. Lincoln's side in the White House, sometimes nearly around the clock. As the funeral train approached Springfield, Mary Lincoln "begged me so hard," Lee wrote, "not to leave her," that she couldn't refuse, though there was much else on Lee's mind: her young son, whom she had to leave in the care of others while she sat by the widow's bedside, her naval commander husband down south, and a lump in her breast that seemed to be growing. After the burial in Springfield, it was time for Mary and the children to leave Washington, and Elizabeth Lee remained a loyal friend throughout the ordeal. "Mrs. Lincoln still sick and miserable," she wrote to her husband, "tired from the effort she is making to get out of the White House." One day in mid-May, Lee found Mary Lincoln "wonderfully better"—over the course of three hours, she had mentioned her husband's death only once, then interrupted herself, saying, "I lived through it. I am now getting well and strong after all those terrible events." A week later, the two women said good-bye as Mary and her sons boarded a train for Chicago. Despite Elizabeth Lee's sense that Mrs. Lincoln's mental health was improving, the president's widow would long remain troubled by grief and emotional instability, never recovering from the loss of her husband and the trauma of witnessing his murder.[7]

9

❧

Nation

AS MUCH AS ALBERT BROWNE thought back over the astounding events of the past weeks, he also looked resolutely ahead, envisioning the nation's future. Mourning the loss of Lincoln also meant reckoning with Lincoln's successor, and Albert admitted that Andrew Johnson's behavior at the president's second inauguration in March 1865 had been questionable, for the vice president had appeared to be inebriated. Nonetheless Albert believed that the new chief executive would nicely finish Lincoln's work on earth. If Johnson could stay sober, Albert reasoned, he would prove to be "all Lincoln was, *and more.*" Sarah Browne looked to the new president approvingly too, confident that he would treat the vanquished enemies properly. "We have faith in Andrew Johnson," she wrote to Albert, "and believe that full measure will be meted out."[1]

When word of Jefferson Davis's capture down south reached Salem, bells rang, flags waved, and guns fired. It was the "great finale of our glorious triumph," Sarah wrote. (She also delighted in reports that Davis had been "disguised in his wife's clothing" when Union forces apprehended him, "underneath which he showed his own boots!!") For Albert's part, he was thrilled that the "arch traitor and wicked man" was now under federal watch and hoped that Davis would be hanged as a step toward vindicating all who had died for the Union cause. Albert worried, though, that Davis would be made a martyr, and nothing infuriated him so much as Confederates who insisted on extolling their self-exiled rebel leader. On a trip to Savannah, he'd had to listen to a southern hostess (a northern-born woman, at that!—Albert had socialized with her family in the past) who called Davis "a *pious* and *good man and patriot.*" That prompted a stern lecture to the entire family (all of whom, in Albert's recounting, listened to him, trembling and aghast), ending with a warning that if he ever heard another apology for Jefferson Davis, he would arrest the speaker, male or female. When the offender's husband tried to apologize, Albert apparently announced that he would never visit again if the man couldn't "bridle the tongue of his she rebel."[2]

Despite that angry encounter with Confederates, when Albert Browne thought about the nation to be formed in the wake of victory, he remained filled with optimism. On Hilton Head Island, he attended a church meeting of African Americans and marveled at the "gathering of a thousand *human beings*" who so recently had been "Chattel *property.*" It astonished him how fast history was being made, right before his eyes. The destruction of slavery, then Union victory, then the assassination: he had lived through the "momentous transactions" of each one. "I can hardly realise the scenes through which I am passing, so important, so astounding, and following in such quick succession," he wrote to Sarah in mid-May. "How fast we all live, how much faster I live than most men." For her part, Sarah connected a sense of involvement in history to faith in God. "A feeling of awe comes over us as we review the events of the last three months," she recorded in her diary. Looking to past and future alike, Sarah shared her husband's optimism. "We see God's hand and feel His power," she wrote.[3]

HAUNTED BY VISIONS OF WHAT was to come, Rodney Dorman spent a good deal of time gazing backward. When he thought about the future, with the Confederacy dismantled and Yankees in charge, it often felt unendurable. Black Union soldiers in Jacksonville served as the first reminder of that humiliation. "The use of them here is an insult & disgrace," he wrote in his diary, "& intended as an insult!" Interference, meddling, tampering—that's how Dorman saw emancipation. Much as he hated the freed slaves and black soldiers (and most especially the slaves-turned-soldiers), Dorman didn't hold them directly accountable. "I do not blame the negroes," he wrote, for they were only "put up to & encouraged in all sorts of impudence, brutality, & wickedness" by their white superiors. Never had black people behaved the way they behaved now, he believed, until the Union army—"these Hell-hounds"—came along to incite insurrection. (That was the way masters had always imagined slave uprisings, in keeping with their fantasies about passive and contented bondspeople.) What "contemptible meanness & baseness," Dorman spat out, "prying into a man's affairs through his servants" (*servants,* too, was a fantasy of the masters, as if enslaved people performed paid labor of their own volition).[4]

Rodney Dorman's venom knew no bounds, and, as usual, he reserved special animosity for the abolitionists, "pitiful, pettifogging scoundrels," their faces "too brazen to blush," whose "sickening sentimentality" did nothing but "beshit & befoul every thing they meddle with." As for the particular Christian missionaries who were in town to teach the former slaves, Dorman found them to be troublemaking fiends whose dastardliness put the devil to shame. What "black hearted devils" were the white "mischief-makers," Dorman proclaimed. Even stupider than the black people they converted, they "out-negro the negro," he wrote. For Rodney Dorman, the post-surrender nation remained a war zone of Yankee invasion. "The outrages are not over," he declared, even "if the war is."[5]

Speaking of outrages, the fact that the federals were pursuing the fleeing Jefferson Davis when the Confederacy had already surrendered only increased Dorman's vexation. True, Davis had been a leader of secession, but according to Dorman, secession had never been a criminal act, not to mention that the abolitionists had started the war in the first place. In the late-arriving northern newspapers, Dorman followed the Union army's hunt for the Confederate president, and when they captured him in mid-May, it only steeled Dorman's conviction that "the day of retribution must come."[6]

IN THE SPRING OF 1865, Union supporters felt themselves palpably immersed in the unfolding of epic events. The fall of Richmond, Lee's surrender, the assassination, the funeral in Washington and the funeral train, the capture and killing of the assassin: here was history in the making, in one's own lifetime, before one's very eyes, at lightning speed, and just like

Albert Browne, Lincoln's mourners wrote themselves into it. For Horatio Nelson Taft, working in the Patent Office in Washington, the past month was not only "*the* most eventful in the History of our Country," but "above all in importance which has occurred in the *world*," for "the President of the United States has been *assassinated*." For the victors-turned-mourners, the events of the past weeks felt like enough for years, or a lifetime, or five hundred years, or "a century of ordinary history." April 1865, wrote Edward Everett Hale, was the "most remarkable month in modern history." Or as one woman told her niece, "You will remember, forever, with satisfaction, that you were alive at this time."[7]

At war's end, with history being made before their eyes, Lincoln's mourners not only looked back, in efforts to make sense of Union victory followed so closely by the assassination, they also looked ahead, as the nation sped into the future. By writing themselves into the historical events taking place around them, the grief-stricken stood ready personally to shape that future, and they did so by bringing politics into everyday life. As the doctor Elizabeth Blackwell wrote to a friend, "Private lives have all become interwoven with the life of the nation," so that "every one seems to live two lives," a personal one and a "great absorbing national one."[8]

This was true not only for white men, who exercised the rights of citizenship and suffrage, but also, and most especially, for black men and women, whose lives were so directly connected to the fate of union and slavery. White women, too, immersed themselves. As Anna Lowell asserted on the day Lincoln died, "We had felt as if we too had cast our votes for him." Children drew themselves into the swirl and fray as well. African American youngsters in the South, who saw the jubilation of emancipation and victory all around them, also heard clearly articulated fears for a future without President Lincoln. Nor could white children remain sheltered, and even some of the youngest grasped the magnitude of events. A week after the assassination, one mother found her son "tired out and very nervous," yet begging to be read the newspaper reports of Booth's capture. For all of Lincoln's mourners, no matter their formal political power, it proved impossible to grieve without also thinking about what kind of nation the victorious United States would become without Lincoln at the helm—whether his absence proved a blessing because of his lenience or a curse because of his statesmanship.[9]

History-making for Confederates felt entirely different, for it was being made in a nation from which they had failed to secede. Amid their spiritual struggles with God's apparent desertion, as they wrestled with the destruction of their land and the pointless loss of so many lives, the vanquished looked back with wistfulness and forward with fear and anger. When they added Lincoln's assassination to their own roster of historic occurrences, it was often only to leaven the gloom. "What exciting, what eventful times we live in!" Emma LeConte had written in her diary when the news arrived. Few of her compatriots were quite so effusive. A musician with a Mississippi regiment glumly reckoned with history as he marched his last fifteen miles home. That day he entitled his diary entry "Reflections upon our situation as a down-fallen people." He then closed his wartime journal with the words, "The end." Except of course it was not the end, for he and everyone else could not help thinking about the future.[10]

The surrender of Robert E. Lee at Appomattox provoked very different visions for the victors and the vanquished, most especially when it came to political rights for black and white southerners. At one extreme lay the restoration of the Union, without legal slavery but with black subordination reinstated, with no interference from the federal government. That was the dream of Rodney Dorman and like-minded Confederates. At the other end of the spectrum lay fully equal rights for African Americans, including voting rights for black men, enforced by federal authorities and coupled with the strict abridgment of the political power of Confederate leaders and elites. That was the hope of Sarah and Albert Browne, of African Americans north and south, and of radical white northerners. In between lay the less clear-cut visions of moderate Republicans, northern Democrats who had supported the war for Union, southern Unionists, and Copperheads.[11]

When Lincoln spoke to the crowd outside the White House on April 11, two days after Lee had surrendered, no one knew that it would be his last speech, that it was the last time he would articulate his ideas about reconstructing the nation. That evening, Lincoln mentioned his personal preference for at least partial black suffrage. Among those who reacted with dismay was John Wilkes Booth, who stood among the listeners ("That means nigger citizenship. Now, by God, I'll put him through"). That evening, Lincoln also told his audience that the process of reconstruction would be "fraught with great difficulty," and so it was proving to be, right from the start.[12]

Four days later, just hours after Lincoln expired, Chief Justice Salmon Chase swore in Andrew Johnson as president. Lincoln allied with the Tennessean as his 1864 running mate for strategic reasons. As an ardent anti-secessionist, Johnson was the only senator from a seceded state to retain his seat in the federal government and therefore a good bet for appealing to northern Democrats. Johnson's background was not so different from Lincoln's own. Lincoln had been born in a dirt-floor cabin in Kentucky, to parents critical of slavery; Johnson had been born to poor and illiterate parents in North Carolina and grew up bitter toward the rich whites of the South. Yet the two men's lives ultimately followed very different trajectories.

When Lincoln's mourners looked ahead to the fate of the nation, they again confronted the paradox of which lesson to draw from the assassination: in the slain chief's kindness and generosity could be found either a divine reason for his death (since he would have treated the defeated rebels too indulgently) or a model for political strategy after his death (because the defeated rebels should in fact be treated with mercy).

Now, with the Confederacy and Lincoln both gone, the future of the nation lay with Andrew Johnson, the man empowered to determine the status of former rebels and former slaves in the postwar nation. For their part, the rebels—including all who rejoiced over the assassination—had to confront a fresh set of anxieties. They had feared Lincoln for his hatred of slavery, and they now feared Johnson for his hatred of slaveholders. It was hard to tell which was more troublesome. "Many think Andy Johnson worse than Lincoln," wrote Kate Stone, a war refugee in Texas, "but that is simply impossible." Emma LeConte shrugged off any distinction, scoffing that a "rail-splitter" had been replaced by a "drunken ass." Most rebels cared little about Johnson's ignoble behavior at the inauguration, though, training their worries instead on the loss of Lincoln, the man they despised and simultaneously imagined would have acted as their best friend after surrender. "All the citizens about here regret the occurance," wrote a Union officer in Virginia after the assassination, "not so much for love of Lincoln as for fear of Johnson."[13]

Warily, Confederate nurse Kate Cumming read a speech the new president had delivered to an Indiana delegation during his first week in office, in which he spoke of the "diabolical and fiendish rebellion" and asserted (to applause) that treason was a crime and traitors should be "punished and impoverished." As for the Confederate leadership, "their social power must be destroyed," Johnson maintained, to ensure that they would never rise again. He even suggested that Confederate property be handed over to Union supporters, including poorer white southerners who had been coerced into the rebellion by powerful elites. As for John Wilkes Booth, Johnson equated him with all the Confederate higher-ups who had tried to "assassinate this nation." After that, Cumming felt sure that the war wasn't yet over, unless Johnson promptly took back everything he had said to the Indianans. The fervent secessionist Edmund Ruffin, before he committed suicide, had recorded his thoughts on the new president, decreeing him an evil traitor who would treat the Confederates even worse than would an abolitionist. A Louisiana planter likewise thought Johnson would "out Herod, Herod." As the black journalist Thomas Morris Chester put it, "From Mr. Johnson they expect no mercy."[14]

A few angry Confederates confronted the new executive personally. The "same spirit," an anonymous rebel wrote to Johnson, "still burns within us, & cannot be crushed." Signing himself "a Southern man," the writer warned that Johnson could either reconcile with white people or "exasperate them" until "*revenge revenge revenge* takes deep root in their hearts." A Confederate in exile in Canada spelled out the consequences. Should Johnson take any untoward action against Lee or Davis, this man wrote (signing himself "A Southerner for life"), "I will shoot you." From the other side, a Virginia Unionist was so sure that Johnson would be assassinated on account of his vigorous stand against the rebels that she implored him to protect himself. "Oh! in Heaven's name & for the sake of our loved country," he should go nowhere without personal security. Fearing for her own life, the woman withheld a signature.[15]

That Andrew Johnson was a man unworthy of shaping the postwar nation was a view shared by a portion of Lincoln's mourners, though for entirely different reasons. African Americans and their allies were the first to voice concerns, their political anxieties running concurrent with their faith that God, in his mysterious ways, had taken Lincoln for the good of the nation. Along with the enormous outpouring of joy over Union victory, some African Americans had in fact expressed reservations about the future even before Lincoln's death. Recall that just after the fall of Richmond, Frederick Douglass had warned, "Hereafter, at the South, the negro will be looked upon with a fiercer and intenser hate than ever before," and the editors of the *New York Anglo-African* had explained, just after Lee's surrender, that their people felt "less disposed to join in the shouts of victory" because "with the cessation of the war our anxieties begin." Legal freedom, they made clear, still left plenty of room for "oppressions akin to slavery." Then, after the assassination, Andrew Johnson appeared as an uncertain ally. Freedpeople in a Norfolk classroom had worried right away that the new president "might not be as friendly toward the colored race" as his predecessor.[16]

Still, most African Americans remained hopeful, at least out loud. Whether sincerely or strategically (or some of each), community leaders offered reassurance, albeit with a dash of circumspection. "As colored men, we have entire confidence in President Johnson," wrote the editor of the *New Orleans Black Republican,* tempering that statement with the tepid assertion that the loss of Lincoln was "in some degree softened" by the new chief executive. If Lincoln had been Moses, "let us hope for a Joshua in Andrew Johnson," wrote a black soldier, referring cautiously (*let us hope*) to the biblical figure who ultimately led the Jews across the Jordan River into the Promised Land.[17]

African Americans addressed President Johnson directly during his first weeks in office as they reflected on the future of a nation in which they now envisioned themselves as full citizens. The founders of the *Colored Tennessean* sent an issue of their newspaper to the White House, calling Johnson "a freind of our '*race,*'" even as they counseled the new leader to "sanction our course." Those who could not speak directly to the president had their voices heard through community spokesmen. John Mercer Langston, lawyer, Union army recruiter, and head of the National Equal Rights League, visited Johnson with a delegation of prominent black men three days after Lincoln's death. Proclaiming that "our liberty and rights will be fully protected and sustained," the men made two requests: "complete emancipation" and "full equality before American law." These demands referred most immediately to the treatment of African Americans in the wake of Confederate defeat, as former slaves became the victims of stepped-up white violence. For their part, black residents of Alexandria, Virginia, delivered a petition to Johnson requesting that control of their city remain in the hands of the federal government, lest they suffer yet more brutality from the angry white people around them. Here was Frederick Douglass's prediction of "fiercer and intenser hate than ever before."[18]

Long-range political policies mattered in the face of Confederate anger and violence. Notably, in their visions of the reconstructed nation, African Americans looked to the slain president, invoking in their petitions what they imagined Lincoln would have accomplished. To make emancipation and equality effective, freedpeople needed education and land, and to make that a sustainable plan, they needed the franchise. African Americans from New Bern, North Carolina, accordingly petitioned Johnson for voting rights "for all loyal men, without regard to color." Johnson's black supplicants in fact repeatedly reminded him that they had been loyal supporters of the Union from the first, displaying "heroic patriotism," naming in their petitions battles like Fort Wagner and Port Hudson. Pointedly, the North Carolinians drew attention to the injustice of denying the vote to "men who have been fighting for the country" while giving it to "men who have just returned from four years fighting against it," and that was the crux of the matter: Would disloyal white men be permitted to vote in the states of the former Confederacy while loyal black men would not? Now the men from North Carolina invoked Lincoln, referring to him as a friend and noble agent of liberty, in hopes, they told Johnson, that "the mantle of our murdered friend and father may have fallen upon your shoulders." These delegates and their allies seized on the Emancipation Proclamation (a cautious legal document that had technically freed slaves only in areas beyond the control of the Union) and the mild April 11 speech, though neither was any guarantee of black freedom and political rights after the war was over.[19]

"In what new skin will the old snake come forth?" That question served as the title of a speech Frederick Douglass delivered to the American Anti-Slavery Society in New York City as the organization was deciding whether to disband at war's end. It was mid-May, and Douglass's concerns were precisely those of the freedpeople who had wondered aloud about reenslavement immediately after the assassination. This was no exaggerated anxiety but rather a real legal possibility, one also recognized by Republican lawmakers as the war drew to a close. As long as the word *white* still appeared in southern laws, Douglass told his audience, the work of abolitionists was not done, for those laws could make "a mockery" of emancipation. Citizenship, and in particular enfranchisement, was the answer, and Douglass believed that antislavery organizations must remain active as long as black men could not vote. Douglass went so far as to predict that without black suffrage, white southerners would replicate the very conditions of slavery in the post-surrender nation. Then he and his comrades would see, he told his listeners, "what new form this old monster will assume" and in "what new skin this old snake will come forth next."[20]

Radical members of the Republican Party shared these concerns, including Chief Justice Salmon Chase, who met repeatedly with President Johnson to underscore the same point. When Chase toured the southern coastal states in May, he wrote letters to Johnson describing meetings with African Americans in North Carolina, South Carolina, Georgia, and Florida, all of whom made clear to him the "very great importance to the right of voting." Stopping in Jacksonville, Chase listened as the city's white residents made equally clear that they hoped to keep political power out of the hands of black men. "It is curious to observe," the Chief Justice reported, "how little they seem to realize that any change in personal or political relations has been wrought by the war." (In his diary, Rodney Dorman noted Chase's appearance, maligning him for blemishing the "dignity & legal ability" of Chief Justice Roger Taney, author of the 1857 Dred Scott decision, which called African Americans "beings of an inferior order" with "no rights which the white man was bound to respect.")[21]

President Johnson's answers to his visitors and petitioners proved far from satisfying, offering either vague assurances of a "guaranty of my future conduct toward your people" or dismissals like "It is not necessary for me to give you any assurance of what my future course will be." Indeed, rather than promising a bright future, Johnson instead referred to the past. He made his most transparent statement at a May meeting with the Reverend Edmund Turney and other black ministers, informing his guests that although he was a native of a slave state and had possessed slaves (he had once owned five), he had never sold one. He then defended slaveholders, who he claimed cared as much for slaves as did any northerner, and lectured the men not to "become loafers and depend upon the Government." When Johnson deplored the state of "notorious concubinage" in which, he implied, all four million enslaved people had willfully lived (with not a word about the illegality of slave marriages, the rape of black women by white men, or the breeding of slaves by their masters), he further taunted the men by adding, "You know what I say is true."[22]

Finally, in the most galling vision of the post–Civil War nation, Johnson alluded to sending all black people off to Africa: "The time may soon come when you shall be gathered together, in a clime and country suited to you," is how he put it. When escaped slave William Gould read those words in the newspapers that arrived on his Union navy ship, he was incensed. "We see by the papers that the President in A speech intimates Colinization for the colard people of the United States," Gould wrote in his diary, a policy that he believed must be firmly resisted, for his people were "born under the Flag of the Union" and would never "know no other." The policy of shipping freed slaves to colonies beyond the bounds of the United States had offended African Americans before the war. Now, having fought and died for the Union, such a vision constituted a yet graver affront, for not only had they been born in the United States for generations, they had also fought mightily for the nation's endurance.[23]

In contrast to Lincoln's black mourners, only a small portion of white mourners criticized Andrew Johnson's leadership in the immediate aftermath of the assassination, and the skepticism they displayed was mild at best. "Will he be equal to its responsibilities & duties?" Anna Ferris wondered. "Every body asks the question & none can answer." An Iowa soldier didn't trust Johnson to deal justly with the nation's traitors. "I had rather have seen Lincoln finish them than any man in the world," he wrote home. Some reserved their chagrin mostly for the commonly held notions that the new president's wife had taught him to read (not true) and that he had been drunk at Lincoln's second inauguration (possibly true). "Andrew Johnson, the *drunken* boasting plebian is President of the United States," scoffed a Washington woman.[24]

Much more commonly, white mourners who consoled themselves that God had taken Lincoln away because of his kind disposition felt sure that Andrew Johnson was the better man for the task of reconstructing the nation. In marked contrast to African Americans, these mourners looked to the future with confidence. On the day Lincoln died, Washington telegrapher David Homer Bates wrote in his diary with great sorrow for the beloved president, with whom he had conversed nearly every day for the past four years. But Bates at once conceded that Lincoln's lenience "may have given the rebels courage & power & at some future time caused another rebellion," a fate he was convinced would be avoided under Johnson's rule. James Ward, one of a group of white ministers who met with the new president two days after Lincoln's death, found himself "most favorably impressed," sure that the terrible calamity of the assassination would be overtaken by good. Such convictions followed not only from ideas about Lincoln's lenience but also from Johnson's own early affirmations of draconian policies toward the defeated enemy (like the speech before the Indiana delegation that made Confederate Kate Cumming so uneasy), coupled with his swift repudiation of the overly indulgent Sherman-Johnston negotiations.[25]

Where black mourners approached the new executive with caution, most bereaved whites exhibited full trust, envisioning Johnson as "a sterner man," a "more radical man," a man of "*less yielding* nature" than Lincoln. He would "give traitors their deserts, a stout rope and a clear swing" and even reward the Copperheads with "a Hemp Nectie," proclaimed Union soldier John Burrud. Georgia Treadway enthused that he would "put on no *silk gloves*," for the word *amnesty* wasn't even "in Johnsons *dictionary*." Even the most radical white abolitionists trusted the new president at the outset, including the otherwise farsighted Lydia Maria Child, who thought that Lincoln's departure from earth was "necessary for the completion of the great work." Never before, she gushed to fellow abolitionist John Greenleaf Whittier, had she known the "finger of God" to be "so plainly visible." Whittier couldn't agree more, since beloved President Lincoln would no doubt have gone too far "to smooth the way of defeated rebellion back to allegiance." When Wendell Phillips declared that God had orchestrated Lincoln's death at the exact moment "when his star touched its zenith," he explained that the moment of death was also the moment in which "the nation needed a sterner hand."[26]

Andrew Johnson's roots as a poor white southerner at least in part led black and white mourners to their divergent conclusions. Lincoln's black mourners, recall, knew that impoverished Confederates (just the same as their better-off compatriots) believed that black people were "made to be slaves," as one journalist put it, and could not, wrote another, be "emancipated from negro-hate." The same could be said, moreover, of many of the South's white Unionists, for even if they were not Confederates, they were still white. A soldier with the Twenty-Seventh U.S. Colored Troops hence wrote with trepidation that President Johnson might well pardon the "prejudiced loyal white man of the South."[27]

By contrast, Johnson's initially harsh pronouncements struck Lincoln's white mourners as fully in keeping with his lowly family origins, and led them to the opposite conclusion. "We plebeins, the majority of the U.S. have great confidence in your ability and sympathy," a Philadelphia man wrote to the new president, since "you were once one of us who toil." At the other end of the class spectrum, Boston Brahmin Edward Everett Hale took heart that Johnson despised the southern aristocracy as could only "a poor white, from the ranks." Lydia Maria Child likewise believed that Johnson's background would work to bring southern poor whites over to the side of the Yankees who were so eager to reform the war-torn region. Karl Marx himself agreed, writing to Friedrich Engels that the murder of Lincoln was the "greatest piece of folly" for Confederates, since Johnson "as a former poor white has a deadly hatred of the oligarchy." If that kind of optimism was understandable in light of Johnson's early assertions, his dealings with African Americans in the weeks immediately following the assassination made clear that his dislike for southern oligarchs was over-ruled by his virulent racism. Indeed, on the all-important question of black suffrage, Johnson would continually read the U.S. Constitution through the lens of white supremacy, professing that the federal government had no power to implement such a policy.[28]

Divergent experiences down south also occasioned a divide between Lincoln's more sanguine white mourners and his more distrustful black mourners. To begin with, some white Union soldiers found themselves moved by the disastrous conditions of ruined rebeldom. Ebenezer Gilpin had once entertained thoughts of avenging Lincoln's murder ("I'm in for making them suffer," he wrote in his diary), but on his way back to Iowa he suddenly felt sorry for the homeless and hungry enemy veterans he en-countered in Georgia. Gilpin, and others like him, were counting on those conditions to make the Confederates compliant, imagining that they would soon embrace the laws of the United States in letter and spirit alike. North-ern white soldiers who struck up conversations with their defeated foes also felt encouraged to exchange their earlier feelings of vengeance for mercy. Confederate officers in Virginia confessed that they were "ready to become good citizens again," one Yankee wrote to his wife, and even the "very ultra Rebels" would "submit gracefully" for the good of the nation. In North Carolina, Confederates told the white northern soldiers trekking through the South on their way home that they were "completely whipped" and glad for peace. Another northern soldier heard from two of Lee's paroled men, heading home to Florida, that they were glad the war was over and "hoped that we would forget the past."[29]

White mourners who wanted to treat the Confederates gently drew on religious convictions about mercy. Ohio soldier Chauncey Welton had expressed intense anguish at the assassination yet advocated pardons for Confederates from the lowest rank to the highest, since he felt sure that all former rebels would embrace the victorious Union. In the name of God and Christ, Welton would not "eaven disfranchise a single man," he wrote in a soliloquy of reconciliation, for generosity would both exemplify the true principles of the Union and further "conciliate the animosity of the two sections." Welton wrote all of this just after Easter Sunday, during which northern ministers confusingly maintained that Lincoln's own kindness— the very fault for which God had ended his reign on earth—should serve as a model for the treatment of the guilty enemies.[30]

At the same time, however, other soldiers, both black and white, along with freedpeople and northern missionaries in the South, found their former battlefield enemies a threatening presence after the assassination. On Easter Sunday in Richmond, a Union soldier saw men from Lee's army returning home, "as bold and defiant as though they were lord of all," giving their conquerors withering looks and pushing them in the street. As Lincoln's funeral train set off from Washington, a missionary among the freedpeople in Virginia worried about the large numbers of rebels out and about. "We have been obliged to suspend night-school for a few days till the proper guard can be established," she wrote. As the funeral train made its way across the country, such apprehensions continued. A white Union officer with a black regiment thought the rebels were "not subdued and humbled as they ought to be," and as the city of Portsmouth, Virginia, filled up with returning men in gray, it became dangerous to go out at night. In Natchez, Mississippi, the freedpeople and their northern allies were subject to the lethal enmity of local whites, and a teacher in Richmond feared that "if Mr. Lincoln was not safe who is?"[31]

The challenge was how to welcome Confederates into a nation rebuilding amid the ashes of racial slavery. The reformer Martha Coffin Wright thought she had a solution. Deeply dissatisfied with President Johnson just a month after Lincoln's death, Wright condemned the "fatal policy of conciliation." She was also among the few white mourners who disputed the innocence of the white southern masses, since plenty of "subordinates" were "as guilty as the chiefs," she asserted. Wright feared reconciliation with the rebels, invoking the former slave and leader of the Haitian Revolution, in hopes that "a Toussaint will be ready when the right time comes, as come it must." Few stronger articulations of racial equality could be found in the personal writings of white mourners, yet Wright also expressed mercy in two ways. First, she was relieved that John Wilkes Booth had been killed rather than having to suffer as a prisoner; second, she found herself moved by a "genuine Christian sentiment" of forgiveness when she read a sermon delivered by the Unitarian minister Octavius Frothingham. Frothingham had spoken of the "horrible and fiendish" murder of Lincoln to be sure, but he also waxed eloquent about tears washing away vengeance and softened hearts replacing bloodthirsty rage. Like many, Frothingham also looked to the slain president's temperament for guidance. Lincoln had been "gentle, kind, forgiving," a "reconciler" and a "forgetter," and reverence for him should dictate charity. Here, once again, came the paradox of Lincoln's presumed lenience as either the reason God had taken him away or as the example of how the victors should treat the vanquished. Martha Wright's solution was to implement political consequences first, and mercy second. First the rebels must be deprived of political power. Then their conquerors could forgive them.[32]

WHILE UNION SUPPORTERS COMPARED THEIR new president to the man they mourned, they also considered what they would like done to the president of the defeated rebels. Jefferson Davis stood first in line in the minds of mourners who blamed Confederate leaders for both the war and the assassination. With the fall of the capital in early April, Davis had fled Richmond, moving south and west in hopes of continuing combat: first to Danville and Greensboro by railroad, next by horse and wagon to

Charlotte, where he arrived on the day of Lincoln's funeral in Washington. Soon Davis's movements shifted toward escape. Because he was a suspect in the conspiracy leading to the assassination, the Union army was on his trail, with President Johnson offering a reward of one hundred thousand dollars for his capture. Davis had not entirely given up the Confederate cause when he reached Abbeville, South Carolina, in early May, even if his military commanders had. With the enemy army close behind, Davis and a small entourage crossed into Georgia and soon met up with his wife, Varina, and their children. On May 10, 1865, in the town of Irwinsville, regiments from Michigan and Wisconsin finally caught up with the fugitives.

Two-inch headlines, telegraph dispatches, and the cries of newsboys spread word north and west, and Yankees celebrated with bells, cannons, and fireworks—the joyous kind that hadn't been heard since Lee's surrender—even as the festivities "*mingled* with sorrow when we think of our *own* loved President," as one mourner wrote in her diary. Another piece of the story meanwhile took on a life of its own. With Union cavalry closing in, Davis had attempted to disguise himself in an effort to dupe the search party coming into camp. Donning cloak and shawl he had feigned an innocent amble toward a nearby stream, as if to fill the bucket slung over his arm. Union general James Harrison Wilson, commanding the cavalry forces, admitted in a personal communication that Varina Davis had exclaimed something along the lines of, "Oh! do let us pass with our poor old mother who is so frightened and fears to be killed," before her husband's boots gave him away. The northern press expanded on this information, spinning a tale of the Confederate president dressed in petticoats, hoopskirt, and bonnet, with his army footgear peeking out below. Just as Sarah Browne recorded that Davis had been caught "disguised in his wife's clothing underneath which he showed his own boots!!" so too did many Union supporters seize on the narrative of the emasculation of the southern aristocracy. It was ridiculous. It was ludicrous. Women tut-tutted that Jefferson Davis had disgraced their garments. For Edgar Dinsmore of the Fifty-Fourth Massachusetts, the "fall of King Jeff" was utterly comical. Just as "a southerner always relys on the women," Dinsmore wrote, Davis had left "Mrs. Southerner" to "face the music." Even more gleefully, Ellis Hughes of Maryland crowed into his journal, "*Jeff* was a *woman*!!!" mocking "chivalry in petticoats & frocks!" Cartoonists put their talents to work,

FINALE of the "JEFF DAVIS DIE-NASTY."
"Last Scene of all, that ends this strange eventful History."

Jefferson Davis, dressed in hoopskirt and military boots, hangs above an open grave. This 1865 cartoon lithograph, entitled "Freedom's Immortal Triumph!" and "Finale of the 'Jeff Davis Die-Nasty,'" shows a glowering sour apple tree upon which nooses await "Confederate Mourners," with Robert E. Lee first in line and John Wilkes Booth bringing up the rear. The ground is littered with broken artillery, skulls, and copperhead snakes, while the figures of Liberty and Justice hover above. A man breaking the chains of slavery stands between a grieving soldier and sailor, and angels escort President Lincoln to heaven. *LC-USZ62-88772, Prints and Photographs Division, Library of Congress.*

and shopkeepers placed caricatures in their windows for brisk sales. Poetry and sheet music soon followed.[33]

Levity aside, there remained the matter of Jefferson Davis's fate. "Shall not his life atone (however poorly) for Abraham Lincoln's?" asked one mourner. The death of Davis, thought another, would "in a small measure compensate us for the loss of our beloved President." Edgar Dinsmore hoped to see him hanged—"fitted with a hempen cravat," as he phrased it, "cut in the latest fashion." Drawing on a verse from the song "John Brown's Body" (*Hang Jeff Davis to a sour apple tree*), runaway slave William Gould hoped the apple tree would be "all ready." The song from which Gould repeated these lyrics was enormously popular with Union soldiers; all embraced the message of fighting and marching onward, while the antislavery

In his diary on May 15, 1865, Maryland professor Ellis Hughes drew a picture of Jefferson Davis in a dress. "*Jeff* was a *woman*!!!" Hughes wrote, followed by the words, "playing Nancy & Sally, or the French Woman / feminizing / chivalry in petticoats & frocks! / crinolining & Horses laughed at him! The last Ditch found!" The first line may refer to Nancy Hanks Lincoln and Sally Bush Lincoln, the president's mother and stepmother, with Nancy also a popular epithet for an effeminate man. References to chivalry, petti-coats, and crinoline were ubiquitous in the mocking imagery and popular songs that followed Davis's capture at Irwinsville, Georgia, on May 10, 1865.
Ellis Hughes diary, May 15, 1865, Hughes-Gray Family Papers, David M. Rubenstein Rare Book and Manuscript Library, Duke University.

men among them reveled in portraying the executed white leader of the failed 1859 slave uprising as inspiring them from his grave. Abolitionist mourners made the same claims for President Lincoln: slavery had caused his death, and his death would inspire black equality. The Confederate president, by contrast, should be hanged as a traitor, and an effeminate one at that. Fourteen-year-old Sarah Putnam wanted Davis not only executed but also, she wrote in her diary, "roasted, starved, burnt, and skinned." Ab-olitionist Lydia Maria Child, who opposed capital punishment, decided that as long as execution was legal, Davis should suffer that way, or else "no other man in the country ever ought to be hung."[34]

Unless, of course, hanging would make Jefferson Davis a martyred hero equal to John Brown and Abraham Lincoln. From Venice, U.S. consul William Dean Howells reasoned that he didn't want "the force of Davis's capture in his wife's clothes, taken away by the tragedy of his execution." In London, U.S. consul Charles Francis Adams found his Confederate-leaning British friends "too anxious about the fate of *poor* Jefferson Davis!" At receptions and garden parties, Adams heard endless consternation over the suggestion that Davis had been part of the assassination conspiracy, leading Adams to worry that the death penalty would only martyr him. A better solution, one Union soldier reckoned, would be for Davis to commit suicide.[35]

Though plenty of Confederates were fed up with their president by war's end, neither the gallows nor suicide proved necessary to turn Davis into a martyr, for his imprisonment—he was even shackled in irons for a few days—readily did so. In South Carolina, Emma LeConte had been studying her German lessons when her father came in to impart news of the capture. In despair, she laid her head on the table, thinking that the only hope now was either a foreign war or a guerrilla war. Or maybe hope lay in another war with the Yankees in years to come, she wrote in her diary, to "renew the struggle and throw off the hateful yoke." LeConte was not alone in her imagined scenario. If Lincoln's white mourners thought Confederates would return to the nation as willing patriots, they very soon found themselves gravely mistaken.[36]

AS MAY DREW TO A close, it was time for a public display of Union glory. On Tuesday and Wednesday, May 23 and 24, three weeks after Lincoln's burial in Illinois, visitors again poured into the capital, filling hotels and sleeping in horsecars, this time to watch soldiers march in the Grand Review in celebration of their victorious armies. The event's very name implied the process of looking back in appraisal, but the idea of a review, especially a grand one, also signaled a shining future. Despite the assassination of Abraham Lincoln, and however undefined that future remained, the capital would witness a magnificent performance.[37]

The weather was splendid. On a viewing stand in front of the White

House stood President Andrew Johnson, surrounded by cabinet members and military men. With a long view from the Capitol dome, Commissioner of Public Buildings Benjamin Brown French could see "troops by the thousands in every direction," with Pennsylvania and Maryland Avenues entirely filled. Up close, it was imposing in a different way. From any one spot, it might take six hours for all the troops to pass by. Walt Whitman described it to his mother as soldiers "just marching steady all day long for two days, without intermission, one regiment after another, real war-worn *soldiers,* that have been marching & fighting for years," including "great battalions of blacks, with axes & shovels & pick axes." The black men Whitman saw were not soldiers but laborers. The regiments of the U.S. Colored Troops were encamped too far from Washington to return for the affair, but former slaves in the capital joined the march spontaneously, and on the first day, the band played "John Brown's Body." Observers both black and white also noticed the tattered regimental flags, their broken staffs and ragged fringes testifying to bravery on the battlefield.[38]

Again came the sense of participation in history. Commissioner French felt sure that future generations would never see such a sight. Navy mathematician Simon Newcomb thought it the "greatest military display of the Western Hemisphere," and the minister James Ward believed it the greatest show "on this continent, if not in the world." Spectators choked up at the thought of the men returning home and choked up again at the thought of those who would never come back from the war. Secretary of the Navy Gideon Welles found it a "magnificent and imposing spectacle," yet couldn't help thinking of Abraham Lincoln's absence—indeed, "All felt this," he wrote in his diary. As a Maine volunteer told his sweetheart, the only note of sadness came in the wish that the beloved Lincoln "should have lived to see this." Or as one onlooker recorded, "It was a strange feeling to be so intensely happy and triumphant, and yet to feel like crying."[39]

The marchers were General George Meade's men from the eastern Army of the Potomac (on Tuesday) and General Sherman's men from the western Army of the Tennessee and Army of Georgia (on Wednesday). Some among the troops marveled too. As officer Stephen Weld of the Fifty-Sixth Massachusetts passed the Capitol, he sensed the Statue of Freedom atop the dome "looking down on us with triumph." Others had a rougher time. The Thirty-Sixth Wisconsin marched twenty miles to Washington and back in one day, which Guy Taylor thought was a "perlite way to kill" the soldiers left in the Union army. Speaking of going home, that's all the men wanted to do, rather than being led around like "wild beasts for a mear show." He was not, Taylor assured his wife, alone in his sentiments, for it was the "talk ov evry soldier that I have talked to." Rufus Mead, a Connecticut volunteer whose regiment wasn't taking part, went over to Pennsylvania Avenue to catch a glimpse but didn't stay long. "We are tired & sick of Reviews already & never wish to see another as long as we live," he confided to his diary.[40]

Confederates expressed discontent with the Grand Review for entirely different reasons. "What do you think I want to see all them devilish yankees for," a Virginia man snapped to his wife when she asked if he would attend. "I can see more than I want to see at home!" Magnificent it may have been, but plenty of the defeated had no intention of joining the patriotism on display, either then or any time soon—or ever. The nation that emerged victorious in the war was not their own, and justice for the vanquished seemed unlikely unless they could find a way to bring the past with them into the future. Meanwhile, even for those who shared in the glory of victory, the future remained unsettled and uncertain, and for African Americans and their more radical white allies, the fruits of that victory were already beginning to seem elusive.[41]

Relics

AS THE VICTORS-TURNED-MOURNERS FORGED AHEAD, they also looked back, collecting Lincoln memorabilia from the first instant. By gathering and preserving relics, the bereaved sought confirmation of the cataclysmic event, wrote themselves into the history they had witnessed, and enshrined the past for the future.

Images of the president were the most ubiquitous commodity, ranging from twenty-cent postcards sold on the street to medals and photographic portraits sold in shops to custom-ordered engravings. Lincoln was pictured alongside the First Lady, his son Tad, Andrew Johnson, and George Washington. Perhaps surprisingly, images of the assassin also went on sale, and while Confederates collected Booth memorabilia to honor their hero, mourners snapped them up too, as part of the preservation of history. To the same end, they collected copies of Lincoln's speeches, early biographies of the president, funeral sermons, and memorial books that gathered together the Emancipation Proclamation, the Gettysburg Address, and the second inaugural. A *Memorial Record of the Nation's Tribute to Abraham Lincoln,* published in 1865, included both of his inaugural addresses, accounts of his "last day on earth" and the "dying scene," transcriptions of sermons and prayers delivered at services along the route of the funeral train, and national and international tributes.[1]

Anna Lowell, who wrote privately about the assassination a good deal longer than most, continued to collect mementos far past the first rush. Among these were multiple copies of a memorial booklet that she planned to give away as presents—but first she read the compendium from cover to cover, filled with "renewed veneration & admiration & love." Only in late June did Lowell finally dispose of the mourning drapery with which she had decorated her home, offering it to a poorer neighbor in need of fabric.[2]

Scrapbook-making had become an ever more popular activity during the Civil War, and tributes to the slain chief often served as the final chapter of Union volumes. Whether the handiwork of African Americans in the South or white farmers or well-to-do women in the North, these were often little more than collections of newspaper clippings. A few compilers put in greater effort, like the New Yorker who walked miles along the city's thoroughfares in the days after the assassination, drawing pictures of the banners he saw, thereby preserving sentiments about loss, vengeance, and forgiveness. Candace Carrington of Providence, Rhode Island, also devoted a good deal of time to creating a personal memorial. On April 15, she commenced a scrapbook devoted solely to the assassination, snipping and pasting articles from national and local papers that included coverage of the crime, mourning rituals, and the funeral, along with related poems, drawings, and musical compositions. Within two weeks, she began a second volume, this one home to a fifty-page section entitled "Round the World," with coverage from Canada, South America, Europe, Russia, and Africa. (Carrington would give the set, in elegant red bindings, to her son on his nineteenth birthday, in 1871.)[3]

Artifacts also felt precious, and collection began on the night of April 14, at Ford's Theatre. A government clerk who encountered the crowds on Tenth Street made his way into the playhouse while everyone else was exiting, climbed up to the presidential box, and pocketed Lincoln's discarded bloody collar. A War Department employee who accompanied the president's body across the street to Petersen House swiped a blood-soaked towel. The theater itself, closed in the immediate aftermath, became something of a pilgrimage site. Marian Hooper and Annette Rogers, in town from New England for the Grand Review, made their way around back to study the spot where Booth had mounted his horse to escape, and struck up a conversation with a resident of the alley, a black woman who told them she had seen the assassin arrive and depart on the night of the crime. When Catherine Lansing traveled from Albany for the Grand Review, she also toured the White House and the Capitol, attended part of the conspirators' trial, and stopped to look at Ford's from the outside, a "very *very* crestfallen experience," she wrote. James Moore, a white doctor whose black regiment had marched at the head of Lincoln's funeral procession in Washington, tucked into an envelope a scrap of the crape tied to his sword and made his way to the theater and Petersen House, places that he knew would become—indeed had already become—historic.[4]

Petersen's was open for business, and Marian Hooper went there too, peering into the tiny room where Lincoln had died, taking in the sight of the blood-soaked pillow, more than six weeks later "left just as it was on that night," she wrote to a friend. Heartbreaking as it felt, there were two reasons she wanted to survey the frozen scene. First, it was "an historical fact." Second, it made everything—that even now still seemed unbelievable—"so vivid."[5]

10

Justice

THE WORD *REBELLION* IN PRESIDENT Andrew Johnson's amnesty proclamation rankled Rodney Dorman. Whether or not the new president pardoned Confederates, he was now "surpassing the demons of Hell in wickedness" just by saying that white southerners had ever been *in rebellion*. As a lawyer, Dorman firmly believed that the Confederacy had acted constitutionally, since "the people alone," he wrote in his diary, "have a right to revolutionize & change their government." In Dorman's reading, it was the Yankees who were the rebels and who deserved death for their traitorous violations of the nation's principles. "A thousand hangings" for every Union official couldn't vindicate all their crimes, and yet, he spluttered, they pronounced Confederates guilty of treason. With each stroke of Dorman's pen, *Lincon,* the unfortunately recovering William Seward, Andrew Johnson, the Freedmen's Bureau agents, the freedpeople, and of course the abolitionists became "damned fools & asses," "sharks & harpies," "ninnyhammers," "blaspheming, hypocritical priests," "craven hearted knaves," and "contemptible pukes & cowards." When Dorman compared the U.S. marshal in Jacksonville to a dog, he apologized to dogs.[1]

As for Confederates swearing loyalty to the United States, that was nothing but "flummery" and "trash." In mid-May, Union general B. C. Tilghman had come to Jacksonville to announce that Confederates who wished to conduct business would have to take the oath of allegiance, and now Dorman despaired as he observed his compatriots obeying, even if it was only out of fear of starvation or a way to get back their confiscated property. On that note, the fact that the return of property didn't include slaves struck Dorman as one of the greatest injustices of all. Jacksonville was crowded with African Americans that spring and summer, many of them refugees who had made their way to the city, and in Dorman's view, the U.S. government had stolen them from their masters. The way he saw it, Yankees had forced enslaved men into the Union army in the first place, and now the agents of the federal Freedmen's Bureau, along with the northern missionaries and "other theives," were acting as fanatical "inciters of insurrection," making submissive black people into copies of their horrific Yankee selves. Education was a major culprit, as the northerners made ignorant black people "still more ignorant," more "insolent, wicked & depraved," just like themselves. "What worse than the fiends of Hell, these Yankees, & their governments," Dorman wrote with anguish, remaining silent about the white-on-black violence taking place in the city around him.[2]

Still intensely galling to Dorman were the occupying black men in uniform, now the "worst, most criminal" of all. William Johnson, with the Third U.S. Colored Troops, felt "great changes" in the making, he wrote from Jacksonville in June, even as he saw the local Confederates "die very hard at the idea of having black troops to guard them." Accordingly, Dorman raged into his diary over those *great changes*. General Tilghman had announced that Jacksonville's black population could go to work for their former masters for wages—a clear recipe for failure, Dorman believed, since the natural inclination of black people was to "enjoy themselves without labor or care." In freedom, as opposed to slavery, they would have to "labor harder & get less," he reckoned, and would only find "less comfort & enjoyment." When Dorman wrote fervently of his wish to end "tyranny & oppression of all kinds," he remained resolutely blind to any dimension of injustice in the southern institution of racial slavery.[3]

Living in temporary quarters beyond the destroyed center of the city, his precious law books gone, his house and personal property burned, Rodney Dorman poured the humiliation of Confederate defeat into the pages of his companionate journal. One June day, he took a walk, tramping seventeen miles into the countryside, taking in the torn-up and burned-out homes of the white people who had once lived there. "All their negroes, nearly every head of their cattle, all their horses & hogs were gone," he wrote, slaves and farm animals all the same to him. If this was peace, he fumed, then "war, with all its horrors, is preferable," for war would always be preferable to black freedom. In any case, the reconstructed nation would never know anything but a "one sided treacherous peace," a peace that was "no better than war." Even the surrender of Kirby Smith's forces west of the Mississippi at the end of May made no difference. "Now, as the war is over, as they pretend," he wrote, "the war has but just commenced."[4]

FOR ALBERT BROWNE, THE WAR was over and done with, and it was time to see that justice came to pass. To that end, he wanted to "disfranchise *forever*" everyone who had ever participated in the rebellion. "Allow them no political privileges, no ballot," unless there was definitive proof that a person had been "unwillingly dragged in," he wrote home. In Albert's calculus, the highest Confederate authorities should be hanged, the ones beneath them forever expatriated, and the next rung down forever barred from holding office. Then all property should be confiscated from those who were "at all active and earnest in rebellion, *male and female.*" African Americans, the only truly loyal southerners, should be citizens of the postwar nation, and black men should be voters, or at least all who could read and write (and, for that matter, white men should also have to prove literacy in order to vote). "A ballot now is as useful as a bullet was six weeks since," he wrote that spring. "Let us fire ballots at these secessionists."[5]

As for the freedpeople, Albert Browne found them "a wonder to all thoughtful minds." As slaves, they had "supported a corrupt, proud, lazy, wicked aristocracy" and so would have no trouble supporting themselves in freedom, once given access to education, land, citizenship, and suffrage. Albert envisioned independent cultivation on allotments of twenty or forty acres per family, with two years of economic assistance to cover tools and seeds, or as he once proclaimed to Sarah and the children, he wanted the freedpeople, led by armed black soldiers, to "*demand of their former masters 2/3 of the produce of the soil.*"[6]

For all his revolutionary zeal, Albert Browne also exhibited common strains of northern racism, fully on display in his letters. With education and land, the freedpeople would show the world that "human nature, even under a black skin, and repulsive features is still human nature, and capable of progressing in Knowledge and goodness," he wrote. All men were lazy, Albert believed, though "the negro man emphatically so." Although Albert didn't "fancy the negro," as did some of his friends, he would "depend and uphold him as I would all the oppressed," he boasted, explaining, "It is my nature, I can't help it." Another time he told Sarah, "I dont love 'niggers as niggers' but I support their rights as men, or loyal citizens." Sarah expressed similar racist assumptions, if in milder terms. During the family's 1864 sojourn in Jacksonville, the Brownes had spent time among the U.S. Colored Troops, at one point attending a service with the "earnest men" of a regiment organized in Baltimore. "Almost all were slaves in Maryland!" she marveled. "What gifted seer a few years ago could have predicted this event!" Giving away the limits of her abolitionism, she professed amazement at the "black but brave men"—notice the *but*—"armed & equipped to fight the battles of Freedom." Now, at war's end, she filled with hope. Toward the end of May, on a beautiful day in Salem, Sarah breakfasted with her son Albert Jr., discussing current events and the "dear, sweet heavenly Peace which is again to bless our land." Her heart felt light, as she saw God's hand in the world around her.[7]

IMMEDIATELY FOLLOWING THE assassination, questions of justice preoccupied Lincoln's allies and antagonists alike. For mourners, this encompassed not only the proper punishment for the assassin's conspirators but also the price to be paid for the bloody rebellion born of slavery and—for the more radical among them—the redress to be paid to African Americans for generations of slavery, followed by their patriotism and bravery during the war. For Lincoln's defeated antagonists, on the other hand, justice meant the right to shape the reunited nation—in which legal slavery seemed no longer to exist—to their own satisfaction.

When Lincoln died, his mourners likened him to George Washington, Moses, and Jesus, and the slain president's near-instantaneous elevation was nowhere more apparent than in black mourners' reflections on the fate of emancipation, equality, and political empowerment. Before Lincoln's death, black and white abolitionists and the radical Republicans in Congress had criticized the president's wartime plans for reconstruction precisely because those plans left power in the hands of white southerners and relegated decisions about black suffrage to the individual states. Then came the April 11 speech from the White House balcony, in which Lincoln mixed a conservative conciliation toward the Confederates with more radical ideas. On the one hand, that speech contained only the most meager hints at black citizenship. On the other, it contained enough radicalism that it prompted John Wilkes Booth to plot murder.

Four days later, Lincoln was dead, and that tentative if potentially radical speech was all his abolitionist mourners had to go on. Radical Republicans, who had once expressed quiet relief at Lincoln's demise owing to his seemingly lenient stance toward the Confederates, now followed the lead of African Americans. In response to the egregious actions of President Andrew Johnson, black mourners and their white friends martialed Lincoln's April 11 words as a forceful counterpoint to the alarming unfolding of events. That spring evening in Washington, Lincoln had acknowledged that some of his supporters found it "unsatisfactory" that the new state constitution of Louisiana did not extend the vote to black men. Deferentially, he had also stated his personal preference ("I would myself prefer") that suffrage be extended to two particular groups of African Americans: the "very intelligent" and those who had fought for the Union. If some form of black suffrage were not permitted, Lincoln stated, the "cup of liberty" held to the lips of former slaves would be dashed to the ground. Moreover, what was true for Louisiana should "apply generally to other States." All told, it wasn't a lot, but precisely because Lincoln was murdered and martyred, his black mourners and their white allies were free to extend those ideas however they saw fit in order to accomplish the goals of justice.[8]

Even in the face of President Johnson's dismissals, some of Lincoln's black mourners continued to express optimism over the ultimate fruits of Union victory, at least in their public pronouncements. Thomas Morris Chester, the war correspondent in Richmond, believed that the "inexorable logic of events" was "fast dissipating all ideas of slavery, all delusions of State rights, and all dreams of a Southern Confederacy." The editors of the *San Francisco Elevator* professed to look toward the nation's reconstruction and the advent of suffrage with confidence, and a reader wrote in to say that soon would come a movement to press Congress for "our right of franchise." The nation, a minister from Philadelphia wrote to the *Christian*

The last photograph of Abraham Lincoln, taken by Alexander Gardner in February 1865, shows the president's careworn face near war's end.
LC-USZ62-11896, Prints and Photographs Division, Library of Congress.

Recorder, had now "awakened to sympathy and humanity through her late Chief Magistrate, Abraham Lincoln, the champion of freedom."[9]

But alongside such hopes, African Americans voiced serious apprehensions. If they had articulated forebodings about the future of the nation from the moment Richmond fell, then their anxieties multiplied after Lincoln's assassination. Freedman and Union army chaplain Garland White wrote a personal letter to the recovering Secretary of State William Seward, asking him to be extra mindful of the Confederates or, as White called them, the "many enemies yet to be arested who must be watched with a vigolent eye." A reader likewise wrote to the *New Orleans Black Republican,* appalled to think that following the murder of "'our' noble President," Confederates would return home to the ballot box ("because they are white") while loyal African American soldiers possessed no such power ("because they are black").[10]

As black mourners cast Lincoln as a champion of freedom, his successor was rapidly turning out to be just the opposite. Ten days after the assassination, President Andrew Johnson addressed himself to the population he called "loyal southerners"—by which he meant white, not black, southerners— thinking largely of those outside the upper classes. Johnson first declared his intentions to mete out "justice toward the leaders," then made clear his wish to extend "amnesty, conciliation, clemency, and mercy" to the many thousands who had been "deceived or driven into this infernal rebellion," thereby echoing the idea that nonslaveholding whites had been duped and coerced into the war.[11]

A little more than a month later, just after the Grand Review in Washington, President Johnson issued his first pardon proclamation, the one that so frustrated Rodney Dorman by invoking the phrase *in rebellion.* It was May 29, a little over three weeks after Lincoln's burial and three days after the surrender of General Kirby Smith in the Trans-Mississippi Department made the end of the war that much more official. Congress would not be back in session until later in the year, and so the new president acted on his own. His proclamation decreed amnesty, including the restoration of all property except slaves, to "all persons who have, directly or indirectly, participated in the existing rebellion," on the condition of taking the oath of allegiance. Dorman may have cringed at Johnson's choice of words and chafed at the required oath, but the fact was, Johnson had just granted voting rights to the white men who had fought against the United States while leaving the black men who had fought for the Union without access to land or political rights.[12]

To be sure, the proclamation came with a lengthy list of exceptions, encompassing Confederate leaders both military and political, as well as economic stipulations intended to exclude the wealthiest planters. But any excluded individual had the right to apply for a personal pardon, and these the new president would grant liberally, including to property-holding women of the elite classes who wanted to protect their assets—a far cry from Albert Browne's dream of confiscating the property of all rebellious men and women. As the runaway slave William Gould wrote ominously in his shipboard diary, "We see that the Rebels are being pardon'd verry fast." Right away, the editors of the *San Francisco Elevator* worried that Confederate leaders would pay few or no consequences for secession and rebellion. The Union victors, they feared, would let most of them escape, and "after a few years they will be pardoned, and return and re-commence their treason anew." In his April 11 speech, President Lincoln had told his listeners that "we, the loyal people, differ among ourselves" as to the best plans for reconstructing the nation. Unlike President Johnson, however, Lincoln included African Americans among the *loyal people*.[13]

Andrew Johnson's late May pardon proclamation exacerbated the apprehensions of African Americans, its terms clearly disregarding the petitions they had brought before him when he assumed office. Now, after the proclamation, black spokesmen continued to bring their concerns to the new executive. Pointedly beckoning the ghost of Lincoln, they called Johnson their "best friend," the phrase so many had chosen to describe their relationship to the slain chief. A public meeting in Richmond yielded a June delegation reminding Johnson that black people alone had welcomed Lincoln to the fallen Confederate capital and that they alone among their city's residents had mourned his death. Now again, the petitioners called attention to white violence and repeated the imperative of black suffrage. A group of men from Louisville visited the White House in June to request a "Political Settlement," asking Johnson to retain martial law in the state of Kentucky, without which whites would continue to treat black residents "with four fold the Venom and Malignanty" as they had before surrender. The Richmonders likewise informed Johnson that the "negro laws" of Virginia, still on the books, gave license to the bitter Confederates who took "special pleasure in persecuting and oppressing us." A petition from nearly fifteen hundred "coloured Citizens" of South Carolina in late June named suffrage as the sole means of "protecting ourselves and our interest, against oppression." Patiently again, African Americans made clear that their men had enlisted to fight for the Union and "poured out their blood lavishly," and that their women on the home front had assisted the Union army. For his part, Johnson continued to brush them off, telling them impatiently not to "expect progress to be too rapid" or asserting that there were "a great many things we would all prefer to have different" in the immediate aftermath of the war.[14]

Pardons had already been going forward at a nice clip, at least for Confederates who had exiled themselves during the war. Charles Francis Adams, minister of the U.S. legation in London, was a moderate Republican from Massachusetts who performed his duties with Assistant Secretary Benjamin Moran, a Pennsylvania Democrat and militant Unionist. Stunned by Lincoln's death, Adams joined many of the president's mourners in naming slavery as the cause. "It was fitting that what began with perjury, fraud, and treachery should end in private assassination," Adams wrote in his diary, since that was only "the fruit of the seed that was sown in the slavery of the African race." Yet when it came to treatment of the Confederates, Adams was more interested in "rehabilitation" than punishment, for retribution should "extend only to a few" rather than "the many." Slavery had killed Lincoln, Adams believed, and the southern aristocracy alone was to blame.[15]

In his London office, Adams therefore dealt quite liberally with a steady stream of Confederates hoping to take the oath of allegiance in order to gain passports for their return to the United States. Even before they had gotten word of President Johnson's May 29 pardon proclamation, both Adams and Moran freely obliged their applicants, sympathetic to the stories they told. A Confederate army veteran, who explained himself as an "old Whig" carried along by "popular passion," now struck Adams as "moderate and reasonable." A Tennessean who had fought for the Confederacy before becoming a blockade runner in Britain also struck Adams as "moderate and reasonable." A Virginian who announced his secessionist status with all frankness got his way too; "having been fairly whipped he now yielded," Moran wrote in his diary. Adams and Moran also encountered a brother and sister from Mobile who claimed they had changed their minds since Union victory. The woman "shuddered at the oath," Moran recorded, "but finally took it, and I gave them both passports." Conversing with the captain of a Confederate ship, Moran was sure the man was "tired of secession and regrets ever having gone into it." There was also a drunk

Alabamian, once a rebel, "but being beaten has returned to his allegiance" and even professed sympathy "with Mrs. Lincoln in her loss." Adams and Moran either never asked their supplicants where they stood on policies toward the freedpeople among whom they would be living back at home or, if they did, they were satisfied with the answers. One petitioner had supported the rebellion "to protect his property," Adams wrote in his diary, adding, "Of course this was a plantation and slaves though he did not say so." The man promised to "go home and deport himself as an obedient citizen," and Adams issued him the requisite papers. Thus did men of the U.S. legation concern themselves with justice for white southerners rather than black southerners.[16]

Adams and Moran had an even easier time after the London consulate got word of President Johnson's May 29 proclamation. Two native Virginians who had emigrated to England, for instance, now struck Adams as suffering a "sacrifice of pride" merely by setting foot in the London office. All in all, Adams wanted the U.S. government to be "lenient and merciful" with the Confederates, who he believed had suffered enough in four years of terrible war. That was a very different view of justice than the one put forth by African Americans in their petitions to the president. To black men and their communities, the idea that white men who casually swore loyalty to the Union suffered a "sacrifice of pride" was not only irrelevant but dangerous, since by such actions the white men regained their political rights. "I saw no difficulty in the way of their restoration under the amnesty," Adams wrote in his diary after reviewing Johnson's proclamation. "My rule is to treat them all gently," he elaborated, even as he carried out his duty to "question them closely." Those interrogations, careful as they may have been, apparently did not include serious consideration of the petitioners' opinions on black freedom and citizenship.[17]

On the same day as the May 29 pardon proclamation came Johnson's policies for readmitting former rebellious states into the Union, further vindicating the decisions taking place at the London consulate. North Carolina would be the first, with a proclamation that called on white men professing loyalty to the United States to convene a state constitutional convention. African Americans remained excluded by a provision that deliberately limited the franchise to those who had been voters before secession, and by midsummer the same procedure was in place for Mississippi, Georgia,

Texas, Alabama, South Carolina, and Florida. All of this raised the hopes of some Confederates, like the Tennessean who wrote to tell the new president that he wanted to see "a *white* Mans Government in America." Thanking Johnson, he assured him that "the White People will sustain you."[18]

To page through the black *Christian Recorder* in the summer of 1865 was to learn just how much Lincoln's African American mourners tempered the optimism of Union victory with keen awareness of white southern determination to reverse emancipation. "*Slavery is not dead,*" wrote a man from Natchez in the face of tremendous white violence. Hadn't the federal government known that "enmity between the master and slave would be doubly deepened, and that they could not live together in harmony again?" In North Carolina, J. H. Payne of the Twenty-Seventh U.S. Colored Troops understood that "trouble and destitution, as well as hatred and revenge, await our poor people in these Southern States," making it feel as if they were "under slavery's cruel power still." The death of slavery, wrote another, was simply "a mistaken idea."[19]

As for Lincoln's white mourners, some moderates still could not quite envision President Johnson's actions as obstructing black freedom, even after the May 29 pardon proclamation. Union officer Henry Halleck believed that the rebels would return to the nation with no difficulty over the "Slave question," as long as northern radicals didn't make "extremist" demands. "The negroes know that they are *free,* and there is no power at the South that can *reenslave* them," he asserted in direct contradiction to black voices. Other moderates, though, found themselves vexed. No policy that "would please the South would agree with enlightened opinion in the North," Sidney Fisher wrote in his Philadelphia diary. Uneasy about black suffrage and the exercise of federal power alike, Fisher saw "no way out of these difficulties" that would be "consistent with the preservation of the Union & free government." Maine volunteer Abial Edwards, still in the army that summer, had fought against slavery yet did not believe black men should be voters until they became more accustomed to freedom. Soon, though, Edwards noticed something else: President Johnson quickly taking away "all we have gained in our years of toil & strife." Former Confederates with the rights of citizenship, Edwards now worried, would only rise up against the Union once again.[20]

More radical white mourners easily envisioned the gruesome portrait drawn by their black friends. For General Carl Schurz, the trouble lay in the fact that white southerners hadn't "abandoned their proslavery sentiments." Schurz worried that once the seceded states were back in the Union, "the status of the former slaves will be fixed in a way as near slavery as possible." To his wife, Schurz wrote that white southerners were "unquestionably thinking of subjecting the negroes to some kind of slavery again," following the withdrawal of Union troops. After Johnson's proclamation, Martha Coffin Wright likewise felt sure that slavery was "not abolished & never will be," unless there was no amnesty for any Confederate, with or without an oath of allegiance. As a white commander of black troops wrote home from New Orleans in early summer, "If Andy doesn't put his foot on slavery hard, they will try to start it again somehow."[21]

Here were the echoes of Frederick Douglass's prediction, made weeks before Johnson's pardon proclamation, which in turn echoed the fears of the freedpeople immediately upon Lincoln's assassination. "In what new skin will the old snake come forth?" Douglass had asked then. "Slavery is not abolished until the black man has the ballot," he asserted. The former Confederates "would not call it slavery," he warned, "but some other name." Indeed, the end of the year would bring the Black Codes, southern state laws designed to replicate the conditions of bondage in the absence of legal enslavement.[22]

THE FIRST OF JUNE BROUGHT yet another historic occasion, this one somber rather than grand. President Johnson appointed that Thursday to be a national day of humiliation and prayer for Abraham Lincoln. In the South, freedpeople paused yet again to try to make sense of the assassination in light of recent dismaying developments, while Confederates looked on with exasperation at the federal command to unite in prayer to request God's blessing. "I am sorry enough that Lincoln was assassinated," Eliza Andrews wrote in her Georgia diary, "but this public fast is a political scheme gotten up to throw reproach on the South, and I wouldn't keep it if I were ten times as sorry as I am." A Methodist clergyman in Kentucky scoffed at the directive, since he did "not think the assassination of Mr. Lincoln a national sin." In Richmond, Hattie Powell was delighted at her minister's solution. "My friends we have been ordered to meet here, by those in authority, for humiliation & prayer on account of the death of

Lincoln," the man told the handful of worshippers who showed up, before adding, "Having met, we will now be dismissed." As summer approached, Lincoln's foes hoped this episode would be the last in the drawn-out fuss over the Yankee martyr.[23]

Up north, meanwhile, mustering the required awe yet again proved an effort for some of Lincoln's mourners. Although it was indeed likely to be the last of the public ceremonies, Caroline White found the whole thing tiring, not to mention that it seemed "more like a festival" than a day of grief. Other mourners agreed that June 1 was all too much "a show & holiday" or just a poor imitation of the two-week funeral ceremonies. For their part, children enjoyed the time off. "No work to-day, it is fast day," wrote fifteen-year-old Alpheus Kenyon in Connecticut. "I have been swimming." After church in Newport, Rhode Island, sisters Kate and Carrie Hunter played croquet and went sailing for a "most glorious & *jolly* time." Grownups followed suit. Men played chess. Women played backgammon. Soldiers did nothing for a change, dreaming of home. Weariness with public performances did not, however, mean that people had stopped grieving. Anna Lowell didn't feel like facing the crowds in Boston, so she observed the day in her heart instead, "more truly," she believed, than those who showed up for the civic rituals. In Michigan, a soldier reflected on God's will and wisdom, writing in his diary that Lincoln "still lives within our hearts." For many the day was sacred, even if not everyone could put aside their responsibilities. "National Fast Day," another mourner recorded, along with the notation, "Tom & the man hauling logs to mill."[24]

For those willing to attend abolitionist-themed observances, the rituals were accompanied by reflections on the challenges ahead for the post-victory, post-assassination nation. In New York, Frederick Douglass offered a eulogy, painting a portrait of the slain president in all his complexity. "Abraham Lincoln, while unsurpassed in his devotion to the welfare of the white race," Douglass claimed, was also "the black man's President: the first to show any respect to their rights as men." In Massachusetts, Martha Anderson listened to her minister speak of the "real cause" of Lincoln's death, "*slavery*," advocating to "do justice to the blacks by giving them the ballot." Lucretia Hale was in the audience at Boston's mourning-draped Music Hall when Senator Charles Sumner made the same appeal, emphasizing, Hale related to her brother in her own words, that without black suffrage, "the slave power would rise again, and it would all have to be done over again."[25]

JUST AS AFRICAN AMERICANS AND their white allies looked to President Andrew Johnson with trepidation, invoking Abraham Lincoln to make sure he had not died in vain, the vanquished Confederates also looked to Johnson with dread, still hoping that rebel soldiers had not died in vain either. When a white preacher in North Carolina asked his listeners (echoing the words of Lincoln's second inaugural) to lay aside "all malice, and hatred, and wrath," the man recorded his parishioners' reaction in his diary: "Exception, I learn has been taken to it." For twenty-one-year-old Sarah Wadley in Louisiana, talk of reconstructing the nation made her livid —"How hateful are the words, yes hateful!" she wrote in her journal, for never would she call herself a citizen of the United States. Gloating Yankees were particularly hard to take. For Elizabeth Alsop, it was nearly unbearable to see them walking the streets of Fredericksburg, forcing men to take the oath of allegiance. Not only that, but now she had to live among free black people, which, as one Georgia man described to his wife, was as horrific as the sight of "the exulting & tyrannical Yankee."[26]

One mid-May night, Emma LeConte and her family took a walk, picking their way through the shattered walls and broken chimneys of the former mansions of Columbia, South Carolina. Only by the lack of moss and vines could they tell that the ruins were not ancient. Her family's home had been spared, but LeConte still had to endure the sight of white Union men fraternizing with black residents, not to mention Yankees standing right in front of her house, their blue uniforms filling her with "such horrid feelings" that she closed the front blinds and hid away in the back parlor. In Alexandria, Virginia, Anne Frobel likewise recoiled: "In a few years," the white Yankees had chillingly told her, "we will have a negro President."[27]

The victors, both black and white, invoked the violent language of slavery at war's end, speaking of "whipped and cowed" rebels and a "badly whipped" people (at the London consulate, Benjamin Moran accordingly described the southern petitioners as "whipped" and "beaten"). Confederates used the same language to describe themselves, like the homeward-bound soldiers who told their conquerors they were "completely whipped," and many now extended the metaphor. Just as four years earlier, secessionists had cast themselves as slaves of the North in their fevered appeals for disunion, in 1865 the defeated spoke of their own bondage and oppression. As Captain Henry Chambers had written in his diary the day after surrender, "Nature weeps over Liberty's death." On the home front back then, Caroline Thornton had referred to her compatriots as "a *subjugated people.*" These kinds of depictions multiplied as spring turned to summer. Recall the laments of Cornelia Spencer, wondering whether Confederate marriages would be legally recognized and describing her ransacked home without furniture or silverware, and "*flies* every where in doors," all without a word about the conditions of the enslaved. Spencer was far from alone in the imagery she invoked.[28]

For the vanquished to imagine themselves as slaves while simultaneously bemoaning the loss of their own human chattel (whom, like Rodney Dorman, they tended to call *servants*) no doubt struck freedpeople as absurd or at best ironic. Yet to the speakers it was neither. Rather than a careless metaphor, enslavement was precisely the point. For white people who believed that God had intended them to be masters, it was intolerable to live under the domination of others. To those who had so recently owned slaves themselves, it made perfect sense to invoke the condition of bondage, for nothing better captured their imagined post-surrender condition. Defeat, Kate Stone wrote in her Texas diary, served only to "rivet more firmly the chains that bind us." Another woman proclaimed that white southerners now lived in "bondage worse than slavery." Ellen House, a Tennessean in exile in Georgia, declared that the white people of the South were "slaves—to the vilest race that ever disgraced humanity," thereby casting Yankees, both white and black, together into a separate racial category. In an exemplary description of the daily dissemblance once required of enslaved people for the sake of survival, Edmund Ruffin (who also described the Yankees as a separate race) wrote that secessionists not only had to obey their conquerors, they had to do so "without sullenness or apparent dislike, & play their parts of obedient subjects & slaves to Yankee power with cheerfulness & smiling faces."[29]

Given such dire circumstances, Confederates resisted giving up the fight. From the moment of Lee's surrender, diehard rebels among the soldiers had vowed to wage war to the last. An army surgeon in Texas wrote to his wife, admitting that the thought of "Yankee Masters" and "Negro equality" made him want to "fight on a little longer." Some of the vanquished went to Europe, or made homes for themselves in Brazil or Cuba, where slavery still existed, and a few, like Edmund Ruffin, committed suicide. But most white southerners could not afford to leave the country, and few acted on suicidal fantasies. Instead, the vanquished tried to envision a time when the future would look more like the past.[30]

Retribution, many Confederates felt certain, would eventually be theirs. Among Edmund Ruffin's final thoughts before he killed himself was the hope that outrage would endure in his people long enough for payback. In South Carolina, Charles Hutson, for whom living permanently under Yankee rule with black freedom was out of the question, urged his countrymen to "bear our fate manfully & keep ever ready to renew the struggle, when the right moment comes" (Hutson soon departed for a sojourn in Paris). John Henderson, a North Carolina law student, looked ahead to "years and years" of the "most intense and bitter animosity," until one day ("May the time soon come!") when the Yankees would be "reduced to our condition." A soldier in Lee's army, making his way home through the wreckage of Richmond, reflected gloomily on the future, then reconsidered, for, he wrote in his diary, something told him that the war "was not all passed through in vain."[31]

Confederate women displayed equal or greater vehemence. Cloe Whittle dreamed of a "*second* war for independence"—which was, ironically, just what the Civil War had been for African Americans, excluded as they were from the nation's original revolutionary ideals. Baptist missionary Martha Crawford echoed and inverted Lincoln's 1858 speech in which he had claimed (paraphrasing Mark 3:25), "A house divided against itself cannot stand." In a letter home from China in the summer of 1865, Crawford wrote, "The two countries *cannot* continue as one." With that conviction, she felt sure her fellow rebels would "await our opportunity and try them again." Nor would Elizabeth Collier consent to considering the Confederacy part of the United States. "*Reconstruction!*": she underlined the word in her journal, capping it off with an indignant exclamation point—"how the very word galls." God may have decreed defeat for the moment, but her people were "bound to rise again." (Confederate men used that phrase too. "Sooner than submit to wholesale confiscation," one wrote, "the south will rise again.") To those mourning defeat, there was one key distinction between themselves and their former slaves: the slaves had been incited to insurrection by the Yankees, whereas white southerners would rise up to fight for freedom on their own.[32]

Envisioning a future white uprising, former Confederates rewrote the war's outcome and meaning to ensure that their cause was not lost. Recall the words of Kate Stone when contemplating the colossal casualties among her people: "The best and bravest of the South sacrificed—and for nothing," she had written in her diary. "Yes, worse than nothing." Reckoning with end-of-war desertion, the dwindling will of the soldiers, and war-weariness on the home front, white southerners nevertheless appropriated the sentiments that Robert E. Lee had put forth in his farewell address, swiftly crafting a story of a noble and honorable fight for independence. For Henry Berkeley, a private in Lee's army who was imprisoned at Fort Delaware, Confederates should always be proud of this part of their history. "We put up a bully fight, if we did go under," he wrote. Julia Watson, in exile in England, promised that if she ever returned to the United States, she would educate her children to "venerate the memory of those who fell so gloriously in the great strife for liberty." That was part of future justice too: reshaping the story so that all Confederates on the battlefield, both the survivors and the fallen, had fought gloriously after all.[33]

WAR, AS THE PRUSSIAN THEORIST Karl von Clausewitz famously stated, is politics by other means. Politics, as the eminent Civil War historian James McPherson has crisply put it, is war by other means. This was to be the battle from the moment of Lee's surrender: determined African Americans and white radicals who wanted what Frederick Douglass called an "abolition peace" against bitter Confederates who wanted their old world back. God had taken Lincoln away, his more radical mourners now came to believe, in order to alert the victors to the enduring intransigence of their vanquished enemies, most especially the rebel leaders and their elite followers, whom Union supporters had always held responsible for the war. Now these mourners wanted land, education, and voting rights for African Americans—*not* as vengeance for the assassination but rather to avenge secession and war. By ensuring the fruits of freedom, they wanted also to avenge the cause of the war: slavery, which they understood as well to be the root cause of Lincoln's assassination. The assassination had opened the eyes of these radicals, both black and white, to the necessity for revolutionary policies following Confederate defeat on the battlefield, because defeated Confederates who held political power could still win the war off the battlefield.[34]

Recall that African Americans had issued warnings of an unvanquished rebel spirit even before Lincoln was killed. This was Frederick Douglass's "fiercer and intenser hate than ever before." This was the call of the *New York Anglo-African* that "with the cessation of the war our anxieties begin." Soon after surrender, visions of subdued Confederates obediently rejoining the Union had shattered, as soldiers and other Union supporters down south witnessed the insubordination all around them. The murder of President Lincoln, coming fast on the heels of surrender, had not subdued the rebels in the least. And that made strikingly clear to Lincoln's mourners the absence of Confederate contrition in the face of defeat.[35]

Here again was God's providence. Frederick Douglass had always hoped the rebels would be punished for slavery as well as for treason. Speaking extemporaneously in Rochester's City Hall on the day Lincoln died, Douglass had surmised that the assassination was God's way of creating the circumstances necessary to provoke the harsh treatment that the enemy had all along deserved, God's way of warning the Union not to readmit into the nation the "spirit which gave birth to Booth." As the white Unitarian minister James Freeman Clarke told his congregants on Easter Sunday, "As Abraham Lincoln saved us, while living, from the open hostility and deadly blows of the slaveholders and secessionists, so, in dying, he may have saved us from their audacious craft, and their poisonous policy." On he went: "The revenge we shall take for the murder of Lincoln," he said, would be to deny power to the leaders of the rebellion, and to make voters of loyal southern African Americans. *Revenge.* Clarke had uttered that word, but he did not mean a mere settling of scores or a simple exchange of Lincoln's life for Confederate disempowerment. His language could not have been clearer. Without the assassination, the Union "might not have insisted on these conditions"—black suffrage and the disfranchisement of slaveholders, he meant. Thus had it been "necessary for Lincoln to die," Clarke explained, "to bring the nation to the point of mandating them." Here was the meaning of God's mysterious design.[36]

Politicians put forward the same message, bringing the argument about

Lincoln's lenience full circle. God had permitted the assassination because Lincoln was not the right man to reconstruct the nation. Lincoln was not the right man to reconstruct the nation because he would have treated the vanquished rebels with too much kindness. Lincoln's assassination at the hand of John Wilkes Booth, as inspired by the rebels and permitted by God, signaled to the victors that their fallen enemies had never intended to rejoin the post–Civil War nation willingly and had never intended willingly to participate in the destruction of slavery. On the day Lincoln died, the radical Republican George Julian wrote in his diary that the assassination eradicated "every vestige of humanitarian weakness" so that "justice shall be done and the righteous ends of the war made sure." Without the signal of Lincoln's death, he meant, Union treatment of the rebels would have been too forgiving. On the Sunday after Easter, the abolitionist Wendell Phillips told his listeners that land and ballots for loyal black men was the "lesson God teaches us in the blood of Lincoln," not as payback for the assassination, he made clear, but rather "to teach the nation in unmistakable terms, the terrible foe with which it has to deal." If Lincoln's mourners hoped to avenge slavery, secession, and the war that resulted, then the best plan was to ensure the political impotence of slaveholders, coupled with the political power of former slaves.[37]

Lincoln's mourners understood that slavery—and Lincoln's antislavery statements in particular—had caused both secession and the assassination. Now, in the political struggles that followed Union victory, the abolitionists among them wanted to complete the circle by seeking rights for African Americans and the abridgment of rights for Confederate leaders and elites. Lincoln needed to be "stricken down by the slaveholder's bullet," reflected Bronson Alcott, "to rouse the people to vigilance" in policing the actions of their now-vanquished enemies. On the brink of conciliation with Confederates, John Greenleaf Whittier wrote, the nation "needed one more terrible lesson." That lesson had come in the assassination, which would prevent the victors from treating the rebels too generously. Even a moderate like Republican Francis Lieber wanted complete exile, and for the same reason. "Drive the fiends from our soil," he advised, until the Confederates "offer themselves, re-revolutionized, back to the Union, freed from Slavery and assassins," those last two transgressions one and the same.[38]

For Lincoln's mourners, his assassination symbolized the unwillingness of the defeated to give in and give up. The enduring recalcitrance of Confederates forced mourners to transform the meaning of Lincoln's wartime moderation and diplomacy. No longer a model for postwar political strategy, the slain chief's kindly disposition now became, without question, the explanation for God's purpose in permitting his death at war's end. Then, paradoxically, with Lincoln gone, his mourners could cast their martyred leader as a political radical. Mourning for Lincoln, African Americans north and south, along with their white allies, wanted to ensure justice with the weapons of freedom, equality, and political power. Mourning the end of slavery and their failed nation, enraged Confederates displayed the greater thirst for vengeance, and Lincoln's successor took their side. In the end, revenge and its fruits came more readily, not to Lincoln's mourners, but to his enemies.

Peace

AS THE BATTLEFIELD FIGHTING CAME to an end, visions of a nation at peace tempered the grief of Lincoln's mourners yet could hardly assuage all anxieties. African Americans welcomed the end of the war, but some also stood at the ready. If the U.S. government favored the rights of Confederates over the rights of his people, asserted a soldier in the Third U.S. Colored Troops, stationed near Jacksonville, "*We will fight it out on this line* until to all be distributed an equal share." Other mourners expressed sorrow that President Lincoln would never witness the fruits of his victory. "It looks as though peace was near us," wrote a white Union soldier in Florida ten days after Lincoln died, "and what a happy people we should be if we only had our beloved President to help inaugurate its reign." Still others found relief and good cheer even while mourning. On the southern home front, even in the face of white violence, northern teachers and missionaries working among the freedpeople detected "renewed hope and energy" at the "prospect of Peace." In camp, white soldiers especially rejoiced. With the "smoke of Battle" gone, one man soothed himself with thoughts of the war's end, "so long dreamed of." Another, who had written of grief "too sad for utterance" now recorded his emotions at the dawning of peace: joy "too deep for utterance." White people on the home front rejoiced too. A

Pennsylvania farmer lamented that "poor old Abraham is gone," grateful nonetheless that the war was over, and a woman in Boston was happy just to be able to "talk about other things than wars and fightings." All spring and into the summer, relief mixed with lingering sorrow and newfound anxieties.[1]

Pardoning the Confederates who came to the London consulate, Assistant Secretary Benjamin Moran wrote in his diary, "Peace is what all want." Moran's superior, Charles Francis Adams, felt the same way, except that one thing troubled him: were it not for Lincoln's assassination, Adams mused to one of his sons, "we might have been on the road to an era of good feelings." Both men were wrong, for the defeated did not want peace, and it was not the assassination alone—far from it—that had ushered in ill will between victor and vanquished. Rather, the bitterness of the defeated was immeasurably compounded by their refusal to accept black freedom. In North Carolina, Elizabeth Collier knew her people could never embrace peace, she wrote in her diary, with the "desecrators of our homes & the murderers of our Fathers, Brothers & Sons—*Never.*" In South Carolina, Emma LeConte agreed with Rodney Dorman. "I used to dream about peace—to pray for it," she wrote in her journal, "but this is worse than war," and when she contemplated the future, she could write only, "Oh God! it is too horrible."[2]

Lincoln's last reflections on peace had come in his White House speech on April 11. Confederate surrender, he said then, offered "hope of a righteous and speedy peace whose joyous expression can not be restrained." But the two adjectives Lincoln invoked, *righteous* and *speedy,* would not sit easily together. For peace to be righteous, it had to reach beyond the formal laying down of arms to encompass true freedom and equality.[3]

Lincoln had also spoken of peace in his second inaugural on March 4, 1865. "Fondly do we hope—fervently do we pray," he told his listeners that day, "that this mighty scourge of war may speedily pass away." Yet Lincoln had followed those words with the warning that God intended the war to continue until all the blood shed by slaves at the hands of their masters would be repaid by blood on the battlefield. Lincoln closed with the words that mourners constantly invoked after the assassination, words they etched onto signs and carried with them to funeral processions: "with malice toward none" and "with charity for all." When freedpeople in Washington honored Lincoln later that summer with a banner bearing those already famous phrases, they must have interpreted them to apply less to the defeated Confederates and more to themselves: as a command from Lincoln to treat African Americans with the humanity they deserved after two centuries of slavery and four years of patriotism and sacrifice. If that's what Lincoln meant, in his characteristic subtlety and diplomacy, then the idea of *malice toward none* and *charity for all* fit perfectly with the near-last lines of his address that day: to "strive on to finish the work we are in" meant to achieve "a just, and a lasting peace." In order to endure, the peace that followed the Civil War would have to be infused with justice toward those once enslaved, and now free.[4]

Summer 1865 and Beyond

SARAH BROWNE FOLLOWED THE TRIAL of Booth's conspirators from its start in mid-May to the verdicts rendered in early July. She felt no special sympathy for the lone woman among them, Mary Surratt, whom she described in her diary as "defiant & unrelenting." Instead, Sarah thought execution "too merciful," death "too lenient for the Authors of these great Crimes," as she wrote to Albert, adding, "Let them be exposed to the burning sun and heavy dews, all unsheltered." Thinking of the terrible conditions of the most notorious Confederate prison, Sarah wanted the guilty "unclothed—unprotected and fed after the manner in which the sufferers at Andersonville lived and died." Only then would there be "righteous retribution." After that, God alone would "deal with the wicked."[1]

As Sarah's thoughts lingered over the assassination, Albert Browne was nearing the end of his southern sojourn. In the late summer and early fall of 1865, he toured the Union army's Department of the South, along the way recording his impressions in letters to the abolitionist Wendell Phillips. In South Carolina, Georgia, and Florida, Albert heard war-weary white southerners express resentment toward Confederate leaders, with some professing to accept the end of slavery. But they seemed "in a sort of stupor," Albert wrote, with loyalty emanating "from the lips only, not from the heart." In any case, most were angry and bitter, and it proved difficult to find any "genuine Union men" anywhere among the white population.[2]

Chaos reigned before Albert's eyes, and the freedpeople felt it most keenly. They were hungry and lacked sufficient clothing (he saw women with only "a bunch of rags around their waists"), and worst of all African Americans found themselves "at the mercy of their former Masters," he wrote home, a circumstance of "*extreme* cruelty." Albert was investigating the case of one paroled rebel soldier who had ambushed a freedman with birdshot, striking him fifty-seven times before running him over with a horse. Albert also had in his possession a cowhide whip with which the wife of a former Confederate senator had lashed a black girl. Some people told him they didn't even know if they were slave or free.[3]

Clearly, Albert Browne told his friend Wendell Phillips, white southerners must not be permitted to rule themselves, and a "*strong military government should be upon this people for years to come.*" He underlined every single word of that imperative. When it came to white-on-black violence, though, Albert saw something else too. In Savannah and Charleston, white Union soldiers sometimes collaborated with "rebel rowdies," ganging up on freedpeople. Union officers might also side with former Confederates (one such man was "a pig headed martinet with no sympathy for the negro") as they beat up black men and sexually assaulted black women. Any self-defense on the part of the victims would be matched with yet harsher white violence. Albert was currently intervening in the case of a boy slapped hard in the face by a Union officer for speaking up to contradict the account of a lying white aggressor. Although Union authorities talked about justice and equality, Albert could tell that some of them had "no more love for the negro than the devil has for holy water." Indeed, Union authorities had briefly arrested Albert himself for calling out the officer who slapped the boy. Albert found too that some of the officers themselves initiated violence against the men of the Fifty-Fourth Massachusetts, then suppressed the incidents. He could think of only one solution. No white soldiers at all should be part of the Union army forces occupying the conquered Confederacy. Only black soldiers should be permitted, and their white officers must be abolitionists fully committed to racial equality.[4]

But Albert was also tired, and the future looked bleak, despite Union victory. His old friend Henry Ward Beecher, with whom he had so mov-

ingly clasped hands when news of Lincoln's assassination reached them
at Fort Sumter, had already expressed his support for President Johnson.
In October, Albert Browne would close up his Treasury Department office
and head home to Massachusetts.[5]

JACKSONVILLE WAS ONE OF THE stops on Albert Browne's final southern circuit, though if Rodney Dorman was aware of the treasury agent's
presence, he did not write about it. Like Sarah Browne up north, Dorman
followed the trial of the conspirators, training his attention on a different set
of facts: the armed soldiers guarding the courtroom, the barred windows,
the hooded prisoners bound at wrist and ankle. It was all "bastard, corrupt proceedings," Dorman spat, with one witness a "sycophantic nincompoop," another a "monkey fool-general," another a "booby nobody." As for
Judge Advocate General Joseph Holt, in charge of the whole affair, he was
merely another "nincompoop knave & prostituter of law." Holt's circle of
judges, "monsters in human shape," were, Dorman wrote, "one thousand
times guilty of infamous crimes." For Dorman, it was the defendants who
were the true "martyrs for freedom," and when the conspirators' sentences
were handed down in early July, he was particularly outraged that Mary
Surratt was among those sent to the gallows. Surratt "certainly did not kill
Lincon," Dorman fumed, as usual intentionally misspelling the president's
name, but had she done so, "it would have been a deed of heroism & patriotism."[6]

As Dorman filled multiple pages of his diary with a torrent of words
about the illegal and corrupt execution of Mrs. Surratt, he consoled himself with visions of eventual retribution, hoping for a "complete & total"
overthrow that would someday wipe out everything Union victory had
wrought. "Oh! for a thunderbolt to exterminate them all," he cried yet
again. The state convention met in Tallahassee that fall to nullify secession,
but even as the white delegates denied voting rights to black men, Dorman wished he could leave the country forever. Instead, he could only rail
against the "northern, worthless, vagabond whites" and "their negroes" all
around him.[7]

As winter came, Dorman continued to feel like "a stranger & mere temporary sojourner in a strange place." A white resident who had fled Jacksonville during the war came back only to find the city "a desolate looking

place, compared to what it used to be." For Christmas 1865, observed Esther Hawks, a northern doctor and missionary working among Jacksonville's freedpeople, there was "no demonstration of festivity among the white inhabitants." They didn't have "much heart for merry-making," she wrote, while "the colored folks seem to be having a good time." Dorman never wrote about white violence in his city, possibly even at his own hands, but Hawks did. "We are hearing reports, every week," she recorded, "of the shooting of negroes by infuriated white men, and no account is made of it." In the meantime, Rodney Dorman remained in despair about his own life. "I really have no home," he wrote three days before Christmas.[8]

LINCOLN'S MOURNERS ALSO THOUGHT ABOUT home and homeward journeys. Enslaved African Americans had escaped to Union lines all through the war, and now the pace quickened as former slaves set out in search of loved ones from whom slave traders and masters had separated them, often many years before. They traveled on foot, on horseback, by carriage, and by train. Even with no fixed destination, and even as many encountered hunger, sickness, and disappointment on the road or in Union army refugee camps, the journey into freedom was still something of a journey toward home.

For Union troops, the literal journey home was a happy occasion. All through the war, black and white soldiers had struggled with homesickness in the form of loneliness and melancholy—in the nineteenth century, the medical diagnosis was called *nostalgia*. The men had sung the verses of sentimental songs like "Do They Miss Me at Home?" imagining loved ones weeping in their absence. Now even those who had fervently wished to keep fighting after the assassination, and those who had experienced the most intense sorrow over the loss of Lincoln, turned from the battlefield with relief. As Edgar Dinsmore of the Fifty-Fourth Massachusetts put it, he was "very, very happy at the thought of soon returning home." On the day Lincoln died, a Union soldier in Virginia counted "only 17 Sundays more in the army," and the day before Lincoln's funeral in Washington, an Iowa soldier wrote in his diary that the "next campaign will be Homeward." Another soldier had a single word to describe his feelings for starting home: "joy." But for the hundreds of thousands who had died in battle, on the march, in army hospitals, and in camp, there was often no journey to parallel that of Lincoln's body, for only a small number of Union corpses would ever return to their hometowns. With the expense of embalming and transportation out of reach for most, the ceremonies for President Lincoln had to substitute for the rituals of more intimate losses.[9]

Union soldiers still in the field as summer arrived now anticipated their return in time for the Fourth of July. Before the Civil War, Independence Day celebrations had been marked in North and South alike by black boycotts and white violence, as well as by fears among white southerners that the holiday would rouse the enslaved to envision their own freedom. In 1852, Frederick Douglass had reminded a white New York audience of his own past as a slave, asking them, "Are the great principles of political freedom and of natural justice, embodied in that Declaration of Independence, extended to us?" The day was a "sham" and a "hollow mockery," Douglass had thundered, filled as it was with "bombast, fraud, deception, impiety, and hypocrisy." Now, on July 4, 1865, Lincoln's mourners across the nation saw both heady celebrations and clashes with former Confederates.[10]

In Washington, a black minister read the Declaration of Independence —indeed, Lincoln himself had once invoked both this founding document and his own untimely death in the same breath. In 1861, speaking at Independence Hall in Philadelphia on his way to the capital to assume the presidency, Lincoln had referred to the Declaration and spoken of saving the divided nation by extending liberty to all men. If the nation could not endure except by renouncing the principles embodied in that document, Lincoln told his audience, "I was about to say I would rather be assassinated on this spot than to surrender it."[11]

Now, four years later, a black journalist in Washington extolled the "first Fourth of July of the colored people." The main orator was a young man named William Howard Day, who spoke of "a sorrow unlike any, nationally, we have ever known," as the shadow of Lincoln's death overlay the joy of freedom. Breaking from the jubilation, Day described the circumstances as "ominous." The monument they would build to Lincoln would be a tribute to liberty, and over the coffin of their late president, Day's people would resist tyranny, whether in the form of the "iron manacles of the slave" or the "unjust written manacles for the free." From his home in Rochester, Douglass sent a letter to the cautious black revelers, with the message that "immediate, complete, and universal enfranchisement of the colored people" was the key to independence. For Douglass, justice demanded black suffrage, and black suffrage was the only road toward "permanent peace." For the ceremonies, Washington freedpeople inscribed Lincoln's words *with malice toward none* and *with charity for all* on a banner, more than likely intending them as both appeal and command for their own treatment in the fraught process of reconstructing the nation.[12]

Across the South that day, victors and vanquished divided sharply. Communities of freedpeople and their white allies celebrated with processions, flags, speeches, prayers, picnics, brass bands, dancing, toasts, fireworks, and illuminations. In Augusta, Georgia, as elsewhere, the ceremonies included a "most glowing tribute to the memory of President Lincoln." In Wilmington, North Carolina, it was a "glorious fourth," wrote a member of the occupying black troops, while the white residents "made a failure in their efforts to get up a celebration." Indeed, Emma LeConte was beside herself that the festivities in Columbia took place in the same building where young white men had once gathered to pledge loyalty to the Confederacy. "Such horrid degradation!" she exploded. In Athens, Georgia, it was the "miserable fourth" for a woman grieving for her husband and "greatly inconvenienced" by the departure of her slaves. In Montgomery, Alabama, "Yankees & negroes" celebrated with readings of the Declaration of Independence and the Emancipation Proclamation, along with a "pyrotechnic display"; former Confederates participated, but a Wisconsin soldier thought it "highly ludicrous to hear them bluster & blow," since nearly all had so recently been vocal secessionists. Elsewhere, local whites shuddered when the celebrators called Lee and Davis traitors or thanked God that the Union had survived and slavery had not. In some places, celebrations were more muted, "on account of the shadow of the President's assassination," as one observer put it. For Alonzo Carr, a white Yankee in the South Carolina Sea Islands, sober feelings arose from a related thought: "It seems that many of the Rebels are to again be citizens of the United States with their former privileges."[13]

Up north, noisy festivities made reference to the victorious Union, Confederate defeat, and the end of slavery. In Gorham, Maine, someone hung a likeness of Jefferson Davis in hoopskirt and boots, topped by an image of a black woman holding an American flag. "What a blessed 4th," wrote Elizabeth Cabot of Boston. "Slavery gone. War at an end. Victory achieved."

But notes of warning still sounded in the North. At an abolitionist picnic in Massachusetts, the writer and escaped slave William Wells Brown declared in counterpoint that the war had ended too soon, for without suffrage would come a "new form of slavery," his people "at the mercy of the tyrants of the South." Frances Harper, the activist and poet (born a free woman in Maryland), together with Wendell Phillips, vowed, "No reconstruction without negro suffrage." Among African Americans north and south, there were few celebrations without reference to justice as yet unfulfilled.[14]

More immediate justice could be found in the verdicts rendered upon Booth's conspirators on July 5, 1865. The seven men and Mary Surratt had been held in custody since late April, and their trial had begun in Washington soon after Lincoln's burial, in a courtroom adjacent to the prisoners' cells. Like Sarah Browne and Rodney Dorman, people everywhere followed the proceedings closely. "The great Conspiracy Trial is still in progress," wrote the minister James Ward in his diary, with "every day's proceedings developing facts of thrilling interest, and showing more and more plainly the diabolical nature and purposes of the Rebellion." Marian Hooper had come from Boston to watch the Grand Review and on the same visit attended the trial two days in a row, squeezing into the crowd of spectators. "The evidence is not very interesting," she wrote, "but it is to see the prisoners." Mary Surratt hid her face behind a fan, Hooper noted, while Lewis Powell appeared "handsome but utterly brutal." On the other side, Confederates were infuriated when Judge Holt attempted to prove that Jefferson Davis and other leaders were behind the plot. "If this thing goes on, women will be hanged for having Booth's photograph in their possession," one rebel fumed.[15]

All eight defendants were pronounced guilty. The military tribunal sentenced four of them to death: George Atzerodt, the man who lost his nerve to kill Vice President Johnson; Lewis Powell, Seward's attacker; David Herold, the man who had guarded Powell's horse that night; and Mary Surratt, the widowed boardinghouse-keeper. Three more were sentenced to life in prison: Samuel Mudd, the doctor who set Booth's broken bone after he escaped from Ford's Theatre; and plotters Samuel Arnold and Michael O'Laughlen. Edman Spangler, who had held Booth's horse outside the theater, was sentenced to six years behind bars. (John Surratt, Mary's son, would be arrested in 1866, with a trial ending in a hung jury. In 1869,

President Johnson would pardon Arnold and Mudd; by then, O'Laughlen had died of yellow fever. That same year, Johnson granted permission for the body of John Wilkes Booth to be released to his family, who reinterred him in a Baltimore cemetery.)

The four executions took place on July 7, before a small, ticketed crowd on the grounds of the Washington Arsenal, with Mary Surratt the first woman to be executed by the federal government. Lincoln's mourners divided over her guilt, but for Confederates and Copperheads all the verdicts were yet another blow. Proslavery Washingtonian William Owner called the hangings a shocking tragedy, while from Cincinnati an anonymous Copperhead wrote to Andrew Johnson to say that the new president had proven himself "not worth a god dam more then old Lincoln Was." Judge Holt had failed to implicate Confederate leaders, but the verdicts still felt like a triumph for Lincoln's mourners. "What a sanguinary tribute to the merciful Lincoln!" Anna Lowell wrote in her diary. She remained troubled, though, and not only because of her opposition to capital punishment. The executions could neither bring back the slain chief nor "compensate for the unjust & weak policy" of President Johnson. His plans for reconstructing the rebel states, she wrote, might well "nullify all our victories."[16]

MOURNERS WANTED TO BELIEVE THAT God had permitted the assassination of Abraham Lincoln so that an even more glorious nation could emerge from the ashes of the Civil War, but the immediate postwar world without Lincoln was turning out to be anything but glorious. "Let us not be in too much haste in the work of restoration," Frederick Douglass had warned on the very day of the president's death. "Let us not remember our enemies and disenfranchise our friends," he had said then, but that was exactly what was coming to pass in the former Confederate states under Johnson's program of Presidential Reconstruction, with voting rights reserved for white men only. On Saint Helena Island, free black men and women saw their former masters, once refugees, returning under Johnson's pardon proclamation. "They no longer pray for the President—*our* President, as they used to call Lincoln," a northern teacher wrote that autumn. "They keep an ominous silence and are very sad and troubled." Anna Ferris had welcomed Union troops home to Delaware over the summer, grateful for peace, but by winter she was disgusted with Johnson's "infamous treach-

Four of the conspirators swing from the gallows in Washington, on July 7, 1865. This photograph shows the hooded and bound George Atzerodt (assigned to kill Vice President
Johnson), Lewis Powell (William Seward's attacker), David Herold (who waited outside
the Seward residence until the screams inside scared him away), and Mary Surratt, far
left (the widow whose properties sheltered the conspirators). With the execution completed, the small crowd of nonmilitary onlookers begins to depart.
LC-DIG-cwpb-04230, Prints and Photographs Division, Library of Congress.

ery," discouraged over the renewed "armed antagonism," and immensely
anxious for the nation's future.[17]

If Lincoln's mourners were unhappy, so too were his antagonists. The
president's gleeful enemies had tried to convince themselves that the assassination would vindicate their defeat on the battlefield, maybe even that it
was God's doing, but now it seemed they had been wrong, for the postwar
world, even without the tyrant Lincoln, was turning out to be a dreadful
place—maybe the late president would have been their best friend after all.
Just as Albert Browne observed on his coastal tour, some white southerners
were exhausted and ready to give up. "I do not write often now," South
Carolina plantation mistress Mary Chesnut explained to her diary in the
summer of 1865, "not for want of something to say, but from a loathing of
all I see and hear. Why dwell upon it?" Others could not help but dwell

upon it. "Oh! Oh! Just to contemplate the miserable changes that four years have brought to our happy country," Amanda Edmunds exclaimed in her Virginia journal, writing as if the Confederacy still existed. It was "enough to run the strongest crazy." In Louisiana, Sarah Wadley had no choice but to perform her own household labor now that her slaves had left, and she did so in a cloud of sadness. "Oh melancholy months, months in which we have learned what it is to be subjugated, to lose our country and the great glory of freedom," she wrote, following the pattern of casting her people as the slaves of Yankee rulers. That summer too, John Henderson, studying law in North Carolina, picked up the diary he had neglected for six months. "Last December I was a citizen of a free country," he wrote, "now I am a subject of a most grinding despotism."[18]

At the same time, though, other erstwhile Confederates believed that the glee over Lincoln's death had been well placed, that something better was indeed in store for those suffering God's chastisement in defeat. Zillah Brandon hadn't written in her diary since late 1864 when she picked up the volume again in the summer of 1865. Four of her sons had fought in the war, and two had died, and now Brandon extolled the noble soldiers in gray, so recently "fighting for our countrys rights, the liberties of their wives and children"—and therein lay her hope: the fight was not yet over. True, Brandon described her countrymen and women as "despoiled of every right claimed by a free people" in the face of northern occupation, but she also proclaimed that the "patriotism of 76 is burning in our souls," confident that God remained on the side of white people fighting for revolutionary freedom, a freedom that depended on black subjugation.[19]

Former Confederates knew they would have to work hard to re-create the world they had lost when they lost the war. "I have been talking with some of our best citizens here and they are very uneasy about the state of affairs," William Carter wrote to his father from Petersburg, Virginia, in the late summer of 1865. The Carters had been wealthy planters, and President Johnson now seemed to be the "only hope of the South," he wrote. Carter worried, however, about the way the Republican Congress was crossing Johnson, and he knew that white southerners would have to stand up for the new executive in the face of pressure from the radicals. With foreboding, he warned his father, "I will tell you when I see you what I do not like to write." At the end of 1865, the Thirteenth Amendment would become part of the U.S. Constitution, legally abolishing slavery; perhaps Carter intended to speak to his father about the white violence necessary to suppress black freedom.[20]

Lincoln's assassination continued to figure in the white-on-black violence in the South after Appomattox. Black soldiers occupying Memphis in the spring of 1866 were giving a cheer for the slain president when a white policeman taunted them with the words, "Your old father, Abe Lincoln, is dead and damned." That confrontation touched off a riot and massacre in which nearly fifty African Americans died, half again as many were wounded, and white men made the rape of black women a tactic of intimidation. By 1866 too, the Ku Klux Klan, created by Confederate veterans, was riding through southern states, its members drawn from all classes of white southerners. In these ways did rebel dreams of retribution begin to come to fruition.[21]

Yet the era of Reconstruction simultaneously brought unprecedented gains for Lincoln's black mourners and their most radical white allies. In 1867, in the face of so much recalcitrance and brutality, moderate and radical Republicans in Congress joined forces against Andrew Johnson, exchanging Presidential Reconstruction for a much more far-reaching program that would establish black suffrage and political participation, labor contracts and education, all overseen by the Union army and the federal Freedmen's Bureau. Here—if at times faltering from northern racism—was realized much of the vision of African Americans, as formulated in their petitions to President Johnson in the wake of Lincoln's assassination. Here was the "*strong military government*" that Albert Browne had wanted "*for years to come.*" By 1870, the Fourteenth and Fifteenth Amendments had become part of the U.S. Constitution, enshrining the rights of citizenship for all African Americans and the right of suffrage for all black men.

With the radical program fully under way, Sarah Browne excoriated President Johnson as an odious and disloyal criminal; at the end of 1868, Lincoln's successor had lived up to Sarah's worst fears by pardoning all Confederates once and for all, including Jefferson Davis and Robert E. Lee. Meanwhile, white southerners met radical Reconstruction with horrific violence, and Sarah read the newspapers with mounting dread, writing in her diary about "Kuklux Klan outrages." In Florida, the Klansmen called themselves the "Young Men's Democratic Club," and when President Ulysses S. Grant

launched an investigation across the South in the early 1870s, African American men and women from Jacksonville came to testify about the gruesome
terrorism they had suffered. Whether or not Rodney Dorman joined in, he
no doubt appreciated the activities of his white compatriots. Although Dorman had intended to cease his diary-keeping when the war ended, he kept
on writing and kept on vilifying the Yankees, still dissatisfied with their
"outrages, monstrosities, & knaveries." Jacksonville hadn't yet become a
comfortable home, and with the "new order of things," as he put it, Dorman found no solace anywhere. In 1873, he wanted only to "go away &
hide."[22]

In November 1876 came the presidential election that would overturn
the mighty experiment of radical Reconstruction. By then Rodney Dorman was again working as an attorney and a judge, and before the election
he headed north to visit friends and relatives he hadn't seen in decades.
Autumn found him at the Centennial Exhibition in Philadelphia, fulminat-
ing into his diary about the Yankee braggarts and their World's Fair, their
pompous ideas about progress and civilization on full display in a lavish
spectacle. A sculpture entitled *Freed Slave* surely infuriated him, but Dorman might have found satisfaction in the concession called "The South,"
which offered musical entertainment by "old-time plantation 'darkies.'" In
October he was ready to head home, "or what I call so," he added with his
customary dejection.[23]

Republican Rutherford B. Hayes ran for president on the twin vows of
black equality and national peace, which by then were nothing less than a
fantastical, oxymoronic impossibility. His Democratic opponent, Samuel
Tilden, won the vote count, but there had been so much violent intimidation at the polls that Republicans disputed the outcome in South Carolina,
Louisiana, and Florida. In the hammered-out compromise, Hayes took office on the condition that the last federal troops in the old Confederacy
be rendered inactive. The South was "redeemed" from Yankee rule and
Reconstruction was over, yet even then Rodney Dorman railed against the
"lost presidential election," furious that Tilden had been denied office.
Nor did Democrats earn his praise for their "imbecility" in agreeing to the
compromise. Up in Salem, Sarah Browne was no less anxious about the nation's future. "I fear for the oppressed, whose shackles are hardly broken,"

she wrote. "Would peace & harmony could reign!" she cried, only hoping that President Hayes would act honorably.[24]

The end of Reconstruction left white southerners free to reassert unchecked violence for the sake of restoring the world they had never stopped fighting to get back. What was more, many exhausted white northerners now complied, eager for reconciliation. Even Albert Browne's zeal had run its course. By 1877, he had given up on the idea of black soldiers and abolitionist white officers ruling the former Confederacy. Thoroughly disenchanted with the so-called carpetbaggers (northerners in the South) and scalawags (southern white Republicans), Albert condemned them all as corrupt, the "vilest of the vile." By then his ideals about the natural virtues of free-labor capitalism had been eclipsed too by a wage-labor proletariat at war with men of industry, nowhere more apparent than in the railroad strikes that roiled the nation in 1877, with workers fighting the might of their employers in the streets. Albert had been tired in the autumn of 1865, but now he was entirely worn out, ready to reconcile with the old Confederates, "showing them," he wrote to Sarah while on a trip to New York, "that we are *at one* with them in trying to build them up & restore prosperity." Whether he understood that the prosperity of white southerners would leave some African Americans in conditions akin to enslavement is unclear. While Sarah hoped meekly for the best for former slaves, Albert hoped only that President Hayes would step up to fight government corruption. Though preferable to the Democratic Party that represented still-enraged former Confederates, the Party of Lincoln now changed course, turning away from racial equality.[25]

The restoration of white supremacy turned out to be a protracted process. Although the majority of Lincoln's white mourners were too tired, too apathetic, or ultimately too bound by racism to match the determination of their former enemies, African Americans and their radical white friends continued to fight valiantly for justice, thereby forestalling the visions of former Confederates—those who were determined to rise again after defeat, to seek retribution in a "*second* war for independence," as Cloe Whittle had put it, to "renew the struggle and throw off the hateful yoke," in Emma LeConte's words. For this reason, Rodney Dorman's rage burned on past the end of Reconstruction. When Thomas Wentworth Higginson visited

Jacksonville in 1878, he found African Americans maintaining their own church and school in the bustling city. He saw black men working in the fishing and lumber trades, and black families working their own land on the Saint Johns River. In the mid-1880s, Charlotte Forten came to Jacksonville with her husband, the minister Francis Grimké. Forten was the black student who had befriended Nellie Browne as a schoolgirl in Salem in the 1850s. As a young woman during the war, Forten had traveled to the Sea Islands to work with the freedpeople, and now she arrived in Jacksonville to teach black children, work with a freedmen's committee, and organize black women into a missionary society, while her husband preached at a black church.[26]

All of that no doubt infuriated Rodney Dorman too, and even as he traveled north to visit relatives for a second time, he continued to write in his diary about ongoing "warfare" with Yankees, portraying the new northerners in town as even worse than the abolitionists and missionaries he had so deeply despised twenty years earlier. As for the black men who continued to exercise their right to vote until the turn of the century—when whites effected near-complete black disfranchisement in the South—Dorman could surmise only that they were political slaves of the Republican Party. Rodney Dorman lived in Jacksonville for the rest of his life but never again made a home for himself there. Though he eventually moved back to the center of town, he only rented rooms in various boardinghouses. He last appeared in the city directory in 1887, at seventy years old.[27]

Like Dorman, who reread and added commentary to his past diary entries during the post-Reconstruction decades, others who had once despaired at defeat also turned back the pages of their wartime journals. For Martha Crawford, word of Lee's surrender had left her "stunned" and "crushed," her heart torn with grief. "The two countries *cannot* continue as one," she had written in 1865, vowing that "we'll await our opportunity and try them again." Sixteen years later, as Crawford reviewed her own words, she paused. "How time and reflection modify our opinions and soften our emotions!" she wrote in 1881. Though time and reflection no doubt played a role, Crawford's uplifted heart resulted more from the fact that her compatriots were by then on the road to re-creating a regime of white supremacy. In the 1890s, Richmond resident Lucy Fletcher perused her end-of-war diary, where she had written in despair about "negro & Yankee, Yankee & negro, ad nauseam." Nearly thirty years later, Fletcher took a mo-

ment to explain that her bitterness had arisen from the "cruel injustice &
unreasonable persecution to which we were subjected during those days of
Reconstruction, that 'Decade of Horror' worse even than the war itself." To
Fletcher's satisfaction, the 1890s saw the near-complete process of segregation and disfranchisement, along with the height of the lynching epidemic,
which activist Ida B. Wells (born into slavery during the war) explained
was the result of white fury for "giving the Afro-American his freedom, the
ballot box and the Civil Rights Law." Confederate veteran John Johnston,
leafing through his Civil War diary in 1905, came across an entry from April
1865 in which he had prayed to God that the rumors of Lincoln's assassination were true. Forty years later, Johnston added a note: "This was a sincere
prayer," he wrote, "and, I think, included Lincoln's death and all."[28]

Sarah and Albert Browne thought back too. For Sarah, the most personally significant aspect of the Civil War years was the loss of her daughter
Nellie, in 1864. Forever after, Sarah continued to record Nellie's birthday
and the anniversary of her death, each time punctuated with phrases like
"Oh! God!" or "agony—our Gethsemane." One year Sarah wrote of reliving
"each one of the closing days of our darling's precious life," while Albert
recorded the "*very hour!*" of Nellie's passing, making note of his restless
sleep and troubled dreams, as he struggled still with the incomprehensible
will of God. For her part, even as she gazed in pain at a photograph of her
daughter frozen in youth, Sarah tried to assure herself that the angel Nellie
had been spared all earthly trials and that they would meet once again in
the world beyond. "Oh! the agony of that surrender!" she wrote in 1881, on
the seventeenth anniversary of Nellie's death.[29]

Sarah Browne also wrote about politics, though in all the many postwar
volumes of her diaries, there is only a single commemoration of Abraham
Lincoln, when, for an unexplained reason, she noted his birthday in 1878.
When Republican James Garfield narrowly won the presidency in 1880,
Sarah exclaimed into her journal, "Our anxieties over! The country saved!"
The following summer, soon after Sarah had recorded what would have
been Nellie's fortieth birthday, President Garfield was shot in a Washington
railway station. Wounded gravely, he lingered until September, and when
he died, Sarah called up a gloom that should have felt familiar. "We are
all sad—sad—sad," she wrote, naming Garfield as "him, who was so dear
to the nation—to the whole world." All around her, people could "read—
talk—think of nothing but our heavy loss!" she claimed, likening the presi-

dent to a father or brother. Sarah recorded the progress of the funeral train that carried Garfield's body from his deathbed on the New Jersey shore to the capital, and then from the capital home to Ohio. "Never before was so much sad earnestness shown," she wrote, as if entirely forgetting the sorrow that had seemed universal in the spring of 1865. She didn't even mention Abraham Lincoln.[30]

Three years later, in 1884, Sarah celebrated the election of Grover Cleveland, the first Democrat to occupy the White House since the Civil War. It had been a close vote, and Cleveland won by the slimmest of margins, dwelling as he did on Republican corruption. "The electoral count in New York is over and Cleveland is elected!" Sarah wrote. "Let the people now be one family—no north, no south. Let us give a full meaning to the word 'United.'" Sarah had nothing to say about race or violence in the South, or, for that matter, in the North either. She had nothing to say about abolition or emancipation or freedom, nothing to say about black landownership or education, citizenship or suffrage. Sarah and Albert Browne both died in 1885, she near seventy-five, he near eighty.[31]

BACK IN DECEMBER 1865, FREDERICK Douglass had written out a speech about Abraham Lincoln, opening with thoughts of the "ominous clouds that hang on the political sky." Douglass described the horror of the assassination, the reversal from the "wildest joy and exultation of victory" to the "dust and ashes of sorrow and mourning." With the year drawing to a close, white mourners were now exchanging their "justly kindled wrath" for "clemency and forgiveness towards the rebels," Douglass wrote. Slavery had been at the root of Lincoln's murder, he maintained, and the assassination could still serve the causes of black freedom and equality by inspiring mourners to stand vigilant against the reassertion of white supremacy. Toward the end of his remarks, Douglass turned to Lincoln's second inaugural address. Bypassing the oft-invoked directives about malice and charity, he instead wrote down the sentence about peace: "Fondly do we hope, fervently do we pray that this mighty scourge of war shall soon pass away." Douglass kept writing, pulling the sentences from memory. "Yet if God wills it continue till all the treasure piled by two hundred and fifty years of the bondman's unrequited toil shall have been wasted," and "each drop of blood drawn by the lash shall have been paid for by one drawn by the sword," then "the judgments of the Lord are true and righteous altogether." By those words, Douglass knew, Lincoln had meant that God would not let the war end until slavery ended.[32]

"Had Mr. Lincoln lived," Frederick Douglass reflected that December, things would have turned out differently. Invoking Lincoln's April 11 speech, with its endorsement of suffrage for black soldiers and intelligent black men, Douglass offered an assessment of the late president. "He was a progressive man, a humane man, an honorable man, and at heart an antislavery man," Douglass wrote. "He had exhausted the resources of conciliation upon rebels and slaveholders and now looked to the principles of Liberty and justice, for the peace, security, happiness and prosperity of his country." Then Douglass moved forcefully away from the providential story in which God had permitted Lincoln's death for the sake of a more glorious future. "I assume therefore, had Abraham Lincoln been spared to see this day," he wrote, "the negro of the South would have more than a hope of enfranchisement and no rebels would hold the reins of Government in any one of the late rebellious states." Had Lincoln lived, Douglass now declared, black men would be voters in the South and former Confederates would not be back in power. Mourners must still stand vigilant against white supremacy, but optimism about divine designs had given way to a different view: Lincoln's assassination was just plain tragic.[33]

Had Lincoln lived, African Americans would have petitioned him and visited him in the White House, advancing the same demands for equality and rights that they asked of his successor. The difference was that Lincoln would have answered without Johnson's defensiveness, ridicule, and dismissal. Lincoln's record of words and actions all during the war, even if marked by slow deliberation, indicated that he would have listened to, absorbed, and responded to the demands of African Americans. Perhaps Douglass was right that Lincoln would ultimately have taken political power from former Confederates and given it to former slaves. No matter, with Lincoln gone, he and other radical mourners were free to reimagine Lincoln's politics in their own image.

Whoever else mourned for Abraham Lincoln, Frederick Douglass concluded in December 1865, "to the colored people of the country, his death is an unspeakable calamity." Decades later, former slaves thought back to the assassination. "Abraham Lincoln!" exclaimed eighty-five-year-old Octavia George in Oklahoma City. "I wouldn't miss a morning getting my black arm band and placing it on in remembrance of Abraham, who was the best friend the Negroes ever had." In Tarrant County, Texas, Ann Edwards called up that time too. "I can't describe the emotions of the people," she said, except that it felt "as if everyone had suddenly experienced the death of their most beloved child." In Mississippi, James Lucas remembered the fears of reenslavement, and in Alabama, Louis Meadows recalled the freedpeople around him vowing never to return to slavery. In light of the post-Reconstruction decades of Jim Crow segregation, disfranchisement, and lynching, Lincoln's assassination was tragic indeed.[34]

And had Lincoln lived? The elderly African Americans speaking in the 1930s thought back on that question too. Louis Meadows believed that "things was hurt by Mr. Lincoln getting killed." John Matheus, in Ohio, thought that if Lincoln had remained president, "he would have done lots of good for the colored people." William Irving, about fifteen years old when the war ended, likewise felt sure that his people would have had an easier time of it with Lincoln as president. George Conrad of Oklahoma City said simply, "I don't think his work was finished." In Arkansas, near one hundred years old, Rosa Ingram was sure that Lincoln had been murdered for freeing the slaves.[35]

For Lincoln's antagonists, the assassination was either the work of a lone madman, an act of heroic patriotism, or God's design for eventual Confederate retribution. For Lincoln's mourners, the meaning of the assassination became more complicated in the post-Reconstruction world, the question *Why?* becoming unanswerable once again. If slavery had indeed been the root cause of the assassination, had God intended Lincoln's death as a means to ensure enduring equality by showing the victors that they must remain vigilant over their vindictive enemies? Or was the assassination, as Frederick Douglass conceded, nothing more than a catastrophe that slowed the long journey toward justice?

Mourners knew that Lincoln's assassination had changed the world irrevocably, but no one could know what would have happened had he lived. The blast of the derringer at Ford's Theatre on the night of April 14, 1865, was the first volley of the war that came after Appomattox—a war on black freedom and equality. That war still ebbs and flows in American history, a century and a half after the assassination of President Abraham Lincoln.

Note on Method

TO WRITE THIS BOOK, I read through perhaps a thousand diaries, collections of letters, and other relevant writings from the spring and summer of 1865. That left thousands of relevant sources unconsulted, and indeed I could have researched this book for another decade, with published letters and diaries alone occupying me for years to come, not to mention the ever-increasing volume of digitized primary sources. I stopped not only in the interest of producing the book in a timely manner but also because I reached a point where new material no longer altered or challenged the patterns I had identified.

In any archive, my starting points were collections that included the writings of Civil War soldiers and officers, along with collections of personal and family papers that held letters or diaries from the spring of 1865. This meant that I asked librarians and archivists to retrieve untold numbers of boxes and folders that I quickly sent back, if, say, a soldier's wartime diary ended in 1864 or a family's papers skipped from March to September 1865. Still, my research unearthed far more relevant diary entries and letters than appear here, and the totality of the sources I read deeply informed both the evidence I ultimately selected for my narrative and my interpretations and conclusions. When I invoke phrases like "many of Lincoln's mourners" or "some Confederates," the words *many* and *some* are not random; rather, they stem from my immersion in personal responses to Lincoln's assassination. Citations in the endnotes must stand in for many more that would have made the notes unwieldy. For certain topics—for example, shock and sorrow at the assassination or the persistence of everyday life—there is comparable evidence from uncountable numbers of sources.

The voluminous number of real-time personal responses to Lincoln's assassination nonetheless presented challenges. First among these was submerged voices, since only certain people possessed the skills of literacy and the time to write. I originally hoped to include a sustained African American voice as one of my protagonists, but that proved more difficult than I'd imagined. It's an old story. The archival papers of men in black Civil War regiments turned out to be the papers of the white officers. The papers of black Reconstruction politicians did not begin until after 1865. In Charlotte Forten's detailed diary, the year 1865 does not exist, and much of Frederick Douglass's personal writings burned in a fire. Because black experiences are central to the story I tell, I turned to two kinds of sources to augment the comparatively small number of personal writings: letters and editorials published in black newspapers, and the writings of whites who related black people's words and sentiments (for example, northern missionaries who taught school to freedpeople down south).

Personal responses to Lincoln's assassination are not the same as private responses. Though ostensibly more private than letters, diaries can nonetheless be deceptive in this regard. Not all diarists wrote for themselves alone. The most religious wrote for the eyes of God, while others crafted their prose for real or imagined audiences. Boston businessman Amos Lawrence, for example, betrayed the presumption of privacy by indexing his volumes (including an entry for "Lincoln, Abraham"), implying a readership of posterity, biographers, or both, while fellow Bostonian Anna Lowell littered her pages with enough cross-outs and rewordings to suggest imagined readers. As for letters, their degree of intimacy varied widely. Business correspondence presumed a certain public quality, and personal letters could also be composed for an audience beyond the named recipient, for example, if a writer knew that a missive would be passed around among relatives or neighbors. Personal responses to Lincoln's assassination also include words spoken aloud in public or semipublic settings, never intended to be private. When I worked with evidence of spoken responses (notably when mourners recounted gleeful commentary), I made every effort to bypass stories based on hearsay, for maximum accuracy using only eyewitness accounts unless writing specifically about rumors.[1]

Another challenge lay in the fact that many writers recorded unadorned facts without reference to thoughts or feelings ("Heard of the assassination of Lincoln" or "The President's funeral today"). People wrote down only that John Wilkes Booth remained at large or that William Seward was re-covering from his wounds; some merely transcribed the headlines. Civil War–era sentimentalism presented a different challenge. In the eighteenth century, diarists most commonly penned chronicles of daily life, whereas by the end of the nineteenth century, the nature of diaries had been heavily influenced by Romanticism and a focus on the individual self. The Civil War years saw a transition from the older pattern of tersely recorded infor-mation to the newer art of effusive introspection. Both sorts of journals can be found in the archives of personal responses to Lincoln's assassination. Though the latter sort may strike modern readers as overwrought, I have approached these documents as reflecting the writer's emotions.[2]

A few notes about word choices and quotations are in order. I have re-ferred to Rodney Dorman by his last name, as I did for all historical actors, but because Sarah and Albert Browne shared a last name, I have referred to them by their respective first names. I have used the words *diary* and *journal* interchangeably. I have described my white southern actors as *Confederates,* rather than *former Confederates,* almost all the way through; although their identity became more ambiguous as the war drew to a close, they continued to think of themselves as members of their own nation. When writing from the perspective of a nineteenth-century actor, I have occasionally used *Negro* without quotation marks.

When quoting sources, I have not corrected spelling or punctuation, except for the sake of readability if it left the meaning unchanged: insert-ing a period at the end of a sentence, adding a comma where absolutely necessary, removing excessive commas for the sake of clarity (Rodney Dor-man was particularly dedicated to the comma), exchanging upper- and lowercase letters, omitting quotation marks within quotation marks, or occasionally adding an apostrophe. (Note also that commas, periods, and dashes are not always easy to distinguish in manuscript sources, and some nineteenth-century writers used dashes as stand-ins for periods.) When people wrote *Johnson* in reference to Confederate general Joseph E. John-ston, I have made a silent correction so as not to confuse the general with the new president. Likewise, where the name of a person was rendered with different spellings, I have chosen a single one (the Brownes, for example, mostly spelled their daughter's name as *Nellie* but occasionally rendered it *Nelly*). In selecting published diaries and letters, I did my very best to reject those that were heavily revised or polished, either by the writers or by later editors.

In two instances, I have taken a bit more liberty with the sources. First, when writers recounted conversations or other spoken words, I corrected spelling and punctuation, or changed capitalization, in order to reflect what people heard, rather than how they captured the words on paper. Second, when white people wrote down the words of African Americans in dialect, I silently corrected the spelling, on the theory that everyone speaks with an accent, including upper-class New Englanders and elite white southerners. Because those variant pronunciations are rarely transcribed with improper spelling, nor should be the spoken words of African Americans; to write *was* when spoken by a white person, and *wuz* when spoken by a black person, makes no sense beyond racist stereotyping. (It was refreshing indeed to read the journalist Thomas Morris Chester, whose dispatches spelled the words of his fellow African Americans properly.)

Finally, a word about Rodney Dorman's diary. The journals in the Library of Congress manuscript collection are anonymous—that is, no author's name appears anywhere on or in them. The collection's donor believed the writer to be her great uncle Orloff M. Dorman, whom she described in 1936 as a northern man living in Jacksonville during the Civil War. As I began to work with the diary, however, I realized that the writer could not be Orloff Dorman, a Unionist who had once met with President Lincoln and asked for an appointment as the provisional wartime governor of Florida. A search in the digital American Historical Newspapers for the words "Jacksonville" and "Dorman" yielded an article in the *National Intelligencer* that listed the names of those whose homes had burned in the 1863 Union attack on the city. Among them was a "Judge Dorman," and the 1860 federal census recorded an attorney named Rodney Dorman, who turned out to be the brother of Orloff, confirmed by the database Ancestry. com. Then, in a search through Confederate Papers Relating to Citizens or Business Firms, in the National Archives and available in the online database Fold3.com, I found Rodney Dorman's 1863 lost-property claim. The handwriting there perfectly matched the handwriting of the anonymous journals in the Library of Congress.[3]

Notes

Abbreviations

AAS: American Antiquarian Society, Worcester, Mass.

ACWLD: The American Civil War: Letters and Diaries, Alexander Street Press, alexander street.com/products/american-civil-war-letters-and-diaries

ADAH-AWD-South: Alabama Department of Archives and History, American Women's Diaries: Southern Women, Readex Newsbank, microform

AMA: American Missionary Association Archives, Amistad Research Center, Tulane University, New Orleans, microform

BAP: Black Abolitionist Papers, ProQuest, bap.chadwyck.com

BFP: Browne Family Papers, Schlesinger Library on the History of Women in America, Radcliffe Institute for Advanced Study, Harvard University, Cambridge, Mass.

BHS: Brooklyn Historical Society, Brooklyn, N.Y.

Brown: John Hay Library, Brown University, Providence, R.I.

Chicago: Special Collections Research Center, University of Chicago

CHM: Chicago History Museum Research Center

Columbia: Rare Book and Manuscript Library, Columbia University, New York

Cornell: Division of Rare and Manuscript Collections, Cornell University Library, Ithaca, N.Y.

CP: College of Physicians, Philadelphia

CWF-RSP: Colonial Williamsburg Foundation Library, Records of Ante-Bellum Southern Plantations from the Revolution through the Civil War, University Publications of America, microform

CWL: Roy P. Basler, ed., *The Collected Works of Abraham Lincoln,* 8 vols. (New Brunswick, N.J.: Rutgers University Press, 1953–55)

DHS: Delaware Historical Society, Wilmington

DocSouth: Documenting the American South, University Library, University of North Carolina, Chapel Hill, docsouth.unc.edu

Dorman diary: Anonymous diary [Rodney Dorman], "Memoranda of Events that transpired at Jacksonville, Florida, & in its vicinity; with some remarks & comments thereon," Orloff M. Dorman Papers, Manuscript Division, Library of Congress, Washington, D.C.

Duke: David M. Rubenstein Rare Book and Manuscript Library, Duke University, Dur-
   ham, N.C.
Duke-SWF: David M. Rubenstein Rare Book and Manuscript Library, Duke University,
   Southern Women and Their Families in the Nineteenth Century: Papers and Dia-
   ries, University Publications of America, microform
FDP: John W. Blassingame and John R. McKivigan, eds., *The Frederick Douglass Papers*
   (New Haven: Yale University Press, 1979–92)
FHL: Friends Historical Library, Swarthmore College, Swarthmore, Pa.
GLC-NYHS: Gilder Lehrman Collection, Gilder Lehrman Institute of American History,
   Patricia D. Klingenstein Library, New-York Historical Society, New York
GWBW: G. W. Blunt White Library, Mystic Seaport, Mystic, Conn.
HL: Huntington Library, San Marino, Calif.
HLH: Houghton Library, Harvard University, Cambridge, Mass.
HLS: Historical and Special Collections, Harvard Law School Library, Harvard Univer-
   sity, Cambridge, Mass.
Howard: Moorland-Spingarn Research Center, Howard University, Washington, D.C.
HSP: Historical Society of Pennsylvania, Philadelphia
LC: Manuscript Division, Library of Congress, Washington, D.C.
LSU-CMM: Louisiana State University Libraries, Confederate Military Manuscripts,
   University Publications of America, microform
LSU-RSPE: Louisiana State University Libraries, Records of Southern Plantations from
   Emancipation to the Great Migration, University Publications of America, micro-
   form
LSU-SWF: Louisiana State University Libraries, Southern Women and Their Families
   in the Nineteenth Century: Papers and Diaries, University Publications of America,
   microform
MDAH-RSP: Mississippi Department of Archives and History, Records of Ante-Bellum
   Southern Plantations from the Revolution through the Civil War, University Publi-
   cations of America, microform
MDHS: H. Furlong Baldwin Library, Maryland Historical Society, Baltimore
MHS: Massachusetts Historical Society, Boston
ML: Morgan Library and Museum, New York
NARA: National Archives and Records Administration, Washington, D.C.
NAWLD: North American Women's Letters and Diaries, Alexander Street Press,
   alexanderstreet.com/products/north-american-womens-letters-and-diaries
NHS-NWF: Newport Historical Society, New England Women and Their Families in
   the Eighteenth and Nineteenth Centuries: Personal Papers, Letters, and Diaries,
   University Publications of America, microform
NYHS: Patricia D. Klingenstein Library, New-York Historical Society, New York
NYPL: Manuscripts and Archives Division, New York Public Library
NYSL: Manuscripts and Special Collections, New York State Library, Albany
PAJ: Leroy P. Graf, ed., *The Papers of Andrew Johnson,* vol. 7: *1864–1865* (Knoxville: Uni-

versity of Tennessee Press, 1986), and Paul H. Bergeron, ed., *The Papers of Andrew Johnson,* vol. 8: *May–August 1865* (Knoxville: University of Tennessee Press, 1989)

Princeton: Rare Books and Special Collections, Princeton University, Princeton, N.J.

RG94-NARA: Records of the Adjutant General's Office, Record Group 94, National Archives and Records Administration, Washington, D.C.

RG109-NARA: War Department Collection of Confederate Records, Record Group 109, National Archives and Records Administration, Washington, D.C.

RG125-NARA: Records of General Courts-Martial and Courts of Inquiry of the Navy Department, Records of the Office of the Judge Advocate General (Navy), Record Group 125, National Archives and Records Administration, Washington, D.C.

RG153-NARA: Court-Martial Case Files, entry 15, Records of the Office of the Judge Advocate General (Army), Record Group 153, National Archives and Records Administration, Washington, D.C.

RIHS-NWF: Rhode Island Historical Society, New England Women and Their Families in the Eighteenth and Nineteenth Centuries: Personal Papers, Letters, and Diaries, University Publications of America, microform

Schomburg: Manuscripts, Archives and Rare Books Division, Schomburg Center for Research in Black Culture, New York Public Library

SHC: Southern Historical Collection, University of North Carolina, Chapel Hill

SHC-AWD-South: Southern Historical Collection, University of North Carolina, Chapel Hill, American Women's Diaries: Southern Women, Readex Newsbank, microform

SHC-RSP: Southern Historical Collection, University of North Carolina, Chapel Hill, Records of Ante-Bellum Southern Plantations from the Revolution through the Civil War, University Publications of America, microform

SHC-SWF: Southern Historical Collection, University of North Carolina, Chapel Hill, Southern Women and Their Families in the Nineteenth Century: Papers and Diaries, University Publications of America, microform

SL: Schlesinger Library on the History of Women in America, Radcliffe Institute for Advanced Study, Harvard University, Cambridge, Mass.

SSC: Sophia Smith Collection, Smith College, Northampton, Mass.

UTA-CMM: University of Texas, Austin, Confederate Military Manuscripts, University Publications of America, microform

UTA-SWF: University of Texas, Austin, Southern Women and Their Families in the Nineteenth Century: Papers and Diaries, University Publications of America, microform

Utah-AWD-West: Utah State Historical Society, American Women's Diaries: Western Women, Readex Newsbank, microform

UVA-CMM: University of Virginia Library, Confederate Military Manuscripts, University Publications of America, microform

UVA-RSP: University of Virginia Library, Records of Ante-Bellum Southern Plantations from the Revolution through the Civil War, University Publications of America, microform

UVA-SWF: University of Virginia Library, Southern Women and Their Families in
    the Nineteenth Century: Papers and Diaries, University Publications of America,
    microform

VHS-CMM: Virginia Historical Society, Confederate Military Manuscripts, University
    Publications of America, microform

VHS-SWF: Virginia Historical Society, Southern Women and Their Families in the
    Nineteenth Century: Papers and Diaries, University Publications of America,
    microform

WM-AWD-South: College of William and Mary, American Women's Diaries: Southern
    Women, Readex Newsbank, microform

WM-SWF: College of William and Mary, Southern Women and Their Families in the
    Nineteenth Century: Papers and Diaries, University Publications of America,
    microform

Yale-Beinecke: Beinecke Rare Book and Manuscript Library, Yale University, New Haven

Yale-Sterling: Manuscripts and Archives, Sterling Memorial Library, Yale University, New
    Haven

Good Friday, 1865

1. **advertisement:** *Washington Evening Star,* Apr. 14, 1865, pp. 1, 2; **citizenship:** William H. Herndon and Jesse W. Weik, *Abraham Lincoln: The True Story of a Great Life,*
2 vols. (New York: D. Appleton, 1900), 2:289 ("Frederick Stone, counsel for Harold [sic]
after Booth's death, is authority for the statement"); **Stanton's words:** Adam Gopnik,
"Angels and Ages: Lincoln's Language and Its Legacy," *New Yorker,* May 28, 2007, and
Gopnik, *Angels and Ages: A Short Book about Darwin, Lincoln, and Modern Life* (New
York: Vintage, 2009).

For primary accounts of the events in and around Ford's Theatre and Petersen House,
see Charles F. Conant to "Hattie," Washington, D.C., Apr. 15, 1865, ML; Albert Daggett to
"Julie," Apr. 15, 1865, in Timothy S. Good, *We Saw Lincoln Shot: One Hundred Eyewitness Accounts* (Jackson: University Press of Mississippi, 1995), 45–47; James S. Knox
to father, Washington, D.C., Apr. 15, 1865, ser. 3: General Correspondence, Abraham
Lincoln Papers, LC, available at memory.loc.gov/ammem/alhtml/alser.html; Charles A.
Sanford to Edward Payson Goodrich, Washington, D.C., Apr. 15, 1865, in "Two Letters
on the Event of April 14, 1865," *Bulletin of the William L. Clements Library of American
History* 47 (Feb. 12, 1946), facsimile, n.p.; Frederick A. Sawyer, "Account of what I saw of
the Death of Mr. Lincoln written April 15, 1865," in "An Eyewitness Account of Abraham
Lincoln's Assassination," ed. Ronald D. Rietveld, *Civil War History* 22 (1976), 62–68;
George B. Todd to Henry P. Todd, Washington, D.C., Apr. 15, 1865, McClellan Lincoln
Collection, Brown; Gideon Welles diary, Apr. 15, 1865, Welles Papers, LC; W. R. Batch-
elder to mother, Washington, D.C., Apr. 16, 1865, NYHS; Augustus Clark to S. M. Allen,
Washington, D.C., Apr. 16, 1865, accompanying scrap of bloodstained towel used for
Abraham Lincoln at Ford's Theatre, Special Collections, MHS; Helen A. Du Barry to
mother, Washington, D.C., Apr. 16, 1865, in "Eyewitness Account of Lincoln's Assassi-

nation," *Journal of the Illinois State Historical Society* 39 (1946), 366–69; R. B. Milliken to "Friend Byron," Washington, D.C., Apr. 16, 1865, #54, Lincoln Room Miscellaneous Papers, HLH; Julia Adelaide Shepard to father, near Washington, D.C., Apr. 16, 1865, in "Lincoln's Assassination Told by an Eye-Witness," *Century Magazine* 77 (1909), 917–18; and Clara Harris to "Mary," Washington, D.C., Apr. 25, 1865, NYHS.

2. **I hope:** Henry Gawthrop diary, Apr. 8, 1865, with addition from 1914–15, DHS.

For rationales for avoiding memoirs, see William A. Dobak, *Freedom by the Sword: The U.S. Colored Troops, 1862–1867* (Washington, D.C.: Center of Military History, 2011), 507; J. Tracy Power, *Lee's Miserables: Life in the Army of Northern Virginia from the Wilderness to Appomattox* (Chapel Hill: University of North Carolina Press, 1998), xiv–xv; and James M. McPherson, *What They Fought For, 1861–1865* (1994; reprint, New York: Doubleday, 1995), 69; see also Don E. Fehrenbacher and Virginia Fehrenbacher, *Recollected Words of Abraham Lincoln* (Stanford, Calif.: Stanford University Press, 1996), xliii–liv.

3. **deeper:** Joseph A. Prime, "Sermon Preached in the Liberty Street Presbyterian Church (Colored)," in *A Tribute of Respect by the Citizens of Troy to the Memory of Abraham Lincoln* (Troy, N.Y.: Young and Benson, 1865), 155; **swept, sea:** "The Great Calamity," Apr. 16, 1865, *Sacramento Daily Union*, published May 17, 1865, in *Lincoln Observed: Civil War Dispatches of Noah Brooks*, ed. Michael Burlingame (Baltimore: Johns Hopkins University Press, 1998), 187, 192; **universal feeling:** Lucretia Hale to Charles Hale, Brookline, Mass., June 2, 1865, box 50, Hale Family Papers, SSC; **North & South:** Mary Peck to Henry J. Peck, Jonesville, N.Y., Apr. 16, 1865, Peck Correspondence, NYSL; **bitter:** F. J. Douglass to George Whipple, Eliot, Jamaica, Apr. 25, 1865, #F1-3837-40, reel 231, AMA; **even:** William L. Avery to U.S. Secretary of the Interior, Cape Town, South Africa, June 13, 1865, Letters Received Relating to Judges and Arbitrators of Mixed Courts at New York, Cape Town, and Sierra Leone, Records of the Office of the Secretary of the Interior Relating to the Suppression of the African Slave Trade and Negro Colonization, M160, roll 7, RG48, NARA; **everyone:** Elizabeth Gaskell to Charles Eliot Norton, London, Apr. 28, 1865, in *Letters of Mrs. Gaskell and Charles Eliot Norton, 1855–1865*, ed. Jane Whitehill (London: Oxford University Press, 1932), 122; **join:** Philip Alexander Bell et al., [no title], *San Francisco Elevator*, Apr. 21, 1865, #4828, BAP.

4. For Albert Browne's work, see Albert Gallatin Browne Papers, MHS; **shrewd, beg:** William T. Sherman, *Memoirs of General William T. Sherman*, 2 vols. (New York: D. Appleton, 1875), 2:231; **now:** Brenda Stevenson, ed., *The Journals of Charlotte Forten Grimké* (New York: Oxford University Press, 1988), 443 (Jan. 31, 1863, entry).

5. **household:** U.S. federal census, Salem, Essex County, Mass., 1860; **house:** photograph, fol. 108, BFP; **Albert Jr.:** *Report of the Harvard Class of 1853 . . . Issued on the Sixtieth Anniversary for the Use of the Class and Its Friends, Commencement 1913* (Cambridge, Mass.: University Press, 1913), 46–51.

6. **Albert Jr.:** *Report of the Harvard Class of 1853*, 46–47; **Forten:** Stevenson, *Journals of Charlotte Forten Grimké*, 157 (June 18, 1856, conservative), 98 (Sept. 3, 1854, insulting), 369 (July 6, 1862, pariah), 140 (Sept. 12, 1855, kind), 139–40 (Sept. 12, 1855, Nellie), 141 (Sept.

[n.d.], 1855, society), 173 (Dec. 16, 1856, lonesome), 196 (Feb. 25, 1857, sorry). Nellie's full name was Sarah Ellen Browne, and Forten referred to her as "Sarah Brown," without the *e* (Forten also wrote about a friend named Nellie, but her last name began with *A*).

7. U.S. federal census and slave schedules, Jacksonville, Duval County, Fla., 1850, 1860; see also Frank Mortimer Hawes, "New Englanders in the Florida Census of 1850," *New England Historical and Genealogical Register* 76 (1922), 49. In the U.S. federal census, Jacksonville, Duval County, Fla., 1860, the census-taker ticked off the box for "Married within the year," though no one else was listed in Dorman's household; in the U.S. federal census, Jacksonville, Duval County, Fla., 1880, Dorman claimed the status of single, rather than married, widowed, or divorced. I have located no marriage record for Rodney Dorman or Stephen Rodney Dorman, as his name appears in his birth records. See also Stephen Rodney Dorman, listed in Wilbraham, Town and City Clerks of Massachusetts, *Massachusetts Town and Vital Records,* Ancestry.com.

8. **home:** Thomas Frederick Davis, *History of Early Jacksonville Florida* (Jacksonville, Fla.: H. and W. B. Drew, 1911), 105 (map), 108–9 (Pine Street).

9. **many:** Christopher Looby, ed., *The Complete Civil War Journal and Selected Letters of Thomas Wentworth Higginson* (Chicago: University of Chicago Press, 1999), 109 (Mar. 13, 1863, entry); **bitterly:** Susie King Taylor, *Reminiscences of My Life in Camp with the 33d United States Colored Troops, Late 1st S.C. Volunteers* (1902; reprint, New York: Arno Press and New York Times, 1968), 23. Dorman diary, Feb. 7, 1864 (Higginson's). See also Thomas Wentworth Higginson, "The reoccupation of Jacksonville, Florida, in 1863," undated ms., #19, Higginson Additional Papers, HLH; "Report of Col. T. W. Higginson, First South Carolina Infantry (Union)," onboard *Ben De Ford,* Feb. 1, 1863, U.S. War Department, *War of the Rebellion: A Compilation of the Official Records of the Union and Confederate Armies,* ser. 1, 53 vols. (Washington, D.C.: Government Printing Office, 1880–1898), 14:195–98; "Our Port Royal Correspondence," *New York Times,* Mar. 25, 1863; "The Negro Troops in Florida," *New York Times,* Apr. 21, 1863. Daniel L. Schafer, *Thunder on the River: The Civil War in Northeast Florida* (Gainesville: University Press of Florida, 2010), 137, notes that a significant number of volunteers were between the ages of forty and sixty.

10. **withdrawal:** Stevenson, *Journals of Charlotte Forten Grimké,* 466 (Mar. 26, 1863, entry); **claim:** "Statement and Schedule of Losses" and "Schedule of property of Rodney Dorman at Jacksonville Florida stolen & destroyed & burned by the enemy in March 1863," July 3, 1863, Rodney Dorman, Citizens File, Confederate Papers Relating to Citizens or Business Firms, RG109-NARA, available at Fold3.com. See also correspondence between Dorman and the U.S. tax collector L. D. Stickney, Mar. 24, Apr. 23, May 7, 1866, copied into Dorman diary, vol. 3, "Note B, page 164," 607–15; "The Ruins of Jacksonville, (Fla.)," *Daily National Intelligencer,* Apr. 27, 1863.

11. Dorman diary, Apr. 29, May 20, 23, 1864, Apr. 16, 1865 (oath), May 23, 1864 (pass). **heaps:** George Heimach, "For the Christian Recorder," near Jacksonville, Fla., Apr. 1, 1864, *Christian Recorder,* published Apr. 16, 1864; **mistresses, hospitals:** Rufus Sibb Jones, "Florida Expedition," Jacksonville, Fla., Apr. 16, 1864, *Christian Recorder,* pub-

lished May 7, 1864; **glad:** Abraham Lincoln to David Hunter, Washington, D.C., Apr. 1, 1863, *War of the Rebellion,* ser. 1, 14:435–36.

On passes, see also Justus M. Silliman to brother, Volusia, Fla., May 16, 1864, in *A New Canaan Private in the Civil War: Letters of Justus M. Silliman, 17th Connecticut Volunteers,* ed. Edward Marcus (New Canaan, Conn.: New Canaan Historical Society, 1984), 68. For Orloff Dorman, see U.S. federal census, Saint Johns County, Saint Augustine, Fla., 1860; Orloff Mather Dorman, U.S. Civil War Soldier Records and Profiles, 1861–1865, Ancestry.com; Matthew Pinsker, *Lincoln's Sanctuary: Abraham Lincoln and the Soldiers' Home* (New York: Oxford University Press, 2003), 34, 208n31; Michael Burlingame and John R. Turner Ettlinger, eds., *Inside Lincoln's White House: The Complete Civil War Diary of John Hay* (Carbondale: Southern Illinois University Press, 1997), 145 (Jan. 20, 1864, entry), 300n37.

12. Dorman diary, May 7, 1864 (raid); Sarah Browne diary, Apr. 25–May 9 (Jacksonville), Apr. 26, 1864 (havoc), May 1, 1865 (mementoes), BFP. For correspondence between Rodney Dorman and L. D. Stickney, see n10, above.

Chapter 1. Victory and Defeat

1. Sarah Browne diary, Apr. 3, 4 (wild), 5 (rebels), 6 (Sheridan), 7, 8 (joy), 1865, BFP.

2. Sarah Browne diary, Apr. 10, 11, 12 (disappointed), 13, 1865, BFP.

3. Albert Browne to "Dear Ones," Charleston, S.C., Apr. 16, 1865 (fast); Albert Browne to "Dear Ones," Hilton Head Island, S.C., Apr. 12, 1865 (grand, glorious, man), both BFP.

4. Albert Browne to "Dear Ones," Charleston, S.C., Apr. 15 (grand, unspeakable), 16 (sights), 1865, BFP.

5. Dorman diary, Apr. 16, 29 (conditions), 22 (nonsensical), 16 (defeat, blacker, if North), 20 (negro, thunder bolt), 1865.

6. Dorman diary, Apr. 20, 25 (Carthage, Irish), 16 (summer), 1865.

7. Dorman diary, Apr. 22, 1865.

newspapers: Justus M. Silliman to mother, Jacksonville, Fla., Apr. 20, 1865, in *A New Canaan Private in the Civil War: Letters of Justus M. Silliman, 17th Connecticut Volunteers,* ed. Edward Marcus (New Canaan, Conn.: New Canaan Historical Society, 1984), 99.

8. **Babylon:** Thomas Day Seymour to Nathan Seymour, Richmond, Va., Apr. 3, 1865, Seymour Family Papers, Yale-Sterling; **at last:** Chester dispatch, Richmond, Va., Apr. 4, 1865, in *Thomas Morris Chester: Black Civil War Correspondent—His Dispatches from the Virginia Front,* ed. R. J. M. Blackett (Baton Rouge: Louisiana State University Press, 1989), 290; **slavery:** Frederick Douglass, "Nemesis," *Douglass' Monthly,* May 1861, in *Frederick Douglass: Selected Speeches and Writings,* ed. Philip S. Foner and Yuval Taylor (Chicago: Lawrence Hill Books, 1999), 451; **sold, violence:** Emmeline Yelland to Albert Yelland, Galena, Ill., May 29, 1865, Yelland Family Correspondence, Duke.

Countless sources convey the joyous crowds of African Americans; see, e.g., John C. Brock, "A Soldier's Letter," *Christian Recorder,* Apr. 29, 1865, and Allen H. Babcock diary, Apr. 4, 1865, Babcock Papers, NYSL.

9. **Norfolk classroom:** Hope R. Daggett to George Whipple, Norfolk, Va., Apr. [n.d.],

1865, #H1-7058; Annie C. Woodbury to George Whipple, Norfolk, Va., Apr. [n.d.], 1865, #H1-7060; Mary E. Watson [mislabeled Hope R. Daggett] to George Whipple, Norfolk, Va., May 1, 1865, #H1-7070, reel 210, AMA; **songs:** Irwin Silber, ed., *Songs of the Civil War* (New York: Bonanza Books, 1960), 17–19, 320–21; American Song Sheets, Duke, available at library.duke.edu/digitalcollections/songsheets; "'A Jubilee of Freedom': Freed Slaves March in Charleston, South Carolina, March, 1865," History Matters, American Social History Project, Center for Media and Learning (Graduate Center, CUNY) and Roy Rosenzweig Center for History and New Media, George Mason University, available at historymatters.gmu.edu/d/6381.

10. **Richmond:** Chester dispatches, Richmond, Va., Apr. 6, 9, 1865, in Blackett, *Thomas Morris Chester,* 294–300 (**citizens,** 296); "The Richmond Freedmen: Their Visit to the President," *New York Daily Tribune,* June 17, 1865; Garland H. White, "Letter from Richmond," City Point, Va., Apr. 12, 1865, *Christian Recorder,* published Apr. 22, 1865.

11. **thought:** Annie G. Dudley Davis diary, Apr. 10, 1865, HL.

12. **hats, shoes:** Narrative of Appomattox Campaign, Apr. 9, 1865, in *The Civil War Letters of General Robert McAllister,* ed. James I. Robertson Jr. (1965; reprint, Baton Rouge: Louisiana State University Press, 1993), 608; **jove:** Charles S. Brown to mother and "Etta," near Haywood, N.C., Apr. 18, 1865, Brown Papers, Duke; **muskets, cannons:** Edward W. Benham to Jennie Benham, Goldsboro, N.C., Apr. 9, 1865, ts., Benham Papers, Duke; **cheers, firecrackers, music:** Theodore St. John to Jane Harries, New Bern, N.C., Apr. 12, 1865, St. John Papers, LC; **9 a.m.:** Rufus Mead Jr. to "Dear Folks at Home," near Goldsboro, N.C., Apr. 7, 1865, and Rufus Mead Jr. diary, Apr. 6, 1865, Mead Papers, LC; **jump, dance, music, whiskey:** Peter Eltinge to Edmund Eltinge, Morehead City, N.C., Apr. 7, 1865, ts., Eltinge-Lord Family Papers (Peter Eltinge Papers), Duke; **liquor:** William C. McLean diary, Apr. 8, 1865, ts., McLean Family Papers, NYSL, and Thomas Day Seymour to Nathan Seymour, Richmond, Va., Apr. 3, 1865, Seymour Family Papers, Yale-Sterling; **glory:** Lyman P. Spencer diary, Apr. 3, 1865, Spencer Papers, LC; **cannon:** "Lydia" to "Anna," Clarksville, Tenn., Apr. 7, 1865, "Miscellaneous letters and fragments," Adam C. Higgins Papers, HL; **pain:** Annie G. Dudley Davis diary, Apr. 3, 1865, HL.

13. **wild:** countless sources invoke this word; see, e.g., Wesley Talley diary, Apr. 3, 1865, DHS; **crazy:** Thomas Francis Johnson diary, Apr. 5, 1865, Johnson Family Papers, MDHS; **agog:** Ellis Hughes diary, Apr. 3, 1865, Hughes-Gray Family Papers, Duke; **Wilmington:** Samuel Canby diary, Apr. 3, 1865, DHS; Anna M. Ferris diary, Apr. 3, 1865, Ferris Family Papers, FHL; Wesley Talley diary, Apr. 3, 1865, DHS; **New York:** Julia Anna Hartness Lay diary, Apr. 3, 1865, NYPL; **Cincinnati:** *"Maggie!": Maggie Lindsley's Journal, Nashville, Tennessee, 1864, Washington, D.C., 1865* (Southbury, Conn.: Muriel Davies Mackenzie, 1977), 82 (Apr. 11, 1865, entry); **Chicago:** Stephen Thurston Farwell diary, Apr. 3, 1865, Farwell Collection, Princeton; **Sacramento:** Frederick G. Niles diary, Apr. 5, 6, 1865, HL; **crowds:** John Thayer to Lorin Low Dame, Dedham, Mass., Apr. 5, 1865, Dame Papers, MHS; **classroom:** Sarah Hale to Charles Hale, Brookline, Mass., Apr. 7, 1865, box 11, Hale Family Papers, SSC; **Washington:** *Diary of Gideon Welles, Secretary of the Navy under Lincoln and Johnson,* 3 vols. (Boston: Houghton Mifflin, 1911), 2:272–73 (Apr. 3,

1865, entry); Charles T. Cotton diary, Apr. 3, 5, 1865, Columbia; Simon Newcomb diary, Apr. 3, 1865, Newcomb Papers, LC; Elizabeth Blair Lee to Samuel Phillips Lee, Washington, D.C., Apr. 4, 1865, in *Wartime Washington: The Civil War Letters of Elizabeth Blair Lee,* ed. Virginia Jean Laas (Urbana: University of Illinois Press, 1991), 489; Benjamin Brown French, *Witness to the Young Republic: A Yankee's Journal, 1828–1870,* ed. Donald B. Cole and John J. McDonough (Hanover, N.H.: University Press of New England, 1989), 468 (Apr. 6, 1865, entry); James Thomas Ward diary, Apr. 3, 1865, Ward Papers, LC; **resplendent, tiers:** Mary Henry diary, Apr. 5, 1865, Smithsonian Institution Archives, available at siarchives.si.edu/history/exhibits/stories/end-civil-war-april-3-10-1865.

14. **Richmond:** Emilie Davis diary, Apr. 3, 1865, HSP and davisdiaries.villanova. edu; **New Year's:** Margaret B. Howell diary, Apr. 3, 1865, HSP; for Philadelphia, see also Mary Dreer diary, Apr. 3, 1865, Edwin Greble Papers, LC; Nicholas B. Wainwright, ed., *A Philadelphia Perspective: The Diary of Sidney George Fisher . . . , 1834–1871* (Philadelphia: Historical Society of Pennsylvania, 1967), 490 (Apr. 5, 1865, entry); **boys:** Lucy Pierce Hedge to Charlotte Hedge, Brookline, Mass., Apr. 4, 1865, Poor Family Papers, SL; Susan Heath diary, Apr. 3, 1865, Heath Family Papers, MHS; **legislature:** John Wolcott Phelps commonplace book, Apr. 10, 1865, Phelps Papers, NYPL; **Weaverville:** Franklin Augustus Buck to Mary Sewall Bradley, Weaverville, Calif., Apr. 27, 1865, Buck Papers, HL; **handshaking:** William Dean Howells to William Cooper and Mary Dean Howells, Venice, Apr. 27, 1865, 1784.13(15), Howells Family Papers, HLH.

15. **corner stone:** John Prentiss journal, Apr. 8, 1865, Prentiss Papers, AAS; **great truth:** Alexander H. Stephens, "Cornerstone Address," in *Southern Pamphlets on Secession: November 1860–April 1861,* ed. Jon L. Wakelyn (Chapel Hill: University of North Carolina Press, 1996), 406.

16. **entire:** *Diary of Gideon Welles,* 2:273 (Apr. 3, 1865, entry); **yankeedom:** Henry Robinson Berkeley diary, Apr. 4, 1865, Berkeley Papers, ser. A, reel 2, VHS-CMM; **sour:** "Sanford" to Mary Peck, near Petersburg, Va., Apr. 7, 1865, Peck Correspondence, NYSL; **Confederates:** Chester dispatches, Richmond, Va., Apr. 4, 6, 1865, in Blackett, *Thomas Morris Chester,* 289, 296; **heavy, followed:** Michael Bedout Chesson and Leslie Jean Roberts, eds., *Exile in Richmond: The Confederate Journal of Henri Garidel* (Charlottesville: University Press of Virginia, 2001), 368, 370 (Apr. 3, 4, 1865, entries); **contemptable:** Malcolm Canfield to Harriett Canfield, New York, Apr. 5, 1865, Canfield Papers, NYSL.

For Copperhead sentiment, see also Caroline Dunstan diary, Apr. 8, 1865, NYPL, and Mary Jane Church to Dennis Church, New York, Apr. 5, 1865, Church Letters, Cornell.

17. **world:** Creed Thomas Davis diary, Apr. 2, 1865, ser. A, reel 13, VHS-CMM; **blues:** Amanda (Edmonds) Chappelear diary, Apr. 7, 1865, Chappelear Papers, ser. D, part 3, reel 9, VHS-SWF; **Yankee glee:** Nimrod Porter diary, Apr. 3, 1865, Porter Papers, SHC; **will not:** Emma F. LeConte diary, Apr. 13, 1865, reel 22, SHC-AWD-South; **fool:** Samuel A. Harrison journal, Apr. 4, 1865, MDHS.

18. **isn't so:** Henry M. Whitney to "Al," City Point, Va., Apr. 4, 1865, Whitney Correspondence, MHS; **Fitzhugh:** Abram Verrick Parmenter diary, Apr. 7, 8, 1865, Parmenter Papers, LC; **Wilmington:** Anna M. Ferris diary, Apr. 7, 1865, Ferris Family Papers, FHL;

bogus: Anna Cabot Lowell diary, Apr. 8, 1865, MHS; **heartsickening:** Henry Robinson Berkeley diary, Apr. 9, 1865, Berkeley Papers, ser. A, reel 2, VHS-CMM; **Lee:** William Williston Heartsill, *Fourteen Hundred and 91 Days in the Confederate Army,* ed. Bell Irvin Wiley (1876; reprint, Jackson, Tenn.: McCowat-Mercer, 1954), 240 (Apr. 20, 1865, entry), ACWLD.

19. **farmer:** Nimrod Porter diary, Apr. 10, 1865, Porter Papers, SHC; **lady:** Caroline Curtis diary, Apr. 10, 1865, Cary Family Papers III, MHS.

For continued skirmishing after surrender, see E. B. Long and Barbara Long, *The Civil War Day by Day: An Almanac, 1861–1865* (Garden City, N.Y.: Doubleday, 1971), 675–91.

20. **road:** James Herbert George to "My dear home," Appomattox, Va., Apr. 14, 1865, George Letters, HL; **impossible:** Chester dispatch, Richmond, Va., Apr. 10, 1865, in Blackett, *Thomas Morris Chester,* 303–4; **promenade:** Thomas Day Seymour to Nathan Seymour, Richmond, Va., Apr. 10, 1865, and Thomas Day Seymour to Sarah Parsons, Richmond, Va., Apr. 12, 1865, Seymour Family Papers, Yale-Sterling; **clothing, John Brown, children:** Lucy Muse (Walton) Fletcher diary, Apr. 25, 1865, Fletcher Papers, Duke; **shouts:** Chesson and Roberts, *Exile in Richmond,* 375 (Apr. 9, 1865, entry); **Roanoke:** P. B. S. Nichuston [?] to George Whipple, Roanoke Island, N.C., Apr. 22, 1865, #100001, reel 169, AMA; **Charleston:** Gerald Schwartz, ed., *A Woman Doctor's Civil War: Esther Hill Hawks' Diary* (Columbia: University of South Carolina Press, 1984), 129 (Apr. 12, 1865, entry).

21. **throats:** John S. Sanford to mother, Appomattox Court House, Va., Apr. 10, 1865, Sanford Papers, Duke; **toasts:** James Herbert George to "My dear home," Appomattox, Va., Apr. 14, 1865, George Letters, HL; **Meade:** Kiliaen Van Rensselaer to W. P. Van Rensselaer, City Point, Va., Apr. 23, 1865, ts., Erving-King Papers, NYHS; **row:** Peter Eltinge to Edmund Eltinge, Goldsboro, N.C., Apr. 14, 1865, ts., Eltinge-Lord Family Papers (Peter Eltinge Papers), Duke; **newspapers:** Hastell P. Lyons to "Dear Friends at Home," Kinston, N.C., Apr. 8–12, 1865, Lyons Papers, GWBW.

22. **kicked, hurrahed:** James Otis Moore to sister, near Petersburg, Va., Apr. 15, 1865, Moore Papers, Duke; **handstands, mud:** Lucius F. Hubbard to aunt, Montgomery, Ala., May 3, 1865, in N. B. Martin, "Letters of a Union Officer: L. F. Hubbard and the Civil War," *Minnesota History* 35 (1957), 318; **mud:** Manning Ferguson Force to "Mr. Kebler" [?], Raleigh, N.C., Apr. 16, 1865 (letters copied into journal), Force Papers, LC; **liquor:** Thomas S. Howland to sister, Raleigh, N.C., Apr. 16, 1865, Howland Papers, MHS; John Swift to sister, White River, Ark., Apr. 21, 1865, in "Letters from a Sailor on a Tinclad," ed. Lester L. Swift, *Civil War History* 7 (1961), 62; **double-shuffle** John Payson Slocum diary, Apr. 9, 1865, Slocum Family Papers, NYSL; **musicians:** John B. Burrud to Ocena Burrud, Winchester, Va., Apr. 10, 1865 (part of Apr. 9 letter), Burrud Papers, HL; **tree:** R. P. Tanner to Charles A. Tanner, Raleigh, N.C., Apr. 14, 1865, Tanner Papers, SHC; **battle:** John Wesley Marshall diary, Apr. 10, 1865, LC; **hospital:** Rose Pickard to family, Alexandria, Va., Apr. 10, 1865, Pickard Papers, LC; **incredible:** James J. Higginson to Anne E. Heath, Burkeville, Va., Apr. 16, 1865, Heath Family Papers, MHS; **impression:** Stephen Minot

Weld to Hannah Weld, City Point, Va., Apr. 24, 1865, in *War Diary and Letters of Stephen Minot Weld, 1861–1865* (Cambridge, Mass.: Riverside Press, 1912), 396; **whipping post:** Rufus Mead Jr. diary, Apr. 12, 1865, Mead Papers, LC.

23. **thunderbolt:** David Gregg McIntosh diary, Apr. 9, 1865, McIntosh Papers, ser. A, reel 25, VHS-CMM; **gloom:** Heartsill, *Fourteen Hundred and 91 Days,* 240 (Apr. 23, 1865, entry), ACWLD; **intense:** Henry Robinson Berkeley diary, Apr. 11, 1865, Berkeley Papers, ser. A, reel 2, VHS-CMM; **hearts:** E. L. Cox diary, Apr. 10, 1865, ser. A, reel 13, VHS-CMM; **sinking:** Henry Robinson Berkeley diary, Apr. 11, 1865, Berkeley Papers, ser. A, reel 2, VHS-CMM; **saddest:** Kena King Chapman diary, Apr. 9, 1865, SHC; **minutes, sick:** John Johnston, "Personal Reminiscence of the Civil War, 1861–1865," diary transcriptions, May 4, Apr. 28, 1865, Johnston Papers, SHC; **rivers:** Junius Newport Bragg to Anna J. G. Bragg, near Marshall, Tex., Apr. 23, 1865, in Bragg, *Letters of a Confederate Surgeon, 1861–65,* ed. Helen Bragg Gaughan (Camden, Ark.: Hurley, 1960), 272, ACWLD; **ain't:** John L. Smith to Hannah Smith, near Burkeville, Va., Apr. 18, 1865, Smith Papers, HSP; **bitter:** Henry A. Chambers diary, Apr. 10, 1865, Chambers Papers, SHC.

24. **broke down:** J. E. Whitehorne diary, Apr. 9, 1865, ts., SHC; **dry eye:** John Walters, *Norfolk Blues: The Civil War Diary of the Norfolk Light Artillery Blues,* ed. Kenneth Wiley (Shippensburg, Pa.: Burd Street Press, 1997), 223 (Apr. 9, 1865, entry); see also C. Vann Woodward, ed., *Mary Chesnut's Civil War* (1981; reprint, New Haven: Yale University Press, 1993), 788 (Apr. 7, 1865, entry); **heart, ailments, unhappiness:** Chesson and Roberts, *Exile in Richmond,* 376, 381, 385 (Apr. 10, 18, 21, 1865, entries).

25. **enjoying, nauseum, anxious:** Lucy Muse (Walton) Fletcher diary, Apr. 25, 9, 1865, Fletcher Papers, Duke; **wild:** Mary (Cabell) Early diary, Apr. 17, 10, 1865, Early Family Papers, ser. D, part 3, reel 14, VHS-SWF, and Elizabeth (Alsop) Wynne diary, Apr. 22, 1865, Wynne Family Papers, ser. D, part 3, reel 52, VHS-SWF ("The past two or three weeks seem like a dream, & yet I feel as if they had been years"); **revulsion:** Eliza F. Andrews, *The War-Time Journal of a Georgia Girl, 1864–1865* (New York: D. Appleton, 1908), 171 (Apr. 21, 1865, entry), DocSouth, docsouth.unc.edu/fpn/andrews/menu.html; **give up:** Emma F. LeConte diary, Apr. 20, 1865, reel 22, SHC-AWD-South.

David Herbert Donald writes, "Nearly every Southern manuscript collection for the period echoes the note of unbelief that defeat had really happened"; see "A Generation of Defeat," in *From the Old South to the New: Essays on the Transitional South,* ed. Walter J. Fraser Jr. and Winfred B. Moore Jr. (Westport, Conn.: Greenwood, 1981), 9.

On Confederates' thoughts of suicide, see chap. 7, below.

26. **thousand:** Anna M. Ferris diary, Apr. 10, 1865, Ferris Family Papers, FHL; **Lexington:** Joseph Cabell Breckinridge diary, Apr. 10, 1865, Breckinridge Family Papers, LC; **Baltimore:** Thomas Francis Johnson diary, Apr. 10, 1865, Johnson Family Papers, MDHS; William Owner diary, Apr. 14, 1865, LC; **caboodles:** "Joe" to [Christian A. Fleetwood?], Baltimore, Apr. 9, 1865, Fleetwood Papers, LC.

27. **victors:** see, e.g., Lucretia Hale to Charles Hale, Brookline, Mass., Apr. 14, 1865, box 50, Hale Family Papers, SSC ("everybody"); **light, midnight:** Julia Adelaide Shepard to father, near Washington, D.C., Apr. 16, 1865, in "Lincoln's Assassination Told by an

Eye-Witness," *Century Magazine* 77 (1909), 918; **candles:** Henry I. Colyer to mother, Washington, D.C., Apr. 15, 1865, in Justin G. Turner, "April 14, 1865: A Soldier's View," *American Book Collector* 15 (1965), 9; **Chicago:** Stephen Thurston Farwell diary, Apr. 10, 11, 1865, Farwell Collection, Princeton; **Hartford:** Mary Bushnell Cheney to Francis Louise Bushnell, [Hartford, Conn.?], Apr. 15, 1865, ts., Cheney Family Papers, SSC; **New York:** Maria Lydig Daly, *Diary of a Union Lady, 1861–1865,* ed. Harold Earl Hammond (New York: Funk and Wagnalls, 1962), 351 (Apr. 10, 1865, entry).

28. **victory:** Mary Peck to Henry J. Peck, Jonesville, N.Y., Apr. 12, 1865, Peck Correspondence, NYSL; **Cincinnati:** "From Cincinnati," *New York Anglo-African,* Apr. 29, 1865; **Sacramento:** Frederick G. Niles diary, Apr. 12, 1865, HL; **horses:** Hattie Schenck to cousin, Cedar Falls, Iowa, Apr. 22, 1865, Schenck Family Papers, NYSL; **inanimate:** Henry S. Thacher diary, Apr. 10, 1865, Thacher Family Papers, MHS.

29. **depended:** Daniel E. Sutherland, ed., *A Very Violent Rebel: The Civil War Diary of Ellen Renshaw House* (Knoxville: University of Tennessee Press, 1996), 162 (Apr. 23, 1865, entry); **Bible, hard, measure:** Cloe (Whittle) Greene diary, Apr. 11, June 16, 1865, reel 4, WM-AWD-South.

30. **until:** Abraham Lincoln, "Second Inaugural Address," Mar. 4, 1865, *CWL,* 8:333; **hell-born:** Daniel Franklin Child diary, Apr. 10, 1865, Child Papers, MHS; **color:** Caroline Barrett White diary, Apr. 10, 1865, White Papers, AAS; **acquiescent:** Robert H. Williams to Ellen Williams, City Point, Va., Apr. 5, 1865, Goff-Williams Papers, HL; **eager:** Hallock Armstrong to Mary Armstrong, near Petersburg, Va., Apr. 15, 1865, in *Letters from a Pennsylvania Chaplain at the Siege of Petersburg: 1865* (N.p.: Privately published, 1961), 27, ACWLD; **cruel, magnanimity:** Anna M. Ferris diary, Apr. 3, 14, 1865, Ferris Family Papers, FHL.

31. **disposed:** "Lee's Surrender—Peace," *New York Anglo-African,* Apr. 15, 1865; **hereafter:** Frederick Douglass, "The Fall of Richmond: An Address Delivered in Boston, Massachusetts, on 4 April 1865," *FDP,* ser. 1, 4:73.

32. **weary:** Lydia Maria Child to Sarah Blake Shaw, [no place], Apr. [n.d.], 1865, Child Letters, SL; **sidearms:** Anna Cabot Lowell diary, Apr. 10, 1865 (on Mary Putnam), MHS; **mortified:** Caroline Dunstan diary, Apr. 10, 1865, NYPL; **squirm:** William L. Dorr to Sarah Bradley Gamble, South Side Railroad, Va., Apr. 9, 1865, Gamble Papers, SL; **country:** John Wolcott Phelps commonplace book, Apr. 17, 1865, Phelps Papers, NYPL; **lay down:** "Lee's Surrender—Peace," *New York Anglo-African,* Apr. 15, 1865.

33. **killed:** Sarah G. Putnam diary, Apr. 2 [sic], 1865, MHS; **baby, chores, news:** James C. Mohr and Richard E. Winslow, eds., *The Cormany Diaries: A Northern Family in the Civil War* (Pittsburgh: University of Pittsburgh Press, 1982), 542 (Apr. 4, 1865, entry); **surrender, furs:** Elizabeth Rogers Mason Cabot diary, Apr. 10, 1865, MHS; **wood:** John B. Orton diary, Apr. 14, 1865, NYSL; **marrage:** William Benjamin Gould diary, Apr. 21, 1865, MHS.

34. **far less:** Sophia E. Perry diary, Apr. 10, 1865, CP.

35. **heard, worked:** Alden Spooner Forbes diary, Apr. 15, 27, 1865, ts., ser. N, reel 10, MDAH-RSP.

36. **speech:** Abraham Lincoln, "Last Public Address," Apr. 11, 1865, *CWL,* 8:399–405. Lincoln had earlier discussed which black men should vote, writing to the governor of Louisiana; see Abraham Lincoln to Michael Hahn, Washington, D.C., Mar. 13, 1864, *CWL,* 7:243.

37. **noble:** Franklin Boyts to Josiah Boyts, Washington, D.C., Apr. 12, 1865, in Boyts diary, HSP; **subjugation:** John Glenn diary, Apr. 15, 1865, Glenn Papers, MDHS.

38. **citizenship:** William H. Herndon and Jesse W. Weik, *Abraham Lincoln: The True Story of a Great Life,* 2 vols. (New York: D. Appleton, 1900), 2:289 ("Frederick Stone, counsel for Harold [sic] after Booth's death, is authority for the statement"); **country:** John Wilkes Booth, "To Whom It May Concern," Philadelphia, November 1864, in *"Right or Wrong, God Judge Me": The Writings of John Wilkes Booth,* ed. John Rhodehamel and Louise Taper (Urbana: University of Illinois Press, 1997), 125; on April 14, 1865, Booth wrote a letter to the *National Intelligencer* with a similar statement (147). On Booth's white supremacy, see Michael Burlingame, *Abraham Lincoln: A Life,* 2 vols. (Baltimore: Johns Hopkins University Press, 2008), 2:810–16.

39. **alive:** R. B. Milliken to "Friend Byron," Washington, D.C., Apr. 16, 1865, #54, Lincoln Room Miscellaneous Papers, HLH; **illumination:** Charles T. Cotton diary, Apr. 14, 1865, Columbia; **continuous:** "Carrie" to sister, Washington, D.C., Apr. 16, 1865, box 2, fol. 27, Richard John Levy and Sally Waldman Sweet Collection, NYPL; **glory:** James Thomas Ward diary, Apr. 13, 1865, Ward Papers, LC; **blazing:** John B. Stonehouse to John B. Stonehouse Jr., Washington, D.C., Apr. 16, 1865, #00368, GLC-NYHS.

40. **Sumter:** *Programme of the Order of Exercises at the Re-Raising of the United States Flag, on Fort Sumter, Charleston, S.C., April 14th, 1865* (Port Royal, S.C.: New South Office, 1865); **Beecher:** Henry Ward Beecher, *Oration at the Raising of "The Old Flag" at Sumter; and Sermon on the Death of Abraham Lincoln* (Manchester: Alexander Ireland, 1865), 12, 19, 24, 25, 13, 14.

41. **ceremonies:** "Fort Sumter: Restoration of the Stars and Stripes," *New York Times,* Apr. 18, 1865; Albert Browne to "Dear Ones," Charleston, S.C., Apr. 16, 1865, BFP; Wilbert L. Jenkins, *Seizing the New Day: African Americans in Post–Civil War Charleston* (Bloomington: Indiana University Press, 1998), 38–39; **Garrison, Wilson, Thompson:** *The Trip of the Steamer Oceanus to Fort Sumter and Charleston, S.C.* (Brooklyn, N.Y.: "The Union" Steam Printing Press, 1865), 96–114 ("regards," 114); **elated:** William Lloyd Garrison Jr. to Martha Coffin Wright, Boston, Apr. 25, 1865, box 56, Garrison Family Papers, SSC; **cheered:** Laura Towne to unknown, Saint Helena Island, S.C., Apr. 23, 1865, in *Letters and Diary of Laura M. Towne: Written from the Sea Islands of South Carolina, 1862–1884,* ed. Rupert Sargent Holland (1912; reprint, New York: Negro Universities Press, 1969), 159; **gun salute:** John Wesley Marshall diary, Apr. 14, 1865, LC; **other celebrations:** Frank S. Mckey to Samuel W. Very, Boston, Apr. 18, 1865, Blair and Lee Family Papers, Princeton; **same flag:** Samuel Canby diary, Apr. 14, 1865, DHS; **traitors:** Daniel Franklin Child diary, Apr. 14, 1865, Child Papers, MHS.

42. **suppose:** Emma F. LeConte diary, Apr. 13, 1865, reel 22, SHC-AWD-South.

43. **letters:** Nathan Seymour to Thomas Day Seymour, Hudson, Ohio, Apr. 13, 1865,

Seymour Family Papers, Yale-Sterling; **unparalleled:** Caroline Barrett White diary, Apr. 10, 1865, White Papers, AAS; **inscribed:** Amos A. Lawrence diary, Apr. 6, 9, 1865, MHS; **fast, written:** Albert Browne to "Dear Ones," Charleston, S.C., Apr. 16, 1865, BFP; **changes:** Emma F. LeConte diary, Apr. 13, 1865, reel 22, SHC-AWD-South; **brain:** Mary (Cabell) Early diary, Apr. 9, 1865, Early Family Papers, ser. D, part 3, reel 14, VHS-SWF; **never:** Margaret (Brown) Wight diary, Apr. 2, 1865, Wight Family Papers, ser. D, part 1, reel 21, VHS-SWF.

44. **sundown:** *Trip of the Steamer Oceanus*, 84; **above:** Sarah Browne diary, Apr. 14, 1865, BFP; **joy:** Amos A. Lawrence diary, Apr. 17, 1865, MHS.

Interlude: Rumors

1. **grapevine:** Joel Calvin McDiarmid diary, Apr. 5, 1865, in *Voices from Company D: Diaries by the Greensboro Guards, Fifth Alabama Infantry Regiment, Army of Northern Virginia*, ed. G. Ward Hubbs (Athens: University of Georgia Press, 2003), 368; **latest, Madam:** Samuel Pickens diary, Apr. 16, 17, 30, 1865, in Hubbs, *Voices from Company D*, 372, 373; **Madam, grapevine:** Henry Clay Weaver to Cornelia S. Wiley, Raleigh, N.C., Apr. 19, 28, 1865, Weaver Papers, LC; **Grant:** William Hamilton to mother, Nottaway Court House, Va., Apr. 25, 1865 (part of Apr. 24 letter), Hamilton Papers, LC; **Stanton:** William Williston Heartsill, *Fourteen Hundred and 91 Days in the Confederate Army*, ed. Bell Irvin Wiley (1876; reprint, Jackson, Tenn.: McCowat-Mercer, 1954), 242–43 (May 7, 1865, entry), ACWLD; **Sewards:** Numerous letters and diaries discuss the Seward deaths; **Tad:** Samuel Pickens diary, Apr. 16, 1865, in Hubbs, *Voices from Company D*, 372.

2. **shot:** Henry Morrill to C. Henry Albers, Memphis, Tenn., Apr. 15, 1865, Morrill Papers, Western Americana, Yale-Beinecke; **traced:** Lyman P. Spencer diary, Apr. 15, 1865, Spencer Papers, LC; **hardly:** "Civil War Diary of James Wesley Riley: Who Served with the Union Army in the War Between the States, April 22, 1861–June 18, 1865," ts. (C. W. Denslinger, 1960), 103 (Apr. 15, 1865, entry); **hope:** Allen H. Babcock diary, Apr. 16, 1865, Babcock Papers, NYSL; **swore:** Henry J. Peck to Mary Peck, Appomattox Court House, Va., Apr. 16, 1865, Peck Correspondence, NYSL; **Sheridan:** Samuel Comfort to George Comfort, Nottaway Station, Va., Apr. 16, 1865, Comfort Papers, Princeton; **noon:** Thomas Day Seymour to Nathan Seymour, Richmond, Va., Apr. 17, 1865, Seymour Family Papers, Yale-Sterling; **camp story:** Warren Goodale to children, in and around Petersburg, Va., Apr. 15ff., 1865, Goodale Papers, MHS; **rumor makers:** Chauncey Welton to parents, Raleigh, N.C., Apr. 19, 1865, Welton Papers, SHC; **rumor, dead, alive:** E. P. Failing diary, Apr. 17, 18, 1865, Failing-Knight Papers, MHS; **wires:** Mary Ann Anderson, ed., *The Civil War Diary of Allen Morgan Geer: Twentieth Regiment, Illinois Volunteers* (Denver: R. C. Appleman, 1977), 215 (Apr. 17, 1865, entry).

3. **lowered flag:** Creed Thomas Davis diary, Apr. 18, 1865, ser. A, reel 13, VHS-CMM; **slavery:** Norman D. Brown, ed., *One of Cleburne's Command: The Civil War Reminiscences and Diary of Capt. Samuel T. Foster, Granbury's Texas Brigade, CSA* (Austin: University of Texas Press, 1980), 165–66 (Apr. 19, 1865, entry); **April Fools:** Eliza F. Andrews, *The War-Time Journal of a Georgia Girl, 1864–1865* (New York: D. Appleton, 1908), 172 (Apr.

21, 1865, entry), DocSouth, docsouth.unc.edu/fpn/andrews/menu.html; **Johnson:** Samuel A. Agnew diary, Apr. 21, 22, 23, 1865, SHC, available at www2.lib.unc.edu/mss/inv/a/Agnew, Samuel_A.html#, and Heartsill, *Fourteen Hundred and 91 Days,* 242–43 (May 7, 1865, entry), ACWLD; **theatric:** John F. Marszalek, ed., *The Diary of Miss Emma Holmes, 1861–1866* (Baton Rouge: Louisiana State University Press, 1994), 436 (Apr. 22, 1865, entry); **reports:** Kate Cumming, *Kate: The Journal of a Confederate Nurse,* ed. Richard Barksdale Harwell (Baton Rouge: Louisiana State University Press, 1998), 275 (Apr. 22, 1865, entry), NAWLD.

4. **float:** James William Latta diary, Apr. 25, 1865, Latta Papers, LC; **all kinds:** John Whitten diary, Apr. 26, 1865, LC; **unlikeliness:** "From the Regiments," letter from "M.F.," 11th U.S. Heavy Artillery, Fort Banks, La., Apr. 12 [sic], 1865, *New York Anglo-African,* published May 20, 1865; **Congress:** Eleanor H. Cohen diary, Apr. 30, 1865, in *Memoirs of American Jews, 1775–1865,* 3 vols., ed. Jacob Rader Marcus (Philadelphia: Jewish Publication Society of America, 1955), 3:366, NAWLD; **not prove:** John Johnston, "Personal Reminiscence of the Civil War, 1861–1865," diary transcriptions, Apr. 28, 1865, Johnston Papers, SHC.

5. **Grover's:** James Tanner to Henry Walch, Washington, D.C., Apr. 17, 1865, in "Documents: The Assassination of President Lincoln, 1865," *American Historical Review* 29 (1924), 514; **awakened:** Annie G. Dudley Davis diary, Apr. 15, 1865, HL; **messenger:** Gideon Welles diary, Apr. 15, 1865, and "Copy. M. J. Welles. 14 April '65," box 41, fol. marked "Welles, Mary Hale, correspondence," Welles Papers, LC.

6. **Stonehouse:** John B. Stonehouse to John B. Stonehouse Jr., Washington, D.C., Apr. 16, 1865, #00368, GLC-NYHS; **lamp:** photograph of Ford's Theatre, 1865, #LC-B8184-7765, LC.

Chapter 2. Shock

1. Sarah Browne diary, Apr. 15, 16, 1865; Sarah Browne to Albert Browne, Salem, Mass., Apr. 20, 1865, both letters of this date, BFP.

2. Albert Browne to "Dear Ones," Hilton Head Island, S.C., Apr. 18, 1865, BFP.

orders: W. A. Nichols, assistant adjutant general, in B. F. Morris, *Memorial Record of the Nation's Tribute to Abraham Lincoln* (Washington, D.C.: W. H. and O. H. Morrison, 1865), 112.

3. Albert Browne to "Dear Ones," Charleston, S.C., Apr. 21, 1865, BFP.

4. **Harris and Rathbone:** Clara Harris to "Mary," Washington, D.C., Apr. 25, 1865, NYHS. See also "Affidavit of Major Rathbone" and "Affidavit of Miss Harris," Washington, D.C., Apr. 17, 1865, in Morris, *Memorial Record,* 42–44.

5. **reserved:** R. B. Milliken to "Friend Byron," Washington, D.C., Apr. 16, 1865, #54, Lincoln Room Miscellaneous Papers, HLH; **whim:** Charles A. Sanford to Edward Payson Goodrich, Washington, D.C., Apr. 15, 1865, in "Two Letters on the Event of April 14, 1865," *Bulletin of the William L. Clements Library of American History* 47 (Feb. 12, 1946), facsimile, n.p.; **sleeping:** Julia Adelaide Shepard to father, near Washington, D.C., Apr. 16, 1865, in "Lincoln's Assassination Told by an Eye-Witness," *Century Magazine* 77

(1909), 918; **cannot:** Frederick A. Sawyer, "Account of what I saw of the Death of Mr. Lincoln written April 15, 1865," in "An Eyewitness Account of Abraham Lincoln's Assassination," ed. Ronald D. Rietveld, *Civil War History* 22 (1976), 62.

6. **Meigs:** Minerva Rodgers to Robert Rodgers, Washington, D.C., Apr. 15, 1865, Denison-Rodgers Family Papers, Mystic; **hospital:** [M. S. Tilton?] to Georgina Lowell, Washington, D.C., Apr. 15, 1865, Francis Cabot Lowell Papers, MHS.

7. **infantry and cavalry:** J. Thoman to "Henrietta," Washington, D.C., Apr. 15, 1865, in Thomas F. Schwartz, "Grief, Souvenirs, and Enterprise Following Lincoln's Assassination," *Illinois Historical Journal* 83 (1990), 260; [M. S. Tilton?] to Georgina Lowell, Washington, D.C., Apr. 15, 1865, Francis Cabot Lowell Papers, MHS; **commotion:** Augustus Clark to S. M. Allen, Washington, D.C., Apr. 16, 1865, accompanying scrap of bloodstained towel used for Abraham Lincoln at Ford's Theatre, Special Collections, MHS; **cavalry, crowd:** Julia Adelaide Shepard to father, near Washington, D.C., Apr. 16, 1865, in "Lincoln's Assassination," 918; **crowd:** Charles F. Conant to "Hattie," Washington, D.C., Apr. 15, 1865, ML; James S. Knox to father, Washington, D.C., Apr. 15, 1865, ser. 3: General Correspondence, Abraham Lincoln Papers, LC, available at memory.loc. gov/ammem/alhtml/alser.html; **black residents:** Gideon Welles diary, Apr. 15, 1865, Welles Papers, LC; Charles A. Sanford to Edward Payson Goodrich, Washington, D.C., Apr. 15, 1865, in "Two Letters," n.p.

8. **good president, finish war:** Jane Swisshelm to *St. Cloud Democrat,* Washington, D.C., Apr. 17, 1865 (published Apr. 27, 1865), in *Crusader and Feminist: Letters of Jane Grey Swisshelm, 1858–1865,* ed. Arthur J. Larsen (Saint Paul: Minnesota Historical Society, 1934), 287.

9. **dead, intense, painfully:** Gideon Welles diary, Apr. 15, 1865, Welles Papers, LC.

10. **preparations, horror:** Benjamin Brown French to Frank O. French, Washington, D.C., Apr. 15, 24, 1865, French Papers, LC. See also Benjamin Brown French, *Witness to the Young Republic: A Yankee's Journal, 1828–1870,* ed. Donald B. Cole and John J. McDonough (Hanover, N.H.: University Press of New England, 1989), 469–70 (Apr. 15, 1865, entry).

11. **telegraph:** George B. Todd to Henry P. Todd, Washington, D.C., Apr. 15, 1865, McClellan Lincoln Collection, Brown; Ellen Kean to Mary Kean, New York, Apr. 16, 1865, in *Death and Funeral of Abraham Lincoln . . . in Two Long Descriptive Letters from Mrs. Ellen Kean, the Actress, whilst Touring the United States in 1865* (London: Privately printed, 1921), 14; Caroline Dunstan diary, Apr. 15, 1865, NYPL; **terrible news:** *Berkshire Courier,* Apr. 15, 1865.

12. **ma'am:** Ellen Kean to "Miss Sherritt," Baltimore, May 13ff., 1865, in *Death and Funeral of Abraham Lincoln,* 21; **Mr. Clapp:** William Warland Clapp diary, Apr. 15, 1865, Clapp Diaries and Correspondence, HLH; **Mrs. Dall:** Caroline Dall to "John," Boston, Apr. 20, 1865, Dall Papers, SL, and Caroline Dall journal, Apr. 22, 1865, vol. J27, Dall Papers, MHS; for transmission by servants, see also Anna Cabot Lowell diary, Apr. 15, 1865, MHS (a servant "said there were bad news afloat"); "Carrie" to sister, Washington, D.C., Apr. 16, 1865, box 2, fol. 27, Richard John Levy and Sally Waldman Sweet Collection,

NYPL ("The news of the President's Murder by J. Wilkes Booth was brought me by the Servants before daylight yesterday morning"); and Edward Everett Hale to Charles Hale, Boston, Apr. 15, 1865, box 6, Hale Papers, NYSL ("The news was brought into our house by the man who makes the fire"); **telegraphic column:** "Rebecca" to Jane Wigglesworth Grew, Boston, Apr. 16, 1865, Grew Correspondence, MHS; **bells:** Amos A. Lawrence diary, Apr. 14, 1865, MHS; Sarah Hale to children, Brookline, Mass., Apr. 18, 1865, box 10, Hale Family Papers, SSC; Anna Cabot Lowell diary, Apr. 15, 1865, MHS.

13. **neighbors:** Mrs. Bardwell diary, Apr. 15, 1865, Helen Temple Cooke Papers, SL; Emily Watkins to Abiathar Watkins, Jersey City, N.J., Apr. 16, 1865, Watkins Papers, NYPL; **window:** Martha Fisher Anderson diary, Apr. 15, 1865, MHS.

For a rare example of staying inside, see Mary Dreer diary, Apr. 15, 1865, Edwin Greble Papers, LC.

14. **terrible:** Charles H. Mallory diary, Apr. 15, 1865, Mallory Family Collection, GWBW; **horrible:** Lucy McKim to Wendell Phillips Garrison, Philadelphia, Apr. 17, 1865, box 49, Garrison Family Papers, SSC.

15. **heads:** Caroline Dall to "John," Boston, Apr. 20, 1865, Dall Papers, SL, and Caroline Dall journal, Apr. 22, 1865, vol. J27, Dall Papers, MHS; **could see, true:** Anna Cabot Lowell diary, Apr. 15, 1865, MHS; **businessmen:** Otis Norcross diary, Apr. 15, 1865, MHS; **visitors:** see, e.g., Caroline Barrett White diary, Apr. 15, 1865, White Papers, AAS.

16. **northern New England:** John Wolcott Phelps commonplace book, Apr. 15, 1865, Phelps Papers, NYPL; **Mid-Atlantic:** Henry Wirt Shriver diary, Apr. 15, 1865, Shriver Family Papers, MDHS; **Chicago:** "H.H." to cousin, Freeport, Ill., Apr. 15, 1865, Jefferson Hartman Correspondence, Duke; **Kansas:** Susan B. Anthony diary, Apr. 15, 1865, Anthony Papers, LC; **Salt Lake City:** Patty Bartlett Sessions diary, Apr. 15, 1865, ts., reel 15, Utah-AWD-West; **Sacramento:** Frederick G. Niles diary, Apr. 15, 1865, HL; **mining town:** Franklin Augustus Buck to Mary Sewall Bradley, Weaverville, Calif., Apr. 27, 1865, Buck Papers, HL; **Ohio:** Henry W. Pearce to "Lena," Marietta, Ohio, Apr. 16, 1865, #00066.150, GLC-NYHS; **Wisconsin:** C. R. Tolles to uncle, Kenosha, Wis., Apr. 16, 1865, Myron Tolles Papers, Duke; **Minnesota:** Eugene Marshall diary, Apr. 16, 1865, Marshall Papers, Duke; **Santa Fe:** "President Lincoln's Assassination," letter from Santa Fe, N.Mex., May 8, 1865, *New York Anglo-African,* published June 17, 1865; **Utah:** Charles Lowell Walker diary, May 8, 1865, HL; **small town:** Nimrod Porter diary, Apr. 15, 1865, Porter Papers, SHC; **New Orleans:** C. Orrez and Patrick Shields, file OO934, RG153-NARA; **Texas:** William Williston Heartsill, *Fourteen Hundred and 91 Days in the Confederate Army,* ed. Bell Irvin Wiley (1876; reprint, Jackson, Tenn.: McCowat-Mercer, 1954), 240 (Apr. 23, 1865, entry), ACWLD; **Alabama:** Charles Oscar Torrey diary, Apr. 29, 1865, Torrey Papers, LC; **freedpeople:** Gerald Schwartz, ed., *A Woman Doctor's Civil War: Esther Hill Hawks' Diary* (Columbia: University of South Carolina Press, 1984), 133 (Apr. 19, 1865, entry); **flag-lowering:** J. Harry Keyes to Sarah Ogden, City Point, Va., Apr. 30, 1865, #06559.060, GLC-NYHS; Thomas Day Seymour to Nathan Seymour, Richmond, Va., Apr. 17, 1865, Seymour Family Papers, Yale-Sterling; **newspapers:** Julius Ramsdell diary, Apr. 19, 1865, Ramsdell Papers, SHC; Thomas J. Kessler diary, Apr. 16, 19, 1865, #04562, GLC-NYHS;

William Kauffman Scarborough, ed., *The Diary of Edmund Ruffin: A Dream Shattered,*
June, 1863–June, 1865 (Baton Rouge: Louisiana State University Press, 1989), 852, 853
(Apr. 18, 19, 1865, entries); Samuel A. Agnew diary, Apr. 29, 1865, SHC, available at www2.
lib.unc.edu/mss/inv/a/Agnew,Samuel_A.html#; **letters:** [illegible] to "Bliss," Morrisville,
N.C., Apr. 18, 1865, Bancroft-Bliss Families Papers, LC.

17. **ships:** Thomas Day Seymour to Nathan Seymour, Richmond, Va., Apr. 17, 1865,
Seymour Family Papers, Yale-Sterling; **Spain:** William Benjamin Gould diary, Apr. 15,
1865, MHS; **London:** Benjamin Moran diary, Apr. 19, 24, 1865, Moran Papers, LC; **Ja-**
maica: T. B. Penfield to George Whipple, Brainerd, Jamaica, Apr. 28, 1865, #F1-3841, reel
231, AMA; **awful:** William Benjamin Gould diary, May 6, 1865, MHS; **Sierra Leone:**
H. H. Himman to George Whipple, Sherbro Island, Sierra Leone, West Africa, June 16,
1865 (part of June 3 letter), #F1-9664, reel 242, AMA; **China:** Martha Green journal, July
13, 1865, MHS; **Australia:** Lowell H. Harrison, "An Australian Reaction to Lincoln's
Death," *Lincoln Herald* 78 (1976), 12–17.

18. **Egypt:** Charles Hale to Sarah Hale, Ramallah, Egypt, May 8, 1865, box 22, and
Charles Hale to Edward Everett Hale, Alexandria, Egypt, May 13, 1865, box 19, Hale Family Papers, SSC.

19. **astonished:** Alexander Randall diary, Apr. 15, 1865, MDHS; Bruno Trombley diary,
Apr. 19, 1865, Civil War Miscellaneous Letters and Papers, Schomburg; **astounding:**
Samuel A. Harrison journal, Apr. 16, 1865, MDHS; **astounded, calamity:** George Comfort
to Samuel Comfort, Morrisville, Pa., Apr. 16, 1865, Comfort Papers, Princeton; **startled:**
Martha Fisher Anderson diary, Apr. 15, 1865, MHS; **stupefied:** George Bedson to Ichabod
Washburn, Manchester, England, Apr. 29, 1865, Washburn Family Papers, AAS; **thunder-**
struck: William E. Fisher to James C. Parker, [no city], N.C., Apr. 30, 1865, Fisher Letters,
NYSL; Charles Edward French diary, Apr. 15, 1865, French Diaries and Papers, MHS;
Charles H. Mallory diary, Apr. 15, 1865, Mallory Family Collection, GWBW; **calamity:**
Edwin Greble Sr. to Susan Greble, Baltimore, Apr. 16, 1865, Greble Papers, LC; William
Gray Brooks diary, Apr. 15, 17, 18, 1865, Brooks Papers, MHS; Anna Cabot Lowell diary,
Apr. 15, 1865, MHS; "Nannie" to Charles E. Snyder, [no place], Apr. 16, 1865, box 1, Miscel-
laneous Documents Relating to Abraham Lincoln, HLH; **catastrophe:** John G. Nicolay to
Therena Bates, "Chesapeake Bay," Apr. 17, 1865, Nicolay Papers, LC; **dagger:** Charles Oscar
Torrey to Mira Torrey, Montgomery, Ala., May 1, 1865, Torrey Papers, LC; **thunderbolt:**
Julia Anna Hartness Lay diary, Apr. 15, 1865, NYPL; "Albert" [?] to mother, New York, Apr.
17, 1865, box 2, Civil War Collection, AAS; unknown writer, Apr. 15, 1865, #193, Thomas
B. Harned Collection of the Papers of Walt Whitman, LC; **thunderclap:** Carl Schurz
to wife, Raleigh, N.C., Apr. 18, 1865, in *Speeches, Correspondence and Political Papers of*
Carl Schurz, 6 vols., ed. Frederic Bancroft (New York: G. P. Putnam's Sons, 1913), 1:253;
blue sky: Henry W. Pearce to "Lena," Marietta, Ohio, Apr. 16, 1865, #00066.150, GLC-
NYHS; **horrible:** Lydia Stark to Franklin W. Fuller, Baldwinsville, N.Y., Apr. 23, 1865,
#03523.42.56, GLC-NYHS; **terrible:** Sophia E. Perry diary, Apr. 15, 1865, CP; **scarcely:**
Edwin Greble Sr. to Susan Greble, Baltimore, Apr. 16, 1865, Greble Papers, LC; **cannot,**
must not: "Em" to Lewis J. Nettleton, Milford, Conn., Apr. 19, 1865, Nettleton-Baldwin

Family Papers, Duke; **but how:** Ruth Anne Hillborn journal, Apr. 15, 1865, Hillborn Papers, FHL.

20. **could not:** Laura Towne to unknown, Saint Helena Island, S.C., Apr. 29, 1865, in *Letters and Diary of Laura M. Towne: Written from the Sea Islands of South Carolina, 1862–1884,* ed. Rupert Sargent Holland (1912; reprint, New York: Negro Universities Press, 1969), 162; **overwhelming:** John Ritchie journal, Apr. 23, 1865, Records of the Fifty-Fourth Massachusetts Volunteer Infantry Regiment, MHS; **refused:** Enock K. Miller, "A Good Letter from a Chaplain in the Army," Fort Barrancas, Fla., May 17, 1865, *Christian Recorder,* published June 10, 1865; **agitated, worried:** Testimony of Elizabeth Clark and Mary Jones, in Patrick Shields, file OO934, RG153-NARA; **electric:** Mattie J. Jackson, *The Story of Mattie J. Jackson* (Lawrence, Mass.: Sentinel, 1866), in *Six Women's Slave Narratives,* ed. William L. Andrews (New York: Oxford University Press, 1988), 30; **distress:** B.L.D. to editor, Louisville, Ky., Apr. 24, 1865, *Christian Recorder,* published May 6, 1865.

21. **secesh lie:** Mary S. Pond to George Whipple, Portsmouth, Va., May 13, 1865, #H1-7147, reel 210, AMA; **canard:** Edwin Greble Sr. to Susan Greble, Baltimore, Apr. 16, 1865, Greble Papers, LC; **getup:** Charles Edward French diary, Apr. 15, 1865, French Diaries and Papers, MHS; **dreadful:** Caroline Barrett White diary, Apr. 19, 1865, White Papers, AAS; **horrible:** Helen Lansing Grinnell diary, Apr. 15, 1865, NYPL; **play:** [M. S. Tilton?] to Georgina Lowell, Washington, D.C., Apr. 15, 1865, Francis Cabot Lowell Papers, MHS; **last scene:** Elizabeth Cary Agassiz to mother, Rio de Janeiro, Brazil, May 18, 1865, Agassiz Papers, SL; **stunning:** Susan B. Anthony diary, Apr. 15, 1865, Anthony Papers, LC; **dream:** Walt Whitman, "O Captain! My Captain!" in *Sequel to Drum-Taps* (Washington, D.C., 1865–66), 13, available at whitmanarchive.org/published/other/DrumTapsSequel.html.

22. **frantic:** Sarah Browne to Albert Browne, Salem, Mass., Apr. 20, 1865, BFP; **Norfolk:** L. D. Burnett to George Whipple, Norfolk, Va., May 1, 1865, #H1-7068, reel 210, AMA; **Nashville:** Martha J. Patterson to Andrew Johnson, Nashville, Tenn., Apr. 15, 1865, *PAJ,* 7:560 (gala); Richard M. Williams to Robert H. Williams, Nashville, Tenn., Apr. 19, 1865, Goff-Williams Papers, HL (crash); **New Bern:** Mary Ann Starkey to "My dear Friend," New Bern, N.C., Apr. 20, 1865, Edward W. Kinsley Papers, Duke; **Charleston:** Charles Barnard Fox, *Record of the Service of the Fifty-Fifth Regiment of Massachusetts Volunteer Infantry* (Cambridge, Mass.: John Wilson, 1868), 74 (Apr. 19, 1865, diary entry); **Virginia:** L. R. Hyslop to George Whipple, Norfolk, Va., Apr. 28, 1865, #H1-7034, reel 209, AMA.

23. **news:** William A. Spicer diary, re: Apr. 18, 1865, Spicer Papers, Duke.

24. **Chicago:** Elon N. Lee to family, Chicago, Apr. 19, 1865, ts., Lee and Bastin Papers, Chicago; **chiming:** Mary Elizabeth Moore to James Otis Moore, Saco, Me., Apr. 15, 1865, Moore Papers, Duke; **dreadful:** Henry W. Pearce to "Lena," Marietta, Ohio, Apr. 16, 1865, #00066.150, GLC-NYHS; **darker:** "Eliz." to "Geo.," Cambridge, Mass., Apr. 16, 1865, Wigglesworth Family Papers, MHS; **sun:** Caroline Barrett White diary, Apr. 15, 1865, White Papers, AAS; **same:** Edward Everett Hale to Charles Hale, Boston, Apr. 15, 1865, box 6, Hale Papers, NYSL; **while:** David F. Cushman to Caroline D. Cushman, Martins-

burg, Va., Apr. 15, 1865, #250, octavo vol. 1, Civil War Collection, AAS; **shot:** George H. Mellish to parents, near Burkeville Junction, Va., Apr. 16, 1865, Mellish Papers, HL.

25. **navy yard:** Michael Shiner diary, Apr. 15, 1865, LC, available at history.navy.mil/ library/online/shinerdiary.html; **saddest:** James Thomas Ward diary, Apr. 15, 1865, Ward Papers, LC; **face:** Sarah G. Putnam diary, Apr. 15, 1865, MHS.

26. **shot:** William H. Lightner diary, Apr. 14, 1865, MDHS; **killed:** Shirley Brooks diary, Apr. 14, 26, 1865, ML; **send:** Caroline Dall to "John," Boston, Apr. 20, 1865, Dall Papers, SL.

27. **lines:** Samuel Canby diary, Apr. 15, 1865, DHS; **box:** Caroline Barrett White diary, Apr. 14–15, 1865, White Papers, AAS; **calligraphy:** Ruth Anne Hillborn journal, Apr. 15, 1865, Hillborn Papers, FHL; **Pres.:** anonymous account book, Apr. 19, 1865, Anonymous Diaries and Account Books, SL.

28. **shot:** Grenville H. Norcross diary, Apr. 15, 1865, AAS; **laughed, rouse:** Anna Cabot Lowell diary, Apr. 15, 1865, MHS; **three inches:** Mrs. Bardwell diary, Apr. 15, 1865, Helen Temple Cooke Papers, SL; **dress circle:** Horatio Nelson Taft diary, Apr. 30, 1865, LC, available at memory.loc.gov/ammem/tafthtml/; **specifics:** Charles Edward French diary, Apr. 15, 17, 1865, French Diaries and Papers, MHS.

29. **poor:** M. M. Hutchins to "Mr. Whiting," Dover, N.H., Apr. 17, 1865, #75762, reel 117, AMA.

30. **greatest:** Heber Painter to Rebecca Frick, Richmond, Va., Apr. 17, 1865 (part of Apr. 16 letter), #02016.082, GLC-NYHS; **startling:** Margaret B. Howell diary, Apr. 15, 1865, HSP.

31. **excite:** v., definition #5, *Oxford English Dictionary;* **everybody:** Gertrude Dunn to [illegible], [no place], Apr. 20, 1865, on "Memoranda" pages of Dunn diary, Diaries Box, NYPL; **thrown:** J. N. Smith to brother, Washington, D.C., Apr. 16, 1865, box 2, Miscellaneous Documents Relating to Abraham Lincoln, HLH; **state:** Alfred Goldsborough Jones journal, Apr. 15, 1865, NYPL; **most:** Simon Newcomb diary, Apr. 15, 1865, Newcomb Papers, LC; **so excited:** Sawyer, "Account," 62.

32. **gloom:** n., definition #2, *Oxford English Dictionary;* **dreadful:** S. L. Daffin to George Whipple, Wilmington, N.C., Apr. 30, 1865, #100009, reel 169, AMA; **dismay:** Lucy Pierce Hedge to Charlotte Hedge, Brookline, Mass., Apr. 25, 1865, Poor Family Papers, SL; **heavy:** John G. Nicolay to Therena Bates, Washington, D.C., Apr. 18, 1865, Nicolay Papers, LC; **every thing:** Edward J. Bartlett to Martha Bartlett, South Side Railroad, Va., Apr. 16, 1865, Bartlett Letters, MHS; **silent:** W. Springer Menge and J. August Shimrak, eds., *The Civil War Notebook of Daniel Chisholm: A Chronicle of Daily Life in the Union Army, 1864–1865* (New York: Orion, 1989), 81–82 (Apr. 17, 18, 1865, entries).

33. **businesses closing:** John Worthington to Mary Worthington, Cooperstown, N.Y., Apr. 15, 1865, Autograph File, HLH; Ruth Anne Hillborn journal, Apr. 15, 1865, Hillborn Papers, FHL; Frank O. French to Benjamin Brown French, Reading, Mass., Apr. 23, 1865, French Papers, LC; **$100,000:** Anne Baldwin to Charlotte Nettleton, New York, Apr. 17, 1865 (part of Apr. 16 letter), Nettleton-Baldwin Family Papers, Duke; **badges:** Abigail Williams May to Eleanor Goddard May, Washington, D.C., Apr. 22, 1865, May and God-

dard Family Papers, SL; Charles Edward French diary, Apr. 19, 1865, French Diaries and Papers, MHS.

Crape is the nineteenth-century spelling.

34. **if you:** Edwin Greble Sr. to Susan Greble, Baltimore, Apr. 16, 1865, Greble Papers, LC; **buildings, miles:** Charles A. Sanford to Edward Payson Goodrich, Washington, D.C., Apr. 18, 1865, in "Two Letters" n.p.; **I had:** Elizabeth Blair Lee to Samuel Phillips Lee, Washington, D.C., Apr. 15, 1865, in *Wartime Washington: The Civil War Letters of Elizabeth Blair Lee,* ed. Virginia Jean Laas (Urbana: University of Illinois Press, 1991), 495; **posh, poor:** Gideon Welles diary, Apr. 18, 1865, Welles Papers, LC; **African Americans:** Jane Swisshelm to *St. Cloud Democrat,* Washington, D.C., Apr. 17, 1865 (published Apr. 27, 1865), in Larsen, *Crusader and Feminist,* 288; **on and on:** Julia Adelaide Shepard to father, near Washington, D.C., Apr. 16, 1865, in "Lincoln's Assassination," 918.

35. **flags:** Otis Norcross diary, Apr. 15, 1865, MHS; Edwin Greble Sr. to Susan Greble, Baltimore, Apr. 16, 1865, Greble Papers, LC; **half yard:** Asa Fitch diary, Apr. 18, 1865, Fitch Papers, Yale-Sterling; **shawl:** Elizabeth Rogers Mason Cabot diary, Apr. 18, 1865, MHS; **widows:** John Wolcott Phelps to John Hickman, Brattleboro, Vt., Apr. 24, 1865, Phelps Papers, NYPL; **lace:** Elon N. Lee to family, Chicago, Apr. 19, 1865, ts., Lee and Bastin Papers, Chicago; **rags:** Allan Nevins and Milton Halsey Thomas, eds., *The Diary of George Templeton Strong: The Civil War, 1860–1865* (New York: Macmillan, 1952), 588 (Apr. 18, 1865, entry); **servants:** Anna Cabot Lowell diary, Apr. 18, 1865, MHS; **Winter Garden:** Ellen Kean to Mary Kean, New York, Apr. 16, 1865, in *Death and Funeral of Abraham Lincoln,* 17; **hammers:** "Cornelia" to parent(s), New York, Apr. 17–19, 1865, Lincoln Miscellaneous Manuscripts, NYHS; **fringed:** Emmeline Yelland to Albert Yelland, Galena, Ill., May 1, 1865, Yelland Family Correspondence, Duke.

36. **Charleston:** Fox, *Record of the Service of the Fifty-Fifth Regiment,* 74–75 (Apr. 19, 1865, diary entry); **New Orleans:** Testimony of Susan Jones and Eliza Spriggs, in Patrick Shields, file OO934, RG153-NARA; **bit, badges:** S. W. Magill to "Secretaries A.M.A.," Savannah, Ga., May 8, 1865, #19368, reel 30, AMA; **rosettes:** Schwartz, *Woman Doctor's Civil War,* 134 (Apr. 19, 1865, entry); **bonnet:** Laura Towne to unknown, Saint Helena Island, S.C., Apr. 29, 1865, in Holland, *Letters and Diary of Laura M. Towne,* 162; **travel:** Manning Ferguson Force diary, Apr. 23, 1865, Force Papers, LC; **trade:** Rose Pickard to Byron Flagg, Alexandria, Va., Apr. 15, 1865 (part of Apr. 14 letter), Pickard Papers, LC.

37. **saviour:** John C. Brock, "Death of the President," *Christian Recorder,* May 6, 1865; **result:** Schwartz, *Woman Doctor's Civil War,* 139 (May 2, 1865, entry); **masters, government, slaves:** T. Edwin Ruggles to Charles P. Ware, Saint Helena Island, S.C., May 6, 1865, Charles Pickard Ware Collection, Howard; **slaves:** Alonzo A. Carr to brother and sister, Beaufort, S.C., Apr. 21, 1865, Cynthia Anthonsen Foster Papers, SL.

38. **we felt:** Ruth [no last name], "Chicago Correspondence," Chicago, May 3, 1865, *Christian Recorder,* published May 20, 1865; **stricken:** "From Our Indiana Corresponding Editor," New Albany, Ind., Apr. 17, 1865, *Christian Recorder,* published Apr. 29, 1865; **visions:** George Comfort to Samuel Comfort, Morrisville, Pa., Apr. 16, 1865, Comfort Papers, Princeton; **groping:** Anna M. Ferris diary, Apr. 16, 1865, Ferris Family Papers, FHL;

evil: Freeman Bradford to Charles Harris, Auburn, Me., Apr. 15, 1865, Emerson Family Papers, Yale-Beinecke.

39. **froze:** Sarah Browne to Albert Browne, Salem, Mass., Apr. 20, 1865, both letters of this date, BFP.

Interlude: Men Weeping

1. **overcome:** Garland H. White, "Letter from Richmond," City Point, Va., Apr. 12, 1865, *Christian Recorder,* published Apr. 22, 1865.

2. **in spite, sobbing:** Allan Nevins and Milton Halsey Thomas, eds., *The Diary of George Templeton Strong: The Civil War, 1860–1865* (New York: Macmillan, 1952), 586 (Apr. 16, 1865, entry); **scarcely:** Julia Anna Hartness Lay diary, Apr. 15, 1865, NYPL; **in camp:** A.B., "Camp William Penn," Chelton Hill, Pa., Apr. 21, 1865, *Christian Recorder,* published Apr. 28, 1865; **grasped:** Ruth Anne Hillborn journal, Apr. 15, 1865, Hillborn Papers, FHL; **wiping:** Mary Elizabeth Moore to James Otis Moore, Saco, Me., Apr. 15, 1865, Moore Papers, Duke; **violent:** "Meetings of Americans in Foreign Countries," in B. F. Morris, *Memorial Record of the Nation's Tribute to Abraham Lincoln* (Washington, D.C.: W. H. and O. H. Morrison, 1865), 260.

3. **not ashamed:** Lydia Stark to Franklin W. Fuller, Baldwinsville, N.Y., Apr. 23, 1865, #03523.42.56, GLC-NYHS; **clerks:** Emily Watkins to Abiathar Watkins, Jersey City, N.J., Apr. 16, 1865, Watkins Papers, NYPL; **unusual:** "Rev. Mr. Allison," in *In Memoriam; Abraham Lincoln Assassinated at Washington, April 14, 1865, Being a Brief Account of the Proceedings . . . at Buffalo, N.Y.* (Buffalo, N.Y.: Matthews and Warren, 1865), 36; **cursed:** James S. Knox to father, Washington, D.C., Apr. 15, 1865, ser. 3: General Correspondence, Abraham Lincoln Papers, LC, available at memory.loc.gov/ammem/alhtml/alser.html; **no shame:** Charles A. Sanford to Edward Payson Goodrich, Washington, D.C., Apr. 15, 1865, in "Two Letters on the Event of April 14, 1865," *Bulletin of the William L. Clements Library of American History* 47 (Feb. 12, 1946), facsimile, n.p.; **impossible:** unknown writer, Apr. 15, 1865, #193, Thomas B. Harned Collection of the Papers of Walt Whitman, LC; **never wept:** [illegible] to mother, "Potomac River," Apr. 23, 1865, ts., Nathaniel H. Harris Papers, SHC.

4. **child:** Ruth Anne Hillborn journal, Apr. 15, 1865, Hillborn Papers, FHL; **like children:** Henry Hitchcock to Mary Hitchcock, "Chesapeake Bay," Apr. 22, 1865, Hitchcock Papers, LC; **strong:** Julia Adelaide Shepard to father, near Washington, D.C., Apr. 16, 1865, in "Lincoln's Assassination Told by an Eye-Witness," *Century Magazine* 77 (1909), 917–18; **fountain:** Anson G. Henry to wife, Washington, D.C., Apr. 19, 1865, ts., box 4, fol. 8, Lincoln Miscellaneous Manuscripts, Chicago.

Chapter 3. Glee

1. Dorman diary, Apr. 23, 1865. *New York Herald,* Apr. 15, 1865. This edition has been widely reproduced in an altered form; the original bears no portrait of Lincoln on the front page.

merry: Justus M. Silliman to brother, Jacksonville, Fla., Apr. 24, 1865, in *A New Canaan Private in the Civil War: Letters of Justus M. Silliman, 17th Connecticut Volunteers*, ed. Edward Marcus (New Canaan, Conn.: New Canaan Historical Society, 1984), 100.

2. Dorman diary, Apr. 25, 1865.

3. Dorman diary, May 6 (habeas corpus, brains), 26 (hanging), 30 (treason), 23 (deserved), 1865.

4. Dorman diary, Apr. 25 (rags, sycophantic), May 26 (fool or insane), 1865; mourners: W. B. Johnson, "From the Third U.S.C. Troops," Jacksonville, Fla., Apr. 29, 1865, *Christian Recorder*, published May 20, 1865.

5. all over: Oscar Brown Ireland to father, near Berryville, Va., Apr. 18, 1865, Ireland Papers, Duke.

6. hardly: "The Assassination of President Lincoln," *Columbia (S.C.) Phoenix*, Apr. 22, 1865; poor country: William Newton Mercer diary, Apr. 15, 1865, Mercer Papers, ser. B, part 4, reel 10, LSU-RSPE; William J. Minor plantation diary, Apr. 18, 1865, Minor Family Papers, ser. B, part 3, reel 4, LSU-RSPE.

7. anarchy: Francis L'Engle to Edward M. L'Engle, [place illegible], Apr. 29, 1865, L'Engle Papers, SHC.

8. heard: John Taylor Wood diary, Apr. 19, 1865, Wood Papers, SHC; bitter, rumors, confirmed: Henry A. Chambers diary, Apr. 9, 10, 18, 19, 1865, Chambers Papers, SHC; unfortunately: Leonie de Varenne to Mary Susan Ker, New Orleans, Apr. 15, 1865, Ker Papers, ser. A, part 1, reel 2, SHC-SWF; planting: Nimrod Porter diary, Apr. 17, 1865, Porter Papers, SHC; troubles: Louisa G. Mason diary, Apr. 15, 1865, MDHS; of course: Emmy Wellford to "Phil," Richmond, Va., Apr. 20, 1865, John Rutherfoord Papers, ser. H, part 3, reel 42, Duke-SWF.

9. long: James Robert McMichael diary, Apr. 20, 1865, ts., SHC; hiatus: Mary Jeffreys Bethell diary, May 2, 1865, ts., ser. J, part 13, reel 12, SHC-RSP; deplorable: Mrs. J. I. White to "Irene," "Cottage Chamber," [Va.], May 13, 1865, Ada P. Bankhead Collection, ser. G, part 2, reel 1, UVA-SWF.

10. Seward, facts: William Owner diary, Apr. 7, 15, 1865, LC; fear: Marmaduke Shannon to Emma M. Crutcher, Vicksburg, Miss., Apr. 18, 1865 (part of Apr. 14 letter), Crutcher-Shannon Family Papers, ser. F, reel 30, UTA-SWF; buffoon: Lucy Muse (Walton) Fletcher diary, Apr. 22, 1865, Fletcher Papers, Duke; baboon, foul: C. Vann Woodward, ed., *Mary Chesnut's Civil War* (1981; reprint, New Haven: Yale University Press, 1993), 360, 791, 795 (June 4, 1862, Apr. 22, 23, 1865, entries); principle: Francis A. Boyle Books, Apr. 16, 1865, SHC.

11. horrible: Margaret (Brown) Wight diary, Apr. 18, 1865, Wight Family Papers, ser. D, part 1, reel 21, VHS-SWF; liberal: William H. Bagley to Adelaide Worth, Hertford, N.C., Apr. 28, 1865, Jonathan Worth Papers, ser. A, part 8, reel 7, SHC-SWF; mercy: Hannah Ford Turner to William Mason Turner, Philadelphia, Apr. 26, 1865, William Mason Turner Papers, Brown; politically: David Schenck diary, [June, 1865], SHC, available at www2.lib.unc.edu/mss/inv/s/Schenck,David.html#d2e89; know: James Helme Rickard to sister, [near Richmond, Va.], May 11, 1865, Rickard Civil War Letters, AAS; hope:

Thomas Day Seymour to Nathan Seymour, Richmond, Va., Apr. 17, 1865, Seymour Family Papers, Yale-Sterling; **lost:** Elizabeth Blair Lee to Samuel Phillips Lee, Washington, D.C., Apr. 15, 1865, in *Wartime Washington: The Civil War Letters of Elizabeth Blair Lee,* ed. Virginia Jean Laas (Urbana: University of Illinois Press, 1991), 495.

12. **uneasy:** Samuel Pickens diary, Apr. 16, 1865, in *Voices from Company D: Diaries by the Greensboro Guards, Fifth Alabama Infantry Regiment, Army of Northern Virginia,* ed. G. Ward Hubbs (Athens: University of Georgia Press, 2003), 372; **guests:** Mahala (Eggleston) Roach diary, Apr. 18, 1865, ser. D, part 4, reel 10, VHS-SWF; **uneasy:** Bessie B. Caine to unknown, Raleigh, N.C., Apr. 18, 1865 (part of Apr. 16 letter), John Lancaster Bailey Papers, ser. A, part 8, reel 9, SHC-SWF; **mingle:** Chauncey Welton to parents, Raleigh, N.C., Apr. 19, 1865, Welton Papers, SHC; **quiet:** Manley Ebenezer Rice to Elizabeth Day Rice, Fort Gaines, Ala., Apr. 30, 1865, Rice Papers, HL; **secretly:** Samuel Miller Quincy [no salutation], New Orleans, Apr. 19, 1865, Quincy, Wendell, Holmes, Upham Family Papers, MHS.

13. **native:** Gerald Schwartz, ed., *A Woman Doctor's Civil War: Esther Hill Hawks' Diary* (Columbia: University of South Carolina Press, 1984), 134 (Apr. 19, 1865, entry); **sharp:** Thomas Day Seymour to Nathan Seymour, Richmond, Va., Apr. 17, 1865, Seymour Family Papers, Yale-Sterling; **looking:** Alfred Neafie to Anne Neafie, Savannah, Ga., Apr. 19, 1865, Neafie Papers, NYSL; **mighty:** William C. McLean to sister, Raleigh, N.C., Apr. 23, 1865, ts., McLean Family Papers, NYSL.

14. **smitten:** "The Great Calamity," Apr. 16, 1865, *Sacramento Daily Union,* published May 17, 1865, in *Lincoln Observed: Civil War Dispatches of Noah Brooks,* ed. Michael Burlingame (Baltimore: Johns Hopkins University Press, 1998), 192; **draped:** Helen A. Du Barry to mother, Washington, D.C., Apr. 16, 1865, in "Eyewitness Account of Lincoln's Assassination," *Journal of the Illinois State Historical Society* 39 (1946), 368; **fling:** Charles A. Sanford to Edward Payson Goodrich, Washington, D.C., Apr. 18, 1865, in "Two Letters on the Event of April 14, 1865," *Bulletin of the William L. Clements Library of American History* 47 (Feb. 12, 1946), facsimile, n.p.; **gunboat:** Manley Ebenezer Rice to Elizabeth Day Rice, Fort Gaines, Ala., Apr. 30, 1865, Rice Papers, HL; **scantiest:** John Glenn diary, Apr. 19, 1865, Glenn Papers, MDHS; **thankful:** Charles East, ed., *Sarah Morgan: The Civil War Diary of a Southern Woman* (New York: Simon and Schuster, 1992), 608 (Apr. 22, 1865, entry). See also "Carrie" to sister, Washington, D.C., Apr. 16, 1865, box 2, fol. 27, Richard John Levy and Sally Waldman Sweet Collection, NYPL ("Old secessionists cryed, and with all Washington and Georgetown draped their houses"); Alma Baker to George Whipple, Carondelet, Mo., Apr. 17, 1865, #73762, reel 114, AMA ("The Rebs are the first to hang out mourning").

15. **strongest:** Harriet Williams to Lewis J. Williams, Medical Hall, Md., May 9, 1865, Archer-Mitchell-Stump-Williams Family Papers, MDHS; **bitter:** "Henry" to family, Montgomery, Ala., May 1, 1865, in "Death of a President," *Abraham Lincoln Quarterly* 3 (1945), 303; **officers:** Thomas Day Seymour to Nathan Seymour, Richmond, Va., Apr. 23, 1865, Seymour Family Papers, Yale-Sterling; **truthful:** "From Committee of Richmond Blacks," Richmond, Va., June 10, 1865, *PAJ,* 8:211; **feigned:** Chester dispatch, Richmond,

Va., Apr. 24, 1865, in *Thomas Morris Chester: Black Civil War Correspondent—His Dispatches from the Virginia Front,* ed. R. J. M. Blackett (Baton Rouge: Louisiana State University Press, 1989), 321.

For a white skeptic, see Samuel A. Harrison journal, Apr. 16, 23, 1865, MDHS. It is not always possible to tell sincerity from self-protection, as when a minister wrote in his North Carolina diary, "Every good and sensible man depracates the murder" (Robert W. Chaffin journal, Apr. 24, 1865, Washington Sandford Chaffin Papers, Duke).

16. **pity:** William Calder diary, Apr. 24, 1865, Calder Family Papers, SHC; **best:** E. R. Harmanson to "Prince," Red River, La., Apr. 23, 1865, Albert A. Batchelor Papers, ser. B, part 5, reel 1, LSU-RSPE; **passeth:** William H. Ellis diary, Apr. 17, 1865, Ellis Papers, ser. B, reel 5, LSU-CMM; **killing:** Gideon Lincecum to William P. "Sioux" Doran, Long Point, Tex., Apr. 27, 1865, in *Gideon Lincecum's Sword: Civil War Letters from the Texas Home Front,* ed. Jerry Bryan Lincecum et al. (Denton: University of North Texas Press, 2001), 325–26; **deserved, entertaining:** William Kauffman Scarborough, ed., *The Diary of Edmund Ruffin: A Dream Shattered, June, 1863–June, 1865* (Baton Rouge: Louisiana State University Press, 1989), 855, 865 (Apr. 18, 25, 1865, entries).

17. **sick, hurrah:** Emma F. LeConte diary, Apr. 20 and "Friday" [Apr. 21], 1865, reel 22, SHC-AWD-South.

18. **glad:** Cloe (Whittle) Greene diary, Apr. 15, 1865, reel 4, WM-AWD-South; **royal:** Clara Dargan MacLean diary, Apr. 20, 1865, MacLean Papers, Duke; **electrified:** Sarah Lois Wadley diary, Apr. 26, 1865, Wadley Papers, ser. A, part 3, reel 6, SHC-SWF; **glory:** [Helen Ellis?] to John Benjamin Long, Rusk, Tex., Apr. 26, 1865, Long Papers, ser. C, part 1, reel 21, UTA-CMM; **cheering:** "Journal Letter Kept by Miss Charlotte St. J. Ravenel of Pooshee Plantation for Miss Meta Heyward," in *Two Diaries from Middle St. John's, Berkeley, South Carolina, February–May 1865* (Pinopolis, S.C.: Saint John's Hunting Club, 1921), 45 (Apr. 21, 1865, entry).

19. **felt:** Amanda (Edmonds) Chappelear diary, Apr. 21, 1865, Chappelear Papers, ser. D, part 3, reel 9, VHS-SWF; **brave, rejoice:** John Q. Anderson, ed., *Brokenburn: The Journal of Kate Stone, 1861–1868* (1955; reprint, Baton Rouge: Louisiana State University Press, 1995), 333, 341 (Apr. 28, May 15, 1865, entries).

20. **laughed:** Eliza F. Andrews, *The War-Time Journal of a Georgia Girl, 1864–1865* (New York: D. Appleton, 1908), 172 (Apr. 21, 1865, entry), DocSouth, docsouth.unc.edu/fpn/andrews/menu.html; **surrounded:** Harriet E. Gaylord to George Whipple, Natchez, Miss., May 1, 1865, #71762, reel 111, AMA; **loose:** C. P. Day to George Whipple, Hampton, Va., Apr. 29, 1865, #H1-7037, reel 209, AMA; **wrath:** W. L. Coan to M. E. Strieby, Richmond, Va., Apr. 30, 1865, #H1-7050, reel 210, AMA.

21. **since:** W. D. Harris to George Whipple, Portsmouth, Va., May 1, 1865, #H1-7062, reel 210, AMA; **citizens:** Thomas Day Seymour to Nathan Seymour, Richmond, Va., Apr. 17, 1865, Seymour Family Papers, Yale-Sterling; **taunting:** H. B. Greely to George Whipple, Saint Augustine, Fla., Apr. 29, 1865 (misdated 1864), #18655, reel 28, AMA; **Old Lincoln:** Thomas Outten, file MM2544, RG153-NARA; **Shields:** Testimony of Susan Jones, in Patrick Shields, file OO934, RG153-NARA.

22. **expressions:** Edwin J. Moore to M. E. Strieby, Key West, Fla., May 3, 1865, #18656, reel 28, AMA; **celebrate:** Dorman diary, Apr. 25, 1865; **fearing:** John Peter Nelson to George W. Colles, New Orleans, Apr. 20, 1865, Colles Family Papers, NYPL; **strutting:** Chester dispatch, Petersburg, Va., Apr. 19, 1865, in Blackett, *Thomas Morris Chester,* 312–13; **father:** Maria Martin, file OO1235, RG153-NARA; **partying:** Thomas Francis Johnson diary, Apr. 25, 1865, Johnson Family Papers, MDHS; **women:** Burnham Wardwell to Benjamin F. Butler, Richmond, Va., Apr. 19, 1865, in *Private and Official Correspondence of Gen. Benjamin F. Butler, during the Period of the Civil War,* 5 vols. (Springfield, Mass.: Plimpton Press, 1917), 598, ACWLD.

23. **woe:** Albert Browne to "Dear Ones," Charleston, S.C., Apr. 21, 1865, BFP; **bully:** Charles D. Spurlin, ed., *The Civil War Diary of Charles A. Leuschner* (Austin, Tex.: Eakin Press, 1992), 52 (Apr. 15, 1865, entry); **goddamned:** A. J. Hamilton, *A Fort Delaware Journal: The Diary of a Yankee Private,* ed. W. Emerson Wilson (Wilmington: Fort Delaware Society, 1981), 78–79 (Apr. 15, 1865, entry; the writer referred to the victim as a Copperhead, though he was likely a Confederate); Bishop Crumrine to Boyd Crumrine, Fort Delaware, Del., May 1, 1865, in "Notes and Documents: Corporal Crumrine Goes to War," ed. Walter S. Sanderlin, *Topic* 2 (1961), 64; **Fort Jefferson:** Peter Kitts to "Mrs. Case," Fort Jefferson, Fla., Apr. 25, 1865, Samuel F. Case Papers, Duke; Claudius Rider diary, Apr. 22, 1865, NYHS; Henry B. Whitney diary, Apr. 22, 1865, Duke.

24. **laughing:** Mary Jane Cook Chadick diary, Apr. 16, 1865, ts., ser. H, part 2, reel 1, Duke-SWF; **brickbats:** Mary H. and Dallas M. Lancaster, eds., *The Civil War Diary of Anne S. Frobel* (McLean, Va.: EPM, 1992), 218 (Apr. 28, 1865, entry); **fate:** Alma Baker to George Whipple, Carondelet, Mo., Apr. 17, 1865, #73762, reel 114, AMA; **expressing:** George W. Squier to Ellen Squier, Chattanooga, Tenn., Apr. 25, 1865 (part of Apr. 15 letter), in *This Wilderness of War: The Civil War Letters of George W. Squier, Hoosier Volunteer,* ed. Julie A. Doyle et al. (Knoxville: University of Tennessee Press, 1998), 107; **not worth:** Charles H. Cooley diary, Apr. 19, 1865, Duke; **glorious:** James L. Hart, file OO1235, RG153-NARA; **glad:** C. Orrez, file OO934, RG153-NARA; **God:** Testimony of Charlotte Johnson via Nancy Diges, in case of Maria Edwards, Robert Harden, and Fanny Cook, #15674, Apr. 22, 1865, Union Provost Marshals' File of Papers Relating to Two or More Civilians, M416, roll 56, RG109-NARA; **harassed, assaulted:** cases of Patrick Shields, file OO934, and Thomas Outten, file MM2544, RG153-NARA; **more:** Gertrude Allen to parents, Charleston, S.C., Apr. 20, 1865 (part of Apr. 18 letter), "Northern Visions of Race, Region and Reform," AAS, faculty.assumption.edu/aas/Manuscripts/allen4-65.html, online exhibition, 2014.

25. **no reason:** Emma F. LeConte diary, "Friday" [Apr. 21], 1865, reel 22, SHC-AWD-South; **raise:** Caroline S. Jones to Mary Jones, Augusta, Ga., Apr. 30, 1865, in *The Children of Pride: A True Story of Georgia and the Civil War,* ed. Robert Manson Myers (New Haven: Yale University Press, 1972), 1268; **glorious:** Woodward, *Mary Chesnut's Civil War,* 805 (May 7, 1865, entry).

26. **good:** Joe H. Lyman to John Inglis, East Randolph, N.Y., Apr. 19, 1865, Inglis Papers, NYSL; **houses, quit:** Franklin Augustus Buck to Mary Sewall Bradley, Weav-

erville, Calif., Apr. 27, 1865, Buck Papers, HL; **strong:** Mattie Smith diary, Apr. 16, 1865, CHM; **even:** Mary Elizabeth Moore to James Otis Moore, Saco, Me., Apr. 16, 1865, Moore Papers, Duke; **draped:** sister to Samuel Comfort, Morrisville, Pa., Apr. 24, 1865, Comfort Papers, Princeton; **plenty:** Caroline Dunstan diary, Apr. 17, 1865, NYPL; **secretly:** Jesse Mullery to Walt Whitman, [no place], May 3, 1865, Henry W. and Albert A. Berg Collection of English and American Literature, NYPL, available at whitmanarchive.org/biography/correspondence/cw/tei/nyp.00178.html.

27. **dinner:** Joanita Kant, ed., *Maggie: The Civil War Diary of Margaret Wylie Mellette* (Watertown, S.Dak.: Mellette Memorial Association, 1983), 19 (Apr. 15, 1865, entry); **expected:** Eugene Marshall diary, Apr. 20, 1865, Marshall Papers, Duke; **laughing, glad:** Mrs. Samuel Batchelder to Mary (Batchelder) James, Cambridge, Mass., Apr. 17, 1865, James Family Papers, SL; **Celtic:** Allan Nevins and Milton Halsey Thomas, ed., *The Diary of George Templeton Strong: The Civil War, 1860–1865* (New York: Macmillan, 1952), 586 (Apr. 16, 1865, entry).

28. **thousands:** Richard McDermott, file MM2870, RG153-NARA; **doffed:** Elijah Chapman, file MM1936, RG153-NARA; **Negro:** Henry Peters, file OO719, RG153-NARA; **next:** James Simmons, #4050, vol. 141, M273, roll 150, RG125-NARA; **white men:** Max Puhan, file OO1277, RG153-NARA; **goddamn:** John W. Nash, file MM2531, RG153-NARA; **come up:** Patrick O'Donnell, file OO1191, RG153-NARA; **friend:** L. C. Chambers to George Whipple, Saint Catharine's, Canada, May 1, 1865, #F1-724, reel 225, AMA.

29. **bloodthirsty:** Francis Brooks journal, Apr. 18, 1865, MHS; **ready:** Mary Butler Reeves to Caroline Butler Laing, Germantown, Pa., Apr. 16, 1865, Butler-Laing Family Papers, NYHS; **dangling:** Edwin Greble Sr. to Susan Greble, Baltimore, Apr. 16, 1865, Greble Papers, LC; **killed:** Caroline Dall journal, Apr. 22, 1865, vol. J27, Dall Papers, MHS; **indignant:** Elon N. Lee to family, Chicago, Apr. 19, 1865, ts., Lee and Bastin Papers, Chicago; **dirty:** John Worthington to Mary Worthington, Cooperstown, N.Y., Apr. 15, 1865, Autograph File, HLH; **knock:** "Em" to Lewis J. Nettleton, part of Henry Cornwall to Lewis J. Nettleton, Milford, Conn., Apr. 16, 1865, Nettleton-Baldwin Family Papers, Duke.

30. **exile:** Martha Coffin Wright to William P. Wright, Auburn, N.Y., Apr. 21, 1865, box 268, Garrison Family Papers, SSC; Charles Edward French diary, Apr. 16, 1865, French Diaries and Papers, MHS; "H.H." to cousin, Freeport, Ill., Apr. 15, 1865, Jefferson Hartman Correspondence, Duke; Sarah Gould to Charles A. Gould, Lexington, Mass., Apr. 18, 1865, Gould Papers, Duke; **recant:** John Wolcott Phelps commonplace book, Apr. 15, 1865, Phelps Papers, NYPL; **tarred:** Maria Lydig Daly, *Diary of a Union Lady, 1861–1865,* ed. Harold Earl Hammond (New York: Funk and Wagnalls, 1962), 357 (Apr. 25, 1865, entry); **swore:** Mary Butler Reeves to Caroline Butler Laing, Germantown, Pa., Apr. 16, 1865, Butler-Laing Family Papers, NYHS; **police:** William Gray Brooks diary, May 6, 1865, Brooks Papers, MHS; **threatened:** Gayle Thornbrough and Paula Corpuz, eds., *The Diary of Calvin Fletcher,* vol. 9 (Indianapolis: Indiana Historical Society, 1983), 68 (Apr. 15, 1865, entry); **attacked:** Frederick Law Olmstead to father, Bear Valley, Calif., Apr. 29, 1865, Olmsted Papers, LC.

31. **store:** Charles Edward French diary, Apr. 15, 1865, French Diaries and Papers, MHS; **tarred, roughly:** William Gray Brooks diary, Apr. 16, 15, 1865, Brooks Papers, MHS; **factory, brain:** Lucy Pierce Hedge to Charlotte Hedge, Brookline, Mass., Apr. 25, 1865, Poor Family Papers, SL; **violent:** Francis R. Rives to unknown, New York, Apr. 15, 1865, William Cabell Rives Papers, LC; **boy:** John Glenn diary, Apr. 15, 1865, Glenn Papers, MDHS; **almost dead:** "Albert" [?] to mother, New York, Apr. 17, 1865, box 2, Civil War Collection, AAS; **crushed:** George Comfort to Samuel Comfort, Morrisville, Pa., Apr. 16, 1865, Comfort Papers, Princeton; **good enough:** John Henry Wilson to wife, Washington, D.C., Apr. 16, 1865, in "A Letter on the Death of Abraham Lincoln, April 16, 1865," ed. Frederick C. Drake, *Lincoln Herald* 84 (1982), 237; **shot:** Elon N. Lee diary, Apr. 15, 1865, ts., Lee and Bastin Papers, Chicago; **warning:** Eugene Marshall diary, Apr. 20, 1865, Marshall Papers, Duke.

32. **all:** Saran Browne to Albert Browne, Salem, Mass., Apr. 20, 1865, BFP; **served right:** "Albert" [?] to mother, New York, Apr. 17, 1865, box 2, Civil War Collection, AAS; John Henry Wilson to wife, Washington, D.C., Apr. 16, 1865, in Drake, "Letter on the Death of Abraham Lincoln," 237; **mob law:** Martha Coffin Wright to William P. Wright, Auburn, N.Y., Apr. 21, 1865, box 268, Garrison Family Papers, SSC; **purged:** Henry W. Pearce to "Lena," Marietta, Ohio, Apr. 16, 1865, #00066.150, GLC-NYHS; **sane:** Frederick A. Sawyer, "Account of what I saw of the Death of Mr. Lincoln written April 15, 1865," in "An Eyewitness Account of Abraham Lincoln's Assassination," ed. Ronald D. Rietveld, *Civil War History* 22 (1976), 68.

33. **Stanton:** David McMurtrie Gregg journal, Apr. 21, 1865, Gregg Papers, Yale-Beinecke; **building:** Samuel White, files MM2092 and NN3708, RG153-NARA; **damned:** Samuel Peacock, file NN3708, RG153-NARA; **few more:** Robert Brown, file MM2110, RG153-NARA; **walk, ignorant:** Chat Helms, May 29, 1865, Union Provost Marshal Citizens File, entry 213, "Various States, Bonds, Oaths of Allegiance, Miscellaneous Amnesty Papers," box 14, RG109-NARA; **General Order No. 27:** Matthew P. Deady, *Reports of Cases Determined in the Circuit and District Courts of the United States of Oregon and California, 1859–1869* (San Francisco: A. L. Bancroft, 1872), 236–37.

34. **expressed:** John W. Haley, *The Rebel Yell and the Yankee Hurrah: The Civil War Journal of a Maine Volunteer,* ed. Ruth L. Silliker (Camden, Me.: Down East Books, 1985), 269 (Apr. 16, 1865, entry); **searved:** Holiday Ames to wife, Decatur, Ala., Apr. 23, 1865, in "Waiting for the War's End: The Letter of an Ohio Soldier in Alabama," ed. Louis Filler, *Ohio History* 74 (1965), 55–62 (quotation, 58).

35. **profound:** Edwin M. Stanton, General Orders No. 66, War Department, Washington, D.C., Apr. 16, 1865, in B. F. Morris, *Memorial Record of the Nation's Tribute to Abraham Lincoln* (Washington, D.C.: W. H. and O. H. Morrison, 1865), 111; **Fifth Article:** *Articles of War, Military Laws, and Rules and Regulations for the Army of the United States* ([Washington, D.C.]: Adjutant and Inspector General's Office, 1817), 9–10; **crape:** Marshall Mortimer Miller to family, New Bern, N.C., Apr. 28, 1865, ts. (p. 114 out of order), Miller Papers, LC; **not sad:** Barney Lowrie, file MM2190, RG153-NARA; **small loss:** William E. Dinan, file OO1191, RG153-NARA; **suffer:** Nicholas Dale, file OO1076, RG153-NA;

sight: Elijah Chapman, file MM1936, RG153-NARA; **good:** James Corner, file MM2379, RG153-NARA; **celebrate:** Patrick O'Donnell, file OO1191, RG153-NARA; **laughter:** Thomas Jackson, #3920, vol. 133, M273, roll 142, RG125-NARA; **cheering, cap:** Frederick Bodmer, file MM1997, RG153-NARA; **joviality:** Patrick O'Donnell, file OO1191, RG153-NARA; **ditties:** Eli Smith, file OO1173, RG153-NARA; **hurrah:** Max Puhan, file OO1277, RG153-NARA.

36. **damned:** John W. Nash, file MM2531, RG153-NARA; **hell:** John H. Casey, file OO908, RG153-NARA; **cur:** Henry Lopshire, file MM2145, RG153-NARA; **son of a bitch:** John McCarty, file MM2226, RG153-NARA; **damned son of a bitch:** Eli Smith, file OO1173, RG153-NARA; **slab-sided:** James Walker, file MM2771, RG153-NARA; **whore-master:** John Ryman, file OO1129, RG153-NARA; **shit:** Thomas Smith, #4082, vol. 146, M273, roll 155, RG125-NARA; **bold:** Thomas Jackson, #3920, vol. 133, M273, roll 142, RG125-NARA; **right:** John Largest, file MM2047, RG153-NARA; **sorry:** Daniel Couilard, #3961, vol. 135, M273, roll 144, RG125-NARA; **target:** Daniel Heeden, file MM2145, RG153-NARA.

37. **Johnny fashion:** James Tozier, #4103, vol. 147, M273, roll 156, RG125-NARA. For an unusually harsh ten-year sentence for verbal insults, see John McCarty, file MM2226, RG153-NARA.

38. **loyal:** "Meeting of Colored Citizens," and Kentucky and Missouri tributes, all in Morris, *Memorial Record,* 153, 137, 141; **think:** John Worthington to Mary Worthington, Cooperstown, N.Y., Apr. 15, 1865, Autograph File, HLH; **few:** Henry S. Thacher diary, Apr. 17, 1865, Thacher Family Papers, MHS.

39. **leaders, universal:** "George W. Julian's Journal—The Assassination of Lincoln," *Indiana Magazine of History* 11 (1915), 335 (Apr. 15, 1865, entry); **as long:** Zachariah Chandler to Letitia Chandler, Washington, D.C., Apr. 23, 1865, Chandler Papers, LC.

Interlude: Public Condolences

1. **condolences:** Charles Francis Adams diary, Apr. 27, 28, 1865, Adams Papers, MHS; **Jews, Mauritian:** Charles Francis Adams to William Hunter, London, May 4, Letter-books, Adams Papers, MHS; **cried, bores:** Benjamin Moran diary, Apr. 27, May 2, 1865, Moran Papers, LC; **boor, ogre:** Charles Francis Adams to Charles Francis Adams Jr., London, Apr. 28, 1865, Chronological Papers, Adams Papers, MHS; **returned:** Charles Francis Adams to William Hunter, London, May 11, 1865, Letterbooks, Adams Papers, MHS; **somersault:** Benjamin Moran diary, May 5, 1865, Moran Papers, LC.

2. **secret:** Benjamin Moran diary, Apr. 26, 1865, Moran Papers, LC; **Hull:** J. T. Upton to Charles Francis Adams, Hull, England, Apr. 29, 1865, Chronological Papers, Adams Papers, MHS; **swallow:** Adeline Tyler to Charles Francis Adams, "Westbourne Grove," Apr. 25, 1865, Chronological Papers, Adams Papers, MHS; **my dear:** Benjamin Moran diary, Apr. 29, 1865, Moran Papers, LC; **crocodile:** Henry S. Thacher diary, May 8, 1865, Thacher Family Papers, MHS; **bootlicking:** Charles Woodward Hutson to "My dear friend," Paris, [day illegible], 1865, Hutson Papers, SHC.

3. **regret, kingdom:** Charles Francis Adams to British Consuls, London, May 2, 1865,

and Charles Francis Adams to Mary Lincoln, London, May 19, 1865, Letterbooks, Adams Papers, MHS.

4. **tributes:** *The Assassination of Abraham Lincoln, Late President of the United States of America . . . Expressions of Condolence and Sympathy Inspired by These Events* (Washington, D.C.: Government Printing Office, 1867), 75 (Creoles), 736 (Polish); **French, Italian, Hanseatic, German:** B. F. Morris, *Memorial Record of the Nation's Tribute to Abraham Lincoln* (Washington, D.C.: W. H. and O. H. Morrison, 1865), 245, 254, 253, 152. And see Morris, *Memorial Record,* 123–54, and C. C. Carrington, "Assassination and Funeral of President Lincoln," scrapbook, 2 vols., 1865–71, section entitled "Round the World," compilation of international responses, 2:123–77, McLellan Lincoln Collection, Brown.

Chapter 4. God

1. Dorman diary, Apr. 23 (time), 25 (what, perverted, tremble), 1865.

2. Dorman diary, May 26 (ministers, ill-shapen), 30 (prayer), June 27 (swallowed), 1865.

3. Sarah Browne to Albert Browne, Salem, Mass., Apr. 20, 1865, BFP.

4. Albert Browne to "Dear Ones," Charleston, S.C., Apr. 15, 1865 (God); Albert Browne to "Dear Ones," Charleston, S.C. , Apr. 24, 1865 (sparrow, believe, gloomy); Albert Browne to "Dear Ones," Hilton Head, S.C., Apr. 18, 1865 (shadow); Albert Browne to "Dear Ones," Charleston, S.C. , Apr. 21, 1865 (reproach), all BFP.

5. **royal:** Clara Dargan MacLean diary, Apr. 20, 1865, MacLean Papers, Duke; **at last:** *"Maggie!": Maggie Lindsley's Journal, Nashville, Tennessee, 1864, Washington, D.C., 1865* (Southbury, Conn.: Muriel Davies Mackenzie, 1977), 86 (Apr. 23, 1865, entry); **very day:** Elizabeth (Alsop) Wynne diary, Apr. 22, 1865, Wynne Family Papers, ser. D, part 3, reel 52, VHS-SWF.

6. **alarm:** unknown to Harriet Powell, Richmond, Va., Apr. 18, 1865, Powell Family Papers, ser. C, reel 6, WM-SWF; **foes:** Eleanor H. Cohen diary, Apr. 30, 1865, in *Memoirs of American Jews, 1775–1865,* 3 vols., ed. Jacob Rader Marcus (Philadelphia: Jewish Publication Society of America, 1955), 3:366, NAWLD; **use:** Cloe (Whittle) Greene diary, Apr. 15, 1865, reel 4, WM-AWD-South; **work out:** Eliza (French) Smith diary, Apr. 19, 1865, ts., Wynne Family Papers, ser. D, part 3, reel 54, VHS-SWF; **judgment:** Francis R. Rives to unknown, New York, Apr. 15, 1865, William Cabell Rives Papers, LC; **side:** Franklin Augustus Buck to Mary Sewall Bradley, Weaverville, Calif., Apr. 27, 1865, Buck Papers, HL.

7. **trouble:** Dorman diary, May 20, 26, 1865; **bitter:** Thomas Day Seymour to Nathan Seymour, Richmond, Va., Apr. 30, 1865, Seymour Family Papers, Yale-Sterling.

8. **cushions, bells:** Thomas Day Seymour to Nathan Seymour, Richmond, Va., Apr. 17, 1865, Seymour Family Papers, Yale-Sterling; **sunny:** Kate Cumming, *Kate: The Journal of a Confederate Nurse,* ed. Richard Barksdale Harwell (Baton Rouge: Louisiana State University Press, 1998), 269 (Apr. 16, 1865, entry), NAWLD; **what:** Dorman diary, Apr. 25, 1865.

9. **glorious:** Mrs. Samuel Batchelder to Mary (Batchelder) James, Cambridge, Mass., Apr. 17, 1865, James Family Papers, SL.

10. **aisles, choir:** Allan Nevins and Milton Halsey Thomas, eds., *The Diary of George*

Templeton Strong: The Civil War, 1860–1865 (New York: Macmillan, 1952), 585 (Apr. 16, 1865, entry); **settees:** Anna Cabot Lowell diary, Apr. 16, 1865, MHS; **pews, settees:** Charles Edward French diary, Apr. 16, 1865, French Diaries and Papers, MHS; **settees, galleries, entries:** Clara Allen to Walter Allen, Worcester, Mass., Apr. 16, 1865, Weston-Allen Papers, SSC; **army:** Edward Williams Morley to Sardis Morley, Fortress Monroe, Va., Apr. 18, 1865, Morley Papers, LC.

For much less common examples of those who preferred to be alone, see Annie G. Dudley Davis diary, Apr. 16, 1865, HL; William G. Wise to James Perkins Walker, Auburn, N.Y., Apr. 24, 1865, Walker Papers, Princeton; and Joanita Kant, ed., *Maggie: The Civil War Diary of Margaret Wylie Mellette* (Watertown, S.Dak.: Mellette Memorial Association, 1983), 18 (Apr. 15, 1865, entry).

11. **all:** M. J. Gonsalves to Mary (Goodridge) Gilbert, Baton Rouge, La., May 27, 1865, Gilbert-Cheever Family Papers, Yale-Sterling; **people:** Eugene Marshall diary, Apr. 19, 1865, Marshall Papers, Duke; **saddest:** Mary Ingham Emerson diary, Apr. 27, 1865, Emerson Family Papers, NYPL; **threw:** "James H." to William P. Corthell, Goldsboro, N.C., Apr. 24, 1865, box 1, Civil War Collection, AAS; **struck down, crest fallen:** Heber Painter to Rebecca Frick, Richmond, Va., Apr. 17, 1865 (part of Apr. 16 letter), #02016.082, GLC-NYHS; **defeat:** Bela T. St. John to J. and J. H. St. John, Mobile, Ala., Apr. 23, 1865, St. John Papers, LC, and see Franklin Boyts to Hiram Boyts, Washington, D.C., Apr. 17, 1865, in Boyts diary, HSP ("The loss of our armies would not have been so great"); **weeping:** William H. Gilbert diary, Apr. 15, 1865, Gilbert-Cheever Family Papers, Yale-Sterling; **sunshine:** Samuel Miller Quincy [no salutation], New Orleans, Apr. 19, 1865, Quincy, Wendell, Holmes, Upham Family Papers, MHS; **trees:** *Fourteenth Annual Report of the Rochester Ladies' Anti-Slavery Society* (Rochester, N.Y., 1865), 6.

12. **heartfelt:** Hope R. Daggett to George Whipple, Norfolk, Va., Apr. [n.d.], 1865, #H1-7058, reel 210, AMA; **troubled, cried:** E. P. Worthington to George Whipple, Portsmouth, Va., May 1, 1865, #H1-7072, reel 210, AMA; **very great:** W. T. Richardson to S. S. Jocelyn, Beaufort, S.C., Apr. 21, 1865, #H5575, reel 187, AMA; **wept:** Gerald Schwartz, ed., *A Woman Doctor's Civil War: Esther Hill Hawks' Diary* (Columbia: University of South Carolina Press, 1984), 133 (Apr. 19, 1865, entry); **numb:** Martha L. Kellogg to George Whipple, Portsmouth, Va., May 2, 1865, #H1-7087, reel 210, AMA; **deranged:** P. B. S. Nichuston [?] to George Whipple, Roanoke Island, N.C., Apr. 22, 1865, #100001, reel 169, AMA; **loss:** Edgar Dinsmore to Carrie Drayton, Saint Andrews Parish, S.C., May 29, 1865, Dinsmore Papers, Duke; **half:** "From the Regiments," letter from Charles Davis, 108th U.S.C.T., Rock Island Barracks, Ill., Apr. 23, 1865, *New York Anglo-African*, published May 13, 1865; **sad, impossibility:** James Otis Moore to Mary Elizabeth Moore, Washington, D.C., Apr. 20, 1865, and James Otis Moore to Mary Elizabeth Moore, "Potomac River," Apr. 19, 1865, Moore Papers, Duke; **unfeigned, undisguised:** Chester dispatches, Petersburg, Va., Apr. 19, 1865, in *Thomas Morris Chester: Black Civil War Correspondent—His Dispatches from the Virginia Front*, ed. R. J. M. Blackett (Baton Rouge: Louisiana State University Press, 1989), 312, 318; **slaves:** Mary S. Pond to George Whipple, Portsmouth, Va., May 13, 1865, #H1-7147, reel 210, AMA.

13. **deeper:** Henry Baker, "An Expression by the Colored People of New Orleans," in *Louisiana's Tribute to the Memory of Abraham Lincoln . . . April 22, 1865* (New Orleans: Picayune, 1881), 37; **keenly:** Joseph A. Prime, "Sermon Preached in the Liberty Street Presbyterian Church (Colored)," in *A Tribute of Respect by the Citizens of Troy to the Memory of Abraham Lincoln* (Troy, N.Y.: Young and Benson, 1865), 155; **more than:** Jacob Thomas, "Sermon Preached in the African Methodist Episcopal Zion Church," in *Tribute of Respect*, 44; **dusky:** "From Baltimore," *New York Anglo-African*, May 6, 1865; **people:** "From the Regiments," letter from Richard H. Black, 3rd U.S.C.T., Fernandina, Fla., *New York Anglo-African*, May 27, 1865; **personal:** Frederick Douglass, "Our Martyred President: An Address Delivered in Rochester, New York, on 15 April 1865," *FDP*, ser. 1, 4:76; **colored:** Gideon Welles diary, Apr. 19, 1865, Welles Papers, LC; **white:** J. G. Holland, *The Nation Weeping for Its Dead: Observances at Springfield, Massachusetts, on President Lincoln's Funeral Day* (Springfield, Mass.: Samuel Bowles, 1865), 25; **intense:** Theodore L. Cuyler, "Sermon IX," in *Our Martyr President, Abraham Lincoln: Voices from the Pulpit of New York and Brooklyn. Oration by Hon. Geo. Bancroft, Oration at the Burial, by Bishop Simpson* (New York: Tibbals and Whiting, 1865), 170; **pity:** S. H. Fowler to "Mr. Whiting," Headley, Mass., Apr. 21, 1865, #57688, reel 91, AMA; see also M. M. Hutchins to "Mr. Whiting," Dover, N.H., Apr. 17, 1865, #75762, reel 117, AMA ("How the poor Freedmen will mourn").

14. **smudging:** Julia Anna Hartness Lay diary, Apr. 16, 1865, NYPL; **sorrowful:** Emily Watkins to Abiathar Watkins, Jersey City, N.J., Apr. 16, 1865, Watkins Papers, NYPL; **horror:** Lindsley, *"Maggie!,"* 83 (Apr. 15, 1865, entry); **broke down:** John Worthington to Mary Worthington, Cooperstown, N.Y., Apr. 15, 1865, Autograph File, HLH; **teachers:** Grenville H. Norcross diary, Apr. 16, 1865, AAS; **boys:** Anna Cabot Lowell diary, Apr. 16, 1865, MHS.

15. **scarcely:** Douglass, "Our Martyred President," *FDP*, ser. 1, 4:76; **none:** "From the Regiments," letter from Richard H. Black, 3rd U.S.C.T., Fernandina, Fla., *New York Anglo-African*, May 27, 1865; **sign:** Baker, "An Expression by the Colored People of New Orleans," in *Louisiana's Tribute*, 37; **express:** Mary Elizabeth Moore to James Otis Moore, Saco, Me., Apr. 15, 1865, Moore Papers, Duke; **describe:** William L. Mead to Louisa White, Charleston, S.C., Apr. 19, 1865, ts., George Cornwell Correspondence, MDHS; **dull:** Nicholas B. Wainwright, ed., *A Philadelphia Perspective: The Diary of Sidney George Fisher . . . , 1834–1871* (Philadelphia: Historical Society of Pennsylvania, 1967), 492 (Apr. 15, 1865, entry); **wildly:** Edward Peacock to Caroline Dall, [England], Apr. 27, 1865, box 4, Dall Papers, MHS.

16. **heard:** "Mary" to mother, Norton, Mass., Apr. 16, 1865, Nye Family Papers, Duke; **shake:** Carl Schurz to wife, Raleigh, N.C., Apr. 18, 1865, in *Speeches, Correspondence and Political Papers of Carl Schurz,* 6 vols., ed. Frederic Bancroft (New York: G. P. Putnam's Sons, 1913), 1:252; **awful:** George E. Ellis diary, Apr. 15, 1865, Ellis Papers, MHS; **Fanny, sad:** Elizabeth R. Child diary, Apr. 3, 16, 1865, Richards-Child Family Papers, MHS.

17. **not feel:** Margaret B. Howell diary, Apr. 17, 1865, HSP; **so bad:** Holiday Ames to wife, Decatur, Ala., Apr. 23, 1865, in "Waiting for the War's End: The Letter of an Ohio

Soldier in Alabama," ed. Louis Filler, *Ohio History* 74 (1965), 56; **sleep:** Susannah A. Milner-Gibson to Jane Poultney Bigelow, Folkestone, England, Apr. 28, 1865, Bigelow Family Papers, NYPL; **lightheaded:** John Langdon Sibley diary, Apr. 15, 1865, in "Harvard and the Tragedy of 1865," *Harvard Alumni Bulletin* 42 (1940), 900; **headache:** Winthrop Henry Phelps diary, Apr. 18, 1865, LC; **trembling:** Horace O. Gilmore to Lucy Gilmore, Petersburg, Va., Apr. [15], 1865, Gilmore Papers, NYSL; **prostration:** Edwin Emerson diary, Apr. 27, 1865, Emerson Family Papers, NYPL; **indefinable:** Mary Elizabeth Moore to James Otis Moore, Saco, Me., May 4, 1865, Moore Papers, Duke; **surgeon:** Moses A. Cleveland diary, Apr. 17, 21, 1865, MHS; **forget:** Henry Gawthrop diary, Apr. 16, 1865, DHS.

18. **new birth:** Abraham Lincoln, "Address Delivered at the Dedication of the Cemetery at Gettysburg," Nov. 19, 1863, *CWL,* 7:23.

19. **Almighty:** Abraham Lincoln, "Second Inaugural Address," Mar. 4, 1865, *CWL,* 8:333.

20. **cannot:** Newton Perkins to mother, New York, Apr. 16, 1865, Montgomery Family Papers, LC; **drifting:** Levi S. Graybill diary, Apr. 17, 1865, Graybill Papers, HL; **atrocity:** Anna M. Ferris diary, Apr. 16, 1865, Ferris Family Papers, FHL; **not shake:** Lydia Maria Child to Sarah Blake Shaw, [no place], Apr. [n.d.], 1865, Child Letters, SL.

21. **hopeless:** Gideon Welles diary, Apr. 16, 1865, Welles Papers, LC; **consolation:** "Cosmorama," letter to the editor, *San Francisco Elevator,* May 12, 1865, #4999, BAP; **more:** Thomas, "Sermon Preached in the African Methodist Episcopal Zion Church," in *Tribute of Respect,* 46; **hope:** Philip Alexander Bell et al., [no title], *San Francisco Elevator,* Apr. 21, 1865, #4828, BAP; **Liberty:** Chauncey Leonard to Lorenzo Thomas, Alexandria, Va., Apr. 30, 1865, Letters Received, #287L, M619, roll 374, RG94-NARA.

22. **all:** Martha Fisher Anderson diary, Apr. 23, 1865, MHS; **doeth, permitted:** William J. Gould diary, Apr. 21, 1865, Gould Papers, LC; **wise:** James Otis Moore to Mary Elizabeth Moore, "Chapel Pt.," May 7, 1865, Moore Papers, Duke; **unfathomable:** Richard G. Lay to Carrie Lay, "Burks station," Va., Apr. 19, 1865, Lay Letters, NYPL; **everybody:** Abigail Williams May to Eleanor Goddard May, Boston, Apr. 16, 1865, May and Goddard Family Papers, SL.

23. **may be:** Douglass, "Our Martyred President," *FDP,* ser. 1, 4:78; **some way:** W. T. Richardson to George Whipple, Beaufort, S.C., Apr. 21, 1865, #H5576, reel 187, AMA; **doubtless:** Gail Hamilton to "My Dear," Hamilton, Mass., Apr. 15, 1865, in *Gail Hamilton's Life in Letters,* 2 vols., ed. H. August Dodge (Boston: Lee and Shepard, 1901), 1:495; **cloud:** J. H. Elliot to Robert Anderson, Brattleboro, Vt., Apr. 25, 1865, Anderson Papers, LC.

24. **stricken:** Minute Book, Apr. 18, 1865, in "Mourning Observance for Abraham Lincoln by the B'nai B'rith Lodge of Marysville, California," *Western States Jewish Historical Quarterly* 1 (1967), 172; **must be:** Mary Ann Starkey to "My dear Friend," New Bern, N.C., Apr. 20, 1865, Edward W. Kinsley Papers, Duke; **view:** "Rebecca" to Jane Wigglesworth Grew, Boston, Apr. 18, 1865 (part of Apr. 16 letter), Grew Correspondence, MHS; **understand:** Charlotte A. Blech notebook, Apr. 16, 1865, Blech-Meyer-Dowd Papers, SL; **seems:** Georgia Treadway to Newton Perkins, New Haven, Conn., Apr. 16, 1865, Montgomery Family Papers, LC.

25. **triumph:** Edward Everett Hale to Charles Hale, Boston, Apr. 15, 1865, box 6, Hale Papers, NYSL; **dawn:** James Thomas Ward diary, Apr. 16, 1865, Ward Papers, LC.

26. **expressed:** Mattie Smith diary, Apr. 16, 1865, CHM.

27. **where:** *Rochester Ladies' Anti-Slavery Society,* 6; **O why:** Mary Elizabeth Moore to James Otis Moore, Saco, Me., Apr. 15, 1865, Moore Papers, Duke; **Why did God, O God:** Lindsley, *"Maggie!,"* 86, 83 (Apr. 23, 15, 1865, entries).

28. **God knows:** Henry S. Thacher diary, Apr. 23, 1865, Thacher Family Papers, MHS; **sinfully, lived:** Mary Elizabeth Moore to James Otis Moore, Saco, Me., Apr. 15, 1865, and James Otis Moore to Mary Elizabeth Moore, Washington, D.C., Apr. 20, 1865, Moore Papers, Duke; **trust:** Henry W. Pearce to "Lena," Marietta, Ohio, Apr. 16, 1865, #00066.150, GLC-NYHS; **save:** H. C. Percy to George Whipple, Norfolk, Va., May 7, 1865, #H1-7112-16, reel 210, AMA.

29. **freedom:** "Cosmorama," letter to the editor, *San Francisco Elevator,* May 12, 1865, #4999, BAP; **nation:** Douglass, "Our Martyred President," *FDP,* ser. 1, 4:76; **inspire:** Montgomery Blair to Samuel L. M. Barlow, Washington, D.C., Apr. 18, 1865, box 56, Barlow Papers, HL; **seal:** Wendell Phillips, "The Lesson of President Lincoln's Death: A Speech of Wendell Phillips at the Tremont Temple, on Sunday Evening, April 23, 1865," in *Universal Suffrage, and Complete Equality in Citizenship, the Safeguards of Democratic Institutions* (Boston: Rand and Avery, 1865), 14.

30. **killed:** Harriet Anne Severance diary, Apr. 16, 1865, SL; **who:** Elizabeth Rogers Mason Cabot diary, Apr. 15, 1865, MHS; **why:** "Em" to Lewis J. Nettleton, Milford, Conn., Apr. 19, 1865, Nettleton-Baldwin Family Papers, Duke; **reconcile:** Mary Elizabeth Moore to James Otis Moore, Saco, Me., Apr. 16, 1865, Moore Papers, Duke; **slight:** Edgar Dinsmore to Carrie Drayton, Saint Andrews Parish, S.C., May 29, 1865, Dinsmore Papers, Duke.

31. **anxiety:** William Lloyd Garrison Jr. to Martha Coffin Wright, Boston, Apr. 25, 1865, box 56, Garrison Family Papers, SSC; **providential:** Evander C. Kennedy to mother, Petersburg, Va., May 1, 1865, Kennedy Letters, MHS; **weak:** Mary Elizabeth Moore to James Otis Moore, Saco, Me., Apr. 16, 1865, Moore Papers, Duke.

32. **wonderful:** Lydia Maria Child to Sarah Blake Shaw, [no place], Apr. [n.d.], 1865, Child Letters, SL; **lenient:** David Homer Bates diary, Apr. 15, 1865, Bates Papers, LC; **policy:** Anna M. Ferris diary, Apr. 16, 1865, Ferris Family Papers, FHL; **star:** Phillips, "Lesson of President Lincoln's Death," 14–15.

33. **sometimes:** editorial, *San Francisco Elevator,* Apr. 21, 1865, #4827, BAP; **cast off:** J. S. Smith to "My Dear Sir," Buchanan, Liberia, Aug. 11, 1865, Incoming Correspondence, Letters from Liberia, box I: B13, reel 160, American Colonization Society Papers, LC; **sorry, honest:** Ellis Hughes diary, Apr. 23, 19, 1865, Hughes-Gray Family Papers, Duke.

Robert S. Harper writes that northern newspapers "poured forth a torrent of adulation and eulogy" and that it was "no longer possible to determine the politics of a newspaper by what it said about Lincoln"; see *Lincoln and the Press* (New York: McGraw-Hill, 1951), 352.

34. **prepared:** John Glenn diary, Apr. 17, 1865, Glenn Papers, MDHS; **disgusted:** William Kauffman Scarborough, ed., *The Diary of Edmund Ruffin: A Dream Shattered, June, 1863–June, 1865* (Baton Rouge: Louisiana State University Press, 1989), 859 (Apr. 21, 1865, entry); **noble:** Chauncey Welton to parents, Raleigh, N.C., Apr. 19, 1865, Welton Papers, SHC.

35. **immortal:** Henry S. Thacher diary, Apr. 15, 1865, Thacher Family Papers, MHS; **statesman:** Evander C. Kennedy to mother, Petersburg, Va., May 1, 1865, Kennedy Letters, MHS; **memorial:** J. N. Whitney to B. F. Whitten, Raymond, Me., Apr. 15, 1865, box 2, Miscellaneous Documents Relating to Abraham Lincoln, HLH; **savior:** John Greenleaf Whittier to F. W. Lincoln, Amesbury, Mass., May, 22, 1865, John Greenleaf Whittier Manuscript Collection, FHL; **man:** Charles Edward French diary, Apr. 23, 1865, French Diaries and Papers, MHS; **liberty:** Alonzo A. Carr to brother and sister, Beaufort, S.C., Apr. 21, 1865, Cynthia Anthonsen Foster Papers, SL; **live on:** James Williams to sister, New York, May 6, 1865, Simon Gratz Autograph Collection, HSP; **Moses, elevation:** Philip Alexander Bell et al., [no title], and editorial, both in *San Francisco Elevator,* Apr. 21, 1865, #4828, 4827, BAP; **Moses:** Thomas, "Sermon Preached in the African Methodist Episcopal Zion Church," in *Tribute of Respect,* 45; **beautiful:** Mary Elizabeth Moore to James Otis Moore, Saco, Me., Apr. 16, 1865, James Otis Moore Papers, Duke.

36. **degree:** editorial, *San Francisco Elevator,* Apr. 21, 1865, #4827, BAP; **more:** P. B. S. Nichuston [?] to George Whipple, Roanoke Island, N.C., Apr. 22, 1865, #100001, reel 169, AMA; **died:** Laura Towne to unknown, Saint Helena Island, S.C., Apr. 29, 1865, in *Letters and Diary of Laura M. Towne: Written from the Sea Islands of South Carolina, 1862–1884,* ed. Rupert Sargent Holland (1912; reprint, New York: Negro Universities Press, 1969), 162; **mankind:** [illegible] to mother, "Potomac River," Apr. 23, 1865, Nathaniel H. Harris Papers, SHC; **no equal:** Robert H. Williams to David and Carrie Thurber, City Point, Va., Apr. 29, 1865, Goff-Williams Papers, HL.

37. **benefit:** "Our Domestic Correspondence," letter from H. O. Waggner, Chicago, Apr. 16, 1865, *New York Anglo-African,* published Apr. 29, 1865; **dark:** James Freeman Clarke, "Who Hath Abolished Death," in *Sermons Preached in Boston on the Death of Abraham Lincoln* (Boston: J. E. Tilton, 1865), 92, 100; **crucifixion:** Montgomery Blair to Samuel L. M. Barlow, Washington, D.C., Apr. 18, 1865, box 56, Barlow Papers, HL; **killed:** Cuyler, "Sermon IX," in *Our Martyr President,* 171; **dead:** C. L. Woodworth to M. E. Strieby, Amherst, Mass., Apr. 17, 1865, #57681, reel 91, AMA.

38. **250:** John Wesley Marshall diary, Apr. 20, 1865, LC; **jumping:** William J. Gould diary, Apr. 22, 25, 1865, Gould Papers, LC; **hope:** Garland H. White to William H. Seward, City Point, Va., Apr. [n.d.], 1865, William H. Seward Papers, University of Rochester (I thank Christopher Hager, Trinity College, Hartford, Conn., for transcribing and sharing this document); **aside:** George Gaskell to sister, Plaquemine, La., Apr. 23, 1865, ts. box 86, fol. 9, Materials Unrelated to Spanish American War, Spanish-American War Veterans Survey Collection, U.S. Army Military History Institute, Carlisle, Pa.; **though:** Douglass, "Our Martyred President," *FDP,* ser. 1, 4:76.

39. **calamity:** John B. Burrud to Ocena Burrud, Washington, D.C., Apr. 25–27, 1865,

Burrud Papers, HL; **full:** Samuel Foster Haven to Caroline Dall, Worcester, Mass., May 2, 1865, box 4, Dall Papers, MHS; **nation:** William Boardman Richards diary, Apr. 16, 1865, Richards Family Papers, MHS.

40. **headache:** Edward Everett Hale diary, Apr. 24, 1865, box 54, Hale Papers, NYSL; **tired, heart:** Anna Cabot Lowell diary, Apr. 18, 23, 1865, MHS; **not:** Rudolph Rey to Lizzie DeVoe, near Raleigh, N.C., Apr. 29, 1865, Rey Letters, NYHS; **hang:** Elizabeth Blackwell to Barbara Bodichon, New York, May 23, 1865, Blackwell Letters, Columbia.

41. **bow:** M. R. Delany, "Monument to President Lincoln," Charleston, S.C., Apr. 20, 1865, *Christian Recorder,* published May 20, 1865; **even:** Lydia Maria Child to John Greenleaf Whittier, May 1865, fragment, Child Letters, SL.

Interlude: Love

1. **never:** Henry J. Peck to Mary Peck, Burkeville Junction, Va., Apr. 20, 1865, Peck Correspondence, NYSL; **good:** Anna Cabot Lowell diary, Apr. 15, 1865, MHS.

2. **fought:** Theodore Lyman diary, Apr. 15, 1865, ts., Lyman Papers, MHS; **no man:** Frederick A. Sawyer, "Account of what I saw of the Death of Mr. Lincoln written April 15, 1865," in "An Eyewitness Account of Abraham Lincoln's Assassination," ed. Ronald D. Rietveld, *Civil War History* 22 (1976), 68; **raised:** Josephine E. Strong to M. E. Strieby, Portsmouth, Va., May 3, 1865, #8853, reel 15 (misfiled with Connecticut), AMA.

3. **personally:** Anne Baldwin to Charlotte Nettleton, New York, Apr. 16, 1865, Nettleton-Baldwin Family Papers, Duke; **dear:** Annie P. Chadwick diary, Apr. 15, 1865, Chadwick Family Papers, NYSL; **beloved:** "New York," letter to the editor, *San Francisco Elevator,* Apr. 28, 1865, #4917, BAP; **us of:** George Gaskell to sister, Plaquemine, La., Apr. 23, 1865, ts., box 86, fol. 9, Materials Unrelated to Spanish American War, Spanish-American War Veterans Survey Collection, U.S. Army Military History Institute, Carlisle, Pa.; **kindred:** "From the Regiments," letter from "M.F.," 11th U.S. Heavy Artillery, Fort Banks, La., Apr. 12 [sic], 1865, *New York Anglo-African,* published May 20, 1865; **could not:** J. Harry Keyes to Sarah Ogden, City Point, Va., Apr. 30, 1865, #06559.060, GLC-NYHS; **everywhere:** Lucy McKim to Wendell Phillips Garrison, Philadelphia, Apr. 17, 1865, box 49, Garrison Family Papers, SSC; **private:** William Lloyd Garrison Jr. to Martha Coffin Wright, Roxbury, Mass., Apr. 16, 1865, box 56, Garrison Family Papers, SSC; **almost:** Mattie Smith diary, Apr. 16, 1865, CHM.

4. **mighty:** Charles Barnard Fox, *Record of the Service of the Fifty-Fifth Regiment of Massachusetts Volunteer Infantry* (Cambridge, Mass.: John Wilson, 1868), 75 (Apr. 19, 1865, diary entry); **claimed:** Franklin Boyts to Hiram Boyts, Washington, D.C., Apr. 17, 1865, in Boyts diary, HSP; **orphans:** Caroline Barrett White diary, May 14, 1865, White Papers, AAS; **could not:** Harry S. Rimhold to George W. Hensel, Philadelphia, Apr. 15, 1865, box 2, Miscellaneous Documents Relating to Abraham Lincoln, HLH; **sorrowfully:** Mary Ingham Emerson diary, May 28, 1865, Emerson Family Papers, NYPL; **father and mother:** P. B. S. Nichuston [?] to George Whipple, Roanoke Island, N.C., Apr. 22, 1865, #100001, reel 169, AMA.

5. **rather die:** Emory M. Thomas, *Robert E. Lee: A Biography* (New York: W. W. Norton,

1995), 362; Thomas writes, "Surrender was death raised to an enormous power" (366); **illustrious:** William H. Ellis diary, Apr. 12, 1865, Ellis Papers, ser. B, reel 5, LSU-CMM; **dear:** Mary (Cabell) Early diary, Apr. 9, 1865, Early Family Papers, ser. D, part 3, reel 14, VHS-SWF.

Chapter 5. Blame

1. Sarah Browne diary, Apr. 15, 1865 (unparalleled); Sarah Browne to Albert Browne, Salem, Mass., Apr. 20, 1865 (enough, fathers), both BFP.

2. Albert Browne to "Dear Ones," Charleston, S.C., Apr. 21, 1865 (dastardly, tree, savage, serpent, heap); Albert Browne to "Dear Ones," off Georgetown, S.C., Apr. 25, 1865 (deluded, extermination), both BFP.

3. Dorman diary, May 6 (molest), 7 (beshit; this is an oft-repeated phrase in the diary), July 10 (Booth), 1865.

4. Dorman diary, May 7 (benevolent, instances, barbarity, force, double), 12 (servants, blaming abolitionists), 23 (beyond); on blaming abolitionists, see also Apr. 16, May 16, 1865.

5. **wrath:** Manning Ferguson Force diary, Apr. 17, 1865, Force Papers, LC.

6. **honor:** Sarah Browne to Albert Browne, Salem, Mass., Apr. 20, 1865, one of two letters of this date, BFP; **mixed:** J. Madison Bell, "Poem: In commemoration of the death of Abraham Lincoln, delivered at the great Public Meeting of Colored Citizens," *San Francisco Elevator,* Apr. 21, 1865, #4831 BAP; **amazement:** "Rebecca" to Jane Wigglesworth Grew, Boston, Apr. 16, 1865, Grew Correspondence, MHS; **fired:** Lucy Pierce Hedge to Charlotte Hedge, Brookline, Mass., Apr. 18, 1865, Poor Family Papers, SL; **crushed:** Mary Butler Reeves to Caroline Butler Laing, Germantown, Pa., Apr. 16, 1865, Butler-Laing Family Papers, NYHS; **wild:** David Homer Bates diary, Apr. 16, 1865, Bates Papers, LC; **hatred:** Alfred Neafie to Anne Neafie, Savannah, Ga., Apr. 19, 1865, Neafie Papers, NYSL.

7. **oath:** Joseph Warren Keifer to Eliza Keifer, Burkeville, Va. Apr. 15, 1865, Keifer Papers, LC; **forgiven:** A. J. Hamilton, *A Fort Delaware Journal: The Diary of a Yankee Private,* ed. W. Emerson Wilson (Wilmington: Fort Delaware Society, 1981), 79 (Apr. 15, 1865, entry); **preparing:** Mary Bushnell Cheney to Francis Louise Bushnell, [Hartford, Conn.?], Apr. 15, 1865, ts., Cheney Family Papers, SSC; **murderous:** Henry Cornwall to Lewis J. Nettleton, Milford, Conn., Apr. 16, 1865, Nettleton-Baldwin Family Papers, Duke; **infernal:** James Otis Moore to Mary Elizabeth Moore, "Potomac River," Apr. 19, 1865, Moore Papers, Duke; **caps:** Heber Painter to Rebecca Frick, Richmond, Va., Apr. 17, 1865 (part of Apr. 16 letter), #02016.082, GLC-NYHS.

8. **a man:** John N. Ferguson diary, Apr. 17, 1865, LC; **spirit:** Newton Perkins to mother, New York, Apr. 16, 1865, Montgomery Family Papers, LC; **butchered:** anonymous Union soldier to parents, Burkeville, Va., Apr. 18, 1865, #08618, GLC-NYHS; **kill:** Samuel Miller Quincy [no salutation], New Orleans, Apr. 20, 1865 (part of Apr. 19 letter), Quincy, Wendell, Holmes, Upham Family Papers, MHS.

9. **just:** Jane Swisshelm to *St. Cloud Democrat,* Washington, D.C., Apr. 17, 1865 (published Apr. 27, 1865), in *Crusader and Feminist: Letters of Jane Grey Swisshelm, 1858–*

1865, ed. Arthur J. Larsen (Saint Paul: Minnesota Historical Society, 1934), 287; **forgotten, don't let:** Manning Ferguson Force diary, Apr. 18, 1865; Manning Ferguson Force to "Mr. Kebler" [?], Raleigh, N.C., Apr. 20, 1865; Manning Ferguson Force to "Mrs. Perkins," Raleigh, N.C., Apr. 21, 1865 (letters copied into journal), Force Papers, LC; **wish:** Carl Schurz to wife, Raleigh, N.C., Apr. 18, 1865, in *Speeches, Correspondence and Political Papers of Carl Schurz,* 6 vols., ed. Frederic Bancroft (New York: G. P. Putnam's Sons, 1913), 1:253; **surrender:** "Tom" to mother, Raleigh, N.C., Apr. 19, 1865, box 2, Miscellaneous Documents Relating to Abraham Lincoln, HLH; **prolonged:** anonymous Union soldier to parents, Burkeville, Va., Apr. 18, 1865, #08618, GLC-NYHS; **better:** Franklin Augustus Buck to Mary Sewall Bradley, Weaverville, Calif., Apr. 27, 1865, Buck Papers, HL.

10. **driven:** "From the Regiments," letter from Richard H. Black, 3rd U.S.C.T., Fernandina, Fla., *New York Anglo-African,* May 27, 1865; **burn:** Edward J. Bartlett to Martha Bartlett, South Side Railroad, Va., Apr. 16, 1865, Bartlett Letters, MHS; **sory:** Chauncey Welton to parents, Raleigh, N.C., Apr. 19, 1865, Welton Papers, SHC; **slay:** Newton Perkins to mother, New York, Apr. 16, 1865, Montgomery Family Papers, LC; **Attila:** Carl Schurz to wife, Raleigh, N.C., Apr. 18, 1865, in Bancroft, *Speeches, Correspondence,* 1:253.

11. **extirminate:** George W. Squier to Ellen Squier, Chattanooga, Tenn., Apr. 15, 1865, in *This Wilderness of War: The Civil War Letters of George W. Squier, Hoosier Volunteer,* ed. Julie A. Doyle et al. (Knoxville: University of Tennessee Press, 1998), 104; **no more:** H. Worthey Hooper to William Schouler, Georgetown, S.C., Apr. 27, 1865, vol. 1, Letters Sent, Records of the Fifty-Fourth Massachusetts Infantry Regiment (Colored), M1659, roll 1, RG94-NARA; **badly:** Henry J. Peck to Mary Peck, Richmond, Va., May 1, 1865, Peck Correspondence, NYSL; **extermination:** Alonzo Pickard to Byron Flagg, Alexandria, Va., Apr. 17, 1865, part of Rose Pickard to Byron Flagg, Apr. 14, 1865, Pickard Papers, LC; **shoot:** William E. Park to "Mr. Newton" (addendum to cousin), Fort Spanish, Ala., Apr. 21, 1865, #01545.05, GLC-NYHS; **willing:** Francis G. Barnes to Frances M. Barnes, near Mobile, Ala., May 19, 1865, ts., p. 365, Barnes Letters, NYSL.

12. **mutterings:** J. Thoman to "Henrietta," Washington, D.C., Apr. 15, 1865, in Thomas F. Schwartz, "Grief, Souvenirs, and Enterprise following Lincoln's Assassination," *Illinois Historical Journal* 83 (1990), 261; **lieutenant:** Henry Robinson Berkeley diary, Apr. 15, 1865, Berkeley Papers, ser. A, reel 2, VHS-CMM; **very hard:** Allen H. Babcock diary, Apr. 18, 1865, Babcock Papers, NYSL; **get up:** Marmaduke Shannon to Emma M. Crutcher, Vicksburg, Miss., Apr. 18, 1865 (part of Apr. 14 letter), Crutcher-Shannon Family Papers, ser. F, reel 30, UTA-SWF; **guards:** Edward W. Benham to Jennie Benham, Goldsboro, N.C., Apr. 20, 1865, ts., Benham Papers, Duke; **vent:** Carl Schurz to wife, Raleigh, N.C., Apr. 18, 1865, in Bancroft, *Speeches, Correspondence,* 1:253, and on this incident, see also Chauncey Welton to parents, Raleigh, N.C., Apr. 19, 1865, Welton Papers, SHC, and Henry Hitchcock to Mary Hitchcock, "Chesapeake Bay," Apr. 22, 1865, Hitchcock Papers, LC.

13. **hardly:** Franklin Boyts to Hiram Boyts, Washington, D.C., Apr. 17, 1865, in Boyts diary, HSP; **burn:** Newton T. Colby to Merrill Colby, Washington, D.C., Apr. 15, 1865, in *The Civil War Papers of Lt. Colonel Newton T. Colby, New York Infantry,* ed. William E. Hughes (Jefferson, N.C.: McFarland, 2003), 293; **earnest:** Benjamin Brown French to

Frank O. French, Washington, D.C., Apr. 15, 1865, French Papers, LC; **lynch:** Annie G. Dudley Davis diary, Apr. 15, 1865, HL; **exterminate:** J. Madison Bell, "Poem: In commemoration of the death of Abraham Lincoln, delivered at the great Public Meeting of Colored Citizens," *San Francisco Elevator,* Apr. 21, 1865, #4831, BAP; **feeling:** George Comfort to Samuel Comfort, Morrisville, Pa., Apr. 16, 1865, Comfort Papers, Princeton; **actually:** Alfred W. Ellet to "Mary," Union Grove, Ill., May 8, 1865, Cabell-Ellet Papers, ser. D, part 1, reel 8, UVA-CMM; **clemency:** Anne Neafie to Alfred Neafie, Ellenville, N.Y., Apr. 20, 1865, Neafie Papers, NYSL; **crushed:** Sarah Browne to Albert Browne, Salem, Mass., Apr. 20, 1865, BFP; **death:** Mary Butler Reeves to Caroline Butler Laing, Germantown, Pa., Apr. 16, 1865, Butler-Laing Family Papers, NYHS.

14. **traitors:** T. M. D. Ward, "Our California Letter," San Francisco, Apr. 21, 1865, *Christian Recorder,* published May 20, 1865; **mercy:** Edward Williams Morley to Sardis Morley, Fortress Monroe, Va., Apr. 18, 1865, Edward Williams Morley Papers, LC.

15. **feeling:** Lucy Pierce Hedge to Charlotte Hedge, Brookline, Mass., Apr. 25, 1865, Poor Family Papers, SL; **merit:** Augustus W. Weeks to George Whipple, Fortress Monroe, Va., Apr. 18, 1865, #H1-7010, reel 209, AMA; **dam:** Alvin Palmer to uncle and aunt, Orfordville, N.H., May 7, 1865, Palmer Family Papers, Duke.

16. **great:** Dorman diary, Apr. 23, 1865; **gleeful:** see, e.g., E. R. Harmanson to "Prince," Red River, La., Apr. 23, 1865, Albert A. Batchelor Papers, ser. B, part 5, reel 1, LSU-RSPE; [Helen Ellis?] to John Benjamin Long, Rusk, Tex., Apr. 26, 1865, Long Papers, ser. C, part 1, reel 21, UTA-CMM; Amanda (Edmonds) Chappelear diary, Apr. 21, 1865, Chappelear Papers, ser. D, part 3, reel 9, VHS-SWF; John Q. Anderson, ed., *Brokenburn: The Journal of Kate Stone, 1861–1868* (1955; reprint, Baton Rouge: Louisiana State University Press, 1995), 333 (Apr. 28, 1865, entry); Sarah Lois Wadley diary, Apr. 26, 1865, Wadley Papers, ser. A, part 3, reel 6, SHC-SWF; **crazy:** Eliza F. Andrews, *The War-Time Journal of a Georgia Girl, 1864–1865* (New York: D. Appleton, 1908), 216 (May 5, 1865, entry), DocSouth, docsouth.unc.edu/fpn/andrews/menu.html; **private:** John Peter Nelson to George W. Colles, New Orleans, Apr. 20, 1865, Colles Family Papers, NYPL; **lunatic:** Lucy Muse (Walton) Fletcher diary, Apr. 19, 1865, Fletcher Papers, Duke; **tyrannicidal:** Francis R. Rives to unknown, New York, Apr. 15, 1865, William Cabell Rives Papers, LC; **fanatics:** Ellen Kean to Mary Kean, New York, Apr. 16, 1865, in *Death and Funeral of Abraham Lincoln . . . in Two Long Descriptive Letters from Mrs. Ellen Kean, the Actress, whilst Touring the United States in 1865* (London: Privately printed, 1921), 17; **desperadoes:** François Joinville to Gustavus V. Fox, "Orleans house," Apr. 28, 1865, Gustavus-Fox Papers, NYHS.

17. **do not:** Cloe (Whittle) Greene diary, Apr. 16, 1865, reel 4, WM-AWD-South; **northern:** Caroline Dunstan diary, Apr. 15, 1865, NYPL; **curse:** Francis G. Barnes to Frances M. Barnes, Tombigbee River, Ala., Apr. 25, 1865, ts., p. 358, Barnes Letters, NYSL; **traitors:** anonymous Union soldier to parents, Burkeville, Va., Apr. 18, 1865, #08618, GLC-NYHS; **rants:** John B. Burrud to Ocena Burrud, Washington, D.C., Apr. 25–27, 28, May 5, 1865, and Charlestown, Va., Apr. 19, 1865, Burrud Papers, HL; **drunken:** unknown writer, Apr. 15, 1865, #193, Thomas B. Harned Collection of the Papers of Walt Whitman, LC.

18. **vile, wretch:** editorials, *San Francisco Elevator,* Apr. 21, 1865, #4827, #4811, BAP; **scoundrel:** David F. Cushman to Caroline D. Cushman, Martinsburg, Va., Apr. 15, 1865, #250, octavo vol. 1, Civil War Collection, AAS; **fiend:** Helen Lansing Grinnell diary, Apr. 15, 1865, NYPL; R. B. Milliken to "Friend Byron," Washington, D.C., Apr. 16, 1865, #54, Lincoln Room Miscellaneous Papers, HLH; **dog:** John Worthington to Mary Worthington, Cooperstown, N.Y., Apr. 15, 1865, Autograph File, HLH; **demon:** Edgar B. Jones to Theresa H. Perkins, City Point, Va., Apr. 22, 1865, Montgomery Family Papers, LC; **gift:** Gareth Wilkinson to "Mr. Linton," London, Apr. 27, 1865, #07749.02, GLC-NYHS; **blood:** James Otis Moore to Mary Elizabeth Moore, Washington, D.C., Apr. 20, 1865, Moore Papers, Duke; Mary Butler Reeves to Caroline Butler Laing, Germantown, Pa., Apr. 16, 1865, Butler-Laing Family Papers, NYHS; **tortured:** Clara Allen to Walter Allen, Worcester, Mass., Apr. 16, 1865, Weston-Allen Papers, SSC; **lamppost, cut:** R. B. Milliken to "Friend Byron," Washington, D.C., Apr. 16, 1865, #54, Lincoln Room Miscellaneous Papers, HLH; **flog:** Asa Fitch diary, Apr. 28, 1865, Fitch Papers, Yale-Sterling; **shoot:** C. B. Pyne to unknown, Diamond Creek, Va., May 12, 1865, #07206, GLC-NYHS; **burn:** J. N. Smith to brother, Washington, D.C., Apr. 16, 1865, box 2, Miscellaneous Documents Relating to Abraham Lincoln, HLH; **resuscitate:** John W. Haley, *The Rebel Yell and the Yankee Hurrah: The Civil War Journal of a Maine Volunteer,* ed. Ruth L. Silliker (Camden, Me.: Down East Books, 1985), 268 (Apr. 16, 1865, entry); **Cincinnati:** L. S. Currier to H. C. Rowley, Cincinnati, Apr. 15, 1865, Currier and Co. Papers, AAS.

19. **wanted:** broadside, "$100,000 reward! The murderer of our late beloved President, Abraham Lincoln, is still at large," 1865, Rare Book and Special Collections, LC, available at loc.gov/pictures/resource/cph.3g05341; **noose:** John Swift to sister, White River, Ark., Apr. 21, 1865, in "Letters from a Sailor on a Tinclad," ed. Lester L. Swift, *Civil War History* 7 (1961), 62; **till:** Charles J. Harris to parents, [Georgetown?], S.C., [late Apr.], 1865, Harris Letters, Duke; **fry:** Haley, *Rebel Yell,* 268 (Apr. 16, 1865, entry); **tear:** John Worthington to Mary Worthington, Cooperstown, N.Y., Apr. 15, 1865, Autograph File, HLH; on the travel accounts, see Elliott J. Gorn, "'Gouge and Bite, Pull Hair and Scratch': The Social Significance of Fighting in the Southern Backcountry," *American Historical Review* 90 (1985), 18–43.

20. **another:** Chester dispatch, Richmond, Va., Apr. 17, 1865, in *Thomas Morris Chester: Black Civil War Correspondent—His Dispatches from the Virginia Front,* ed. R. J. M. Blackett (Baton Rouge: Louisiana State University Press, 1989), 311; **spurred:** Samuel A. Harrison journal, Apr. 18, 23, 1865, MDHS; **villain:** Emilie Davis diary, "Miscellaneous" pages at back, dated Apr. 14, 1865, HSP and davisdiaries.villanova.edu; **rebels:** Sarah G. Putnam diary, Apr. 27, 1865, MHS.

21. **devilish:** Francis Lieber to Henry W. Halleck, New York, Apr. 16, 1865, box 28, Lieber Papers, HL; **thug:** Ellis Hughes diary, Apr. 25, 1865, Hughes-Gray Family Papers, Duke; **whole:** J. and J. H. St. John to Bela T. St. John, Genesee, Ill., Apr. 24, 1865, St. John Papers, LC; **because:** "General Hancock's Appeal to the Colored People," Washington, D.C., Apr. 24, 1865, in B. F. Morris, *Memorial Record of the Nation's Tribute to Abraham Lincoln* (Washington, D.C.: W. H. and O. H. Morrison, 1865), 117.

22. **Africa:** George H. Mellish to parents, Danville, Va., May 2, 1865, Mellish Papers, HL; **shoot:** John L. Smith to Hannah Smith, near Washington, D.C., July 2, 1865, Smith Papers, HSP; **martyrs:** Frederick A. Sawyer, "Account of what I saw of the Death of Mr. Lincoln written April 15, 1865," in "An Eyewitness Account of Abraham Lincoln's Assassination," ed. Ronald D. Rietveld, *Civil War History* 22 (1976), 67; **slavery:** Francis Lieber to Henry W. Halleck, New York, Apr. 15, 1865, box 28, Lieber Papers, HL; **sacrificed:** Susan E. Parsons Brown Forbes diary, Apr. 15, 1865, AAS; **agent:** Charles H. Mallory diary, Apr. 15, 1865, Mallory Family Collection, GWBW; **hate:** Anna M. Ferris diary, Apr. 15, 1865, Ferris Family Papers, FHL; **fruit:** Charles Francis Adams diary, Apr. 26, 1865, Adams Family Papers, MHS.

23. **slavery:** Joseph A. Prime, "Sermon Preached in the Liberty Street Presbyterian Church (Colored)," in *A Tribute of Respect by the Citizens of Troy to the Memory of Abraham Lincoln* (Troy, N.Y.: Young and Benson, 1865), 155; **agent:** "Fragment of commentary on Lincoln's death," John Morgan Walden Papers, Chicago; **expiate:** Philip Alexander Bell et al., [no title], *San Francisco Elevator,* Apr. 21, 1865, #4828, BAP; **localized, offence:** Abraham Lincoln, "Second Inaugural Address," Mar. 4, 1865, *CWL,* 8:332, 333.

24. **fruit:** Geo. Booth and Chas. Cuthbert, "Proceedings of the Colored Citizens of Sacramento," *San Francisco Elevator,* Apr. 28, 1865, #4992, BAP; **outcrop:** "Assassination of President Lincoln," *New Orleans Black Republican,* Apr. 22, 1865, #5841, BAP; **one word:** Edward Morris to "My Dear Friend," Philadelphia, Apr. 20, 1865, Incoming Correspondence, box I: A179, reel 97, American Colonization Society Papers, LC; **deepley:** A. H. Barnes to Lewis Tappan, Sakets Harbor, N.Y., Apr. 17, 1865, #88580, reel 136, AMA; **slayer:** John Glenn diary, Apr. 29, 1865, Glenn Papers, MDHS.

25. **foe:** Horace Greeley to [E. C. Doughty?], New York, Apr. 21, 1865, #18, Lincoln Room Miscellaneous Papers, HLH; **depravity:** George White diary, Apr. 16, 1865, vol. 32, Special Collections, HLS; Joseph Warren Keifer to Eliza Keifer, Burkeville, Va., Apr. 15, 1865, Keifer Papers, LC; **perverted:** Francis Lieber to Henry W. Halleck, New York, Apr. 22, 1865, box 28, Lieber Papers, HL; **another, appalling:** Pennsylvania and Ohio tributes, in Morris, *Memorial Record,* 132, 134; **pistol, embodied:** *Proceedings of the Union League of Philadelphia Regarding the Assassination of Abraham Lincoln* (Philadelphia: Ashmead, 1865), 11, 12.

26. **loyalty:** Lyman Trumbull, "Furnished by Mr. Lincoln & copied into my remarks to be made at the celebration at Springfield, Ill. Nov. 20, 1860," in "A Lincoln Correspondence," ed. William H. Lambert, *Century Magazine* 77 (1909), 625–26.

27. **crew:** Elbert Johnson diary (labeled "E. M. Johnson's Reminiscences of the War"), Apr. 15, 1865, Johnson Papers, NYSL; **some:** William H. Brown to George W. Brown, Philadelphia, Apr. 15, 1865, Brown Letters, Brown.

28. **slaveholders:** Alonso H. Quint, "Southern Chivalry, and What the Nation Ought to Do With It," Apr. 16, 1865, in Quint, *Three Sermons Preached in the North Congregational Church, New Bedford, Mass., Fast Day, April 13, and Sunday, April 16, 1865* (New Bedford, Mass.: Mercury, 1865), 31–45; **level:** Georgia Treadway to Newton Perkins, New Haven, Conn., Apr. 16, 1865, Montgomery Family Papers, LC; **connection:** "What Has Jefferson Davis Done?" *New York Anglo-African,* May 27, 1865.

29. **dont see:** Henry Robinson Berkeley diary, Apr. 15, 1865, Berkeley Papers, ser. A, reel 2, VHS-CMM; **spirit:** William Kauffman Scarborough, ed., *The Diary of Edmund Ruffin: A Dream Shattered, June, 1863–June, 1865* (Baton Rouge: Louisiana State University Press, 1989), 859 (Apr. 21, 1865, entry); **villainous:** Eliza F. Andrews, *The War-Time Journal of a Georgia Girl, 1864–1865* (New York: D. Appleton, 1908), 238 (May 10, 1865, entry), DocSouth, docsouth.unc.edu/fpn/andrews/menu.html.

30. **leading:** "Rebecca" to Jane Wigglesworth Grew, Boston, Apr. 18, 1865 (part of Apr. 16 letter), Grew Correspondence, MHS; **secession:** William Gray Brooks diary, Apr. 16, 1865, Brooks Papers, MHS; **upper:** Francis Cabot Lowell to brother, Boston, Apr. 17, 1865, Francis Cabot Lowell Papers, MHS; **hot-headed:** Hatsell P. Lyons to "Mary," Kinston, N.C., May 15, 1865, Lyons Papers, GWBW; **leaders:** W.H.C., "Our California Letter," San Francisco, Apr. 21, 1865, *Christian Recorder,* published May 20, 1865; **John Brown:** Mary Mellish to George H. Mellish, Woodstock, Vt., Apr. 19, 1865, Mellish Papers, HL; **list:** George White diary, Apr. 17, 18, 1865, HLS; **pity:** Quint, "Southern Chivalry," 41; **she-devils:** Hallock Armstrong to Mary Armstrong, near Petersburg, Va., Apr. 19, 1865, in *Letters from a Pennsylvania Chaplain at the Siege of Petersburg: 1865* (N.p.: Privately published, 1961), 31, ACWLD; **worse:** Edgar B. Jones to Theresa H. Perkins, City Point, Va., Apr. 22, 1865, Montgomery Family Papers, LC.

31. **masses:** see, e.g., Charles W. Morrell to brother, Richmond, Va., Apr. 17, 1865, ts., Morrell Letters, LC; **common:** Henry Ward Beecher, *Oration at the Raising of "The Old Flag" at Sumter; and Sermon on the Death of Abraham Lincoln* (Manchester: Alexander Ireland, 1865), 24.

32. **people:** Henry S. Thacher diary, Apr. 6, 1865, Thacher Family Papers, MHS; **aristocracy:** Hallock Armstrong to Mary Armstrong, near Petersburg, Va., Apr. 8, 1865, in *Letters from a Pennsylvania Chaplain,* 21, ACWLD; **think:** Edward W. Benham to Jennie Benham, near Falling Creek, Va., May 8, 1865, ts., Benham Papers, Duke; **miserably:** William H. Ellis diary, Apr. 14, 1865, Ellis Papers, ser. B, reel 5, LSU-CMM; **not because:** Robert H. Williams to Ellen Williams, City Point, Va., Apr. 5, 1865, Goff-Williams Papers, HL; **starving:** John H. Francis to William E. Conrow, "Camp 7th N.Y. Indpt. Battery," Apr. 10, 1865 (in folder of James E. McBeth Letters), Francis Letters, NYHS.

33. **ignorantly:** Quint, "Southern Chivalry," 42; **masses:** "Funeral Oration by Bishop Simpson," in B. F. Morris, *Memorial Record,* 236; **unwilling:** Henry Hitchcock to Mary Hitchcock, Raleigh, N.C., Apr. 25, 1865, Hitchcock Papers, LC; **inflaming:** Samuel A. Harrison journal, Apr. 16, 1865, MDHS.

34. **guilty:** Alfred Neafie to Anne Neafie, Savannah, Ga., Apr. 20, 1865, Neafie Papers, NYSL; **always:** Alonzo Pickard to Byron Flagg, Alexandria, Va., Apr. 17, 1865, part of Rose Pickard to Byron Flagg, Apr. 14, 1865, Pickard Papers, LC.

35. **friends, foes:** Frederick Douglass, "Our Martyred President: An Address Delivered in Rochester, New York, on 15 April 1865," *FDP,* ser. 1, 4:78–79; **poor:** "Emancipation of the White Man," *New York Anglo-African,* July 23, 1865; **class:** "The Blacks and the Ballot," *Christian Recorder,* May 27, 1865.

36. **poor:** Hallock Armstrong to Mary Armstrong, near Petersburg, Va., Apr. 10, 8,

1865, in *Letters from a Pennsylvania Chaplain*, 25, 22, ACWLD; **instruct:** Anna Cabot Lowell diary, Apr. 18, 1865, MHS; **trash:** John Greenleaf Whittier, "The Question of To-Day," *Liberator*, May 26, 1865.

37. **feeling:** Anna M. Ferris diary, Apr. 19, 1865, Ferris Family Papers, FHL; **judge:** William L. Mead to Louisa White, Charleston, S.C., Apr. 19, May 4, 1865, ts., George Cornwell Correspondence, MDHS; **God:** James Thomas Ward diary, Apr. 28, 1865, Ward Papers, LC; **vengeance:** Caroline Butler Laing to Mary Butler Reeves, Brooklyn, N.Y., Apr. 21, 1865, Butler-Laing Family Papers, NYHS.

38. **malice, bind:** Lincoln, "Second Inaugural," Mar. 4, 1865, *CWL*, 8:333; **even:** Jacob Thomas, "Sermon Preached in the African Methodist Episcopal Zion Church," in *Tribute of Respect*, 46; **Christian:** J. G. Holland, *The Nation Weeping for Its Dead: Observances at Springfield, Massachusetts, on President Lincoln's Funeral Day* (Springfield, Mass.: Samuel Bowles, 1865), 28–29.

39. **do all, all knew, blood:** Lincoln, "Second Inaugural," Mar. 4, 1865, *CWL*, 8:332–33.

40. **sublimely:** Anna Cabot Lowell diary, Apr. 23, 1865, MHS; **remember:** Ruth [no last name], "Chicago Correspondence," Chicago, May 3, 1865, *Christian Recorder*, published May 20, 1865.

Interlude: Best Friend

1. **best friend:** Otis Norcross diary, Apr. 15, 1865, MHS; **murdered:** "Our Domestic Correspondence," letter from H. O. Waggner, Chicago, Apr. 16, 1865, *New York Anglo-African*, published Apr. 29, 1865; **editors:** "Our National Sacrifice," *Christian Recorder*, Apr. 22, 1865; editorial, *San Francisco Elevator*, Apr. 21, 1865, #4811, BAP; **ministers:** Edwin Greble Sr. to Susan Greble, Richmond, Va., Apr. 18, 1865, Greble Papers, LC; **cabinet:** John P. Usher to wife, Washington, D.C., Apr. 16, 1865, ts., Usher letter, LC; **generals:** Carl Schurz to wife, Raleigh, N.C., Apr. 18, 1865, in *Speeches, Correspondence and Political Papers of Carl Schurz*, 6 vols., ed. Frederic Bancroft (New York: G. P. Putnam's Sons, 1913), 1:253; **officers:** Francis G. Barnes to Frances M. Barnes, Tombigbee River, Ala., Apr. 25, 1865, ts., p. 359, Barnes Letters, NYSL; **soldiers:** Franklin Boyts to Hiram Boyts, Washington, D.C., Apr. 17, 1865, in Boyts diary, HSP; **women:** Caroline Butler Laing to Mary Butler Reeves, Brooklyn, N.Y., Apr. 21, 1865, Butler-Laing Family Papers, NYHS; **dastardly:** Albert Browne to "Dear Ones," Charleston, S.C., Apr. 21, 1865, BFP.

2. **greatest:** Dorman diary, Apr. 26, 1865; **lost:** Samuel Miller Quincy [no salutation], New Orleans, Apr. 19, 1865, Quincy, Wendell, Holmes, Upham Family Papers, MHS; **warm:** Hannah Ford Turner to William Mason Turner, Philadelphia, Apr. 20, 1865, Turner Papers, Brown; **horrible:** Kate Johnson to William Fell Johnson II, Rockland Estate, Md., Apr. 21, 1865, box 47, Johnson Family Papers, MDHS.

3. **ever:** Laura Towne to unknown, Saint Helena Island, S.C., Apr. 29, 1865, in *Letters and Diary of Laura M. Towne: Written from the Sea Islands of South Carolina, 1862–1884*, ed. Rupert Sargent Holland (1912; reprint, New York: Negro Universities Press, 1969), 162; **earthly:** L. R. Hyslop to George Whipple, Norfolk, Va., Apr. 28, 1865, #H1-7034, reel 209, AMA; **emancipator:** Field Cook, "Meeting in Richmond, Va.," *Christian*

Recorder, Apr. 29, 1865; **brothers:** "Meeting in Richmond," *New York Anglo-African,* May 6, 1865; **greatest:** "Assassination of President Lincoln," *New Orleans Black Republican,* Apr. 22, 1865, #5841, BAP.

Chapter 6. Funeral

1. Dorman diary, May 2, 1865.

2. Dorman diary, May 14 (start, dastardly), 2 (law), 1865.

3. Sarah Browne diary, Apr. 19, 1865, BFP.

4. Sarah Browne diary, Apr. 17 (Albert Jr., embalmed), 19, 20, 24, May 5 (ceremonies, funeral), 11 (Lincolns), Apr. 25 (astonishing), 1865; Albert Browne to "Dear Ones," Georgetown, S.C., Apr. 25, 1865, both BFP.

5. For arguments about the funeral and funeral train unifying Americans, see Gary Laderman, *The Sacred Remains: American Attitudes toward Death, 1799–1883* (New Haven: Yale University Press, 1996), 157–63, and Barry Schwartz, "Mourning and the Making of a Sacred Symbol: Durkheim and the Lincoln Assassination," *Social Forces* 70 (1991), 343–64.

6. **lining up:** David Homer Bates diary, Apr. 18, 1865, Bates Papers, LC; **most:** Helen Varnum Hill McCalla diary, Apr. 18, 1865, LC; *Fourteenth Annual Report of the Rochester Ladies' Anti-Slavery Society* (Rochester, N.Y., 1865), 7; **surface:** unknown writer, Apr. 20, 1865, #193, Thomas B. Harned Collection of the Papers of Walt Whitman, LC; **fabric:** "Bills for President Lincoln's Funeral," in Margaret Leech, *Reveille in Washington, 1860–1865* (New York: Harper and Brothers, 1941), 422.

7. **quiet:** James G. Randall, ed., *The Diary of Orville Hickman Browning,* 2 vols. (Springfield: Illinois State Historical Library, 1933), 2:20, 22 (Apr. 17, 1865, entry; see also Apr. 15); **perfectly:** Benjamin Brown French, *Witness to the Young Republic: A Yankee's Journal, 1828–1870,* ed. Donald B. Cole and John J. McDonough (Hanover, N.H.: University Press of New England, 1989), 471 (Apr. 17, 1865, entry).

8. **last:** Ellis Hughes diary, Apr. 18, 1865, Hughes-Gray Family Papers, Duke; **rush, guards:** Charles A. Sanford to Edward Payson Goodrich, Washington, D.C., Apr. 18, 1865, in "Two Letters on the Event of April 14, 1865," *Bulletin of the William L. Clements Library of American History* 47 (Feb. 12, 1946), facsimile, n.p.; **jammed:** Rose Pickard to Angeline Flagg, Alexandria, Va., Apr. 24, 1865, Pickard Papers, LC; **wait:** Helen Varnum Hill McCalla diary, Apr. 18, 1865, LC; **turned away:** James Thomas Ward diary, Apr. 18, 1865, Ward Papers, LC.

9. **saddest:** Anson G. Henry to wife, Washington, D.C., Apr. 19, 1865, ts., box 4, fol. 8, Lincoln Miscellaneous Manuscripts, Chicago.

10. **sermon:** Phineas D. Gurley, "Funeral Address," in B. F. Morris, *Memorial Record of the Nation's Tribute to Abraham Lincoln* (Washington, D.C.: W. H. and O. H. Morrison, 1865), 85–91; **men weeping:** James Thomas Ward diary, Apr. 19, 1865, Ward Papers, LC.

11. **vile:** Allan Nevins and Milton Halsey Thomas, eds., *The Diary of George Templeton Strong: The Civil War, 1860–1865* (New York: Macmillan, 1952), 589 (Apr. 19, 1865, entry).

12. **represent:** James Otis Moore to Mary Elizabeth Moore, "Potomac River," Apr. 19, 1865, Moore Papers, Duke; on the 22nd U.S.C.T., see also Charles Griswold Gurley Merrill diary, Apr. 17, 19, Merrill Papers, Yale-Sterling; Levi S. Graybill Papers, Apr. 19, 1865, HL; **negro & white:** Harry Gibbons to Samuel Bancroft Jr., Washington, D.C., Apr. 19, 1865, Bird-Bancroft Collection, DHS; **promiscuous:** Ellis Hughes diary, Apr. 19, 1865, Hughes-Gray Family Papers, Duke.

13. **memorable:** Nevins and Thomas, *Diary of George Templeton Strong,* 590 (Apr. 19, 1865, entry); **splendid:** Gertrude Dunn diary, Apr. 19, 1865, Diaries Box, NYPL; **solemn:** Selden Connor to sister, Washington, D.C., Apr. 19, 1865, Connor Papers, Brown; **great:** William Owner diary, Apr. 19, 1865, LC.

14. **biggest:** Amory K. Allen to wife, Washington, D.C., Apr. 23, 1865, in "Civil War Letters of Amory K. Allen," *Indiana Magazine of History* 31 (1935), 386; **roasted:** Simon Newcomb diary, Apr. 19, 1865, Newcomb Papers, LC; **excellent:** William H. Gilbert diary, Apr. 19, 1865, Gilbert-Cheever Family Papers, Yale-Sterling; **dark:** Sarah Browne diary, Apr. 19, 1865, BFP.

15. **serious:** John Wolcott Phelps commonplace book, Apr. 19, 1865, Phelps Papers, NYPL; **holy:** editorial, *San Francisco Elevator,* Apr. 21, 1865, #4807, BAP; **dreadful:** Harriet Anne Severance diary, Apr. 19, 1865, SL; **headache:** Anna Cabot Lowell diary, Apr. 19, 1865, MHS; **faint:** Caroline Dall journal, Apr. 22, 1865, vol. J27, Dall Papers, MHS; **lovely:** Caroline Barrett White diary, Apr. 19, 1865, White Papers, AAS.

16. **took:** Anna Cabot Lowell diary, Apr. 19, 1865, MHS; **Cincinnati:** Wallace Shelton, *Discourse upon the Death of Abraham Lincoln . . . Delivered in Zion Baptist Church, Cincinnati, Wednesday, April 19, 1865* (Newport, Ky.: W. S. Baily, 1865), 3, 6; **thy will:** Lucy Pierce Hedge to Charlotte Hedge, Brookline, Mass., Apr. 20, 1865 (part of Apr. 18 letter), Poor Family Papers, SL; **God works:** Martha Coffin Wright to William P. Wright, Auburn, N.Y., Apr. 21, 1865, box 268, Garrison Family Papers, SSC; **got over:** "Em" to Lewis J. Nettleton, Milford, Conn., Apr. 19, 1865, Nettleton-Baldwin Family Papers, Duke; **felt:** Caroline Butler Laing to Mary Butler Reeves, Brooklyn, N.Y., Apr. 21, 1865, Butler-Laing Family Papers, NYHS; **too much:** Kate Hunter journal, Apr. 19, 1865, Hunter Family Papers, ser. B, part 2, reel 27, NHS-NWF; **delightful:** Ruth Anne Hillborn journal, Apr. 19, 1865, Hillborn Papers, FHL.

17. **Altoona:** Doug Phillips to Aaron S. Crosby, Fallen Timber, Pa., Apr. 23, 1865, box 1, Miscellaneous Documents Relating to Abraham Lincoln, HLH; **San Francisco:** "The Day of the Obsequies," *San Francisco Elevator,* Apr. 21, 1865, #4812, BAP; **camp:** William H. Richards to "Anna," Camp Lowell, Va., Apr. 20, 1865, Brown Family Papers, NYSL; **marched:** Zoe J. Campbell diary, Apr. 22, 1865, ser. E, reel 5, LSU-SWF (translation from French by Martha Hodes); **rebeldom, claims:** "From the Regiments," letter from Richard H. Black, 3rd U.S.C.T., Fernandina, Fla., *New York Anglo-African,* May 27, 1865.

18. **worst:** Caroline Butler Laing to Mary Butler Reeves, Brooklyn, N.Y., Apr. 21, 1865, Butler-Laing Family Papers, NYHS; **universal:** Anna M. Ferris diary, Apr. 19, 1865, Ferris Family Papers, FHL; **free states:** Ezra Stiles Gannett daily journal, Gannett Papers, Apr. 19, 1865, MHS; **Union:** Henry S. Thacher diary, Apr. 19, 1865, Thacher Family Papers,

MHS; **dare:** Mary Jane Church to Dennis Church, New York, Apr. 20, 1865, Church Letters, Cornell; **trunk:** Louisa G. Mason diary, Apr. 19, 1865, MDHS; **ape:** Kena King Chapman diary, Apr. 19, 1865, SHC; **bristled:** John V. L. Pruyn diary, Apr. 19, 1865, Pruyn Papers, NYSL; **during:** John Glenn diary, Apr. 21, 1865, Glenn Papers, MDHS; **bitter:** Anna Cabot Lowell diary, Apr. 19, 1865, MHS; **importens:** diary fragments, "Point Lookout, Md.," Apr. 19, 1865, Prison Papers, Confederate States of America Papers, Duke.

19. **notables:** Charles Larrabee to Mary Ann Larrabee, [no place], Apr. 27, 1865, HM46981, HL; **in-between stops:** see, e.g., Jennie M. Smith to Mercy Schenck, Syracuse, N.Y., May 7, 1865, Schenck Family Papers, NYSL.

20. **lonesome:** W. A. Barkalow to brother, Kokomo, Ind., Apr. 30, 1865, in *Wanted— Correspondence: Women's Letters to a Union Soldier,* ed. Nancy L. Rhoades and Lucy E. Bailey (Athens: Ohio University Press, 2009), 305; **tide:** Anna M. Ferris diary, Apr. 22, 1865, Ferris Family Papers, FHL; **100,000:** Samuel S. Halsey to Joseph J. Halsey, Morristown, N.J., May 1, 1865, Morton-Halsey Papers, ser. E, part 1, reel 37, UVA-RSP; **faint:** Asa Fitch diary, Apr. 26, 1865, Fitch Papers, Yale-Sterling; **Springfield:** see, e.g., Robert Steele to "Mrs. Wood," Cairo, Ill., May 9, 1865, box 2, Miscellaneous Documents Relating to Abraham Lincoln, HLH.

21. **Liberty Bell:** Martin S. Nowak, *The White House in Mourning: Deaths and Funerals of Presidents in Office* (Jefferson, N.C.: McFarland, 2010), 76; **Lord and Taylor:** James Williams to sister, New York, May 6, 1865, Simon Gratz Autograph Collection, HSP; **nation, heart:** "Funeral Honors on the Route from Washington to Springfield," in Morris, *Memorial Record,* 195, 200, 183; **death:** "Notebook containing drawings and transcriptions of memorial tributes to Abraham Lincoln displayed in New York, N.Y. and other places in the aftermath of his assassination," McLellan Lincoln Collection and Center for Digital Scholarship, Brown; see also Ted Widmer, "New York's Lincoln Memorial," Op-Archive: Lincoln Memorial Diary, *New York Times,* Apr. 17, 2009, available at nytimes. com/2009/04/17/opinion/17widmer.html.

22. **imposing:** James Williams to sister, New York, May 6, 1865, Simon Gratz Autograph Collection, HSP; **notable:** Gayle Thornbrough and Paula Corpuz, eds., *The Diary of Calvin Fletcher,* vol. 9 (Indianapolis: Indiana Historical Society, 1983), 84 (May 2, 1865, entry); **gratify:** Ellen Kean to "Miss Sherritt," Baltimore, May 13ff., 1865, in *Death and Funeral of Abraham Lincoln . . . in Two Long Descriptive Letters from Mrs. Ellen Kean, the Actress, whilst Touring the United States in 1865* (London: Privately printed, 1921), 22; **show:** William M. Myers to William H. Henshaw, Danville, Ill., May 12, 1865, Ann Henshaw Gardiner Papers, Duke; **baby:** Nancy Ann (Atwood) Sprague diary, Apr. [n.d.], 1865, Sprague Papers, SL.

23. **twenty:** Ellen Kean to "Miss Sherritt," Baltimore, May 13ff., 1865, in *Death and Funeral of Abraham Lincoln,* 23; **dark:** Mary Dreer diary, Apr. 22, 1865, Edwin Greble Papers, LC; **sea:** Ruth Anne Hillborn journal, Apr. 22, 1865, Hillborn Papers, FHL; **flash:** Anna M. Ferris diary, Apr. 22, 1865, Ferris Family Papers, FHL; **beat:** Alexander M. Thackara to Benjamin Thackara, Philadelphia, Apr. 24, 1865, Sherman Thackara Collection, available at digital.library.villanova.edu/Item/vudl:27010; **fumbling:** anonymous diary,

Apr. 23, 1865, John L. Smith Papers, HSP; **impersonal:** Lucy McKim to Wendell Phillips Garrison, Philadelphia, Apr. 23, 1865, box 49, Garrison Family Papers, SSC.

24. **president, sight:** Emilie Davis diary, Apr. 22, 23, 24, 1865, HSP, and davisdiaries.villa nova.edu; **believe:** Mattie J. Jackson, *The Story of Mattie J. Jackson* (Lawrence, Mass.: Sentinel, 1866), in *Six Women's Slave Narratives,* ed. William L. Andrews (New York: Oxford University Press, 1988), 30.

25. **rushed:** Bishop Crumrine to Boyd Crumrine, Fort Delaware, Del., May 1, 1865, in "Notes and Documents: Corporal Crumrine Goes to War," ed. Walter S. Sanderlin, *Topic* 2 (1961), 64; **ineffectual:** James Williams to sister, New York, May 6, 1865, Simon Gratz Autograph Collection, HSP.

26. **wan:** Helen Lansing Grinnell diary, Apr. 24, 1865, NYPL; **shrunken:** Saul Ames to mother, Brooklyn, N.Y., Apr. 25, 1865, letter pasted in C. C. Carrington, "Assassination and Funeral of President Lincoln," scrapbook, 2 vols., 1865–71, 1:166, McLellan Lincoln Collection, Brown; **lead:** Asa Fitch diary, Apr. 25, 1865, Fitch Papers, Yale-Sterling; **fancied:** Elon N. Lee to family, Chicago, May 3, 1865, ts., Lee and Bastin Papers, Chicago; **Sally:** Mary Henry diary, Apr. 18, 1865, Smithsonian Institution Archives, available at siarchives.si.edu/history/exhibits/stories/death-abraham-lincoln-april-15-26-1865; **funeral:** Clara Barton diary, Apr. 19, 1865, Barton Papers, LC; **glad:** William S. C. Webster to Charles Webster, [no place], May 3, 1865, Webster Collection, Princeton.

27. **confounding:** Caroline Barrett White diary, Apr. 24, 1865, White Papers, AAS.

28. **inglorious:** Abram Verrick Parmenter diary, Apr. 19, 1865, Parmenter Papers, LC; **startling:** Anna Cabot Lowell diary, Apr. 23, 1865, MHS; **hardly:** Henry S. Thacher diary, Apr. 24, 1865, Thacher Family Papers, MHS; **stupendous:** Martha Coffin Wright to Frank Wright, Auburn, N.Y., Apr. 26, 1865, box 268, Garrison Family Papers, SSC; **ass:** Malcolm Canfield to Harriett Canfield, New York, Apr. 24, 1865, Canfield Papers, NYSL; **ignoramus:** Anne Neafie to Alfred Neafie, Ellenville, N.Y., Apr. 26, 1865, Neafie Papers, NYSL; **woman:** Francis Lieber to Henry W. Halleck, New York, Apr. 26, 1865, box 28, Lieber Papers, HL; **language:** Lydia Maria Child to Sarah Blake Shaw, [no place], Apr. [n.d.], 1865, Child Letters, SL.

29. **if Sherman:** Robert H. Williams to David and Carrie Thurber, City Point, Va., Apr. 29, 1865, Goff-Williams Papers, HL; **proclaimed:** Charles Hale to Sarah Hale, Alexandria, Egypt, May 27, 1865, box 22, Hale Family Papers, SSC.

30. **shot:** Shirley Brooks diary, May 11, 1865, ML; **well done:** Susan E. Parsons Brown Forbes diary, Apr. 27, 1865, AAS; **die:** William Gray Brooks diary, Apr. 28, 1865, Brooks Papers, MHS; **tortured:** "Lizzie" to "Charlie," [no place], Apr. 30, 1865, box 1, Miscellaneous Documents Relating to Abraham Lincoln, HLH; **cruel:** Newton Perkins to mother, onboard *Star of the South,* Apr. 27, 1865, Montgomery Family Papers, LC; **same way:** Elizabeth Bancroft to "Lou," New York, Apr. 26, 1865, Bancroft-Bliss Families Papers, LC; **dare:** Sarah Hale to Charles Hale, Brookline, Mass., Apr. 28, 1865, box 11, Hale Family Papers, SSC; **restless:** Martha Coffin Wright to Marianna Pelham Mott, Auburn, N.Y., May 4, 1865, box 265, Garrison Family Papers, SSC; **fanatical:** Ambrose A. White to Thomas H. White, Baltimore, Apr. 27, 1865, Lucas-White Papers, MDHS; **sorry:** Lizzie Hamilton

to Albert Batchelor, [no place], May 21, 1865, Batchelor Papers, ser. B, part 5, reel 1, LSU-RSPE.

31. **think:** James Williams to sister, New York, May 6, 1865, Simon Gratz Autograph Collection, HSP; **rested:** Elon N. Lee to family, Chicago, May 3, 1865, ts., Lee and Bastin Papers, Chicago.

32. **ends:** Martha Fisher Anderson diary, Apr. 30, 1865, MHS; **so now:** Frances Owens diary, May 2, 1865, ts., CHM.

33. **damned:** James Flint, file MM2344, RG153-NARA; **better:** Henry Brainard, file MM2011, RG153-NARA; **done right:** James Hall, file MM2092, RG153-NARA; **glad:** John Craig, file OO893, RG153-NARA; **sit:** David J. Parsons, file OO940, RG153-NARA; **added:** Charles N. Niles to father, Baltimore, Apr. 22, 1865, Niles Family Papers, NYSL.

34. **leaned:** "Reception of the Remains of Abraham Lincoln," *New York Daily Tribune,* Apr. 25, 1865; **Irish:** "The Day of the Obsequies," *San Francisco Elevator,* Apr. 21, 1865, #4812, BAP; **Emancipation Proclamation:** "Oration by the Hon. Geo. Bancroft," in Morris, *Memorial Record,* 171; **bar:** J. Sella Martin, "Colored People Excluded from the Funeral Procession," *Liberator,* May 5, 1865, #2863, BAP; **curious:** Ellen Kean to "Miss Sherritt," Baltimore, May 13ff., 1865, in *Death and Funeral of Abraham Lincoln,* 23; **utterly:** John Glenn diary, Apr. 21, 1865, Glenn Papers, MDHS.

35. **come out:** "Prayer," in Morris, *Memorial Record,* 226; **oration:** "Funeral Oration by Bishop Simpson," in Morris, *Memorial Record,* 230, 236; **none:** Chas. S. Jacobs, "Letter from Decatur, Illinois," May 5, 1865, *Christian Recorder,* published May 20, 1865.

36. **to day:** Caroline Dunstan diary, May 4, 1865, NYPL; **remains:** William Boardman Richards diary, Apr. 28, 1865, Richards Family Papers, MHS; **continued:** James Thomas Ward diary, May 4, 1865, Ward Papers, LC; **hearts:** Caroline Barrett White diary, May 4, 1865, White Papers, AAS; **world:** Elon N. Lee to family, Chicago, May 3, 1865, ts., Lee and Bastin Papers, Chicago.

37. **noisy:** George W. Squier to Ellen Squier, Chattanooga, Tenn., May 4, 1865, in *This Wilderness of War: The Civil War Letters of George W. Squier, Hoosier Volunteer,* ed. Julie A. Doyle et al. (Knoxville: University of Tennessee Press, 1998), 111; **hope:** Mary H. and Dallas M. Lancaster, ed., *The Civil War Diary of Anne S. Frobel* (McLean, Va.: EPM, 1992), 224 (May 4, 1865, entry).

38. **jog:** Benjamin Brown French to Frank O. French, Washington, D.C., May 8, 1865, French Papers, LC; **absorbing:** William M. Myers to William H. Henshaw, Danville, Ill., May 12, 1865, Ann Henshaw Gardiner Papers, Duke; **Philadelphia:** F. C. Chambers diary, Apr. 28, 1865, Chambers Family Diaries, Princeton; **Indianapolis:** Lyman P. Spencer diary, May 30, 1865, Spencer Papers, LC.

Interlude: Springtime

1. **humiliating:** Virginia Ingraham Burr, ed., *The Secret Eye: The Journal of Ella Gertrude Clanton Thomas, 1848–1889* (Chapel Hill: University of North Carolina Press, 1990), 261 (May 1, 1865, entry); **troubled:** Kate Cumming, *Kate: The Journal of a Confederate Nurse,* ed. Richard Barksdale Harwell (Baton Rouge: Louisiana State University

Press, 1998), 276 (May 1, 1865, entry), NAWLD; **life:** Hannah Ford Turner to William Mason Turner, Philadelphia, Apr. 20, 1865, Turner Papers, Brown; **national:** Caroline Kean (Hill) Davis diary, May 14, 1865, ser. D, part 1, reel 5, VHS-SWF; **flowers:** Elizabeth (Alsop) Wynne diary, May 18, 1865, Wynne Family Papers, ser. D, part 3, reel 52, VHS-SWF.

2. **loveliest:** Lucretia Hale to Charles Hale, Brookline, Mass., Apr. 28, 1865, box 50, Hale Family Papers, SSC; **gloomy:** Douglass S. Taylor to Elizabeth H. Taylor, Washington, D.C., May 14, 1865, Taylor Family Correspondence, HL; **mourn'd:** Walt Whitman, "When Lilacs Last in the Dooryard Bloom'd," in *Sequel to Drum-Taps* (Washington, D.C., 1865–66), 3, available at whitmanarchive.org/published/other/DrumTapsSequel .html.

3. **world:** James J. Higginson to Anne E. Heath, Burkeville, Va., Apr. 25, 1865, Heath Family Papers, MHS; **everything:** Samuel Canby diary, Apr. 25, 1865, DHS; **cannot:** Harriet Williams to Lewis J. Williams, Medical Hall, Md., Apr. 24, 1865, Archer-Mitchell-Stump-Williams Family Papers, MDHS; **exquisite:** Anna Cabot Lowell diary, May 24, 1865, MHS; **life:** Sarah Browne diary, May 2, 1865, BFP.

Chapter 7. Everyday Life

1. Sarah Browne diary, Apr. 19, 1865; Albert Browne to Edward Browne, Charleston, S.C., Apr. 20, 31 [sic], 1865; Sarah Browne to Albert Browne, Salem, Mass., Apr. 20, 1865, one of two letters of this date, all BFP.

2. Sarah Browne diary, Apr. 20, 25 (Booth), 23, 30 (Latin, French), May 1 (picnic, closet), 13 (cleaning), 10 (proclamation, Alice), 1865; Sarah Browne to Albert Browne, Salem, Mass., May 14, 1865 (minister, wages), both letters of this date, all BFP.

3. Dorman diary, May 25, 1865.

4. Dorman diary, Apr. 16 (protection), May 6 (what), 26 (black-hearted), 23 (revolution), 1865.

5. Dorman diary, May 13 (familiar), 8 (begging), 25 (wish), June 22 (stay), 1865.

6. **nothing:** Thomas Bradford Drew diary, Apr. 16, 1865, MHS; **anything:** Georgia Treadway to Newton Perkins, New Haven, Conn., Apr. 16, 1865, Montgomery Family Papers, LC; **heart:** Julia Adelaide Shepard to father, near Washington, D.C., Apr. 16, 1865, in "Lincoln's Assassination Told by an Eye-Witness," *Century Magazine* 77 (1909), 918; **halt:** "Funeral Oration by Bishop Simpson," in B. F. Morris, *Memorial Record of the Nation's Tribute to Abraham Lincoln* (Washington, D.C.: W. H. and O. H. Morrison, 1865), 229; **still:** Edward Everett Hale to Charles Hale, Boston, May 2, 1865, box 6, Hale Papers, NYSL.

7. As Franz Kafka wrote in his diary in August 1914, "Germany has declared war on Russia.—Swimming in the afternoon"; see Max Brod, ed., *The Diaries of Franz Kafka, 1914–23* (1949; reprint, New York: Schocken Books, 1965), 75.

8. **journalists:** Scott D. Trostel, *The Lincoln Funeral Train: The Final Journey and National Funeral for Abraham Lincoln* (Fletcher, Ohio: Cam-Tech, 2002), 66 ("Newspapers reported that from the time they left Harrisburg until they reached Philadelphia, not

a person in sight was engaged in labor"); **obsequies:** anonymous account book, Apr. 19, 1865, Anonymous Diaries and Account Books, SL.

9. **gardens:** Abbie Clarke Stimson diary, Apr. 14, 1865, ser. C, part 2, reel 16, RIHS-NWF; Patty Bartlett Sessions diary, Apr. 17, 1865, ts., reel 15, Utah-AWD-West; **socks:** Mary Dreer diary, Apr. 18, 1865, Edwin Greble Papers, LC; **ironing:** Mrs. Bardwell diary, Apr. 19, 1865, Helen Temple Cooke Papers, SL; **walls:** Ann Buckingham diary, Apr. 22, 1865, box 7, vol. 15, Shaker Collection, NYSL; **dyeing:** Omelia Bouton diary, Apr. 18, 1865, Bouton Family Diaries, NYSL; **chimneys, poultices:** Elizabeth Rogers Mason Cabot diary, Apr. 20, May 4, 1865, MHS; **curtains:** Sarah Lydia Gilpin diary, Apr. 29, 1865, #06846.05, GLC-NYHS; **injuries:** Lydia Lyman Paine diary, Apr. 27, 1865, Robert Treat Paine Papers II, MHS; **ploughing:** F. C. Chambers diary, Apr. 20, 1865, Chambers Family Diaries, Princeton.

10. **fainted:** Mary Elizabeth Moore to James Otis Moore, Saco, Me., Apr. 15, 1865, Moore Papers, Duke; **feel like, sew:** Margaret B. Howell diary, Apr. 17, 18, 1865, HSP; **cleaning:** Caroline Dall journal, Apr. 22, 1865, vol. J27, Dall Papers, MHS; **busy:** Caroline Barrett White diary, Apr. 20, 1865, White Papers, AAS; **dare not:** Harriett Canfield to Malcolm Canfield, Sunderland, Vt., Apr. 16, 1865, NYSL; **gave out:** James C. Mohr and Richard E. Winslow, eds., *The Cormany Diaries: A Northern Family in the Civil War* (Pittsburgh: University of Pittsburgh Press, 1982), 543, 545 (Apr. 15, 21, 1865, entries).

11. **planted, funeral:** Ebenezer Paul diary, Apr. 14, 19, 1865, vol. 2, Henry F. Howe Collection II, MHS.

12. **shipbuilder:** James A. Latham journal, Apr. 14, 19, passim, 1865, Latham Papers, GWBW; **lawyer:** Porter and Warren to George Frisbie Hoar, Boston, Apr. 18, 1865, Hoar Papers, MHS; **writer:** Bayard Taylor to George Palmer Putnam, Kennett Square, Pa., Apr. 28, 1865, HM14640, HL; **presume:** L. S. Currier to H. C. Rowley, Cincinnati, Apr. 15, 1865, Currier and Co. Papers, AAS; **how much:** Edward Everett Hale to Charles Hale, Boston, May 2, 1865, box 6, Hale Papers, NYSL.

13. **died:** William H. Lightner diary, Apr. 15, 1865, MDHS; **rations:** George H. Butler diary, Apr. 17, 18, 19, 1865, #00794, GLC-NYHS; **lame:** Henry O. Perry diary, Apr. 17, 1865, NYHS; **hospital:** Henry B. James diary, Apr. 15, 1865, James Papers, MHS.

14. **news, Lisbon, politics:** William Benjamin Gould diary, May 6, 7, June 14, 16, 1865, MHS.

15. **Susie:** J. Thoman to "Henrietta," Washington, D.C., Apr. 15, 1865, in Thomas F. Schwartz, "Grief, Souvenirs, and Enterprise following Lincoln's Assassination," *Illinois Historical Journal* 83 (1990), 259.

16. **undershirts:** Alfred Neafie to Anne Neafie, Savannah, Ga., Apr. 19, 1865, Neafie Papers, NYSL; **sugar:** La Motte K. Devendorf to Jerusha Devendorf, Morehead City, N.C., Apr. 23, 1865, Devendorf Family Papers, NYSL; **boots:** Jacob Henry Enders to parents and sister, Summit Point, Va., Apr. 20, 1865, ts., Enders Papers, NYSL; **farm:** Horace O. Gilmore to Lucy Gilmore, Petersburg, Va., Apr. [15], 1865, Gilmore Papers, NYSL; **arm:** E. P. Grover to Josiah Wood, Washington, D.C., May 12, 1865, Wood Papers, Duke; **overcoat:** Kiliaen Van Rensselaer to parents, City Point, Va., Apr. 20, 1865, ts., Erving-King

Papers, NYHS; **snake:** James McHue to family, Pleasant Valley, Md., Apr. 17, 1865, McHue Letters, NYSL.

17. **relate:** D. H. Jacques, *How to Write: A Pocket Manual of Composition and Letter-Writing* (New York: Fowler and Wells, 1857), 65; **too deep:** "Rebecca" to Jane Wigglesworth Grew, Boston, May 14, 1865, Grew Correspondence, MHS; **minutiae:** Martha Coffin Wright to Ellen W. Garrison, Auburn, N.Y., Apr. 19, 1865, box 261, Garrison Family Papers, SSC.

18. **nervous, finished:** Helen A. Du Barry to mother, Washington, D.C., Apr. 25, 1865, in "Eyewitness Account of Lincoln's Assassination," *Journal of the Illinois State Historical Society* 39 (1946), 369, 370.

19. **heart:** Charles Nye to mother, Worcester, Mass., Apr. 18, 1865, Nye Family Papers, Duke; **refuses:** "Eliz." to "Geo.," Cambridge, Mass., Apr. 16, 1865, Wigglesworth Family Papers, MHS; **mania:** Martha Thomas, "Synopsis of Record," case #3245, entry 66, July 16, 1872, box 11, stack area 12W2A, RG418, Records of Saint Elizabeths Hospital, NARA (I thank Ashley Bowen-Murphy, Brown University, for transcribing and sharing this document); **poor, troubled:** Emily Watkins to Abiathar Watkins, Jersey City, N.J., Apr. 16, May 11, 1865, Watkins Papers, NYPL.

20. **black line:** "Carrie" to sister, Washington, D.C., Apr. 16, 1865, box 2, fol. 27, Richard John Levy and Sally Waldman Sweet Collection, NYPL; **cease:** "Rebecca" to Jane Wigglesworth Grew, Boston, Apr. 18, 1865 (part of Apr. 16 letter), Grew Correspondence, MHS; **written:** Helen M. Blake to Mary Ingham Emerson, Brussels, Belgium, May 4, 1865, Emerson Family Papers, NYPL.

21. **prevented, hardly:** Sarah Hale to Charles Hale, Brookline, Mass., Apr. 28, June 9, 1865, box 11, Hale Family Papers, SSC.

22. **Ellie, last week:** William Lloyd Garrison Jr. diary, Apr. 15, 16, 1865, box 34, and William Lloyd Garrison Jr. to Martha Coffin Wright, Roxbury, Mass., Apr. 16, 1865, box 56, Garrison Family Papers, SSC.

23. **wrong:** Harriett Canfield to Malcolm Canfield Sunderland, Vt., Apr. 16, 1865, Canfield Papers, NYSL; **trifling:** Caroline Butler Laing to Mary Butler Reeves, Brooklyn, N.Y., Apr. 21, 1865, Butler-Laing Family Papers, NYHS; **sacrilege:** James Garfield to Lucretia Garfield, New York, Apr. 17, 1865, in *Crete and James: Personal Letters of Lucretia and James Garfield,* ed. John Shaw (East Lansing: Michigan State University Press, 1994), 218.

24. **very sad:** Emilie Davis diary, Apr. 15, 1865, and see Apr. 17–19, 24–26, 1865, HSP and davisdiaries.villanova.edu.

25. **whist:** Annie P. Chadwick diary, Apr. 18, 1865, Chadwick Family Papers, NYSL; **croquet, jackstraws:** William Lloyd Garrison Jr. diary, Apr. 24, May 3, 1865, box 34, Garrison Family Papers, SSC; **shopping:** F. C. Chambers diary, May 1865, Chambers Family Diaries, Princeton; **dances, balls:** Martha Fisher Anderson diary, Apr. 22, 1865, MHS; Margaret B. Howell diary, Apr. 26, 1865, HSP; **circus:** Charles Edward French diary, Apr. 25, 1865, French Diaries and Papers, MHS; **solemn, billiards:** Mary S. Elliot diary, Apr. 19, 20, 21, 1865, Robinson-Elliot Papers, DHS; **evil:** James Thomas Ward diary, Apr. 14, 21, 1865, Ward Papers, LC; **resist:** Ellis Hughes diary, Apr. 19, 1865, Hughes-Gray Family

Papers, Duke; **grief:** Ellen Kean to Mary Kean, New York, Apr. 16, 1865, in *Death and Funeral of Abraham Lincoln . . . in Two Long Descriptive Letters from Mrs. Ellen Kean, the Actress, whilst Touring the United States in 1865* (London: Privately printed, 1921), 17.

26. **weeping, funniest:** Lizzie Niles diary, Apr. 16, 17, 1865, NYSL; **talk, dream:** Joanita Kant, ed., *Maggie: The Civil War Diary of Margaret Wylie Mellette* (Watertown, S.Dak.: Mellette Memorial Association, 1983), 20, 22 (Apr. 16, 19, 1865, entries); **delightful:** Henry Wirt Shriver diary, Apr. 16, 1865, Shriver Family Papers, MDHS; **how sad:** Maria H. Thomas diary, May 28, 1865, NYSL.

27. **flirtation:** Edgar Dinsmore to Carrie Drayton, Saint Andrews Parish, S.C., May 29, 1865, Dinsmore Papers, Duke.

28. **fair:** William L. Mead to Louisa White, Charleston, S.C., Apr. 19, 1865, ts., George Cornwell Correspondence, MDHS; **summers:** Nelson Palmer to Mercy Schenck, [no place], Apr. 23, 1865, Schenck Family Papers, NYSL; **Miss Montgomery:** Henry Adams to "Caro amico mio" [Charles Milnes Gaskell], Rome and Florence, May 10, 1865 (part of Apr. 23 letter), in *The Letters of Henry Adams,* ed. J. C. Levenson et al. (Cambridge, Mass.: Harvard University Press, 1982), 493.

29. **shut:** "Frank" to Henry C. Morgan, Tiffin, Ohio, Apr. 19, 1865, Morgan-Parry Family Papers, BHS.

30. **midst:** Nathan Appleton Jr. to Harriet Appleton, Nottoway Court House, Va., Apr. 25, 1865, Appleton Family Papers, MHS; **much:** Henry Adams to "Caro amico mio" [Charles Milnes Gaskell], Rome and Florence, May 10, 1865 (part of Apr. 23 letter), in Levenson et al., *Letters of Henry Adams,* 493.

31. **infinite:** Walt Whitman, "When Lilacs Last in the Dooryard Bloom'd," in *Sequel to Drum-Taps* (Washington, D.C., 1865-66), 8, available at whitmanarchive.org/published/other/DrumTapsSequel.html.

32. **blues:** John Johnston, "Personal Reminiscence of the Civil War, 1861-1865," diary transcriptions, May 17, 1865, Johnston Papers, SHC.

33. **produce:** E. R. Harmanson to "Prince," Red River, La., Apr. 23, 1865, Albert A. Batchelor Papers, ser. B, part 5, reel 1, LSU-RSPE; **delightful:** Daniel E. Sutherland, ed., *A Very Violent Rebel: The Civil War Diary of Ellen Renshaw House* (Knoxville: University of Tennessee Press, 1996), 165 (May 25, 1865, entry); **engaged:** niece to aunt, Charlottesville, Va., June 14, 1865 (part of May 15 letter), Minor-Wilson Family Papers, ser. G, part 2, reel 33, UVA-SWF; **distraction, heart:** Elizabeth (Alsop) Wynne diary, May 29, June 14, 26, 1865, Wynne Family Papers, ser. D, part 3, reel 52, VHS-SWF.

34. **mourning, property, free, restless:** Nancy McDougall Robinson diary, undated late May entry ["Friday"?], May 29, June 7, July 1, 1865, Robinson Collection, ser. N, reel 17, MDAH-RSP; **dark:** Eva B. Jones to Mary Jones, Augusta, Ga., June 13, 1865, in *The Children of Pride: A True Story of Georgia and the Civil War,* ed. Robert Manson Myers (New Haven: Yale University Press, 1972), 1273-74.

35. **life, chair:** Cornelia Spencer journal, May 7, June 8, 1865, Spencer Papers, ser. A, part 7, reel 16, SHC-SWF; **rooms:** "Frank" to Henry C. Morgan, Tiffin, Ohio, Apr. 19, 1865, Morgan-Parry Family Papers, BHS.

36. **heaven:** Elizabeth (Alsop) Wynne diary, Apr. 22, 1865 (see also July 12, 1865), Wynne Family Papers, ser. D, part 3, reel 52, VHS-SWF; **drive:** Creed Thomas Davis diary, May 5, 1865, ser. A, reel 13, VHS-CMM; **suicide:** William Kauffman Scarborough, ed., *The Diary of Edmund Ruffin: A Dream Shattered, June, 1863–June, 1865* (Baton Rouge: Louisiana State University Press, 1989), 884, 892, 873, 935, 946 (May 9, 16, 1, June 16–18, 1865, entries).

Interlude: Young Folk

1. **Uncle Sam:** Edward Williams Morley to Sardis Morley, Fortress Monroe, Va., Apr. 18, 1865, Morley Papers, LC; **ceasing:** Mary S. Pond to George Whipple, Portsmouth, Va., May 13 1865, #H1-7147, reel 210, AMA; **tearful, weight:** H. C. Percy to George Whipple, Norfolk, Va., May 7, 1865, #H1-7112-16, reel 210, AMA; **dead:** Lizzie [no last name], "Letter from Morristown, Ohio," *Christian Recorder,* May 27, 1865.

2. **ball:** Edward Sanford Martin diary, Apr. 19, 1865, Throop and Martin Family Papers, Princeton; **books, houses:** Grenville H. Norcross diary, Apr. 15, 1865, AAS.

3. **try:** Harriett Canfield to Malcolm Canfield, Sunderland, Vt., Apr. 16, 1865, Canfield Papers, NYSL; **good:** "Rebecca" to Jane Wigglesworth Grew, Boston, May 24, 1865, Grew Correspondence, MHS; **ain't, dead:** Frances Owens diary, May 2, 1865, ts., CHM.

Johnson: Hope R. Daggett to George Whipple, Norfolk, Va., Apr. [n.d.], 1865, #H1-7058, reel 210, AMA; **catch:** *"Maggie!": Maggie Lindsley's Journal, Nashville, Tennessee, 1864, Washington, D.C. 1865* (Southbury, Conn.: Muriel Davies Mackenzie, 1977), 86 (Apr. 23, 1865, entry).

4. **dismal:** Carrie Hunter to Kate Hunter, Newport, R.I., Apr. 15, 1865, Hunter Family Papers, ser. B, part 2, reel 36, NHS-NWF; **weeping, flirtation:** Georgiana Gordon King diary, Apr. 15, 17, 1865, King Family Papers, ser. B, part 2, reel 40, NHS-NWF.

5. **sit:** Emma F. LeConte diary, May 17, 1865, reel 22, SHC-AWD-South.

Chapter 8. Everyday Loss

1. Dorman diary, May 2, 1865. Drew Gilpin Faust writes, "Confederate men died at a rate three times that of their Yankee counterparts; one in five white southern men of military age did not survive the Civil War"; see "Death and Dying," available at nps.gov/history/nr/travel/national_cemeteries/death.html.

2. Dorman diary, May 4, 1865.

3. Albert Browne to "Dear Ones," Charleston, S.C., Apr. 31 [sic], 1865 (part of Apr. 24 letter), BFP.

4. Sarah Browne diary, Apr. 17, 21, 22, 1864; Nellie Browne to Albert Browne Jr., Beaufort, S.C., May 14, 1864; Albert Browne Jr. to Nellie Browne, Boston, May 26, 1864; and see correspondence between Nellie Browne and Lewis Weld, May 1864, all BFP.

5. Sarah Browne diary, May 26, 27, 1865; Alice Browne to Lewis Weld, Salem, Mass., June 27, 1864; Albert Browne to Lewis Weld, Beaufort, S.C., June 1, 1865; Lewis Weld to Nellie Browne, Jacksonville, Fla., June 3, 1864, one of two letters of this date; and see "In

Memoriam: Miss Nellie Browne. Beaufort, S.C., June 2, 1864," clipping from the *Free South,* Beaufort, S.C., July 2, 1864 (giving her age as twenty-three), all BFP.

6. Albert Browne Jr. to Lewis Weld, Salem, Mass., June 12, 1864 (God); Sarah Browne diary, June 6, 26, Aug. 28, 1864; Alice Browne to Lewis Weld, Salem, Mass., June 27, 1864, all BFP; and see "Walking with God," in *The Life and Works of William Cowper,* vol. 8, ed. T. S. Grimshawe (London: Saunders and Otley, 1835), 97. Albert Browne to Lewis Weld, Salem, Mass., June 21, 1864 (thunder bolt); Albert Browne to Lewis Weld, Salem, Mass., June 30, 1864 (blessed), both BFP. Albert Browne to "Rev. Wilson," Beaufort, S.C., Dec. 6, 1864, Browne Family Additional Papers, SL.

7. Sarah Browne diary, Apr. 6, May 2, 30, 1865; Sarah Browne to Albert Browne, Salem, Mass., May 31, 1865; Sarah Browne to Albert Browne, Salem, Mass., May 14, 1865; and see Nellie Browne to Albert Browne Jr., Beaufort, S.C., May 14, 1865, all BFP.

8. Albert Browne to "Dear Ones," Charleston, S.C., June 1, 1865, one of two letters of this date, BFP.

9. **fondly, blood:** Abraham Lincoln, "Second Inaugural Address," Mar. 4, 1865, *CWL,* 8:333; **ultimate:** Drew Gilpin Faust, *This Republic of Suffering: Death and the American Civil War* (New York: Alfred A. Knopf, 2008), 156.

10. **hardest:** Albert Browne Jr. to Lewis Weld, Boston, June 28, 1864, BFP; **apaling:** Gayle Thornbrough and Paula Corpuz, eds., *The Diary of Calvin Fletcher,* vol. 9 (Indianapolis: Indiana Historical Society, 1983), 68 (Apr. 15, 1865, entry); **horrid, distress:** Edward Lear diary, Apr. 26, May 4, 1865, HLH; **should:** George W. Van Horne to John Bigelow, Marseille, France, May 9, 1865, John Bigelow Papers, NYPL.

11. **rather:** Jane Swisshelm to *St. Cloud Democrat,* Washington, D.C., Apr. 17, 1865 (published Apr. 27, 1865), in *Crusader and Feminist: Letters of Jane Grey Swisshelm, 1858–1865,* ed. Arthur J. Larsen (Saint Paul: Minnesota Historical Society, 1934), 287; **never:** Laudie Henderson to "Luth," James River, Va., Apr. 18, 1865, Duke.

For other comparisons see P. B. S. Nichuston [?] to George Whipple, Roanoke Island, N.C., Apr. 22, 1865, #100001, reel 169, AMA (father and mother), and Mary Ingham Emerson diary, May 28, 1865, Emerson Family Papers, NYPL (father). For a rare expression of Lincoln's death as worse than a private loss, see Harriett Canfield to Malcolm Canfield, Sunderland, Vt., Apr. 16, 1865, Canfield Papers, NYSL ("This great national calamity overpowers private grief").

12. **take:** Wallace Shelton, *Discourse upon the Death of Abraham Lincoln . . . Delivered in Zion Baptist Church, Cincinnati, Wednesday, April 19, 1865* (Newport, Ky.: W. S. Baily, 1865), 4; **Alfred:** Emilie Davis diary, Dec. 20–23, 1865, HSP and davisdiaries.villanova.edu.

13. **highest:** Chester dispatch, Richmond, Va., Apr. 10, 1865, in *Thomas Morris Chester: Black Civil War Correspondent—His Dispatches from the Virginia Front,* ed. R. J. M. Blackett (Baton Rouge: Louisiana State University Press, 1989), 303.

14. **assassinated, five, man, another:** Henry B. James diary, Apr. 15, 20, May 9, 13, 1865, James Papers, MHS; **funerals:** H. H. B. Chambers diary, Apr. 28, 1865, and F. C. Chambers diary, Apr. 23, 1865, Chambers Family Diaries, Princeton; **perfectly:** Walt Whitman to

"Mrs. Irwin," Washington, D.C., May 1, 1865, available at whitmanarchive.org/biography/correspondence/cw/tei/med.00310.html.

Ronald C. White Jr. writes that ministers declared Lincoln "the Civil War's final casualty"; see *A. Lincoln: A Biography* (New York: Random House, 2009), 675.

15. **whipped, warmest:** John Payne to W. W. Thomas, near Mobile, Ala., May 26, 1865, and John Payne to uncle, Alexandria, La., July 11, 1865, Payne Papers, Civil War Miscellaneous Letters and Papers, Schomburg; on Payne and his friend Mathias Hutchison of the 32nd Iowa, see Civil War Soldiers and Sailors database, nps.gov/civilwar/soldiers-and-sailors-database.htm; **one, left:** Henry J. Peck to Mary Peck, Richmond, Va., May 23, 1865, and Mary Peck to Henry J. Peck, Jonesville, N.Y., May 26, 1865, Peck Correspondence, NYSL; **strike:** Abial H. Edwards to Anna L. Conant, Darlington, S.C., Sept. 15, 1865, in *"Dear Friend Anna": The Civil War Letters of a Common Soldier from Maine,* ed. Beverly Hayes Kallgren and James L. Crouthamel (Orono: University of Maine Press, 1992), 137; **bodies, bones:** Heber Painter to Rebecca Frick, Richmond, Va., Apr. 16, 1865, #02016.082, GLC-NYHS; William C. McLean diary, May 15, 1865, ts., McLean Family Papers, NYSL; William H. Gilbert diary, May 1–5, 1865, Gilbert-Cheever Family Papers, Yale-Sterling; Rufus Mead Jr. diary, May 15, 1865, Mead Papers, LC; **world:** James Thomas Ward diary, May 1, 1865, Ward Papers, LC.

16. **sad:** Edward J. Bartlett to Martha Bartlett, South Side Railroad, Va., Apr. 16, 1865, Bartlett Letters, MHS; **many:** D. M. Corthell to William P. Corthell, Savannah, Ga., May 8, 1865, box 1, Civil War Collection, AAS.

17. "Break It Gently" and "Let Me Kiss Him": Irwin Silber, comp. and ed., *Songs of the Civil War* (New York: Bonanza, 1960), 116, 117.

18. **brother:** Rose Pickard to Alonzo Pickard, Stockton, N.Y., May [n.d.], 1865, and Rose Pickard to Byron Flagg, Alexandria, Va., Apr. 17, 1865 (part of Apr. 14 letter), Pickard Papers, LC.

19. **deep:** Mary Mellish to George H. Mellish, Woodstock, Vt., Apr. 16, 1865, Mellish Papers, HL; **never:** Elizabeth Blair Lee to Samuel Phillips Lee, Washington, D.C., Apr. 20, 1865, in *Wartime Washington: The Civil War Letters of Elizabeth Blair Lee,* ed. Virginia Jean Laas (Urbana: University of Illinois Press, 1991), 498; **a live:** Wesley Shaw to parents, Burkeville, Va., Apr. 18, 1865, Shaw Letters, NYSL; **you are:** Emily Watkins to Abiathar Watkins, Jersey City, N.J., Apr. 16, 1865, Watkins Papers, NYPL.

20. **vacancies:** Edward W. Benham to Jennie Benham, Washington, D.C., May 28, 1865, ts., Benham Papers, Duke; **bringing:** William Benjamin Gould diary, May 24, 1865, MHS; **brother:** J. and J. H. John to Bela T. St. John. Genesee, Ill., Mar. 5, Apr. 9, 24, June 5, 1865.

21. **April 15 deaths:** Amos A. Lawrence diary, Apr. 15, 1865, MHS; **Hale:** Edward Everett Hale diary, Apr. 16, 19, 22, 1865, box 54, Hale Papers, NYSL; **depressed:** William Gray Brooks diary, Apr. 22, 1865, Brooks Papers, MHS. For another related suicide, see E. Gould to John Mead Gould, Portland, Me., Apr. 17, 1865, Gould Papers, Duke.

22. **Mifflin:** Ruth Anne Hillborn journal, Apr. 22, 1865, Hillborn Papers, FHL; **Otis:**

Jennie M. Smith to Mercy Schenck, Syracuse, N.Y., May 7, 1865, Schenck Family Papers, NYSL.

23. **applicable:** Anna Cabot Lowell diary, Apr. 23, 1865, MHS; **vividly:** William Gray Brooks diary, Apr. 29, 1865, Brooks Papers, MHS; **doubly:** Sarah Gould to Charles A. Gould, Lexington, Mass., Apr. 18, 1865, Gould Papers, Duke; **sacrifice:** Ruth Anne Hillborn journal, Apr. 19, 1865, Hillborn Papers, FHL.

24. **two years:** Laura Rhoades Lamson diary, Apr. 15, 1865, ts., Lamson Papers, SL; **very sad:** Sarah Lydia Gilpin diary, Apr. 19, 20, 24, 1865, #06846.05, GLC-NYHS.

25. **other:** Sarah Hale to children, Brookline, Mass., Apr. 18, 1865, box 10, Hale Family Papers, SSC; **Neafies:** Anne Neafie to Alfred Neafie, Ellenville, N.Y., Apr. 26, 28, May 1 (part of Apr. 28 letter), 18, 1865, and Alfred Neafie to Anne Neafie, Savannah, Ga., May 5, 13, 1865, Neafie Papers, NYSL.

26. **husband:** Louisa Walter Bishop Hughes diary, Jan. 15, Apr. 10, 16, 1865, ts., Hughes Papers, SL; **heavy, hope:** Mary Russell to Eunice Stone, Claremont, N.H., Apr. 16, 1865, Margaret Russell to Eunice Stone, Claremont, N.H., Apr. 19, 1865, Lois Wright Richardson Davis Papers, Duke; on this family, see Martha Hodes, *The Sea Captain's Wife: A True Story of Love, Race, and War in the Nineteenth Century* (New York: W. W. Norton, 2006).

27. **overwhelming:** Robert E. Lee, "General Order No. 9," Appomattox, Va., Apr. 10, 1865 (farewell address to the Army of Northern Virginia), Lee Letters and Documents, Museum of the Confederacy, Richmond, Va., available at moc.org/lee-jackson/lee-letters-and-documents-1865-15; **so many:** C. Vann Woodward, ed., *Mary Chesnut's Civil War* (1981; reprint, New Haven: Yale University Press, 1993), 796 (Apr. 23, 1865, entry); **best:** John Q. Anderson, ed., *Brokenburn: The Journal of Kate Stone, 1861–1868* (1955; reprint, Baton Rouge: Louisiana State University Press, 1995), 340 (May 15, 1865, entry).

28. **depth:** William Gordon plantation journal, May 1, 1865, Gordon Family Papers, ser. E, part 1, reel 35, UVA-RSP; **sit:** Nimrod Porter diary, Apr. 29, 1865, Porter Papers, SHC.

29. **bitterer:** Martha E. Foster Crawford diary, June 17, 1865, ser. H, part 2, reel 21, Duke-SWF; **feel:** Cornelia Spencer journal, May 4, 1865, Spencer Papers, ser. A, part 7, reel 16, SHC-SWF; **hardships:** Henry Robinson Berkeley diary, June 24, 1865, Berkeley Papers, ser. A, reel 2, VHS-CMM.

30. **language:** Samuel Thomas McCullough to brother, Johnson's Island, Ohio, Apr. 24, 1865, Hotchkiss-McCullough Manuscripts, LC.

31. **avenged:** E. A. Aglionby to cousin, London, May 13, 1865, Frances Walker Yates Aglionby Papers, ser. H, part 3, reel 1, Duke-SWF; and see *Encyclopedia Virginia*, s.v. "John Y. Beall," EncyclopediaVirginia.org/Beall_John_Y_1835-1865; **agony:** Elizabeth (Alsop) Wynne diary, Apr. 22, 1865, Wynne Family Papers, ser. D, part 3, reel 52, VHS-SWF; **unreturning:** Henry Robinson Berkeley diary, June 24, 1865, Berkeley Papers, ser. A, reel 2, VHS-CMM; **prisoner:** Creed Thomas Davis diary, May 4, 7, 1865, ser. A, reel 13, VHS-CMM; **could not:** [L. C. Gilmore?] to Susan (Dabney) Taylor, "Ingleside," July 6, 1865, Saunders Family Papers, ser. D, part 3, reel 42, VHS-SWF; **drink:** Cloe (Whittle) Greene diary, Apr. 11, 1865, reel 4, WM-AWD-South.

Interlude: Mary Lincoln

1. **Poor Mrs. Lincoln:** John Downing Jr. to "My Dear Friend," [no place], Apr. 26, 1865, in Timothy S. Good, *We Saw Lincoln Shot: One Hundred Eyewitness Accounts* (Jackson: University Press of Mississippi, 1995), 68; Helen A. Du Barry to mother, Washington, D.C., Apr. 25, 1865, in "Eyewitness Account of Lincoln's Assassination," *Journal of the Illinois State Historical Society* 39 (1946), 370; Sarah Hale to children, Brookline, Mass., Apr. 18, 1865, box 10, Hale Family Papers, SSC; Samuel Phillips Lee to Elizabeth Blair Lee, Cairo, Ill., Apr. 25, 1865, Blair and Lee Family Papers, Princeton; Susannah A. Milner-Gibson to Jane Poultney Bigelow, Folkestone, England, Apr. 28, 1865, Bigelow Family Papers, NYPL; Maria Lydig Daly, *Diary of a Union Lady, 1861–1865,* ed. Harold Earl Hammond (New York: Funk and Wagnalls, 1962), 357 (Apr. 25, 1865, entry), xli (Uncle Ape).

2. **how sad:** Mary Elizabeth Moore to James Otis Moore, Saco, Me., Apr. 16, 1865, Moore Papers, Duke; **Mr. Welles:** Gideon Welles diary, Apr. 15, 1865, Welles Papers, LC; **Tad:** Anna Cabot Lowell diary, Apr. 20, 1865, MHS; **tears:** Caroline Barrett White diary, May 4, 1865, White Papers, AAS.

3. **depth:** Elizabeth Gaskell to Charles Eliot Norton, London, Apr. 28, 1865, in *Letters of Mrs. Gaskell and Charles Eliot Norton, 1855–1865,* ed. Jane Whitehill (London: Oxford University Press, 1932), 123; **sat:** Nellie S. DeLamater to "My Dear Friend," Schenectady, N.Y., Apr. 24, 1865, box 2, fol. 27, Richard John Levy and Sally Waldman Sweet Collection, NYPL.

4. **agonizing:** Mrs. Bardwell diary, Apr. 15, 1865, Helen Temple Cooke Papers, SL; **funeral:** Martha Fisher Anderson diary, Apr. 21, 1865, MHS; **train:** William Gray Brooks diary, Apr. 29, 1865, Brooks Papers, MHS; **pistol:** Edgar Welles to George Harrington, Washington, D.C., Apr. [20?], 1865, Harrington Papers, HL; **colored:** "Mansion for Mrs. Lincoln," *San Francisco Elevator,* Apr. 21, 1865, #4809, BAP.

5. **happy:** Anne Neafie to Alfred Neafie, Ellenville, N.Y., Apr. 28, 1865, Neafie Papers, NYSL; **above:** William Dean Howells to William Cooper and Mary Dean Howells, Venice, Apr. 27, 1865, 1784.13(15), Howells Family Papers, HLH; **better:** Rachel Ann Cope to John Cope, [no place], Apr. 17, 1865, John Cope Papers, LC; **shore:** J. G. Holland, *The Nation Weeping for Its Dead: Observances at Springfield, Massachusetts, on President Lincoln's Funeral Day* (Springfield, Mass.: Samuel Bowles, 1865), 29.

6. **no-one:** Queen Victoria to Mary Lincoln, "Osborne," Apr. 29, 1865, in Justin G. Turner and Linda Levitt Turner, *Mary Todd Lincoln: Her Life and Letters* (New York: Alfred A. Knopf, 1972), 231n4; **catalog:** Charles Francis Adams to William Hunter, London, May 4, 1865, Letterbooks, Adams Papers, MHS.

7. **visits:** Elizabeth Blair Lee to Samuel Phillips Lee, Washington, D.C., Apr. 17, 19, 20, 22, 25, 1865, in *Wartime Washington: The Civil War Letters of Elizabeth Blair Lee,* ed. Virginia Jean Laas (Urbana: University of Illinois Press, 1991), 496–501 ("begged," May 4, 1865, p. 500n1); **sick:** Elizabeth Blair Lee to Samuel Phillips Lee, Washington, D.C., May 12, 1865, Blair and Lee Family Papers, Princeton; **wonderfully:** Elizabeth Blair Lee to Samuel Phillips Lee, Silver Spring, Md., May 15, 1865, Blair and Lee Family Papers,

Princeton; **good-bye:** Elizabeth Blair Lee to Samuel Phillips Lee, Washington, D.C., May 22, 1865, Blair and Lee Family Papers, Princeton.

Chapter 9. Nation

1. Albert Browne to "Dear Ones," Hilton Head Island, S.C., Apr. 18, 1865; Sarah Browne to Albert Browne, Salem, Mass., May 14, 1865, both BFP.

2. Sarah Browne to Albert Browne, Salem, Mass., May 14, 1865 (finale); Sarah Browne diary, May 14 (Salem), 15 (disguised), 1865; Albert Browne to Sarah Browne, Savannah, Ga., May 16, 1865 (traitor); Albert Browne to "Dear Ones," Summerville, S.C., May 24, 1865 (part of May 18 letter), all BFP.

3. Albert Browne [no salutation], Hilton Head Island, S.C., May 15, 1865, part of Charleston, S.C., May 11, 1865 (gathering); Albert Browne to Sarah Browne, Savannah, Ga., May 16, 1865 (momentous, hardly); Sarah Browne to Albert Browne, Salem, Mass., May 14, 1865, all BFP.

4. Dorman diary, May 10 (insult), Apr. 16 (blame, Hell-hounds), May 12 (contemptible), 1865.

5. Dorman diary, May 12 (pitiful, outrages), 7 (beshit), Apr. 16 (black-hearted), May 16 (mischief, out-negro), 1865.

6. Dorman diary, May 25 (not criminal), June 14 (retribution), 1865.

7. **eventful:** Horatio Nelson Taft diary, Apr. 30, 1865, LC, available at memory.loc.gov/ammem/tafthtml; **years:** James Helme Rickard to sister, [near Richmond, Va.], May 11, 1865, Rickard Civil War Letters, AAS; **lifetime:** Manning Ferguson Force to "Mr. Kebler" [?], Raleigh, N.C., Apr. 20, 1865 (letter copied into journal), Force Papers, LC; Franklin Augustus Buck to Mary Sewall Bradley, Weaverville, Calif., Apr. 27, 1865, Buck Papers, HL; **500:** Nathan Seymour to Thomas Day Seymour, Hudson, Ohio, Apr. 13, 1865, Seymour Family Papers, Yale-Sterling; **century:** Anna M. Ferris diary, Apr. 22, 1865, Ferris Family Papers, FHL; **remarkable:** Edward Everett Hale to Charles Hale, Boston, May 9, 1865, box 23, Hale Papers, NYSL; **remember:** Abigail Williams May to Eleanor Goddard May, Boston, Apr. 16, 1865, May and Goddard Family Papers, SL.

8. **private:** Elizabeth Blackwell to Barbara Bodichon, New York, May 23, 1865, Blackwell Letters, Columbia.

9. **had felt:** Anna Cabot Lowell diary, Apr. 15, 1865, MHS; **tired:** Anne Baldwin to Charlotte Nettleton, New York, Apr. 25, 1865, Nettleton-Baldwin Family Papers, Duke.

10. **exciting:** Emma F. LeConte diary, "Friday" [Apr. 21], 1865, reel 22, SHC-AWD-South; **reflections:** Albert Quincy Porter diary, May 30, 1865, ts., LC.

11. As James Oakes notes, union and slavery were inseparable for both radical and moderate Republicans during the war; see *Freedom National: The Destruction of Slavery in the United States* (New York: W. W. Norton, 2013), 108, 117, 200, 242.

12. **citizenship:** William H. Herndon and Jesse W. Weik, *Abraham Lincoln: The True Story of a Great Life,* 2 vols. (New York: D. Appleton, 1900), 2:289 ("Frederick Stone, counsel for Harold [sic] after Booth's death, is authority for the statement"); **fraught:** Abraham Lincoln, "Last Public Address," Apr. 11, 1865, *CWL,* 8:400.

13. **worse:** John Q. Anderson, ed., *Brokenburn: The Journal of Kate Stone, 1861–1868* (1955; reprint, Baton Rouge: Louisiana State University Press, 1995), 341 (May 15, 1865, entry); **rail-splitter:** Emma F. LeConte diary, "Friday" [Apr. 21], 1865, reel 22, SHC-AWD-South; **all:** Edward J. Bartlett to Martha Bartlett, South Side Railroad, Va., Apr. 23, 1865, Bartlett Letters, MHS.

14. **diabolical:** "Speech to Indiana Delegation," Apr. 21, 1865, *PAJ*, 7:610–15; **over:** Kate Cumming, *Kate: The Journal of a Confederate Nurse*, ed. Richard Barksdale Harwell (Baton Rouge: Louisiana State University Press, 1998), 290 (May 15, 1865, entry), NAWLD; **traitor:** William Kauffman Scarborough, ed., *The Diary of Edmund Ruffin: A Dream Shattered, June, 1863–June, 1865* (Baton Rouge: Louisiana State University Press, 1989), 865 (Apr. 25, 1865, entry); **Herod:** Daniel Dudley Avery to Dudley Avery, "Petit Ance Island," May 12, 1865, Avery Family Papers, ser. J, part 5, reel 11, SHC-RSP; **from:** Chester dispatch, Richmond, Va., May 15, 1865, in *Thomas Morris Chester: Black Civil War Correspondent—His Dispatches from the Virginia Front*, ed. R. J. M. Blackett (Baton Rouge: Louisiana State University Press, 1989), 347.

15. **same:** "a Southern Man" to Andrew Johnson, Saint Louis, Mo., May 31, 1865, *PAJ*, 8:159; **shoot:** "A Southerner for life" to Andrew Johnson, "Canada," June 1, 1865, *PAJ*, 8:166; **heaven's:** "From a Loyal Woman of Virginia" to Andrew Johnson, Baltimore, Apr. 15, 1865, *PAJ*, 7:559.

16. **hereafter:** Frederick Douglass, "The Fall of Richmond: An Address Delivered in Boston, Massachusetts, on 4 April 1865," *FDP*, ser. 1, 4:73; **less:** "Lee's Surrender—Peace," *New York Anglo-African*, Apr. 15, 1865; **might not:** Hope R. Daggett to George Whipple, Norfolk, Va., Apr. [n.d.], 1865, #H1-7058, reel 210, AMA.

17. **colored:** "Andrew Johnson President of the United States," *New Orleans Black Republican*, Apr. 22, 1865, #15222, BAP; **hope:** "From the Regiments," letter from Richard H. Black, 3rd U.S.C.T., Fernandina, Fla., *New York Anglo-African*, May 27, 1865.

18. **freind:** William B. Scott and William B. Scott Jr. to President Johnson, Nashville, Tenn., May 27, 1865, *PAJ*, 8:120; **liberty:** "Response to John Mercer Langston," *PAJ*, 7:585–86n2; **control:** "Petition from the Colored People of Alexandria," Alexandria, Va., Apr. 29, 1865, *PAJ*, 7:656–58.

19. **loyal, fighting, mantle:** "From North Carolina Blacks," New Bern, N.C., May 10, 1865, *PAJ*, 8:58; **heroic:** "From Committee of Richmond Blacks," Richmond, Va., June 10, 1865, *PAJ*, 8:210.

20. **new skin:** Frederick Douglass, "In What New Skin Will the Old Snake Come Forth?: An Address Delivered in New York, New York, on 10 May 1865," *FDP*, ser. 1, 4:83, 85.

21. **very, curious:** Salmon P. Chase to Andrew Johnson, Hilton Head Island, S.C., May 17, 1865, and Salmon P. Chase to Andrew Johnson, Fernandina, Fla., May 21, 1865, in James E. Sefton, "Chief Justice Chase as an Advisor on Presidential Reconstruction," *Civil War History* 13 (1967), 253, 261; **dignity:** Dorman diary, May 18, 1865; **inferior:** *Dred Scott v. Sandford*, 60 U.S. 393 (1857).

22. **guaranty:** "Response to John Mercer Langston," Apr. 18, 1865, *PAJ*, 7:585; **necessary, native, loafers:** "Reply to Delegation of Black Ministers," May 11, 1865, *PAJ*, 8:63, 62.

A minority of ardent white southern Unionists joined African Americans in directly confronting President Johnson, demanding black suffrage as a way to curtail the power of the aristocracy; see James E. Hamilton to Andrew Johnson, New York, May 3, 1865, and Joseph Noxon to Andrew Johnson, New York, May 27, 1865, *PAJ,* 8:20, 119.

23. **time:** "Reply to Delegation of Black Ministers," May 11, 1865, *PAJ,* 8:63; **we see:** William Benjamin Gould diary, June 14, 1865, MHS.

24. **equal:** Anna M. Ferris diary, Apr. 16, 1865, Ferris Family Papers, FHL; **rather:** Henry Morrill to C. Henry Albers, Memphis, Tenn., Apr. 20, 1865, Morrill Papers, Western Americana, Yale-Beinecke; **read:** *"Maggie!": Maggie Lindsley's Journal, Nashville, Tennessee, 1864, Washington, D.C., 1865* (Southbury, Conn.: Muriel Davies Mackenzie, 1977), 84 (Apr. 15, 1865, entry); **drunken:** "Carrie" to sister, Washington, D.C., Apr. 16, 1865, box 2, fol. 27, Richard John Levy and Sally Waldman Sweet Collection, NYPL.

25. **given:** David Homer Bates diary, Apr. 15, 1865, Bates Papers, LC; **favorably:** James Thomas Ward diary, Apr. 17, 1865, Ward Papers, LC.

26. **sterner:** Samuel Comfort to Susan Comfort, Petersburg, Va., Apr. 21, 1865, Comfort Papers, Princeton; **radical:** Hallock Armstrong to Mary Armstrong, near Petersburg, Va., Apr. 16, 1865, in *Letters from a Pennsylvania Chaplain at the Siege of Petersburg: 1865* (n.p.: Privately published, 1961), 28, ACWLD; **yielding:** Caroline Butler Laing to Mary Butler Reeves, Brooklyn, N.Y., Apr. 21, 1865, Butler-Laing Family Papers, NYHS; **traitors:** Selden Connor to father, Washington, D.C., Apr. 18, 1865, Connor Papers, Brown; **hemp:** John B. Burrud to Ocena Burrud, Charlestown, Va., Apr. 19, 1865, Burrud Papers, HL; **silk:** Georgia Treadway to Newton Perkins, New Haven, Conn., Apr. 16, 1865, Montgomery Family Papers, LC; **necessary:** Lydia Maria Child to John Greenleaf Whittier, May 1865, fragment, Child Letters, SL; **smooth:** John Greenleaf Whittier, "The Question of To-Day," *Liberator,* May 26, 1865; **star:** Wendell Phillips, "The Lesson of President Lincoln's Death: A Speech of Wendell Phillips at the Tremont Temple, on Sunday Evening, April 23, 1865," in *Universal Suffrage, and Complete Equality in Citizenship, the Safeguards of Democratic Institutions* (Boston: Rand and Avery, 1865), 14–15.

27. **made:** "The Blacks and the Ballot," *Christian Recorder,* May 27, 1865; **emancipated:** "Emancipation of the White Man," *New York Anglo-African,* July 23, 1865; **prejudiced:** J. H. Payne, "Letter from Wilmington," Wilmington, N.C., Aug. 12, 1865, *Christian Recorder,* published Aug. 19, 1865.

28. **plebeins:** Stephen M. Barbour to Andrew Johnson, Philadelphia, May 1, 1865, *PAJ,* 8:3; **poor:** Edward Everett Hale to Charles Hale, Boston, Apr. 25, 26, 1865, box 6, Hale Papers, NYSL; **background:** Lydia Maria Child to Sarah Blake Shaw, Apr. [n.d.], 1865, Child Letters, SL; **greatest:** Karl Marx to Friedrich Engels, May 1, 1855, in Karl Marx and Friedrich Engels, *The Civil War in the United States* (New York: International Publishers, 1937), 275.

29. **suffer, sorry:** Ebenezer N. Gilpin diary, Apr. 24, May 5, 16, 1865, Gilpin Papers, LC; **ready:** Richard G. Lay to Carrie Lay, Danville, Va., May 3, 1865, Lay Letters, NYPL; **completely, peace:** William C. McLean diary, May 2, Apr. 30, 1865, ts., McLean Family Papers, NYSL; **hoped:** Theophilus M. Magaw diary, Apr. 21, 1865, Magaw Papers, HL.

30. **disfranchise:** Chauncey Welton to parents, Raleigh, N.C., Apr. 19, 1865, Welton Papers, SHC.

31. **bold:** Heber Painter to Rebecca Frick, Richmond, Va., Apr. 16, 1865, #02016.082, GLC-NYHS; **obliged:** C. P. Day to George Whipple, Hampton, Va., Apr. 21, 1865, #H1-7022, reel 209, AMA; **not subdued:** Warren Goodale to children, Petersburg, Va., Apr. 20, 1865, Goodale Papers, MHS; **dangerous:** W. D. Harris to George Whipple, Portsmouth, Va., May 1, 1865, #H1-062, reel 210, AMA; **lethal:** Harriet E. Gaylord to George Whipple, Natchez, Miss., May 1, 1865, #71762, reel 111, AMA; **Mr. Lincoln:** W. L. Coan to M. E. Strieby, Richmond, Va., Apr. 30, 1865, #H1-7050, reel 210, AMA.

32. **fatal, Booth, genuine, forgive:** Martha Coffin Wright to Marianna Pelham Mott, Auburn, N.Y., May 4, 1865, box 265, Garrison Family Papers, SSC; **subordinates:** Martha Coffin Wright to David Wright, Roxbury, Mass., May 24, 1865, box 267, Garrison Family Papers, SSC; **Toussaint:** Martha Coffin Wright to sisters, Auburn, N.Y., June 25, 1865, box 266, Garrison Family Papers, SSC; **horrible, gentle:** Octavius B. Frothingham, "The Saints Coming from the Graves," *National Anti-Slavery Standard,* Apr. 29, 1865, pp. 2–3.

33. **headlines:** Benjamin Brown French to Frank O. French, Washington, D.C., May 15, 1865, French Papers, LC; **telegraph:** Frederick G. Niles diary, May 16, 1865, HL; **newsboys:** Anna Cabot Lowell diary, May 14, 1865, MHS; **celebrations:** Asa Fitch diary, May 15, 1865, Fitch Papers, Yale-Sterling; Silas W. Haven to Jane Haven, Montgomery, Ala., May 17, 1865, in *"A Punishment on the Nation": An Iowa Soldier Endures the Civil War,* ed. Brian Craig Miller (Kent, Ohio: Kent State University Press, 2012), 178; **mingled:** Harriet Anne Severance diary, May 15, 1865, SL; **let us pass:** James Harrison Wilson to "Ad," Macon, Ga., May 13, 1865, Adam Badeau Civil War Letters, Princeton; **disguised:** Sarah Browne diary, May 15, 1865, BFP; **ridiculous:** Annie G. Dudley Davis diary, May 15, 1865, HL; **ludicrous:** Thomas Bradford Drew diary, May 14, 1865, MHS; **disgraced:** Lucretia Hale to Charles Hale, Brookline, Mass., May 19, 1865, box 50, Hale Family Papers, SSC; Emmeline Yelland to Albert Yelland, [no place], May 23, 1865, Yelland Family Correspondence, Duke; **king:** Edgar Dinsmore to Carrie Drayton, Saint Andrews Parish, S.C., May 29, 1865, Dinsmore Papers, Duke; **woman:** Ellis Hughes diary, May 15, 1865, Hughes-Gray Family Papers, Duke; **images:** Simon Newcomb diary, June 7, 1865, Newcomb Papers, LC; **sales:** Sarah Lydia Gilpin diary, May 24, 1865, #06846.05, GLC-NYHS; Caroline Dunstan diary, May 25, 1865, NYPL.

34. **shall:** Samuel May almanac, Apr. 12, 1865, May Papers, MHS; **measure:** Charles Edward French diary, May 14, 1865, French Diaries and Papers, MHS; **fitted:** Edgar Dinsmore to Carrie Drayton, Saint Andrews Parish, S.C., May 29, 1865, Dinsmore Papers, Duke; **ready:** William Benjamin Gould diary, June 16, 1865, MHS; **roasted:** Sarah G. Putnam diary, Apr. 27, 1865, MHS; **no other:** Lydia Maria Child to John Greenleaf Whittier, May 1865, fragment, Child Letters, SL.

35. **force:** William Dean Howells to William Cooper Howells, Venice, June 6, 1865, 1784.1.2(78), Howells Family Papers, HLH; **anxious:** Charles Francis Adams to John G. Palfrey, London, June 6, 1865, Letterbooks, Adams Papers, MHS; **consternation:** Charles Francis Adams diary, May 27, June 14, 1865, and Adams to William Hunter, London, June

15, 1865, Letterbooks, Adams Papers, MHS; **martyr:** Charles Francis Adams to Charles Francis Adams Jr., London, May 26, 1865, Letters Received and Other Loose Papers, Adams Papers, MHS; **suicide:** William H. Stewart diary, May 11, 1865, ts., SHC.

36. **renew:** Emma F. LeConte diary, "Thursday" [May 18], 1865, reel 22, SHC-AWD-South.

37. **horsecars:** Marian Hooper to Mary Louisa Shaw, Boston, May 28, 1865, in *The Letters of Mrs. Henry Adams, 1865–1883,* ed. Ward Thoron (Boston: Little, Brown, 1936), 5.

38. **weather:** Charles T. Cotton diary, May 23, 24, 1865, Columbia; **troops:** Benjamin Brown French, *Witness to the Young Republic: A Yankee's Journal, 1828–1870,* ed. Donald B. Cole and John J. McDonough (Hanover, N.H.: University Press of New England, 1989), 478 (May 24, 1865, entry); **hours:** Samuel Canby diary, May 24, 1865, DHS; **marching:** Walt Whitman to Louisa Van Velsor Whitman, Washington, D.C., May 25, 1865, available at whitmanarchive.org/biography/correspondence/cw/tei/wwh.00008.html; **"John Brown":** Marian Hooper to Mary Louisa Shaw, Boston, May 28, 1865, in Thoron, *Letters of Mrs. Henry Adams,* 7; **flags:** Annie G. Dudley Davis diary, May 28, 1865, HL.

For observations of African Americans marching, see also Marian Hooper to Mary Louisa Shaw, Boston, May 28, 1865, in Thoron, *Letters of Mrs. Henry Adams,* 8. On black troops, see Noah Brooks, "The Grand Review—First Day," Washington, D.C., May 23, 1865, in *Mr. Lincoln's Washington: Selections from the Writings of Noah Brooks, Civil War Correspondent,* ed. P. J. Staudenraus (South Brunswick, N.J.: Thomas Yoseloff, 1967), 475.

39. **generations, return:** French, *Witness to the Young Republic,* 479 (May 24, 1865, entry); **greatest:** Simon Newcomb diary, May 24, 1865, Newcomb Papers, LC; **continent, never return:** James Thomas Ward diary, May 23, 1865, Ward Papers, LC; **magnificent, all:** *Diary of Gideon Welles, Secretary of the Navy under Lincoln and Johnson,* 3 vols. (Boston: Houghton Mifflin, 1911), 2:310 (May 22–23, 1865, entry); **should:** Abial H. Edwards to Anna L. Conant, Washington, D.C., May 26, 1865, in *"Dear Friend Anna": The Civil War Letters of a Common Soldier from Maine,* ed. Beverly Hayes Kallgren and James L. Crouthamel (Orono: University of Maine Press, 1992), 128; **strange:** Marian Hooper to Mary Louisa Shaw, Boston, May 28, 1865, in Thoron, *Letters of Mrs. Henry Adams,* 7.

40. **looking:** Stephen Minot Weld to Hannah Weld, near Alexandria, Va., May 25, 1865, in *War Diary and Letters of Stephen Minot Weld, 1861–1865* (Cambridge, Mass.: Riverside Press, 1912), 399; **perlite:** Guy C. Taylor to Sarah Taylor, near Washington, Va., May 20, 1865, in *Letters Home to Sarah: The Civil War Letters of Guy C. Taylor, Thirty-Sixth Wisconsin Volunteers,* ed. Kevin Alderson and Patsy Alderson (Madison: University of Wisconsin Press, 2012), 263; **tired:** Rufus Mead Jr. diary, May 24, 1865, Mead Papers, LC.

41. **devilish:** Mary H. and Dallas M. Lancaster, eds., *The Civil War Diary of Anne S. Frobel* (McLean, Va.: EPM, 1992), 230 (May 22, 1865, entry).

Interlude: Relics

1. **postcards, First Lady:** "Cornelia" to parent(s), New York, Apr. 17–19, 1865, Lincoln Miscellaneous Manuscripts, NYHS; **medal:** Frances Owens diary, May 3, 1865, CHM;

Johnson: F. C. Chambers diary, Apr. 24, 1865, Chambers Family Diaries, Princeton; **Washington:** Caroline Dunstan diary, May 29, 1865, NYPL; **photographs:** William Gray Brooks diary, May 9, 1865, Brooks Papers, MHS; Harriet Anne Severance diary, July 1, 1865, SL; Margaret B. Howell diary, May 9, 1865, HSP; **Tad, speeches, memorial book:** Anna Cabot Lowell diary, May 5, 15, 13, 1865, MHS; **Booth, biography:** Susan E. Parsons Brown Forbes diary, Apr. 18, 1865, AAS; **Booth:** E. Gould to John Mead Gould, Portland, Me., Apr. 17, 1865, Gould Papers, Duke; **sermons:** William Gray Brooks diary, May 9, 1865, Brooks Papers, MHS; **memorial:** B. F. Morris, *Memorial Record of the Nation's Tribute to Abraham Lincoln* (Washington, D.C.: W. H. and O. H. Morrison, 1865).

Victor Searcher writes, "The memorabilia of Lincoln's passing—the badges, pamphlets, posters, books, special newspaper editions, magazine features, sketches, engravings, photographs and other souvenirs—is beyond belief"; see *The Farewell to Lincoln* (New York: Abingdon, 1965), 294.

2. **renewed, drapery:** Anna Cabot Lowell diary, May 13, June 26, 1865, MHS.

3. **scrapbooks:** scrapbook compiled by J. W. H. Cathcart, 24-S12, ser. K, Cromwell Family Papers, Schomburg; Samuel Canby diary, May 1865, DHS; **New Yorker:** "Notebook containing drawings and transcriptions of memorial tributes to Abraham Lincoln displayed in New York, N.Y. and other places in the aftermath of his assassination," McLellan Lincoln Collection and Center for Digital Scholarship, Brown; see also Ted Widmer, "New York's Lincoln Memorial," Op-Archive: Lincoln Memorial Diary, *New York Times,* Apr. 17, 2009, available at nytimes.com/2009/04/17/opinion/17widmer.html; **Carrington:** C. C. Carrington, "Assassination and Funeral of President Lincoln," scrapbook, 1865–71, 2 vols., McLellan Lincoln Collection, Brown.

4. **collar:** Newton Ferree diary, Apr. 14, 1865, in "Eyewitness to History: Newton Ferree, the Lincoln Assassination and the Close of the Civil War in Washington," ed. John K. Lattimer and Terry Alford, *Lincoln Herald* 58 (1956), 97; **towel:** Augustus Clark to S. M. Allen, Washington, D.C., Apr. 16, 1865, accompanying scrap of bloodstained towel used for Abraham Lincoln at Ford's Theatre, Special Collections, MHS; **alley:** Marian Hooper to Mary Louisa Shaw, Boston, May 28, 1865, in *The Letters of Mrs. Henry Adams, 1865–1883,* ed. Ward Thoron (Boston: Little, Brown, 1936), 8; **crestfallen:** Catherine Gansevoort Lansing diary, May 23–28, 1865, box 255, Gansevoort-Lansing Papers, NYPL; **crape, theater, Petersen's:** James Otis Moore to Mary Elizabeth Moore, "Chapel Pt.," May 7, 1865, and James Otis Moore to Mary Elizabeth Moore, Washington, D.C., Apr. 20, 1865, Moore Papers, Duke.

5. **left:** Marian Hooper to Mary Louisa Shaw, Boston, May 28, 1865, in Thoron, *Letters of Mrs. Henry Adams,* 8.

Chapter 10. Justice

1. Dorman diary, June 20 (rebellion, surpassing), May 30 (people, thousand), 2 (damned), June 7 (sharks, contemptible), 9 (ninnyhammers, blaspheming, craven), 24 (dogs), 1865.

2. Dorman diary, June 20 (flummery, starvation), 27 (property, education), 18 (theives),

May 23 (inciters), 16 (ignorant, insolent), 28 (worse), 1865; on slave property, see also May 12, 1865.

oath: Justus Silliman to brother, Jacksonville, Fla., May 18, 1865, in *A New Canaan Private in the Civil War: Letters of Justus M. Silliman, 17th Connecticut Volunteers,* ed. Edward Marcus (New Canaan, Conn.: New Canaan Historical Society, 1984), 108.

3. Dorman diary, June 10 (worst), 3 (enjoy), Apr. 26 (tyranny), 1865.

changes, die: William B. Johnson, "Florida Correspondence," Jacksonville, Fla., June 22, 1865, *Christian Recorder,* published July 8, 1865.

4. Dorman diary, June 27 (negroes), May 15 (war, one sided), 14 (no better), 30 (over), 1865.

5. Albert Browne to Sarah Browne, Savannah, Ga., May 16, 1865 (disfranchise, literacy); Albert Browne to "Dear Ones," Charleston, S.C., Apr. 28, 1865 (part of Apr. 24 letter) (active); Albert Browne, [no salutation], Charleston, S.C., May 11, 1865 (loyal, ballot), all BFP.

6. Albert Browne to "Dear Ones," Charleston, S.C., Apr. 28, 1865 (part of Apr. 24 letter) (wonder, acres); Albert Browne, [no salutation], Charleston, S.C., May 11, 1865 (supported); Albert Browne to "Dear Ones," Charleston, S.C., Apr. 27, 1865 (part of Apr. 24 letter) (demand), all BFP.

7. Albert Browne to "Dear Ones," Charleston, S.C., Apr. 28, 1865 (part of Apr. 24 letter) (human nature, fancy); Albert Browne, [no salutation], Charleston, S.C., May 11, 1865 (dont love); Sarah Browne diary, May 1, 1864 (earnest), May 26, 1865 (dear), all BFP.

8. **unsatisfactory, cup:** Abraham Lincoln, "Last Public Address," Apr. 11, 1865, *CWL,* 8:403, 404.

9. **inexorable:** Chester dispatch, Richmond, Va., May 19, 1865, in *Thomas Morris Chester: Black Civil War Correspondent—His Dispatches from the Virginia Front,* ed. R. J. M. Blackett (Baton Rouge: Louisiana State University Press, 1989), 348–49; **confidence:** "The Duties of the Nation," *San Francisco Elevator,* May 19, 1865, #4997, BAP; **right:** "Box," letter to the editor, May 28, 1865, *San Francisco Elevator,* published July 7, 1865, #4993, BAP; **awakened:** "Emancipation Celebration at Bath, Pennsylvania," *Christian Recorder,* Aug. 12, 1865.

10. **enemies:** Garland H. White to William H. Seward, City Point, Va., Apr. [n.d.], 1865, William H. Seward Papers, University of Rochester (I thank Christopher Hager, Trinity College, Hartford, Conn., for transcribing and sharing this document); **noble:** John H. Winston, letter to the editor, *New Orleans Black Republican,* Apr. 22, 1865, #3405, BAP.

11. **loyal:** Andrew Johnson, "Address to Loyal Southerners," Apr. 24, 1865, *PAJ,* 7:631.

12. **pardon:** Andrew Johnson, "Amnesty Proclamation," May 29, 1865, , *PAJ,* 8:128–31.

13. For a clear summary of the proclamation, see James M. McPherson, *Ordeal by Fire: The Civil War and Reconstruction* (New York: Alfred A. Knopf, 1982), 498–99; **we see:** William Benjamin Gould diary, July 11, 1865, MHS; **after:** "Will Justice Be Done?" *San Francisco Elevator,* June 2, 1865, #5477, BAP; **differ:** Lincoln, "Last Public Address," Apr. 11, 1865, *CWL,* 8:401.

14. **best friend:** "The Richmond Freedmen: Their Visit to the President," *New York Daily Tribune,* June 17, 1865; **welcomed, laws, women, many:** "From Committee of Richmond Blacks," Richmond, Va., June 10, 1865, *PAJ,* 8:210–14 and n6; **political, poured:** "From Delegation Representing the Black People of Kentucky," Washington, D.C., June 9, 1865, *PAJ,* 8:203–5; **protecting:** "From South Carolina Black Citizens," [no city], June 29, 1865, *PAJ,* 8:317; **expect:** *Chicago Tribune,* June 15, 1865, cited in *PAJ,* 8:205n8.

15. **fitting:** Charles Francis Adams diary, Apr. 26, 1865, Adams Papers, MHS; **rehabilitation:** Charles Francis Adams to Charles Francis Adams Jr., London, May 12, 1865, Letters Received and Other Loose Papers, Adams Papers, MHS.

16. **Whig:** Charles Francis Adams diary, May 25, 1865, Adams Papers, MHS; **blockade:** Charles Francis Adams to William Hunter, London, May 25, 1865, Letterbooks, Adams Papers, MHS; **whipped, shuddered, tired, beaten:** Benjamin Moran diary, Apr. 17, May 26, 31, 17, 1865, Moran Papers, LC; **protect:** Charles Francis Adams diary, May 26, 1865, Adams Papers, MHS.

17. **sacrifice, no difficulty:** Charles Francis Adams diary, July 10, 1865, Adams Papers, MHS; **lenient:** Charles Francis Adams to William Hunter, London, May 25, 1865, Letterbooks, Adams Papers, MHS.

18. **readmitting:** "Proclamation Establishing Government for North Carolina," May 29, 1865, *PAJ,* 8:136–38; **white:** John W. Gorham to Andrew Johnson, Clarksville, Tenn., June 3, 1865, *PAJ,* 8:173.

19. **not dead:** P. Houston Murray, "Negro Suffering and Suffrage in the South," Natchez, Miss., June 10, 1865, *Christian Recorder,* published July 1, 1865; **trouble:** J. H. Payne, "Letter from Wilmington," Wilmington, N.C., Aug. 12, 1865, *Christian Recorder,* published Aug. 19, 1865; **mistaken:** J. J. Wright, "Reconstruction," *Christian Recorder,* July 8, 1865.

20. **question:** Henry W. Halleck to Francis Lieber, Richmond, Va., June 14, 1865, box 10, Lieber Papers, HL; **please:** Nicholas B. Wainwright, ed., *A Philadelphia Perspective: The Diary of Sidney George Fisher . . . , 1834–1871* (Philadelphia: Historical Society of Pennsylvania, 1967), 499 (June 8, 1865, entry); **voters, gained:** Abial H. Edwards to Marcia Edwards, Darlington, S.C., Aug. 13, 1865, and Abial H. Edwards to Anna L. Conant, Darlington, S.C., Oct. 22, 1865, in *"Dear Friend Anna": The Civil War Letters of a Common Soldier from Maine,* ed. Beverly Hayes Kallgren and James L. Crouthamel (Orono: University of Maine Press, 1992), 135, 140.

21. **abandoned, unquestionably:** Carl Schurz to Frederick Althaus, Bethlehem, Pa., June 25, 1865, and Carl Schurz to wife, Savannah, Ga., July 30, 1865, in *Intimate Letters of Carl Schurz, 1841–1869,* trans. and ed. Joseph Schafer (Madison: State Historical Society of Wisconsin, 1928), 341, 345; **not abolished:** Martha Coffin Wright to sisters, Auburn, N.Y., June 25, 1865, box 266, Garrison Family Papers, SSC; **Andy:** Samuel Miller Quincy to mother, New Orleans, June 28, 1865, Quincy, Wendell, Holmes, Upham Family Papers, MHS.

22. **slavery:** Frederick Douglass, "In What New Skin Will the Old Snake Come Forth?: An Address Delivered in New York, New York, on 10 May 1865," *FDP,* ser. 1, 4:83, 85.

23. **freedpeople:** David Todd to George Whipple, Pine Bluff, Ark., May 31, 1865,

#4608, reel 8, AMA; **sorry:** Eliza F. Andrews, *The War-Time Journal of a Georgia Girl, 1864–1865* (New York: D. Appleton, 1908), 281–82 (June 1, 1865, entry), DocSouth, docsouth.unc.edu/fpn/andrews/menu.html; **not think:** Richard L. Troutman, ed., *The Heavens Are Weeping: The Diaries of George Richard Browder, 1852–1886* (Grand Rapids, Mich.: Zondervan, 1987), 199 (June 1, 1865, entry); **friends:** Hattie Powell to Nina Powell, Richmond, Va., June 15, 1865, Powell Family Papers, ser. C, reel 6, WM-SWF.

    24. **festival:** Caroline Barrett White diary, June 1, 1865, White Papers, AAS; **show:** George E. Ellis diary, June 1, 1865, Ellis Papers, MHS; **imitation:** Ezra Stiles Gannett daily journal, June 1, 1865, Gannett Papers, MHS; **work:** Alpheus B. Kenyon diary, June 1, 1865, GWBW; **glorious:** Kate Hunter journal, June 1, 1865, Hunter Family Papers, ser. B, part 2, reel 27, NHS-NWF; **chess:** Simon Newcomb to wife, Washington, D.C., June 1, 1865, Newcomb Papers, LC; **backgammon:** Mary Dreer diary, June 1, 1865, Edwin Greble Papers, LC; **soldiers:** William D. Guernsey to Emeline Guernsey, Atlanta, Ga., June 1, 1865, Guernsey Family Papers, HL; **more truly:** Anna Cabot Lowell diary, June 1, 1865, MHS; **still lives:** Abram Verrick Parmenter diary, June 1, 1865, Parmenter Papers, LC; **sacred:** Mary (Jackson) Darlington to William S. Jackson, Elkdale, Pa., June 1, 1865, Alger Family Papers, SL; **hauling:** F. C. Chambers diary, June 1, 1865, Chambers Family Diaries, Princeton.

    25. **unsurpassed:** Frederick Douglass eulogy on Abraham Lincoln, June 1, 1865, holograph document, #177, digital ID #al0177, Frederick Douglass Papers, LC, available at loc.gov/exhibits/lincoln/lincoln-and-frederick-douglass.html; **real:** Martha Fisher Anderson diary, June 1, 1865, MHS; **slave power:** Lucretia Hale to Charles Hale, Brookline, Mass., June 2, 1865, box 50, Hale Family Papers, SSC.

    26. **malice:** Robert W. Chaffin journal, May 14, 1865, Washington Sandford Chaffin Papers, Duke; **hateful:** Sarah Lois Wadley diary, May 13, 1865, Wadley Papers, ser. A, part 3, reel 6, SHC-SWF; **unbearable:** Elizabeth (Alsop) Wynne diary, Apr. 22, 1865, Wynne Family Papers, ser. D, part 3, reel 52, VHS-SWF; **exulting:** Samuel A. Burney to wife, Wooten's Station, Ga., Apr. 26, 1865, in *A Southern Soldier's Letters Home: The Civil War Letters of Samuel A. Burney, Cobb's Georgia Legion, Army of Northern Virginia*, ed. Nat S. Turner III (Macon, Ga.: Mercer University Press, 2003), 293.

    27. **walk, horrid:** Emma F. LeConte diary, May 17 and "Thursday" [May 18], 1865, reel 22, SHC-AWD-South; **negro president:** Mary H. and Dallas M. Lancaster, eds., *The Civil War Diary of Anne S. Frobel* (McLean, Va.: EPM, 1992), 226 (May 10, 1865, entry).

    28. **cowed:** John Payne to W. W. Thomas, near Mobile, Ala., May 26, 1865, Payne Papers, Civil War Miscellaneous Letters and Papers, Schomburg; **badly:** Henry J. Peck to Mary Peck, Richmond, Va., May 1, 1865, Peck Correspondence, NYSL; **whipped, beaten:** Benjamin Moran diary, Apr. 17, May 17, 1865, Moran Papers, LC; **completely:** William C. McLean diary, May 2, 1865, ts., McLean Family Papers, NYSL; **nature:** Henry A. Chambers diary, Apr. 10, 1865, Chambers Papers, SHC; **subjugated:** Caroline Thornton diary, Apr. 9, 1865, Green Family Papers, ser. D, part 3, reel 16, VHS-SWF; **flies:** Cornelia Spencer journal, June 8, 1865, Spencer Papers, ser. A, part 7, reel 16, SHC-SWF.

    29. **rivet:** John Q. Anderson, ed., *Brokenburn: The Journal of Kate Stone, 1861–1868* (1955; reprint, Baton Rouge: Louisiana State University Press, 1995), 340 (May 15, 1865,

entry); **bondage:** sister to "Fannie," "Willowdew," June 6, 1865, Graves Family Papers, ser. A, part 5, reel 11, SHC-SWF; **vilest:** Daniel E. Sutherland, ed., *A Very Violent Rebel: The Civil War Diary of Ellen Renshaw House* (Knoxville: University of Tennessee Press, 1996), 165 (May 25, 1865, entry); **race, without:** William Kauffman Scarborough, ed., *The Diary of Edmund Ruffin: A Dream Shattered, June, 1863–June, 1865* (Baton Rouge: Louisiana State University Press, 1989), 884, 889 (May 9, 13, 1865, entries).

For a rare Confederate voice articulating that former masters "have now changed in their opinions" about slavery because of God's punishment through war, see Norman D. Brown, ed., *One of Cleburne's Command: The Civil War Reminiscences and Diary of Capt. Samuel T. Foster, Granbury's Texas Brigade, CSA* (Austin: University of Texas Press, 1980), 171 (Apr. 30, 1865, entry), and see 176 (May 16, 1865, entry), professing readiness to submit.

30. **Yankee:** Junius Newport Bragg to Anna J. G. Bragg, near Marshall, Tex., Apr. 23, 1865, in Bragg, *Letters of a Confederate Surgeon, 1861–65,* ed. Helen Bragg Gaughan (Camden, Ark.: Hurley, 1960), 272, ACWLD; **Europe:** Charles Woodward Hutson to "My dear friend," Paris, [day illegible], 1865, Hutson Papers, SHC.

For Latin America, see Matthew Pratt Guterl, *American Mediterranean: Southern Slaveholders in the Age of Emancipation* (Cambridge, Mass.: Harvard University Press, 2008), 79–113, and Cyrus B. Dawsey and James M. Dawsey, eds., *The Confederados: Old South Immigrants in Brazil* (Tuscaloosa: University of Alabama Press, 1995).

31. **outrage:** Scarborough, *Diary of Edmund Ruffin,* 946 (June 16–18, 1865, entries); **bear:** Charles Woodward Hutson diary, Apr. 18, 1865, Hutson Papers, SHC; **years:** John Steele Henderson diary, July 23, 1865, ts., Henderson Papers, ser. J, part 13, reel 25, SHC-RSP; **not all:** Henry Robinson Berkeley diary, June 24, 1865, Berkeley Papers, ser. A, reel 2, VHS-CMM.

32. **second:** Cloe (Whittle) Greene diary, Apr. 19, 1865, reel 4, WM-AWD-South; **two:** Martha E. Foster Crawford diary, June 17, 1865, ser. H, part 2, reel 21, Duke-SWF, and see Abraham Lincoln, "'A House Divided': Speech at Springfield, Illinois," June 16, 1858, in *CWL,* 2:461; **Reconstruction:** Elizabeth Collier diary, Apr. 25, 1865, ts., SHC; **sooner:** E. S. Mallory to Edward J. Garnet, Liberty, Va., May 12, 1865, Flora Morgan McCabe Papers, LC.

33. **best:** Anderson, *Brokenburn,* 340 (May 15, 1865, entry); **bully:** Henry Robinson Berkeley diary, May 20, 1865, Berkeley Papers, ser. A, reel 2, VHS-CMM; **venerate:** Julia Watson to Katherine Douglas Meares, Lexington, England, June 15, 1865, De Rosset Family Papers, ser. A, part 8, reel 16, SHC-SWF.

34. **Clausewitz:** James M. McPherson, "War and Politics," in Geoffrey C. Ward, *The Civil War: An Illustrated History* (New York: Vintage, 1994), 282, writing about the year 1864.

35. **fiercer:** Frederick Douglass, "The Fall of Richmond: An Address Delivered in Boston, Massachusetts, on 4 April 1865," *FDP,* ser. 1, 4:73, and Douglass made the same point yet earlier, in "Emancipation, Racism, and the Work before Us: An Address Delivered in Philadelphia, Pennsylvania on 4 December 1863," *FDP,* ser. 1, 4:605 ("the bitter revenge which shall crystalize all over the South"); **cessation:** "Lee's Surrender— Peace," *New York Anglo-African,* Apr. 15, 1865 (published before news of the assassination arrived).

36. **spirit:** Frederick Douglass, "Our Martyred President: An Address Delivered in Rochester, New York, on 15 April 1865," *FDP,* ser. 1, 4:78; **saved:** James Freeman Clarke, "Who Hath Abolished Death," in *Sermons Preached in Boston on the Death of Abraham Lincoln* (Boston: J. E. Tilton, 1865), 101–2.

Scholars have implied that the victors made Reconstruction harsher as a result of Lincoln's assassination. For example, John Fabian Witt writes, "After John Wilkes Booth assassinated Lincoln on April 14, a mere five days after the courtly meeting of military commanders at Appomattox, northern sentiment tipped toward a fierce justice for the postwar world"; see *Lincoln's Code: The Laws of War in American History* (New York: Free Press, 2012), 286–87. William C. Harris writes that "the spirit of vengeance that swept the North following Lincoln's murder greatly complicated postwar reconstruction"; see *With Charity for All: Lincoln and the Restoration of the Union* (Lexington: University Press of Kentucky, 1997), 265. Don E. Fehrenbacher writes that Lincoln's assassination "undoubtedly helped set the emotional tone for a harsher reconstruction policy"; see "The Death of Lincoln," in *Lincoln in Text and Context: Collected Essays* (Stanford, Calif.: Stanford University Press, 1987), 170.

37. **vestige:** "George W. Julian's Journal—The Assassination of Lincoln," *Indiana Magazine of History* 11 (1915), 335 (Apr. 15, 1865, entry); **lesson:** Wendell Phillips, "The Lesson of President Lincoln's Death: A Speech of Wendell Phillips at the Tremont Temple, on Sunday Evening, April 23, 1865," in *Universal Suffrage, and Complete Equality in Citizenship, the Safeguards of Democratic Institutions* (Boston: Rand and Avery, 1865), 16, 14. See also S. W. Magill to "Secretaries A.M.A.," Savannah, Ga., May 8, 1865, #19368, reel 30, AMA: a white missionary working among freedpeople understood Lincoln's death as divine providence, since the crime brought the nation to "a sharper & better tone in regard to the punishment of traitors, and the carrying out of the great measures for which Mr. Lincoln became a martyr."

38. **stricken:** Odell Shepard, ed., *The Journals of Bronson Alcott* (Boston: Little, Brown, 1938), 372 (Apr. 19, 1865, entry); **needed:** John Greenleaf Whittier, "The Question of To-Day," *Liberator,* May 26, 1865; **drive:** Francis Lieber to Henry W. Halleck, New York, Apr. 15, 1865, box 28, Lieber Papers, HL.

Interlude: Peace

1. **fight:** "From the Regiments," letter from Richard H. Black, 3rd U.S.C.T., Fernandina, Fla., *New York Anglo-African,* May 27, 1865; **looks:** Peter Kitts to "Mrs. Case," Fort Jefferson, Fla., Apr. 25, 1865, Samuel F. Case Papers, Duke; **renewed:** Robert Harris to George Whipple, near Norfolk, Va., Apr. 29, 1865, #H1-7036, reel 209, AMA; **smoke:** Norman Leslie Snow to "Dear Friend," Camp near Summit Point, Va., Apr. 18, 1865, Snow Letters, NYSL; **sad, deep:** Rufus Mead Jr. diary, Apr. 17, 19, 1865, Mead Papers, LC; **poor:** John Mowry to Bob Flinigan and Hamilton Mowry, Newburg, Pa., Apr. 25, 1865, Humer Family Correspondence, HL; **talk:** "Rebecca" to Jane Wigglesworth Grew, Boston, May 24, 1865, Grew Correspondence, MHS.

2. **peace:** Benjamin Moran diary, May 22, 1865, Moran Papers, LC; **might:** Charles Francis Adams to Charles Francis Adams Jr., London, May 19, 1865, Letters Received and

Other Loose Papers, Adams Papers, MHS; **desecrators:** Elizabeth Collier diary, Apr. 25, 1865, ts., SHC; **dream:** Emma F. LeConte diary, Apr. 20, 1865, reel 22, SHC-AWD-South.

3. **hope:** Abraham Lincoln, "Last Public Address," Apr. 11, 1865, *CWL,* 8:399.

4. **fondly, blood, malice, just:** Abraham Lincoln, "Second Inaugural Address," Mar. 4, 1865, *CWL,* 8:333; **banner:** "Washington Correspondence," *Christian Recorder,* July 15, 1865. I have found no other interpretation of "malice toward none" and "charity for all" pertaining to African Americans rather than Confederates.

Summer 1865 and Beyond

1. Sarah Browne diary, May 11, 1865 (defiant); Sarah Browne to Albert Browne, Salem, Mass., May 14, 1865, one of two letters of this date (merciful), both BFP.

2. Albert Browne to Wendell Phillips, Hilton Head Island, S.C., Sept. 17, 1865 (stupor); Albert Browne to Wendell Phillips, Hilton Head Island, S.C., July 16, 1865 (genuine), both #328, Phillips Papers, HLH.

3. Albert Browne to Wendell Phillips, Savannah River, Ga., Sept. 8, 1865 (rags, mercy, free); Albert Browne to Wendell Phillips, Hilton Head Island, S.C., Sept. 17, 1865 (case, whip), both #328, Phillips Papers, HLH.

4. Albert Browne to Wendell Phillips, Savannah River, Ga., Sept. 8, 1865 (strong); Albert Browne to Wendell Phillips, Hilton Head Island, S.C., July 16, 1865 (rowdies, martinet, no more, 54th, solution); Albert Browne to Wendell Phillips, Hilton Head Island, S.C., Sept. 17, 1865 (boy), all #328, Phillips Papers, HLH.

Frederick Douglass had earlier noted, "You will need the black man there as a watchman and patrol; and you may need him as a soldier"; see "Emancipation, Racism, and the Work before Us: An Address Delivered in Philadelphia, Pennsylvania on 4 December 1863," *FDP,* ser. 1, 3:605.

5. Albert Browne to Wendell Phillips, Hilton Head Island, S.C., Sept. 17, 1865, #328, Phillips Papers, HLH.

6. Dorman diary, June 6 (trial, monsters, thousand), May 12 (bastard), July 24 (sycophantic, monkey, booby, knave, certainly, heroism), June 18 (martyrs), 1865.

7. Dorman diary, June 3 (complete), July 9 (thunderbolt), Oct. 7 (leave), Nov. 6 (whites, negroes), 1865.

8. Dorman diary, Dec. 22, 1865.

desolate: Otis Keene diary, Jan. 16, 1866, Department of Special Collections and Area Studies, George A. Smathers Libraries, University of Florida, available at ufdc.ufl.edu/UF00076636/00004/3j; **demonstration, hearing:** Gerald Schwartz, ed., *A Woman Doctor's Civil War: Esther Hill Hawks' Diary* (Columbia: University of South Carolina Press, 1984), 234, 243 (Dec. 25, 1865, Jan. 14, 1866, entries).

9. **songs:** Irwin Silber, ed., *Songs of the Civil War* (New York: Bonanza Books, 1960), 131–33; **happy:** Edgar Dinsmore to Carrie Drayton, Saint Andrews Parish, S.C., May 29, 1865, Dinsmore Papers, Duke; **Sundays:** David F. Cushman to Caroline D. Cushman, Martinsburg, Va., Apr. 15, 1865, #250, octavo vol. 1, Civil War Collection, AAS; **next:** John N. Ferguson diary, Apr. 18, 1865, LC; **joy:** Alfred Baker Smith diary, Apr. 29, 1865, NYHS.

10. **principles:** Frederick Douglass, "What to the Slave Is the Fourth of July?: An Address Delivered in Rochester, New York, on 5 July 1852," *FDP,* ser. 1, 2:367, 371.

11. **about:** Abraham Lincoln, "Speech in Independence Hall, Philadelphia, Pennsylvania," Feb. 22, 1861, *CWL,* 4:240.

12. **first, banner:** "Washington Correspondence," *Christian Recorder,* July 15, 1865; **Day, Douglass:** *Celebration by the Colored People's Educational Monument Association in Memory of Abraham Lincoln, on the Fourth of July, 1865* (Washington, D.C.: McGill and Withernow, 1865), 10, 18, 11, 16.

13. **glowing:** "The Freedmen's Celebration," *Christian Recorder,* July 29, 1865; **glorious:** James H. Payne, "Letter from Wilmington," Wilmington, N.C., July 4, 1865, *Christian Recorder,* published July 15, 1865; **horrid:** Emma F. LeConte diary, July 5, 1865, reel 22, SHC-AWD-South; **miserable:** Mrs. William Gaston Delony to Maria Osbourne Delony, Athens, Ga., July 4, 1865, J. W. Gunnison Papers, HL; **Yankees:** Samuel Pickens diary, July 4, 1865, in *Voices from Company D: Diaries by the Greensboro Guards, Fifth Alabama Infantry Regiment, Army of Northern Virginia,* ed. G. Ward Hubbs (Athens: University of Georgia Press, 2003), 390; **ludicrous:** James K. Newton to sister, ca. July 5, 1865, in *A Wisconsin Boy in Dixie: Civil War Letters of James K. Newton,* ed. Stephen E. Ambrose (1961; reprint, Madison: University of Wisconsin Press, 1989), 164; **shadow:** Anna M. Ferris diary, July 4, 1865, Ferris Family Papers, FHL; **seems:** Alonzo A. Carr to unknown, fragment, after July 4, 1865, Cynthia Anthonsen Foster Papers, SL.

14. **north:** see, e.g., Anna Cabot Lowell diary, July 4, 1865, MHS; **Davis:** Sophia E. Perry diary, July 4, 1865, CP; **blessed:** Elizabeth Rogers Mason Cabot diary, July 4, 1865, MHS; **Brown, Harper, Phillips:** "Anti-Slavery Celebration at Framingham, July 4th, 1865," *Liberator,* July 14, 1865.

15. **great:** James Thomas Ward diary, May 30, 1865, Ward Papers, LC; **evidence:** Marian Hooper to Mary Louisa Shaw, Boston, May 28, 1865, in *The Letters of Mrs. Henry Adams, 1865–1883,* ed. Ward Thoron (Boston: Little, Brown, 1936), 10 (referring to Powell by his alias last name, "Paine"); **if this:** John Glenn diary, July 6, 1865, Glenn Papers, MDHS.

16. **Surratt:** Annie G. Dudley Davis diary, June 4, 1865, HL (innocent); Benjamin Brown French, *Witness to the Young Republic: A Yankee's Journal, 1828–1870,* ed. Donald B. Cole and John J. McDonough (Hanover, N.H.: University Press of New England, 1989), 483 (July 8, 1865, entry) (guilty); Anna Cabot Lowell diary, July 8, 1865, MHS (uncertain); **tragedy:** William Owner diary, July 8, 1865, LC; **not worth:** "K.W.R." to Andrew Johnson, Cincinnati, July 8, 1865, *PAJ,* 8:375; **sanguinary:** Anna Cabot Lowell diary, July 8, 1865, MHS.

17. **haste, remember:** Frederick Douglass, "Our Martyred President: An Address Delivered in Rochester, New York, on 15 April 1865," *FDP,* ser. 1, 4:78, 79; **no longer:** Laura Towne to unknown, Saint Helena Island, S.C., Oct. 15, 1865, in *Letters and Diary of Laura M. Towne: Written from the Sea Islands of South Carolina, 1862–1884,* ed. Rupert Sargent Holland (1912; reprint, New York: Negro Universities Press, 1969), 167; **peace, infamous:** Anna M. Ferris diary, July 14, 1865, Sept. 3, 1866 (second entry of this date), Ferris Family Papers, FHL.

18. **do not:** C. Vann Woodward, ed., *Mary Chesnut's Civil War* (1981; reprint, New Haven: Yale University Press, 1993), 834 (July 26, 1865, entry); **contemplate:** Amanda (Edmonds) Chappelear diary, Sept. 6, 1865, Chappelear Papers, ts., ser. D, part 3, reel 8, VHS-SWF; **melancholy:** Sarah Lois Wadley diary, Sept. 26, 1865, Wadley Papers, ser. A, part 3, reel 6, SHC-SWF; **citizen:** John Steele Henderson diary, July 23, 1865, ts., Henderson Papers, ser. J, part 13, reel 25, SHC-RSP.

19. **fighting:** Zillah Brandon diary, July 5, 1865, reel 13, ADAH-AWD-South.

20. **talking:** William Fitzhugh Carter to Hill Carter, Petersburg, Va., Aug. 12, 1865, Shirley Plantation Collection, ser. K, reel 10, CWF-RSP.

21. **old father:** "Memphis Riots and Massacres," 39th Cong., 1st sess., House of Representatives, Report No. 101, July 25, 1866, p. 7.

22. Sarah Browne diary, Apr. 1 (odious), 7 (Kuklux), 1868, BFP; **pardons:** Andrew Johnson, "Fourth Amnesty Proclamation," Dec. 25, 1868, in *The Papers of Andrew Johnson*, vol. 15: *September 1868–April 1869,* ed. Paul H. Bergeron (Knoxville: University of Tennessee Press, 1998), 332; **Klan:** *Testimony Taken by the Joint Select Committee to Inquire into the Condition of Affairs in the Late Insurrectionary States: Miscellaneous and Florida* (Washington, D.C.: Government Printing Office, 1872); **Dorman:** Dorman diary, vol. 5, [ca. 1866], p. 5 (outrages); vol. 7, [ca. 1875–76], p. 311 (new order); vol. 6, [ca. 1873], p. 4 (go away).

23. Dorman diary, vol. 7, Sept. 10–21 (Centennial), 28 (what), Oct. 7 (return), 1876.

24. Dorman diary, vol. 7, Dec. [n.d.], 1877, pp. 435, 451 (lost, imbecility); Sarah Browne diary, Nov. 13 (fear), Dec. 5, 1876 (peace), Feb. 17, 1877 (Hayes), BFP.

25. Albert Browne to Sarah Browne, New York, Feb. 17 (vilest), 24 (showing), 1877, BFP.

26. **second:** Cloe (Whittle) Greene diary, Apr. 19, 1865, reel 4, WM-AWD-South; **renew:** Emma F. LeConte diary, "Thursday" [May 18], 1865, reel 22, SHC-AWD-South; **Jacksonville:** Thomas Wentworth Higginson, "Some War Scenes Revisited," *Atlantic Monthly* 42 (July 1878), 1, 3; Brenda Stevenson, ed., *The Journals of Charlotte Forten Grimké* (New York: Oxford University Press, 1988), 515–37 (November 1885–January 1889 entries).

27. Dorman diary, vol. 8, May 30, 1883, p. 173 (warfare, worse), and [ca. March 1885], p. 279 (slaves); U.S. federal census, Jacksonville, Duval County, Fla., 1800; Jacksonville City Directories, 1876–77 (p. 76), 1878–79 (p. 99), 1882 (p. 79), 1884 (p. 94), 1886 (p. 108), 1887 (p. 87); 1885 Florida state census.

28. **stunned, two, time:** Martha E. Foster Crawford diary, Aug. 22, June 17, 1865, ser. H, part 2, reel 21, Duke-SWF; **negro, cruel:** Lucy Muse (Walton) Fletcher diary, Apr. 25, 1865, and note at back of diary, Fletcher Papers, Duke; **giving:** Ida B. Wells, "Southern Horrors: Lynch Law in All Its Phases" (1892), in *Southern Horrors and Other Writings: The Anti-Lynching Campaign of Ida B. Wells, 1892–1900,* ed. Jacqueline Jones Royster (Boston: Bedford, 1997), 60; **prayed, sincere:** John Johnston, "Personal Reminiscence of the Civil War, 1861–1865," diary transcriptions, Apr. 28, 1865, with 1905 annotation, Johnston Papers, SHC.

29. Sarah Browne diary, Apr. 9, 1866 (God; this was the anniversary of the family's

departure for the south), June 2, 1869 (agony), June 2, 1870 (closing), June 2, 1881 (agony); Albert Browne to "Dear Ones," Brooklyn, N.Y., June 2, 1870 (hour). See also Sarah Browne diary, July 9, 1875; July 9, 1876; June 2, July 9, 1877; July 2, July 9, 1878; July 9, 1879; June 2, 1880, all BFP.

30. Sarah Browne diary, Feb. 12, 1878 (Lincoln), Nov. 3, 1880 (anxieties), July 9 (40th), Sept. 19 (sad), 27 (never), 1881, BFP.

31. Sarah Browne diary, Nov. 15, 1884, BFP.

32. **ominous:** Frederick Douglass, "Abraham Lincoln, a Speech," late December 1865, Douglass Papers, LC, available at hdl.loc.gov/loc.mss/mfd.22015. Douglass's wording of Lincoln's second inaugural is slightly different from that preserved in *CWL,* 8:333.

33. **lived:** Frederick Douglass, "Abraham Lincoln, a Speech," late December 1865, Douglass Papers, LC, available at hdl.loc.gov/loc.mss/mfd.22015. For Douglass's 1866 meeting with Andrew Johnson, see "The Claims of Our Race: An Interview with President Andrew Johnson in Washington, D.C., on 7 February 1866," *FDP,* ser. 1, 4:96–106. That month, Douglass said that "had Mr. Lincoln been living to-day, he would have stood with those who stand foremost, and gone with those who go farthest, in the cause of equal and universal suffrage"; see "The Assassination and Its Lessons: An Address Delivered in Washington, D.C., on 13 February 1866," *FDP,* ser. 1, 4:111.

34. **colored:** Douglass, "Abraham Lincoln, a Speech," late December 1865, Douglass Papers, available at LC, hdl.loc.gov/loc.mss/mfd.22015; **thought back:** George P. Rawick, ed., *The American Slave: A Composite Autobiography,* 18 vols.; supplement ser. 1, 12 vols.; supplement ser. 2, 10 vols. (Westport, Conn.: Greenwood, 1972–79): **wouldn't miss:** vol. 7:114; **can't describe:** suppl. 2, vol. 4, part 3:1271; **fears:** suppl. 1, vol. 8, part 3:1345; **vowing:** suppl. 1, vol. 1:257.

35. **Lincoln lived:** Rawick, *American Slave:* **hurt:** suppl. 1, vol. 1:257; **lots:** vol. 16, part 4:72; **easier:** suppl. 2, vol. 5, part 4:1874; **work:** vol. 7:44; **murdered:** vol. 8:113.

Note on Method

1. **index:** Amos A. Lawrence diary, vol. 8, MHS; **cross-outs, rewordings:** Anna Cabot Lowell diaries, MHS, vols. 195–97.

2. **heard, funeral:** William M. Beauchamp diary, Apr. 15, 19, 1865, Beauchamp Papers, NYSL.

On sentimentality in Civil War–era writings, Drew Glipin Faust writes, "The predominant response to the unexpected carnage was in fact a resolute sentimentality that verged at times on pathos"; see *This Republic of Suffering: Death and the American Civil War* (New York: Alfred A. Knopf, 2008), 194. James M. McPherson writes, "What seems like bathos or platitudes to us were real pathos and convictions for them"; see *What They Fought For, 1861–1865* (1994; reprint, New York: Doubleday, 1995), 13.

3. Flora M. Gardner to Ernest Cushing Richardson, Evanston, Ill., Oct. 27, 1936, administrative file, Orloff M. Dorman Papers, LC; the Library of Congress commented that "the work has doubtful value . . . . It is worth preserving here but belongs far down on the lower shelf" (Thomas P. Martin to "Dr. Jameson," Washington, D.C., July 20,

1937). "The Ruins of Jacksonville, (Fla.)," *National Intelligencer,* Apr. 27, 1863. Because the collection was named for Orloff Dorman, scholars have reasonably taken him to be the diarist; see Richard A. Martin and Daniel L. Schafer, *Jacksonville's Ordeal by Fire: A Civil War History* (Jacksonville: Florida Publishing, 1984), and Schafer, *Thunder on the River: The Civil War in Northeast Florida* (Gainesville: University Press of Florida, 2010). For Dorman's claim, see "Statement and Schedule of Losses" and "Schedule of property of Rodney Dorman at Jacksonville Florida stolen & destroyed & burned by the enemy in March 1863," July 3, 1863, Rodney Dorman, Citizens File, Confederate Papers Relating to Citizens or Business Firms, RG109-NARA, available at Fold3.com.

Essay on Sources

The secondary sources on the Civil War era, Lincoln's assassination, and related topics are voluminous. The sources here represent a sampling of recent and influential works.

Antebellum United States

For **Republican Party ideology,** see the classic and enduring Eric Foner, *Free Soil, Free Labor, Free Men: The Ideology of the Republican Party before the Civil War* (1970; reprint, New York: Oxford University Press, 1995). On **abolitionism,** see Manisha Sinha, *The Slave's Cause: Abolition and the Origins of American Democracy* (New Haven: Yale University Press, 2015); David Brion Davis, *The Problem of Slavery in the Age of Emancipation* (New York: Alfred A. Knopf, 2014); Andrew Delbanco, *The Abolitionist Imagination* (Cambridge, Mass.: Harvard University Press, 2012), including responses by John Stauffer, Manisha Sinha, Darryl Pinckney, and Wilfred M. McClay; Stephen Kantrowitz, *More Than Freedom: Fighting for Black Citizenship in a White Republic, 1829–1889* (New York: Penguin, 2012); Seymour Drescher, *Abolition: A History of Slavery and Antislavery* (New York: Cambridge University Press, 2009); Julie Roy Jeffrey, *Abolitionists Remember: Antislavery Autobiographies and the Unfinished Work of Emancipation* (Chapel Hill: University of North Carolina Press, 2008); Steven Mintz and John Stauffer, eds., *The Problem of Evil: Slavery, Freedom, and the Ambiguities of American Reform* (Amherst: University of Massachusetts Press, 2007); Manisha Sinha, "Coming of Age: The Historiography of Black Abolitionism," in *Prophets of Protest: Reconsidering the History of American Abolitionism,* ed. Timothy Patrick McCarthy and John Stauffer (New York: New Press, 2006), 23–38; John Stauffer, *The Black Hearts of Men: Radical Abolitionists and the Transformation of Race* (Cambridge, Mass.: Harvard University Press, 2002); Victor B. Howard, *Religion and the Radical Republican Movement, 1860–1870* (Lexington: University Press of Kentucky, 1990); James Brewer Stewart, *Holy Warriors: The Abolitionists and American Slavery* (1976; reprint, New York: Hill and Wang, 1997); James M. McPherson, *The Abolitionist Legacy: From Reconstruction to the NAACP* (1975; reprint, Princeton, N.J.: Princeton University Press, 1995); and James M. McPherson, *The Struggle for Equality: Abolitionists and the Negro in the Civil War and Reconstruction* (1964; reprint, Princeton, N.J.: Princeton University Press, 1992). On the song **"John Brown's Body,"** see

John Stauffer and Benjamin Soskis, *The Battle Hymn of the Republic: A Biography of the Song That Marches On* (New York: Oxford University Press, 2013); Franny Nudelman, *John Brown's Body: Slavery, Violence, and the Culture of War* (Chapel Hill: University of North Carolina Press, 2004); and Boyd B. Stutler, "John Brown's Body," *Civil War History* 4 (1958), 251–60. On **proslavery ideology**, see Lacy K. Ford, *Deliver Us from Evil: The Slavery Question in the Old South* (New York: Oxford University Press, 2009); and Manisha Sinha, *The Counter-Revolution of Slavery: Politics and Ideology in Antebellum South Carolina* (Chapel Hill: University of North Carolina Press, 2000). On the idea of slaves as incapable of rebellion, see Michel-Rolph Trouillot, "An Unthinkable History," in Trouillot, *Silencing the Past: Power and the Production of History* (Boston: Beacon Press, 1995), 70–107. On **the toll of slavery**, see Jim Downs, *Sick from Freedom: African-American Illness and Suffering during the Civil War and Reconstruction* (New York: Oxford University Press, 2012); Kidada E. Williams, *They Left Great Marks on Me: African American Testimonies of Racial Violence from Emancipation to World War I* (New York: New York University Press, 2012); and Nell Irvin Painter, "Soul Murder and Slavery: Toward a Fully Loaded Cost Accounting," in *U.S. History as Women's History: New Feminist Essays*, ed. Linda K. Kerber, Alice Kessler-Harris, and Kathryn Kish Sklar (Chapel Hill: University of North Carolina Press, 1995), 15–39. On **dissemblance**, see James C. Scott, *Domination and the Arts of Resistance: Hidden Transcripts* (New Haven: Yale University Press, 1990); and Darlene Clark Hine, "Rape and the Inner Lives of Black Women in the Middle West," *Signs* 14 (1989), 912–20. On **the coming of the Civil War**, see James Oakes, *The Scorpion's Sting: Antislavery and the Coming of the Civil War* (New York: W. W. Norton, 2014); Michael E. Woods, "What Twenty-First-Century Historians Have Said about the Causes of Disunion: A Civil War Sesquicentennial Review of the Recent Literature," *Journal of American History* 99 (2012), 415–39; Adam Goodheart, *1861: The Civil War Awakening* (New York: Alfred A. Knopf, 2011); Elizabeth R. Varon, *Disunion! The Coming of the American Civil War, 1789–1859* (Chapel Hill: University of North Carolina Press, 2008); and Charles B. Dew, *Apostles of Disunion: Southern Secession Commissioners and the Causes of the Civil War* (Charlottesville: University Press of Virginia, 2001).

Abraham Lincoln

On **Lincoln and slavery**, see especially Eric Foner, *The Fiery Trial: Abraham Lincoln and American Slavery* (New York: W. W. Norton, 2010). And see John Burt, *Lincoln's Tragic Pragmatism: Lincoln, Douglas, and Moral Conflict* (Cambridge, Mass.: Harvard University Press, 2013); Brian R. Dirck, *Abraham Lincoln and White America* (Lawrence: University Press of Kansas, 2012); Henry Louis Gates Jr., ed., *Lincoln on Race and Slavery* (Princeton, N.J.: Princeton University Press, 2009); James Oliver Horton, "Naturally Anti-Slavery: Lincoln, Race, and the Complexity of American Liberty," in *The Best American History Essays on Lincoln*, ed. Sean Wilentz (New York: Palgrave Macmillan, 2009); George M. Fredrickson, *Big Enough to Be Inconsistent: Abraham Lincoln Confronts Slavery and Race* (Cambridge, Mass.: Harvard University Press, 2008); Manisha Sinha, "Allies for Emancipation? Lincoln and Black Abolitionists," in *Our Lincoln: New*

Perspectives on Lincoln and His World, ed. Eric Foner (New York: W. W. Norton, 2008), 167–96; James Oakes, *The Radical and the Republican: Frederick Douglass, Abraham Lincoln, and the Triumph of Antislavery Politics* (New York: W. W. Norton, 2007); Lerone Bennett Jr., *Forced into Glory: Abraham Lincoln's White Dream* (1999; reprint, Chicago: Johnson, 2007); James M. McPherson, *Abraham Lincoln and the Second American Revolution* (New York: Oxford University Press, 1991); and Benjamin Quarles, *Lincoln and the Negro* (New York: Oxford University Press, 1962). On **Lincoln and civil liberties,** see William A. Blair, *With Malice toward Some: Treason and Loyalty in the Civil War Era* (Chapel Hill: University of North Carolina Press, 2014); John Fabian Witt, *Lincoln's Code: The Laws of War in American History* (New York: Free Press, 2012); Mark E. Neely Jr., *Lincoln and the Triumph of the Nation: Constitutional Conflict in the American Civil War* (Chapel Hill: University of North Carolina Press, 2011); and Mark E. Neely Jr., *The Fate of Liberty: Abraham Lincoln and Civil Liberties* (New York: Oxford University Press, 1991). **Lincoln's second inaugural address** is treated in works on Lincoln and slavery (see above) and Lincoln biographies (see below); I have found none that interpret Lincoln's ideas about malice and charity as pertaining to African Americans rather than Confederates. On the speech, see especially Ronald C. White Jr., *Lincoln's Greatest Speech: The Second Inaugural* (New York: Simon and Schuster, 2002); Mark A. Noll, *America's God: From Jonathan Edwards to Abraham Lincoln* (New York: Oxford University Press, 2002). And see James Tackach, *Lincoln's Moral Vision: The Second Inaugural Address* (Jackson: University of Mississippi Press, 2002); Nicholas Parrillo, "Lincoln's Calvinist Transformation: Emancipation and War," *Civil War History* 46 (2000), 227–53; Allen C. Guelzo, *Abraham Lincoln, Redeemer President* (Grand Rapids: William B. Eerdmans, 1999); Garry Wills, "Lincoln's Greatest Speech," *Atlantic,* September 1, 1999, available at theatlantic.com; and Ronald C. White Jr., "Lincoln's Sermon on the Mount: The Second Inaugural," in *Religion and the American Civil War,* ed. Randall M. Miller et al. (New York: Oxford University Press, 1998), 208–25. See also Richard Carwardine, "Lincoln's Religion," in *Our Lincoln: New Perspectives on Lincoln and His World,* ed. Eric Foner (New York: W. W. Norton, 2008), 223–48; and Glen E. Thurow, "Abraham Lincoln and American Political Religion," in *The Historian's Lincoln: Pseudohistory, Psychohistory, and History,* ed. Gabor S. Boritt (Urbana: University of Illinois Press, 1988), 125–43. On **Lincoln's plans for Reconstruction,** see William C. Harris, *With Charity for All: Lincoln and the Restoration of the Union* (Lexington: University Press of Kentucky, 1997); and LaWanda Cox, *Lincoln and Black Freedom: A Study in Presidential Leadership* (Columbia: University of South Carolina Press, 1981).

The Civil War

On **the Civil War era,** see Bruce Levine, *The Fall of the House of Dixie: The Civil War and the Social Revolution That Transformed the South* (New York: Random House, 2013); Allen C. Guelzo, *Fateful Lightning: A New History of the Civil War and Reconstruction* (New York: Oxford University Press, 2012); Gary W. Gallagher, *The Union War* (Cambridge, Mass.: Harvard University Press, 2011); Harry S. Stout, *Upon the Altar of the*

Nation: A Moral History of the Civil War (New York: Viking Penguin, 2006); Gary W.
Gallagher, *The Confederate War* (Cambridge, Mass.: Harvard University Press, 1997);
James M. McPherson, *Battle Cry of Freedom: The Civil War Era* (New York: Oxford
University Press, 1988); James M. McPherson, *Ordeal by Fire: The Civil War and
Reconstruction* (New York: Alfred A. Knopf, 1982); James M. McPherson, *The Negro's
Civil War: How American Blacks Felt and Acted during the War for the Union* (1965;
reprint, New York: Random House, 2008); and Benjamin Quarles, *The Negro in the Civil
War* (1953; reprint, New York: Da Capo, 1989). See also E. B. Long and Barbara Long,
The Civil War Day by Day: An Almanac, 1861–1865 (New York: Doubleday, 1971). On
Civil War soldiers, see William A. Dobak, *Freedom by the Sword: The U.S. Colored Troops,
1862–1867* (Washington, D.C.: Center of Military History, 2011); Thomas J. Ward Jr., "Enemy
Combatants: Black Soldiers in Confederate Prisons," *Army History* 78 (Winter 2011),
32–41; Chandra Manning, *What This Cruel War Was Over: Soldiers, Slavery, and the
Civil War* (New York: Alfred A. Knopf, 2007); Martin H. Blatt et al., eds., *Hope and
Glory: Essays on the Legacy of the 54th Massachusetts Regiment* (Amherst: University of
Massachusetts Press, 2001); William C. Davis, *Lincoln's Men: How President Lincoln
Became Father to an Army and a Nation* (New York: Free Press, 1999); James M.
McPherson, *For Cause and Comrades: Why Men Fought in the Civil War* (New York:
Oxford University Press, 1997); James M. McPherson, *What They Fought For, 1861–1865*
(1994; reprint, New York: Doubleday, 1995); Joseph T. Glatthaar, *Forged in Battle: The
Civil War Alliance of Black Soldiers and White Officers* (New York: Free Press, 1990); Ira
Berlin et al., eds., *The Black Military Experience* (New York: Cambridge University Press,
1982); Dudley Taylor Cornish, *The Sable Arm: Negro Troops in the Union Army, 1861–
1865* (1956; reprint, Lawrence: University Press of Kansas, 1987); Bell Irvin Wiley, *The Life
of Billy Yank: The Common Soldier of the Union* (1952; reprint, Baton Rouge: Louisiana
State University Press, 2008); and Bell Irvin Wiley, *The Life of Johnny Reb: The Common
Soldier of the Confederacy* (1943; reprint, Baton Rouge: Louisiana State University Press,
2008). On **combat stress,** see Diane Miller Sommerville, "'A Burden Too Heavy to Bear':
War Trauma, Suicide, and Confederate Soldiers," *Civil War History* 59 (2013), 453–91;
Diane Miller Sommerville, "'Will They Ever Be Able to Forget?' Confederate Soldiers in
the Defeated South," in *Weirding the War: Stories from the Civil War's Ragged Edges,* ed.
Stephen Berry (Athens: University of Georgia Press, 2011), 321–39; Bertram Wyatt-Brown,
"Honor Chastened," in Brown, *The Shaping of Southern Culture: Honor, Grace, and
War, 1760s–1890s* (Chapel Hill: University of North Carolina Press, 2001), 255–69; Eric T.
Dean Jr., *Shook over Hell: Post-Traumatic Stress, Vietnam, and the Civil War* (Cambridge,
Mass: Harvard University Press, 1997); and Drew Gilpin Faust, "Christian Soldiers: The
Meaning of Revivalism in the Confederate Army," in Faust, *Southern Stories: Slaveholders
in Peace and War* (Columbia: University of Missouri Press, 1992), 88–109. On **Washington,
D.C., during the Civil War era,** see Kate Masur, *An Example for All the Land: Emancipa-
tion and the Struggle over Equality in Washington, D.C.* (Chapel Hill: University of North
Carolina Press, 2012); and Robert Harrison, *Washington during Civil War and Reconstruction: Race and Radicalism* (New York: Cambridge University Press, 2011). On **religion and the**

Civil War, see Timothy L. Wesley, *The Politics of Faith during the Civil War* (Baton Rouge: Louisiana State University Press, 2013); Sean A. Scott, *A Visitation of God: Northern Civilians Interpret the Civil War* (New York: Oxford University Press, 2011); George C. Rable, *God's Almost Chosen Peoples: A Religious History of the American Civil War* (Chapel Hill: University of North Carolina Press, 2010); Nicholas Guyatt, *Providence and the Invention of the United States, 1607–1876* (New York: Cambridge University Press, 2007); Mark A. Noll, *The Civil War as a Theological Crisis* (Chapel Hill: University of North Carolina Press, 2006); Gary Dorrien, *The Making of American Liberal Theology: Imagining Progressive Religion, 1805–1900* (Louisville, Ky.: Westminster John Knox Press, 2001); and Steven E. Woodworth, *While God Is Marching On: The Religious World of Civil War Soldiers* (Lawrence: University Press of Kansas, 2001). On **civil religion,** see Robert N. Bellah, "Civil Religion in America," *Daedalus* 96 (Winter 1967), 1–21. On **women and the Civil War,** see Stephanie McCurry, *Confederate Reckoning: Power and Politics in the Civil War South* (Cambridge, Mass.: Harvard University Press, 2010); Thavolia Glymph, *Out of the House of Bondage: The Transformation of the Plantation Household* (New York: Cambridge University Press, 2008); Nina Silber, *Daughters of the Union: Northern Women Fight the Civil War* (Cambridge, Mass.: Harvard University Press, 2005); and Drew Gilpin Faust, *Mothers of Invention: Women of the Slaveholding South in the American Civil War* (Chapel Hill: University of North Carolina Press, 1996). On **nonslaveholding white southerners,** see Stephanie McCurry, *Confederate Reckoning: Power and Politics in the Civil War South* (Cambridge, Mass.: Harvard University Press, 2010); Samuel C. Hyde Jr., "Plain Folk Reconsidered: Historiographical Ambiguity in Search of Definition," *Journal of Southern History* 71 (2005), 803–30; Adam Rothman, "The 'Slave Power' in the United States, 1783–1865," in *Ruling America: A History of Wealth and Power in a Democracy,* ed. Steve Fraser and Gary Gerstle (Cambridge, Mass.: Harvard University Press, 2005), 64–91; Stephanie McCurry, *Masters of Small Worlds: Yeoman Households, Gender Relations, and the Political Culture of the Antebellum South Carolina Low Country* (New York: Oxford University Press, 1995); Charles C. Bolton, *Poor Whites of the Antebellum South: Tenants and Laborers in Central North Carolina and Northeast Mississippi* (Durham, N.C.: Duke University Press, 1994); Daniel W. Crofts, *Reluctant Confederates: Upper South Unionists in the Secession Crisis* (Chapel Hill: University of North Carolina Press, 1989); Steven Hahn, *The Roots of Southern Populism: Yeoman Farmers and the Transformation of the Georgia Upcountry* (New York: Oxford University Press, 1983); and Eugene D. Genovese, "Yeoman Farmers in a Slaveholders' Democracy," *Agricultural History* 49 (1975), 331–42. On **Herrenvolk democracy,** see George M. Fredrickson, *The Black Image in the White Mind: The Debate on Afro-American Character and Destiny, 1817–1914* (New York: Harper and Row, 1971). On **emancipation,** see James Oakes, *Freedom National: The Destruction of Slavery in the United States, 1861–1865* (New York: W. W. Norton, 2013); Louis P. Masur, *Lincoln's Hundred Days: The Emancipation Proclamation and the War for the Union* (Cambridge, Mass.: Harvard University Press, 2012); Steven Hahn, *The Political Worlds of Slavery and Freedom* (Cambridge, Mass.: Harvard University Press, 2009); Edna Greene Medford,

"Imagined Promises, Bitter Realities: African Americans and the Meaning of the Emancipation Proclamation," in *The Emancipation Proclamation: Three Views*, ed. Harold Holzer et al. (Baton Rouge: Louisiana State University Press, 2006), 1–47; Allen C. Guelzo, *Lincoln's Emancipation Proclamation: The End of Slavery in America* (New York: Simon and Schuster, 2004); and Ira Berlin et al., *Slaves No More: Three Essays on Emancipation and the Civil War* (New York: Cambridge University Press, 1992). On **the Copperheads,** see Jennifer L. Weber, "Lincoln's Critics: The Copperheads," *Journal of the Abraham Lincoln Association* 32 (Winter 2011), 33–47; and Jennifer L. Weber, *Copperheads: The Rise and Fall of Lincoln's Opponents in the North* (New York: Oxford University Press, 2006). See also Sidney Blumenthal, "Romanticizing the Villains of the Civil War," *Atlantic*, July 22, 2013, available at theatlantic.com. On **colonization,** see Eric Foner, "Lincoln and Colonization," in *Our Lincoln: New Perspectives on Lincoln and His World*, ed. Foner (New York: W. W. Norton, 2008), 135–66; Eric Burin, *Slavery and the Peculiar Solution: A History of the American Colonization Society* (Gainesville: University Press of Florida, 2005); Claude A. Clegg III, *The Price of Liberty: African Americans and the Making of Liberia* (Chapel Hill: University of North Carolina Press, 2004); and Bruce Dorsey, *Reforming Men and Women: Gender in the Antebellum City* (Ithaca, N.Y.: Cornell University Press, 2002). On **Great Britain during the Civil War,** see Amanda Foreman, *A World on Fire: Britain's Crucial Role in the American Civil War* (New York: Random House, 2010); and J. R. Pole, *Abraham Lincoln and the Working Classes of Britain* (London: English Speaking Union, 1912).

The End of the Civil War

On **the end of the Confederacy,** see Stephanie McCurry, *Confederate Reckoning: Power and Politics in the Civil War South* (Cambridge, Mass.: Harvard University Press, 2010); Paul F. Paskoff, "Measures of War: A Quantitative Examination of the Civil War's Destructiveness in the Confederacy," *Civil War History* 54 (2008), 35–62; Jason Phillips, *Diehard Rebels: The Confederate Culture of Invincibility* (Athens: University of Georgia Press, 2007); Anne Sarah Rubin, *A Shattered Nation: The Rise and Fall of the Confederacy, 1861–1868* (Chapel Hill: University of North Carolina Press, 2005); Wolfgang Schivelbusch, *The Culture of Defeat: On National Trauma, Mourning, and Recovery,* trans. Jefferson Chase (London: Granta, 2001); Stephen V. Ash, *When the Yankees Came: Conflict and Chaos in the Occupied South, 1861–1865* (Chapel Hill: University of North Carolina Press, 1995); Drew Gilpin Faust, "Altars of Sacrifice: Confederate Women and the Narratives of War," *Journal of American History* 76 (1990), 1200–1228; Gaines M. Foster, *Ghosts of the Confederacy: Defeat, the Lost Cause, and the Emergence of the New South* (New York: Oxford University Press, 1987); and David Herbert Donald, "A Generation of Defeat," in *From the Old South to the New: Essays on the Transitional South,* ed. Walter J. Fraser Jr. and Winfred B. Moore Jr. (Westport, Conn.: Greenwood, 1981), 3–20. On **the fall of Richmond and Confederate surrender,** see Elizabeth R. Varon, *Appomattox: Victory, Defeat, and Freedom at the End of the Civil War* (New York: Oxford University Press, 2014); Joan Waugh, "'I Only Knew What Was in My Mind': Ulysses S.

Grant and the Meaning of Appomattox," *Journal of the Civil War Era* 2 (2012), 307–36; Nelson Lankford, *Richmond Burning: The Last Days of the Confederate Capital* (New York: Viking Penguin, 2002); Jay Winik, *April 1865: The Month That Saved America* (New York: HarperCollins, 2001); J. Tracy Power, *Lee's Miserables: Life in the Army of Northern Virginia from the Wilderness to Appomattox* (Chapel Hill: University of North Carolina Press, 1998); and Ernest B. Furgurson, *Ashes of Glory: Richmond at War* (New York: Alfred A. Knopf, 1996). On **Lincoln in Richmond,** see Richard Wightman Fox, "'A Death-Shock to Chivalry, and a Mortal Wound to Caste': The Story of Tad and Abraham Lincoln in Richmond," *Journal of the Abraham Lincoln Association* 33 (Summer 2012), 1–19; and Richard Wightman Fox, "Lincoln's Practice of Republicanism: Striding through Richmond, April 4, 1865," in *The Living Lincoln,* ed. Thomas A. Horrocks et al. (Carbondale: Southern Illinois University Press, 2011), 131–51. On **the Sherman-Johnston negotiations,** see Mark L. Bradley, *This Astounding Close: The Road to Bennett Place* (Chapel Hill: University of North Carolina Press, 2000); and Craig L. Symonds, *Joseph E. Johnston: A Civil War Biography* (New York: W. W. Norton, 1992). See also Eric Rauchway, "What Did Lincoln Say to Sherman at City Point?" Chronicle Blog Network, *Chronicle of Higher Education,* April 9, 2008, chronicle.com/blognetwork/edgeofthe west/2008/04/09/what-did-lincoln-say-to-sherman-at-city-point. On **oaths of allegiance,** see Bradley R. Clampitt, "'Not Intended to Dispossess Females': Southern Women and Civil War Amnesty," *Civil War History* 56 (2010), 325–49; and Harold Melvin Hyman, *Era of the Oath: Northern Loyalty Tests during the Civil War and Reconstruction* (Philadelphia: University of Pennsylvania Press, 1954). On **the post-Appomattox nation,** see Gregory P. Downs, *After Appomattox: Military Occupation and the Ends of War* (Cambridge, Mass.: Harvard University Press, 2015); and Michael Vorenberg, *The Appomattox Myth: Struggling to Find the End of the American Civil War,* forthcoming. On **the departure of freedpeople and the search for family,** see Sydney Nathans, *To Free a Family: The Journey of Mary Walker* (Cambridge, Mass.: Harvard University Press, 2012); Yael A. Sternhell, *Routes of War: The World of Movement in the Confederate South* (Cambridge, Mass.: Harvard University Press, 2012); Heather Andrea Williams, *Help Me to Find My People: The African American Search for Family Lost in Slavery* (Chapel Hill: University of North Carolina Press, 2012); and Leon F. Litwack, *Been in the Storm So Long: The Aftermath of Slavery* (New York: Alfred A. Knopf, 1979). On **the Grand Review,** see Gary W. Gallagher, *The Union War* (Cambridge, Mass.: Harvard University Press, 2011). On **the Fourth of July,** see Matthew Dennis, *Red, White, and Blue Letter Days: An American Calendar* (Ithaca, N.Y.: Cornell University Press, 2002); and Leonard I. Sweet, "The Fourth of July and Black Americans in the Nineteenth Century: Northern Leadership Opinion within the Context of the Black Experience," *Journal of Negro History* 61 (1976), 256–75.

The Assassination

By a 2011 count, there were fewer than ten books about Lincoln's assassination written by professional historians out of ten dozen such books (Edward Steers Jr., review of Bill

O'Reilly and Martin Dugard, *Killing Lincoln: The Shocking Assassination That Changed America Forever,* in *North and South: The Official Magazine of the Civil War Society* 13 [November 2011], 61). On **Lincoln's assassination,** see Richard Wightman Fox, *Lincoln's Body: A Cultural History* (New York: W. W. Norton, 2015); Thomas A. Bogar, *Backstage at the Lincoln Assassination: The Untold Story of the Actors and Stagehands at Ford's Theatre* (Washington, D.C.: Regnery History, 2013); Frederick Hatch, *Protecting President Lincoln: The Security Effort, the Thwarted Plots and the Disaster at Ford's Theatre* (Jefferson, N.C.: McFarland, 2011); Harold Holzer et al., eds., *The Lincoln Assassination: Crime and Punishment, Myth and Memory* (New York: Fordham University Press, 2010); Edward Steers Jr., *The Lincoln Assassination Encyclopedia* (New York: Harper Perennial, 2010); James L. Swanson, *Manhunt: The Twelve-Day Chase for Lincoln's Killer* (New York: HarperCollins, 2006); Thomas Goodrich and Debra Goodrich, *The Darkest Dawn: Lincoln, Booth, and the Great American Tragedy* (Bloomington: Indiana University Press, 2005); Michael W. Kauffman, *American Brutus: John Wilkes Booth and the Lincoln Conspiracies* (New York: Random House, 2004); Elizabeth D. Leonard, *Lincoln's Avengers: Justice, Revenge, and Reunion after the Civil War* (New York: W. W. Norton, 2004); Edward Steers Jr., *Blood on the Moon: The Assassination of Abraham Lincoln* (Lexington: University Press of Kentucky, 2001); Richard Bak, *The Day Lincoln Was Shot: An Illustrated Chronicle* (Dallas, Tex.: Taylor, 1998); Carolyn L. Harrell, *When the Bells Tolled for Lincoln: Southern Reaction to the Assassination* (Macon, Ga.: Mercer University Press, 1997); Don E. Fehrenbacher, "The Death of Lincoln," in Fehrenbacher, *Lincoln in Text and Context: Collected Essays* (Stanford, Calif.: Stanford University Press, 1987), 164–77; Dorothy Meserve Kunhardt and Philip B. Kunhardt Jr., *Twenty Days: A Narrative in Text and Pictures of the Assassination of Abraham Lincoln and the Twenty Days and Nights That Followed* (North Hollywood, Calif.: Newcastle, 1985); William Hanchett, *The Lincoln Murder Conspiracies* (Urbana: University of Illinois Press, 1983); Thomas Reed Turner, *Beware the People Weeping: Public Opinion and the Assassination of Abraham Lincoln* (Baton Rouge: Louisiana State University Press, 1982); and George S. Bryan, *The Great American Myth: The True Story of Lincoln's Murder* (1940; reprint, Chicago: Americana House, 1990). See also Bill O'Reilly and Martin Dugard, *Killing Lincoln: The Shocking Assassination That Changed America Forever* (New York: Henry Holt, 2011), in tandem with Edward Steers Jr.'s review in *North and South: The Official Magazine of the Civil War Society* 13 (November 2011), 61–63. And see the in-progress online collection of primary sources (created too late for my research), "Remembering Lincoln: A Digital Collection of Responses to His Assassination," Ford's Theatre, Washington, D.C., fords .org/remembering-lincoln.

For books on other topics that treat the assassination in some depth, see John McKee Barr, *Loathing Lincoln: An American Tradition from the Civil War to the Present* (Baton Rouge: Louisiana State University Press, 2014); John R. Neff, *Honoring the Civil War Dead: Commemoration and the Problem of Reconciliation* (Lawrence: University Press of Kansas, 2005); William C. Harris, *Lincoln's Last Months* (Cambridge, Mass.: Harvard University Press, 2004); Barry Schwartz, *Abraham Lincoln and the Forge of National*

Memory (Chicago: University of Chicago Press, 2000); Merrill D. Peterson, *Lincoln in American Memory* (New York: Oxford University Press, 1994); and Michael Davis, *The Image of Lincoln in the South* (Knoxville: University of Tennessee Press, 1971).

For biographies and other books about Lincoln that treat the assassination briefly, see Eric Foner, *The Fiery Trial: Abraham Lincoln and American Slavery* (New York: W. W. Norton, 2010); Catherine Clinton, *Mrs. Lincoln: A Life* (New York: HarperCollins, 2009); Ronald C. White Jr., *A. Lincoln: A Biography* (New York: Random House, 2009); Michael Burlingame, *Abraham Lincoln: A Life,* 2 vols. (Baltimore: Johns Hopkins University Press, 2008); Richard Carwardine, *Lincoln: A Life of Purpose and Power* (New York: Alfred A. Knopf, 2006); Doris Kearns Goodwin, *Team of Rivals: The Political Genius of Abraham Lincoln* (New York: Simon and Schuster, 2005); William E. Gienapp, *Abraham Lincoln and Civil War America* (New York: Oxford University Press, 2002); and David Herbert Donald, *Lincoln* (New York: Simon and Schuster, 1995).

For related articles, see Chandra Manning, "The Shifting Terrain of Attitudes toward Abraham Lincoln and Emancipation," *Journal of the Abraham Lincoln Association* 34 (Winter 2013), 18–39; Thomas P. Lowry, "Not Everybody Mourned Lincoln's Death," in *The Lincoln Assassination: Crime and Punishment, Myth and Memory,* ed. Harold Holzer et al. (New York: Fordham University Press, 2010), 95–114; Justin Carisio, "'Every Soul Shudders': Delaware Reacts to Lincoln's Death," *Delaware History* 32 (2008), 171–86; Steven J. Ramold, "'We Should Have Killed Them All': The Violent Reaction of Union Soldiers to the Assassination of Abraham Lincoln," *Journal of Illinois History* 10 (2007), 27–48; Jeffry D. Wert, "'A Silent Gloom Fell upon Us Like a Pall,'" *Civil War Times* 44 (January 2006), 50–56; Roger Platizky, "Abraham Lincoln's Assassination in Victorian England and America," *Lamar Journal of the Humanities* 27 (2002), 23–31; Roger L. Rosentreter, "'Our Lincoln Is Dead,'" *Michigan History Magazine* 84 (March/April 2000), 28–39; James Marten, "'I Think It's Just as Mean as It Can Be': Northern Children Respond to Lincoln's Assassination," *Lincoln Herald* 101 (1999), 117–21; Trevor K. Plante, "The Shady Side of the Family Tree: Civil War Union Court-Martial Case Files," *Prologue* 30 (Winter 1998), archives.gov/publications/prologue/1998/winter/union-court-mar tials.html; Mark H. Dunkelman, "Alas! He Is Gone," *Lincoln Herald* 94 (1992), 46–48; Barry Schwartz, "Mourning and the Making of a Sacred Symbol: Durkheim and the Lincoln Assassination," *Social Forces* 70 (1991), 343–64; Barry Schwartz, "The Reconstruction of Abraham Lincoln," in *Collective Remembering,* ed. David Middleton and Derek Edwards (London: Sage, 1990), 81–107; John M. Barr, "The Tyrannicide's Reception: Responses in Texas to Lincoln's Assassination," *Lincoln Herald* 91 (1989), 58–64; Don E. Fehrenbacher, "The Anti-Lincoln Tradition," in Fehrenbacher, *Lincoln in Text and Context: Collected Essays* (Stanford, Calif.: Stanford University Press, 1987), 197–213; R. L. Reid, "Louisiana and Lincoln's Assassination: Reactions in a Southern State," *Southern Historian* 6 (1985), 20–27; Allan Peskin, "Putting the 'Baboon' To Rest: Observations of a Radical Republican on Lincoln's Funeral Train," *Lincoln Herald* 79 (1977), 26–28; Lowell H. Harrison, "An Australian Reaction to Lincoln's Death," *Lincoln Herald* 78 (1976), 12–17; Kathe van Winden, "The Assassination of Abraham Lincoln: Its Effect in California," *Journal of the*

West 4 (April 1965), 211–30; James P. Jones, "'Lincoln's Avengers': The Assassination and Sherman's Army," *Lincoln Herald* 64 (1962), 185–90; Martin Abbott, "Southern Reaction to Lincoln's Assassination," *Abraham Lincoln Quarterly* 7 (1952), 111–27; Bell Irvin Wiley, "Billy Yank and Abraham Lincoln," *Abraham Lincoln Quarterly* 6 (1950), 103–20; and [Editorial Department], "The Assassination of Abraham Lincoln," *Annals of Iowa* 4 (1900), 467–68.

On **Ford's Theatre,** see Patrick O'Brien, "Ford's Theatre and the White House," *White House History* 30 [n.d.], 23–33. On **Henry Rathbone and Clara Harris,** see Mark E. Neely Jr., *The Abraham Lincoln Encyclopedia* (New York: McGraw Hill, 1982), 256–57; and [no author], "Major Rathbone and Miss Harris: Guests of the Lincolns in the Ford's Theatre Box," *Lincoln Lore* 1602 (August 1971), 1–3; and see Thomas Mallon's wonderful historical novel *Henry and Clara* (New York: Houghton Mifflin, 1994). On **William Seward,** see Walter Stahr, *Seward: Lincoln's Indispensable Man* (New York: Simon and Schuster, 2012). On **the trial and fates of the conspirators,** see Elizabeth D. Leonard, *Lincoln's Avengers: Justice, Revenge, and Reunion after the Civil War* (New York: W. W. Norton, 2004); and Elizabeth D. Leonard, "Mary Surratt and the Plot to Assassinate Abraham Lincoln," in *The War Was You and Me: Civilians in the American Civil War,* ed. Joan E. Cashin (Princeton, N.J.: Princeton University Press, 2002), 286–309. Arguing for an official Confederate conspiracy, see William A. Tidwell, *April '65: Confederate Covert Action in the American Civil War* (Kent, Ohio: Kent State University Press, 1995), and William A. Tidwell et al., *Come Retribution: The Confederate Secret Service and the Assassination of Lincoln* (Jackson: University Press of Mississippi, 1988). On **the 1861 attempt to assassinate Lincoln,** see Daniel Stashower, *The Hour of Peril: The Secret Plot to Murder Lincoln before the Civil War* (New York: Minotaur, 2013).

On **communication and rumors,** see Richard R. John, *Network Nation: Inventing American Telecommunications* (Cambridge, Mass.: Harvard University Press, 2010); Daniel Walker Howe, *What Hath God Wrought: The Transformation of America, 1815–1848* (New York: Oxford University Press, 2007); Alice Fahs, "Northern and Southern Worlds of Print," in *Perspectives in American Book History,* ed. Scott Casper et al. (Amherst: University of Massachusetts Press, 2002), 195–222; and Jean-Noël Kapferer, *Rumors: Uses, Interpretations, and Images* (New Brunswick: Transaction, 1990). On **the telegraph,** see David Hochfelder, *The Telegraph in America, 1832–1920* (Baltimore: Johns Hopkins University Press, 2012); Robert Luther Thompson, *Wiring a Continent: The History of the Telegraph Industry in the United States* (Princeton, N.J.: Princeton University Press, 1947); and David Homer Bates, *Lincoln in the Telegraph Office: Recollections of the United States Military Telegraph Corps during the Civil War* (New York: Century, 1907). On **imagined universality,** see Benedict Anderson, *Imagined Communities: Reflections on the Origin and Spread of Nationalism,* rev. ed. (New York: Verso, 1991). On **reading faces in the nineteenth century,** see Karen Halttunen, *Confidence Men and Painted Women: A Study of Middle-Class Culture in America, 1830–1870* (New Haven: Yale University Press, 1982), 153–90. On **assassination sermons,** see David B. Chesebrough, *"No Sorrow Like Our Sorrow": Northern Protestant Ministers and the Assassination of Lincoln* (Kent,

Ohio: Kent State University Press, 1994); Rollin W. Quimby, "Lincoln's Character as Described in Sermons at the Time of His Death," *Lincoln Herald* 69 (1967), 178–86 (with an objectionable last line excoriating the radical Republicans); Charles J. Stewart, "The Pulpit and the Assassination of Lincoln," *Quarterly Journal of Speech* 50 (1964), 299–307; Jay Monaghan, "An Analysis of Lincoln's Funeral Sermons," *Indiana Magazine of History* 41 (1945), 31–44; and Chester Forrester Dunham, *The Attitude of the Northern Clergy toward the South, 1860–1865* (Toledo, Ohio: Gray, 1942). On **Easter decorations,** see Leigh Eric Schmidt, "The Easter Parade: Piety, Fashion, and Display," *Religion and American Culture* 4 (1994), 135–64. On **memorabilia and relics,** see Teresa Barnett, *Sacred Relics: Pieces of the Past in Nineteenth-Century America* (Chicago: University of Chicago Press, 2013); Ellen Gruber Garvey, *Writing with Scissors: American Scrapbooks from the Civil War to the Harlem Renaissance* (New York: Oxford University Press, 2013); Michael DeGruccio, "Letting the War Slip through Our Hands: Material Culture and the Weakness of Words in the Civil War Era," in *Weirding the War: Stories from the Civil War's Ragged Edges,* ed. Stephen Berry (Athens: University of Georgia Press, 2011), 15–35; Helen R. Purtle, "Lincoln Memorabilia in the Medical Museum of the Armed Forces Institute of Pathology," *Bulletin of the History of Medicine* 32 (1958), 68–74; and Matthew Dennis, *American Relics and the Politics of Public Memory,* forthcoming. On **Lincoln's birthday,** see Matthew Dennis, *Red, White, and Blue Letter Days: An American Calendar* (Ithaca, N.Y.: Cornell University Press, 2002). On **the assassination of President James A. Garfield,** see Candice Millard, *Destiny of the Republic: A Tale of Madness, Medicine, and the Murder of a President* (New York: Doubleday, 2011); on **the assassination of President John F. Kennedy,** see Martha Hodes, "'Where Were You When You Heard?'" in *The Day Kennedy Died: Fifty Years Later: LIFE Remembers the Man and the Moment* (New York: Time Home Entertainment, 2013), 96–99; Ellen Fitzpatrick, *Letters to Jackie: Condolences for a Grieving Nation* (New York: HarperCollins, 2010); John B. Jovich, *Reflections on JFK's Assassination: 250 Famous Americans Remember November 22, 1963* (Kensington, Md.: Woodbine House, 1968); William Manchester, *The Death of a President: November 20–November 25, 1863* (New York: Harper and Row, 1967); Theodore H. White, *The Making of the President 1964* (New York: Atheneum, 1965); and "Walter Cronkite Announces Death of JFK," youtube.com/watch?v=RE-TCzIHrLI. For **September 11, 2001, headlines,** see "Today's Front Pages, Wednesday September 12, 2001," Newseum.org, newseum.org/todaysfrontpages/default_archive.asp?fpArchive=091201.

Death and Mourning

On **death in the Civil War,** see especially Drew Gilpin Faust, *This Republic of Suffering: Death and the American Civil War* (New York: Alfred A. Knopf, 2008). And see Ian Finseth, "The Civil War Dead: Realism and the Problem of Anonymity," *American Literary History* 25 (2013), 535–62; J. David Book, "'Death Is Every Where Present,'" *Vermont History* 79 (2011), 26–57; Mark S. Schantz, *Awaiting the Heavenly Country: The Civil War and America's Culture of Death* (Ithaca, N.Y.: Cornell University Press, 2008); and John R. Neff, *Honoring the Civil War Dead: Commemoration and the Problem of Rec-*

onciliation (Lawrence: University Press of Kansas, 2005). See also Megan Kate Nelson, *Ruin Nation: Destruction and the American Civil War* (Athens: University of Georgia Press, 2012); and Frances M. Clarke, *War Stories: Suffering and Sacrifice in the Civil War North* (Chicago: University of Chicago Press, 2011). On the numbers of Civil War dead, see J. David Hacker, "A Census-Based Count of the Civil War Dead," *Civil War History* 57 (2011), 307–48, including James M. McPherson, "Commentary on 'A Census-Based Count of the Civil War Dead'"; note that it has proven impossible to estimate Union versus Confederate numbers. See also Nicholas Marshall, "The Great Exaggeration: Death and the Civil War," *Journal of the Civil War Era* 4 (2014), 3–27. On mourning practices and ideas about death, see Sarah Nehama, *In Death Lamented: The Tradition of Anglo-American Mourning Jewelry,* exh. cat. (Boston: Massachusetts Historical Society, 2012); Suzanne E. Smith, *To Serve the Living: Funeral Directors and the African American Way of Death* (Cambridge, Mass.: Harvard University Press, 2010); Vincent Brown, *The Reaper's Garden: Death and Power in the World of Atlantic Slavery* (Cambridge, Mass.: Harvard University Press, 2008); Lucy E. Frank, ed., *Representations of Death in Nineteenth-Century U.S. Writing and Culture* (Burlington, Vt.: Ashgate, 2007); Robert V. Wells, *Facing the 'King of Terrors': Death and Society in an American Community, 1750–1990* (New York: Cambridge University Press, 2000); Pat Jalland, *Death in the Victorian Family* (New York: Oxford University Press, 1996); Gary Laderman, *The Sacred Remains: American Attitudes toward Death, 1799–1883* (New Haven: Yale University Press, 1996); Colleen McDannell and Bernhard Lang, *Heaven: A History* (1988; reprint, New Haven: Yale University Press, 2001); Lou Taylor, *Mourning Dress: A Costume and Social History* (London: Allen and Unwin, 1983); Karen Halttunen, *Confidence Men and Painted Women: A Study of Middle-Class Culture in America, 1830–1870* (New Haven: Yale University Press, 1982), 124–52; Philippe Ariès, *The Hour of Our Death,* trans. Helen Weaver (New York: Alfred A. Knopf, 1981); David R. Roediger, "And Die in Dixie: Funerals, Death, and Heaven in the Slave Community, 1700–1865," *Massachusetts Review* 22 (1981), 163–83; Martha V. Pike and Janice Gray Armstrong, eds., *A Time to Mourn: Expressions of Grief in Nineteenth-Century America* (Stony Brook, N.Y.: Museums at Stony Brook, 1980); Philippe Ariès, *Western Attitudes toward Death: From the Middle Ages to the Present,* trans. Patricia M. Ranum (Baltimore: Johns Hopkins University Press, 1974); Ann Douglas, "Heaven Our Home: Consolation Literature in the Northern United States, 1830–1880," *American Quarterly* 26 (1974), 496–515; and Lewis O. Saum, "Death in the Popular Mind of Pre–Civil War America," *American Quarterly* 26 (1974), 477–95. On embalming, see Glenna R. Schroeder-Lein, *The Encyclopedia of Civil War Medicine* (Armonk, N.Y.: M. E. Sharpe, 2008); Edward C. Johnson et al., "The Origin and History of Embalming," in *Embalming: History, Theory, and Practice,* ed. Robert G. Mayer (New York: McGraw-Hill, 2000); and F. L. Sarmiento, "Ancient and Modern Embalming," *Beadle's Monthly: A Magazine of To-Day* 3 (January 1867), 408–15. On the funeral of George Washington, see Jerry Hawn, "The Funeral of George Washington," *Mall Times* 1 (September 2007), 1; and Gerald E. Kahler, "Washington in Glory, America in Tears: The Nation Mourns the Death of George Washington, 1799–1800" (PhD diss.,

College of William and Mary, 2003). See also Sarah J. Purcell, "All That Remains of Henry Clay," *Common-Place* 12 (April 2012), common-place.org/vol-12/no-03/purcell/. On **Lincoln's funeral in Washington and the funeral train,** see, in addition to sources about the assassination, Martin S. Nowak, *The White House in Mourning: Deaths and Funerals of Presidents in Office* (Jefferson, N.C.: McFarland, 2010); Richard E. Sloan, "Abraham Lincoln's New York City Funeral," in *The Lincoln Assassination: Crime and Punishment, Myth and Memory,* ed. Harold Holzer et al. (New York: Fordham University Press, 2010), 55–93; Scott D. Trostel, *The Lincoln Funeral Train: The Final Journey and National Funeral for Abraham Lincoln* (Fletcher, Ohio: Cam-Tech, 2002); Ralph G. Newman, *"In This Sad World of Ours, Sorrow Comes to All": A Timetable for the Lincoln Funeral Train* (Springfield: State of Illinois, 1965); and Victor Searcher, *The Farewell to Lincoln* (New York: Abingdon, 1965). On **the railroads,** see Richard White, *Railroaded: The Transcontinentals and the Making of Modern America* (New York: W. W. Norton, 2011); and Douglas J. Puffert, "The Standardization of Track Gauge on North American Railways," *Journal of Economic History* 60 (2000), 933–60.

Everyday Life

On **the study of everyday life,** my ideas were deeply influenced by Robin Bernstein and Samuel Zipp's seminar, "Everyday Life: The Textures and Politics of the Ordinary, Persistent, and Repeated," Charles Warren Center for Studies in American History, Harvard University, 2012–13. See Paul Steege et al., "The History of Everyday Life: A Second Chapter," *Journal of Modern History* 80 (2008), 358–78; Geoff Eley, "Labor History, Social History, 'Alltagsgeschichte': Experience, Culture, and the Politics of the Everyday—A New Direction for German Social History?" *Journal of Modern History* 61 (1989), 297–343; and Alf Lüdtke, ed., *The History of Everyday Life: Reconstructing Historical Experiences and Ways of Life,* trans. William Templer (1989; Princeton, N.J.: Princeton University Press, 1995). More specifically, see Peter John Brownlee et al., eds., *Home Front: Daily Life in the Civil War North* (Chicago: University of Chicago Press, 2013); James Marten, ed., *Children and Youth during the Civil War Era* (New York: New York University Press, 2012); Anya Jabour, *Topsy-Turvy: How the Civil War Turned the World Upside Down for Southern Children* (Chicago: Ivan R. Dee, 2010); Alice Fahs, *The Imagined Civil War: Popular Literature of the North and South, 1861–1865* (Chapel Hill: University of North Carolina Press, 2001); James Marten, *The Children's Civil War* (Chapel Hill: University of North Carolina Press, 1998); and J. Matthew Gallman, *The North Fights the Civil War: The Home Front* (Chicago: Ivan R. Dee, 1994).

Emotion

On **the history of emotion,** see Susan J. Matt and Peter N. Stearns, eds., *Doing Emotions History* (Champaign: University of Illinois Press, 2014); Nicole Eustace et al., "AHR Conversation: The Historical Study of Emotions," *American Historical Review* 117 (2012), 1487–1531; Ruth Leys, "The Turn to Affect: A Critique," *Critical Inquiry* 37 (2011), 434–72;

William E. Connolly, "The Complexity of Intention," *Critical Inquiry* 37 (2011), 791–98; Ruth Leys, "Affect and Intention: A Reply to William E. Connolly," *Critical Inquiry* 37 (2011), 799–805; Nicole Eustace, *Passion Is the Gale: Emotion, Power, and the Coming of the American Revolution* (Chapel Hill: University of North Carolina Press, 2008); Martha Tomhave Blauvelt, *The Work of the Heart: Young Women and Emotion, 1780–1830* (Charlottesville: University of Virginia Press, 2007); Andrew R. L. Cayton, "*In*sufficient Woe: Sense and Sensibility in Writing Nineteenth-Century History," *Reviews in American History* 31 (2003), 331–41; Barbara H. Rosenwein, "Worrying about Emotions in History," *American Historical Review* 107 (2002), 821–45; William M. Reddy, *The Navigation of Feeling: A Framework for the History of Emotions* (New York: Cambridge University Press, 2001); Peter N. Stearns and Jan Lewis, *An Emotional History of the United States* (New York: New York University Press, 1998); and Carol Zisowitz Stearns and Peter N. Stearns, *Anger: The Struggle for Emotional Control in America's History* (Chicago: University of Chicago Press, 1986). On **homesickness**, see David Anderson, "Dying of Nostalgia: Homesickness in the Union Army during the Civil War," *Civil War History* 56 (2010), 247–82; Frances Clarke, "So Lonesome I Could Die: Nostalgia and Debates over Emotional Control in the Civil War North," *Journal of Social History* 41 (2007), 253–82; and Susan J. Matt, "You Can't Go Home Again: Homesickness and Nostalgia in U.S. History," *Journal of American History* 94 (2007), 469–97.

Reconstruction

On **Reconstruction,** see especially Eric Foner, *Reconstruction: America's Unfinished Revolution, 1863–1877* (New York: Harper and Row, 1988); see also the books under "Civil War," above. And see Douglas R. Egerton, *The Wars of Reconstruction: The Brief, Violent History of America's Most Progressive Era* (New York: Bloomsbury, 2014); Carole Emberton, *Beyond Redemption: Race, Violence, and the American South after the Civil War* (Chicago: University of Chicago Press, 2013); Hugh Davis, *"We Will Be Satisfied with Nothing Less": The African American Struggle for Equal Rights in the North during Reconstruction* (Ithaca, N.Y.: Cornell University Press, 2011); Hannah Rosen, *Terror in the Heart of Freedom: Citizenship, Sexual Violence, and the Meaning of Race in the Postemancipation South* (Chapel Hill: University of North Carolina Press, 2009); Charles Lane, *The Day Freedom Died: The Colfax Massacre, the Supreme Court, and the Betrayal of Reconstruction* (New York: Henry Holt, 2008); Michael W. Fitzgerald, *Splendid Failure: Postwar Reconstruction in the American South* (Chicago: Ivan R Dee, 2007); Edward J. Blum, *Reforging the White Republic: Race, Religion, and American Nationalism, 1865–1898* (Baton Rouge: Louisiana State University Press, 2005); Steven Hahn, *A Nation under Our Feet: Black Political Struggles in the Rural South from Slavery to the Great Migration* (Cambridge, Mass.: Harvard University Press, 2003); Heather Cox Richardson, *The Death of Reconstruction: Race, Labor, and Politics in the Post–Civil War North, 1865–1901* (Cambridge, Mass.: Harvard University Press, 2001); Laura F. Edwards, *Gendered Strife and Confusion: The Political Culture of Reconstruction* (Urbana: University of Illinois Press, 1997); John Hope Franklin, *Reconstruction after the Civil War,* 2nd ed. (Chicago: University of Chicago Press, 1994); Julie Saville, *The Work of Reconstruction: From Slave to Wage Labor in South Carolina, 1860–1870* (New York: Cambridge University Press, 1994); Dan T. Carter, *When the War Was Over: The Failure of Self-Reconstruction in the South, 1865–1867* (Baton Rouge: Louisiana State University Press, 1985); George C. Rable, *But There Was No Peace: The Role of Violence in the Politics of Reconstruction* (Athens: University of Georgia Press, 1984); James M. McPherson, *Ordeal by Fire: The Civil War and Reconstruction* (New York: Alfred A. Knopf, 1982); Leon F. Litwack, *Been in the Storm So Long: The Aftermath of Slavery* (New York: Alfred A. Knopf, 1979); Allen W. Trelease, *White Terror: The Ku Klux Klan Conspiracy and Southern Reconstruction* (Baton Rouge: Louisiana State University Press, 1971); and W. E. B. Du Bois, *Black Reconstruction in America, 1860–1880* (1935; reprint, New York: Free Press, 1998). On **Andrew Johnson,** see Paul H. Bergeron, *Andrew Johnson's Civil War and Reconstruction* (Knoxville: University of Tennessee Press, 2011); Annette Gordon-Reed, *Andrew Johnson* (New York: Henry Holt, 2011); Hans L. Trefousse, *Andrew Johnson: A Biography* (New York: W. W. Norton, 1989); Paul C. Brownlow, "The Northern Protestant Pulpit and Andrew Johnson," *Southern Speech Communication Journal* 39 (1974), 248–59; and Eric L. McKitrick, *Andrew Johnson and Reconstruction* (Chicago: University of Chicago Press, 1960). On the **1876 World's Fair,** see Bruno Giberti, *Designing the Centennial: A History of the 1876 International Exhibition in Philadelphia* (Lexington: University Press of Kentucky, 2002); and Robert W. Rydell, *All the World's a Fair: Visions of Empire at American International Expositions, 1876–1916* (Chicago: University of Chicago Press, 1984). On the **railroad strike of 1877,** see Michael A. Bellesiles, *1877: America's Year of Living Violently* (New York: New Press, 2010).

Post-Reconstruction

On the **nation after Reconstruction,** see Amy Louise Wood, *Lynching and Spectacle: Witnessing Racial Violence in America, 1890–1940* (Chapel Hill: University of North Carolina Press, 2011); Crystal N. Feimster, *Southern Horrors: Women and the Politics of Rape and Lynching* (Cambridge, Mass.: Harvard University Press, 2009); Douglas A. Blackmon, *Slavery by Another Name: The Re-Enslavement of Black Americans from the Civil War to World War II* (New York: Doubleday, 2008); Steven Hahn, *A Nation under Our Feet: Black Political Struggles in the Rural South from Slavery to the Great Migration* (Cambridge, Mass.: Harvard University Press, 2003); Heather Cox Richardson, *The Death of Reconstruction: Race, Labor, and Politics in the Post–Civil War North, 1865–1901* (Cambridge, Mass.: Harvard University Press, 2001); Leon F. Litwack, *Trouble in Mind: Black Southerners in the Age of Jim Crow* (New York: Alfred A. Knopf, 1998); Tera W. Hunter, *To 'Joy My Freedom: Southern Black Women's Lives and Labors after the Civil War* (Cambridge, Mass.: Harvard University Press, 1997); Alex Lichtenstein, *Twice the Work of Free Labor: The Political Economy of Convict Labor in the New South* (New York: Verso, 1996); Matthew J. Mancini, *One Dies, Get Another: Convict Leasing in the American South, 1866–1928* (Columbia: University of South Carolina Press, 1996); David M. Oshinsky, *"Worse Than Slavery": Parchman Farm and the Ordeal of Jim Crow Justice*

(New York: Free Press, 1996); Edward L. Ayers, *The Promise of the New South: Life after Reconstruction* (New York: Oxford University Press, 1992); and C. Vann Woodward, *The Strange Career of Jim Crow* (1955; reprint, New York: Oxford University Press, 2002). For **counterfactuals**, see James L. Huston, "Reconstruction as It Should Have Been: An Exercise in Counterfactual History," *Civil War History* 51 (2005), 358–63; Roger L. Ransom, "Reconstructing Reconstruction: Options and Limitations to Federal Policies on Land Distribution in 1866–67," *Civil War History* 51 (2005), 364–77; Heather Cox Richardson, "A Marshall Plan for the South?: The Failure of Republican and Democratic Ideology during Reconstruction," *Civil War History* 51 (2005), 378–87; William Blair, "The Use of Military Force to Protect the Gains of Reconstruction," *Civil War History* 51 (2005), 388–402; James L. Huston, "An Alternative to the Tragic Era: Applying the Virtues of Bureaucracy to the Reconstruction Dilemma," *Civil War History* 51 (2005), 403–15; Michael Vorenberg, "Imagining a Different Reconstruction Constitution," *Civil War History* 51 (2005), 416–26; Robert F. Engs, "The Missing Catalyst: In Response to Essays on Reconstructions That Might Have Been," *Civil War History* 51 (2005), 427–31; C. Vann Woodward, "Reconstruction: A Counterfactual Playback," in Woodward, *The Future of the Past* (New York: Oxford University Press, 1989), 183–200; and LaWanda Cox, *Lincoln and Black Freedom: A Study in Presidential Leadership* (Columbia: University of South Carolina Press, 1981).

Memory and Legacies

On **memories of the Civil War**, see especially David W. Blight, *Race and Reunion: The Civil War in American Memory* (Cambridge, Mass.: Harvard University Press, 2001). And see Caroline E. Janney, *Remembering the Civil War: Reunion and the Limits of Reconciliation* (Chapel Hill: University of North Carolina Press, 2013); Caroline E. Janney, *Burying the Dead but Not the Past: Ladies' Memorial Associations and the Lost Cause* (Chapel Hill: University of North Carolina Press, 2008); Mitch Kachun, *Festivals of Freedom: Memory and Meaning in African American Emancipation Celebrations, 1808–1915* (Amherst: University of Massachusetts Press, 2003); David Goldfield, *Still Fighting the Civil War: The American South and Southern History* (Baton Rouge: Louisiana State University Press, 2002); and Nina Silber, *The Romance of Reunion: Northerners and the South, 1865–1900* (Chapel Hill: University of North Carolina Press, 1993). On **the 1930s interviews with former slaves,** see John Barr, "African American Memory and the Great Emancipator," in *Lincoln's Enduring Legacy: Perspectives from Great Thinkers, Great Leaders, and the American Experiment,* ed. Robert P. Watson et al. (Lanham, Md.: Rowman and Littlefield, 2010), 133–64.

Individuals

On **Henry Ward Beecher**, see Debby Applegate, *The Most Famous Man in America: The Biography of Henry Ward Beecher* (New York: Doubleday, 2006); and William G. McLoughlin, *The Meaning of Henry Ward Beecher: An Essay on the Shifting Values of*

Mid-Victorian America, 1840–1870 (New York: Alfred A. Knopf, 1970). On **Emilie Davis,** see "Emilie: Memorable Days—The Emilie Davis Diaries," davisdiaries.villanova.edu; Judith Giesberg, ed., *Emilie Davis's Civil War: The Diaries of a Free Black Woman in Philadelphia, 1863–1865* (University Park: Penn State University Press, 2014); and Karsonya Wise Whitehead, *Notes from a Colored Girl: The Civil War Pocket Diaries of Emilie Frances Davis* (Columbia: University of South Carolina Press, 2014). On **Jefferson Davis,** see William J. Cooper Jr., *Jefferson Davis, American* (New York: Alfred A. Knopf, 2000); William C. Davis, *Jefferson Davis: The Man and His Hour* (New York: Harper-Collins, 1991); Mark E. Neely Jr., Harold Holzer, Gabor S. Boritt, *The Confederate Image: Prints of the Lost Cause* (Chapel Hill: University of North Carolina Press, 1987); Chester D. Bradley, "Was Jefferson Davis Disguised as a Woman When Captured?" *Journal of Mississippi History* 36 (1974), 243–68; and David M. Potter, "Jefferson Davis and the Political Factors in Confederate Defeat," in *Why the North Won the Civil War,* ed. David Herbert Donald (Baton Rouge: Louisiana State University Press, 1960), 91–114. On **Frederick Douglass,** see especially David W. Blight, *Frederick Douglass: A Life* (Simon and Schuster, forthcoming). And see James Oakes, *The Radical and the Republican: Frederick Douglass, Abraham Lincoln, and the Triumph of Antislavery Politics* (New York: W. W. Norton, 2007); William S. McFeely, *Frederick Douglass* (New York: W. W. Norton, 1991); and David W. Blight, *Frederick Douglass' Civil War: Keeping Faith in Jubilee* (Baton Rouge: Louisiana State University Press, 1989). On **William Benjamin Gould,** see Christopher Hager, *Word by Word: Emancipation and the Act of Writing* (Cambridge, Mass.: Harvard University Press, 2013); and William Benjamin Gould, *Diary of a Contraband: The Civil War Passage of a Black Sailor,* ed. William B. Gould IV (Stanford, Calif.: Stanford University Press, 2002), and "Diary of a Contraband," goulddiary.stanford.edu. On **Robert E. Lee,** see Joseph T. Glatthaar, "Robert E. Lee, the Army of Northern Virginia, and Confederate Surrender," in *How Fighting Ends: A History of Surrender,* ed. Holger Afflerbach and Hew Strachan (New York: Oxford University Press, 2012), 239–52; Emory M. Thomas, *Robert E. Lee: A Biography* (New York: W. W. Norton, 1995); and Alan T. Nolan, *Lee Considered: General Robert E. Lee and Civil War History* (Chapel Hill: University of North Carolina Press, 1991). On **Mary Lincoln,** see Catherine Clinton, *Mrs. Lincoln: A Life* (New York: HarperCollins, 2009); Catherine Clinton, "Wife versus Widow: Clashing Perspectives on Mary Lincoln's Legacy," *Journal of the Abraham Lincoln Association* 28 (Winter 2007), 1–19; Jean H. Baker, *Mary Todd Lincoln: A Biography* (New York: W. W. Norton, 1987); and Justin G. Turner and Linda Levitt Turner, *Mary Todd Lincoln: Her Life and Letters* (New York: International Publishing, 1987). On **Edmund Ruffin,** see David F. Allmendinger Jr., *Ruffin: Family and Reform in the Old South* (New York: Oxford University Press, 1990). On **Walt Whitman,** see Donald D. Kummings, *A Companion to Walt Whitman* (Malden, Mass.: Blackwell, 2006); Helen Vendler, "Poetry and the Mediation of Value: Whitman on Lincoln," *Michigan Quarterly Review* 39 (2000), 1–18; Roy Morris Jr., *The Better Angel: Walt Whitman in the Civil War* (New York: Oxford University Press, 2000); and R. W. French, "When Lilacs Last in the Dooryard Bloom'd," in *Walt Whitman: An Encyclopedia,* ed. J. R. LeMaster and Donald D. Kummings (New York:

Garland, 1998); both the poem and French's analysis are available at "The Walt Whitman Archive," ed. Ed Folsom and Kenneth M. Price, whitmanarchive.org.

Sarah and Albert Browne and Rodney Dorman

On **Salem, Massachusetts,** during the Civil War, see D. Hamilton Hurd, *History of Essex County, Massachusetts,* vol. 1 (Philadelphia: J. W. Lewis, 1888), 200–208; and T. J. Hutchinson and Ralph Childs, *Patriots of Salem* (Salem: T. J. Hutchinson, 1877). On **abolitionism in Salem,** see Laura Rundell and Emily A. Murphy, "African American Heritage Sites in Salem: A Guide to Salem's History" (1998; rev. ed., Salem Maritime National Historical Site, National Park Service, U.S. Department of the Interior, 2008), nps.gov/sama/history culture/upload/SalemAfAmsitessm.pdf; Julie Roy Jeffrey, *The Great Silent Army of Aboli- tionism: Ordinary Women in the Antislavery Movement* (Chapel Hill: University of North Carolina Press, 1998); and Shirley J. Yee, *Black Women Abolitionists: A Study in Activism, 1828–1860* (Knoxville: University of Tennessee Press, 1992). On **the Brownes' church,** see *The First Centenary of the North Church and Society, in Salem, Massachusetts* (Salem, Mass.: North Church, 1873). On **Florida and Jacksonville in the Civil War era,** see Larry Eugene Rivers, *Rebels and Runaways: Slave Resistance in Nineteenth-Century Florida* (Urbana: University of Illinois Press, 2012); Daniel L. Schafer, *Thunder on the River: The Civil War in Northeast Florida* (Gainesville: University Press of Florida, 2010); Calvin L. Robinson, *A Yankee in a Confederate Town: The Journal of Calvin L. Robinson,* ed. Anne Robinson Clancy (Sarasota, Fla.: Pineapple Press, 2002); Lewis N. Wynne and Robert Taylor, *Florida in the Civil War* (Charleston, S.C.: Arcadia, 2002); Larry Eugene Rivers, *Slavery in Florida: Territorial Days to Emancipation* (Gainesville: University Press of Florida, 2000); Daniel L. Schafer, "'A Class of People Neither Freemen nor Slaves': From Spanish to American Race Relations in Florida, 1821–1861," *Journal of Social History* 26 (1993), 587–609; Richard A. Martin and Daniel L. Schafer, *Jacksonville's Ordeal by Fire: A Civil War History* (Jacksonville: Florida Publishing, 1984); Joe M. Richardson, "Florida Black Codes," *Florida Historical Quarterly* 47 (1969), 365–79; Russell Garvin, "The Free Negro in Florida before the Civil War," *Florida Historical Quarterly* 46 (1967), 1–17; and Thelma Bates, "The Legal Status of the Negro in Florida," *Florida Historical Quarterly* 6 (1928), 159–81. On **the March 1863 expedition,** see especially Stephen V. Ash, *Firebrand of Liberty: The Story of Two Black Regiments That Changed the Course of the Civil War* (New York: W. W. Norton, 2008).

Method

On **diaries and diary keeping,** see Christine Nelson, "Writing for an Imagined Audience," Room for Debate, *New York Times,* November 26, 2012, nytimes.com/room fordebate/2012/11/25/will-diaries-be-published-in-2050/digital-and-paper-diaries-are-writ ten-for-an-imagined-audience; "The Diary: Three Centuries of Private Lives," Morgan Library and Museum exhibition, New York, January 21–May 22, 2011, themorgan.org/ exhibitions/exhibition.asp?id=42; Alexandra Johnson, *A Brief History of Diaries: From*

Pepys to Blogs (London: Hesperus, 2011); Molly McCarthy, "A Pocketful of Days: Pocket Diaries and Daily Record Keeping among Nineteenth-Century New England Women," *New England Quarterly* 73 (2000), 274–96; Cinthia Gannett, *Gender and the Journal: Diaries and Academic Discourse* (Albany: State University of New York Press, 1992); Laurel Thatcher Ulrich, *A Midwife's Tale: The Life of Martha Ballard, Based on Her Diary, 1785–1812* (New York: Alfred A. Knopf, 1990); Margo Culley, *A Day at a Time: The Diary Literature of American Women Writers from 1764 to the Present* (New York: Feminist Press, 1985); and Thomas Mallon, *A Book of One's Own: People and Their Diaries* (New York: Ticknor and Fields, 1984). On **letters and letter writing,** see Konstantin Dierks, *In My Power: Letter Writing and Communications in Early America* (Philadelphia: University of Pennsylvania Press, 2009); Thomas Mallon, *Yours Ever: People and Their Letters* (New York: Random House, 2009); and Nigel Hall, "The Materiality of Letter Writing: A Nineteenth-Century Perspective," in *Letter Writing as a Social Practice,* ed. David Barton and Nigel Hall (Amsterdam: John Benjamins, 2000), 83–108. On **literacy,** see Christopher Hager, *Word by Word: Emancipation and the Act of Writing* (Cambridge, Mass.: Harvard University Press, 2013); and Edward E. Gordon and Elaine H. Gordon, *Literacy in America: Historic Journey and Contemporary Solutions* (Westport, Conn.: Praeger, 2003).

Acknowledgments

Most historians work with a single collection of archival papers for weeks at a time, but the nature of this project required me to request as many as ten or twenty collections in a day of research. For their assistance and patience, I thank the librarians in archives across the country who fetched thousands of letters and diaries from the vaults, thereby bringing alive the spring and summer of 1865. For transporting me back in time, I also thank Sarah Jencks for an extra-special tour of Ford's Theatre and Petersen House.

For engaging with ideas at key junctures, I thank Louis Masur and the Trinity College American Studies Department, and Laura Gotkowitz and the University of Pittsburgh Humanities Center, for two wonderful extended visits filled with intellectual enthusiasm. I thank equally keen audiences at Bowdoin College, the Charles Warren Center at Harvard University, the Massachusetts Historical Society, Brown University's Nineteenth-Century Workshop, the German Historical Institute in Washington, the "Writing the History of Everyday Life" workshop at NYU-Berlin, the New York Military Affairs Symposium, the Gathering Place in Swarthmore, Pennsylvania, the Society of Civil War Historians, and the graduate student–designed conference at New York University, "Against Recovery: Slavery, Freedom, and the Archive."

For a fellowship year of paradise, I thank the Charles Warren Center for Studies in American History at Harvard University, where I joined a group of scholars exploring the theme of everyday life, and the Massachusetts Historical Society, where I held a National Endowment for the Humanities fellowship (the views and conclusions in this book do not necessarily reflect those of the NEH). At Harvard, I thank Robin Bernstein and Samuel Zipp for creating and nurturing an exceptional community. Thank you Robin, Sandy, Luis Alvarez, Jayna Brown (special thanks for our lunch at Sandrine's that day), Bruce Dorsey, Karen Hansen, David Jaffee, Ann Pellegrini, Kyla Wazana Tompkins, Sara Warner, and Harvey Young for persistent, repeated, and extraordinary interchange. Sincere gratitude also to Nancy Cott and Lizabeth Cohen, and to Arthur Patton-Hock and Larissa Kennedy. At the Massachusetts Historical Society, Conrad Wright and the entire staff offered generous attention, steady writing time, and ongoing edifying exchange in a glittering array of events. My fellow long-term fellows, Matthew Dennis and Kristin Collins, kept our hallway humming with productivity, and the endnotes to this book attest to the remarkable richness of the MHS collections. Together, Harvard, the Massachusetts Historical Society, and the NEH gave me the gift of a year that Bruce Dorsey and I had long conjured: all the time in the world to write, followed by time to talk about writing—on the skylit top floor of Emerson Hall, in our bright and cozy Avon Street home, on miles-at-a-time walks, and over coffee at Simon's or Bloc 11.

That imagined paradise could not have come true without the mighty senior scholars who magnanimously supported my work. James McPherson long ago awakened my passion for studying race, the Civil War, and Reconstruction in his luminous seminars and lectures at Princeton University and remains a steadfast presence in my intellectual life, from every book he produces to our lunches at Prospect House, where we talked about Lincoln's assassination. David Blight has lit up my path with his brilliance and warmth—as someone so aptly put it after attending a lecture by David, "You just want to hang out with him forever." I am fortunate indeed to hang out with him every so often. Drew Faust has been an ally since the earliest years of my career and remains unstintingly generous, even as she has scaled to the top of the world. Martha Sandweiss and I began to talk about writing during the book before this one, and her ideas continue to dazzle me (special thanks also for introducing me to Wendy Strothman). Thomas Bender's enduring wisdom and encouragement across two decades of collegiality continue to shape my scholarship (Tom was also the neighbor who walked with me on the morning of September 12, 2001, in search of a newspaper). James Goodman has inspired me from the first line of his dissertation all those many years ago to our conversation over coffee last week. Thank you all for your time and letters. Sincere thanks as well to Richard Wightman Fox, who welcomed me to the world of Lincoln's assassination and happily discussed our parallel projects.

I thank New York University's Global Research Initiative for a sublime month in Berlin, where I wrote every day, with a beautiful view of Prenzlauer Berg, and together with Bruce Dorsey hosted a stirring workshop on "Writing the History of Everyday Life"; thank you, Ryan Wu, Gabriella Etmektsoglou, Maya Jex, Katherine Fleming, and our fellow everydaylifers: Grace Hale, Sebastian Jobs, Nora Kreuzenbeck, Jürgen Martschukat, and Silvan Niedermeier. Back home at NYU, I thank colleagues and friends Thomas Bender, Jane Burbank, Herrick Chapman, Fred Cooper, Hasia Diner, Nicole Eustace, Ada Ferrer, Linda Gordon, Fiona Griffiths, Karen Kupperman, Michele Mitchell, Maria Montoya, Jennifer Morgan, Molly Nolan (especially for our Berlin days that June), David Oshinsky, Joanna Waley-Cohen, and Barbara Weinstein. Thank you to the undergraduates in my 2011 Experimental History seminar, Brendan Check, Megan Dran, Lara Gomes da Costa, Sarah Kolinovsky, Zachary Leibman, Caroline Marris, Jed Portman, and Sheena Yap, who indulged me as I completed the course's writing assignments along with them, experimenting with different ways to tell the story of mourning Lincoln. My phenomenal PhD advisees—some out in the world, others soon to launch—inspire me more than they can imagine: Emilie Connolly, Sarah Cornell, Ben Davidson, Kendra Field, Taja-Nia Henderson, Alex Manevitz, Rachel Mattson, Melissa Milewski, Max Mishler, Samantha Seeley, and Peter Wirzbicki.

My agent, Wendy Strothman, helped me figure out this book. With her sharp-eyed toughness, she brainstormed ideas, shaped the proposal, thought up the title, and hurried me along. In the rapidly changing world of publishing, Wendy knows everything and everyone and hence united me with Steve Wasserman at Yale University Press, who charmed me from the moment we met. Spotting him at his special table at the Union Square Café, in dapper attire and reading a book, I'd barely taken my seat before he exclaimed upon the beauty of a particular sentence he'd just encountered. Ever since (and always at the same lovely table), Steve has treated me to a stream of thrilling and thought-provoking conversation about reading, writing, and writers—that invariably sent me skipping back to my desk. At Yale University Press, editorial assistants Erica Hanson and Eva Skewes remained gallantly attentive and obliging throughout the production process and beyond. Laura Jones Dooley graciously answered my countless questions about grammar and style and, best of all, taught me about compound predicates.

Freelance editor Susan Whitlock had at the manuscript when it was a tortuous second draft, upon which she performed a first-class, five-star, blue-chip, top-of-the-line redraft. Susan's expert artistry can make the tired words of anyone shimmer and dance, and I recommend her to all scholars and writers. Louis Masur provided a terrifically thoughtful and spot-on reading of the penultimate draft in record time. To an anonymous reader I give my utmost gratitude, not least for saving me from factual errors that could have been corrected only by someone with a vast knowledge of the Civil War era—I venture to say that your luminous name has already appeared in these acknowledgments. James Goodman, scholar and writer par excellence, cheerfully volunteered to read the whole thing at nearly the eleventh hour, giving me a host of insights and a genius correction in the very first line that no one else had noticed. Eva Moseley, archivist and writer, volunteered a read-through at the eleventh-and-three-quarters hour, and I am grateful indeed for her gift of linguistic rigor and precision. Bruce Dorsey read every word twice and many words ten times, rattled off whole bibliographies of context, and helped me identify the author of the anonymous diary as Rodney Dorman. Most of all, Bruce offered so many interpretations of the evidence that had never occurred to me that I regularly suggested coauthorship, which he stubbornly refused every time. Accordingly, each person in this paragraph is responsible only for the good parts of the book, and I alone for the rest.

I am grateful to my community of friends in Swarthmore and Philadelphia: to Laurie Bernstein and Robert Weinberg, and especially for my walks with Laurie, which always left me breathless, not only from the hills climbed but also from the content of our conversations; to Mary Marissen, for our steady and soothing get-togethers across so many years; and to Ben Yagoda and Gigi Simeone, Sharon Ullman, and Bryant Simon, for friendship and much-needed good times, with special thanks to Ben and Bryant for always-sage reflections on writing. In New York, James Goodman provided hours of inspiring conversation, and along with Jenny McFeely provided respite from everything. Susan Whitlock is not only a stupendous editor but a precious friend as well—we met many years ago working on the *Let's Go Europe* travel guides, and how happy I am that she is now a fellow New Yorker.

The glorious year in Cambridge was enhanced yet more by Elizabeth Reis and Matthew Dennis serendipitously living up the street, and Shane Minkin and Heiko Reinhard in Somerville (thank you for the driveway), with the late, great Frankie and, at the very end, beloved Harry. It was utterly delightful to spend time again with Eva Moseley, and with Thomas Battle and Margaret Waters, and to make a new friend, Carla Kaplan, who instantly felt like an old friend. Thanks as well to Heather Sullivan and to our lovely downstairs neighbor, Ruth Beckwith.

As always, I thank Jody Goodman and Marc Fisher for making my Washington research so much more enjoyable, and Jody for a depth of dialogue that would be impossible with anyone else. The scholars and writers who double as good friends have my heartfelt gratitude as well: Barbara Walker, Dick Meyer, Judith Weisenfeld, Woody Register and Julie Berebitsky, Konstantin Dierks and Sarah Knott, Laura Gotkowitz and Michel Gobat, Kevin Mumford, Leslie Harris, Jürgen Martschukat, and Greg Downs. I also thank a number of longtime dear friends who had less to do with this book but whose friendships are ever-important: Marsha Rich, Lisa Tessler, Sheba Veghte, Sharon Achinstein, and Jamie Jamieson. Three people in particular listened with sympathy to the difficulties of meeting a sesquicentennial deadline: Linda Hodes (thank you for the homemade "Abe's Night Out" card), Laurie Bernstein, and Bruce Dorsey.

An extended family has long sustained me. I thank my father, Stuart Hodes, Martha Graham dancer-turned-writer, at ninety; my mother, Linda Hodes, Martha Graham dancer-turned-artist; my ever-inspiring sisters, Catherine Hodes and Tal Ben-David; and Dalen Cole, Stephen Margolies, Elizabeth Hodes, Jack Gescheidt and Amy Pfaffman, Andy Gescheidt and Karen Balacek, Kevin Brady, Holly Richardson, Ken Tosti and David O'Keefe, Danielle Abrams, Betty and Dave Dorsey, Connie Cashman, Ruth and Chris Purcell, and Jon and Stacy Dorsey, plus the amazing next generation, Tim Dorsey and Sarah Dorsey, Matthew Choi, Julietta Cole, Quinn Brady, Katie Purcell, Tyler Dorsey, Evan Dorsey, Danielle Dorsey, Brian Kalousek and Holley Biroczky, Scott Kalousek, and Kailee Dorsey (with a special shout-out to Matt and Tim, whose childhood cast-offs became my muses).

I've saved the best for last. Bruce Dorsey understands my preoccupation with loss and grief as no one else ever will. His unending love and immeasurable kindness make me the luckiest person in the world and make my world radiant every day.

Index

Page numbers in *italics* indicate illustrations.

Alabama, 17, 45, 55, 84, 101, 139, 244, 274.
    See also specific locations
Albany, N.Y., 34, 233; Lincoln's funeral in,
    149, 153, 156, 159, 201
Alcott, Bronson, 252
Alexandria, Egypt, 55–56, 159
Alexandria, Va., 81, 164, 218, 247
Allen, Clara, 126
Alsop, Elizabeth, 96, 183, 184, 205, 247,
    289n25
Altoona, Pa., 148
amnesty, Confederate, 40, 158, 221, 223,
    234, 240–45, 255, 264, 267
anarchy, fear of, 66, 73, 104, 105, 173
Anderson, Martha, 161, 246
Andersonville Prison, 257
Andrews, Eliza, 33, 132, 245
anger: of mourners toward Booth, 125–26;
    of mourners toward Confederates, 90,
    129–30, 134, 136, 137–38, *154;* of mourn-
    ers toward Copperheads, 90, *86, 154,*
    162; as response to assassination, 5, 16,
    46, 117–23, 145, 201–2; as response to
    Confederate defeat, 24, 71, 183, 184–85,
    214, 218
Anthony, Susan B., 57
anti-slavery ideology, 13, 15, 25, 108, 134, 218,
    219, 252, 273. *See also* abolitionists; slavery
Appleton, Nathan, 182
Appomattox, 30–31, 32–33, 41, 116, 158,
    214, 267, 274. *See also* Lee, Robert E.;
    surrender
April 11, 1865, speech by Lincoln, 4, 23,
    38–39, 214–15, 218, 238, 241, 255, 273;
    and Booth, 4, 38–39, 214, 238; and
    Douglass, 273
Arkansas, 17, 274
Armory Square Hospital, 49, 196
Armstrong, Hillock, 35, 133, 135
Army of Georgia, 229
Army of Northern Virginia, 29, 30–31,
    79–80, 158, 205, 223

Army of the Potomac, 30, 229
Army of the Tennessee, 158, 229
Arnold, Samuel, 124, 263, 264. *See also*
    conspirators
assassination, act of, 1–3, *2, 3;* as God's
    will, Confederate view, 11, 70–71, 114; as
    God's will, mourner's view, 11, 102–10,
    105–9, 113–14, 119, 143, 145, 147, 182, 215;
    spread of news of, 3, 5, 10, 49, 52–56;
    studying personal responses to, 8–9, 11,
    21, 275–77; timing of, 42, 47, 48, 57–58,
    110. *See also* Davis, Jefferson; Doug-
    lass, Frederick; eyewitnesses; Ford's
    Theatre; Lee, Robert E.; newspapers;
    Petersen House; Reconstruction;
    rumors; sermons; slavery; telegraph
assassination, personal responses to. *See*
    African Americans; anger; Confeder-
    ates; Copperheads; everyday life; fear;
    glee; grief; hope; horror; hospitals;
    indignation; mercy; mourning; opti-
    mism; physical symptoms; provi-
    dence; shock; silence; trauma; "why"
    question; whites
Athens, Ga., 262
Atzerodt, George, 4, 124, 263, *265. See also*
    conspirators
Augusta, Ga., 262
Australia, 55
Austria, 44

Baker, Alma, 302n14
Baltimore: Confederates in, 74, 77, 80, 148;
    Copperheads in, 85, 87, 162; Lincoln's
    funeral in, 148, 149, 150, 153, 163; news
    of assassination in, 57; reburial of
    Booth in, 264; and Union victory,
    33–34; Unionists in, 77, 80
Bancroft, George, 162
Barnes, Francis, 122, 139
Barton, Clara, 156–57
Bates, David Homer, 109, 220–21

Shannon, Marmaduke, 75

Shepard, Julia, 34, 49, 64, 170

Sheridan, Philip, 22, 30, 43, 83

Sherman, William Tecumseh, 14, 31, 44, 79, 83, 98, 113, 121, 139; and Johnston, 141, 142–43, 158–59

Shields, Patrick, 80, 81

Shiner, Michael, 58–59

shock, as response to assassination, 4, 5, 7, 9, 10, 16, 46–48, 56–58, 59, 59, 62, 65, 66, 68, 90, 93, 97, 98, 101, 113, 116, 117, 146, 147, 168, 170, 175, 195, 199; as response to Confederate defeat, 33, 68, 183, as response to death of loved ones, 202

Shriver, Henry, 180

Sierra Leone, 55

silence, as response to assassination: Confederates, 70, 74–75, 76, 82, 162; Copperheads, 83, 88, 90, 148, 162; mourners, 47, 63, 68, 100, 147, 161, 264

Simpson, Matthew, 134, 145–46, 163–64, 170

Sixteenth New York Cavalry, 160

slave holders. *See* planter classes

slavery: as cause of assassination, 108, 117, 118, 128–30, 131, 137–38, 227, 242, 246, 250–52, 272, 274; as cause of Civil War, 25, 28–29, 35, 40, 71, 73, 82–83, 108, 112–13, 128, 130–32, 137, 145, 194, 205, 237, 238, 251, 252, 262, 272–73; Confederates compare to defeat, 183–84, 247–48, 249–50, 266; and Johnson, 215, 219–20, 221–22; and Lincoln, 35, 79, 103, 108, 111, 129, 130, 137, 145, 194, 215, 218, 238, 250–52, 255–56, 273; and poor white southerners, 132–36, 221–22, 240; and reenslavement, 35–36, 50, 66, 73, 80, 99, 212–13, 217, 218–19, 244–45, 246–47, 263, 274; and second inaugural address, 35, 103, 129, 137, 194, 255–56, 272–73. *See also* abolitionists; African Americans; anti-slavery ideology;

Douglass, Frederick; Emancipation Proclamation; proslavery ideology; second inaugural address

Slidell, John, 132

Smalls, Robert, 39

Smith, Eli, 89

Smith, Jennie, 200

Smith, John, 129

Smith, Kirby, 236, 240

songs, 197, 260. *See also* "John Brown's Body"; "Star-Spangled Banner"

South Africa, 10

South Carolina, 17–18, 244, 268; African Americans in, 121, 219, 228, 241; Confederates in, 44, 45, 72, 77, 79, 82, 203, 249, 255, 257, 265. *See also specific locations*

Spain, 44. *See also* Cádiz

Spangler, Edman, 124, 263. *See also* conspirators

Spencer, Cornelia, 183–84, 204, 248

Spencer, Magnus, 204

Springfield, Ill., 134; Lincoln's burial in, 143, 163–64, 170, 197, 207; Lincoln's funeral in, 149, 150, 153

Stanton, Edwin, 22, 43, 46, 56, 87, 129; and Booth, 160; and Lincoln's funeral, 163; at Petersen House, 5, 131

"Star-Spangled Banner" (song), 31

Starkey, Mary Ann, 57, 106

Stephens, Alexander, 28–29

Stickney, Lyman, 20

Stone, Eunice, 202

Stone, Kate, 79, 203, 215, 248, 250

Stonehouse, John, 45

Strong, George Templeton, 68, 145–46, 163

suffrage. *See* voting rights

suicide, 195, 202; as response to assassination, 187, 200; as response to Confederate defeat, 33, 184–85, 204, 205, 228, 249

Sumner, Charles, 71, 246–47

Surratt, John 124, 127, 263. *See also* conspirators